Android™

HOW TO PROGRAM

THIRD EDITION

with an Introduction to Java™

Deitel® Series Page

How To Program Series

Android™ How to Program, 3/E
C++ How to Program, 9/E
C How to Program, 7/E
Java™ How to Program, Early Objects Version, 10/E
Java™ How to Program, Late Objects Version, 10/E
Internet & World Wide Web How to Program, 5/E
Visual Basic® 2015 How to Program, 7/E
Visual C#® 2015 How to Program, 6/E

Deitel® Developer Series

Android™ 6 for Programmers: An App-Driven Approach, 3/E
C for Programmers with an Introduction to C11
C++11 for Programmers
C# 2015 for Programmers
iOS® 8 for Programmers: An App-Driven Approach with Swift™
Java™ for Programmers, 3/E
JavaScript for Programmers
Swift™ for Programmers

Simply Series

Simply C++: An App-Driven Tutorial Approach
Simply Java™ Programming: An App-Driven Tutorial Approach
(continued in next column)

(continued from previous column)
Simply C#: An App-Driven Tutorial Approach
Simply Visual Basic® 2010: An App-Driven Approach, 4/E

CourseSmart Web Books

www.deitel.com/books/CourseSmart/

C++ How to Program, 8/E and 9/E
Simply C++: An App-Driven Tutorial Approach
Java™ How to Program, 9/E and 10/E
Simply Visual Basic® 2010: An App-Driven Approach, 4/E
Visual Basic® 2015 How to Program, 7/E
Visual Basic® 2012 How to Program, 6/E
Visual C#® 2015 How to Program, 6/E
Visual C#® 2012 How to Program, 5/E

LiveLessons Video Learning Products

www.deitel.com/books/LiveLessons/

Android™ 6 App Development Fundamentals, 3/e
C++ Fundamentals
Java™ Fundamentals, 2/e
C# 2015 Fundamentals
C# 2012 Fundamentals
iOS® 8 App Development Fundamentals, 3/e
JavaScript Fundamentals
Swift™ Fundamentals

To receive updates on Deitel publications, Resource Centers, training courses, partner offers and more, please join the Deitel communities on

- Facebook®—facebook.com/DeitelFan
- Twitter®—twitter.com/deitel
- Google+™—google.com/+DeitelFan
- YouTube™—youtube.com/DeitelTV
- LinkedIn®—linkedin.com/company/deitel-&-associates

and register for the free *Deitel® Buzz Online* e-mail newsletter at:

www.deitel.com/newsletter/subscribe.html

To communicate with the authors, send e-mail to:

deitel@deitel.com

For information on *Dive-Into® Series* on-site seminars offered by Deitel & Associates, Inc. worldwide, write to us at deitel@deitel.com or visit:

www.deitel.com/training/

For continuing updates on Pearson/Deitel publications visit:

www.deitel.com
www.pearsonhighered.com/deitel/

Visit the Deitel Resource Centers, which will help you master programming languages, software development, Android and iOS app development, and Internet- and web-related topics:

www.deitel.com/ResourceCenters.html

Android™

HOW TO PROGRAM

THIRD EDITION

**with an
Introduction
to Java™**

Paul Deitel • Harvey Deitel
Deitel & Associates, Inc.

DEITEL®

PEARSON

Boston   Columbus   Indianapolis   New York   San Francisco   Upper Saddle River
Amsterdam   Cape Town   Dubai   London   Madrid   Milan   Munich   Paris   Montreal   Toronto
Delhi   Mexico City   Sao Paulo   Sydney   Hong Kong   Seoul   Singapore   Taipei   Tokyo

Vice President, Editorial Director: *Marcia Horton*
Acquisitions Editor: *Tracy Johnson*
Editorial Assistant: *Kristy Alaura*
VP of Marketing: *Christy Lesko*
Director of Field Marketing: *Tim Galligan*
Product Marketing Manager: *Bram Van Kempen*
Field Marketing Manager: *Demetrius Hall*
Marketing Assistant: *Jon Bryant*
Director of Product Management: *Erin Gregg*
Team Lead, Program and Project Management: *Scott Disanno*
Program Manager: *Carole Snyder*
Project Manager: *Robert Engelhardt*
Senior Specialist, Program Planning and Support: *Maura Zaldivar-Garcia*
Cover Design: *Paul Deitel, Harvey Deitel, Chuti Prasertsith*
R&P Manager: *Rachel Youdelman*
R&P Project Manager: *Timothy Nicholls*
Inventory Manager: *Meredith Maresca*
Cover Art: *Oleksiy Mark / Shutterstock*

Credits and acknowledgments borrowed from other sources and reproduced, with permission, in this textbook appear on page vi.

Library of Congress Cataloging-in-Publication Data
On file

ISBN-10: 0-13-444430-2
ISBN-13: 978-0-13-444430-7

To the Android software-engineering community:

For creating and evolving a platform that challenges app developers to test the limits of their imagination

Paul and Harvey Deitel

Trademarks

DEITEL, the double-thumbs-up bug and DIVE-INTO are registered trademarks of Deitel & Associates, Inc.

Java is a registered trademark of Oracle and/or its affiliates. Other names may be trademarks of their respective owners.

Google, Android, Google Play, Google Maps, Google Wallet, Nexus, YouTube, AdSense and AdMob are trademarks of Google, Inc.

Microsoft and/or its respective suppliers make no representations about the suitability of the information contained in the documents and related graphics published as part of the services for any purpose. All such documents and related graphics are provided "as is" without warranty of any kind. Microsoft and/or its respective suppliers hereby disclaim all warranties and conditions with regard to this information, including all warranties and conditions of merchantability, whether express, implied or statutory, fitness for a particular purpose, title and non-infringement. In no event shall Microsoft and/or its respective suppliers be liable for any special, indirect or consequential damages or any damages whatsoever resulting from loss of use, data or profits, whether in an action of contract, negligence or other tortious action, arising out of or in connection with the use or performance of information available from the services.

The documents and related graphics contained herein could include technical inaccuracies or typographical errors. Changes are periodically added to the information herein. Microsoft and/or its respective suppliers may make improvements and/or changes in the product(s) and/or the program(s) described herein at any time. Partial screen shots may be viewed in full within the software version specified.

Microsoft® and Windows® are registered trademarks of the Microsoft Corporation in the U.S.A. and other countries. Screen shots and icons reprinted with permission from the Microsoft Corporation. This book is not sponsored or endorsed by or affiliated with the Microsoft Corporation.

Throughout this book, trademarks are used. Rather than put a trademark symbol in every occurrence of a trademarked name, we state that we are using the names in an editorial fashion only and to the benefit of the trademark owner, with no intention of infringement of the trademark.

Contents

2 Welcome App 37

Android Studio: Introducing Visual GUI Design, Layouts, Accessibility and Internationalization

3 Tip Calculator App

Introducing GridLayout, EditText, SeekBar, Event Handling, NumberFormat, Customizing the App's Theme and Defining App Functionality with Java

4   Flag Quiz App   110

Fragments, Menus, Preferences, Explicit Intents, Handler, AssetManager, Tweened Animations, Animators, Toasts, Color State Lists, Layouts for Multiple Device Orientations, Logging Error Messages for Debugging

5 Doodlz App 173

*2D Graphics, **Canvas**, **Bitmap**, Accelerometer, **SensorManager**, Multitouch Events, MediaStore, Printing, Android 6.0 Permissions, Gradle*

6 Cannon Game App   228

Manual Frame-By-Frame Animation, Graphics, Sound, Threading,
SurfaceView and SurfaceHolder, Immersive Mode and Full-Screen

7 WeatherViewer App   270

REST Web Services, AsyncTask, HttpUrlConnection, Processing JSON Responses, JSONObject, JSONArray, ListView, ArrayAdapter, ViewHolder Pattern, TextInputLayout, FloatingActionButton

8 Twitter® Searches App 302

SharedPreferences, SharedPreferences.Editor, Implicit Intents, Intent Choosers, RecyclerView, RecyclerView.Adapter, RecyclerView.ViewHolder, RecyclerView.ItemDecoration

9   Address Book App   341

FragmentTransactions and the Fragment Back Stack, SQLite, SQLiteDatabase, SQLiteOpenHelper, ContentProvider, ContentResolver, Loader, LoaderManager, Cursor and GUI Styles

10 Google Play and App Business Issues 405

A Introduction to Java Applications 427

B Introduction to Classes, Objects, Methods and Strings 451

C Control Statements 473

D   Methods: A Deeper Look   518

E   Arrays and ArrayLists   547

F Classes and Objects: A Deeper Look   593

G Object-Oriented Programming: Inheritance and Polymorphism   622

H   Exception Handling: A Deeper Look   686

I   GUI Components and Event Handling   707

Preface

Welcome to the dynamic world of Android *smartphone* and *tablet* app development with the Android Software Development Kit (SDK), the Java™ programming language and the rapidly evolving Android Studio Integrated Development Environment (IDE). *Android How to Program, 3/e* presents leading-edge mobile computing technologies for upper-level college courses. Many of the Android techniques we present also apply to Android Wear and Android TV app development, so after reading this book, you'll be well prepared to investigate how to develop apps for these platforms.

The opportunities for Android app developers are enormous. Sales of Android devices and app downloads have been growing exponentially. The first-generation Android phones were released in October 2008. According to IDC, as of June 2015, Android had 82.8% of the global smartphone market share, compared to 13.9% for Apple and 2.6% for Microsoft.[1] Over one billion Android devices shipped in 2014 alone.[2] At the 2015 Google I/O conference, Google announced that in the prior 12 months there had been 50 billion app installs from Google Play™—Google's marketplace for Android apps.[3] Fierce competition among popular mobile platforms and carriers is leading to rapid innovation and falling prices. In addition, competition among the hundreds of Android device manufacturers is driving hardware and software innovation within the Android community.

Architecture of *Android How to Program, 3/e*

Android How to Program, 3/e was formed by merging

- our professional book *Android 6 for Programmers: An App-Driven Approach, 3/e*, published by the Pearson Technology Group

- condensed, introductory object-oriented Java programming content from our college textbook *Java How to Program, 9/e*, published by Pearson Higher Education

- hundreds of Android short-answer questions and app-development exercises we created for this book—most are in the book and many of the short-answer questions are in the test-item file for instructors.

We scoured the Android material, especially the fully coded Android apps, and enumerated the Java features that you'll need to build these and similar apps. Then we extracted the corresponding Java content from *Java How to Program, 9/e*. That's a 1500-page book, so it was challenging to whittle down that much content and keep it friendly for programming novices.

---

1. http://www.idc.com/prodserv/smartphone-os-market-share.jsp.
2. http://www.businessinsider.com/android-1-billion-shipments-2014-strategy-analytics-2015-2.
3. http://bit.ly/2015GoogleIOKeynote.

When you study the Android content, you'll be thinking like a developer from the start. You'll build real stuff and you'll face the kinds of challenges professional developers must deal with. We'll point you to the online documentation and forums where you can find additional information and get answers to your questions. We also encourage you to read, modify and enhance open-source code as part of your learning process.

App-Driven Approach

At the heart of the book is our *app-driven approach*—we present concepts in the context of *eight complete working Android apps*. We begin each of the app chapters with an *introduction* to the app, an app *test-drive* showing one or more *sample executions*, and a *technologies overview*. We build the app's *GUI* and *resource files*. Then we proceed with a detailed *code walkthrough* of the app's source code in which we discuss the programming concepts and demonstrate the functionality of the Android APIs used in the app. All the source code is available at http://www.deitel.com/books/AndroidHTP3 and at the book's Companion Website http://www.pearsonhighered.com/deitel. We recommend that you have the source code open in the IDE as you read the book. Figure 1 lists the book's apps and the key technologies we used to build each.

App	Technologies
Chapter 2, **Welcome** App	Android Studio, visual GUI design, layouts, TextViews, ImageViews, accessibility, internationalization.
Chapter 3, **Tip Calculator** App	GridLayout, EditText, SeekBar, event handling, NumberFormat, customizing themes, defining app functionality with Java.
Chapter 4, **Flag Quiz** App	Fragments, Menus, Preferences, explicit Intents, Handler, AssetManager, tweened animations, Animators, Toasts, color state lists, layouts for multiple device orientations, logging error messages for debugging.
Chapter 5, **Doodlz** App	Two-dimensional graphics, Canvas, Bitmap, accelerometer, SensorManager, multitouch events, MediaStore, printing, Android 6.0 permissions.
Chapter 6, **Cannon Game** App	Manual frame-by-frame animation, graphics, sound, threading, SurfaceView and SurfaceHolder, immersive mode and full-screen layouts.
Chapter 7, **Weather Viewer** App	REST web services, AsyncTask, HttpUrlConnection, processing JSON, JSONObject, JSONArray, ListView, ArrayAdapter, ViewHolder pattern, TextInputLayout, FloatingActionButton.
Chapter 8, **Twitter® Searches** App	SharedPreferences, SharedPreferences.Editor, implicit Intents, Intent Choosers, RecyclerView, RecyclerView.Adapter, RecyclerView.ViewHolder, RecyclerView.ItemDecoration.
Chapter 9, **Address Book** App	FragmentTransactions and the Fragment back stack, SQLite, SQLiteDatabase, SQLiteOpenHelper, ContentProvider, ContentResolver, Loader, LoaderManager, Cursor and GUI Styles

Fig. 1 | *Android How to Program, 3/e* apps.

Intended Audiences

There are several audiences for this book. Most commonly, it will be used in upper-level elective college courses and industry professional courses for people familiar with object-oriented programming but who may or may not know Java and want to learn Android app development.

Uniquely, the book can also be used in introductory courses like CS1, intended for programming novices. We recommend that schools typically offering many sections of CS1 in Java consider designating one or two sections for ambitious students who have at least some prior programming experience and who want to work hard to learn a good amount of Java and Android in an aggressively paced one-semester course. The schools may want to list the courses with "honors" or "accelerated" designations. The book will work especially well in two-semester introductory programming sequences where the introduction to Java is covered first.

Instructor Resources

The following **supplements are available to qualified college instructors only** through Pearson Education's Instructor Resource Center (http://www.pearsonhighered.com/irc):

- *PowerPoint® slides* containing the code and figures in the text.
- *Test Item File* of short-answer questions.
- *Solutions Manual* with solutions to the end-of-chapter **short-answer exercises** for *both* the Java and Android content. For the Java content, solutions also are provided for *most* of the programming exercises.

   The suggested Android app-development project exercises are *not* typical homework problems. These tend to be *substantial* projects—many of which could require weeks of effort, possibly with students working in teams, as is common in industry. We do not provide solutions for these exercises. Please contact us at deitel@deitel.com if you have any questions.

Please do not write to us requesting access to the Pearson Instructor's Resource Center. Access is restricted to qualified college instructors teaching from the book. Instructors may obtain access *only* through their Pearson representatives. If you're not a registered faculty member, contact your Pearson representative or visit

   http://www.pearsonhighered.com/educator/replocator/

Before You Begin: Software Used in *Android How to Program, 3/e*

For information on configuring your computer so that you can develop apps with Java and Android, see the Before You Begin section that follows this Preface.

Getting up to Speed in Java and XML

The Android portion of this book assumes that you already know Java and object-oriented programming. We use only complete, working apps, so if you don't know Java but have object-oriented programming experience in a C-based language such as C++, C#, Swift or Objective-C you should be able to master the material quickly, learning a good amount of Java and Java-style object-oriented programming along the way.

If you do not know Java or another object-oriented programming language, the appendices provide a friendly introduction to Java and the object-oriented programming techniques you'll need to develop Android apps. If you're interested in learning Java in more depth, you may want to check out the comprehensive treatment in our textbook *Java How to Program, 10/e* (http://www.deitel.com/books/jhtp10). If you're not familiar with XML, many free online tutorials are available, including:

- http://bit.ly/DeitelXMLBasics
- http://bit.ly/StructureXMLData

App-Development Courses

In 2007, Stanford University offered a new course called Creating Engaging Facebook Apps. Students worked in teams developing apps, several of which landed in Facebook's top 10, earning some of the student developers millions of dollars.[4] This course gained wide recognition for encouraging student creativity and team-oriented app development. Scores of colleges now offer app-development courses across many social media and mobile platforms such as Android and iOS. We encourage instructors to read the online mobile app development syllabi and check out the YouTube™ videos created by instructors and students for many of these courses.

Key Topics

Here are some of this book's other key topics:

Android 6 SDK. We cover various new Android 6 Software Development Kit (SDK) features.

Android Studio IDE. The free Android Studio (based on IntelliJ IDEA Community Edition) is now Google's preferred IDE for Android app development (the original Android development tools were based on the Eclipse IDE). Android Studio, combined with the free Android Software Development Kit (SDK) and the free Java Development Kit (JDK), provide all the software you'll need to create, run and debug Android apps, export them for distribution (e.g., upload them to Google Play™) and more. See the Before You Begin section after this Preface for download and installation instructions for all this software.

Material Design. With Android 5, Google introduced its new Android look-and-feel, based on their material design specification:

> http://www.google.com/design/spec/material-design/introduction.html

In the specification, Google presents material design's goals and principles, then provides details on animation techniques, styling on-screen elements, positioning elements, uses of specific user-interface components, user-interaction patterns, accessibility, internationalization and more. Google uses material-design principles in its mobile and browser-based apps.

Material design is a massive topic. In this book, we focus on the following aspects:

- Using Android's built-in *Material themes*—these give Android's built-in user-interface components a look-and-feel consistent with material design principles.

---

4. http://www.businessinsider.com/these-stanford-students-made-millions-taking-a-class-on-facebook-2011-5.

- Using built-in Android Studio *app templates*—these are designed by Google to adhere to material design principles.

- Using *user-interface components*, as appropriate, that are recommended by the material design guidelines for specific purposes, such as `FloatingActionButtons`, `TextInputLayouts` and `RecyclerViews`.

In addition to Google's material design specification, you may want to read the book *Android User Interface Design: Implementing Material Design for Developers, 2nd Edition*:

    http://bit.ly/IanCliftonMaterialDesign

by our professional colleague and past *Android for Programmers* reviewer Ian Clifton. From Ian: "Google announced the material design guidelines in 2014, creating a design system that suggested how an app should look as well as behave. The goal was to provide a design framework that would improve the visual appearance of all apps and create a behavioral consistency that did not exist previously across apps. *Android User Interface Design: Implementing Material Design for Developers, 2nd Edition* covers material design in detail, making user-centered design, color theory, typography, interaction patterns and other aspects of design accessible to all developers."

Support and App Compatibility Libraries. A big challenge developers face when using new Android features is backward compatibility with earlier Android platforms. Many new Android features are now introduced via support libraries. These enable you to use new features in apps targeting current *and* past Android platforms. One such library is the App-Compat library. Android Studio's app templates have been updated to use the `AppCompat` library and its themes, enabling the new apps you create to run on most Android devices. By creating apps with the `AppCompat` library from the start, you avoid having to reimplement your code if you decide to support older Android versions to target a wider audience.

In addition, at the 2015 Google I/O developer conference, Google introduced the Android Design Support Library

    http://android-developers.blogspot.com/2015/05/android-design-
    support-library.html

for using material design in Android 2.1 and higher. Material design support also is built into most of Android Studio's app templates.

REST Web Services and JSON. Chapter 7 presents our **Weather Viewer** app, which demonstrates how to invoke REST (Representational State Transfer) web services—in this case, the 16-day weather-forecast web service from `OpenWeatherMap.org`. This service returns the weather forecast in JSON (JavaScript Object Notation)—a popular text-based data-interchange format used to represent objects as key–value pairs of data. The app also uses classes from the `org.json` package to process the web service's JSON response.

Android 6.0 Permissions. Android 6.0 has a new permissions model that's designed for a better user experience. Before Android 6.0, a user was required at installation time to grant *in advance* all permissions that an app would ever need, which often discouraged users from installing apps. With the new model, the app is installed without asking for any permissions. Instead, the user is asked to grant a permission only the *first* time the corresponding feature is used. Chapter 5 introduces the new permissions model and uses it to request permission from the user to store an image on the device's external storage.

Fragments. Starting with Chapter 4, we use `Fragments` to create and manage portions of each app's GUI. You can combine several fragments to create user interfaces that take advantage of tablet screen sizes. Also, you can easily interchange fragments to make your GUIs more dynamic, as you'll do in Chapter 9.

View-Holder Pattern, `ListView` and `RecyclerView`. The apps in Chapters 7–9 each display scrollable lists of data. Chapter 7 presents the data in a `ListView` and introduces the view-holder pattern, which improves scrolling performance by reusing GUI components that scroll off-screen. With `ListView`s, using the view-holder pattern is recommended. Chapters 8 and 9 each present a list of data in the more flexible and more efficient `RecyclerView` for which the view-holder pattern is required.

Printing. We demonstrate class `PrintHelper` from Android's printing framework for printing from an app (Chapter 5). Class `PrintHelper` provides a user interface for selecting a printer, has a method for determining whether a given device supports printing and provides a method for printing a `Bitmap`. `PrintHelper` is part of the Android Support Library.

Immersive Mode. Chapter 6's **Cannon Game** app uses immersive mode to hide the system bars at the screen's top and bottom, allowing the game to fill the screen. Users can access the system bars by swiping down from the top of the screen.

Testing on Android Smartphones, Tablets and the Android Emulator. For the best app-development experience and results, you should test your apps on actual Android smartphones and tablets. You can still have a meaningful experience using just the Android emulator (see the Before You Begin section); however, it's processor intensive and can be slow, particularly with games that have a lot of moving parts. In Chapter 1, we mention some Android features that are not supported on the emulator.

Cloud Test Lab. Google is working on a new *Cloud Test Lab*—an online site for testing your apps across a wide range of devices, device orientations, locales, spoken languages and network conditions. You'll be able to run automated tests and receive detailed reports containing screenshots and videos of your app in action, as well as error logs to help you find problems and improve your apps. For more information and to sign up to be notified when Cloud Test Lab becomes available, visit:

```
http://developers.google.com/cloud-test-lab/
```

Android Wear and Android TV. Android Wear runs on smart watches. Android TV runs directly on some smart TVs and on media players that you can connect to your TV (typically via HDMI cables). Many Android techniques we present also apply to Android Wear and Android TV app development. The Android SDK provides Android Wear and Android TV emulators, so you can test your apps for these platforms, even if you don't have devices. To learn more about these technologies from the developer perspective, visit:

```
http://developer.android.com/wear/index.html
```

for Android Wear and

```
http://developer.android.com/tv/index.html
```

for Android TV.

Multimedia. The book's apps use a range of Android multimedia capabilities, including graphics, images, frame-by-frame animation and audio.

Uploading Apps to Google Play. Chapter 10, Google Play and App Business Issues, discusses Google Play and setting up a merchant account so you can sell your apps. You'll learn how to prepare apps for submission to Google Play, find tips for pricing your apps, and find resources for monetizing them with in-app advertising and in-app sales of virtual goods. You'll also find resources for marketing your apps. Chapter 10 can be read after Chapter 1.

Java Exception Handling. We integrate basic exception handling early in the Java content then present a richer treatment in Appendix H; we use exception handling throughout the Android chapters.

Classes `Arrays` and `ArrayList`; Collections. Appendix E covers class `Arrays`—which contains methods for performing common array manipulations—and generic class `Array-List`—which implements a dynamically resizable array-like data structure. Appendix J introduces Java's generic collections that are used frequently in our Android treatment.

Java Multithreading. Maintaining app responsiveness is a key to building robust Android apps and requires extensive use of Android multithreading. Appendix J introduces multithreading fundamentals so that you can understand our use of the Android `AsyncTask` class in Chapter 7.

GUI Presentation. Appendix I introduces Java GUI development. Android provides its own GUI components, so this appendix presents a few Java GUI components and focuses on nested classes and anonymous inner classes, which are used extensively for event-handling in Android GUIs.

Pedagogic Features

Syntax Shading. For readability, we syntax shade the code, similar to Android Studio's use of syntax coloring. Our syntax-shading conventions are as follows:

```
comments appear like this
keywords appear like this
constants and literal values appear like this
all other code appears like this
```

Code Highlighting. We emphasize the key code segments in each program by enclosing them in light gray rectangles.

Using Fonts for Emphasis. We use various font conventions:

- The defining occurrences of key terms appear in **bold** for easy reference.
- On-screen IDE components appear in **bold Helvetica** (e.g., the **File** menu).
- Program source code appears in Lucida (e.g., int x = 5;).

In this book you'll create GUIs using a combination of visual programming (point-and-click, drag-and-drop) and writing code. We use different fonts when we refer to GUI elements in program code versus GUI elements displayed in the IDE:

- When we refer to a GUI component that we create in a program, we place its class name and object name in a Lucida font—e.g., Button saveContactButton.

- When we refer to a GUI component that's part of the IDE, we place the component's text in a **bold Helvetica** font and use a plain text font for the component's type—e.g., "the **File** menu" or "the **Run** button."

Using the > Character. We use the > character to indicate selecting a menu item from a menu. For example, we use the notation **File > New** to indicate that you should select the **New** menu item from the **File** menu.

Source Code. The book's source code is available for download from the following sites

```
http://www.deitel.com/books/AndroidHTP3
http://www.pearsonhighered.com/deitel
```

Documentation. The Android documentation, which we reference frequently, is available at

```
http://developer.android.com
```

An overview of Android Studio is available at

```
http://developer.android.com/tools/studio/index.html
```

Chapter Objectives. Each chapter begins with a list of learning objectives.

Figures. Numerous tables, source-code listings and screenshots are included.

Software Engineering. We stress program clarity and performance, and we concentrate on building well-engineered, object-oriented software.

Self-Review Exercises and Answers. Extensive self-review exercises *and* answers are included for self study.

Exercises with a Current Flair. We've worked hard to create topical Android app-development exercises. You'll create apps using a broad array of current technologies. All of the Android programming exercises require the implementation of complete apps. You'll be asked to enhance the existing chapter apps, develop similar apps, use your creativity to develop your own apps that use the chapter technologies and build new apps based on open-source apps available on the Internet (**be sure to read and comply with the open-source code-license terms for any app you modify**). The Android exercises also include short-answer fill-in and true/false questions.

In the Java exercises, you'll be asked to recall important terms and concepts; indicate what code segments do; indicate what's wrong with a portion of code; write Java statements, methods and classes; and write complete Java programs.

Index. We include an extensive index for reference. The page number of the defining occurrence of each key term in the book is highlighted in the index in **bold**.

Working with Open-Source Apps

The numerous free, open-source Android apps available online are excellent resources for learning Android app development. We encourage you to download open-source apps and read their source code to understand how they work. Some of the apps in the programming exercises can be implemented by modifying or enhancing existing open-source apps. Our goal is to give you handles on interesting problems that may also inspire you to create new apps using the same technologies.

Caution: The terms of open source licenses vary considerably. Some allow you to use the app's source code freely for any purpose, while others stipulate that the code is available for personal use only—not for creating for-sale or publicly available apps. **Be sure to read the licensing agreements carefully. If you wish to create a commercial app based on an open-source app, you should consider having an intellectual property attorney read the license; be aware that these attorneys charge significant fees.**

Copyright Notice and Code License

All of the Android code and Android apps in the book are copyrighted by Deitel & Associates, Inc. The sample Android apps in the book are licensed under a Creative Commons Attribution 3.0 Unported License (http://creativecommons.org/licenses/by/3.0), *with the exception that they may not be reused in any way in educational tutorials and textbooks, whether in print or digital format.*

Additionally, the authors and publisher make no warranty of any kind, expressed or implied, with regard to these programs or to the documentation contained in this book. The authors and publisher shall not be liable in any event for incidental or consequential damages in connection with, or arising out of, the furnishing, performance, or use of these programs. You're welcome to use the apps in the book as shells for your own apps, building on their existing functionality (within the terms of the preceding license). If you have any questions, contact the authors at deitel@deitel.com.

Android 6 App-Development Fundamentals LiveLessons Video Training

Our *Android 6 App-Development Fundamentals, Parts I and II* LiveLessons videos show you what you need to know to start building robust, powerful Android apps with Android 6, the Java programming language and Android Studio. Included are approximately 16–20 hours of expert training synchronized with this book's Before You Begin section, Section 1.9 and the apps presented in Chapters 2–9. For additional information about Deitel LiveLessons video products, visit

    http://www.deitel.com/livelessons

or contact us at deitel@deitel.com. You also can access our LiveLessons videos if you have a subscription to SafariBooksOnline.com. For a free 10-day trial, register at

    http://www.safaribooksonline.com/register

Join the Deitel & Associates, Inc. Social Media Communities

To receive updates on this and our other publications, online Resource Centers, instructor-led on-site training courses and more, join the Deitel social media communities on

- Facebook®—http://facebook.com/DeitelFan
- Twitter®—http://twitter.com/deitel
- LinkedIn®—http://bit.ly/DeitelLinkedIn
- YouTube®—http://youtube.com/DeitelTV
- Google+™—http://google.com/+DeitelFan

and subscribe to the *Deitel® Buzz Online* newsletter

    http://www.deitel.com/newsletter/subscribe.html

Contacting the Authors

We'd sincerely appreciate your comments, criticisms, corrections and suggestions for improvement. Please address all questions and other correspondence to

    deitel@deitel.com

We'll respond promptly and post corrections and clarifications as Android evolves at:

    http://www.deitel.com/books/AndroidHTP3

and on Facebook, LinkedIn, Twitter, Google+ and the *Deitel® Buzz Online*.
Visit http://www.deitel.com to

- download code examples
- check out our growing list of online programming Resource Centers
- receive updates for this book by subscribing to the free *Deitel® Buzz Online* e-mail newsletter at http://www.deitel.com/newsletter/subscribe.html
- receive information on our instructor-led programming-language training courses offered at customer sites worldwide.

Acknowledgments

Thanks to Barbara Deitel for long hours devoted to this project—she created all of our Android Resource Centers and patiently researched hundreds of technical details.

We're fortunate to have worked with the dedicated team of publishing professionals at Pearson Higher Education. We appreciate the guidance, wisdom and energy of Tracy Johnson, Executive Editor, Computer Science. Tracy and her team publish our college textbooks. We also appreciate the efforts and 20-year mentorship of our friend and professional colleague Mark L. Taub, Editor-in-Chief of the Pearson Technology Group. Mark and his team publish all of our professional books and LiveLessons video products. Michelle Housley recruited distinguished members of the Android community to review the manuscript. We selected the cover art and Chuti Prasertsith designed the cover. Bob Engelhardt did a wonderful job bringing the book to publication.

We'd like to thank Alexander Wald, a Deitel summer intern and co-author of our professional book, *Android 6 for Programmers: An App-Driven Approach*. He helped us convert the previous edition of that book and our Android apps from Android 4.3 and 4.4 using Eclipse to Android 6 using Android Studio. Alexander is currently pursuing a B.S. in Computer Science at Worcester Polytechnic Institute with a minor in Electrical Engineering. He became interested in mathematics and the sciences at an early age and has been writing code for approximately nine years. He's motivated by his passion to be creative and innovative and his interest in sharing his knowledge with others.

We'd also like to thank Michael Morgano, a former colleague of ours at Deitel & Associates, Inc., now an Android developer at PHHHOTO, who co-authored the first editions of this book and our book, *iPhone for Programmers: An App-Driven Approach*. Michael is an extraordinarily talented software development professional.

Finally, thanks to Abbey Deitel, former President of Deitel & Associates, Inc., and a graduate of Carnegie Mellon University's Tepper School of Management where she received a B.S. in Industrial Management. Abbey managed the business operations of Deitel & Associates, Inc. for 17 years, along the way co-authoring a number of our publications, including the previous *Android How to Program* editions' versions of Chapters 1 and 10.

Reviewers of the Content from Android How to Program *and* Android 6 for Programmers: An App-Driven Approach *Recent Editions*

We'd like to thank the following academics and professionals who reviewed this book and/ or its previous editions. They scrutinized the text and the code and provided countless suggestions for improving the presentation: Paul Beusterien (Principal, Mobile Developer Solutions), Eric J. Bowden, COO (Safe Driving Systems, LLC), Tony Cantrell (Georgia Northwestern Technical College), Ian G. Clifton (Independent Contractor, Android App Developer and author of *Android User Interface Design: Implementing Material Design for Developers, 2nd Edition*), Daniel Galpin (Android Advocate and author of *Intro to Android Application Development*), Jim Hathaway (Application Developer, Kellogg Company), Douglas Jones (Senior Software Engineer, Fullpower Technologies), Charles Lasky (Nagautuck Community College), Enrique Lopez-Manas (Lead Android Architect, Sixt, and Computer Science Teacher at the University of Alcalá in Madrid), Sebastian Nykopp (Chief Architect, Reaktor), Michael Pardo (Android Developer, Mobiata), Luis Ramirez (Lead Android Engineer at Reverb), Ronan "Zero" Schwarz (CIO, OpenIntents), Arijit Sengupta (Wright State University), Donald Smith (Columbia College), Jesus Ubaldo Quevedo-Torrero (University of Wisconsin, Parkside), Dawn Wick (Southwestern Community College) and Frank Xu (Gannon University).

Well, there you have it! *Android How to Program, 3/e* will quickly get you started developing Android apps with Android 6 and Android Studio. We hope you enjoy reading the book as much as we enjoyed writing it!

Paul Deitel
Harvey Deitel

About the Authors

Paul Deitel, CEO and Chief Technical Officer of Deitel & Associates, Inc., has over 30 years experience in computing and is a graduate of MIT, where he studied Information Technology. He holds the Java Certified Programmer and Java Certified Developer designations and is an Oracle Java Champion. Paul was named as a Microsoft® Most Valuable Professional (MVP) for C# in 2012–2014. Through Deitel & Associates, Inc., he has delivered hundreds of programming courses worldwide to clients, including Cisco, IBM, Siemens, Sun Microsystems, Dell, Fidelity, NASA at the Kennedy Space Center, the National Severe Storm Laboratory, White Sands Missile Range, Rogue Wave Software, Boeing, SunGard, Nortel Networks, Puma, iRobot, Invensys and many more. He and his co-author, Dr. Harvey Deitel, are the world's best-selling programming-language textbook/ professional book/video authors.

Dr. Harvey Deitel, Chairman and Chief Strategy Officer of Deitel & Associates, Inc., has over 50 years of experience in the computer field. Dr. Deitel earned B.S. and M.S. degrees in Electrical Engineering from MIT and a Ph.D. in Mathematics from Boston University—he studied computing in each of these programs before they spun off Computer Science departments. He has extensive college teaching experience, including earning tenure and serving as the Chairman of the Computer Science Department at Boston College before founding Deitel & Associates, Inc., in 1991 with his son, Paul. The Deitels' publications have earned international recognition, with translations published in Japanese, German, Russian, Spanish, French, Polish, Italian, Simplified Chinese, Traditional Chinese, Korean, Portuguese, Greek, Urdu and Turkish. Dr. Deitel has delivered hundreds of programming courses to corporate, academic, government and military clients.

About Deitel & Associates, Inc.

Deitel & Associates, Inc., founded by Paul Deitel and Harvey Deitel, is an internationally recognized authoring and corporate training organization, specializing in Android and iOS app development, computer programming languages and Internet and web software technology. The company's clients include many of the world's largest corporations, as well as government agencies, branches of the military, and academic institutions. The company offers instructor-led training courses delivered at client sites worldwide on major programming languages and platforms, including Android app development, iOS app development, Java™, Swift™, C++, C, Visual C#®, Visual Basic®, and Internet and web programming.

Through its 40-year publishing partnership with Prentice Hall/Pearson, Deitel & Associates, Inc., publishes leading-edge programming professional books, college textbooks, e-books, interactive e-learning and *LiveLessons* video courses. Deitel & Associates, Inc. and the authors can be reached at:

> deitel@deitel.com

To learn more about Deitel's Corporate Training curriculum, visit

> http://www.deitel.com/training

To request a proposal for worldwide on-site, instructor-led training at your organization, send an e-mail to deitel@deitel.com.

Individuals wishing to purchase Deitel publications can do so via links posted at http://www.deitel.com and through http://informit.com, http://amazon.com, http://barnesandnoble.com and other major booksellers. Bulk orders by corporations, the government, the military and academic institutions should be placed directly with Pearson. For more information, visit

> http://www.informit.com/store/sales.aspx

In this section, you'll set up your computer for use with this book. Google frequently updates the Android™ development tools, so before reading this section, check

> http://www.deitel.com/books/AndroidHTP3

to see if we've posted an updated version of this Before You Begin section.

Software and Hardware System Requirements

To develop Android apps, you need a Windows®, Linux® or Mac® OS X® system. To view the latest operating-system requirements visit

> http://developer.android.com/sdk/index.html#Requirements

We developed the apps in this book using the following software:

- Java SE Software Development Kit (JDK)
- Android Studio 1.4 Integrated Development Environment (IDE)
- Android 6 SDK (API 23)

You'll see how to obtain each of these in the following sections.

Installing the Java Development Kit (JDK)

Android versions 5 and higher require the Java Development Kit version 7 (JDK 7). All Java language features in JDK 7 are supported in Android Studio, however the try-with-resources statement is supported only for Android platform versions with API levels 19 (Android 4.4) and higher. To download JDK 7 for Windows, OS X or Linux, go to

> http://www.oracle.com/technetwork/java/javase/downloads/java-
>   archive-downloads-javase7-521261.html

Choose the appropriate 32-bit or 64-bit version for your computer hardware and operating system. Be sure to follow the installation instructions at

> http://docs.oracle.com/javase/7/docs/webnotes/install/index.html

Android does not yet support Java 8 language features, such as lambda expressions, new interface features and the stream APIs. You can use JDK 8 (as we did when developing this book's apps), provided that you do not use any Java 8 language features in your code.

Setting the PATH Environment Variable

The PATH environment variable on your computer designates which directories the computer searches when looking for applications, such as the applications that enable you to compile and run your Java applications (called javac and java, respectively). *Carefully fol-*

low the installation instructions for Java on your platform to ensure that you set the PATH environment variable correctly. The steps for setting environment variables differ by operating system and sometimes by operating system version (e.g., Windows 7 vs. Windows 10). Instructions for various platforms are listed at:

```
http://www.java.com/en/download/help/path.xml
```

If you do not set the PATH variable correctly on Windows and some Linux installations, when you use the JDK's tools, you'll receive a message like:

```
'java' is not recognized as an internal or external command,
operable program or batch file.
```

In this case, go back to the installation instructions for setting the PATH and recheck your steps. If you've downloaded a newer version of the JDK, you may need to change the name of the JDK's installation directory in the PATH variable.

JDK Installation Directory and the bin Subdirectory

The JDK's installation directory varies by platform. The directories listed below are for Oracle's JDK 7 update 80 (the most current version at the time of this writing):

- 32-bit JDK on Windows:
  `C:\Program Files (x86)\Java\jdk1.7.0_80`

- 64-bit JDK on Windows:
  `C:\Program Files\Java\jdk1.7.0_80`

- Mac OS X:
  `/Library/Java/JavaVirtualMachines/jdk1.7.0_80.jdk/Contents/Home`

- Ubuntu Linux:
  `/usr/lib/jvm/java-7-oracle`

The JDK installation folder's name might differ if you're using a different update of JDK 7 or using JDK 8. For Linux, the install location depends on the installer you use and possibly the version of Linux that you use. We used Ubuntu Linux.

The PATH environment variable must point to the JDK installation directory's bin subdirectory. When setting the PATH, be sure to use the proper installation-directory name for the *version of the JDK you installed*. As JDK updates become available, the installation-directory name changes to include the *updated version number*.

Setting the CLASSPATH Environment Variable

If you attempt to run a Java program and receive a message like

```
Exception in thread "main" java.lang.NoClassDefFoundError: YourClass
```

then your system has a CLASSPATH environment variable that must be modified. To fix the preceding error, follow the steps in setting the PATH environment variable to locate the CLASSPATH variable, then edit the variable's value to include the local directory—typically represented as a dot (.). On Windows add

```
.;
```

at the beginning of the CLASSPATH's value (with no spaces before or after these characters). On other platforms, replace the semicolon with the appropriate path separator characters—typically a colon (:).

Installing Android Studio

Android Studio comes with the latest Android Software Development Kit (SDK) and is based on the popular Java IDE from JetBrains called IntelliJ® IDEA. To download, go to

```
http://developer.android.com/sdk/index.html
```

and click the **Download Android Studio** button. When the download completes, run the installer and follow the on-screen instructions to complete the installation. If you previously installed an earlier Android Studio version, a **Complete Installation** window will appear at the end of the install process and give you the option to import your previous settings. At the time of this writing, Android Studio 1.4 is the current released version and Android Studio 1.5 is available as an early access release.

Configure Android Studio to Show Line Numbers

By default, Android Studio does not show line numbers next to the code that you write. To turn on line numbers to make it easier to follow our line-numbered code examples:

1. Open Android Studio ( ).

2. When the **Welcome to Android Studio** window appears, click **Configure**, then click **Settings** to open the **Default Settings** window. If the **Welcome to Android Studio** window does not appear, use the menus on Mac to select **Android Studio > Preferences…** or on Windows/Linux to select **File > Other Settings > Default Settings….**

3. Expand the **Editor > General** node and select **Appearance**, then ensure that **Show line numbers** is selected and click **OK**.

Configure Android Studio to Disallow Code Folding

By default, Android Studio's code-folding feature is enabled. This feature collapses multiple lines of code into a single line so you can focus on other aspects of the code. For example, all the import statements in a Java source-code file can be collapsed into a single line to hide them, or an entire method can be collapsed into a single line. You can expand these lines if you need to look at the code in detail. We disabled this feature in our IDE. If you wish to do so, follow the steps in the preceding section, then under **Editor > General > Code Folding** uncheck **Show code folding outline**.

Android 6 SDK

This book's code examples were written using Android 6. At the time of this writing, the Android 6 SDK was bundled with Android Studio. As new Android versions are released, the latest version will be bundled, which may prevent our apps from compiling properly. When you work with this book, we recommend using Android 6. You can install prior Android platform versions as follows:

1. Open Android Studio ( ).

2. When the **Welcome to Android Studio** window appears, click **Configure**, then click **SDK Manager** to display the **Android SDK** manager. If a project window appears rather than the **Welcome to Android Studio** window, you can access the **Android SDK** manager via **Tools > Android > SDK Manager**.

3. In the SDK Platforms tab, check the versions of Android you wish to install, then click **Apply** and **OK**. The IDE then downloads and installs the additional platform versions. The IDE also will help you keep your installed versions up to date.

Creating Android Virtual Devices (AVDs)

The Android SDK's **Android emulator** allows you to test apps on your computer rather than on an Android device—this is essential, of course, if you do not have Android devices. To do so, you create Android Virtual Devices (AVDs) that run in the emulator. The emulator can be slow, so most Android developers prefer testing on actual devices. Also, the emulator does not support various features, including phone calls, USB connections, headphones and Bluetooth. For the latest emulator capabilities and limitations, visit

> http://developer.android.com/tools/devices/emulator.html

That page's **Using Hardware Acceleration** section discusses features that can improve emulator performance, such as using the computer's graphics processing unit (GPU) to increase graphics performance, and using the Intel HAXM (hardware accelerated execution manager) emulator to increase overall AVD performance. There are also faster third-party emulators, such as Genymotion.

After you've installed the Android Studio and before you run an app in the emulator, you must create at least one **Android Virtual Device (AVD)** for Android 6. Each AVD defines the characteristics of the device you wish to emulate, including

- its screen size in pixels
- its pixel density
- its screen's physical size
- the size of the SD card for data storage
- and more.

To test your apps for multiple Android devices, you can create AVDs that emulate each unique device. You also can use Google's new Cloud Test Lab

> https://developers.google.com/cloud-test-lab/

a website that will enable you to upload your app and test it on many of today's popular Android devices. By default, Android Studio creates for you one AVD that's configured to use the version of Android bundled with the IDE. For this book, we use AVDs for two of Google's Android reference devices—the Nexus 6 phone and the Nexus 9 tablet—which run standard Android without the modifications made by many device manufacturers. It's easiest to create AVDs in Android Studio once you already have a project open in the IDE. For this reason, we'll show how to create the Android 6 AVDs in Section 1.9.

Setting Up an Android Device for Testing Apps

Testing apps on Android devices tends to be quicker than using AVDs. In addition, recall that there are some features you can test only on actual devices. To execute your apps on Android devices, follow the instructions at

```
http://developer.android.com/tools/device.html
```

If you're developing on Microsoft Windows, you'll also need the Windows USB driver for Android devices that you installed earlier in this Before You Begin section. In some cases on Windows, you may also need the manufacturer's device-specific USB drivers. For a list of USB driver sites for various device brands, visit

```
http://developer.android.com/tools/extras/oem-usb.html
```

Downloading the Book's Code Examples

The source code for *Android How to Program, 3/e* is available for download at

```
http://www.deitel.com/books/AndroidHTP3/
```

Click the **Download Code Examples** link to download a ZIP archive file containing the examples to your computer. Depending on your operating system, double click the ZIP file to unzip the archive or right click and select the option to extract the archive's contents. Remember where the extracted files are located on your system so you can access them later.

A Note Regarding Android Studio and the Android SDK

If you import one of our apps into Android Studio and receive an error message, this could be the result of updates to Android Studio or the Android platform tools. For such issues, please check Android questions and answers on StackOverflow at:

```
http://stackoverflow.com/questions/tagged/android
```

and the Google+ Android Development community at:

```
http://bit.ly/GoogleAndroidDevelopment
```

or write to us at

```
deitel@deitel.com
```

You've now installed all the software and downloaded the code examples you'll need to study Android app development with *Android How to Program, 3/e* and to begin developing your own apps. Enjoy!

Introduction to Android

1

Objectives

In this chapter you'll be introduced to:

- The history of Android and the Android SDK.
- Google Play Store for downloading apps.
- The Android packages used in this book to help you create Android apps.
- A quick refresher of object-technology concepts.
- Key software for Android app development, including the Android SDK, the Java SDK and the Android Studio Integrated Development Environment (IDE).
- Important Android documentation.
- Test-driving an Android tip-calculator app in Android Studio.
- Characteristics of great Android apps.

1.1 Introduction

Welcome to Android app development! We hope that working with *Android How to Program* will be an informative, challenging, entertaining and rewarding experience for you.

The Android portion of this book is geared toward people who know *Java object-oriented programming*. If you do not know Java or another object-oriented programming language, the appendices provide a friendly introduction to Java and the object-oriented programming techniques you'll need to develop Android apps. We use only complete working Android apps, so if you have object-oriented programming experience in another language, such as C#, Objective-C/Cocoa or C++ (with class libraries), you should be able to master the material quickly, learning a good amount of Java and Java-style object-oriented programming as you learn Android app development.

App-Driven Approach

We use an **app-driven approach**—new features are discussed in the context of complete working Android apps, with one app per chapter. For each app, we first describe it, then have you *test-drive* it. Next, we briefly overview the key **Android Studio IDE** (Integrated Development Environment), Java and **Android SDK** (Software Development Kit) technologies we use to implement the app. For apps that require it, we walk through designing the GUI using Android Studio. Then we provide the complete source-code listing, using line numbers, *syntax shading* and *code highlighting* to emphasize the key portions of the code. We also show one or more screenshots of the running app. Then we do a detailed code walkthrough, emphasizing the new programming concepts introduced in the app. You can download the source code for all of the book's apps from

http://www.deitel.com/books/AndroidHTP3/

1.2 Android—The World's Leading Mobile Operating System

Android device sales are growing quickly, creating enormous opportunities for Android app developers.

- The first-generation Android phones were released in October 2008. As of June 2015, Android had 82.8% of the global smartphone market share, compared to 13.9% for Apple and 2.6% for Microsoft.[1]

- Billions of apps have been downloaded from Google Play and more than one billion Android devices were shipped worldwide in 2014.[2]

- According to *PC World*, approximately 230 million tablets shipped in 2014 of which 67.3% were Android tablets, compared to 27.6% for iOS and 5.1% for Microsoft Windows.[3]

- Android devices now include smartphones, tablets, e-readers, robots, jet engines, NASA satellites, game consoles, refrigerators, televisions, cameras, health-care devices, smartwatches, automobile in-vehicle "infotainment" systems (for controlling the radio, GPS, phone calls, thermostat, etc.) and more.[4]

- A recent report says that mobile app revenue (across all mobile platforms) is expected to reach reach $99 billion by 2019.[5]

1.3 Android Features

Openness and Open Source

One benefit of developing Android apps is the openness of the platform. The operating system is *open source* and free. This allows you to view Android's source code and see how its features are implemented. You can contribute to Android by reporting bugs:

http://source.android.com/source/report-bugs.html

or by participating in the Open Source Project discussion groups

http://source.android.com/community/index.html

Numerous open-source Android apps from Google and others are available on the Internet (Fig. 1.1). Figure 1.2 shows you where you can get the Android source code, learn about the philosophy behind the open-source operating system and get licensing information.

---

1. http://www.idc.com/prodserv/smartphone-os-market-share.jsp.
2. http://www.cnet.com/news/android-shipments-exceed-1-billion-for-first-time-in-2014/.
3. http://www.pcworld.com/article/2896196/windows-forecast-to-gradually-grab-tablet-market-share-from-ios-and-android.html.
4. http://www.businessweek.com/articles/2013-05-29/behind-the-internet-of-things-is-android-and-its-everywhere.
5. http://www.telecompetitor.com/mobile-app-forecast-calls-for-revenue-of-99-billion-by-2019/.

URL	Description

`http://en.wikipedia.org/wiki/`
`List_of_open_source_Android`
`_applications`
	Extensive list of open-source apps, organized by category (e.g., games, communication, emulators, multimedia, security).

`http://developer.android.com/` `tools/samples/index.html`	Instructions for accessing Google's sample apps for the Android platform; includes approximately 100 apps and games demonstrating various Android capabilities.
`http://github.com`	GitHub allows you to share your apps and source code and contribute to others' open-source projects.
`http://f-droid.org`	Hundreds of free and open-source Android apps.
`http://www.openintents.org`	Open-source libraries that can be used to enhance app capabilities.
`http://www.stackoverflow.com`	Stack Overflow is a question-and-answer website for programmers. Users can vote on each answer, and the best responses rise to the top.

Fig. 1.1 | Open-source Android app and library resource sites.

Title	URL
Get Android Source Code	`http://source.android.com/source/downloading.html`
Licenses	`http://source.android.com/source/licenses.html`
FAQs	`http://source.android.com/source/faqs.html`

Fig. 1.2 | Resources and source code for the open-source Android operating system.

The openness of the platform spurs rapid innovation. Unlike Apple's *proprietary* iOS, which is available only on Apple devices, Android is available on devices from dozens of original equipment manufacturers (OEMs) and through numerous telecommunications carriers worldwide. The intense competition among OEMs and carriers benefits customers.

Java

Android apps are developed with Java—one of the world's most widely used programming languages. Java was a logical choice for the Android platform, because it's powerful, free, open source and used by millions of developers. Experienced Java programmers can quickly dive into Android development, using Google's Android APIs (Application Programming Interfaces) and others available from third parties.

Java is object oriented and has access to extensive class libraries that help you quickly develop powerful apps. GUI programming in Java is *event driven*—in this book, you'll write apps that respond to various user-initiated *events* such as *screen touches*. In addition to directly programming portions of your apps, you'll also use the Android Studio IDE to conveniently drag and drop predefined objects such as buttons and textboxes into place on your screen, and label and resize them. Using Android Studio, you can create, run, test and debug Android apps quickly and conveniently.

Multitouch Screen

Android smartphones wrap the functionality of a mobile phone, Internet client, MP3 player, gaming console, digital camera and more into a handheld device with full-color *multitouch screens*. With the touch of your fingers, you can navigate easily between using your phone, running apps, playing music, web browsing and more. The screen can display a keyboard for typing e-mails and text messages and entering data in apps (some Android devices also have physical keyboards).

Gestures

The multitouch screens allow you to control the device with *gestures* involving one touch or multiple simultaneous touches (Fig. 1.3).

Gesture name	Physical action	Used to
Touch	Tap the screen once.	Open an app, "press" a button or a menu item.
Double touch	Tap the screen twice.	Zoom in on pictures, Google Maps and web pages. Tap the screen twice again to zoom back out.
Long press	Touch the screen and hold your finger in position.	Select items in a view—for example, checking an item in a list.
Swipe	Touch the screen, then move your finger in the swipe direction and release.	Flip item-by-item through a series, such as photos. A swipe automatically stops at the next item.
Drag	Touch and drag your finger across the screen.	Move objects or icons, or scroll through a web page or list.
Pinch zoom	Pinch two fingers together, or spread them apart.	Zoom in and out on the screen (e.g., resizing text and pictures).

Fig. 1.3 | Some common Android gestures.

Built-in Apps

Android devices come with several default apps, which may vary, depending on the device, the manufacturer or the mobile service carrier. Some apps commonly included are **Phone**, **Contacts**, **Messenger**, **Browser**, **Calculator**, **Calendar**, **Clock** and **Photos**.

Web Services

Web services are software components stored on one computer that can be accessed by an app (or other software component) on another computer over the Internet. With web services, you can create **mashups**, which enable you to rapidly develop apps by quickly *combining* complementary web services, often from different organizations and possibly other forms of information feeds. For example, 100 Destinations

        http://www.100destinations.co.uk

combines the photos and tweets from Twitter with the mapping capabilities of Google Maps to allow you to explore countries around the world through the photos of others.

Programmableweb

> http://www.programmableweb.com/

provides a directory of over 14,000 APIs and mashups, plus how-to guides and sample code for creating your own mashups. Figure 1.4 lists some popular web services. We use OpenWeatherMap.org's weather web services in Chapter 7.

Web services source	How it's used
Google Maps	Mapping services
Twitter	Microblogging
YouTube	Video search
Facebook	Social networking
Instagram	Photo sharing
Foursquare	Mobile check-in
LinkedIn	Social networking for business
Netflix	Movie rentals
eBay	Internet auctions
Wikipedia	Collaborative encyclopedia
PayPal	Payments
Amazon eCommerce	Shopping for books and lots of other products
Salesforce.com	Customer Relationship Management (CRM)
Skype	Internet telephony
Microsoft Bing	Search
Flickr	Photo sharing
Zillow	Real-estate pricing
Yahoo Search	Search
WeatherBug	Weather

Fig. 1.4 | Some popular web services (http://www.programmableweb.com/category/all/apis).

1.4 Android Operating System

The Android operating system was developed by Android, Inc., which was acquired by Google in 2005. In 2007, the Open Handset Alliance™

> http://www.openhandsetalliance.com/oha_members.html

was formed to develop, maintain and evolve Android, driving innovation in mobile technology and improving the user experience while reducing costs.

In this section, we walk through the evolution of the Android operating system, showing its versions and their key functionality. The Android marketplace is fragmented—many devices still use older Android versions—so it's helpful for you to be aware of the features introduced in each version.

Android Version Naming Convention
Each new version of Android is named after a dessert, going in alphabetical order (Fig. 1.5).

Android version	Name	Android version	Name
Android 1.5	Cupcake	Android 4.0	Ice Cream Sandwich
Android 1.6	Donut	Android 4.1–4.3	Jelly Bean
Android 2.0–2.1	Eclair	Android 4.4	KitKat
Android 2.2	Froyo	Android 5.0–5.1	Lollipop
Android 2.3	Gingerbread	Android 6.0	Marshmallow
Android 3.0–3.2	Honeycomb		

Fig. 1.5 | Android version numbers and the corresponding names.

1.4.1 Android 2.2 (Froyo)

Android 2.2 (also called **Froyo**, released in May 2010) introduced external storage, allowing you to store apps on an external memory device rather than just in the Android device's internal memory. It also introduced the **Android Cloud to Device Messaging (C2DM)** service. **Cloud computing** allows you to use software and data stored in the "cloud"—i.e., accessed on remote computers (or servers) via the Internet and available on demand—rather than having it stored on your desktop, notebook computer or mobile device. Cloud computing gives you the flexibility to increase or decrease computing resources to meet your resource needs at any given time, making it more cost effective than purchasing expensive hardware to ensure that you have enough storage and processing power for occasional peak levels. Android C2DM allows app developers to send data from their servers to their apps installed on Android devices, even when the apps are *not* currently running. The server notifies the apps to contact it directly to receive updated app or user data.[6] C2DM is now deprecated in favor of Google Cloud Messaging, which was introduced in 2012.

For information about additional Android 2.2 features—OpenGL ES 2.0 graphics capabilities, the media framework and more—visit

```
http://developer.android.com/about/versions/android-2.2-
    highlights.html
```

1.4.2 Android 2.3 (Gingerbread)

Android 2.3 (**Gingerbread**), released later in 2010, added more user refinements, such as a redesigned keyboard, improved navigation capabilities, increased power efficiency and more. It also added several developer features for communications (e.g., technologies that make it easier to make and receive calls from within an app), multimedia (e.g., new audio and graphics APIs) and gaming (e.g., improved performance and new sensors, such as a gyroscope for better motion processing).

One of the most significant new features in Android 2.3 was support for **near-field communication (NFC)**—a short-range wireless connectivity standard that enables com-

---

6. `http://code.google.com/android/c2dm/`.

munication between two devices within a few centimeters. NFC support and features vary by Android device. NFC can be used for payments (for example, touching your NFC-enabled Android device to a payment device on a soda machine), exchanging data such as contacts and pictures, pairing devices and accessories and more. For more Android 2.3 developer features, see

```
http://developer.android.com/about/versions/android-2.3-
    highlights.html
```

1.4.3 Android 3.0 through 3.2 (Honeycomb)

Android 3.0 (Honeycomb) included user-interface improvements specifically for large-screen devices (e.g., tablets), such as a redesigned keyboard for more efficient typing, a visually appealing 3D user interface, easier navigation between screens within an app and more. New Android 3.0 developer features included:

- fragments, which describe portions of an app's user interface and can be combined into one screen or used across multiple screens
- a persistent Action Bar at the top of the screen providing users with options for interacting with apps
- the ability to add large-screen layouts to existing apps designed for small screens to optimize your app for use on different screen sizes
- a visually attractive and more functional user interface, known as "Holo" for its holographic look and feel
- a new animation framework
- improved graphics and multimedia capabilities
- ability to use multicore processor architectures for enhanced performance
- increased Bluetooth support (e.g., enabling an app to determine if there are any connected devices such as headphones or a keyboard)
- and an animation framework for animating user-interface or graphics objects.

For a list of Android 3.0 user and developer features and platform technologies, go to

```
http://developer.android.com/about/versions/android-3.0-
    highlights.html
```

1.4.4 Android 4.0 through 4.0.4 (Ice Cream Sandwich)

Android 4.0 (Ice Cream Sandwich), released in 2011, merged Android 2.3 (Gingerbread) and Android 3.0 (Honeycomb) into one operating system for use on all Android devices. This allowed you to incorporate into your smartphone apps Honeycomb's features that previously were available only on tablets—the "Holo" user interface, a new launcher (used to customize the device's home screen and launch apps) and more—and easily scale your apps to work on different devices. Ice Cream Sandwich also added several APIs for improved communication between devices, accessibility for users with disabilities (e.g., vision impairments), social networking and more (Fig. 1.6). For a complete list of Android 4.0 APIs, see

```
http://developer.android.com/about/versions/android-4.0.html
```

Feature	Description
Face detection	Using the camera, compatible devices can determine the positioning of the user's eyes, nose and mouth. The camera also can track the user's eye movement, allowing you to create apps that change perspective, based on where the user is looking.
Virtual camera operator	When filming video of multiple people, the camera will automatically focus on the person who is speaking.
Android Beam	Using NFC, **Android Beam** allows you to touch two Android devices to share content (e.g., contacts, pictures, videos).
Wi-Fi Direct	Wi-Fi P2P (peer-to-peer) APIs allow you to connect multiple Android devices using Wi-Fi. The devices can communicate wirelessly at a greater distance than when using Bluetooth.
Social API	Access and share contact information across social networks and apps (with the user's permission).
Calendar API	Add and share events across multiple apps, manage alerts and attendees and more.
Accessibility APIs	Use the new Accessibility Text-to-Speech APIs to enhance the user experience of your apps for people with disabilities such as vision impairments and more. The explore-by-touch mode allows users with vision impairments to touch anywhere on the screen and hear a voice description of the touched content.
Android@Home framework	Use the **Android@Home framework** to create apps that control appliances in users' homes, such as, thermostats, irrigation systems, networked light bulbs and more.
Bluetooth health devices	Create apps that communicate with Bluetooth health devices such as scales, heart-rate monitors and more.

Fig. 1.6 | Some Android Ice Cream Sandwich developer features (`http://developer.android.com/about/versions/android-4.0.html`).

1.4.5 Android 4.1–4.3 (Jelly Bean)

Android Jelly Bean, released in 2012, focused on many behind-the-scenes platform improvements, such as better performance, accessibility, support for international users and more. Other new features included support for enhanced Bluetooth connectivity (Bluetooth LE was introduced in Android 4.3), external displays, support for multiple users on one tablet, restricted user profiles, improved security, appearance enhancements (e.g., resizable app widgets, lock screen widgets, and expandable notifications), optimized location and sensor capabilities, better media capabilities (audio/video), and more seamless switching between apps and screens (Fig. 1.7). In addition, Google introduced new APIs that are developed separately from Android platform versions:

- Google Cloud Messaging—a cross-platform solution that enables developers to deliver messages to devices
- Google Play Services—a set of APIs for incorporating Google functionality into your apps.

For the Jelly Bean features list, see

```
http://developer.android.com/about/versions/jelly-bean.html
```

Feature	Description
Android Beam	Enhanced to enable communication via Bluetooth in addition to NFC.
Lock screen widgets	Create widgets that appear on the user's screen when the device is locked, or modify your existing home-screen widgets so that they're also visible when the device is locked.
Photo Sphere	APIs for working with the new panoramic photo features that enable users to take 360-degree photos, similar to those used for Google Maps Street View.
Daydreams	Daydreams are interactive screensavers that are activated when a device is docked or charging. Daydreams can play audio and video and respond to user interactions.
Language support	New features help your apps reach international users, such as bidirectional text (left-to-right or right-to-left), international keyboards, additional keyboard layouts and more.
Developer options	Several new tracking and debugging features help you improve your apps, such as bug reports that include a screenshot and device state information.

Fig. 1.7 | Some Android Jelly Bean features (`http://developer.android.com/about/versions/jelly-bean.html`).

1.4.6 Android 4.4 (KitKat)

Android 4.4 KitKat, released in October 2013, includes several performance improvements that make it possible to run the operating system on all Android devices, including older, memory-constrained devices, which are particularly popular in developing countries.[7]

Enabling more users to update to KitKat reduced the "fragmentation" of Android versions in the market, which has been a challenge for developers who previously had to design apps to run across multiple versions of the operating system, or limit their potential market by targeting their apps to a specific version of the operating system.

Android KitKat also includes security and accessibility enhancements, improved graphics and multimedia capabilities, memory-use analysis tools and more. Figure 1.8 lists some of the key KitKat features. For a complete list, see

```
http://developer.android.com/about/versions/kitkat.html
```

---

7. `http://techcrunch.com/2013/10/31/android-4-4-kitkat-google/`.

Feature	Description
Immersive mode	The status bar at the top of the screen and the menu buttons at the bottom can be hidden, allowing your apps to fill more of the screen. Users can access the status bar by swiping down from the top of the screen, and the system bar (with the back button, home button and recent apps button) by swiping up from the bottom.
Printing framework	Build printing functionality into your apps, including locating available printers over Wi-Fi or the cloud, selecting the paper size and specifying which pages to print.
Storage access framework	Create document storage providers that allow users to browse, create and edit files (e.g., documents and images) across multiple apps.
SMS provider	Create SMS (Short Message Service) or MMS (Multimedia Messaging Service) apps using the new SMS provider and APIs. Users can now select their default messaging app.
Transitions framework	The new framework makes it easier to create transition animations.
Screen recording	Record video of your app to create tutorials and marketing materials.
Enhanced accessibility	The captioning manager API allows apps to check the user's captioning preferences (e.g., language, text styles and more).
Chromium WebView	Supports the latest standards for displaying web content including HTML5, CSS3 and a faster version of JavaScript.
Step detector and step counter	Create apps that detect whether the user is running, walking or climbing stairs and count the number of steps.
Host Card Emulator (HCE)	HCE enables any app to perform secure NFC transactions (e.g., mobile payments) without the need for a secure element on the SIM card controlled by the wireless carrier.

Fig. 1.8 | Some Android KitKat features (`http://developer.android.com/about/versions/kitkat.html`).

1.4.7 Android 5.0 and 5.1 (Lollipop)

Android Lollipop—released in November 2014—was a major update with thousands of API enhancements for phones and tablets, and new capabilities that enable developers to create apps for wearables (e.g., smart watches), TVs and cars. One of the biggest changes was **material design**—a complete user-interface redesign (also used in Google's web apps). Other features included: a new Android runtime, notification enhancements (enabling users to interact with a notification without leaving the current app), networking enhancements (Bluetooth, Wi-Fi, cellular and NFC), high-performance graphics (OpenGL ES 3.1 and the Android Extension Pack), better audio capabilities (capture, multichannel mixing, playback and support for USB peripherals), enhanced camera capabilities, screen sharing, new sensor support, enhanced accessibility features, multiple SIM card support and more. Figure 1.9 lists some of the key Lollipop features. For a complete list, see

```
http://developer.android.com/about/versions/lollipop.html
http://developer.android.com/about/versions/android-5.0.html
http://developer.android.com/about/versions/android-5.1.html
```

Feature	Description
Material design	Google's new look-and-feel for Android and web applications was the key new feature in Lollipop. Material design helps you create apps with nice transition effects, shadows that add depth to the user interface and emphasize actionable components, customization capabilities and more. For details, visit `https://www.google.com/design/spec/material-design/introduction.html`.
ART runtime	Google replaced the original Android runtime with the new 64-bit compatible ART runtime, which uses a combination of interpretation, ahead-of-time (AOT) compilation and just-in-time (JIT) compilation to improve performance.
Concurrent documents and activities in the recent apps screen	Apps can now specify that multiple activities and documents should appear on the recent apps screen. For example, if the user has multiple tabs open in a web browser or multiple documents open in a text-editing app, when the user touches the recent apps button (▣), each browser tab or document can appear as a separate item that the user can select.
Screen capturing and sharing	Apps can now capture the device's screen and share the contents with other users across a network.
Project Volta	Features that help preserve battery life, including the new `JobScheduler` that can execute asynchronous tasks when the device is charging, connected to an unmetered network (i.e., use Wi-Fi vs. cellular data) or idle.

Fig. 1.9 | Some Android Lollipop features (`http://developer.android.com/about/versions/lollipop.html`).

1.4.8 Android 6 (Marshmallow)

Android Marshmallow, released in September 2015, is the current version of Android at the time of this writing. Some new features include Now on Tap (for getting Google Now information in the context of an app), Doze and App Standby (for saving battery), a new permissions model to make apps easier to install, fingerprint authentication, better data protection, better text-selection support, 4K display support, new audio and video capabilities, new camera capabilities (flashlight and image-reprocessing APIs) and more. Figure 1.10 lists some of the key Lollipop features. For a complete list, see

```
http://developer.android.com/about/versions/marshmallow/android-
    6.0-changes.html
```

Feature	Description
Doze	Using software and sensors, Android determines when a device is stationary for a period of time—such as when you place it on a table overnight—and defers background processes that drain the battery.

Fig. 1.10 | Some Android Marshmallow features (`http://developer.android.com/about/versions/marshmallow/android-6.0-changes.html`). (Part 1 of 2.)

Feature	Description
App Standby	For apps that a user has open but has not interacted with recently, Android defers background network activity.
Now on Tap	Tap and hold the home button while inside any app and Google Now inspects what's on the screen and presents relevant information in the form of cards. For example, in a text message discussing a movie, a card containing information about that movie is displayed. Similarly, in a text message mentioning a restaurant name, a card with the ratings, location and phone number appears.
New permissions model	Before Android 6.0, a user was required at installation time to grant in advance all permissions that an app would ever need—this caused many people not to install certain apps. With the new model, the app is installed without asking for any permissions. Instead, the user is asked to grant a permission only the first time the corresponding feature is used.
Fingerprint authentication	For devices with fingerprint readers, apps can now authenticate users via their fingerprints.
App linking	Enables developers to associate apps with their own web domains and craft web links that launch specific apps from the same developer.
Automatic backup	Android can automatically backup and restore an app's data.
Direct Share	You can define direct share targets in your app that enable users to share data via other apps, directly from your app.
Voice Interaction API	Enables apps to respond to voice interactions.
Bluetooth stylus support	Apps can respond to pressure-sensitive interactions from a Bluetooth stylus—for example, in a drawing app, pressing the stylus against the screen harder could result in a thicker line.

Fig. 1.10 | Some Android Marshmallow features (`http://developer.android.com/about/versions/marshmallow/android-6.0-changes.html`). (Part 2 of 2.)

1.5 Downloading Apps from Google Play

At the time of this writing, there were over 1.6 million apps in **Google Play**, and the number is growing quickly.[8] Figure 1.11 lists some popular free and fee-based apps in various categories. You can download apps through the **Play Store** app installed on your Android device. You also can log into your Google Play account at

> `http://play.google.com`

then specify the Android device on which to install the app. It will then download via the device's Wi-Fi or 3G/4G connection. In Chapter 10, Google Play and App Business Issues, we discuss additional app stores, offering your apps for free or charging a fee, app pricing and more.

---

8. `http://www.statista.com/statistics/266210/number-of-available-applications-in-the-google-play-store/`.

Google Play category	Some popular apps in the category
Books and Reference	WolframAlpha, Dictionary.com, Audible for Android, Kindle
Business	Polaris Office, OfficeSuite 8, QuickBooks Online, PayPal Here
Communication	Snapchat, LinkedIn, Pinterest, Instagram, WeChat, Line
Education	Google Classroom, Star Tracker, Sight Words, Math Tricks
Entertainment	Showtime Anytime, History Channel, Discovery Channel
Finance	PayPal, Credit Karma, Google Wallet, Chase Mobile
Games	Pac-Man 256, Angry Birds 2, Fruit Ninja, Tetris, Solitaire
Health & Fitness	RunKeeper, ViewRanger GPS, Calorie Counter
Lifestyle	Assistant, Horoscope, Food Network, Starbucks
Live Wallpaper	Facebook, Next Launcher 3D Shell, Weather Live
Media & Video	VHS Camera Recorder, VivaVideo Pro, musical.ly, GIF Keyboard
Medical	Feed Baby Pro, CareZone, FollowMyHealth, Essential Anatomy
Music & Audio	SoundCloud, Spotify, Beats Music, Pandora, iHeartRadio
News & Magazines	BBC News, CBS News, NPR News, Reuters, NBC News
Photography	Google Camera, Instagram, Retrica, GoPro App, Pencil Sketch
Productivity	Pocket, Wunderlist, Microsoft Word, Google Docs, SwiftKey
Shopping	Zappos, Groupon, JackThreads, Fancy, Etsy, Home Depot
Social	Snapchat, Instagram, Meetup, textPlus, Pinterest, Tumblr
Sports	Fox Sports, theScore, NBA 2015–16, ESPN, CBS Sports
Tools	CM Security Antivirus, Clean Master, Google Translate
Transportation	Uber, Lyft, MarrineTraffic, BringGo, DigiHUD Speedometer
Travel & Local	Priceline, Google Earth, Eat24, GasBuddy, Hotels.com
Weather	AccuWeather, Weather Underground, Yahoo Weather
Widgets	Facebook, Pandora, Pocket Casts, Tasker, Weather Timeline

Fig. 1.11 | Some popular Android apps in Google Play.

1.6 Packages

Android uses a collection of *packages*, which are named groups of related, predefined classes. Some of the packages are Android specific, some are Java specific and some are Google specific. These packages allow you to conveniently access Android OS features and incorporate them into your apps. The Android packages help you create apps that adhere to Android's unique look-and-feel conventions and style guidelines,

```
http://developer.android.com/design/index.html
```

Figure 1.12 lists many of the packages we discuss in this book. For a complete list of Android packages, see

```
http://developer.android.com/reference/packages.html
```

Several of the packages we use are from the Android Support libraries, which enable you to use newer Android features in apps that run on current and older platforms. For an overview of the key features in the Android Support libraries, visit:

https://developer.android.com/tools/support-library/features.html

Package	Description
android.animation	Classes for property animation. (Chapter 4's **Flag Quiz** app and Chapter 5's **Doodlz** app.)
android.app	Includes high-level classes in the Android app model. (Chapter 4's **Flag Quiz** app and Chapter 5's **Doodlz** app.)
android.content	Access and publish data on a device. (Chapter 6's **Cannon Game** app.)
android.content.res	Classes for accessing app resources (e.g., media, colors, drawables, etc.), and device-configuration information affecting app behavior. (Chapter 4's **Flag Quiz** app.)
android.database	Handling data returned by the content provider. (Chapter 9's **Address Book** app.)
android.database.sqlite	SQLite database management for private databases. (Chapter 9's **Address Book** app.)
android.graphics	Graphics tools used for drawing to the screen. (Chapter 4's **Flag Quiz** app and Chapter 5's **Doodlz** app.)
android.graphics. drawable	Classes for display-only elements (e.g., gradients, etc.). (Chapter 4's **Flag Quiz** app.)
android.hardware	Device hardware support. (Chapter 5's **Doodlz** app.)
android.media	Classes for handling audio and video media interfaces. (Chapter 6's **Cannon Game** app.)
android.net	Network access classes. (Chapter 8's **Twitter® Searches** app.)
android.os	Operating-systems services. (Chapter 3's **Tip Calculator** app.)
android.preference	Working with an app's user preferences. (Chapter 4's **Flag Quiz** app.)
android.provider	Access to Android content providers. (Chapter 5's **Doodlz** app.)
android.support. design.widget	Android Design Support Library classes that enable recent GUI enhancements to run on current and older Android platforms. (Chapter 7's **Weather Viewer** app.)
android.support.v4. print	Part of the v4 Android Support Library for use in platform API levels 4 and higher. Includes features for using the Android 4.4 printing framework. (Chapter 5's **Doodlz** app.)
android.support.v7.app	Part of the v7 Android Support Library for use in platform API levels 7 and higher. Includes application-compatibility library components, such as app bars (formerly action bars). (Chapter 7's **Weather Viewer** app.)

Fig. 1.12 | Android and Java packages used in this book, listed with the chapter in which they *first* appear. We discuss additional packages in Volume 2. (Part 1 of 2.)

Package	Description
android.support.v7. widget	Part of the v7 Android Support Library for use in platform API levels 7 and higher. Includes GUI components and layouts. (Chapter 7's **Weather Viewer** app.)
android.text	Rendering and tracking text changes. (Chapter 3's **Tip Calculator** app.)
android.util	Utility methods and XML utilities. (Chapter 4's **Flag Quiz** app.)
android.widget	User-interface classes for widgets. (Chapter 3's **Tip Calculator** app.)
android.view	User interface classes for layout and user interactions. (Chapter 4's **Flag Quiz** app.)

Fig. 1.12 | Android and Java packages used in this book, listed with the chapter in which they *first* appear. We discuss additional packages in Volume 2. (Part 2 of 2.)

1.7 Android Software Development Kit (SDK)

The Android SDK provides the tools you'll need to build Android apps. It gets installed with Android Studio. See the Before You Begin section (after the Preface) for details on downloading the software you'll need to develop Android apps, including Java SE 7 and Android Studio.

Android Studio
Android Studio[9] was announced at the Google I/O developer conference in 2013 and is now Google's preferred Android IDE. The IDE includes:

- GUI designer
- code editor with support for syntax coloring and line numbering
- auto-indenting and auto-complete (i.e., type hinting)
- debugger
- version control system
- refactoring support

and more.

The Android Emulator
The **Android emulator**, included in the Android SDK, allows you to run Android apps in a simulated environment within Windows, Mac OS X or Linux, without using an actual Android device. The emulator displays a realistic Android user-interface window. It's particularly useful if you do not have access to Android devices for testing. You should certainly test your apps on a variety of Android devices before uploading them to Google Play.

Before running an app in the emulator, you'll need to create an **Android Virtual Device (AVD)**, which defines the characteristics of the device on which you want to test, including the hardware, system image, screen size, data storage and more. If you want to

---

9. Android Studio is based on the JetBrains IntelliJ IDEA Java IDE (http://www.jetbrains.com/idea/).

test your apps for multiple Android devices, you'll need to create separate AVDs to emulate each unique device, or use Google's Cloud Test Lab

```
https://developers.google.com/cloud-test-lab
```

which enables you to test on many different devices.

You can reproduce on the emulator most of the Android gestures (Fig. 1.13) and controls (Fig. 1.14) using your computer's keyboard and mouse. The gestures on the emulator are a bit limited, since your computer probably cannot simulate all the Android hardware features. For example, to test GPS apps in the emulator, you'll need to create files that simulate GPS readings. Also, although you can simulate orientation changes (to *portrait* or *landscape* mode), simulating particular **accelerometer** readings (the accelerometer allows the device to respond to up/down, left/right and forward/backward acceleration) requires features that are not built into the emulator. The emulator can, however, use sensor data from an actual Android device connected to the computer, as described at

```
http://tools.android.com/tips/hardware-emulation
```

Figure 1.15 lists Android functionality that's *not* available on the emulator. You can install your app on an Android device to test these features. You'll start creating AVDs and using the emulator to develop Android apps in Chapter 2's **Welcome** app.

Gesture	Emulator action
Touch	Click the mouse once. Introduced in Chapter 3's **Tip Calculator** app.
Double touch	Double click the mouse.
Long press	Click and hold the mouse. Introduced in Chapter 8's **Twitter® Searches** app.
Drag	Click, hold and drag the mouse. Introduced in Chapter 6's **Cannon Game** app.
Swipe	Click and hold the mouse, move the pointer in the swipe direction and release the mouse. Introduced in Chapter 7's **Weather Viewer** app.
Pinch zoom	Press and hold the *Ctrl* (*Control*) key. Two circles that simulate the two touches will appear. Move the circles to the start position, click and hold the mouse and drag the circles to the end position.

Fig. 1.13 | Android gestures on the emulator.

Control	Emulator action
Back	*Esc*
Call/dial button	*F3*
Camera	*Ctrl-KEYPAD_5*, *Ctrl-F3*
End call button	*F4*
Home	*Home* button
Menu (left softkey)	*F2* or *Page Up* button

Fig. 1.14 | Android hardware controls in the emulator (for additional controls, go to `http://developer.android.com/tools/help/emulator.html`). (Part 1 of 2.)

Control	Emulator action
Power button	F7
Search	F5
* (right softkey)	*Shift-F2* or *Page Down* button
Rotate to previous orientation	*KEYPAD_7, Ctrl-F11*
Rotate to next orientation	*KEYPAD_9, Ctrl-F12*
Toggle cell networking on/off	F8
Volume up button	*KEYPAD_PLUS, Ctrl-F5*
Volume down button	*KEYPAD_MINUS, Ctrl-F6*

Fig. 1.14 | Android hardware controls in the emulator (for additional controls, go to `http://developer.android.com/tools/help/emulator.html`). (Part 2 of 2.)

Android functionality not available on the emulator

- Making or receiving real phone calls (the emulator allows simulated calls only)
- Bluetooth
- USB connections
- Device-attached headphones
- Determining network connected state
- Determining battery charge or power charging state
- Determining SD card insert/eject
- Direct support for sensors (accelerometer, barometer, compass, light sensor, proximity sensor)—it is possible, however, to use sensor data from a USB-connected device

Fig. 1.15 | Android functionality not available in the emulator (`http://developer.android.com/tools/devices/emulator.html#limitations`).

1.8 Object-Oriented Programming: A Quick Refresher

Android uses object-oriented programming techniques, so in this section we review the basics of object technology. We use all of these concepts in this book.

Building software quickly, correctly and economically remains an elusive goal at a time when demands for new and more powerful software are soaring. *Objects*, or more precisely—as we'll see in Chapter 3—the *classes* objects come from, are essentially *reusable* software components. There are date objects, time objects, audio objects, video objects, automobile objects, people objects, etc. Almost any *noun* can be reasonably represented as a software object in terms of *attributes* (e.g., name, color and size) and *behaviors* (e.g., calculating, moving and communicating). Software developers are discovering that using a modular, object-oriented design-and-implementation approach can make software development groups much more productive than they could be with earlier popular techniques like "structured programming"—object-oriented programs are often easier to understand, correct and modify.

1.8.1 The Automobile as an Object

To help you understand objects and their contents, let's begin with a simple analogy. Suppose you want to *drive a car and make it go faster by pressing its accelerator pedal*. What must happen before you can do this? Well, before you can drive a car, someone has to *design* it. A car typically begins as engineering drawings, similar to the *blueprints* that describe the design of a house. These drawings include the design for an accelerator pedal. The pedal *hides* from the driver the complex mechanisms that actually make the car go faster, just as the brake pedal *hides* the mechanisms that slow the car, and the steering wheel *hides* the mechanisms that turn the car. This enables people with little or no knowledge of how engines, braking and steering mechanisms work to drive a car easily.

Just as you cannot cook meals in the kitchen of a blueprint, you cannot drive a car's engineering drawings. Before you can drive a car, it must be *built* from the engineering drawings that describe it. A completed car has an *actual* accelerator pedal to make it go faster, but even that's not enough—the car won't accelerate on its own (hopefully!), so the driver must *press* the pedal to accelerate the car.

1.8.2 Methods and Classes

Let's use our car example to introduce some key object-oriented programming concepts. Performing a task in a program requires a **method**. The method houses the program statements that actually perform its tasks. The method hides these statements from its user, just as the accelerator pedal of a car hides from the driver the mechanisms of making the car go faster. A class houses the methods that perform the class's tasks. For example, a class that represents a bank account might contain one method to *deposit* money to an account, another to *withdraw* money from an account and a third to *inquire* what the account's current balance is. A class is similar in concept to a car's engineering drawings, which house the design of an accelerator pedal, steering wheel, and so on.

1.8.3 Instantiation

Just as someone has to *build a car* from its engineering drawings before you can actually drive a car, you must *build an object* of a class before a program can perform the tasks that the class's methods define. The process of doing this is called *instantiation*. An object is then referred to as an **instance** of its class.

1.8.4 Reuse

Just as a car's engineering drawings can be *reused* many times to build many cars, you can *reuse* a class many times to build many objects. **Reuse** of existing classes when building new classes and programs saves time and effort. Reuse also helps you build more reliable and effective systems, because existing classes and components often have gone through extensive testing, debugging and performance tuning. Just as the notion of *interchangeable parts* was crucial to the Industrial Revolution, reusable classes are crucial to the software revolution that has been spurred by object technology.

1.8.5 Messages and Method Calls

When you drive a car, pressing its gas pedal sends a *message* to the car to perform a task—that is, to go faster. Similarly, you *send messages to an object*. Each message is a **method call** that tells a method of the object to perform its task. For example, a program might call a particular bank-account object's *deposit* method to increase the account's balance.

1.8.6 Attributes and Instance Variables

A car, besides having capabilities to accomplish tasks, also has *attributes*, such as its color, its number of doors, the amount of gas in its tank, its current speed and its record of total miles driven (i.e., its odometer reading). Like its capabilities, the car's attributes are represented as part of its design in its engineering diagrams (which, for example, include an odometer and a fuel gauge). As you drive an actual car, these attributes are carried along with the car. Every car maintains its *own* attributes. For example, each car knows how much gas is in its own gas tank, but *not* how much is in the tanks of *other* cars.

An object, similarly, has attributes that it carries along as it's used in a program. These attributes are specified as part of the object's class. For example, a bank-account object has a *balance attribute* that represents the amount of money in the account. Each bank-account object knows the balance in the account it represents, but *not* the balances of the *other* accounts in the bank. Attributes are specified by the class's **instance variables**.

1.8.7 Encapsulation

Classes **encapsulate** (i.e., wrap) attributes and methods into objects—an object's attributes and methods are intimately related. Objects may communicate with one another, but they're normally not allowed to know how other objects are implemented—implementation details are *hidden* within the objects themselves. This **information hiding** is crucial to good software engineering.

1.8.8 Inheritance

A new class of objects can be created quickly and conveniently by **inheritance**—the new class absorbs the characteristics of an existing one, possibly customizing them and adding unique characteristics of its own. In our car analogy, a "convertible" certainly *is an* object of the more *general* class "automobile," but more *specifically*, the roof can be raised or lowered.

1.8.9 Object-Oriented Analysis and Design (OOAD)

How will you create the code for your programs? Perhaps, like many programmers, you'll simply turn on your computer and start typing. This approach may work for small programs, but what if you were asked to create a software system to control thousands of automated teller machines for a major bank? Or suppose you were asked to work on a team of 1,000 software developers building the next U.S. air traffic control system? For projects so large and complex, you should not simply sit down and start writing programs.

To create the best solutions, you should follow a detailed **analysis** process for determining your project's **requirements** (i.e., defining *what* the system is supposed to do) and developing a **design** that satisfies them (i.e., deciding *how* the system should do it). Ideally, you'd go through this process and carefully review the design (and have your design reviewed by other software professionals) before writing any code. If this process involves analyzing and designing your system from an object-oriented point of view, it's called an **object-oriented analysis and design (OOAD) process**. Languages like Java are object oriented. Programming in such a language, called **object-oriented programming (OOP)**, allows you to implement an object-oriented design as a working system.

1.9 Test-Driving the Tip Calculator App in an Android Virtual Device (AVD)

In this section, you'll run and interact with your first Android app using an Android Virtual Device and, if you have one, an actual Android device. The **Tip Calculator** (Fig. 1.16(a))—which you'll build in Chapter 3—calculates and displays for a restaurant bill the tip amount and the total bill amount. As you enter each digit of the bill amount by touching the numeric keypad, the app calculates and displays the tip and total bill for a tip percentage that you specify with the app's **SeekBar**—we use 15% by default (Fig. 1.16(a)). You can select a tip percentage in the range 0–30% by moving the **Seek-Bar**'s thumb—this updates the tip percentage **TextView** and displays the updated tip and bill total in the **TextViews** below the **SeekBar** (Fig. 1.16(b)).

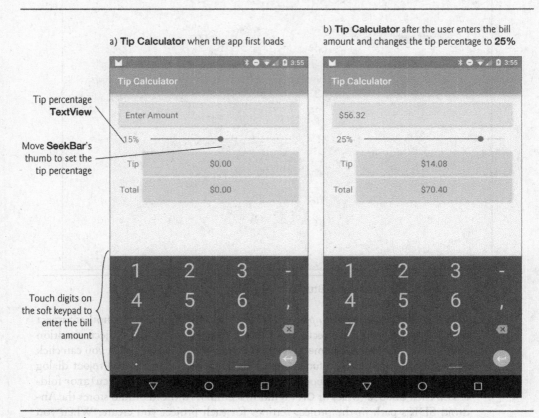

a) **Tip Calculator** when the app first loads

b) **Tip Calculator** after the user enters the bill amount and changes the tip percentage to **25%**

Tip percentage **TextView**

Move **SeekBar**'s thumb to set the tip percentage

Touch digits on the soft keypad to enter the bill amount

Fig. 1.16 | **Tip Calculator** when the app first loads, then after the user enters the bill amount and changes the tip percentage.

1.9.1 Opening the Tip Calculator App's Project in Android Studio

To open the **Tip Calculator** app's project, perform the following steps:

1. *Checking your setup.* If you have not done so already, perform the steps specified in the Before You Begin section.

2. *Opening Android Studio.* Use the Android Studio shortcut

   to open the IDE. On Windows, the shortcut will appear in your **Start** menu or **Start** screen. On OS X, the shortcut is located in your Applications folder. On Linux, the shortcut's location depends on where you extract the ZIP file containing the Android Studio files. Once open Android Studio for the first time, the **Welcome to Android Studio** window appears (Fig. 1.17).

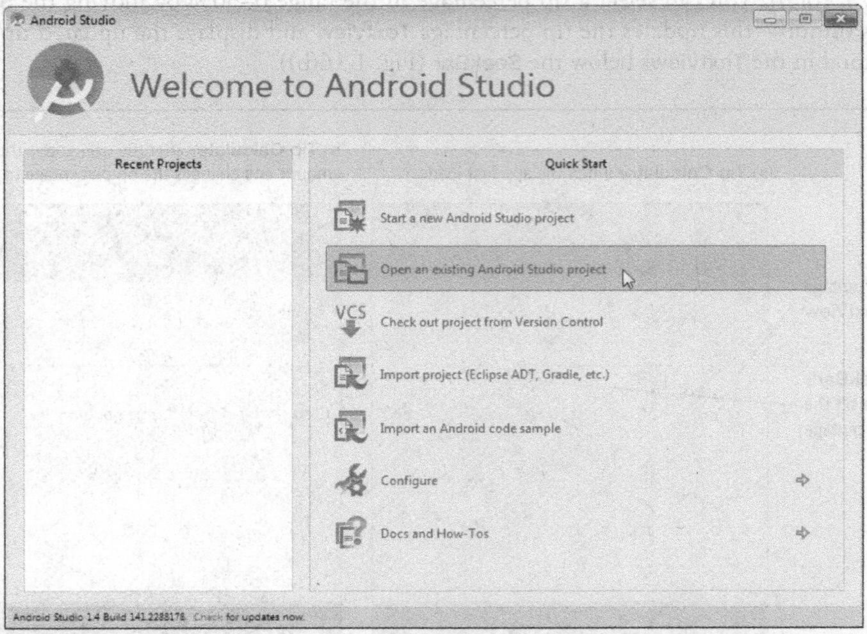

Fig. 1.17 | Welcome to Android Studio window.

3. *Opening the Tip Calculator app's project.* In Android Studio, when another project is already open, you can select **File > Open...** to navigate to that project's location and open it, or in the **Welcome to Android Studio Window** (Fig. 1.17), you can click **Open an existing Android Studio Project** to open the **Open File or Project** dialog (Fig. 1.18). Navigate to the book's examples folder, select the TipCalculator folder and click **Choose** (Mac) or **OK** (Windows/Linux). Android Studio stores the Android SDK's path in the project settings for each project you create. When you open our projects on your system, you'll receive an error message if the SDK on your system is in a different location from ours. Simply click the **OK** button in the

error dialog that appears, and Android Studio will update the project settings to use the SDK on your system. At this point, the IDE opens the project and displays its contents in the **Project** window (Fig. 1.19) at the IDE's left side. If the **Project** window is not visible, you can view it by selecting **View > Tool Windows > Project**.

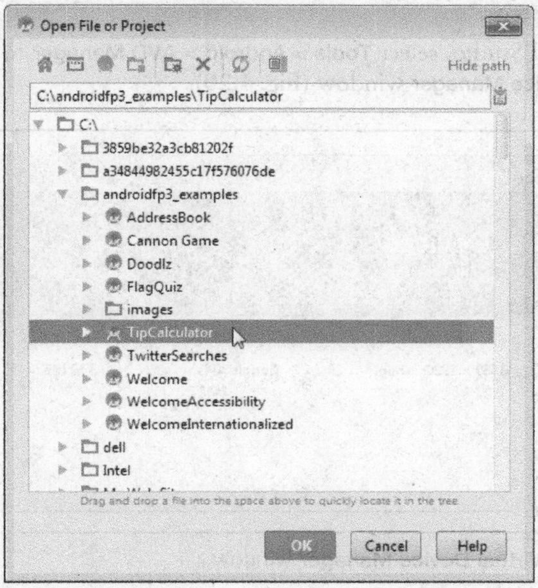

Fig. 1.18 | **Open File or Project** dialog.

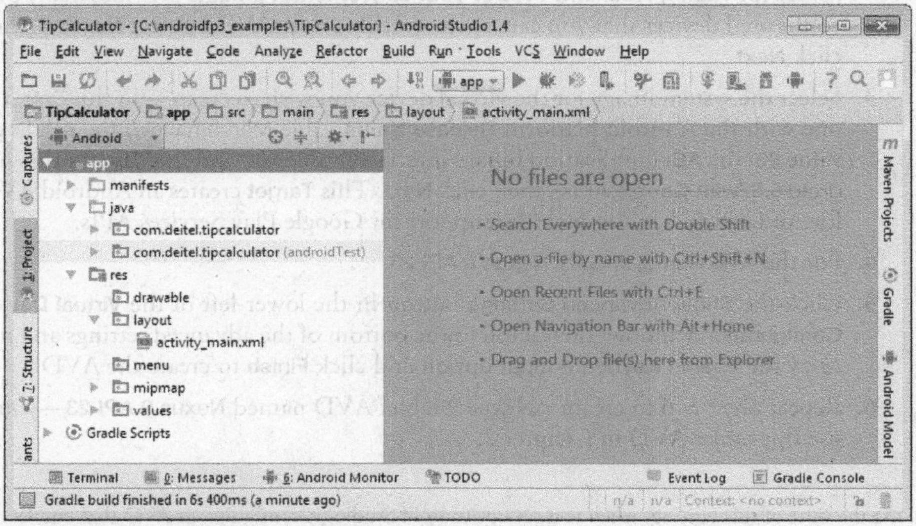

Fig. 1.19 | **Project** window for the **Tip Calculator** project.

1.9.2 Creating Android Virtual Devices (AVDs)

As we discussed in the Before You Begin section, you can test apps for multiple Android devices by creating Android Virtual Devices (AVDs) that emulate each unique device.[10] In this section you'll create Android 6 AVDs for the devices we used to test this book's apps—the Google's Nexus 6 phone and the Nexus 9 tablet. To create these AVDs, perform the following steps:

1. In Android Studio, select **Tools > Android > AVD Manager** to display the **Android Virtual Device Manager** window (Fig. 1.20).

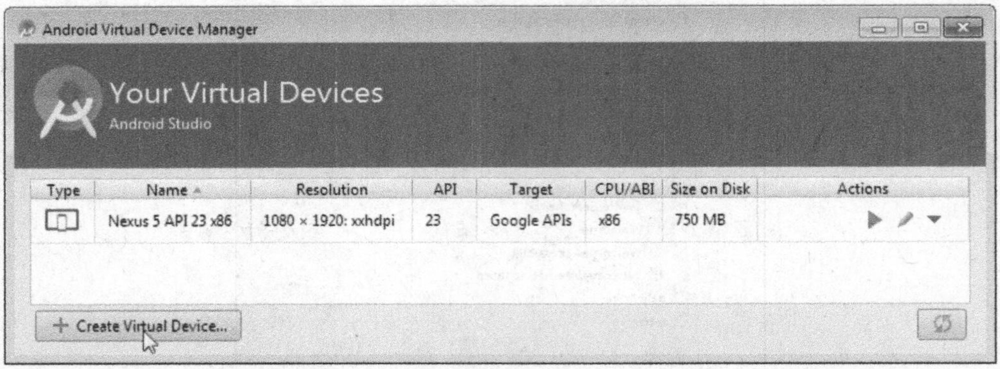

Fig. 1.20 | **Android Virtual Device Manager** window.

2. Click **Create Virtual Device...** to open the **Virtual Device Configuration** window (Fig. 1.21). By default the **Category "Phone"** is selected, but you may also create AVDs for **Tablet, Wear** and **TV**. For your convenience, Google provides many pre-configured devices that you can use to quickly create AVDs. Select **Nexus 6**, then click **Next**.

3. Select the system image for the virtual device you wish to create—in this case, the one with the Android platform **Release Name** value **Marshmallow**, the **API Level** value **23**, the **ABI** (application binary interface) value **x86** and the **Target** value **Android 6.0 (with Google APIs)**, then click **Next**. This **Target** creates an Android AVD for Android 6 that also includes support for Google Play Services APIs.

4. For the **AVD Name**, specify **Nexus 6 API 23**.

5. Click the **Show Advanced Settings** button in the lower-left of the **Virtual Device Configuration** window, then scroll to the bottom of the advanced settings and *uncheck* the **Enable Keyboard Input** option and click **Finish** to create the AVD.

6. Repeat *Steps 1–6* to create a Nexus 9 tablet AVD named **Nexus 9 API 23**—you'll use this tablet AVD in Chapter 2.

---

10. At the time of this writing, when you set up Android Studio, it configures an AVD that emulates a Google Nexus 5 phone running Android 6.0 (Marshmallow). You'll still need to perform Section 1.9.2's steps to create the additional AVDs you need for testing.

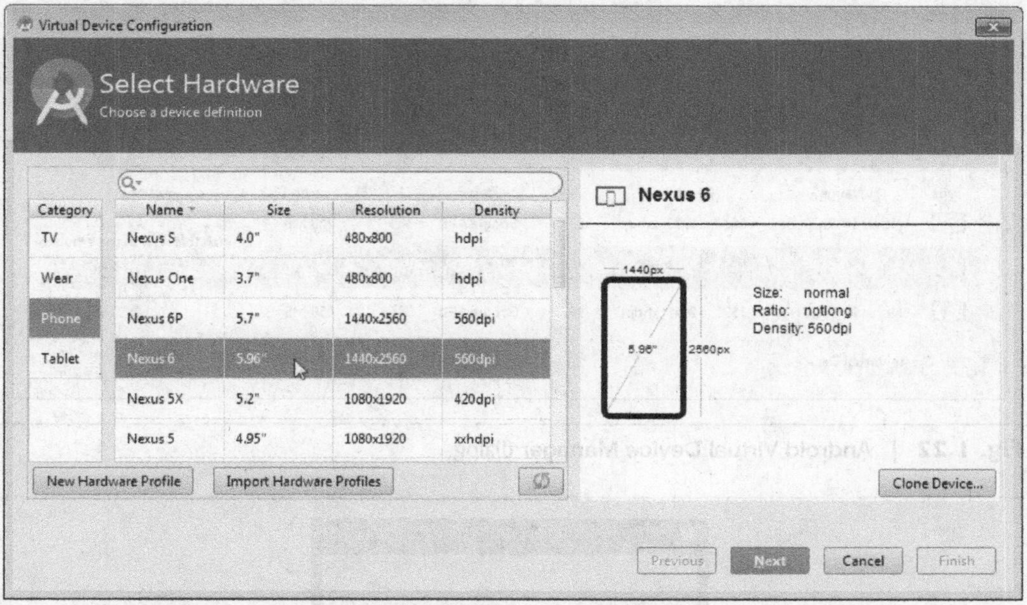

Fig. 1.21 | **Virtual Device Configuration** window.

If you leave the **Enable Keyboard Input** option checked in *Step 5* above, you can use your computer's keyboard to enter data into apps running in the AVD. However, this prevents the soft keyboard shown in the screen captures from displaying.

Each AVD you create has many other options specified in its `config.ini` file. To more precisely match a particular device's hardware configuration, you can modify `config.ini` as described at:

> `http://developer.android.com/tools/devices/managing-avds.html`

1.9.3 Running the **Tip Calculator** App on the Nexus 6 Smartphone AVD

To test-drive the **Tip Calculator** app, perform the following steps:

1. *Checking your setup.* If you have not done so already, perform the steps specified in the Before You Begin section.

2. *Launching the Nexus 6 AVD.* For this test-drive, we'll use the Nexus 6 smartphone AVD that you configured in Section 1.9.2. To launch the Nexus 6 AVD, select **Tools > Android > AVD Manager** to display the **Android Virtual Device Manager** dialog (Fig. 1.22). Click the **Launch this AVD in the emulator button** (▶) in the row for the **Nexus 6 API 23** AVD. An AVD can take some time to load—do not attempt to execute the app until the AVD finishes loading. When it's done loading, the AVD will display the lock screen. On an actual device, you unlock it by swiping up with your finger. You perform the swipe gesture on an AVD by placing the mouse over the AVD's "screen" and dragging up with the mouse. Figure 1.23 shows the AVD after you unlock it.

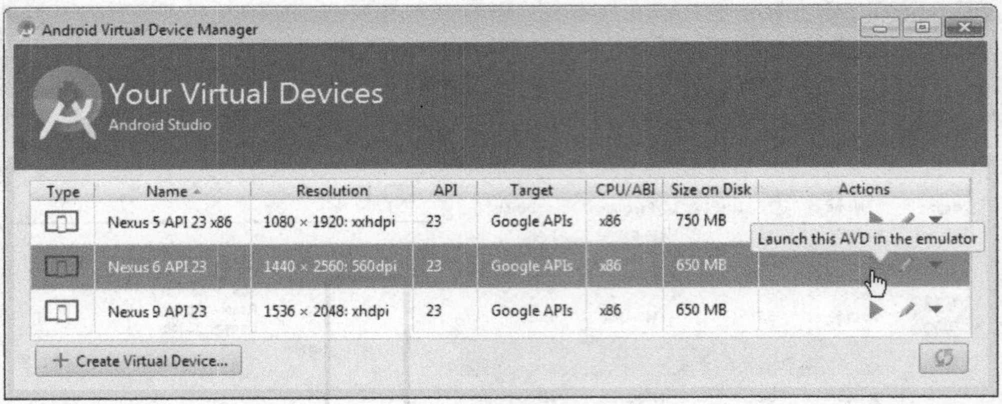

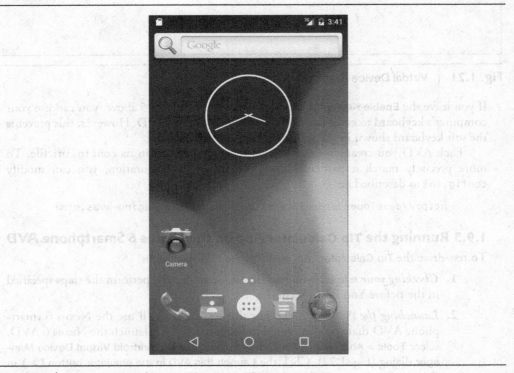

Fig. 1.22 | **Android Virtual Device Manager** dialog.

Fig. 1.23 | Nexus 6 AVD home screen after you unlock the AVD.

3. *Launching the Tip Calculator app.* In Android Studio, select **Run > Run 'app'** or click the **Run 'app'** button (▶) on the Android Studio toolbar. This will display a **Device Chooser** dialog (Fig. 1.24) with the currently running AVD already selected. Click **OK** to run the **Tip Calculator** in the AVD (Fig. 1.25) that you

launched in *Step 2*.[11] As an alternative to opening the **Android Virtual Device** Manager dialog in *Step 2*, you can click the **Run 'app'** button (▶) on the Android Studio toolbar and the **Device Chooser** dialog will appear. You can then use the **Launch emulator** option at the bottom of the dialog to select an AVD to launch, and in which to run the app.

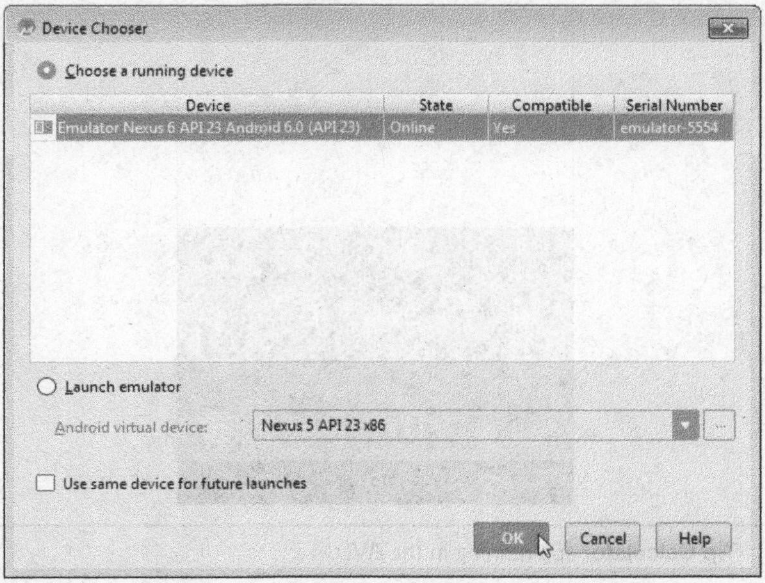

Fig. 1.24 | **Device Chooser** for selecting AVD or device on which to test an app.

4. *Exploring the AVD.* At the AVD screen's bottom are various *soft buttons* that appear on the device's touch screen. You touch these to interact with apps and the Android OS. In an AVD touches are performed by clicking with the mouse. The down button (▼) dismisses the keypad. When there is no keypad on the screen the back button (◀) appears instead. Touching this button takes you back to an app's prior screen, or back to a prior app if you're in the current app's initial screen. The home button (⬤) returns you to the device's home screen. The recent apps button (▣) allows you to view the recently used apps list, so that you can switch back to recent apps quickly. At the screen's top is the app's app bar, which displays the app's name and may contain other app-specific soft buttons—some may appear on the app bar and the rest in the app's **options menu**, which

---

11. The keypad in Fig. 1.25 may differ, based on your AVD's or device's Android version or whether you've installed and selected a custom keyboard. We configured our AVD to display the dark keyboard for better contrast in our screen captures. To do so: Touch the home (⬤) icon on your AVD or device. On the home screen, touch the launcher (⠿) icon, then open the **Settings** app. In the **Personal** section, touch **Language and Input**. On an AVD, touch **Android Keyboard (AOSP)**. On a device, touch **Google Keyboard** (the standard Android keyboard). Touch **Appearance & layouts**, then touch **Theme. Touch Material Dark** to change to the keyboard with the dark background.

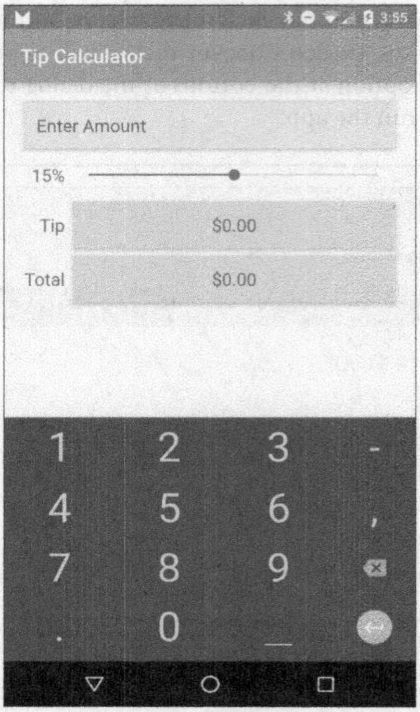

Fig. 1.25 | **Tip Calculator** app running in the AVD.

appears in the app bar at the top of the screen as ⋮. The number of options on the app bar depends on the size of the device—we discuss this in Chapter 5.

5. *Entering a Bill Total.* Enter the bill total 56.32 by touching numbers on the numeric keypad. If you make a mistake, press the delete button (⊠) in the bottom-right corner of the keypad to erase the last digit you entered. Even though the keypad contains a decimal point, the app is configured so that you may enter only the digits 0–9. Each time you touch a digit or delete one, the app reads what you've entered so far and converts it to a number—if you delete all the digits the app redisplays **Enter Amount** in the **TextView** at the top of the app. The app divides the value by 100 and displays the result in the blue **TextView**. The app then calculates and updates the tip and total amounts that are displayed. We use Android's locale-specific currency-formatting capabilities to display monetary values formatted for the device's current locale. For the U.S. locale, as you enter the four digits 5, 6, 3 and 2, the bill total is displayed successively as $0.05, $0.56, $5.63 and $56.32, respectively.

6. *Selecting a Custom Tip Percentage.* The **SeekBar** allows you to select a custom percentage, and the **TextViews** in the right column below the **SeekBar** display the corresponding tip and the total bill. Drag the **SeekBar** thumb to the right until the custom percentage reads **25%**. As you drag the thumb, the **SeekBar** value continuously changes. The app updates the tip percentage, the tip amount and the

bill total accordingly for each **SeekBar** value until you release the thumb. Figure 1.26 shows the app after you've entered the bill amount and selected the tip percentage.

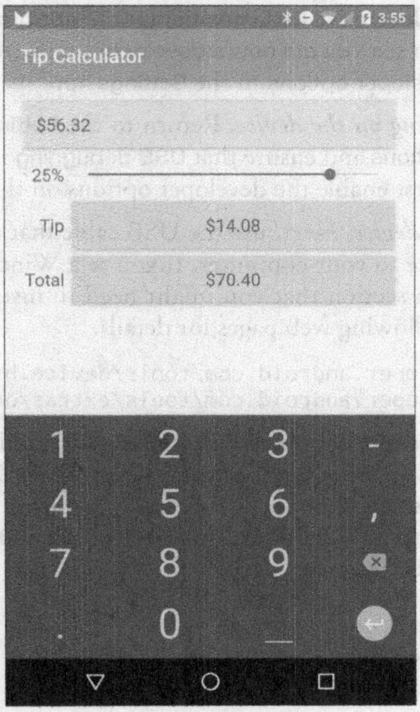

Fig. 1.26 | **Tip Calculator** after entering the bill amount and selecting a 25% tip.

7. *Returning to the home screen.* You can return to the AVD's home screen by tapping the home (⊙) button on the AVD.

Troubleshooting AVD Startup

If you have trouble executing an Android Virtual Device, it might be that too much of your computer's memory is allocated to the AVD. To reduce AVD's memory size:

1. In Android Studio, select **Tools > Android > AVD Manager** to open the **Android Virtual Device Manager** window.

2. You'll see a list of existing AVDs. For the AVD you'd like to reconfigure, click the pencil icon (✐) in the **Actions** column.

3. In the **Virtual Device Configuration** window, click **Show Advanced Settings**, and scroll to the **Memory and Storage** section.

4. Decrease value for **RAM** from the default 1536 MB (1.5 GB) down to 1 GB.

5. Click **Finish** and close the **Android Virtual Device Manager** window.

If you still cannot run the AVD, repeat these steps and reduce the memory to 768 MB.

1.9.4 Running the Tip Calculator App on an Android Device

If you have an Android device, you can easily execute an app on it for testing purposes.

1. *Enabling the developer options on the device.* First, you must enable debugging on the device. To do so, go to the device's **Settings** app, then select **About phone** (or **About tablet**), locate the **Build number** (at the bottom of the list) and tap it seven times until you see **You are now a developer** on the screen. This will enable an entry named **Developer options** in the **Settings** app.

2. *Enabling debugging on the device.* Return to the **Settings** app's main screen, select **Developer options** and ensure that **USB debugging** is checked—this is the default when you first enable the developer options on the device.

3. *Connecting your device.* Next, use the USB cable that came with your device to connect the device to your computer. If you're a Windows user, recall from the Before You Begin section that you might need to install a USB driver for your device. See the following web pages for details:

   ```
   http://developer.android.com/tools/device.html
   http://developer.android.com/tools/extras/oem-usb.html
   ```

4. *Running Tip Calculator on the Android device.* In Android Studio, select **Run > Run 'app'** or click the **Run 'app'** button (▶) on the Android Studio toolbar. This will display the **Device Chooser** dialog that you saw in Fig. 1.24. Select your device from the list of running AVDs and devices. Click **OK** to run the **Tip Calculator** on the AVD or device you selected.

Test-Drives for the Book's Apps

To get a broad sense of the capabilities that you'll learn in this book, check out the test-drives of the book's apps in Chapters 2–9.

Preparing to Distribute Apps

When you build apps for distribution via app stores like Google Play, you should test the apps on as many actual devices as you can. Remember that some features can be tested *only* on actual devices. If you don't have Android devices available to you, create AVDs that simulate the various devices on which you'd like your app to execute—the AVD Manager provides many preconfigured AVD templates. When you configure each AVD to simulate a particular device, look up the device's specifications online and configure the AVD accordingly. In addition, you can modify the AVD's config.ini file as described in the section **Setting hardware emulation options** at

   ```
   http://developer.android.com/tools/devices/managing-avds-
       cmdline.html#hardwareopts
   ```

This file contains options that are not configurable via the **Android Virtual Device Manager**. Modifying these options allows you to more precisely match the hardware configuration of an actual device.

1.10 Building Great Android Apps

With over 1.6 million apps in Google Play,[12] how do you create an Android app that people will find, download, use and recommend to others? Consider what makes an app fun, useful, interesting, appealing and enduring. A clever app name, an attractive icon and an engaging description might lure people to your app on Google Play or one of the many other Android app marketplaces. But once users download the app, what will make them use it regularly and recommend it to others? Figure 1.27 shows some characteristics of great apps.

Characteristics of great apps

Great Games

- Entertaining and fun.
- Challenging.
- Progressive levels of difficulty.
- Show your scores and use leaderboards to record high scores.
- Provide audio and visual feedback.
- Offer single-player, multiplayer and networked versions.
- Have high-quality animations.
- Offloading input/output and compute-intensive code to separate threads of execution to improve interface responsiveness and app performance.
- Innovate with augmented reality technology—enhancing a real-world environment with virtual components; this is particularly popular with video-based apps.

Useful Utilities

- Provide useful functionality and accurate information.
- Increase personal and business productivity.
- Make tasks more convenient (e.g., maintaining a to-do list, managing expenses).
- Make the user better informed.
- Provide topical information (e.g., the latest stock prices, news, severe-storm warnings, traffic updates).
- Use location-based services to provide local services (e.g., coupons for local businesses, best gas prices, food delivery).

General Characteristics

- Up-to-date with the latest Android features, but compatible with multiple Android versions to support the widest possible audience.
- Work properly.
- Bugs are fixed promptly.
- Follow standard Android app GUI conventions.
- Launch quickly.
- Are responsive.

Fig. 1.27 | Characteristics of great apps. (Part 1 of 2.)

---

12. http://www.statista.com/statistics/266210/number-of-available-applications-in-the-google-play-store/.

Characteristics of great apps

General Characteristics (cont.)

- Don't require excessive memory, bandwidth or battery power.
- Are novel and creative.
- Enduring—something that your users will use regularly.
- Use professional-quality icons that will appear in Google Play and on the user's device.
- Use quality graphics, images, animations, audio and video.
- Are intuitive and easy to use (don't require extensive help documentation).
- Accessible to people with disabilities (`http://developer.android.com/guide/topics/ui/accessibility/index.html`).
- Give users reasons and a means to tell others about your app (e.g., you can give users the option to post their game scores to Facebook or Twitter).
- Provide additional content for content-driven apps (e.g., game levels, articles, puzzles).
- Localized (Chapter 2) for each country in which the app is offered (e.g., translate the app's text and audio files, use different graphics based on the locale, etc.).
- Offer better performance, capabilities and ease-of-use than competitive apps.
- Take advantage of the device's built-in capabilities.
- Do not request excessive permissions.
- Are designed to run optimally across a broad variety of Android devices.
- Future-proofed for new hardware devices—specify the exact hardware features your app uses so Google Play can filter and display it in the store for only compatible devices (`http://android-developers.blogspot.com/2010/06/future-proofing-your-app.html`).

Fig. 1.27 | Characteristics of great apps. (Part 2 of 2.)

1.11 Android Development Resources

Figure 1.28 lists some of the key documentation from the Android Developer site. As you dive into Android app development, you may have questions about the tools, design issues, security and more. There are several Android developer newsgroups and forums where you can get the latest announcements or ask questions (Fig. 1.29). Figure 1.30 lists several websites where you'll find Android development tips, videos and resources.

Title	URL
App Components	`http://developer.android.com/guide/components/index.html`
Using the Android Emulator	`http://developer.android.com/tools/devices/emulator.html`
Package Index	`http://developer.android.com/reference/packages.html`
Class Index	`http://developer.android.com/reference/classes.html`

Fig. 1.28 | Key online documentation for Android developers. (Part 1 of 2.)

Title	URL
Android Design	`http://developer.android.com/design/index.html`
Data Backup	`http://developer.android.com/guide/topics/data/backup.html`
Security Tips	`http://developer.android.com/training/articles/security-tips.html`
Android Studio	`http://developer.android.com/sdk/index.html`
Debugging	`http://developer.android.com/tools/debugging/index.html`
Tools Help	`http://developer.android.com/tools/help/index.html`
Performance Tips	`http://developer.android.com/training/articles/perf-tips.html`
Keeping Your App Responsive	`http://developer.android.com/training/articles/perf-anr.html`
Launch Checklist (for Google Play)	`http://developer.android.com/distribute/tools/launch-checklist.html`
Getting Started with Publishing	`http://developer.android.com/distribute/googleplay/start.html`
Managing Your App's Memory	`http://developer.android.com/training/articles/memory.html`
Google Play Developer Distribution Agreement	`http://play.google.com/about/developer-distribution-agreement.html`

Fig. 1.28 | Key online documentation for Android developers. (Part 2 of 2.)

Title	Subscribe	Description
Android Discuss	*Subscribe using Google Groups:* android-discuss *Subscribe via e-mail:* android-discuss-subscribe@googlegroups.com	A general Android discussion group where you can get answers to your app-development questions.
Stack Overflow	`http://stackoverflow.com/questions/tagged/android`	Use this for Android app-development questions and questions about best practices.
Android Developers	`http://groups.google.com/forum/?fromgroups#!forum/android-developers`	Experienced Android developers use this list for troubleshooting apps, GUI design issues, performance issues and more.
Android Forums	`http://www.androidforums.com`	Ask questions, share tips with other developers and find forums targeting specific Android devices.

Fig. 1.29 | Android newsgroups and forums.

Android development tips, videos and resources	URL
Android Sample Code and Utilities from Google	`https://github.com/google` (use the filter "android")
Bright Hub™ website for Android programming tips and how-to guides	`http://www.brighthub.com/mobile/google-android.aspx`
The Android Developers Blog	`http://android-developers.blogspot.com/`
HTC's Developer Center for Android	`http://www.htcdev.com/`
The Motorola Android development site	`http://developer.motorola.com/`
Top Android Users on Stack Overflow	`http://stackoverflow.com/tags/android/topusers`
Android Weekly Newsletter	`http://androidweekly.net/`
Chet Haase's Codependent blog	`http://graphics-geek.blogspot.com/`
Romain Guy's Android blog	`http://www.curious-creature.org/category/android/`
Android Developers Channel on YouTube®	`http://www.youtube.com/user/androiddevelopers`
Google I/O 2015 Developer Conference session videos	`https://events.google.com/io2015/videos`

Fig. 1.30 | Android development tips, videos and resources.

1.12 Wrap-Up

This chapter presented a brief history of Android and discussed its functionality. We provided links to some of the key online documentation and to the newsgroups and forums you can use to connect with the developer community and get your questions answered. We discussed features of the Android operating system. We introduced the Java, Android and Google packages that enable you to use the hardware and software functionality you'll need to build a variety of Android apps. You'll use many of these packages in this book. We also discussed Java programming and the Android SDK. You learned the Android gestures and how to perform each on an Android device and on the emulator. We provided a quick refresher on basic object-technology concepts, including classes, objects, attributes, behaviors, encapsulation, information hiding, inheritance and more. You test-drove the **Tip Calculator** app on the Android emulator for both smartphone and tablet AVDs.

In Chapter 2, you'll build your first Android app in Android Studio. The app will display text and an image. You'll also learn about Android accessibility and internationalization.

Self-Review Exercises

1.1 Fill in the blanks in each of the following statements:
   a) In 2007, the _____ was formed to develop, maintain and evolve Android, driving innovation in mobile technology and improving the user experience while reducing costs.

b) The _____ IDE allows you to create, run and debug Android apps.

c) Multitouch screens allow you to control your Android device with _____ involving one touch or multiple simultaneous touches.

d) With web services, you can create _____, which enable you to rapidly develop apps by quickly combining complementary web services, often from different organizations and possibly other forms of information feeds.

e) Android uses a collection of _____, which are named groups of related, predefined classes.

f) The _____, included in the Android SDK, allows you to run Android apps in a simulated environment within Windows, Mac OS X or Linux.

g) Almost any noun can be reasonably represented as a software object in terms of _____ (e.g., name, color and size) and behaviors (e.g., calculating, moving and communicating).

h) A program unit called a(n) _____ houses the methods that perform its tasks.

i) You send messages to an object. Each message is a(n) _____ that tells a method of the object to perform its task.

1.2   State whether each of the following is *true* or *false*. If *false*, explain why.

a) One benefit of developing Android apps is that the operating system is proprietary to Google.

b) The openness of the Android platform discourages innovation.

c) You can reuse a class many times to build many objects. Reuse of existing classes when building new classes and programs saves time and effort.

d) Attributes are specified by the class's methods.

e) Objects may communicate with one another, but they're normally not allowed to know how other objects are implemented—implementation details are hidden within the objects themselves.

1.3   Fill in the blanks in each of the following statements (based on Section 1.8):

a) Objects have the property of _____—although objects communicate with one another, they're normally not allowed to know how other objects are implemented.

b) The _____ that objects come from are essentially reusable software components; they include attributes and behaviors.

c) The process of analyzing and designing a system from an object-oriented point of view is called _____.

d) With _____, new classes of objects are derived by absorbing characteristics of existing classes, then adding unique characteristics of their own.

e) The size, shape, color and weight of an object are considered _____ of the object's class.

f) A class that represents a bank account might contain one _____ to deposit money to an account, another to withdraw money from an account and a third to inquire what the account's current balance is.

g) You must build an object of a class before a program can perform the tasks that the class's methods define—this process is called _____.

h) The balance of a bank account class is an example of a(n) _____ of that class.

i) Your project's requirements define what the system is supposed to do and your design specifies _____ the system should do it.

Answers to Self-Review Exercises

1.1   a) Open Handset Alliance. b) Android Development Tools (ADT). c) gestures. d) mashups. e) packages. f) Android emulator. g) attributes. h) class. i) method call.

1.2 a) False. The operating system is open source and free. b) False. The openness of the platform spurs rapid innovation. c) True. d) False. Attributes are specified by the class's instance variables. e) True.

1.3 a) information hiding. b) classes. c) object-oriented analysis and design (OOAD). d) inheritance. e) attributes. f) method. g) instantiation. h) attribute. i) how.

Exercises

1.4 Fill in the blanks in each of the following statements:
a) Android apps are developed with _____—one of the world's most widely used programming language, a logical choice because it's powerful, free and open source.
b) GUI programming in Java is _____ driven, so you'll write apps that respond to various user interactions such as screen touches and keystrokes.
c) Touching the screen and holding your finger in position is called a(n) _____.
d) Touching the screen, then moving your finger in one direction and releasing it is called a(n) _____.
e) Before running an app in the emulator, you'll need to create a(n) _____, which defines the characteristics of the device on which you want to test, including the hardware, system image, screen size, data storage and more.
f) Performing a task in a program requires a(n) _____ which houses the program statements that actually perform its tasks.
g) You must build an object of a class before a program can perform the tasks that the class's methods define. The process of doing this is called _____.
h) _____ helps you build more reliable and effective systems, because existing classes and components often have gone through extensive testing, debugging and performance tuning.
i) Classes _____ (i.e., wrap) attributes and methods into objects—an object's attributes and methods are intimately related.
j) A new class of objects can be created quickly and conveniently by _____—the new class absorbs the characteristics of an existing one, possibly customizing them and adding unique characteristics of its own.
k) Unlike actual buttons on a device, _____ buttons appear on the device's touch screen.
l) _____ was the complete user-interface redesign that Google introduced with Android 5.0.
m) Among its many new features, Android 6.0 introduced a new _____ to make apps easier to install.

1.5 State whether each of the following is *true* or *false*. If *false*, explain why.
a) The vast majority of Android development is done in C++.
b) You can reproduce on the emulator most of the Android gestures and controls using your computer's keyboard and mouse.
c) Objects, or more precisely the classes objects come from, are essentially reusable software components.

1.6 One of the most common objects is a wrist watch. Discuss how each of the following terms and concepts applies to the notion of a watch: object, attributes, behaviors, class, inheritance (consider, for example, an alarm clock), messages, encapsulation and information hiding.

Welcome App

Objectives

In this chapter you'll:

- Learn the basics of the Android Studio IDE, which you'll use to write, test and debug your Android apps.

- Use the IDE to create a new app project.

- Design a graphical user interface (GUI) visually (without programming) using the IDE's layout editor.

- Display text and an image in a GUI.

- Edit the properties of views (GUI components).

- Build and launch an app in the Android emulator.

- Make the app more accessible to visually impaired people by specifying strings for use with Android's TalkBack and Explore-by-Touch features.

- Support internationalization so your app can display strings localized in different languages.

Outline

Self-Review Exercises | Answers to Self-Review Exercises | Exercises

2.1 Introduction

In this chapter, you'll build the **Welcome** app that displays a welcome message and an image. You'll use Android Studio to create a simple app (Fig. 2.1) that runs on Android phones and tablets in both portrait and landscape orientations:

- In portrait the device's height is greater than its width.
- In landscape the width is greater than the height.

You'll use Android Studio's layout editor to build the GUI using *drag-and-drop* techniques. You'll also edit the GUI's XML directly. You'll execute your app in the Android *emulator* and on an Android device, if you have one.

    You'll provide descriptive text for the app's image to make the app more *accessible* for people with visual impairments. As you'll see, Android's *Explore by Touch* enables users to touch items on the screen and hear *TalkBack* speak the corresponding descriptive text. We'll discuss how to test these features, which are available only on Android devices.

Android's top system bar shows items including the time, battery indicator, cellular connection status and icons for apps that have sent you notifications

Welcome

Welcome to Android App Development!

TextView component

Client area in which your app's content is displayed

®

ImageView component showing the Deitel bug logo

Android's bottom system bar shows (left-to-right) the *back, home* and *recent apps* buttons

Fig. 2.1 | **Welcome** app running in the Android emulator.

Finally, you'll *internationalize* the app so that you can provide *localized* strings in different languages. You'll then change the locale setting on the Android emulator so that you can test the app in Spanish. When your app executes, Android chooses the correct strings based on the device's locale. We show how to change the locale on a device. We assume that you've read the Preface, Before You Begin and Section 1.9.

2.2 Technologies Overview

This section introduces the technologies you'll use to build the **Welcome** app.

2.2.1 Android Studio

In Section 2.3, you'll use the Android Studio integrated development environment (IDE) to create a new app. As you'll see, the IDE creates a default GUI that contains the text "Hello world!" You'll then use the layout editor's **Design** and **Text** views and the **Properties** window to visually build a simple graphical user interface (GUI) consisting of text and an image (Section 2.5).

2.2.2 LinearLayout, TextView and ImageView

GUI components in Android are called **views**. **Layouts** are views that contain and arrange other views. You'll use a vertical **LinearLayout** to arrange the app's text and image with each occupying half the LinearLayout's vertical space. A LinearLayout also can arrange views horizontally.

This app's text is displayed in a **TextView** and its image is displayed in an **ImageView**. The default GUI created by Android Studio already contains a TextView. You'll modify its properties, including its text, font size and font color and its size relative to the Image-View within the LinearLayout (Section 2.5.5). You'll use the layout editor's **Palette** of views (Fig. 2.11) to drag and drop an ImageView onto the GUI (Section 2.5.11), then configure its properties, including its image source and positioning within the LinearLayout.

2.2.3 Extensible Markup Language (XML)

Extensible Markup Language (XML) is a natural way to express GUIs. XML is human- and computer-readable text and, in the context of Android, helps you specify the layouts and components to use, as well as their attributes, such as size, position, color, text size, margins and padding. Android Studio parses the XML to display your design in the layout editor and to generate the Java code that produces the runtime GUI. You'll also use XML files to store **app resources**, such as strings, numbers and colors (Section 2.2.4).

2.2.4 App Resources

It's considered good practice to define all strings, numeric values and other values in XML resource files that are placed in the subfolders of a project's res folder. In Section 2.5.5, you'll create resources for strings (such as the text on a TextView) and measurements (such as a font's size). For the TextView's font color, you'll create a color resource using a color selected from Google's Material Design color palette:

```
http://www.google.com/design/spec/style/color.html
```

2.2.5 Accessibility

Android provides *accessibility* features to help people with certain disabilities use their devices. People with visual impairments can use Android's **TalkBack** to allow a device to speak screen text or text that you provide to help them understand the purpose and contents of a view. Android's **Explore by Touch** enables the user to touch the screen to hear TalkBack speak what's on the screen near the touch. Section 2.7 shows how to enable these features and configure your app's views for accessibility.

2.2.6 Internationalization

Android devices are used worldwide. To reach the most users with your apps, you should consider customizing them for various *locales* and spoken languages. Configuring your app so that it can be customized for various locales is known as **internationalization**. Customizing your app for a specific locale is known as **localization**. Section 2.8 shows how to provide Spanish text for the **Welcome** app's TextView and the ImageView's accessibility string, and how to test the app on an AVD or device configured for Spanish.

2.3 Creating an App

This book's examples were developed using the Android 6 SDK that was current at the time of this writing. This section shows you how to use Android Studio to create a new project. We introduce additional features of the IDE throughout the book.

2.3.1 Launching Android Studio

As you did in Section 1.9, open Android Studio via its shortcut:

The IDE displays either the **Welcome** window (Fig. 1.17) or the last project you had open.

2.3.2 Creating a New Project

A **project** is a group of related files, such as code files, resource files and images that make up an app. To create an app, you must first create its project. To do so, click **Start a new Android Studio project** in the **Welcome** window or, if a project is open, select **File > New > New Project....** This displays the **Create New Project** dialog (Fig. 2.2).

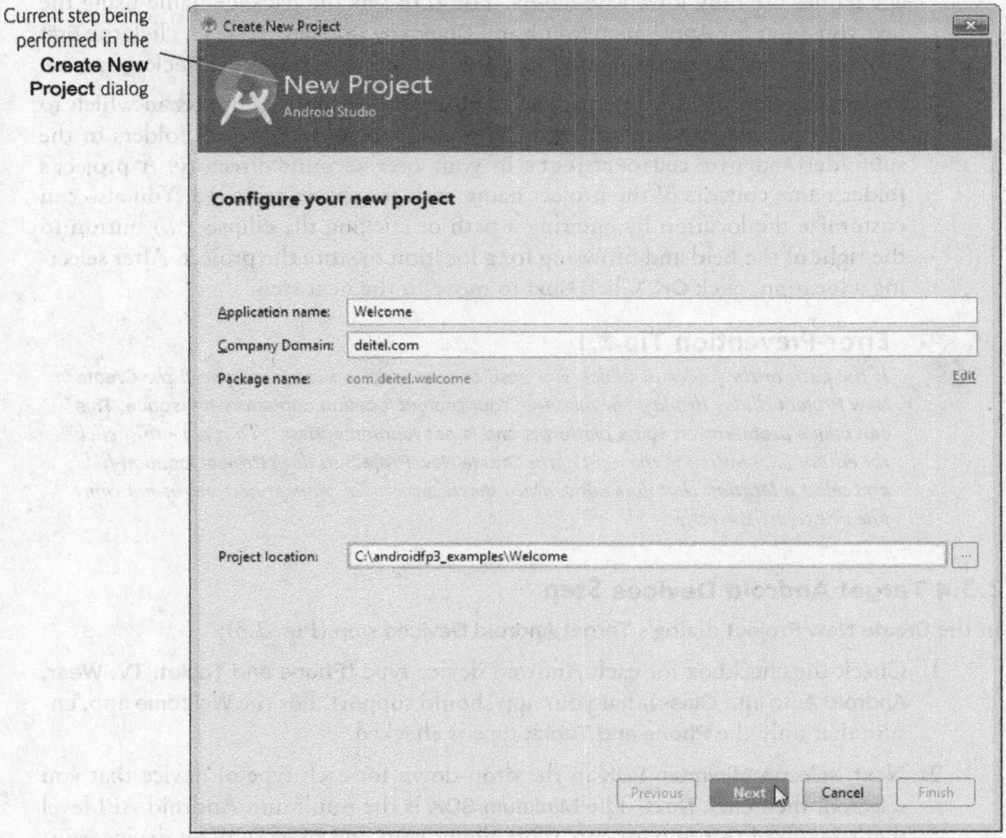
Current step being performed in the Create New Project dialog
Create New Project
New Project
Android Studio
Configure your new project
Application name:
Welcome
Company Domain:
deitel.com
Package name:
com.deitel.welcome
Edit
Project location:
C:\androidfp3_examples\Welcome
...
Previous
Next
Cancel
Finish

Fig. 2.2 | **Create New Project** dialog—**New Project** step.

2.3.3 Create New Project Dialog

In the **Create New Project** dialog's **Configure your new project** step (Fig. 2.2), specify the following information, then click **Next**:

1. **Application name:** field—Your app's name. Enter Welcome in this field.

2. **Company Domain:** field—Your company website's domain name. We used our deitel.com website domain. For learning purposes you can use example.com, but this must be changed if you intend to distribute your app.

3. **Package name:** field—The Java package name for your app's source code. Android and the Google Play store use this as the app's *unique identifier*, which must remain the same in all versions of your app that you upload to the Google Play store. The package name normally begins with your company's or institution's **Company Domain** *in reverse*—our **Company Domain** is deitel.com, so our Java package names begin with com.deitel. This is followed by a dot (.) and the app's name in all lowercase letters with any spaces removed. By convention, package names use only lowercase letters. The IDE sets the package name using the text you enter for **Application Name** and **Company Domain**. You can click the **Edit** link to the right of the generated package name to customize the **Package name**.

4. **Project location:** field—The path of the location on your computer in which to store the project. By default, Android Studio places new project folders in the subfolder AndroidStudioProjects in your user account directory. A project's folder name consists of the project name with the spaces removed. You also can customize the location by entering a path or clicking the ellipsis (...) button to the right of the field and browsing for a location to store the project. After selecting a location, click **OK**. Click **Next** to move to the next step.

Error-Prevention Tip 2.1

If the path to the folder in which you wish to save a project contains spaces, the Create New Project *dialog displays the message* "Your project location contains whitespace. This can cause problems on some platforms and is not recommended." *To resolve this, click the ellipsis (...) button to the right of the* Create New Project *dialog's* Project location *field and select a location that does not contain spaces; otherwise, your project might not compile or execute correctly.*

2.3.4 Target Android Devices Step

In the **Create New Project** dialog's **Target Android Devices** step (Fig. 2.3):

1. Check the checkbox for each Android device type (**Phone and Tablet, TV, Wear, Android Auto** and **Glass**) that your app should support. For the **Welcome** app, ensure that only the **Phone and Tablet** type is checked.

2. Next, select a **Minimum SDK** in the drop-down for each type of device that you selected, then click **Next**. The **Minimum SDK** is the minimum Android API level that's required to run your app. This allows your app to execute on devices supporting that API level and higher. Select **API23: Android 6.0 (Marshmallow)** for this

book's apps and click **Next**. Figure 2.4 shows the Android SDK versions and their API levels—versions not shown here are deprecated and should not be used. The percentage of Android devices running each platform version is shown at

```
http://developer.android.com/about/dashboards/index.html
```

Software Engineering Observation 2.1

*Lower **Minimum SDK** values enable your app to run on more devices—e.g., at the time of this writing, you could reach 94% of devices with API 15. Generally you should target the lowest API level on which your app can run. You must disable newer features that are not available on older platforms when your app is installed on those platforms.*

Create New Project

Target Android Devices

Select the form factors your app will run on

Different platforms may require separate SDKs

☑ **Phone and Tablet**

Minimum SDK   API 23: Android 6.0 (Marshmallow)

Lower API levels target more devices, but have fewer features available. By targeting API 23 and later, your app will run on < 1% of the devices that are active on the Google Play Store.

Help me choose

☐ **Wear**

Minimum SDK   API 21: Android 5.0 (Lollipop)

☐ **TV**

Minimum SDK   API 21: Android 5.0 (Lollipop)

☐ **Android Auto**

☐ Glass (Not Installed)   Download

Minimum SDK

Previous   Next   Cancel   Finish

Fig. 2.3 | **Create New Project** dialog—**Target Android Devices** step.

SDK version	API level	SDK version	API level	SDK version	API level
6.0	23	4.3	18	2.3.3–2.3.7	10
5.1	22	4.2.x	17	2.2	8
5.0	21	4.1.x	16		
4.4	19	4.0.3–4.0.4	15		

Fig. 2.4 | Android SDK versions and API levels. (`http://developer.android.com/about/dashboards/index.html`)

2.3.5 Add an Activity to Mobile Step

In the **Add an Activity to Mobile** step (Fig. 2.5), you'll select an app template. Templates provide preconfigured starting points for common app designs and app logic.

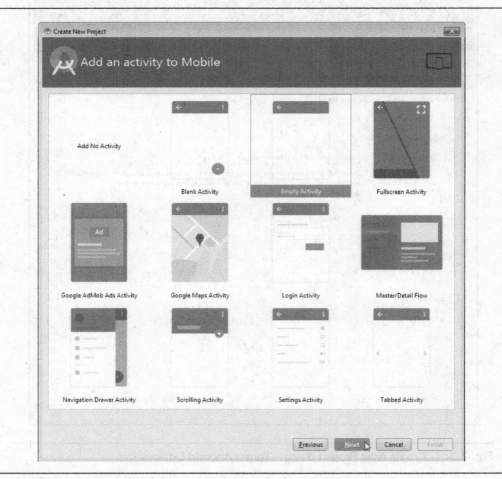

Fig. 2.5 | **Create New Project** dialog—**Add an activity to Mobile** step.

Figure 2.6 briefly describes four commonly used templates from Fig. 2.5. For this app, select **Empty Activity**, then click **Next**. This template defines a one-screen app that displays **Hello World!**. We'll use other templates in later chapters. For multiscreen apps, you also can define a new screen by adding one of the Fig. 2.5 activities to an existing app. For example, in Chapter 4's **Flag Quiz** app, we'll add a **Settings Activity** that provides a screen in which the user can specify the quizzes settings.

Template	Description
Blank Activity	Used for a *single-screen app* in which you build most of the GUI yourself. Provides an *app bar* at the top of the app that displays the app's name and can display controls that enable a user to interact with the app. Also includes a material design FloatingActionButton.
Fullscreen Activity	Used for a *single-screen app* (similar to **Blank Activity**) that occupies the entire screen, but can toggle visibility of the device's status bar and the app's app bar.
Master/Detail Flow	Used for an app that displays a *master list* of items from which a user can choose one item to see its *details*—similar to the built-in **Email** and **Contacts** apps. Includes basic logic for enabling a user to select an item from the master list and display that item in the detail view. For tablets, the master list and details are shown side-by-side on the same screen. For phones, the master list is shown on one screen, and selecting an item displays the item's details in a separate screen.

Fig. 2.6 | Activity templates.

2.3.6 Customize the Activity Step

This step (Fig. 2.7) depends on the template selected in the previous step. For the **Empty Activity** template, this step allows you to specify:

- **Activity Name**—MainActivity is the default name provided by the IDE. This is the name of an Activity subclass that controls the app's execution. Starting in Chapter 3, we'll modify this class to implement the app's functionality.

- **Layout Name**—activity_main is the default name provided by the IDE. This file (which has the .xml extension) stores an XML representation of the app's GUI that you'll build in Section 2.5 using visual techniques.

For this app, keep the default settings, then click **Finish** to create the project.

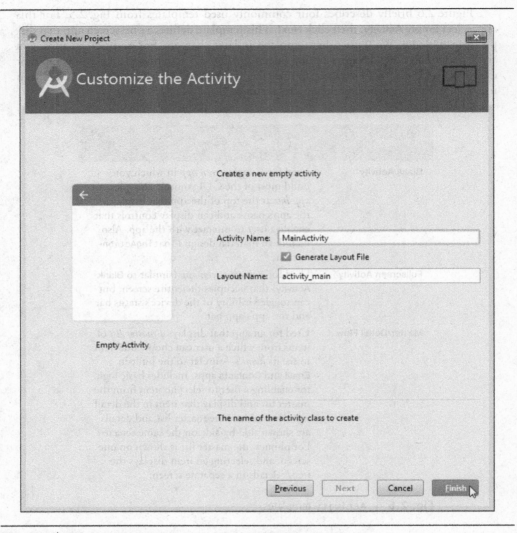

Fig. 2.7 | **Create New Project** dialog—**Customize the Activity** step.

2.4 Android Studio Window

When you finish creating the project, the IDE opens both MainActivity.java and activity_main.xml. Close MainActivity.java so that the IDE appears as shown in Fig. 2.8. The IDE shows the layout editor, so you can begin designing your app's GUI. In this chapter, we discuss only the IDE features we need to build the **Welcome** app. We'll introduce more IDE features throughout the book.

Project window displays the project's files in the **app** node

Editor windows—like the layout and code editors—appear here

Component Tree with the currently selected item properties displayed in the **Properties** window

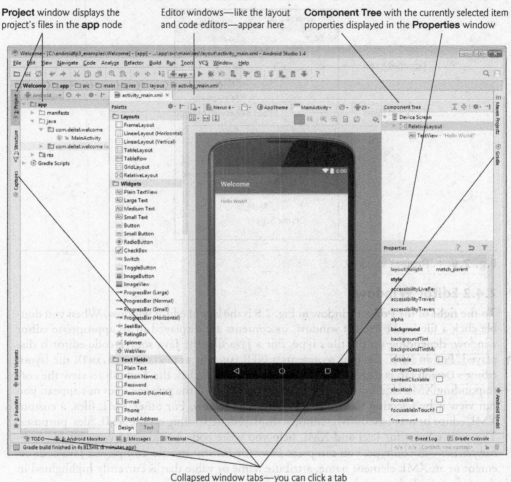

Collapsed window tabs—you can click a tab to expand the corresponding window

Fig. 2.8 | Welcome project open in the Android Studio.

2.4.1 Project Window

The **Project** window provides access to all of the project's files. You can have many projects open in the IDE at once—each in its own window. Figure 2.9 shows the **Welcome** app project's contents in the **Project** window—we expanded the res folder and it's nested layout folder. The app folder contains the files you'll edit to create your apps' GUIs and logic. The app folder's contents are organized into nested folders containing files. In this chapter, you'll use only files located in the res folder, which we discuss in Section 2.4.4—we'll discuss the other folders and files as we use them in later chapters.

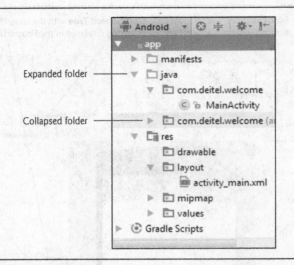

Expanded folder ——

Collapsed folder ——

Fig. 2.9 | **Project** window.

2.4.2 Editor Windows

To the right of the **Project** window in Fig. 2.8 is the layout editor window. When you double click a file in the **Project** window, its contents are displayed in an appropriate editor window, depending on the file's type. For a Java file, the Java source-code editor is displayed. For an XML file that represents a GUI (such as `activity_main.xml`), the layout editor's **Design** tab is displayed by default and you can click the **Text** tab to view the corresponding XML side-by-side with a design preview—if the preview does not appear, you can view it by selecting **View > Tool Windows > Preview**. For other XML files, a custom XML editor or text-based XML editor is displayed, depending on the XML files' purposes. The code editors for Java and XML help you write code quickly and correctly via *code-completion*—as you type, you can press *Enter* (or *Return*) to auto-complete a Java code element or an XML element name, attribute name or value that is currently highlighted in the code-completion window.

2.4.3 Component Tree Window

When the layout editor is open in **Design** view, the **Component Tree** appears at the right side of the IDE (Fig. 2.8). This window shows the *layouts* and *views* (GUI components) that comprise the GUI and their parent-child relationships—for example, a layout (the parent) might contain many nested views (the children), including other layouts.

2.4.4 App Resource Files

Layout files like `activity_main.xml` are app resources and are stored in subfolders of the project's **res** folder. The subfolders contain different resource types. The ones we use in this app are shown in Fig. 2.10, and the others (`menu`, `animator`, `anim`, `color`, `mipmap`, `raw` and `xml`) are discussed as we need them later in the book.

Resource subfolder	Description
drawable	Folder names that begin with drawable typically contain images. These folders may also contain XML files representing shapes and other types of drawables (such as the images that represent a button's *unpressed* and *pressed* states).
layout	Folder names that begin with layout contain XML files that describe GUIs, such as the activity_main.xml file.
values	Folder names that begin with values contain XML files that specify values for *arrays* (arrays.xml), *colors* (colors.xml), *dimensions* (dimens.xml—values such as widths, heights and font sizes), *strings* (strings.xml) and *styles* (styles.xml). These file names are used by convention but are *not* required—actually, you can place all resources of these types in *one* file. It's considered good practice to define the data from hard-coded arrays, colors, sizes, strings and styles as *resources* so they can be modified easily without changing the app's Java code. For example, if a *dimension resource* is referenced from many locations in your code, you can change the dimension's value in the resource file, rather than search for every occurrence of a hard-coded dimension value in your app's Java source files.

Fig. 2.10 | Subfolders of the project's res folder that are used in this chapter.

2.4.5 Layout Editor

When you first create a project, the IDE opens the app's activity_main.xml file in the layout editor (Fig. 2.11). You also can double click activity_main.xml in the res/layout folder to open the file in the layout editor.

Selecting the Screen Type for GUI Design
Android devices can run on many types of devices. In this chapter, you'll design an Android phone GUI. As we mentioned in the Before You Begin section, we use an AVD that emulates the Google Nexus 6 phone for this purpose. The layout editor comes with many device configurations that represent various screen sizes and resolutions that you can use to design your GUI. For this chapter, we use the predefined **Nexus 6**, which you can select in the virtual-device drop-down at the top of the layout editor in Fig. 2.11—**Nexus 4** is selected by default. This does not mean that the app can execute only on a Nexus 6 device—it simply means that the design is for devices similar in screen size and resolution to the Nexus 6. In later chapters, you'll see how to design your GUIs to scale appropriately for a wide range of devices.

The **Palette** contains **Widgets** (views), **Layouts** and other items that can be dragged and dropped onto the canvas

The virtual device drop-down lists devices you can use to design your GUI—select **Nexus 6** for this chapter

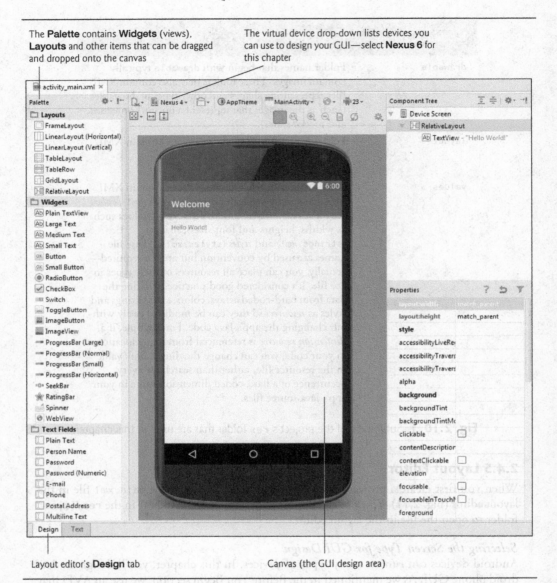

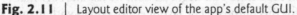

Layout editor's **Design** tab   Canvas (the GUI design area)

Fig. 2.11 | Layout editor view of the app's default GUI.

2.4.6 Default GUI

The default GUI for a **Blank Page** app (Fig. 2.11) consists of a RelativeLayout with a white background and a TextView containing "Hello World!". A **RelativeLayout** arranges views *relative to one another* or *relative to the layout itself*—for example, you can specify that one view should appear *below* another and be *centered horizontally* within the RelativeLayout. For the **Welcome** app, you'll change the RelativeLayout to a vertical LinearLayout in which text and an image will be arranged top-to-bottom on the screen and each will occupy half the layout's height. A TextView displays text. You'll add an ImageView to display the image. We'll say more about each of these in Section 2.5.

2.4.7 XML for the Default GUI

As we mentioned previously, the file activity_main.xml contains the GUI's XML representation. Figure 2.12 shows the initial XML. We reduced the amount of indentation in the default XML for book-publication purposes. You'll edit this XML directly to change the RelativeLayout to a LinearLayout.

```
1   <?xml version="1.0" encoding="utf-8"?>
2   <RelativeLayout xmlns:android="http://schemas.android.com/apk/res/android"
3       xmlns:tools="http://schemas.android.com/tools"
4       android:layout_width="match_parent"
5       android:layout_height="match_parent"
6       android:paddingBottom="@dimen/activity_vertical_margin"
7       android:paddingLeft="@dimen/activity_horizontal_margin"
8       android:paddingRight="@dimen/activity_horizontal_margin"
9       android:paddingTop="@dimen/activity_vertical_margin"
10      tools:context=".MainActivity">
11
12      <TextView
13          android:layout_width="wrap_content"
14          android:layout_height="wrap_content"
15          android:text="@string/hello_world" />
16
17  </RelativeLayout>
```

Fig. 2.12 | Initial contents of the project's activity_main.xml file.

The attribute values that begin with @, such as

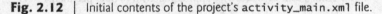

@dimen/activity_vertical_margin

in line 6, are *resources* with values defined in other files. By default, the XML editor displays a resource's literal value (16dp for the resource in line 6) and highlights the value with a light green background (or light gray, if you're using the dark Android Studio theme). This enables you to see the resource's actual value that's used in a particular context. If you click the literal value (16dp for @dimen/activity_vertical_margin), the editor instead displays the corresponding resource name.

2.5 Building the App's GUI with the Layout Editor

You'll now create the **Welcome** app's GUI. The IDE's layout editor allows you to build your GUI by dragging and dropping views—such as TextViews, ImageViews and Buttons—onto the layout editor. By default, the GUI layout for an app based on the **Empty Activity** template is stored in an XML file called **activity_main.xml**, located in the project's res folder in the layout subfolder. In this chapter, we'll use the layout editor and the **Component Tree** window to build the GUI. You'll edit the XML in activity_main.xml only to change the layout used to arrange this app's TextView and ImageView.

2.5.1 Adding an Image to the Project

For this app, you'll need to add an image to the project. We'll use the Deitel bug logo[1] image (bug.png), which is located with the book's examples in the images folder's Welcome subfolder. File names for image resources—and all the other resources you'll use in later chapters—must be in all *lowercase* letters.

drawable *Folders*

Android devices have various *screen sizes*, *resolutions* and *pixel densities* (that is, dots per inch or DPI), so you typically provide images in various resolutions that the operating system chooses based on a device's pixel density. These are placed in drawable folders (in a project's res folder) that store images with different pixel densities (Fig. 2.13). For example, images for devices that are similar in pixel density to the Google Nexus 6 phone (560 dpi) we use in our phone AVD would be placed in the folder drawable-xxxhdpi. Images for devices with lower pixel densities are placed in the other drawable folders—normally the folder that represents the closest pixel density to the actual device.

Density	Description
drawable-ldpi	*Low density*—approximately 120 dots-per-inch.
drawable-mdpi	*Medium density*—approximately 160 dots-per-inch.
drawable-hdpi	*High density*—approximately 240 dots-per-inch.
drawable-xhdpi	*Extra-high density*—approximately 320 dots-per-inch.
drawable-xxhdpi	*Extra-Extra-high density*—approximately 480 dots-per-inch.
drawable-xxxhdpi	*Extra-Extra-Extra-high density*—approximately 640 dots-per-inch.

Fig. 2.13 | Android pixel densities.

Android Studio displays only one drawable folder containing the app's drawable resources, even if your project contains resources for multiple densities. For a resource stored in the project's folder drawable-xxxhdpi on disk, Android Studio displays

> *filename*.xml (xxxhdpi)

in the project's drawable folder.

For this app, we provide only one version of the image. If Android cannot find an image in the drawable folder that most closely matches the device's pixel density, Android will scale the version from another drawable folder up or down as necessary. By default, Android Studio creates only a drawable folder without a DPI qualifier, which we'll use for this initial app. For detailed information on supporting multiple screens and screen sizes in Android, visit:

> http://developer.android.com/guide/practices/screens_support.html

---

1. Before you use any image in an app, you should ensure that you've properly licensed the image. Some image licenses require you to pay for the right to use an image and others provide free open-source or Creative Commons (creativecommons.org) licenses.

Look-and-Feel Observation 2.1

Low-resolution images do not scale well. For images to render nicely, a high-pixel-density device needs highe-resolution images than a low-pixel-density device.

Adding bug.png to the Project

Perform the following steps to add the images to this project:

1. In the **Project** window, expand the project's res folder.

2. In the book's examples folder on your file system, open the images folder, then the Welcome subfolder.

3. Copy the bug.png file, then in Android Studio's **Project** window select res folder's drawable subfolder and paste the file into that subfolder.

4. In the **Copy** dialog that appears, click **OK**.

The image can now be used in the app.

2.5.2 Adding an App Icon

When your app is installed on a device, its icon and name appear with all other installed apps in the launcher, which you can access via the 🔳 icon on your device's home screen. To add the app's launcher icon, right click the res folder, then select **New > Image Asset**. This will open the **Asset Studio** window (Fig. 2.14), which enables you to configure the app's icon from an existing image, a piece of clip art or text.

For this app, we chose the DeitelOrange.png image located in the images folder with the book's examples. To use this image:

1. Click the ellipsis button to the right of the **Image file:** field.

2. Navigate to the images folder in the book's examples folder.

3. Select DeitelOrange.png and click **OK**. Previews of the scaled images are shown in the dialog's **Preview** area.

4. Click **Next**, then click **Finish**.

The IDE creates several scaled versions of the image, each named ic_launcher.png, and places them in the project's mipmap[2] subfolders of the res folder. The mipmap subfolders are similar to the drawable subfolders, but are specifically for the app's icon. When you upload an app to Google Play, you can upload multiple versions of the app for various device sizes and screen resolutions. All images in the mipmap folders are uploaded with every versions of your app, whereas you can remove extra drawable folders for specific pixel densities from a given app version to minimize the total installation size for a particular device.

Look-and-Feel Observation 2.2

Images do not always scale well. For apps that you intend to place in the Google Play store, you might want to have an artist design icons for the appropriate resolutions. In Chapter 10, we discuss submitting apps to the Google Play store and list several companies that offer free and fee-based icon-design services.

---

2. For the origin of the term *mipmap*, see https://en.wikipedia.org/wiki/Mipmap.

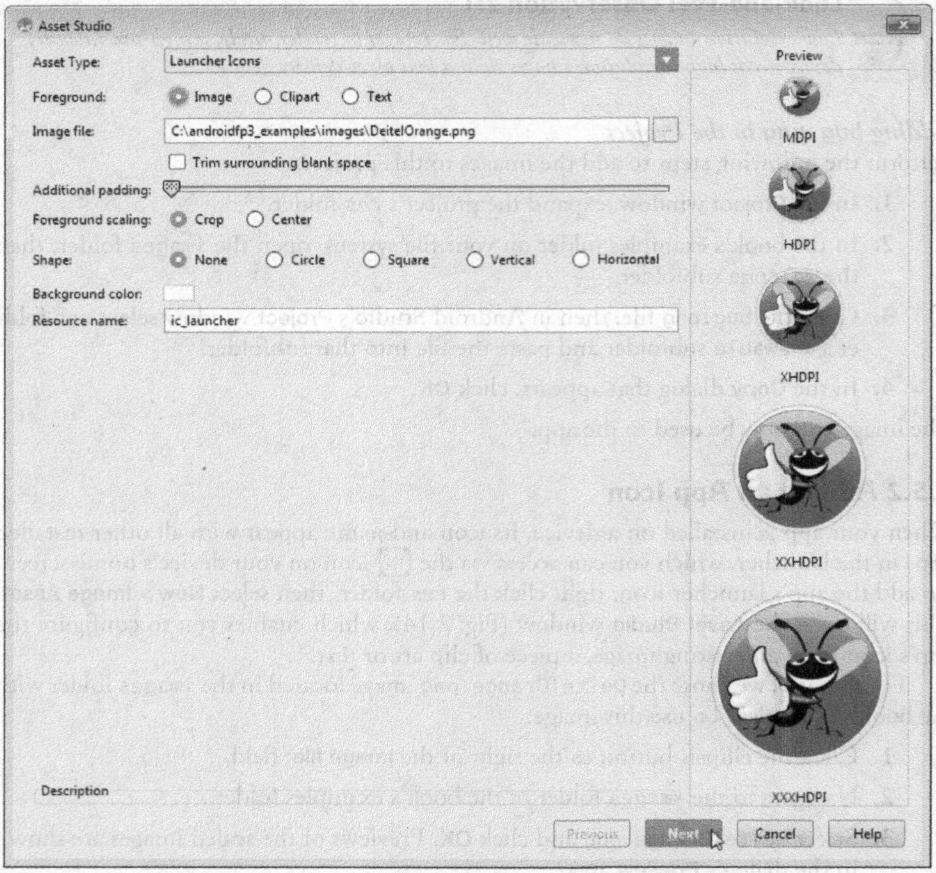

Fig. 2.14 | Configuring the launcher icon in the **Asset Studio** window.

2.5.3 Changing `RelativeLayout` to a `LinearLayout`

When you open a layout XML file, the layout's design appears in the layout editor and the layout's views and their hierarchical relationships appear in the **Component Tree** window (Fig. 2.15). To configure a layout or view, you can select it in the layout editor or in the **Component Tree**, then use the **Properties** window below the **Component Tree** to specify the view's property values without editing the XML directly. When designing and modifying more complex layouts, it's often easier to work directly in the **Component Tree**.

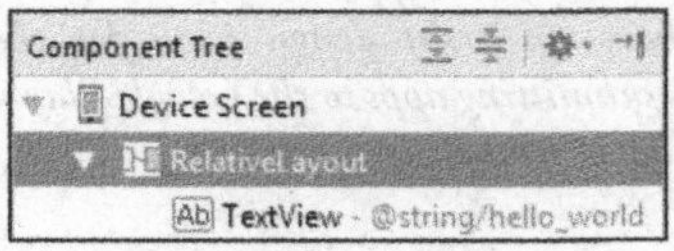

Fig. 2.15 | Hierarchical GUI view in the **Component Tree** window.

For some GUI modifications—such as changing the default `RelativeLayout` to a `LinearLayout`—you must edit the layout's XML directly. (This might change as Google improves the layout editor's capabilities.) To do so:

1. Click the **Text** tab at the bottom of the layout editor to switch from the **Design** view to the layout's XML text.

2. At the top of the XML (line 2 in Fig. 2.12), double click the XML element name `RelativeLayout` to select it, then start typing `LinearLayout`.

3. As you type in line 2, the IDE edits the corresponding ending XML tag (line 17 in Fig. 2.12) simultaneously to keep them in sync, and a code-completion window appears containing element names that begin with the letters you've typed so far. Once `LinearLayout` appears in the code-completion window and is highlighted, press *Enter* (or *Return*) to select `LinearLayout` and enable Android Studio to auto-complete the edit.

4. Save the changes and switch back to the layout editor's **Design** tab.

The **Component Tree** should now appear as in Fig. 2.16.

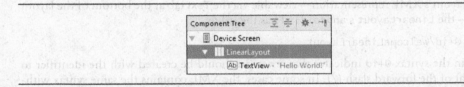

Fig. 2.16 | **Component Tree** after changing from a `RelativeLayout` to a `LinearLayout`.

2.5.4 Changing the `LinearLayout`'s `id` and `orientation`

In this section, you'll customize the `LinearLayout`'s properties. In general, give each layout and component a relevant name. This helps you easily identify each view in the **Component Tree** and enables you to manipulate the views programmatically, as we'll do in subsequent apps.

When a GUI is displayed in the layout editor, you can use the **Properties** window below the **Component Tree** (Fig. 2.8) to configure the selected view's properties. You also can edit a view's most commonly used properties (as you'll do in this section) by double clicking the view in the canvas. The layout editor then displays a small dialog in which you can set the view's `id` property and other properties that depend on the specific view:

- For a `LinearLayout`, you can set the **orientation** to specify whether the layout's children are arranged in `horizontal` or `vertical` orientation.

- For a `TextView`, you can set the **text** that's displayed.

- For an `ImageView`, you can set the **src** (source) of the image to display.

Setting the `LinearLayout`'s orientation and id Properties

To change the `LinearLayout`'s `orientation`, double click the virtual phone screen's white background in the layout editor to display the dialog of common `LinearLayout` properties, then select **vertical** from the **orientation:** drop-down as shown in Fig. 2.17. This sets the property's value and dismisses the dialog. A view's name is defined by setting its **id**

property, which is specified in the layout's XML with the attribute android:id. Double click the virtual phone screen's white background, enter the name welcomeLinearLayout in the id: field, then press *Enter* (or *Return*) to set the value and dismiss the dialog.

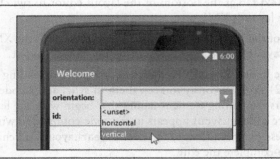

Fig. 2.17 | Setting the LinearLayout's orientation.

The id Property's XML Representation
In the layout's XML representation—viewable via the **Text** tab at the bottom of the layout editor—the LinearLayout's android:id has the value:

```
@+id/welcomeLinearLayout
```

The + in the syntax @+id indicates that a *new* id should be created with the identifier to the right of the forward slash (/). In some cases, the XML contains the same syntax without the + to refer to an existing view—for example, to specify the relationships between views in a RelativeLayout.

2.5.5 Configuring the TextView's id and text Properties
The **Welcome** app's default GUI already contains a TextView, so you'll simply modify its properties.

Setting the TextView's id Property
Double click the TextView in the layout editor, then in the dialog that appears set the **id:** to welcomeTextView and press *Enter* (or *Return*).

Configuring the TextView's text Property Using a String Resource
According to the Android documentation for application resources

```
http://developer.android.com/guide/topics/resources/index.html
```

it's considered good practice to place strings, string arrays, images, colors, font sizes, dimensions and other app resources in XML files within the subfolders of the project's res folder, so these resources can be managed separately from your app's Java code. This is known as *externalizing* the resources. For example, if you externalize color values, all components that use the same color can be updated to a new color simply by changing the color value in a central resource file.

If you wish to *localize* your app in several languages, storing the strings *separately* from the app's code allows you to change them easily. In your project's res folder, the subfolder values contains a `strings.xml` file that's used to store the app's default language strings—English for our apps. To provide localized strings for other languages, you can create separate values folders for each language, as we'll demonstrate in Section 2.8.

To set the TextView's text property, create a new string resource in the `strings.xml` file as follows:

1. Either double click the welcomeTextView in the layout editor or select welcome-TextView and locate its text property in the **Properties** window

2. Click the ellipsis (…) button to the right of the property's value to display the **Resources** dialog.

3. In the **Resources** dialog, click **New Resource**, then select **New String Value…** to display the **New String Value Resource** dialog and fill the **Resource name:** and **Resource value:** fields as shown in Fig. 2.18. Leave the other settings (we'll discuss these in later sections and apps) and click **OK** to create the new string resource named welcome and set it as the value of the TextView's text property.

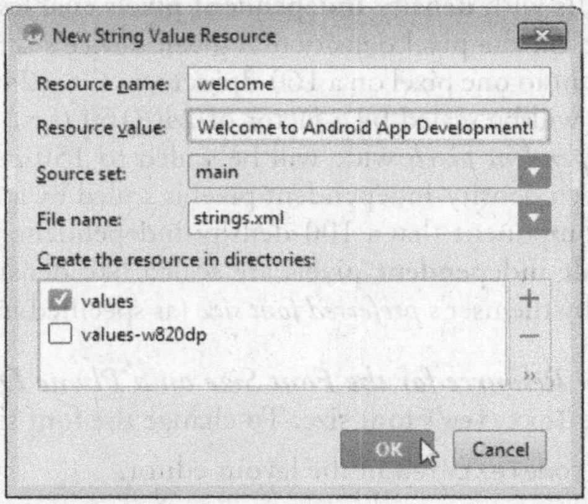

Fig. 2.18 | **New String Value Resource** dialog.

In the **Properties** window, the text property should now appear as in Fig. 2.19. The @string/ prefix indicates that a string resource will be used to obtain the value for the text property and welcome indicates the specific string resource to use. By default, the resource is placed in the `strings.xml` file (located in the project's res/values folder).

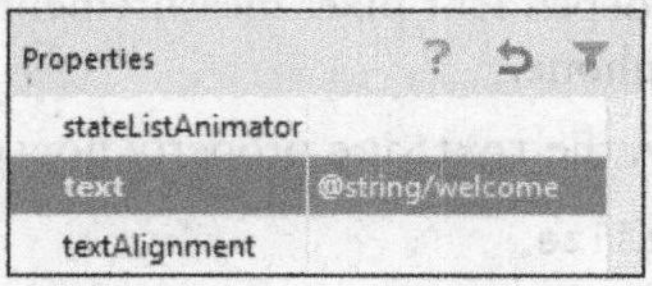

Fig. 2.19 | **Properties** window after changing the TextView's text property.

2.5.6 Configuring the TextView's textSize Property—Scaled Pixels and Density-Independent Pixels

Sizes can be specified in various measurement units (Fig. 2.20). The documentation for supporting multiple screen sizes recommends that you use *density-independent pixels* for dimensions of views and other screen elements, and *scale-independent pixels* for font sizes:

http://developer.android.com/guide/practices/screens_support.html

Unit	Description	Unit	Description
px	pixel	in	inches
dp or dip	density-independent pixel	mm	millimeters
sp	scale-independent pixel		

Fig. 2.20 | Measurement units.

Defining your GUIs with **density-independent pixels** enables the Android platform to *scale* the GUI, based on the pixel density of a given device's screen. One *density-independent pixel* is equivalent to one pixel on a 160-dpi screen. On a 240-dpi screen, each density-independent pixel will be scaled by a factor of 240/160 (i.e., 1.5). So, a component that's 100 *density-independent pixels* wide will be scaled to 150 *actual pixels* wide. On a screen with 120 dpi, each density-independent pixel is scaled by a factor of 120/160 (i.e., 0.75). So, the same component that's 100 density-independent pixels wide will be 75 actual pixels wide. **Scale-independent pixels** are scaled like density-independent pixels, but they're also scaled by the user's *preferred font size* (as specified in the device's settings).

Creating a Dimension Resource for the Font Size on a Phone Device
You'll now increase the TextView's font size. To change the font size:

1. Select the welcomeTextView in the layout editor.

2. Locate the **textSize property**, then click in the right column to reveal the ellipsis (...) button and click the button to display the **Resources** dialog.

3. In the **Resources** dialog, click **New Resource**, then select **New Dimension Value...** to display the **New Dimension Value Resource** dialog.

4. In the dialog that appears, specify welcome_textsize for the **Resource name** and 40sp for the **Resource value**, then click **OK** to dismiss the dialog and return to the **Resources** dialog. The letters sp in the value 40sp indicate that this is a scale-independent pixel measurement. The letters dp in a dimension value (e.g., 10dp) indicate a density-independent pixel measurement. We used the value 40sp for displaying text on a phone.

In the **Properties** window, the textSize property now contains the value:

@dimen/welcome_textsize

The @dimen/ prefix indicates that the textSize property's value is a dimension resource and welcome_textsize indicates the specific dimension resource to use. By default, the resource is placed in the dimens.xml file—located in the project's res/values folder.

Creating a Dimension Resource for the Font Size on a Large Tablet Device

The 40sp font size works well for phone-sized devices, but is small for tablets. Android can automatically choose different resource values based on device sizes, orientations, pixel densities, spoken languages, locales and more. To specify a separate font size for larger devices such as tablets:

1. Reopen the **New Dimension Value Resource** dialog as described above.

2. Enter welcome_textsize for the **Resource name** (the resource names must match for Android to select different resource values automatically) and enter 80sp for the **Resource value**.

3. Next, you'll create a new values resource folder that's specific to larger devices such as tablets that have widths and heights that are each *at least* 600dp. In the **New Dimension Value Resource** dialog, uncheck the **values** checkbox, and click the **Add** button (+) to open the **New Resource Directory** dialog. In this dialog's **Available qualifiers** list, select **Screen Width**, then click the **>>** button to add the screen **Screen Width** qualifier to the **Chosen qualifiers** list. Next, enter 600 in the **Screen width** field.

4. Next, add the **Screen Height** qualifier to the **Chosen qualifiers** list and enter 600 for the **Screen height**.

5. Click **OK** to create a new resource folder named values-xlarge.

6. In the **New Dimension Value Resource** dialog, check the values-w600dp-h600dp checkbox, then click **OK**. This creates another welcome_textsize dimension resource in a dimens.xml file that's stored on disk in the project's res/values-w600dp-h600dp folder. Android will use that resource for devices with extra-large screen widths and heights that are at least 600dp, typical of most Android tablets. The new dimens.xml resource file appears in Android Studio in the project's res/values/dimens.xml node as

   dimens.xml (w600dp-h600dp)

2.5.7 Setting the TextView's textColor Property

When you need custom colors in your apps, Google's Material Design guidelines recommend using colors from the Material Design color palette at:

   http://www.google.com/design/spec/style/color.html

Colors are specified as RGB (red-green-blue) or ARGB (alpha-red-green-blue) values. An RGB value consists of integer values in the range 0–255 that define the amounts of red, green and blue in the color, respectively. Custom colors are defined in *hexadecimal* format, so the RGB components are values in the range 00 (the hexadecimal value for 0) to FF (the hexadecimal value for 255).

Android also supports alpha (transparency) values in the range 00 (completely transparent) to FF (completely opaque). To use alpha, you specify the color as #AARRGGBB, where the first two hexadecimal digits represent the alpha value.

If both digits of each color component are the same, you can use the abbreviated value formats #RGB or #ARGB. For example, the RGB value #9AC is equivalent to #99AACC and the ARGB value #F9AC is equivalent to #FF99AACC.

To set the TextView's **textColor property** to a new color resource:

1. In the **Properties** window click the ellipsis (...) button to display the **Resources** dialog, then click **New Resource** and select **New Color Value...**.

2. In the **New Color Value Resource** dialog, enter welcome_text_color for the **Resource name** and #2196F3 for the **Resource value** (Fig. 2.21), then click **OK**.

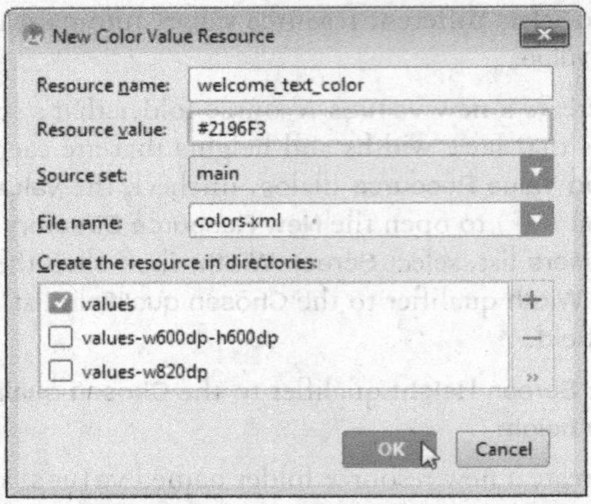

Fig. 2.21 | Creating a **New Color Value Resource** for the TextView's textColor property.

2.5.8 Setting the TextView's gravity Property

To center the text in the TextView if it wraps to multiple lines, you can set its **gravity property** to center. To do so, expand the node for this property, then check the **center** checkbox (Fig. 2.22).

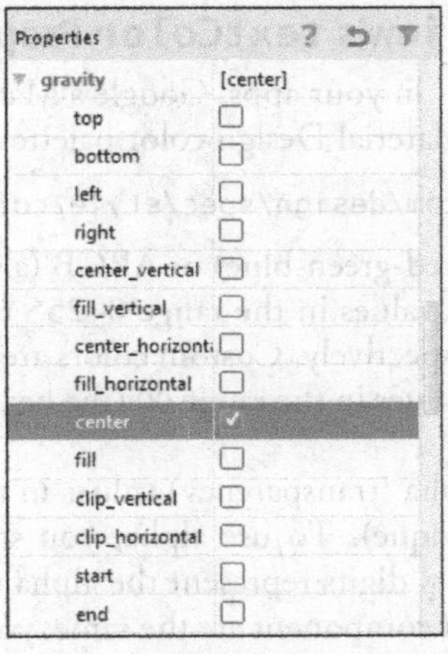

Fig. 2.22 | Options for the **Gravity** property of a TextView.

2.5.9 Setting the TextView's layout:gravity Property

Each view you place in a layout has various layout properties that enable you to customize the view's size and positioning within the layout. When you select a view in the layout editor or **Component Tree**, the **Properties** window lists the layout and style properties at the top, followed by the view-specific properties in alphabetical order (Fig. 2.23).

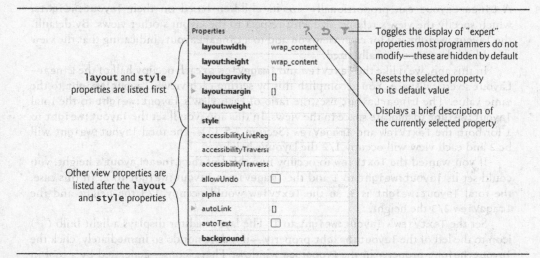

Fig. 2.23 | **Properties** window showing layout and style properties at the top.

In this app, we'd like to center the TextView horizontally within the LinearLayout. To do this, you'll set its **layout:gravity property** to center horizontally as follows:

1. With the TextView selected, expand the layout:gravity property's node in the **Properties** window.

2. Click the value field to the right of the center option that appears, then select the horizontal option (Fig. 2.24).

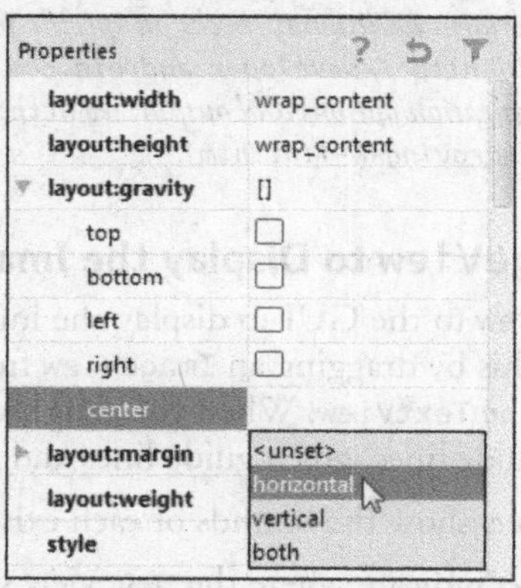

Fig. 2.24 | Setting the layout:gravity for the TextView.

In the layout XML file, layout properties have attribute names that begin with `layout_`. The preceding `layout:gravity` property setting is represented in XML as:

```
android:layout_gravity="center_horizontal"
```

2.5.10 Setting the TextView's `layout:weight` Property

A `LinearLayout` can proportionally size its children based on their **`layout:weights`**, which specify the view's relative size with respect to the layout's other views. By default, the `layout:weight` is 0 for each view you add to a `LinearLayout`, indicating that the view should not be proportionally sized.

In this app, we'd like the `TextView` and `ImageView` to each occupy half of the `Linear-Layout`'s vertical space. You accomplish this by setting each view's `layout:weight` to the same value. The `LinearLayout` uses the ratio of each view's `layout:weight` to the total `layout:weight` to allocate space to the views. In this app, you'll set the `layout:weight` to 1 for both the `TextView` and `ImageView` (Section 2.5.11)—the total `layout:weight` will be 2 and each view will occupy 1/2 the layout's height.

If you wanted the `TextView` to occupy one-third of the `LinearLayout`'s height, you could set its `layout:weight` to 1 and the `ImageView`'s `layout:weight` to 2. In this case, the total `layout:weight` is 3, so the `TextView` would occupy 1/3 the height and the `ImageView` 2/3 the height.

Set the `TextView`'s `layout:weight` to 1. The layout editor displays a light bulb () icon to the left of the `layout:height` property—if it does not do so immediately, click the `layout:height` property in the **Properties** window. These icons—generated by a tool in the IDE known as *Android Lint*—warn you of potential problems and help you fix them. When you click the light bulb, the IDE displays the message, "Use a `layout_height` of `0dp` instead of `wrap_content` for better performance." Click the message to apply the recommendation. This change enables the `LinearLayout` to calculate its children's sizes more efficiently. The layout editor window should now appear as shown in Fig. 2.25.

> **Error-Prevention Tip 2.2**
> *Android Lint checks your project for common errors, and makes suggestions for better security, enhanced performance, improved accessibility, internationalization and more. Some checks occur as you build your apps and write code. You also can select* **Analyze > Inspect Code...** *to perform additional checks on specific files or your entire project. For more information, visit* `http://developer.android.com/tools/help/lint.html`. *For Android Lint's configuration options and output, see* `http://developer.android.com/tools/debugging/improving-w-lint.html`.

2.5.11 Adding an ImageView to Display the Image

Next, you'll add an `ImageView` to the GUI to display the image you added to the project in Section 2.5.1. You'll do this by dragging an `ImageView` from the **Palette**'s **Widgets** section onto the canvas below the `TextView`. When you drag a view onto the canvas, the layout editor displays orange guide lines, green guide lines and a tooltip:

- The *orange guide lines* show the bounds of each existing view in the layout.
- The *green guide lines* indicate where the new view will be placed with respect to the existing views—by default, new views are added at the bottom of a vertical

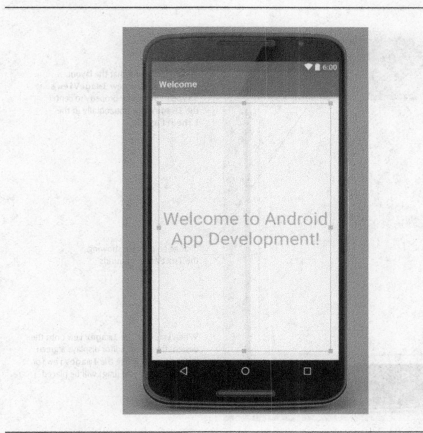

Fig. 2.25 | Layout editor window after configuring the `TextView`.

`LinearLayout`, unless you position the mouse above the orange box that bounds the layout's topmost view.

- The *tooltip* displays how the view will be configured if you drop it at the current position.

To add and configure the `ImageView`:

1. From the **Palette**'s **Widgets** section, drag an `ImageView` onto the canvas as shown in Fig. 2.26. *Before releasing the mouse*, ensure that **center** appears in the tooltip at the top of the design—this indicates that the layout editor will set the `Image-View`'s `layout:gravity` property to center the `ImageView` horizontally in the `LinearLayout`. When you drop the `ImageView` by releasing the mouse, the layout editor assumes that the `ImageView`'s `layout:weight` should be the same as the `TextView`'s and sets the `layout:weight` to 1. It also sets the `layout_height` to 0dp as we did for the `TextView`. The new `ImageView` appears below the `TextView` in the design and below `welcomeTextView` in the **Component Tree**. The `Image-View`'s properties are displayed in the **Properties** window.

Tooltip indicating that the layout editor will set the new **ImageView**'s **layout:gravity** property to center the **ImageView** horizontally in the **LinearLayout**

Orange guide lines showing the **TextView**'s bounds

When you drag the **ImageView** onto the design, the layout editor displays a green line indicating where the **ImageView** (or any other view you drag) will be placed

Fig. 2.26 | Dragging and dropping an **ImageView** onto the GUI.

2. In the **Properties** window, locate the **ImageView**'s **src** property (which specifies the image to display), then click its value field's ellipsis button to display the **Resources** dialog (Fig. 2.27). When the dialog opens, type **bug** to search the list of resources for the image you added in Section 2.5.1, then click **OK**. For every image you place in a **drawable** folder, the IDE generates a unique resource ID (i.e., a resource name) that you can use to reference that image. An image's resource ID is the image's file name without the file-name extension—**bug** for the **bug.png** file.

3. Double-click the **ImageView** in the layout editor and set its **id:** to **bugImageView**.

The GUI should now appear as in Fig. 2.28. If you select the **ImageView** in the layout editor, Android Lint displays a light bulb (💡) next to the **ImageView**—clicking this displays a message indicating that a property is missing for visually impaired users. You'll correct this in Section 2.7.

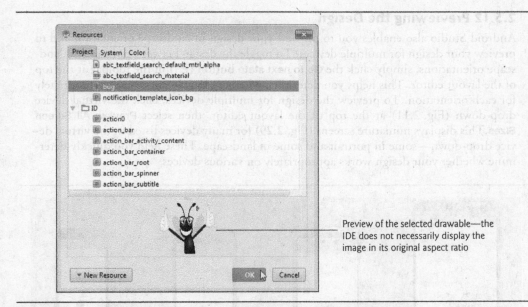

Preview of the selected drawable—the IDE does not necessarily display the image in its original aspect ratio

Fig. 2.27 | Selecting the bug image resource from the **Resources** dialog.

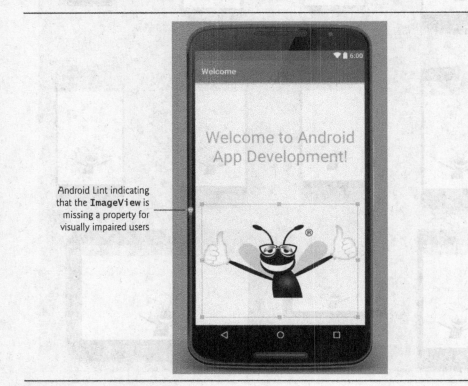

Android Lint indicating that the **ImageView** is missing a property for visually impaired users

Fig. 2.28 | Preview of the completed design.

2.5.12 Previewing the Design

Android Studio also enables you to preview your design in landscape orientation and to preview your design for multiple devices. To toggle the design between portrait and landscape orientations, simply click the **Go to next state** button ( ) in the toolbar at the top of the layout editor. This helps you determine whether your design adjusts appropriately for each orientation. To preview the design for multiple devices, click the virtual device drop-down (Fig. 2.11) at the top of the layout editor, then select **Preview All Screen Sizes**. This displays miniature screens (Fig. 2.29) for many devices listed in the virtual device drop-down—some in portrait and some in landscape. These help you quickly determine whether your design works appropriately on various devices.

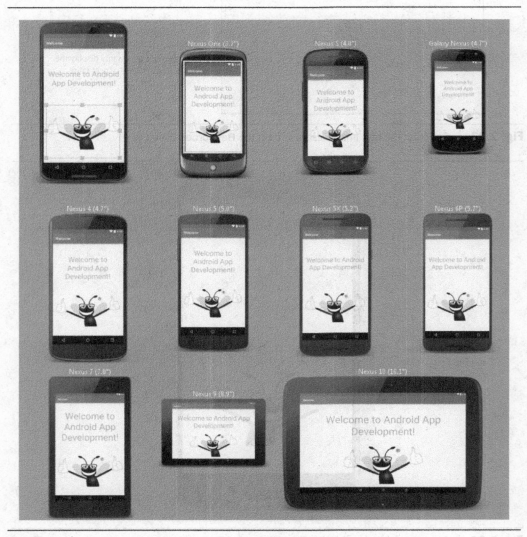

Fig. 2.29 | Previewing various devices for the **Welcome** app's design.

You can return to displaying one device by clicking the virtual device drop-down and selecting **Remove Previews**. You also can preview your design for a particular device be selecting that device in the virtual device drop-down.

2.6 Running the **Welcome** App

You're now ready to run the **Welcome** app. Perform the steps shown in Section 1.9.3 to run the app on the AVDs you configured previously for both the Nexus 6 phone and Nexus 9 tablet. Figures 2.30–2.31 show the app running in the Nexus 6 AVD (in portrait and landscape) and the Nexus 9 AVD (in landscape), respectively. You can toggle an AVD between portrait and landscape orientations by typing *Ctrl + F11* or *control + F11*. Typically, for apps that run on both phones and tablets, you'll also provide a tablet layout that makes better use of the screen's available space, as we'll demonstrate in later chapters. If you have an Android device, you can follow the steps in Section 1.9.4 to run the app on your device.

Fig. 2.30 | **Welcome** app running in the Nexus 6 AVD.

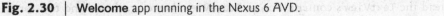

Fig. 2.31 | **Welcome** app running in the Nexus 9 AVD.

2.7 Making Your App Accessible

Android contains *accessibility* features to help people with certain disabilities use their devices. For people with visual disabilities, Android's TalkBack can speak screen text or text that you provide (when designing your GUI or programmatically) to help the user understand the purpose of a view. Android also provides *Explore by Touch*, which enables the user to hear TalkBack speak what's on the screen where the user touches.

When TalkBack is enabled and the user touches a view for which accessibility text is specified, the device vibrates to indicate that the user touched a significant view and TalkBack speaks the views's accessibility text. All standard Android views support accessibility. For those that display text, TalkBack speaks that text by default—e.g., when the user touches a TextView, TalkBack speaks the TextView's text. You enable TalkBack in the **Settings** app under **Accessibility**. From that page, you also can enable other Android accessibility features such as a *larger default text size* and the ability to use *gestures that magnify areas of the screen*. TalkBack is *not* currently supported on AVDs, so you must run this app on a device to hear TalkBack speak the text. When you enable TalkBack, Android walks you through a tutorial on using TalkBack with Explore by Touch.

Enabling TalkBack for the ImageViews
In the **Welcome** app, we don't need more descriptive text for the TextView, because TalkBack will read the TextView's content. For an ImageView, however, there is no text for

TalkBack to speak unless you provide it. It's considered good practice in Android to ensure that *every* view can be used with TalkBack by providing text for the **contentDescription property** of any view that does not display text. For that reason, the IDE warned us that something was wrong by displaying a light-bulb icon (💡—as you saw in Fig. 2.28) in the layout editor next to the ImageView. If you click the light bulb, you'll see the message, "[Accessibility] Missing contentDescription attribute on image." The text you provide should help the user understand the purpose of the component. For an ImageView, the text should describe the image.

To add the ImageView's contentDescription (and eliminate the warning):

1. Select the bugImageView in the layout editor.

2. In the **Properties** window, click the ellipsis button to the right of the contentDescription property to open the **Resources** dialog.

3. Click **New Resource**, then select **New String Value...** to display the **New String Value Resource** dialog.

4. In the **Resource name** field specify deitel_logo and in the **Resource value** field specify "Deitel double-thumbs-up bug logo", then press **OK**. The new string resource is chosen automatically as the contentDescription value.

After you set the ImageView's contentDescription, the layout editor removes the warning light bulb.

Testing the App with TalkBack Enabled
Run this app on a device with TalkBack enabled, then touch the TextView and ImageView to hear TalkBack speak the corresponding text.

Dynamically Created Views
Some apps dynamically create views in response to user interactions. For such views, you can programmatically set the accessibility text. For more information on this and Android's other accessibility features, and for a checklist to follow when developing accessible apps, visit:

```
http://developer.android.com/design/patterns/accessibility.html
http://developer.android.com/guide/topics/ui/accessibility
```

2.8 Internationalizing Your App

To reach the largest possible audience, you should consider designing your apps so that they can be customized for various locales and spoken languages. Then, if you intend to offer your app, for example, in France, you would translate its resources (text, audio files, etc.) into French. You might also choose to use different colors, graphics and sounds based on the *locale*. For each locale, you'll have a separate, customized set of resources. When the user launches the app, Android automatically finds and loads the resources that match the device's locale settings. Designing an app so it can be customized is known as *internationalization*. Customizing an app's resources for each locale is known as *localization*.

2.8.1 Localization

A key benefit of defining your string values as string resources (as we did in this app) is that you can easily *localize* your app by creating additional XML resource files for those string resources in other languages. In each file, you use the same string-resource names, but provide the *translated* string. Android can then choose the appropriate resource file based on the device user's preferred language.

2.8.2 Naming the Folders for Localized Resources

The XML resource files containing localized strings are placed on disk in subfolders of the project's `res` folder. Android uses a special folder-naming scheme to automatically choose the correct localized resources—for example, the folder `values-fr` would contain a `strings.xml` file for French and the folder `values-es` would contain a `strings.xml` file for Spanish. You also can name these folders with region information—`values-en-rUS` would contain a `strings.xml` file for United States English and `values-en-rGB` would contain a `strings.xml` file for United Kingdom English. If localized resources are not provided for a given locale, Android uses the app's *default* resources—that is, those in the `res` folder's `values` subfolder. We discuss these alternative-resource naming conventions in more detail in later chapters.

2.8.3 Adding String Translations to the App's Project

Android Studio provides a **Translations Editor** for quickly and easily adding translations for existing strings in your app. Follow these steps to add translated strings to the project:

1. In the **Project** window, expand the `values` node, then open the `strings.xml` file.

2. In the editor's upper-right corner, click the **Open editor** link to open the **Translations Editor**.

3. In the upper-left corner of the **Translations Editor**, click the **Add Locale** button (⊕), then select **Spanish (es)**—you can search for this entry by typing part of the language name or its abbreviation (es). After you select the locale in the list, a new `strings.xml (es)` file will be created and be placed in the `strings.xml` node in the **Project** window (the file is stored in a `values-es` folder on disk). The **Translations Editor** also displays a new column for the Spanish translations.

4. To add a Spanish translation for a given `String` resource, click the cell for the resource's **Spanish (es)** translation, then in the **Translation:** field at the bottom of the window enter the Spanish text. If a string should not be translated (for example, a string that's never displayed to the user), check the **Untranslatable** checkbox for that `String` resource. For the **Welcome** app, use the translations in Section 2.8.4.

Repeat the preceding steps for each language you wish to support.

2.8.4 Localizing Strings

In this app, the GUI contains one `TextView` that displays a string and one content-description string for the `ImageView`. These strings were defined as string resources in the `strings.xml` file. You can now provide the translated strings that will be stored in the new version of the `strings.xml` file. For this app, you'll replace the strings

```
"Welcome to Android App Development!"
"Deitel double-thumbs-up bug logo"
```

with the Spanish strings

```
"¡Bienvenido al Desarrollo de App Android!"
"El logo de Deitel que tiene el insecto con dedos pulgares
    hacia arriba"
```

In the **Translation Editor** window:

1. Click the cell for the `welcome` resource **Spanish (es)** translation, then in the **Translation:** field at the bottom of the window enter the Spanish string "`¡Bienvenido al Desarrollo de App Android!`". If you cannot type special Spanish characters and symbols on your keyboard, you can copy the Spanish strings from our `res/values-es/strings.xml` file in the final version of the **Welcome** app (located in the `WelcomeInternationalized` folder with the chapter's examples), then paste the Spanish string into the **Translation:** field.

2. Next, click the cell for the `deitel_logo` resource's value and enter in the **Translation:** field "`El logo de Deitel que tiene el insecto con dedos pulgares hacia arriba`".

3. We chose not to translate the resource `app_name`, though we could have. The window should appear as in Fig. 2.32.

4. Save the Spanish `strings.xml` file by selecting **File > Save All** or clicking the **Save All** toolbar button ( ).

Key	Default Value	Untranslatable	Spanish (es)
app_name	Welcome	☐	Welcome
deitel_logo	Deitel double-thumbs-up bug logo	☐	El logo de Deitel que tiene el insecto con dedos pulgares hacia arriba
welcome	Welcome to Android App Development!	☐	¡Bienvenido al Desarrollo de App Android!

Key:	deitel_logo
Default Value:	Deitel double-thumbs-up bug logo
Translation:	El logo de Deitel que tiene el insecto con dedos pulgares hacia arriba

Fig. 2.32 | **Translations Editor** window with the Spanish strings.

2.8.5 Testing the App in Spanish on an AVD

To test the app in Spanish on an AVD, you can use the **Custom Locale** app that's installed on the AVD.

1. Click the home ( ) icon on your AVD.

2. Click the launcher ( ) icon, then locate and click the **Custom Locale** app's icon to open it.

3. Drag the mouse to scroll to the **es - español** option, then click it and click the **SELECT 'ES'** button to change the AVD's locale.

The emulator or device changes its language setting to Spanish.

Next, run the **Welcome** app, which installs and launches the localized app (Fig. 2.33). When the app begins executing, Android checks the AVD's (or device's) language settings, determines that the AVD (or device) is set to Spanish and uses the Spanish `welcome` and `deitel_logo` string resources defined in `res/values-es/strings.xml`. Notice, however, that the app's name still appears in *English* in the app bar at the top of the app. This is because we did *not* provide a localized version of the `app_name` string resource in the `res/values-es/strings.xml` file. If Android cannot find a localized version of a string resource, it uses the default version in the `res/values/strings.xml` file.

Returning the AVD to English
To return your AVD to English:

1. Click the home () icon on your AVD.

2. Click the launcher ( ) icon, then locate and click the **Custom Locale** app's icon to open it.

3. Drag the mouse to scroll to the **en-US - en-us** option, then click it and click the **SELECT 'EN-US'** button to change the AVD's locale.

Fig. 2.33 | **Welcome** app running in Spanish in the Nexus 6 AVD.

2.8.6 Testing the App in Spanish on a Device

To test on a device you must change the language settings for your device. To do so:

1. Touch the home ( ) icon on your device.

2. Touch the launcher ( ) icon, then locate and touch the **Settings** app ( ) icon.

3. In the **Settings** app, scroll to the **Personal** section, then touch **Language & input**.

4. Touch **Language** (the first item in the list), then select **Español (España)** from the list of languages.

The device changes its language setting to Spanish and returns to the **Language & input** settings, which are now displayed in Spanish. Run the app from the IDE to install and run the localized version on your device.

Returning Your Device to English
To return your AVD (or Device) to English:

1. Touch the home (⊙) icon on the emulator or on your device.

2. Touch the launcher (⊞) icon, then locate and touch the **Settings** app (⚙) icon—the app is now called **Ajustes** in Spanish.

3. Touch the item **Idioma e introduccion de texto** to access the language settings.

4. Touch the item **Idioma**, then in the list of languages select **English (United States)**.

2.8.7 TalkBack and Localization

TalkBack currently supports English, Spanish, Italian, French and German. If you run the **Welcome** app on a device with Spanish specified as the device's language and TalkBack enabled, TalkBack will speak the app's Spanish strings as you touch each view.

When you first switch your device to Spanish and enable TalkBack, Android will automatically download the Spanish text-to-speech engine. If TalkBack does *not* speak the Spanish strings, then the Spanish text-to-speech engine has not finished downloading and installing yet. In this case, you should try executing the app again later.

2.8.8 Localization Checklist

For more information on localizing your app's resources, be sure to check out the Android *Localization Checklist* at:

```
http://developer.android.com/distribute/tools/localization-
    checklist.html
```

2.8.9 Professional Translation

App-development companies often have translators on staff or hire other companies to perform translations. In fact, in the Google Play Developer Console—which you use to publish your apps in the Google Play store—you can find translation-services companies, and in the **Translations Editor** window there is an **Order translations...** link. For more information on the Google Play Developer Console, see Chapter 10 and

```
http://developer.android.com/distribute/googleplay/developer-
    console.html
```

For more information regarding translation, see

```
https://support.google.com/l10n/answer/6227218
```

2.9 Wrap-Up

In this chapter, you used Android Studio to build the **Welcome** app that displays a welcome message and an image without writing any code. You created a simple GUI using the IDE's layout editor and configured view properties using the **Properties** window.

In the layout XML file, you changed the default `RelativeLayout` to a `LinearLayout`, which you then configured to arrange views vertically. The app displayed text in a `TextView` and a picture in an `ImageView`. You modified the `TextView` from the default GUI to display the app's text centered in the GUI, with a larger font size and in one of the standard theme colors. You also used the layout editor's **Palette** of GUI controls to drag and drop the `ImageView` onto the GUI. Following good practice, you defined all strings and numeric values in resource files in the project's `res` folder.

You learned that Android has accessibility features to help people with certain disabilities use their devices. We showed how to enable Android's TalkBack to allow a device to speak screen text or speak text that you provide to help the visually impaired user understand the purpose and contents of a view. We discussed Android's Explore by Touch feature, which enables the user to touch the screen to hear TalkBack speak what's on the screen near the touch. For the app's `ImageView`s, you provided content descriptions that could be used with TalkBack and Explore by Touch.

Finally, you learned how to use Android's internationalization features to reach the largest possible audience for your apps. You localized the **Welcome** app with Spanish strings for the `TextView`'s text and the `ImageView`s' accessibility strings, then tested the app on an AVD configured for Spanish.

Android development is a combination of GUI design and Java coding. In the next chapter, you'll develop a simple **Tip Calculator** app by using the layout editor to develop the GUI visually and Java programming to specify the app's behavior.

Self-Review Exercises

2.1 Fill in the blanks in each of the following statements:
  a) Layout files are considered app resources and are stored in the project's _____ folder. GUI layouts are placed within that folder's `layout` subfolder.
  b) When designing an Android GUI, you typically want it to be _____ so that it displays properly on various devices.
  c) You can easily _____ your app by creating additional XML resource files for string resources in other languages.
  d) The two measurement units for density independent pixels are _____ and _____.
  e) _____ enables the user to hear TalkBack speak what's on the screen where the user touches.
  f) Android uses a special folder-naming scheme to automatically choose the correct localized resources—for example, the folder _____ would contain a `strings.xml` file for French and the folder _____ would contain a `strings.xml` file for Spanish.

2.2 State whether each of the following is *true* or *false*. If *false*, explain why.
  a) Android Studio is used to create and test Android apps.
  b) A `RelativeLayout` arranges views relative to one another or relative to their parent container.
  c) A `LinearLayout` arranges views horizontally.
  d) To center the text in the `TextView`, set its `alignment` property to center.

e) Android's accessibility features help people with various disabilities use their devices.

f) For people with visual disabilities, Android's SpeakBack can speak screen text or text that you provide to help the user understand the purpose of a GUI component.

g) It's considered a best practice in Android to ensure that every GUI component can be used with TalkBack by providing text for the contentDescription property of any component that does not display text.

Answers to Self-Review Exercises

2.1 a) res. b) scalable. c) localize. d) dp and dip. e) Explore by Touch. f) values-fr, values-es.

2.2 a) True. b) True. c) False. A LinearLayout arranges views horizontally or vertically. d) False. To center the text in the TextView, set its gravity property to center. e) True. f) False. The feature is named TalkBack. g) True.

Exercises

2.3 Fill in the blanks in each of the following statements:
a) Android Studio's _____ allows you to build GUIs using drag-and-drop techniques.
b) For an app based on the **Empty Activity** template, the GUI layout is stored in an XML file called _____, by default.
c) The default GUI for an app based on the **Empty Activity** template consists of a(n) _____ (layout) and a TextView containing "Hello world!".
d) The documentation for supporting multiple screen sizes recommends that you use density-independent pixels for the dimensions of GUI components and other screen elements and _____ for font sizes.
e) One density-independent pixel is equivalent to one pixel on a screen with 160 dpi (dots per inch). On a screen with 240 dpi, each density-independent pixel will be scaled by a factor of _____.
f) On a screen with 120 dpi, each density-independent pixel is scaled by a factor of _____. So, the same component that's 100 density-independent pixels wide will be 75 actual pixels wide.

2.4 State whether each of the following is *true* or *false*. If *false*, explain why.
a) For images to render nicely, a high-pixel-density device needs lower-resolution images than a low-pixel-density device.
b) It's considered a good practice to "externalize" strings, string arrays, images, colors, font sizes, dimensions and other app resources so that you, or someone else on your team, can manage them separately from your application's code.
c) You can use the **Layout** editor to create a working app without writing any Java code.

2.5 *(Scrapbooking App)* Find three open source images of famous landmarks using websites such as Flickr. Create an app in which you arrange the images in a collage. Add text that identifies each landmark. Recall that image file names must use all lowercase letters.

2.6 *(Scrapbooking App with Accessibility)* Using the techniques you learned in Section 2.7, enhance your solution to Exercise 2.5 to provide strings that can be used with Android's TalkBack accessibility feature. If you have an Android device available to you, test the app on the device with TalkBack enabled.

2.7 *(Scrapbooking App with Internationalization)* Using the techniques you learned in Section 2.8, enhance your solution to Exercise 2.6 to define a set of strings for another spoken language. Use an online translator service, such as translate.google.com to translate the strings and place them in the appropriate strings.xml resource file. Use the instructions in Section 2.8 to test the app on an AVD (or a device if you have one available to you).

3

Tip Calculator App

Objectives

In this chapter you'll:

- Change the default GUI theme.

- Customize the GUI theme's colors.

- Design a GUI using a GridLayout.

- Use the IDE's **Component Tree** window to add views to a GridLayout.

- Use TextViews, an EditText and a SeekBar.

- Use Java object-oriented programming capabilities, including classes, objects, interfaces, anonymous inner classes and inheritance to add functionality to an app.

- Programmatically change the text in a TextView.

- Use event handling to respond to user interactions with an EditText and a SeekBar.

- Specify that the keypad should display by default when the app executes.

- Specify that the app supports only portrait orientation.

Outline

3.1 Introduction

The **Tip Calculator** app (Fig. 3.1(a)) calculates and displays the tip and total for a restaurant bill amount. As you touch the numeric keypad to enter the bill amount's digits, the app calculates and displays the tip and total bill amounts for the current tip percentage (15% by default). You specify a tip percentage from 0% to 30% by moving the `SeekBar` *thumb*—this updates the displayed tip percentage and recalculates the tip and total. All numeric values are displayed using *locale-specific* formatting. Figure 3.1(b) shows the app after the user enters the amount 56.32 and changes the tip percentage to 25%.

You'll begin by test-driving the app. Then we'll overview the technologies you'll use to create the app. You'll build the app's GUI using Android Studio's layout editor and the **Component Tree** window. Finally, we'll present the complete Java code for the app and do a detailed code walkthrough.

Note Regarding the Keyboard in Our Screen Captures
The keypad in Fig. 3.1 may differ, based on your AVD's or device's Android version or whether you've installed and selected a custom keyboard on your device. We configured our AVD to display the *dark keyboard* for better contrast in our screen captures. To do so:

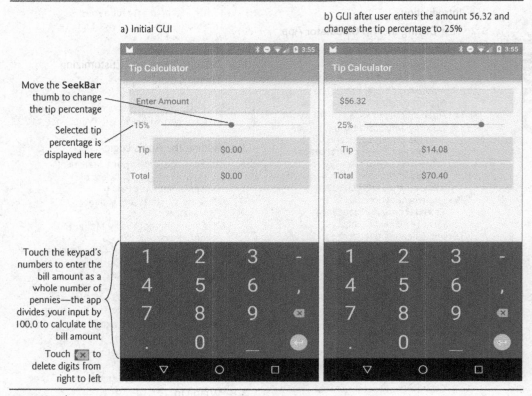

a) Initial GUI

b) GUI after user enters the amount 56.32 and changes the tip percentage to 25%

Move the **SeekBar** thumb to change the tip percentage

Selected tip percentage is displayed here

Touch the keypad's numbers to enter the bill amount as a whole number of pennies—the app divides your input by 100.0 to calculate the bill amount

Touch ⌫ to delete digits from right to left

Fig. 3.1 | Entering the bill total and calculating the tip.

1. Touch the home (◯) icon on your AVD or device.
2. On the home screen, touch the launcher (⁙) icon, then open the **Settings** app.
3. In the **Personal** section, touch **Language and Input**.
4. On an AVD, touch **Android Keyboard (AOSP)**. On a device touch **Google Keyboard**—we assume you're using the standard Android keyboard.
5. Touch **Appearance & layouts**, then touch **Theme**.
6. Touch **Material Dark** to change to the keyboard with the dark background.

3.2 Test-Driving the Tip Calculator App

Opening and Running the App

Perform the steps in Sections 1.9.1– and 1.9.3 to open the **Tip Calculator** app project in Android Studio and run the app on the Nexus 6 AVD. If you prefer, perform the steps in Section 1.9.4 to run the app on an Android phone.

Entering a Bill Total

Enter the bill total 56.32 by touching numbers on the numeric keypad. If you make a mistake, press the keypad's delete button (⌫) to erase the last digit you entered. Even though the keypad contains a decimal point, the app is configured so that you may enter only the digits 0 through 9—other input buttons on the keypad are ignored and an Android device will vibrate to indicate when you touch an invalid input button. Each time you touch a digit or delete a digit, the app reads what you've entered so far, and

- converts it to a number
- divides the number by 100.0 and displays the new bill amount
- recalculates the tip and total amounts, based on the current tip percentage (**15%** by default) and
- displays in the **Tip** and **Total** TextViews the new tip and total amounts.

If you delete all the digits, the app redisplays **Enter Amount** in the blue TextView and displays 0.00 in the orange TextViews. The app divides the value by 100.0 and displays the result in the blue TextView. The app then calculates and updates the tip and total amounts in the orange TextViews.

All monetary amounts are displayed in locale-specific currency formats and the tip percentage is displayed in a locale-specific percentage format. For the U.S. locale, as you enter the four digits 5, 6, 3 and 2, the bill total is displayed successively as **$0.05**, **$0.56**, **$5.63** and **$56.32**, respectively.

Selecting a Tip Percentage
Use the Seekbar—often called a *slider* in other GUI technologies—to specify the tip percentage. Drag the Seekbar's *thumb* until the percentage reads **25%** (Fig. 3.1(b)). As you drag the thumb, the tip and total update continuously. By default, the Seekbar allows you to select values from 0 to 100, but we specified a maximum value of 30 for this app.

3.3 Technologies Overview

This section introduces the IDE and Android features you'll use to build the **Tip Calculator** app. We assume that you're already familiar with Java object-oriented programming—if not, we present Java in the book's appendices. You'll

- use various Android classes to create objects
- call methods on classes and objects
- define and call your own methods
- use inheritance to create a class that defines the **Tip Calculator**'s functionality and
- use event handling, anonymous inner classes and interfaces to process the user's GUI interactions.

3.3.1 Class Activity

Android apps have four types of executable components—*activities, services, content providers* and *broadcast receivers*. In this chapter, we'll discuss activities, which are defined as subclasses of **Activity** (package **android.app**). An app can have many activities, one of which is the first you see after launching the app. You interact with an Activity through views—GUI components that inherit from class **View** (package android.view).

Before Android 3.0, a separate Activity was typically associated with each screen of an app. As you'll see, starting in Chapter 4, an Activity can manage multiple Fragments.

On a phone, each Fragment typically occupies the entire screen and the Activity switches between the Fragments, based on user interactions. On a tablet, activities typically display multiple Fragments per screen to take advantage of the larger screen size.

3.3.2 Activity Lifecycle Methods

Throughout its life, an Activity can be in one of several *states*—*active* (i.e., *running*), *paused* or *stopped*. The Activity transitions between these states in response to various *events*:

- An *active* Activity is *visible* on the screen and "has the focus"—that is, it's in the *foreground*. You can interact with the Activity currently in the foreground.

- A *paused* Activity is *visible* on the screen but *does not* have the focus—such as when an alert dialog is displayed. You cannot interact with the *paused* activity until it becomes active—for example, after the user dismisses an alert dialog.

- A *stopped* activity is *not visible* on the screen—it's in the *background* and is likely to be killed by the system when its memory is needed. An Activity is *stopped* when another Activity enters the *foreground* and becomes *active*. For example, when you answer a phone call, the phone app becomes *active* and the app you previously were using is *stopped*.

As an Activity transitions among these states, the Android runtime calls various Activity *lifecycle methods*—all of which are defined by the Activity class in package android.app. You'll override the **onCreate** method in *every* activity. This method is called by the Android runtime when an Activity is *starting*—that is, when its GUI is about to be displayed so you can interact with the Activity. Other lifecycle methods include onStart, onPause, onRestart, onResume, onStop and onDestroy. We'll discuss most of these in later chapters. Each activity lifecycle method you override *must* call the superclass's version; otherwise, an *exception* will occur. This is required because each lifecycle method in superclass Activity contains code that must execute in addition to the code you define in your overridden lifecycle methods. For more on the Activity lifecycle see

```
http://developer.android.com/reference/android/app/Activity.html
```

3.3.3 AppCompat Library and Class AppCompatActivity

A big challenge developers face when using new Android features is backward compatibility with earlier Android platforms. Google now introduces many new Android features via the *Android Support Library*—a set of libraries that enable you to use newer Android features in apps targeting current and past Android platforms.

One such library is the AppCompat library, which enables apps to provide an app bar (formerly called an action bar) and more on devices running Android 2.1 (API 7) and higher—app bars were originally introduced in Android 3.0 (API 11). Android Studio's app templates have been updated to use the AppCompat library, enabling the new apps you create to run on almost all Android devices.

Android Studio's **Empty Activity** app template defines the app's MainActivity class as a subclass of **AppCompatActivity** (package **android.support.v7.app**)—an indirect subclass of Activity that supports using newer Android features in apps running on current and older Android platforms.

Software Engineering Observation 3.1

By creating apps with the AppCompat library from the start, you avoid having to reimplement your code if you decide to support older Android versions to target a wider potential audience for your app.

Software Engineering Observation 3.2

Some Android features are not available in earlier Android versions, even if you use the AppCompat libraries. For example, Android's printing capabilities are available only in Android 4.4 and higher. If you use such features in your app, you must either restrict the app to the supported platforms or disable those features on Android versions that do not support them.

For more details on Android Support Libraries, including when to use them and how to set them up, visit:

```
http://developer.android.com/tools/support-library
```

3.3.4 Arranging Views with a GridLayout

Recall that you arrange a GUI's views in layouts. We'll use a **GridLayout** (package **android.widget**) to arrange views into cells in a rectangular grid. Cells can occupy *multiple* rows and columns, allowing for complex layouts. Normally, GridLayout requires API level 14 or higher. However, the *Android Support Library* provides alternate versions of GridLayout and many other views and layouts so that you can use them in older Android versions. For more information on this library and how to use it in your apps, visit

```
http://developer.android.com/tools/support-library/index.html
```

We'll cover more layouts and views in later chapters—for a complete list, visit

```
http://developer.android.com/reference/android/widget/package-
   summary.html
```

3.3.5 Creating and Customizing the GUI with the Layout Editor and the Component Tree and Properties Windows

You'll create TextViews, an EditText and a SeekBar using the layout editor (that you used in Chapter 2) and **Component Tree** window, then customize them with the IDE's **Properties** window.

An **EditText**—often called a *text box* or *text field* in other GUI technologies—is a *subclass* of TextView (presented in Chapter 2) that can display text *and* accept text input from the user. You'll specify an EditText for numeric input, allow users to enter only digits and restrict the maximum number of digits that can be entered.

A **SeekBar** represents an integer in the range 0–100 by default and allows the user to select a number in that range by moving the SeekBar's thumb. You'll customize the SeekBar so the user can choose a tip percentage from the more limited range 0 to 30.

3.3.6 Formatting Numbers as Locale-Specific Currency and Percentage Strings

You'll use class **NumberFormat** (package **java.text**) to create *locale-specific* currency and percentage strings—an important part of *internationalizing* your apps. You also can add *accessibility* strings and internationalize the app's other text using the techniques you learned in Sections 2.7–2.8.

3.3.7 Implementing Interface TextWatcher for Handling EditText Text Changes

To respond to events when the user changes the text in this app's EditText, you'll use an *anonymous inner class* to implement the **TextWatcher** *interface* (from package **android.text**). In particular, you'll use method onTextChanged to display the currency-formatted bill amount and to calculate the tip and total as the user enters each digit. If you're not familiar with *anonymous inner classes*, visit

```
http://bit.ly/AnonymousInnerClasses
```

3.3.8 Implementing Interface OnSeekBarChangeListener for Handling SeekBar Thumb Position Changes

You'll use another anonymous inner class to implement the **SeekBar.OnSeekBarChangeListener** interface (from package android.widget) to respond to the user moving the SeekBar's *thumb*. In particular, you'll use method onProgressChanged to display the selected tip percentage and to calculate the tip and total as the user moves the SeekBar's thumb.

3.3.9 Material Themes

A theme gives an app a look-and-feel that's consistent with Android. Projects that you create for Android 5 and higher use themes that adhere to Google's material design guidelines. There are several predefined material design themes:

- The "light" theme has a white app bar, a white app background and text that is black or shades of dark gray.
- The "light" theme with a dark app bar is the same as above, but the app bar is black with white text by default.
- The "dark" has a black app bar, a dark gray app background and text that is white or shades of light gray.

For each of these themes, there is

- a Theme.Material version (e.g., Theme.Material.Light) for apps that do not use any AppCompat libraries and run on Android 5 and higher, and
- a Theme.AppCompat version (e.g., Theme.AppCompat.Light) for apps that use AppCompat libraries and run on Android 2.1 and higher.

When designing a GUI, you can choose from the predefined themes, or even create your own new ones. For this chapter, we'll use **Theme.AppCompat.Light.DarkActionBar**, which is the default theme in Android Studio's app templates. Apps that use the AppCompat libraries must use one of the AppCompat themes; otherwise, some views will not render correctly. For more information about each theme and to see sample screen captures, visit

```
http://www.google.com/design/spec/style/color.html#color-themes
http://developer.android.com/training/material/theme.html
```

Performance Tip 3.1

Many of today's Android phones use AMOLED displays. On such displays, a black pixel is turned off and does not consume power. Apps that use mostly black themes can reduce power consumption by approximately 40% (http://bit.ly/AndroidAMOLEDDisplay).

3.3.10 Material Design: Elevation and Shadows

Google's material design guidelines recommend that objects in your user interfaces cast shadows just as real-world objects do. When you set a view's **elevation property**, Android automatically casts a shadow for that view. Larger elevation values result in more pronounced shadows. For this app, we'll set the elevation of the blue and orange TextViews that display monetary amounts.

The material design guidelines contain elevation recommendations for various on-screen components—for example, a dialog's recommended elevation is 24dp and a menu's is 8dp. For other recommended elevations, see:

        http://www.google.com/design/spec/what-is-material/elevation-
            shadows.html

3.3.11 Material Design: Colors

App developers often customize a theme's colors to match a company's branding. If you need to customize theme colors, Google's material design guidelines for color[1] recommend that you choose a color palette consisting of a primary color—with no more than three hues (shades)—and an accent color. The primary colors typically are used to color the status bar and the app bar at the top of the screen and also can be used in your GUI. The accent color is used to tint various views in your GUI, such as SeekBars, CheckBoxes and RadioButtons. Once you choose a palette, you can use Android Studio's **Theme Editor** (Section 3.5.2) to modify a theme's colors.

You can find recommended sample color swatches from the material design color palette at

        http://www.google.com/design/spec/style/color.html#color-color-
            palette

For palette color recommendations, visit

        http://www.materialpalette.com/

This site enables you to click two colors from Google's material design color palette, then it recommends three shades of the primary color, one secondary color and colors for your app's text and icons.

In this app, we'll use color swatches displayed in the Android Studio **Theme Editor** to select

- a blue *primary color* for app bar's background color
- a darker blue *dark primary color* for the status bar that appears above the app bar, and
- an orange *accent color* used to tint the SeekBar.

---

1. http://www.google.com/design/spec/style/color.html.

For the amount TextView's light blue color and the tip and total TextViews' light orange color, we used Google's material design color palette to choose lighter shades of the primary and accent colors.

3.3.12 AndroidManifest.xml

The **AndroidManifest.xml** file is created by the IDE when you create a new app project. This file contains many of the settings that you specify in the **Create New Project** dialog—the app's name, package name and Activity name(s) and more. You'll edit this file's XML to add a new setting that forces the *soft keyboard* to be displayed when the app begins executing. You'll also specify that the app supports only *portrait orientation*—that is, the device's longer dimension is vertical.

3.3.13 Searching in the Properties Window

The **Properties** window allows you to search for properties by their names or portions of their names, which can help you find and set properties faster. To do so, click the **Properties** window's title bar and begin typing. At the top of the property list, a **Search for** tooltip appears showing what you've typed so far, and Android Studio highlights parts of every property name in the list that matches all or part of what you've typed. Then you can scroll through the list looking at the property names containing highlights.

The window will also scroll to the specific property that best matches what you type. For example, when searching a TextView's properties, if you type "text co" or "textco", the **Properties** window will highlight portions of many properties, but it specifically scrolls to and highlights the textColor property.

3.4 Building the GUI

In this section, we'll show the precise steps for building the **Tip Calculator**'s GUI, including how to customize the Material theme's primary and accent colors.

3.4.1 GridLayout Introduction

This app uses a **GridLayout** (package android.widget) to arrange views into four *rows* and two *columns*, each indexed from 0 like the elements in an array. You can specify a GridLayout's number of rows and columns in the **Properties** window. Each cell can be *empty* or can hold one or more *views*, including layouts *containing* other views. A row's *height* is determined by the row's *tallest* view. Similarly, a column's *width* is defined by the column's *widest* view. Figure 3.2 shows the **Tip Calculator**'s GridLayout labeled by its rows and columns—we drew horizontal lines to delineate the rows and a vertical line to delineate the columns. Views can span *multiple* rows and/or columns—for example, the **Enter Amount** TextView in Fig. 3.2 spans both columns in row 0.

When you drag a view onto a GridLayout in the **Component Tree**, the view occupies the next available grid cell—cells populate the GridLayout left-to-right until a given row is full, then the next view appears in the first column of the next row. As you'll see, you also can specify the exact row and column in which to place a view. We'll discuss other GridLayout features as we present the GUI-building steps.

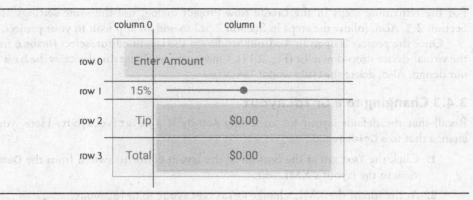

column 0   column 1

row 0   Enter Amount

row 1   15%

row 2   Tip $0.00

row 3   Total $0.00

Fig. 3.2 | **Tip Calculator** GUI's `GridLayout` labeled by its rows and columns.

id Property Values for This App's Views

Figure 3.3 shows the views' `id` property values. For clarity, our naming convention is to use the view's class name in the `id` property and the corresponding Java variable name. In the first row, there are actually *two* components in the *same* grid cell—the `amountTextView` (which initially displays **Enter Amount**) *hides* the `amountEditText` that receives the user input. As you'll soon see, we restrict the user's input to whole-number values entered as integer digits, so the user enters the bill amount $34.56 as 3456. This ensures the user *cannot* enter invalid input. However, this amount should be displayed as *currency*. As the user enters each digit, we divide the amount by 100.0 and display in the `amountTextView` the locale-specific, currency-formatted amount.

`amountTextView` (as you'll soon see, the
`amountEditText` is hidden behind this `TextView`)

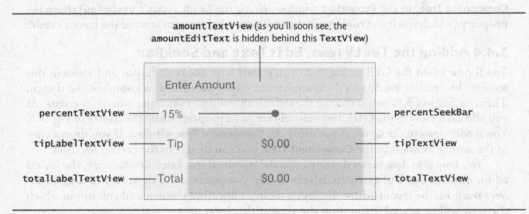

Enter Amount

`percentTextView` —— 15% —————————●——————— `percentSeekBar`

`tipLabelTextView` —— Tip $0.00 —— `tipTextView`

`totalLabelTextView` —— Total $0.00 —— `totalTextView`

Fig. 3.3 | **Tip Calculator** views labeled with their `id` property values.

3.4.2 Creating the TipCalculator Project

Follow the steps in Section 2.3 to create a new project using the **Empty Activity** template. Specify the following values in the **Create New Project** dialog's **New Project** step:

- **Application name:** Tip Calculator
- **Company Domain:** deitel.com (or specify your own domain name)

For the remaining steps in the **Create New Project** dialog, use the same settings as in Section 2.3. Also, follow the steps in Section 2.5.2 to add an app icon to your project.

Once the project is open in Android Studio, in the layout editor, select **Nexus 6** from the virtual-device drop-down list (Fig. 2.11). Once again, we'll use this device as the basis for our design. Also, delete the **Hello world!** TextView.

3.4.3 Changing to a GridLayout

Recall that the default layout for an **Empty Activity** is a RelativeLayout. Here, you'll change that to a GridLayout:

1. Click the **Text** tab at the bottom of the layout editor to switch from the **Design** view to the layout's XML text.

2. At the top of the XML, change RelativeLayout to GridLayout.

3. Switch back to the layout editor's **Design** tab.

Specifying Two Columns and Default Margins for the GridLayout
Recall that the GUI in Fig. 3.2 consists of two columns. To specify this, select GridLayout in the **Component Tree** window, then change its columnCount property to 2—this property appears near the top of the **Properties** window with the other layout properties. You do not need to set the rowCount—it will be increased as we build the GUI.

By default, there are *no margins*—spacing that separates views—around a GridLayout's cells. The material design guidelines recommend 8dp minimum spacing between views:

> http://developer.android.com/design/style/metrics-grids.html.

GridLayout can enforce this recommended spacing. With the GridLayout selected in the **Component Tree**, in the **Properties** window, check the GridLayout's **useDefaultMargins** property (which sets it to true) to use the recommended margins around the layout's cells.

3.4.4 Adding the TextViews, EditText and SeekBar

You'll now build the GUI in Fig. 3.2. You'll start with the basic layout and views in this section. In Section 3.4.5, you'll customize the views' properties to complete the design. Then, in Section 3.5, you'll change the default theme and customize two of its colors. As you add each view to the GUI, immediately set its id property using the names in Fig. 3.3. You'll add views to the GridLayout using the **Component Tree** window. If you drop a view in the wrong location in the **Component Tree**, you can drag it to the correct location.

You may also drag views directly onto the layout editor. For a GridLayout, the layout editor displays a grid of green guidelines to help you position the view. As you drag a view over the grid, the layout editor displays a tooltip indicating the row and column in which the view will be placed if you drop the view at that location.

> **Error-Prevention Tip 3.1**
> *The cells in the layout editor's grid of green guidelines are small. If you drop a view in the wrong location, the layout editor might change the GridLayout's rowCount and column-Count property values and incorrectly set the view's layout:row and layout:column property values, causing your GUI to lay out incorrectly. If so, reset the GridLayout's row-Count and columnCount, based on your design, and change the view's layout:row and layout:column property values to the correct row and column for your design.*

Step 1: Adding Views to the First Row

The first row consists of the amountTextView and the amountEditText—both occupy the same cell and span two columns. Each time you drop a view onto the GridLayout in the **Component Tree** window, the view is placed in the layout's *next open cell*, unless you specify otherwise by setting the view's layout:row and layout:column properties. You'll do that in this step so that the amountEditText and amountTextView appear in the same cell with the amountTextView in the foreground.

This app's TextViews use the *medium*-sized font from the app's theme. The layout editor's **Palette** provides preconfigured TextViews named **Plain Text**, **Large Text**, **Medium Text** and **Small Text** (in the **Widgets** section) for various text sizes. The **Plain Text** TextView uses the theme's default font size. For the others, the IDE configures the TextView's text-Appearance property using the Material theme's styles for the corresponding font sizes.

Perform the following steps to add to the GridLayout an EditText and a TextView for receiving and displaying the bill amount:

1. This app allows you to enter only *nonnegative integers*, which the app divides by 100.0 to display the bill amount. The **Palette**'s **Text Fields** section provides *preconfigured* EditTexts for various forms of input, including person names, passwords, e-mail addresses, phone numbers, times, dates and numbers. When the user interacts with an EditText, an appropriate keyboard is displayed, based on the EditText's *input type*. From the **Palette**'s **Text Fields** section, drag and drop a **Number** EditText onto the GridLayout node in the **Component Tree** window—this creates an EditText with the id editText in the GridLayout. Change the id to amountEditText. The EditText is placed in the *first* column of the GridLayout's *first* row. Set the EditText's layout:column to 0 and the layout:columnSpan to 2—these settings ensure that the TextView spans both columns of row 0.

2. Drag a **Medium Text** TextView from the **Palette**'s **Widgets** section over the amount-EditText in the **Component Tree** window—a horizontal black line appears below amountEditText, indicating that the TextView will be placed after amountEdit-Text. The IDE creates a new TextView named textView and nests it in the Grid-Layout node. The default text "Medium Text" appears in the layout editor. You'll change this in *Step 5* (Section 3.4.5). Change the TextView's id to amountText-View, then set the layout:row to 0, the layout:column to 0 and the layout:columnSpan to 2—these settings ensure that the TextView spans both columns of row 0, as you'll see once we change the TextView's background color.

Step 2: Adding Views to the Second Row

Next, add the percentTextView and percentSeekBar to the GridLayout for displaying and selecting the tip percentage (be sure to set each view's id to the name we specify):

1. Drag a **Medium** TextView (percentTextView) from the **Palette**'s **Widgets** section over the amountTextView in the GridLayout node in the **Component Tree** window. The new view becomes the first view in row 1 (the second row).

2. Drag a SeekBar (percentSeekBar) from the **Palette**'s **Widgets** section over the percentTextView in the GridLayout node in the **Component Tree** window. The new view becomes the second view in row 1.

Step 3: Adding Views to the Third Row

Next, add the `tipLabelTextView` and the `tipTextView` to the `GridLayout` for displaying the tip amount:

1. Drag a **Medium** TextView (`tipLabelTextView`) over the `percentSeekBar` in the `GridLayout` node. The new view becomes the first view in row 2 (the third row).

2. Drag a **Medium** TextView (`tipTextView`) over the `tipLabelTextView` in the `GridLayout` node. The new view becomes the second view in row 2.

Step 4: Adding Views to the Fourth Row

Next, add the `totalLabelTextView` and the `totalTextView` to the `GridLayout` for displaying the tip amount:

1. Drag a **Medium** TextView (`totalLabelTextView`) over the `tipTextView` in the `GridLayout` node. This becomes the first view in row 3 (the fourth row).

2. Drag a **Medium** TextView (`totalTextView`) over the `totalLabelTextView` in the `GridLayout` node. This becomes the second view in row 3.

Reviewing the Layout So Far

The GUI and **Component Tree** window should now appear as shown in Fig. 3.4. The warning symbols shown in the layout editor and the **Component Tree** window will go away as you complete the GUI design in Section 3.4.5.

a) GUI design so far

b) **Component Tree** window showing the **Tip Calculator**'s layout and views

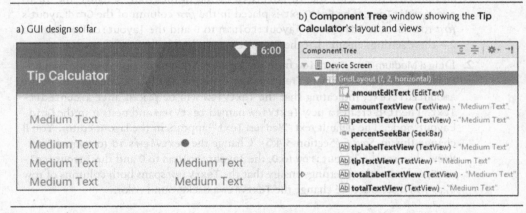

Fig. 3.4 | GUI and the **Component Tree** window after adding the views to the `GridLayout`.

A Note Regarding the EditText's Virtual Keyboard

When the virtual keyboard is displayed, the device's back button (◀) changes to a down button (▼) that enables you to dismiss the keyboard. If you do so, the down button (▼) changes to a back button (◀) that you can touch to return to the previous Activity—possibly a prior app or the device's home screen.

Normally, you'd touch the EditText to redisplay the virtual keyboard. In this app, however, the EditText is hidden behind a TextView. If you were to dismiss this app's keyboard, you'd have to leave the app and return to it to redisplay the keyboard. We could programmatically force the keyboard to stay on the screen, but this would prevent the back button from ever being displayed in this app. This, in turn, would prevent you from returning to the previous Activity—a basic Android feature that every user expects.

We used an Android virtual keyboard to demonstrate how to choose the keyboard displayed for a given EditText. Another approach would be to provide Buttons representing the digits 0–9 that always remain on the screen. We could handle their click events and use String manipulation rather than an EditText to keep track of the user input.

3.4.5 Customizing the Views
You'll now customize additional view properties. As you did in Section 2.5, you'll also create several String, dimension and color resources.

Step 5: Specifying Literal Text
Next, you'll specify the literal text for the amountTextView, percentTextView, tipLabel-TextView and totalLabelTextView. When a TextView's text property is empty, its **hint property**'s value (if you specify one) is displayed—this property is commonly used with an EditText (a subclass of TextView) to help the user understand the EditText's purpose. We're using it similarly in the amountTextView to tell the user to enter a bill amount:

1. In the **Component Tree**, select amountTextView and locate its hint property in the **Properties** window.

2. Click the ellipsis (...) button to the right of the property's value to display the **Resources** dialog.

3. In the dialog, click **New Resource**, then select **New String Value...** to display the **New String Value Resource** dialog and set the **Resource name** to enter_amount and **Resource value** to "Enter Amount". Leave the other settings and click **OK** to create the new String resource and set it as amountTextView's hint.

Repeat these steps to set the text property for the percentTextView, tipLabelTextView and totalLabelTextView using the values shown in Fig. 3.5.

View	Resource name	Resource Value
percentTextView	tip_percentage	15%
tipLabelTextView	tip	Tip
totalLabelTextView	total	Total

Fig. 3.5 | String resource values and names.

Step 6: Right Aligning the TextViews in the Left Column
In Fig. 3.2, the percentTextView, tipLabelTextView and totalLabelTextView are right aligned. You can accomplish this for all three TextViews at once as follows:

1. Select the percentTextView.

2. Hold *Ctrl* on Windows/Linux or *Command* on Mac and click the tipLabelText-View and totalLabelTextView. Now all three TextViews are selected.

3. Expand the layout:gravity property's node and check the right checkbox.

Step 7: Configuring the **amountEditText**
In the final app, the amountEditText is *hidden* behind the amountTextView and is configured to allow only *digits* to be entered by the user. Select the amountEditText and set the following properties:

1. Set the **digits property** to 0123456789—this allows *only* digits to be entered, even though the numeric keypad contains other characters, such as minus (-), comma (,) and period (.).

2. Set the **maxLength property** to 6. This restricts the bill amount to a maximum of *six* digits—so the largest supported bill amount is 9999.99.

Step 8: Configuring the **amountTextView**
To complete the amountTextView's formatting, select it and set the following properties:

1. Delete the default value of the text property ("Medium Text")—we'll programmatically display text here, based on the user's input.

2. Expand the layout:gravity property's node and set the fill to horizontal. This indicates that the TextView should occupy all remaining horizontal space in this GridLayout row.

3. Set the **background property** (which specifies the view's background color) to a new color resource named amount_background with the value #BBDEFB—a light blue color chosen from Google's material design color palette.

4. Add padding around the TextView. A view's **padding** specifies extra space around a view's content. The all property specifies that the padding amount should be applied to the top, right, bottom and left of the view's contents. You may also set the padding for each of these individually. Expand the padding property's node, click the all property, then click the ellipsis button. Create a new dimension resource named textview_padding with the value 12dp. You'll use this resource again shortly.

5. Finally, add a shadow to the view by setting the elevation property to a new dimension resource named elevation with the value 4dp. We chose this value for demonstration purposes to emphasize the shadow effect.

Step 9: Configuring the **percentTextView**
Notice that the percentTextView is aligned higher than the percentSeekBar. This looks better if it's *vertically centered*. To do this, expand the layout:gravity property's node, then set the center value to vertical. Recall that you previously set the layout:gravity to right. The combination of these settings appears in the layout XML as

```
android:layout_gravity="center_vertical|right"
```

A *vertical bar* (|) is used to separate multiple layout:gravity values—in this case indicating that the TextView should be *centered vertically* and *right aligned* within the grid cell.

Step 10: Configuring the **percentSeekBar**
Select percentSeekBar and configure the following properties:

1. By default, a SeekBar's range is 0 to 100 and its current value is indicated by its **progress** property. This app allows tip percentages from 0 to 30 and specifies a

default of 15 percent. Set the SeekBar's **max property** to 30 and the progress property to 15.

2. Expand the layout:gravity property's node and set the fill to horizontal so the SeekBar occupies all horizontal space in the SeekBar's GridLayout column.

3. Set the layout:height property to a new dimension resource (seekbar_height) with the value 40dp to increase vertical space in which the SeekBar is displayed.

Step 11: Configuring the *tipTextView and totalTextView*

To complete the formatting of the tipTextView and totalTextView, select both and set the following properties:

1. Delete the default value of the text property ("Medium Text")—we'll programmatically display the calculated tip and total.

2. Expand the layout:gravity property's node and set the fill to horizontal so each TextView occupies all horizontal space in the TextViews' GridLayout column.

3. Set the background property to a new color resource named result_background with the value #FFE0B2—a light orange color chosen from Google's material design color palette.

4. Set the gravity property to center so the calculated tip and total amounts will be centered within these TextViews.

5. Expand the padding property's node, click the ellipsis button for the all value, then select the dimension resource named textview_padding that you created previously for the amountTextView.

6. Finally, add a shadow to each view by setting the elevation property to the elevation dimension resource you created earlier.

3.5 Default Theme and Customizing Theme Colors

Each app has a theme that defines the default look-and-feel of the standard views you use. The theme is specified in the app's AndroidManifest.xml file (Section 3.7). You can customize aspects of the theme, such those that define an app's color scheme, by defining **style resources** in the styles.xml file located in the in the app's res/values folder.

3.5.1 parent Themes

The style.xml resource file contains a style with the name "AppTheme" that's referenced from the app's AndroidManifest.xml file to specify the app's theme. This style also specifies a parent theme, which is similar to a superclass in Java—the new style inherits its parent theme's attributes and their default values. Just as in a Java subclass, a style can override parent theme attributes with values customized for specific apps. A company might do this, for example, to use the company's branding colors. We'll use this concept in Section 3.5.2 to customize three colors used in the app's theme.

As we mentioned previously, Android Studio's app templates now include support for the AppCompat libraries that enable you to use newer Android features in older Android versions. By default, Android Studio sets the parent theme to

Theme.AppCompat.Light.DarkActionBar

one of several predefined themes from the AppCompat library—apps that use this theme have a light background, except for the dark app bar at the top of the app. Each AppCompat theme uses Google's material design recommendations to style your apps' GUIs.

3.5.2 Customizing Theme Colors

Section 3.3.11 discussed where a theme's primary, dark primary and accent colors are applied in an app's on-screen elements. In this section, you'll use the new Android Studio **Theme Editor** to change the app's primary, dark primary and accent colors, thus overriding the values of the android:colorPrimary, android:colorPrimaryDark and android:colorAccent theme attributes shown in Fig. 3.6. These are three of many theme attributes you can override. For the complete list, visit:

```
http://developer.android.com/reference/android/R.attr.html
```

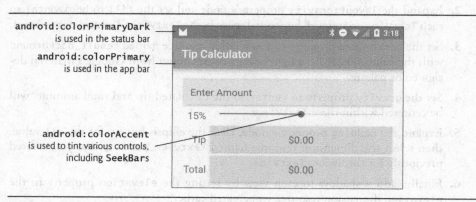

Fig. 3.6 | Theme attributes for the primary, primary dark and accent colors.

Modifying the Theme's Primary, Dark Primary and Accent Colors
To customize the colors:

1. Open styles.xml. In the editor's upper-right corner, click the **Open editor** link to display the **Theme Editor** (Fig. 3.7) showing the current colors for colorPrimary (dark blue), colorPrimaryDark (a darker shade of colorPrimary) and colorAccent (bright pink)—these are the default colors specified in Android Studio's **Empty Activity** app template. For this app, we'll change colorPrimary and colorPrimaryDark to lighter blues and change colorAccent to orange.

2. Customize the app's colorPrimary value by clicking its color swatch (Fig. 3.7) to display the **Resources** dialog (Fig. 3.8). In the dialog, click the **Material Blue 500** color swatch, then click **OK** to change colorPrimary's value—hovering the mouse cursor over a color swatch displays its color name in a tooltip. The number **500** represents a particular shade of the **Material Blue** color. Shades of each color range from 50 (a light shade) to 900 (a dark shade)—you can view samples of each color's shades at

```
https://www.google.com/design/spec/style/color.html#color-
         color-palette
```

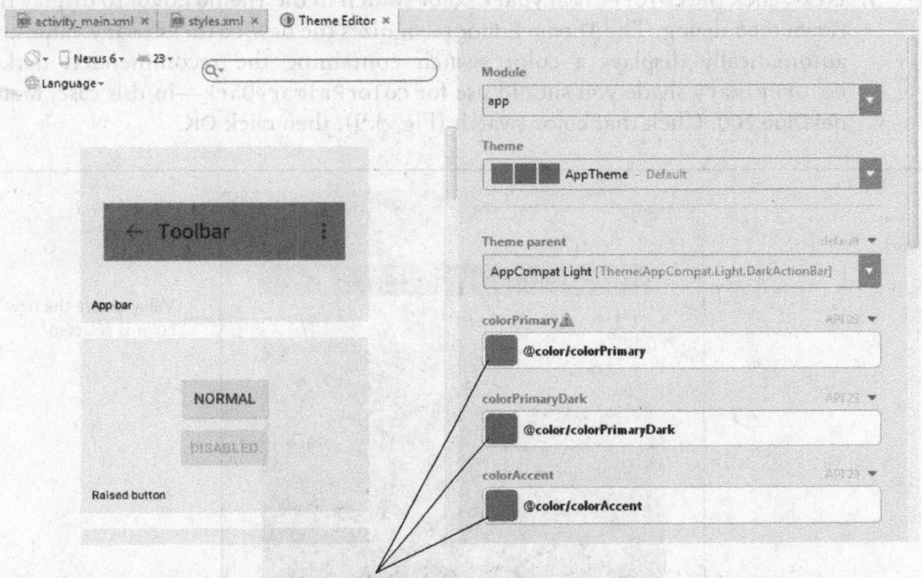

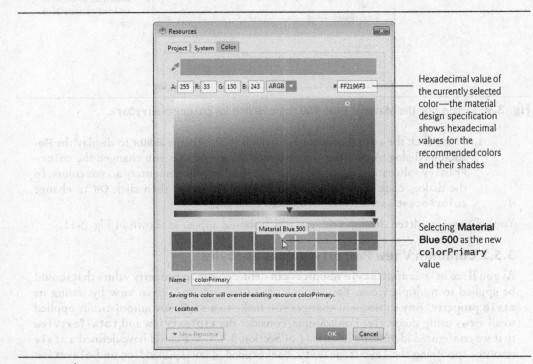

Color swatches for the theme's `colorPrimary`, `colorPrimaryDark` and `colorAccent` attributes

Fig. 3.7 | **Theme Editor** shows styled view previews on the left and theme attributes on the right.

Fig. 3.8 | Selecting the **Material Blue 500** color swatch for `colorPrimary`.

3. Next, click the `colorPrimaryDark` color swatch in the **Theme Editor** to display the **Resources** dialog. The **Theme Editor** recognizes the new `colorPrimary` value and automatically displays a color swatch containing the recommended darker `colorPrimary` shade you should use for `colorPrimaryDark`—in this case, **Material Blue 700**. Click that color swatch (Fig. 3.9), then click **OK**.

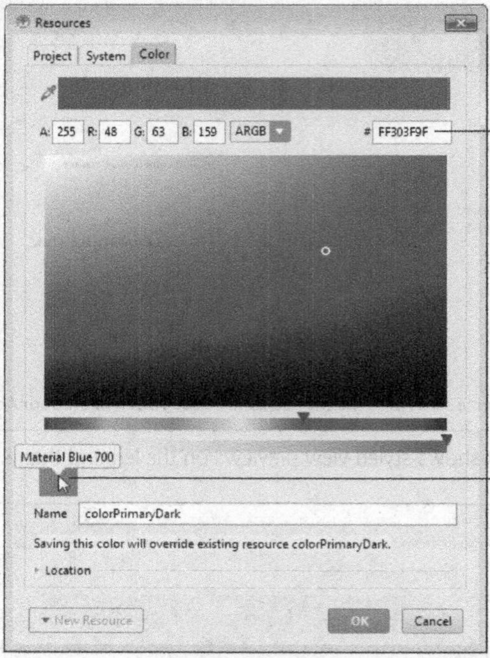

Fig. 3.9 | Selecting the **Material Blue 700** color swatch for `colorPrimaryDark`.

4. Next, click the `colorAccent` color swatch in the **Theme Editor** to display the **Resources** dialog. Again, the **Theme Editor** recognizes that you changed the `colorPrimary` value and displays swatches for various complementary accent colors. In the dialog, click the **Orange accent 400** color swatch, then click **OK** to change `colorAccent`'s value (Fig. 3.10), then click **OK**.

You've now completed the app's design, which should appear as shown in Fig. 3.11.

3.5.3 Common `View` Property Values as Styles

As you'll see in later apps, `style` resources can define common property values that should be applied to multiple views. You apply a `style` resource to a given view by setting its **style property**. Any subsequent changes you make to a `style` are automatically applied to all views using the `style`. For example, consider the `tipTextView` and `totalTextView` that we configured identically in *Step 11* of Section 3.4.5. We could have defined a `style` resource specifying the `layout:gravity`, `background`, `gravity`, `padding` and `elevation` properties' values, then set both `TextViews`' `style` properties to the same `style` resource.

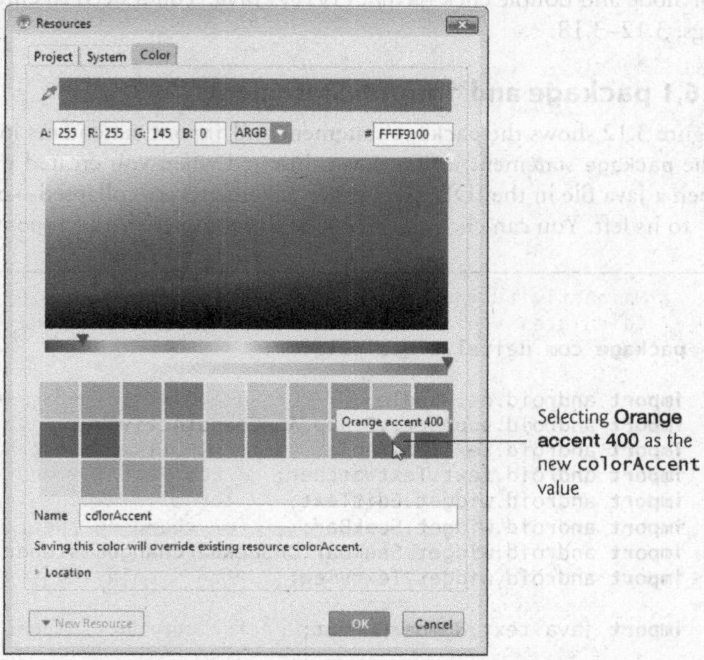

Fig. 3.10 | Selecting the **Orange accent 400** color swatch for `colorAccent`.

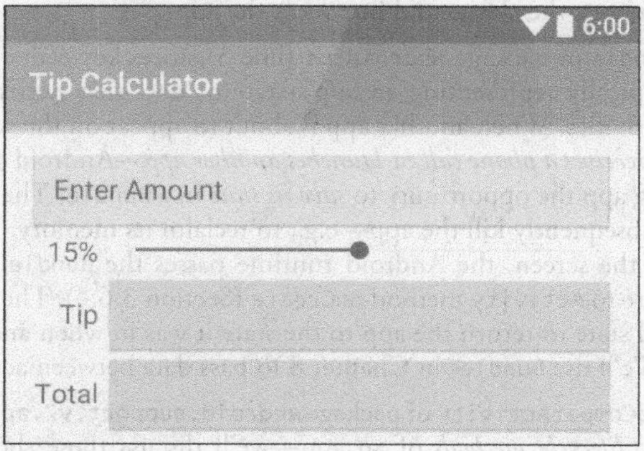

Fig. 3.11 | Completed design.

3.6 Adding the App's Logic

Class `MainActivity` (Figs. 3.12–3.18) implements the **Tip Calculator** app's logic. It calculates the tip and total bill amounts, then displays them in locale-specific currency format. To view the file, in the Project window, expand the app/Java/com.deitel.tipcalculator node and double click `MainActivity.java`. You'll need to enter most of the code in Figs. 3.12–3.18.

3.6.1 package and import Statements

Figure 3.12 shows the package statement and `import` statements in `MainActivity.java`. The package statement in line 3 was inserted when you created the project. When you open a Java file in the IDE, the `import` statements are collapsed—one is displayed with a ⊕ to its left. You can click the ⊕ to see the complete list of `import` statements.

```
 I   // MainActivity.java
 2   // Calculates a bill total based on a tip percentage
 3   package com.deitel.tipcalculator;
 4
 5   import android.os.Bundle; // for saving state information
 6   import android.support.v7.app.AppCompatActivity; // base class
 7   import android.text.Editable; // for EditText event handling
 8   import android.text.TextWatcher; // EditText listener
 9   import android.widget.EditText; // for bill amount input
10   import android.widget.SeekBar; // for changing the tip percentage
11   import android.widget.SeekBar.OnSeekBarChangeListener; // SeekBar listener
12   import android.widget.TextView; // for displaying text
13
14   import java.text.NumberFormat; // for currency formatting
15
```

Fig. 3.12 | `MainActivity`'s package and `import` statements.

Lines 5–14 `import` the classes and interfaces the app uses:

- Class `Bundle` of package `android.os` (line 5) stores key–value pairs of information—typically representing an app's state or data that needs to be passed between activities. When another app is about to appear on the screen—e.g., when the user *receives a phone call* or *launches another app*—Android gives the currently executing app the opportunity to *save its state* in a `Bundle`. The Android runtime might subsequently kill the app—e.g., to reclaim its memory. When the app returns to the screen, the Android runtime passes the `Bundle` of the previously saved state to `Activity` method onCreate (Section 3.6.4). Then, the app can use the saved state to return the app to the state it was in when another app became active. We'll use `Bundle`s in Chapter 8 to pass data between activities.

- Class `AppCompatActivity` of package `android.support.v7.app` (line 6) provides the basic *lifecycle methods* of an app—we'll discuss these shortly. `AppCompatActivity` is an indirect subclass of `Activity` (package `android.app`) that supports using newer Android features apps running on current and older Android platforms.

- Interface `Editable` of package `android.text` (line 7) allows you to modify the content and markup of text in a GUI.

- You implement interface `TextWatcher` of package `android.text` (line 8) to respond to events when the user changes the text in an `EditText`.

- Package android.widget (lines 9, 10 and 12) contains the *widgets* (i.e., views) and layouts that are used in Android GUIs. This app uses EditText (line 9), SeekBar (line 10) and TextView (line 12) widgets.

- You implement interface SeekBar.OnSeekBarChangeListener of package android.widget (line 11) to respond to the user moving the SeekBar's *thumb*.

- Class NumberFormat of package java.text (line 14) provides numeric formatting capabilities, such as *locale-specific* currency and percentage formats.

3.6.2 MainActivity Subclass of AppCompatActivity

Class MainActivity (Figs. 3.13–3.18) is the **Tip Calculator** app's Activity subclass. When you created the TipCalculator project, the IDE generated this class as a subclass of App-CompatActivity (an indirect subclass of Activity) and provided an override of class Activity's inherited onCreate method (Fig. 3.15). Every Activity subclass *must* override this method. We'll discuss onCreate shortly.

```
16    // MainActivity class for the Tip Calculator app
17    public class MainActivity extends Activity {
18
```

Fig. 3.13 | Class MainActivity is a subclass of Activity.

3.6.3 Class Variables and Instance Variables

Figure 3.14 declares class MainActivity's variables. The NumberFormat objects (lines 20–23) are used to format currency values and percentages, respectively. NumberFormat's static method getCurrencyInstance returns a NumberFormat object that formats values as currency using the device's locale. Similarly, static method getPercentInstance formats values as percentages using the device's locale.

```
19        // currency and percent formatter objects
20        private static final NumberFormat currencyFormat =
21            NumberFormat.getCurrencyInstance();
22        private static final NumberFormat percentFormat =
23            NumberFormat.getPercentInstance();
24
25        private double billAmount = 0.0; // bill amount entered by the user
26        private double percent = 0.15; // initial tip percentage
27        private TextView amountTextView; // shows formatted bill amount
28        private TextView percentTextView; // shows tip percentage
29        private TextView tipTextView; // shows calculated tip amount
30        private TextView totalTextView; // shows calculated total bill amount
31
```

Fig. 3.14 | MainActivity class's instance variables.

The bill amount entered by the user into amountEditText will be read and stored as a double in billAmount (line 25). The tip percentage (an integer in the range 0–30) that the user sets by moving the Seekbar *thumb* will be divided by 100.0 to create a double for use in calculations, then stored in percent (line 26). For example, if you select 25 with the SeekBar, percent will store 0.25, so the app will multiply the bill amount by 0.25 to calculate the 25% tip.

> ### Software Engineering Observation 3.3
> *For precise monetary calculations, use class BigDecimal (package java.math)—rather than type double—to represent the monetary amounts and perform calculations.*

Line 27 declares the TextView that displays the currency-formatted bill amount. Line 28 declares the TextView that displays the tip percentage, based on the SeekBar *thumb's* position (see the **15%** in Fig. 3.1(a)). The variables in lines 29–30 will refer to the TextViews in which the app displays the calculated tip and total.

3.6.4 Overriding Activity Method onCreate

The onCreate method (Fig. 3.15)—which is *autogenerated* with lines 33–36 when you create the app's project—is called by the system when an Activity is *started*. Method onCreate typically initializes the Activity's instance variables and views. This method should be as simple as possible so that the app *loads quickly*. In fact, if the app takes longer than five seconds to load, the operating system will display an **ANR (Application Not Responding) dialog**—giving the user the option to *forcibly terminate the app*. You'll learn how to prevent this problem in Chapter 9.

```
32    // called when the activity is first created
33    @Override
34    protected void onCreate(Bundle savedInstanceState) {
35       super.onCreate(savedInstanceState); // call superclass's version
36       setContentView(R.layout.activity_main); // inflate the GUI
37
38       // get references to programmatically manipulated TextViews
39       amountTextView = (TextView) findViewById(R.id.amountTextView);
40       percentTextView = (TextView) findViewById(R.id.percentTextView);
41       tipTextView = (TextView) findViewById(R.id.tipTextView);
42       totalTextView = (TextView) findViewById(R.id.totalTextView);
43       tipTextView.setText(currencyFormat.format(0)); // set text to 0
44       totalTextView.setText(currencyFormat.format(0)); // set text to 0
45
46       // set amountEditText's TextWatcher
47       EditText amountEditText =
48          (EditText) findViewById(R.id.amountEditText);
49       amountEditText.addTextChangedListener(amountEditTextWatcher);
50
51       // set percentSeekBar's OnSeekBarChangeListener
52       SeekBar percentSeekBar =
53          (SeekBar) findViewById(R.id.percentSeekBar);
54       percentSeekBar.setOnSeekBarChangeListener(seekBarListener);
55    }
56
```

Fig. 3.15 | Overriding Activity method onCreate.

onCreate's Bundle *Parameter*

During the app's execution, the user could change the device's configuration—for example, by *rotating the device, connecting to a Bluetooth keyboard* or *sliding out a hard keyboard*. For a good user experience, the app should continue operating smoothly through such configuration changes. When the system calls onCreate, it passes a Bundle argument containing the Activity's saved state, if any. Typically, you save state in Activity methods onPause or onSaveInstanceState (demonstrated in later apps). Line 35 calls the superclass's onCreate method, which is *required* when overriding onCreate.

Generated R Class Contains Resource IDs

As you build your app's GUI and add *resources* (such as strings in the strings.xml file or views in the activity_main.xml file) to your app, the IDE generates a class named **R** that contains *nested classes* representing each type of resource in your project's res folder. The nested classes are declared static, so that you can access them in your code with R.*ClassName*. Within class R's nested classes, the IDE creates static final int constants that enable you to refer to your app's resources programmatically (as we'll discuss momentarily). Some of the nested classes in class R include

- class **R.drawable**—contains constants for any drawable items, such as *images*, that you put in the various drawable folders in your app's res folder
- class **R.id**—contains constants for the *views* in your *XML layout files*
- class **R.layout**—contains constants that represent each *layout file* in your project (such as, activity_main.xml), and
- class **R.string**—contains constants for each String in the strings.xml file.

Inflating the GUI

The call to **setContentView** (line 36) receives the constant **R.layout.activity_main** which indicates the XML file that represents MainActivity's GUI—in this case, the constant represents the activity_main.xml file. Method setContentView uses this constant to load the corresponding XML document, which Android parses and converts into the app's GUI. This process is known as **inflating the GUI**.

Getting References to the Widgets

Once the layout is *inflated*, you can *get references to the individual widgets* so that you can interact with them programmatically. To do so, you use class Activity's findViewById method. This method takes an int constant representing a specific view's **Id** and returns a reference to the view. The name of each view's **R.id** constant is determined by the component's **Id** property that you specified when designing the GUI. For example, amountEditText's constant is R.id.amountEditText.

Lines 39–42 obtain references to the TextViews that we change programmatically in the app. Line 39 obtains a reference to the amountTextView that's updated when the user enters the bill amount. Line 40 obtains a reference to the percentTextView that's updated when the user changes the tip percentage. Lines 41–42 obtain references to the TextViews where the calculated tip and total are displayed.

Displaying Initial Values in the **TextViews**

Lines 43–44 set tipTextView's and totalTextView's text to 0 in a *locale-specific* currency format by calling the currencyFormat object's **format method**. The text in each of these TextViews will change as the user enters the bill amount.

Registering the Event Listeners

Lines 47–49 get the amountEditText and call its addTextChangedListener method to register the TextWatcher object that responds to events generated when the user changes the EditText's contents. We define this listener (Fig. 3.18) as an anonymous-inner-class object and assign it to the amountEditTextWatcher instance variable. Though we could have defined the anonymous inner class in place of amountEditTextWatcher in line 49 of Fig. 3.15, we chose to define it later in the class so that the code is easier to read.

 Software Engineering Observation 3.4

Rather than defining anonymous inner classes in large methods, define them as private final *instance variables to make your code easier to debug, modify and maintain.*

Lines 52–53 get a reference to the percentSeekBar. Line 54 calls the SeekBar's setOnSeekBarChangeListener method to register the OnSeekBarChangeListener object that responds to *events* generated when the user moves the SeekBar's thumb. Figure 3.17 defines this listener as an anonymous-inner-class object that's assigned to the instance variable seekBarListener.

Note Regarding Android 6 Data Binding

Android now has a **Data Binding support library** that you can use with Android apps targeting Android 2.1 (API level 7) and higher. You now can include in your layout XML files data-binding expressions that manipulate Java objects and dynamically update data in your apps' user interfaces.

In addition, each layout XML file that contains views with ids has a corresponding autogenerated class. For each view with an id, the class has a public final instance variable referencing that view. You can create an instance of this "Binding" class to replace all calls to findViewById, which can greatly simplify your onCreate methods in Activity and Fragment classes with complex user interfaces. Each instance variable's name is the id specified in the layout for the corresponding view. The "Binding" class's name is based on the layout's name—for activity_main.xml, the class name is ActivityMainBinding.

At the time of this writing, the Data Binding library is an early beta release that's subject to substantial changes, both in the syntax of data-binding expressions and in the Android Studio tool support. You can learn more about Android data binding at

https://developer.android.com/tools/data-binding/guide.html

3.6.5 MainActivity Method calculate

Method calculate (Fig. 3.16) is called by the EditText's and SeekBar's listeners to update the tip and total TextViews each time the user *changes* the bill amount. Line 60 displays the tip percentage in the percentTextView. Lines 63–64 calculate the tip and total, based on the billAmount. Lines 67–68 display the amounts in currency format.

```
57      // calculate and display tip and total amounts
58      private void calculate() {
59          // format percent and display in percentTextView
60          percentTextView.setText(percentFormat.format(percent));
61
62          // calculate the tip and total
63          double tip = billAmount * percent;
64          double total = billAmount + tip;
65
66          // display tip and total formatted as currency
67          tipTextView.setText(currencyFormat.format(tip));
68          totalTextView.setText(currencyFormat.format(total));
69      }
70
```

Fig. 3.16 | MainActivity Method calculate.

3.6.6 Anonymous Inner Class That Implements Interface OnSeekBarChangeListener

Lines 72–87 (Fig. 3.17) create the *anonymous-inner-class* object that responds to percent-SeekBar's *events*. The object is assigned to the instance variable seekBarListener. Line 54 (Fig. 3.15) registered seekBarListener as percentSeekBar's OnSeekBarChangeListener *event-handling* object. For clarity, we define all but the simplest event-handling objects in this manner so that we do not clutter the onCreate method with this code.

```
71      // listener object for the SeekBar's progress changed events
72      private final OnSeekBarChangeListener seekBarListener =
73          new OnSeekBarChangeListener() {
74              // update percent, then call calculate
75              @Override
76              public void onProgressChanged(SeekBar seekBar, int progress,
77                  boolean fromUser) {
78                  percent = progress / 100.0; // set percent based on progress
79                  calculate(); // calculate and display tip and total
80              }
81
82              @Override
83              public void onStartTrackingTouch(SeekBar seekBar) { }
84
85              @Override
86              public void onStopTrackingTouch(SeekBar seekBar) { }
87          };
88
```

Fig. 3.17 | Anonymous inner class that implements interface OnSeekBarChangeListener.

*Overriding Method **onProgressChanged** of Interface **OnSeekBarChangeListener***
Lines 75–86 (Fig. 3.17) implement interface OnSeekBarChangeListener's methods. Method onProgressChanged is called whenever the SeekBar's thumb position changes. Line 78 calculates the percent value using the method's progress parameter—an int rep-

resenting the SeekBar's *thumb* position. We divide this by 100.0 to get the percentage. Line 79 calls method calculate to recalculate and display the tip and total.

Overriding Methods onStartTrackingTouch and onStopTrackingTouch of Interface OnSeekBarChangeListener

Java requires that you override *every* method in an interface that you implement. This app does not need to know when the user starts moving the SeekBar's thumb (onStartTrackingTouch) or stops moving it (onStopTrackingTouch), so we simply provide an empty body for each (lines 82–86) to fulfill the interface contract.

Android Studio Tools for Overriding Methods

Android Studio can create for you empty methods that override inherited methods from the class's superclasses or that implement interface methods. When you place the cursor in a class's body, then select the **Code > Override Methods...** menu option, the IDE displays a **Select Methods to Override/Implement** dialog that lists every method you can override in the current class. This list includes all the inherited methods in the class's hierarchy and the methods of any interfaces implemented throughout the class's hierarchy.

Error-Prevention Tip 3.2
Using Android Studio's **Code > Override Methods...** *menu option helps you write code faster and with fewer errors.*

3.6.7 Anonymous Inner Class That Implements Interface TextWatcher

Lines 90–114 of Fig. 3.18 create an *anonymous-inner-class* object that responds to amountEditText's *events* and assign it to the instance variable amountEditTextWatcher. Line 49 (Fig. 3.15) registered this object to *listen* for amountEditText's events that occur when the text changes.

```
89    // listener object for the EditText's text-changed events
90    private final TextWatcher amountEditTextWatcher = new TextWatcher() {
91        // called when the user modifies the bill amount
92        @Override
93        public void onTextChanged(CharSequence s, int start,
94            int before, int count) {
95
96            try { // get bill amount and display currency formatted value
97                billAmount = Double.parseDouble(s.toString()) / 100.0;
98                amountTextView.setText(currencyFormat.format(billAmount));
99            }
100           catch (NumberFormatException e) { // if s is empty or non-numeric
101               amountTextView.setText("");
102               billAmount = 0.0;
103           }
104
105           calculate(); // update the tip and total TextViews
106       }
107
```

Fig. 3.18 | Anonymous inner class that implements interface TextWatcher. (Part 1 of 2.)

```
108        @Override
109        public void afterTextChanged(Editable s) { }
110
111        @Override
112        public void beforeTextChanged(
113            CharSequence s, int start, int count, int after) { }
114    };
115 }
```

Fig. 3.18 | Anonymous inner class that implements interface TextWatcher. (Part 2 of 2.)

Overriding Method *onTextChanged of Interface* TextWatcher

The onTextChanged method (lines 92–106) is called whenever the text in the amount-EditText is *modified*. The method receives four parameters. In this example, we use only CharSequence s, which contains a copy of amountEditText's text. The other parameters indicate that the count characters starting at start *replaced* previous text of length before.

Line 97 converts the user input from amountEditText to a double. We allow users to enter only whole numbers in pennies, so we divide the converted value by 100.0 to get the actual bill amount—e.g., if the user enters 2495, the bill amount is 24.95. Line 98 displays the updated bill amount. If an exception occurs, lines 101–102 clear the amountTextView and set the billAmount to 0.0. Lines 105 calls calculate to recalculate and display the tip and total, based on the current bill amount.

Other Methods of the *amountEditTextWatcher* TextWatcher

This app does *not* need to know what changes are about to be made to the text (before-TextChanged) or that the text has already been changed (afterTextChanged), so we simply override each of these TextWatcher interface methods with an *empty* body (lines 108–113) to fulfill the interface contract.

3.7 AndroidManifest.xml

In this section, you'll modify the AndroidManifest.xml file to specify that this app's Activity supports only a device's portrait orientation and that the virtual keyboard should always be displayed when the Activity first appears on the screen or navigates back to the Activity. To open the manifest, double click AndroidManifest.xml in the **Project** window's manifests folder. Figure 3.19 shows the completed manifest with our changes highlighted—the rest of the file was autogenerated by Android Studio when we created the app's project. We'll discuss some aspects of the manifest here. For a list of all the elements a manifest may contain, their attributes and their values, visit

```
http://developer.android.com/guide/topics/manifest/manifest-
    intro.html
```

```
1  <?xml version="1.0" encoding="utf-8"?>
2  <manifest xmlns:android="http://schemas.android.com/apk/res/android"
3      package="com.deitel.tipcalculator" >
4
```

Fig. 3.19 | AndroidManifest.xml contents. (Part 1 of 2.)

```
 5        <application
 6            android:allowBackup="true"
 7            android:icon="@mipmap/ic_launcher"
 8            android:label="@string/app_name"
 9            android:supportsRtl="true"
10            android:theme="@style/AppTheme" >
11            <activity
12                android:name=".MainActivity"
13                android:label="@string/app_name"
14                android:screenOrientation="portrait"
15                android:windowSoftInputMode="stateAlwaysVisible">
16                <intent-filter>
17                    <action android:name="android.intent.action.MAIN" />
18
19                    <category android:name="android.intent.category.LAUNCHER" />
20                </intent-filter>
21            </activity>
22        </application>
23
24    </manifest>
```

Fig. 3.19 | AndroidManifest.xml contents. (Part 2 of 2.)

3.7.1 manifest Element

The **manifest** element (lines 2–24) indicates that this XML file's contents represent the app's manifest. This element's package attribute specifies the app's Java package name that was configured when you created the app's project (Section 3.4.2). Recall that for apps you submit to the Google Play store, the package name is used as the app's unique identifier.

3.7.2 application Element

The manifest element's nested **application** element (lines 5–21) specifies attributes of the application, including

- **android:allowBackup**—Whether or not the app's data should be backed up automatically by Android so that the data can be restored to the device or a new device at a later time.

- **android:icon**—The app icon that you touch in the launcher to execute the app.

- **android:label**—The app's name that's typically displayed below the icon in the launcher and often displayed in the app bar when the app is executing.

- **android:supportsRtl**—Whether or not the app's interface can be flipped horizontally to support right-to-left languages like Arabic and Hebrew.

- **android:theme**—The theme that determines the default look-and-feel of the app's views.

The application element's nested elements define app components, such as activities.

3.7.3 activity Element

The application element's nested **activity** element (lines 10–20) describes an Activity. An app can have many activities, one of which is designated as the Activity that's displayed when the user touches the app's icon in the launcher to execute the app. Each activity element specifies at least the following attributes:

- **android:name**—The Activity's class name. The notation ".MainActivity" is shorthand for "com.deitel.MainActivity" (where com.deitel is the reverse of the domain name you specified when creating the app's project).
- **android:label**—The Activity's name. This is often displayed in the app bar when the Activity is on the screen. For single Activity apps, this name is typically the same as the app's name.

For MainActivity, we added the following attributes:

- **android:screenOrientation**—In general, most apps should support *both* portrait and landscape orientations. In *portrait* orientation, the device's longer dimension is vertical. In *landscape orientation*, the device's longer dimension is horizontal. In the **Tip Calculator** app, rotating the device to landscape orientation on a typical phone would cause the numeric keypad to obscure most of the **Tip Calculator**'s GUI. For this reason, we set this property to "portrait" to support *only* portrait orientation.
- **android:windowSoftInputMode**—In the **Tip Calculator** app, the soft keypad should be displayed immediately when the app executes and should reappear each time the user returns to the **Tip Calculator** app. For this reason we set this property to "stateAlwaysVisible". This will *not* display the soft keyboard if a hard keyboard is present.

3.7.4 intent-filter Element

Intents are Android's mechanism for communicating between executable components—such as activities, background services and the operating system. You *state your intent*, then Android uses **intent messaging** to coordinate the executable components to accomplish what you intend to do. This *loose coupling* makes it easy to mix and match parts of different applications. You tell Android what you want to accomplish, then let Android find the installed applications with activities that can handle the task.

Inter-App Communication
One example of how Intents are used is *coordinating efforts between separate apps*. Consider how photo sharing can be handled in Android:

- Most social-networking Android apps provide their own photo-sharing capabilities. Each app can advertise in its manifest its specific Activity that uploads a photo to the user's account.
- Other apps can use these photo-sharing capabilities, rather than implementing their own. For example, a photo-editing app can provide a **Share Photo** option. The app can respond to a user's photo-sharing request by *stating its intent* to share a photo—that is, creating a photo-sharing Intent and passing it to Android.
- Android looks at the Intent to determine which installed applications provide activities that can share photos.
- If there's only *one* such app, Android executes that app's photo-sharing Activity.

- If there are *many* such apps, Android displays a list of apps and asks the *user to decide* which app's photo-sharing Activity should execute.

A key benefit of this loosely coupled approach is that the photo-editing app's developer does not need to incorporate support for every possible social-networking site. By issuing a photo-sharing Intent, the app automatically supports *any* app that declares a photo-sharing Activity in its manifest, including those apps the user has already installed and any the user chooses to install in the future. For a list of the items that can be used with Intents, visit

```
http://developer.android.com/reference/android/content/
   Intent.html#constants
```

Executing Apps

Another example of how Intents are used is in *launching activities*. When you touch an app's icon in the device's launcher app, your intent is to execute the app. In this case, the launcher issues an Intent to execute that app's main Activity (discussed momentarily). Android responds to this Intent by launching the app and executing the specific Activity designated in the app's manifest as the main Activity.

Determining Which Activity to Execute

Android uses information in the manifest to determine the activities that can respond to Intents and which Intents each Activity can handle. In the manifest, the activity element's nested **intent-filter element** (Fig. 3.19, lines 16–20) determines which Intent types can launch an Activity. If an Intent matches only one Activity's intent-filter, Android executes that Activity. If there are multiple matches, Android presents a list from which the user can choose an app, then executes the appropriate Activity in that app.

Android also passes the Intent to the Activity, because an Intent often contains data the Activity can use to perform its task. For example, a photo-editing app can include in a share-photo Intent the specific photo to share.

The intent-filter element must contain one or more **action elements**. The action "android.intent.action.MAIN" in line 17 of Fig. 3.19 indicates that MainActivity is the Activity to execute when the app launches. The optional **category element** in line 19 specifies what initiates the Intent—for "android.intent.category.LAUNCHER", it's the device's launcher. This category also indicates that the Activity should appear as an icon in the device's launcher with the icons for the user's other installed apps.

We'll discuss and program with Intents in the next chapter. For more information on Intents and Intent filters, visit

```
http://developer.android.com/guide/components/intents-filters.html
```

3.8 Wrap-Up

In this chapter, you created the interactive **Tip Calculator** app. We discussed the app's capabilities, then you test-drove it to calculate the tip and total, based on the bill amount. You built the app's GUI using Android Studio's layout editor, **Component Tree** window and **Properties** window. You also edited the layout's XML and used the **Theme Editor** to customize the Theme.AppCompat.Light.DarkActionBar theme's primary, dark primary and accent colors that were set by the IDE when you created the project. We presented the code for class MainActivity, a subclass of AppCompatActivity (and an indirect subclass of Activity) that defined the app's logic.

In the app's GUI, you used a GridLayout to arrange the views into rows and columns. You displayed text in TextViews and received input from an EditText and a SeekBar.

The MainActivity class required many Java object-oriented programming capabilities, including classes, objects, methods, interfaces, anonymous inner classes and inheritance. We explained the notion of inflating the GUI from its XML file into its screen representation. You learned about Android's Activity class and part of the Activity life-cycle. In particular, you overrode the onCreate method to initialize the app when it's launched. In the onCreate method, you used Activity method findViewById to get references to each of the views the app interacts with programmatically. You defined an anonymous inner class that implements the TextWatcher interface so the app can calculate new tips and totals as the user enters the bill amount in the EditText. You also defined an anonymous inner class that implements the OnSeekBarChangeListener interface so the app can calculate a new tip and total as the user changes the tip percentage by moving the SeekBar's thumb.

Finally, you edited the AndroidManifest.xml file to specify that the MainActivity supports only portrait orientation and that the MainActivity should always display the keypad. We also discussed the other elements that Android Studio placed in the manifest when you created the project.

In Chapter 4, you'll build the **Flag Quiz** app in which the user is shown a graphic of a country's flag and must guess the country from 2, 4, 6 or 8 choices. You'll use a menu and checkboxes to customize the quiz, specifying the number of guess options and limiting the flags to specific regions of the world.

Self-Review Exercises

3.1 Fill in the blanks in each of the following statements:
a) A(n) _____—often called a text box or text field in other GUI technologies—is a subclass of TextView that can display text and accept text input from the user.
b) Use a(n) _____ to arrange GUI components into cells in a rectangular grid.
c) Android Studio's _____ window shows the nested structure of the GUI.
d) Class _____ of package android.os represents an app's state information.
e) You implement interface _____ of package android.text to respond to events when the user interacts with an EditText component.
f) Before Android 3.0, a separate _____ was typically associated with each screen of an app.
g) The method _____ is called by the system when an Activity is starting—that is, when its GUI is about to be displayed so that the user can interact with the Activity.
h) As you build your app's GUI and add resources (such as strings in the strings.xml file or GUI components in a layout XML file) to your app, the IDE generates a class named _____ that contains nested static classes representing each type of resource in your project's res folder.
i) Class _____ (nested in class R) contains constants for any drawable items, such as images, that you put in drawable folder in your app's res folder.
j) Class _____ (nested in class R) contains constants for each String in the strings.xml file.

k) Once the layout is inflated, you can get references to the individual widgets using Activity's _____ method. This method takes an int constant for a specific view (that is, a GUI component) and returns a reference to it.

3.2 State whether each of the following is *true* or *false*. If *false*, explain why.

a) Method onCreate typically initializes the Activity's instance variables and GUI components. This method should be as simple as possible so that the app loads quickly. In fact, if the app takes longer than five seconds to load, the operating system will display an ANR (Application Not Responding) dialog—giving the user the option to forcibly terminate the app.

b) As with all Java programs, Android apps have a main method.

c) An active (or running) activity is visible on the screen and "has the focus"—that is, it's in the background.

d) A stopped activity is visible on the screen and is likely to be killed by the system when its memory is needed.

Answers to Self-Review Exercises

3.1 a) EditText. b) GridLayout. c) **Outline**. d) Bundle. e) TextWatcher. f) activity. g) onCreate. h) R. i) R.drawable. j) R.string. k) findViewById.

3.2 a) True. b) False. Android apps *don't* have a main method. c) False. An active (or running) activity is visible on the screen and "has the focus"—that is, it's in the *foreground*. d) False. A stopped activity is *not* visible on the screen and is likely to be killed by the system when its memory is needed.

Exercises

3.3 Fill in the blanks in each of the following statements:

a) String literals should be placed in the strings.xml file in the app's _____ folder.

b) Class _____ of package android.app provides the basic lifecycle methods of an app.

c) Interface _____ of package android.text allows you to change the content and markup of text in a GUI.

d) You implement interface _____ of package android.widget to respond to the user moving the SeekBar's thumb.

e) Android apps have four types of components—activities, services, content providers and _____.

f) Throughout its life an activity can be in one of several states—active (or running), paused or _____. The activity transitions between these states in response to various events.

g) Class _____ (nested in class R) contains constants for the GUI components in your XML layout files.

h) Method setContentView uses a received constant to load the corresponding XML document, which is then parsed and converted into the app's GUI. This process is known as _____ the GUI.

i) You can use Android Studio's _____ to modify a theme's colors.

3.4 State whether each of the following is *true* or *false*. If *false*, explain why.

a) By default, a Seekbar allows you to select values from 0 to 255.

b) A GUI component can span multiple columns in a GridLayout.

c) Every Activity subclass must override the construct method.

d) A paused activity is visible on the screen and has the focus.

e) Time-consuming initializations should be done in an onCreate method instead of the background process.

f) You override the onStart method to initialize the app when it's launched.

g) AppCompat is an indirect subclass of Activity that supports using newer Android features in apps running on current and older Android platforms.

h) Apps that use the AppCompat libraries must use one of the AppCompat themes; otherwise, some views will not render correctly.

3.5 *(Enhanced Tip Calculator App)* Make the following enhancements to the **Tip Calculator** app:
a) Add an option to calculate the tip based on either the price before tax or after tax.
b) Allow the user to enter the number of people in the party. Calculate and display the amount owed by each person if the bill were to be split evenly among the party members.

3.6 *(Mortgage Calculator App)* Create a mortgage calculator app that allows the user to enter a purchase price, down payment amount and an interest rate. Based on these values, the app should calculate the loan amount (purchase price minus down payment) and display the monthly payment for 10, 20 and 30 year loans. Allow the user to select a custom loan duration (in years) by using a SeekBar and display the monthly payment for that custom loan duration.

3.7 *(College Loan Payoff Calculator App)* A bank offers college loans that can be repaid in 5, 10, 15, 20, 25 or 30 years. Write an app that allows the user to enter the amount of the loan and the annual interest rate. Based on these values, the app should display the loan lengths in years and their corresponding monthly payments.

3.8 *(Car Payment Calculator App)* Typically, banks offer car loans for periods ranging from two to five years (24 to 60 months). Borrowers repay the loans in monthly installments. The amount of each monthly payment is based on the length of the loan, the amount borrowed and the interest rate. Create an app that allows the customer to enter the price of a car, the down-payment amount and the loan's annual interest rate. The app should display the loan's duration in months and the monthly payments for two-, three-, four- and five-year loans. The variety of options allows the user to easily compare repayment plans and choose the most appropriate.

3.9 *(Body Mass Index Calculator App)* The formulas for calculating the BMI are

$$BMI = \frac{weightInPounds \times 703}{heightInInches \times heightInInches}$$

or

$$BMI = \frac{weightInKilograms}{heightInMeters \times heightInMeters}$$

Create a BMI calculator app that allows users to enter their weight and height and whether they are entering these values in English or Metric units, then calculates and displays the user's body mass index. The app should also display the following information from the Department of Health and Human Services/National Institutes of Health so the user can evaluate his/her BMI:

```
BMI VALUES
Underweight: less than 18.5
Normal:      between 18.5 and 24.9
Overweight:  between 25 and 29.9
Obese:       30 or greater
```

3.10 *(Target-Heart-Rate Calculator App)* While exercising, you can use a heart-rate monitor to see that your heart rate stays within a safe range suggested by your trainers and doctors. According to the American Heart Association (AHA), the formula for calculating your *maximum heart rate* in beats per minute is *220 minus your age in years* (http://bit.ly/AHATargetHeartRates). Your *target heart rate* is a range that is 50–85% of your maximum heart rate. [*Note:* These formulas are estimates provided by the AHA. Maximum and target heart rates may vary based on the health, fitness and gender of the individual. Always consult a physician or qualified health care professional before beginning or modifying an exercise program.] Write an app that inputs the person's age, then calculates and displays the person's maximum heart rate and target-heart-rate range.

4

Flag Quiz App

Objectives

In this chapter you'll:

- Use Fragments to make better use of available screen real estate in an Activity's GUI on phones and tablets.

- Display a settings icon on the app bar to enable users to access the app's user preferences.

- Automatically manage and persist an app's settings via a PreferenceFragment.

- Modify key–value pairs settings via a SharedPreferences.Editor.

- Organize image resources in the app's assets subfolders and manipulate them with an AssetManager.

- Define an animation and apply it to a View.

- Use a Handler to schedule a future task to perform on the GUI thread.

- Use Toasts to display messages briefly to the user.

- Launch a specific Activity with an explicit Intent.

- Use collections from the java.util package.

- Define layouts for multiple device orientations.

- Use Android's logging mechanism to log error messages.

4.1 Introduction

The **Flag Quiz** app tests your ability to correctly identify 10 flags from various countries and territories (Fig. 4.1). By default, the app presents a flag image and four country-name Buttons that you click to guess the answer—one is correct and the others are randomly selected, *nonduplicated* incorrect answers. The app displays the user's progress throughout the quiz, showing the question number (out of 10) in a TextView above the current flag image.

Settings icon displayed on the app bar

Quiz progress

Current flag

Guess **Buttons**

Fig. 4.1 | **Flag Quiz** app running on a smartphone in portrait orientation.

As you'll see, the app also allows you to control the quiz difficulty by specifying whether to display two, four, six or eight guess Buttons, and by choosing the world regions that should be included in the quiz. These options are displayed differently, based on the device that's running the app and the orientation of the device—the app supports portrait orientation on *any* device, but landscape orientation only on tablets.

In portrait orientation, the app displays on the app bar a settings icon (⚙). When the user touches this icon, the app displays a separate screen (another Activity) for setting the number of guess Buttons, and the world regions to use in the quiz. On a tablet in landscape orientation (Fig. 4.2), the app uses a different layout that always displays the app's settings and the quiz at the same time.

First you'll test-drive the app. Then we'll overview the technologies we used to build it. Next, you'll design the app's GUI. Finally, we'll present and walk through the app's complete source code, discussing the app's new features in more detail.

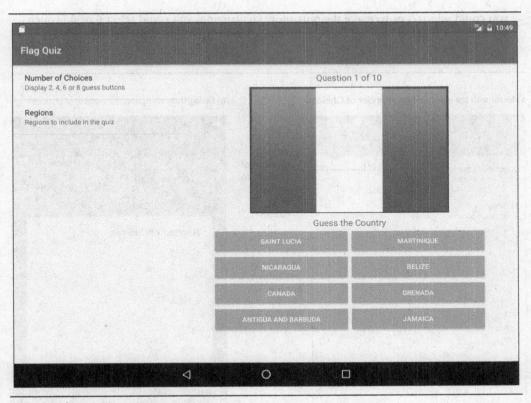

Fig. 4.2 | **Flag Quiz** app running on a tablet in landscape orientation.

4.2 Test-Driving the Flag Quiz App

You'll now test-drive the **Flag Quiz** app. To do so, open Android Studio, open the **Flag Quiz** app from the FlagQuiz folder in the book's examples folder, then execute the app in the AVD or on a device. This builds the project and runs the app (Fig. 4.1 or Fig. 4.2).

4.2.1 Configuring the Quiz's Settings

When you first install and run the app, the quiz is configured to display four guess Buttons and to select flags from *all* of the world's regions. For this test-drive, you'll change the app's options to select flags only from North America and you'll keep the app's default setting of four guess Buttons per flag.

On a phone, a tablet or an AVD in portrait orientation, touch the settings icon (⚙) on the app bar (Fig. 4.1) to view the **Settings** screen (Fig. 4.3(a)). On a tablet device or tablet AVD in *landscape* orientation, the app's settings appear at the left side of the screen (Fig. 4.2). Touch **Number of Choices** to display the dialog for selecting the number of Buttons that should be displayed with each flag (Fig. 4.3(b)). (On a tablet device or tablet AVD in landscape orientation, the entire app is grayed out and the dialog is centered on the screen.) By default, **4** is selected—we used this default setting. To make the quiz easier, you could select 2, or to make the quiz more challenging, you could select **6** or **8**. Touch **CANCEL** (or touch the screen outside the dialog) to return to the **Settings** screen.

a) Menu with the user touching **Number of Choices**   b) Dialog showing options for number of choices

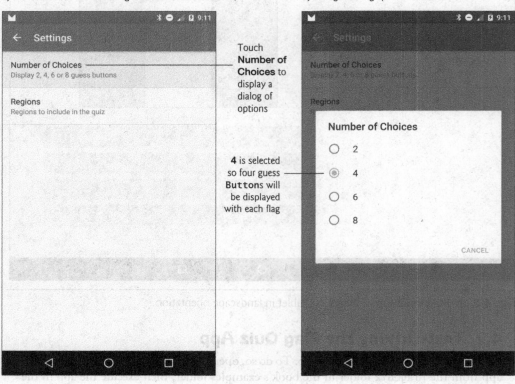

Touch **Number of Choices** to display a dialog of options

4 is selected so four guess **Buttons** will be displayed with each flag

Fig. 4.3 | **Flag Quiz** settings screen and the **Number of Choices** dialog.

Next, touch **Regions** (Fig. 4.4(a)) to display the checkboxes representing the world regions (Fig. 4.4(b)). By default, all regions are enabled when the app first executes, so every flag we provide with the app can be selected randomly for a quiz. Touch the checkboxes next to **Africa**, **Asia**, **Europe**, **Oceania** (Australia, New Zealand and the islands in that vicinity) and **South America** to uncheck them—this excludes those regions' countries from the quiz. Touch **OK** to save your settings. On a phone, a tablet or an AVD in portrait orientation, touch the back button (◀) to return to the quiz screen and start a new quiz with your updated settings. On a tablet device or tablet AVD in landscape orientation, a new quiz with the updated settings is immediately displayed at the right side of the screen.

a) Menu with the user touching **Regions**   b) Dialog showing regions

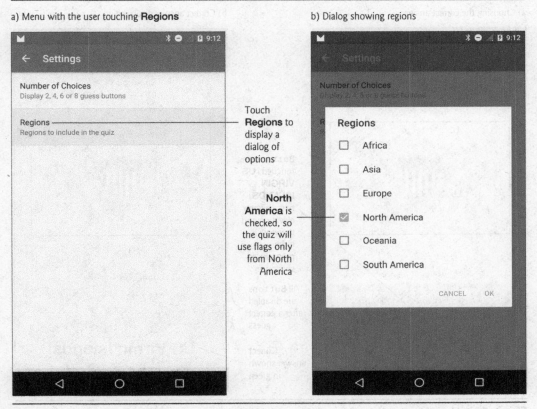

Touch **Regions** to display a dialog of options

North America is checked, so the quiz will use flags only from North America

Fig. 4.4 | Flag Quiz settings screen and the **Regions** dialog (after unchecking **Africa**, **Asia**, **Europe**, **Oceania** and **South America**).

4.2.2 Taking the Quiz

A new quiz starts with the number of answer choices you selected and flags only from the region(s) you selected. Work through the quiz by touching the guess Button for the country that you think matches each flag.

Making a Correct Selection

If the choice is correct (Fig. 4.5(a)), the app disables all the answer Buttons and displays the country name in green, followed by an exclamation point at the bottom of the screen (Fig. 4.5(b)). After a short delay, the app loads the next flag and animates the flag and a new set of answer Buttons onto the screen. The app transitions from the current quiz question to the next with a *circular reveal* animation:

• First, a large-diameter circle shrinks onto the screen until its diameter is zero, thus hiding the current quiz question's flag and guess Buttons.

• Then, the circle's diameter grows from zero until the new question's flag and guess Buttons are fully visible on the screen.

a) Choosing the correct answer   b) Correct answer displayed

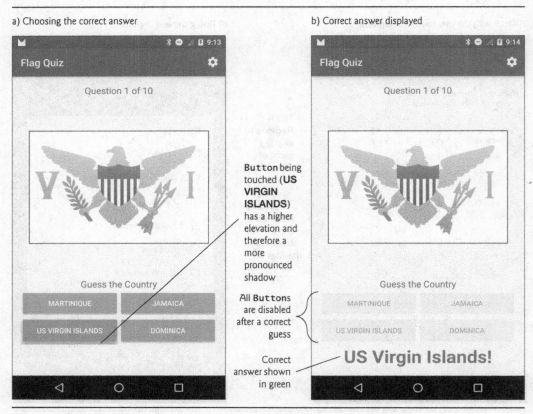

Button being touched (**US VIRGIN ISLANDS**) has a higher elevation and therefore a more pronounced shadow

All **Buttons** are disabled after a correct guess

Correct answer shown in green

Fig. 4.5 | User choosing the correct answer and the correct answer displayed.

Making an Incorrect Selection

For each incorrect country-name Button you touch (Fig. 4.6(a)), the app

- disables the corresponding country name Button
- uses an animation to *shake* the flag horizontally and
- displays **Incorrect!** in red at the bottom of the screen (Fig. 4.6(b)).

Continue guessing until you get the correct answer for that flag.

Completing the Quiz

After you select the 10 correct country names, a popup AlertDialog displays over the app, showing your total number of guesses and the percentage of correct answers (Fig. 4.7). This is a modal dialog, so you must interact with it to dismiss it—for a non-modal dialog, touching the AVD's or device's back button (◀) will dismiss the dialog. When you touch the dialog's **RESET QUIZ** Button, Android dismisses the dialog and a new quiz begins, using the same number of guess options and region(s) as the quiz you just completed.

a) Choosing an incorrect answer

b) **Incorrect!** displayed

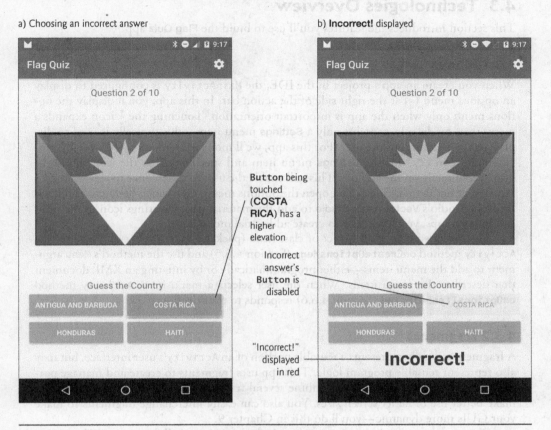

Button being touched (**COSTA RICA**) has a higher elevation

Incorrect answer's **Button** is disabled

"Incorrect!" displayed in red

Fig. 4.6 | Disabled incorrect answer in the **Flag Quiz** app.

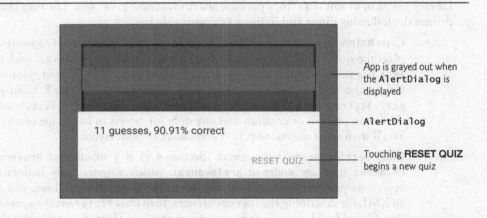

App is grayed out when the **AlertDialog** is displayed

AlertDialog

Touching **RESET QUIZ** begins a new quiz

Fig. 4.7 | Results displayed after quiz completion.

4.3 Technologies Overview

This section introduces the features you'll use to build the **Flag Quiz** app.

4.3.1 Menus

When you create an app's project in the IDE, the MainActivity is configured to display an options menu (⋮) at the right side of the action bar. In this app, you'll display the options menu only when the app is in portrait orientation. Touching the ⋮ icon expands a menu that, by default, contains only a **Settings** menu item—this typically is used to display an app's settings to the user. For this app, we'll modify the menu's XML file by providing an icon (⚙) for the **Settings** menu item and specifying that the icon should be displayed directly on the app bar. This will enable the user to touch once to view the app's settings, rather than having to first open the options menu, then touch **Settings**. You'll use Android Studio's **Vector Asset Studio** to add the material design settings icon to the project. In later apps, you'll see how to create additional menu items.

The options menu is an object of class **Menu** (package android.view). You override Activity method **onCreateOptionsMenu** (Section 4.6.5) and use the method's Menu argument to add the menu items—either programmatically or by inflating an XML document that describes the menu items. When the user selects a menu item, Activity method **onOptionsItemSelected** (Section 4.6.6) responds to the selection.

4.3.2 Fragments

A **fragment** typically represents a reusable portion of an Activity's user interface, but may also represent reusable program logic. This app uses fragments to create and manage portions of the app's GUI. You can combine several fragments to create user interfaces that make better use of tablet screen sizes. You also can easily interchange fragments to make your GUIs more dynamic—you'll do this in Chapter 9.

Class **Fragment** (package android.app) is the base class of all fragments. When using subclasses of AppCompatActivity with Fragments you must use the Android Support Library's version of this class from package android.support.v4.app. The **Flag Quiz** app defines the following direct and indirect Fragment subclasses:

- Class MainActivityFragment (Section 4.7)—a direct subclass of Fragment—displays the quiz's GUI and defines the quiz's logic. Like an Activity, each Fragment has its own layout that's typically defined as an XML layout resource file (GUIs also can be created dynamically). In Section 4.5.2, you'll build MainActivityFragment's GUI. You'll create *two* layouts for MainActivity—one for devices in portrait orientation and one only for tablets in landscape orientation. You'll then reuse the MainActivityFragment in both layouts.

- Class SettingsActivityFragment (Section 4.9) is a subclass of **Preference-Fragment** (package **android.preference**), which automatically maintains an app's user preferences in a file associated with the app. As you'll see, you create an XML file describing the user preferences, then class PreferenceFragment uses that file to build an appropriate preferences GUI (Figs. 4.3–4.4). We discuss preferences more in Section 4.3.5.

- When you finish a quiz, the app creates an anonymous subclass of **DialogFragment** (package android.support.v4.app) and displays an AlertDialog (introduced in Section 4.3.15) containing the quiz results (Section 4.7.10).

Fragments *must* be hosted by an Activity—they cannot execute independently. When this app runs in landscape orientation on a tablet, the MainActivity hosts all of the Fragments. In portrait orientation (on any device), the SettingsActivity (Section 4.8) hosts the SettingsActivityFragment and the MainActivity hosts the others.

4.3.3 Fragment Lifecycle Methods

Like an Activity, each Fragment has a *lifecycle* and provides methods that you can override to respond to *lifecycle events*. In this app, you'll override

- **onCreate**—This method (which you'll override in class SettingsActivityFragment) is called when a Fragment is created. The MainActivityFragment and SettingsActivityFragment are created when the app inflates their parent activities' layouts. The DialogFragment that displays the quiz results is created and displayed dynamically when the user completes a quiz.

- **onCreateView**—This method (which you'll override in class MainActivityFragment) is called after onCreate to build and return a View containing the Fragment's GUI. As you'll see, this method receives a **LayoutInflater**, which you'll use to programmatically inflate a Fragment's GUI from the components specified in a predefined XML layout.

Fragments can add their own menu items to a host Activity's menu. Like class Activity, Fragments also have lifecycle method onCreateOptionsMenu and event-handling method onOptionsItemSelected.

We'll discuss other Fragment lifecycle methods as we encounter them throughout the book. For the complete lifecycle details, visit

```
http://developer.android.com/guide/components/fragments.html
```

4.3.4 Managing Fragments

An Activity manages its Fragments via a **FragmentManager** (package android.app)—accessible via Activity's **getFragmentManager** method. If the Activity needs to interact with a Fragment that's declared in the Activity's layout and has an **id**, the Activity can call FragmentManager method **findFragmentById** to obtain a reference to the specified Fragment. As you'll see in Chapter 9, a FragmentManager can use **FragmentTransactions** to dynamically *add*, *remove* and *transition* between Fragments.

For backward compatibility, subclasses of AppCompatActivity must use the Android Support Library's version of FragmentManager from package android.support.v4.app, rather than the one in package android.app. Class AppCompatActivity inherits method **getSupportFragmentManager** from the Android Support Library's FragmentActivity class to obtain the correct FragmentManager.

4.3.5 Preferences

In Section 4.2.1, you customized the quiz by changing the app's settings. These settings are stored persistently in a file as *key–value* pairs—each *key* enables you to quickly look up a corresponding *value*. The keys in the file must be Strings, and the values can be Strings or primitive-type values. Such a file is manipulated via an object of class **SharedPreferences** (package **android.content**) and the file is accessible only to the app that creates the file.

A PreferenceFragment uses **Preference** objects (package android.preference) to manage app settings and stores those settings in a file via a SharedPreferences object. This app uses Preference subclass **ListPreference** to manage the number of guess Buttons displayed for each flag and Preference subclass **MultiSelectListPreference** to manage the world regions to include in the quiz. A ListPreference creates *mutually exclusive* radio buttons in which only one can be selected (Fig. 4.3(b)). A MultiSelectListPreference creates a GUI containing checkboxes, any number of which can be selected (Fig. 4.4(b)). You'll use a **PreferenceManager** object (package android.preference) to access and interact with the app's default SharedPreferences file.

You'll also interact directly with the app's default SharedPreferences file:

- When starting a quiz, you'll query the app's preferences to determine the number of guess Buttons to display and the region(s) from which to select flags.

- When the user changes the regions preference, the app will ensure that at least one region is selected; otherwise, there would be no flags to include in the quiz. If none is selected, the app edits the regions preference to select North America.

To modify a SharedPreferences file's contents, you'll use a **SharedPreferences.Editor** object (Section 4.6.7).

4.3.6 assets Folder

This app's flag images are loaded into the app only when needed and are located in the app's **assets folder**.[1] To add the images to the project, we copied each region's folder from our file system into the assets folder in the **Project** window (Section 4.4.4). The images are located in the images/FlagQuizImages folder with the book's examples.

Unlike an app's drawable folders, which require their image contents to be at the root level in each folder, the assets folder may contain files of any type and they can be organized in subfolders—we maintain the flag images for each region in a separate subfolder. Files in the assets subfolders are accessed via an **AssetManager** (package android.content.res), which can provide a list of all of the file names in a specified subfolder and can be used to access each asset.

4.3.7 Resource Folders

In Section 2.4.4, you learned about the drawable, layout and values subfolders of an app's res folder. In this app, you'll also use the menu, anim, color and xml resource folders. Figure 4.8 overviews these folders as well as the animator and raw folders.

---

1. We obtained the images from http://www.free-country-flags.com.

Resource subfolder	Description
anim	Folder names that begin with anim contain XML files that define *tweened animations*, which can change an object's *transparency*, *size*, *position* and *rotation* over time. You'll define such an animation in Section 4.4.10, then in Section 4.7.10 you'll play it to create a *shake effect* to provide the user with visual feedback for an incorrect guess.
animator	Folder names that begin with animator contain XML files that define *property animations*, which change the value of an object's property over time. In Java, a property is typically implemented in a class as an instance variable with both *set* and *get* accessors.
color	Folder names that begin with color contain XML files that define color state lists—lists of colors for various states, such as the states of a Button (*unpressed*, *pressed*, *enabled*, *disabled*, and so on). We'll use a color state list to define separate colors for when the guess Buttons are *enabled* or *disabled* in Section 4.4.8.
raw	Folder names that begin with raw contain resource files (such as audio clips) that are read into an app as streams of bytes. We'll use such resources in Chapter 6 to play sounds.
menu	Folder names that begin with menu contain XML files that describe the contents of menus. When you create a project, the IDE automatically defines a menu with a **Settings** option.
xml	Folder names that begin with xml contain XML files that do not fit into the other resource categories—often XML data files used by the app. In Section 4.4.11, you'll create an XML file that represents the preferences displayed by this app's SettingsActivityFragment.

Fig. 4.8 | Other subfolders within a project's res folder.

4.3.8 Supporting Different Screen Sizes and Resolutions

In Section 2.5.1 you learned that Android devices have various *screen sizes*, *resolutions* and *pixel densities* (dots per inch or DPI). You also learned that you typically provide images and other visual resources in multiple resolutions so Android can choose the best resource for a device's pixel density. Similarly, in Section 2.8, you learned how to provide String resources for different languages and regions. Android uses resource folders with *qualified names* to choose the appropriate images, based on a device's pixel density, and the correct language strings, based on a device's locale and region settings. This mechanism also can be used to select resources from any of the resource folders discussed in Section 4.3.7.

For this app's MainActivity, you'll use minimum screen width and orientation qualifiers to determine which layout to use—one for portrait orientation on phones and tablets and another only for tablets in landscape orientation. To do this, you'll define two layouts that present MainActivity's contents:

- content_main.xml is the default layout that displays only the MainActivity-Fragment.
- content_main.xml (sw700dp-land) is used *only* on devices (i.e., tablets) when the app is in landscape (land) orientation.

Qualified resource folder names (on disk) have the format:

name-qualifiers

where *qualifiers* consists of one or more qualifiers separated by dashes (-). There are currently 19 qualifier types that you can use to designate when Android should choose specific resource files. We'll explain other qualifiers as we use them throughout the book. For a complete description of all the res subfolder qualifiers and the rules for the order in which they must be defined in a fully qualified folder's name, visit

```
http://developer.android.com/guide/topics/resources/providing-
        resources.html#AlternativeResources
```

4.3.9 Determining the Device Orientation

In this app, we display the Menu only when the app is running on a phone-sized device or when it's running on a tablet in portrait orientation (Section 4.6.5). To determine this, we'll obtain an object of class **Configuration** (package android.content.res), which contains public instance variable **orientation** containing either ORIENTATION_PORTRAIT or ORIENTATION_LANDSCAPE for the device's current orientation.

4.3.10 Toasts for Displaying Messages

A **Toast** (package android.widget) briefly displays a message, then disappears from the screen. Toasts are often used to display minor error messages or informational messages. We use Toasts as follows:

- To indicate that the quiz will be reset after the user changes the app's settings.

- To indicate that at least one region must be selected if the user deselects all regions—in this case, the app sets North America as the quiz's default region.

4.3.11 Using a `Handler` to Execute a `Runnable` in the Future

When the user makes a correct guess, the app displays the correct answer for two seconds before displaying the next flag. To do this, we use a **Handler** (package android.os). Handler method **postDelayed** receives as arguments a Runnable to execute and a delay in milliseconds. After the delay has passed, the Handler's Runnable executes in the *same thread* that created the Handler.

Error-Prevention Tip 4.1
Operations that interact with or modify the GUI must be performed in the GUI thread (also called the UI thread or main thread), because GUI components are not thread safe.

4.3.12 Applying an Animation to a `View`

When the user makes an incorrect choice, the app shakes the flag by applying an **Animation** (package android.view.animation) to the ImageView. We use **AnimationUtils** static method **loadAnimation** to load the animation from an XML file that describes the animation's options. We also specify the number of times the animation should repeat with Animation method **setRepeatCount** and perform the animation by calling View method **startAnimation** (with the Animation as an argument) on the ImageView.

4.3.13 Using `ViewAnimationUtils` to Create a Circular Reveal Animator

Animations can make an app more visually appealing. In this app, shortly after the user makes a correct choice, the app animates the flag and answer `Button`s off the screen and the next flag and answer `Button`s onto the screen. To do this, in Section 4.7.9, you'll use the `ViewAnimationUtils` class to create a *circular reveal* `Animator` object by calling the `createCircularReveal` method. You'll then set the animation's duration and start the animation by calling `Animator` methods **setDuration** and **start**, respectively. The animation appears as a shrinking or expanding circular window that displays part of a UI element.

4.3.14 Specifying Colors Based on a View's State Via a Color State List

A **color state list resource file** defines a color resource that changes colors based on a `View`'s state. For example, you could define a color state list for a `Button`'s background color that specifies different colors for the `Button`'s *pressed*, *unpressed*, *enabled* and *disabled* states. Similarly, for a `CheckBox`, you could specify different colors for its *checked* or *unchecked* states.

In this app, when the user makes an incorrect guess, the app disables that guess `Button`, and when the user makes a correct guess, the app disables all the guess `Button`s. In a disabled `Button`, the white text is difficult to read. To solve this issue you'll define a **color state list** that specifies a `Button`'s text color, based on the `Button`'s enabled or disabled state (Section 4.4.8). For more information on color state lists, visit

```
http://developer.android.com/guide/topics/resources/color-list-
    resource.html
```

4.3.15 `AlertDialog`

You can display messages, options and confirmations to app users via **AlertDialogs** (package `android.app`). An `AlertDialog` is a **modal dialog**—when it's displayed, the user cannot interact with the app until the dialog is dismissed (closed). As you'll see, you create and configure the `AlertDialog` with an **AlertDialog.Builder** object, then use it to create the `AlertDialog`.

`AlertDialog`s can display buttons, checkboxes, radio buttons and lists of items that the user can touch to respond to the dialog's message. They can also display custom GUIs. A standard `AlertDialog` may have up to three buttons that represent:

- A *negative action*—Cancels the dialog's specified action, often labeled with **CANCEL** or **NO**. This is the leftmost button when there are multiple buttons in the dialog.

- A *positive action*—Accepts the dialog's specified action, often labeled with **OK** or **YES**. This is the rightmost button when there are multiple buttons in the dialog.

- A *neutral action*—This button indicates that the user does not want to cancel or accept the action specified by the dialog. For example, an app that asks the user to register to gain access to additional features might provide a **REMIND ME LATER** neutral button.

We use an AlertDialog at the end of a quiz to display the quiz results to the user (Section 4.7.10) and enable the user to touch a button to reset the quiz. You'll implement the interface **DialogInterface.OnClickListener** (package android.content) to handle the button's event. You can learn more about Android dialogs at

> http://developer.android.com/guide/topics/ui/dialogs.html

4.3.16 Logging Exception Messages

When exceptions occur or when you want to track important aspects of your code's execution, you can *log* messages for debugging purposes with Android's built-in logging mechanism. Android provides class **Log** (package android.util) with several static methods that represent messages of varying detail. Logged messages can be viewed in the bottom of the Android Device Monitor's **LogCat** tab or with the **Android logcat tool**. You can open the Android Device Monitor window from Android Studio by selecting **View > Tool Windows > Android Monitor**. For more details on logging messages, visit

> http://developer.android.com/tools/debugging/debugging-log.html

4.3.17 Launching Another Activity Via an Explicit Intent

As you learned in Section 3.7.4, Android uses a technique known as *intent messaging* to communicate information between activities within one app or activities in separate apps. Each Activity declared in the AndroidManifest.xml file can specify *intent filters* indicating *actions* the Activity is capable of handling. In each app so far, the IDE created an intent filter for the app's only Activity indicating that it could respond to the predefined action named android.intent.action.MAIN, which specifies that the Activity can be used to *launch* the app to begin its execution. An Activity is launched by using an Intent that indicates an *action* to be performed and the *data* on which to perform that action.

Implicit and Explicit Intents

This app uses an **explicit Intent**. When this app runs in portrait orientation, its preferences are displayed *explicitly* in the SettingsActivity (Section 4.8)—the specific Activity that understands how to manage this app's preferences. Section 4.6.6 shows how to use an explicit Intent to launch a specific Activity in the same app.

Android also supports **implicit Intents** for which you do *not* specify explicitly which component should handle the Intent. For example, you can create an Intent to display the contents of a URL and allow Android to launch the most appropriate activity (a web browser), based on the type of data. If *multiple* activities can handle the action and data passed to startActivity, the system will display a *dialog* in which the user can select the activity to use (possibly one of several browsers the user has installed). If the system cannot find an activity to handle the action, then method startActivity throws an Activity-NotFoundException. In general, it's a good practice to handle this exception to prevent your app from crashing. You can also prevent this exception from happening by first using Intent method **resolveActivity** to determine whether there is an Activity to handle the Intent. For a more information on Intents, visit

> http://developer.android.com/guide/components/intents-filters.html

4.3.18 Java Data Structures

This app uses various data structures from the java.util package. The app dynamically loads the image file names for the enabled regions and stores them in an Array-List<String>. We use **Collections** method **shuffle** to randomize the order of the image file names for each new game (Section 4.7.7). We use a second ArrayList<String> to hold the image file names for the countries eligible to be used in the current quiz. We also use a **Set<String>** to store the world regions included in a quiz. We refer to the Array-List<String> object with a variable of interface type List<String>.

> **Software Engineering Observation 4.1**
>
> *Refer to collection objects using variables of the corresponding generic interface type, so you can change data structures easily without affecting the rest of your app's code.*

4.3.19 Java SE 7 Features

Android fully supports Java SE 7. For a complete list of the features introduced in Java SE 7, visit

```
http://www.oracle.com/technetwork/java/javase/jdk7-relnotes-
    418459.html
```

This app uses the following Java SE 7 features:

- Type inference for generic instance creation—If the compiler can infer a generic object's type from the context, you can replace *<type>* with <> when creating the object. For example, in the **Flag Quiz**'s MainActivityFragment code, the instance variable quizCountriesList is declared to be of type List<String>, so the compiler knows the collection must contain Strings. Thus, when we create the corresponding ArrayList object, we can use Java SE 7's *diamond operator* <> as in the following statement, and the compiler infers that <> should be <String>, based on quizCountriesList's declaration:

```
quizCountriesList = new ArrayList<>();
```

- The try-*with-resources* statement—Rather than declaring a resource, using it in a try block and closing it in a finally block, you can use the try-*with-resources* statement to declare the resource in the try block's parentheses and use the resource in the try block. The resource is *implicitly* closed when program control leaves the try block. For example, in the **Flag Quiz**'s MainActivityFragment code, we use an InputStream to read the bytes of the app's flag images and use them to create Drawables (Section 4.7.7):

```
try (InputStream stream =
    assets.open(region + "/" + nextImage + ".png")) {
    // code that might throw an exception
}
```

4.3.20 AndroidManifest.xml

As you learned in Chapter 3, the AndroidManifest.xml file is created for you when you create an app. All activities in an Android app must be listed in the app's manifest file. We'll show you how to add additional activities to the project. When you add the SettingsActivity to the project (Section 4.4.12), the IDE will also add it to the manifest file. For the complete details of AndroidManifest.xml, visit

> http://developer.android.com/guide/topics/manifest/manifest-
>   intro.html

We'll cover various other aspects of the AndroidManifest.xml file in subsequent apps.

4.4 Creating the Project, Resource Files and Additional Classes

In this section, you'll create the project and configure the String, array, color and animation resources used by the **Flag Quiz** app. You'll also create additional classes for a second Activity that enables the user to change the app's settings.

4.4.1 Creating the Project

Follow the steps in Section 2.3 to create a new project. Specify the following values in the **Create New Project** dialog's **New Project** step:

- **Application name:** Flag Quiz
- **Company Domain:** deitel.com (or specify your own domain name)

For the remaining steps in the **Create New Project** dialog, use the same settings as in Section 2.3, but this time in the **Add an activity to Mobile** step, select **Blank Activity** rather than **Empty Activity** and check the **Use a Fragment** checkbox. Keep the default names provided for the **Activity Name**, **Layout Name**, **Title** and **Menu Resource Name**, then click **Finish** to create the project. The IDE will create various Java and resource files, including

- a MainActivity class
- a Fragment subclass called MainActivityFragment that's displayed by the MainActivity
- layout files for the MainActivity and MainActivityFragment, and
- a menu_main.xml file that defines MainActivity's options menu.

Also, follow the steps in Section 2.5.2 to add an app icon to your project.

When the project opens in Android Studio, the IDE displays content_main.xml in the layout editor. Select **Nexus 6** from the virtual-device drop-down list (Fig. 2.11)—once again, we'll use this device as the basis for our design.

4.4.2 Blank Activity Template Layouts

The **Blank Activity** template is a backward-compatible app template (for Android 2.1 and higher) that uses features of the Android Design Support Library. This template can be used with or without a Fragment. When you choose to use the Fragment option, the IDE creates layouts named activity_main.xml, content_main.xml and fragment_main.xml.

activity_main.xml

The layout in activity_main.xml contains a **CoordinatorLayout** (from the package android.support.design.widget in the Android Design Support Library). The CoordinatorLayout layouts defined Android Studio's app templates typically contain an app bar, defined as a Toolbar (package android.support.v7.widget). The templates define the app bar explicitly for backward compatibility with early Android versions that did not support app bars. CoordinatorLayouts also help manage material-design-based interactions with nested views—such as moving a portion of a GUI out of the way when a view animates onto the screen and restoring the GUI to its original location when a view animates off the screen.

The default activity_main.xml layout embeds (via an <include> element in the XML) the GUI defined in content_main.xml. The default layout also contains a FloatingActionButton—a round image button from the Android Design Support Library that has a higher elevation than the GUI's other components, so it "floats" over the GUI. A FloatingActionButton typically emphasizes an important action that the user can perform by touching the button. Each app based on the **Blank Activity** template includes a FloatingActionButton and other material design features. You'll use FloatingActionButtons starting in Chapter 7.

content_main.xml

The content_main.xml layout defines the portion of MainActivity's GUI that appears below the app bar and above the system bar. When you choose the **Blank Activity** template's Fragment option, this file contains only a <fragment> element that displays the MainActivityFragment's GUI defined in fragment_main.xml. If you do not choose the template's Fragment option, this file defines a RelativeLayout containing a TextView, and you'd define MainActivity's GUI here.

fragment_main.xml

The fragment_main.xml layout is defined only when you choose the **Blank Activity** template's Fragment option. When using a Fragment, this is where you define the main GUI.

Preparing to Design the GUI

We don't need the FloatingActionButton for this app, so open the activity_main.xml layout and delete the bright pink button in the layout's bottom-right corner. Also, select the CoordinatorLayout in the **Component Tree** and set the layout's **id** to coordinatorLayout. Open the fragment_main.xml layout and remove the **Hello World!** TextView defined by the app template.

4.4.3 Configuring Java SE 7 Support

We use Java SE 7 programming features in this app. By default, a new Android Studio project uses Java SE 6. To use Java SE 7:

1. Right click the project's app folder and select **Open Module Settings** to open the **Project Structure** window.

2. Ensure that the **Properties** tab is selected at the top of the window.

3. In both the **Source Compatibility** and **Target Compatibility** drop-down lists, select 1.7, then click **OK**.

4.4.4 Adding the Flag Images to the Project

Follow these steps to create an assets folder and add the flags to the project:

1. Right click the app folder in the **Project** window and select **New > Folder > Assets Folder**. In the **Customize the Activity** dialog that appears, click **Finish**.

2. Navigate to the folder on disk containing the book's examples and copy all of the folders located in the `images/FlagQuizImages` folder.

3. Click the `assets` folder in the **Project** window, then paste the folders you copied in the preceding step. In the **Copy** dialog that appears, click **OK** to copy the folders and their images into your project.

4.4.5 `strings.xml` and Formatted String Resources

In Section 3.4.5, you learned how to create a `String` resource using the **Resources** dialog. For this app, we'll create the `String` (and many other) resources in advance, then use them as we design the GUI and from the program's code. You'll now create new `String` resources using the **Translations Editor** that you first saw in Section 2.8:

1. In the **Project** window, expand the `res/values` node, then open `strings.xml`.

2. In the editor's upper-right corner, click the **Open Editor** link to open the **Translations Editor**.

3. In the upper-left corner of the **Translations Editor**, click the **Add Key** button (➕).

4. In the dialog that appears, enter `number_of_choices` for the **Key** and `Number of Choices` for the **Default Value**, then click **OK** to create the new resource.

5. Repeat *Step 4* for each of the remaining string resources listed in the table (Fig. 4.9).

Look-and-Feel Observation 4.1

The Android design guidelines indicate that text displayed in your GUI should be brief, simple and friendly with the important words first. For details on the recommended writing style, see http://developer.android.com/design/style/writing.html.

Key	Default value
number_of_choices_description	Display 2, 4, 6 or 8 guess buttons
world_regions	Regions
world_regions_description	Regions to include in the quiz
guess_country	Guess the Country
results	%1$d guesses, %2$.02f%% correct
incorrect_answer	Incorrect!
default_region_message	One region must be selected. Setting North America as the default region.
restarting_quiz	Quiz will restart with your new settings
question	Question %1$d of %2$d
reset_quiz	Reset Quiz
image_description	Image of the current flag in the quiz
default_region	North_America

Fig. 4.9 | String resources used in the **Flag Quiz** app.

Format Strings as String Resources

The results and question resources are *format Strings*. When a String resource contains multiple format specifiers, you must number them for localization purposes. In the results resource

```
%1$d guesses, %2$.02f%% correct
```

the notation 1$ in %1$d indicates that the *first* value to insert in the String should replace the format specifier %1$d. Similarly, 2$ in %2$.02f indicates that the *second* value to insert in the String should replace the format specifier %2$.02f. The d in the first format specifier formats an integer and the f in the second one formats a floating-point number. In localized versions of strings.xml, the format specifiers %1$d and %2$.02f can be reordered as necessary to properly translate the String resource. The *first* value to insert will replace %1$d—*regardless* of where it appears in the format String—and the *second* value will replace %2$.02f *regardless* of where it appears in the format String.

4.4.6 arrays.xml

Technically, all of your app's resources in the res/values folder can be defined in the *same* file. However, to make it easier to manage different types of resources, separate files are typically used for each. For example, by convention array resources are normally defined in arrays.xml, colors in colors.xml, Strings in strings.xml and numeric values in values.xml. This app uses three String array resources that are defined in arrays.xml:

- regions_list specifies the names of the world regions with their words separated by *underscores*—these values are used to load image file names from the appropriate folders and as the selected values for the world regions the user selects in the SettingsActivityFragment.

- regions_list_for_settings specifies the names of the world regions with their words separated by *spaces*—these values are used in the SettingsActivityFragment to display the region-name checkboxes to the user.

- guesses_list specifies the Strings 2, 4, 6 and 8—these values are used in the SettingsActivityFragment to display the radio buttons that enable the user to select the number of guess Buttons to display.

Figure 4.10 shows the names and element values for these three array resources.

Array resource name	Values
regions_list	Africa, Asia, Europe, North_America, Oceania, South_America
regions_list_for_settings	Africa, Asia, Europe, North America, Oceania, South America
guesses_list	2, 4, 6, 8

Fig. 4.10 | String array resources defined in arrays.xml.

To create `arrays.xml` and configure the array resources, perform the following steps:

1. In the project's res folder, right click the values folder, then select **New > Values resource file** to display the **New Resource File** dialog. Because you right-clicked the values folder, the dialog is preconfigured to add a **Values** resource file in the values folder.

2. Specify `arrays.xml` in the **File name** field and click **OK** to create the file.

3. Android Studio does not provide a `String` resource editor for `String` arrays, so you'll need to edit the XML to create the `String` array resources.

Each `String`-array resource has the following format:

```
<string-array name="resource_name">
    <item>first element value</item>
    <item>second element value</item>
    ...
</string-array>
```

Figure 4.11 shows the completed XML file.

```
1   <?xml version="1.0" encoding="utf-8"?>
2   <resources>
3
4       <string-array name="regions_list">
5           <item>Africa</item>
6           <item>Asia</item>
7           <item>Europe</item>
8           <item>North_America</item>
9           <item>Oceania</item>
10          <item>South_America</item>
11      </string-array>
12
13      <string-array name="regions_list_for_settings">
14          <item>Africa</item>
15          <item>Asia</item>
16          <item>Europe</item>
17          <item>North America</item>
18          <item>Oceania</item>
19          <item>South America</item>
20      </string-array>
21
22      <string-array name="guesses_list">
23          <item>2</item>
24          <item>4</item>
25          <item>6</item>
26          <item>8</item>
27      </string-array>
28
29  </resources>
```

Fig. 4.11 | `arrays.xml` defines `String` array resources used in the **Flag Quiz** app.

4.4.7 colors.xml

This app displays correct answers in green and incorrect answers in red. As with any other resource, color resources should be defined in XML so you can easily change colors without modifying your app's Java source code and so you can use Android's resource-choosing capabilities to provide colors resources for various scenarios (different locales, night and day colors, and so on). Typically, colors are defined in the file colors.xml, which is created for you by most of Android Studio's app templates or created when you define colors using the technique shown in Section 2.5.7; otherwise, you must create the file.

The **Blank Activity** app template already contains a colors.xml file that defines the theme's primary, primary dark and accent color resources. Here you'll add color resources for the correct and incorrect answers and modify the app's accent color. To do so, you'll edit the XML directly, rather than using the **Theme Editor** to modify theme colors, as you did in Section 3.5.

Open colors.xml (Fig. 4.12) from the project's res/values folder and add lines 6 and 7. Also, change the hexadecimal value for the color named colorAccent (line 5) from #FF4081 (the default bright pink defined by the app template) to #448AFF (a lighter shade of blue than those used for colorPrimary and colorPrimaryDark). Notice in the IDE that the XML editor shows a color swatch to the left of each color.

```
1  <?xml version="1.0" encoding="utf-8"?>
2  <resources>
3      <color name="colorPrimary">#3F51B5</color>
4      <color name="colorPrimaryDark">#303F9F</color>
5      <color name="colorAccent">#448AFF</color>
6      <color name="correct_answer">#00CC00</color>
7      <color name="incorrect_answer">#FF0000</color>
8  </resources>
```

Fig. 4.12 | colors.xml defines the app's color resources.

4.4.8 button_text_color.xml

As we discussed in Section 4.3.14, when a color state list resource is provided for a Button color (either foreground or background), the appropriate color from the list of colors is selected, based on the Button's state. For this app you'll define colors for the answer Buttons' text color in the *enabled* and *disabled* states. To create the color state list resource file:

1. Right click the project's res folder, then select **New > Andorid resource file** to display the **New Resource File** dialog.

2. Specify button_text_color.xml as the **File name**.

3. In the **Resource type** drop-down, select **Color**. The **Root element** will automatically change to selector and the **Directory name** will automatically change to color.

4. Click **OK** to create the file. The button_text_color.xml file will be placed in a res/color folder, which the IDE automatically creates with the file.

5. Add the text shown in Fig. 4.13 to the file.

The <selector> element (lines 2–10) contains <item> elements that each specify a color for a particular Button state. In this color state list, we specify the android:state_enabled property in each <item>—once for the *enabled* state (true; lines 3–5) and once for the *disabled* state (false; lines 7–9). The android:color property (lines 4 and 8) specifies the color for that state.

```
1   <?xml version="1.0" encoding="utf-8"?>
2   <selector xmlns:android="http://schemas.android.com/apk/res/android">
3     <item
4         android:color="@android:color/primary_text_dark"
5         android:state_enabled="true"/>
6
7     <item
8         android:color="@android:color/darker_gray"
9         android:state_enabled="false"/>
10  </selector>
```

Fig. 4.13 | button_text_color.xml defines a button's text color for the *enabled* and *disabled* states.

4.4.9 Editing menu_main.xml

In the test-drive, you touched the (⚙) icon to access the app's settings. Here, you'll add this icon to the project, then edit menu_main.xml to display this icon on the app bar. To add the icon to the project:

1. Select **File > New > Vector Asset** to display the **Vector Asset Studio**—this tool enables you to add to your project any of Google's recommended *material design icons* (https://www.google.com/design/icons/). Each icon is defined as a scalable vector graphic that smoothly scales to any size.

2. Click the **Choose** button, then in the dialog that appears, scroll to locate the (⚙) icon, select it and click **OK**. The IDE updates the **Resource name** automatically to match the selected icon—you can edit this name if you wish. Keep the other settings in the dialog as is.

3. Click **Next**, then **Finish** to add to the res/drawable folder the icon's scalable representation—ic_settings_24dp.xml.

4. By default, each icon you add to the project in this manner is black, which would be difficult to see against the dark blue app bar background. To change this, open ic_settings_24dp.xml and change the <path> element's android:fillColor attribute to white, as in

    android:fillColor="@android:color/white"

Next, you'll add the icon to menu_main.xml:

1. Open menu_main.xml in the editor—this file is located in the res/menu folder.

2. In the <item> element, add the following android:icon attribute (a preview of the icon appears in the gray margin to the left of the line):

    android:icon="@drawable/ic_settings_24dp"

3. You can force a menu item to display on the app bar, in which case it's known as an *action*. By default, the action is displayed as the menu item's icon (if there is one); otherwise, the menu item's text is displayed. To force the menu item to appear as an action on the app bar, change the `<item>` element's `app:showAsAction` attribute to

>   app:showAsAction="always"

In the next chapter, you'll see how to specify that menu items should be shown on the app bar only if there is room.

4.4.10 Creating the Flag Shake Animation

In this section, you'll create the animation that shakes the flag when the user guesses incorrectly. We'll show how the app uses this animation in Section 4.7.10. To create the animation:

1. Right click the project's `res` folder, then select **New > Android resource file** to open the **New Resource file** dialog.

2. In the **File name** field, enter `incorrect_shake.xml`.

3. In the **Resource type** drop-down, select **Animation**. The IDE changes the **Root element** to set and the **Directory name** to anim.

4. Click **OK** to create the file. The XML file opens immediately.

The IDE does not provide an editor for animations, so you must modify the XML contents of the file as shown in Fig. 4.14.

```
 I   <?xml version="1.0" encoding="utf-8"?>
 2
 3   <set xmlns:android="http://schemas.android.com/apk/res/android"
 4      android:interpolator="@android:anim/decelerate_interpolator" >
 5
 6      <translate android:duration="100" android:fromXDelta="0"
 7         android:toXDelta="-5%p" />
 8
 9      <translate android:duration="100" android:fromXDelta="-5%p"
10         android:toXDelta="5%p" android:startOffset="100" />
11
12      <translate android:duration="100" android:fromXDelta="5%p"
13         android:toXDelta="-5%p" android:startOffset="200" />
14   </set>
```

Fig. 4.14 | `incorrect_shake.xml` defines a flag animation that's played when the user makes an incorrect guess.

In this example, we use **View animations** to create a *shake effect* that consists of three animations in an **animation set** (lines 3–14)—a collection of animations that make up a larger animation. Animation sets may contain any combination of **tweened animations**—**alpha** (transparency), **scale** (resize), **translate** (move) and **rotate**. Our shake animation consists of a series of three translate animations. A translate animation moves a View within its parent. Android also supports *property animations* in which you can animate any property of any object.

The first translate animation (lines 6–7) moves a View from a starting location to an ending position over a specified period of time. The **android:fromXDelta** attribute is the View's offset when the animation starts and the **android:toXDelta attribute** is the View's offset when the animation ends. These attributes can have

- absolute values (in pixels)
- a percentage of the animated View's size
- a percentage of the animated View's *parent's* size.

For the android:fromXDelta attribute, we specified an absolute value of 0. For the android:toXDelta attribute, we specified the value -5%p, which indicates that the View should move to the *left* (due to the minus sign) by 5% of the parent's width (the p indicates "percent"). To move by 5% of the View's width, simply remove the p. The **android:duration attribute** specifies how long the animation lasts in milliseconds. So the animation in lines 6–7 will move the View to the left by 5% of its parent's width in 100 milliseconds.

The second animation (lines 9–10) continues from where the first finished, moving the View from the -5%p offset to a %5p offset in 100 milliseconds. By default, animations in an animation set are applied simultaneously (i.e., in parallel), but you can use the **android:startOffset attribute** to specify the number of milliseconds into the future at which an animation should begin. This can be used to sequence the animations in a set. In this case, the second animation starts 100 milliseconds after the first. The third animation (lines 12–13) is the same as the second, but in the reverse direction, and it starts 200 milliseconds after the first animation.

4.4.11 preferences.xml for Specifying the App's Settings

In this section, you'll create the preferences.xml file that the SettingsActivityFragment uses to display the app's preferences. To create the file:

1. Right click the project's res folder, then select **New > Android resource file** to open the **New Resource File** dialog.

2. In the **File name** field enter the name preferences.xml.

3. In the **Resource type** drop-down list, select **XML**. The **Root element** will automatically change to PreferenceScreen, which represents a screen in which preferences are displayed. The **Directory name** will automatically change to xml.

4. Click **OK** to create the file. The preferences.xml file will be placed in the xml folder, which is created automatically.

5. If the IDE did not open res/xml/preferences.xml automatically, double click the file to open it.

You'll now add two types of preferences to the file, a **ListPreference** and a **MultiSelectListPreference**. Each preference has properties that we explain in Fig. 4.15 for **ListPreference** and Fig. 4.16 for **MultiSelectListPreference**. To add the preferences and their properties to the file, you'll need to edit the XML. Figure 4.17 shows the completed XML file.

Property	Value	Description
entries	@array/guesses_list	An array of Strings that will be displayed in the list of options.
entryValues	@array/guesses_list	An array of values associated with the options in the **Entries** property. The selected entry's value will be stored in the app's SharedPreferences.
key	pref_numberOfChoices	The name of the preference stored in the app's SharedPreferences.
title	@string/number_of_choices	The title of the preference displayed in the GUI.
summary	@string/number_of_choices_description	A summary description of the preference that's displayed below its title.
persistent	true	Whether the preference should persist after the app terminates—if true, class PreferenceFragment immediately persists the preference value each time it changes.
defaultValue	4	The item in the **Entries** property that's selected by default.

Fig. 4.15 | ListPreference property values.

Property	Value	Description
entries	@array/regions_list_for_settings	An array of Strings that will be displayed in the list of options.
entryValues	@array/regions_list	An array of the values associated with the options in the **Entries** property. The selected entries' values will *all* be stored in the app's SharedPreferences.
key	pref_regionsToInclude	The name of the preference stored in the app's SharedPreferences.
title	@string/world_regions	The title of the preference displayed in the GUI.
summary	@string/world_regions_description	A summary description of the preference that's displayed below its title.
persistent	true	Whether the preference should persist after the app terminates.
defaultValue	@array/regions_list	An array of the default values for this preference—in this case, all of the regions will be selected by default.

Fig. 4.16 | MultiSelectListPreference property values.

```
1    <?xml version="1.0" encoding="utf-8"?>
2    <PreferenceScreen
3      xmlns:android="http://schemas.android.com/apk/res/android">
4
5      <ListPreference
6        android:entries="@array/guesses_list"
7        android:entryValues="@array/guesses_list"
8        android:key="pref_numberOfChoices"
9        android:title="@string/number_of_choices"
10       android:summary="@string/number_of_choices_description"
11       android:persistent="true"
12       android:defaultValue="4" />
13
14     <MultiSelectListPreference
15       android:entries="@array/regions_list_for_settings"
16       android:entryValues="@array/regions_list"
17       android:key="pref_regionsToInclude"
18       android:title="@string/world_regions"
19       android:summary="@string/world_regions_description"
20       android:persistent="true"
21       android:defaultValue="@array/regions_list" />
22
23   </PreferenceScreen>
```

Fig. 4.17 | preferences.xml defines the preferences displayed by the SettingsActivityFragment.

4.4.12 Adding Classes SettingsActivity and SettingsActivityFragment to the Project

In this section, you'll create the SettingsActivity class (discussed in Section 4.8) and the SettingsActivityFragment class (Section 4.9) by adding to the project a new **Blank Activity** that uses a Fragment. To add the SettingsActivity and SettingsActivityFragment (and their layouts) to the project, perform the following steps:

1. Right click the app folder and select **New > Activity > Blank Activity** to open the **New Android Activity** dialog.

2. In the **Activity Name** field, enter SettingsActivity. The **Layout Name** and **Title** will automatically update based on what you enter in the **Activity Name** field.

3. Specify Settings in the **Title** field to add a new String resource to strings.xml that will be displayed in the SettingsActivity's app bar.

4. Check **Use a Fragment** which will create the SettingsActivityFragment class and its corresponding layout.

5. Select MainActivity as the **Hierarchical Parent** of the new SettingsActivity (use the ... button to the right of the drop-down list). This tells Android Studio to generate code that places in the activity's app bar a button that the user can touch to return to the parent activity (i.e., MainActivity). This button is known as the *up button*.

6. Click **Finish** to create the new classes and layouts.

The IDE creates the layout files `activity_settings.xml`, `content_settings.xml` and `fragment_settings.xml` in the app's `res/layout` folder, and the code files `Settings-Activity.java` and `SettingsActivityFragment.java` in the app's Java package folder. Open the `activity_settings.xml` layout and delete the `FloatingActionButton` as you did in Section 4.4.2 for `activity_main.xml`.

4.5 Building the App's GUI

In this section, you'll build the **Flag Quiz** app's user interface. In the two previous chapters, you saw how to create a GUI and configure component properties, so Sections 4.5.1–4.5.4 focus primarily on new features. Many of the component properties you need to set are specified in tables.

4.5.1 `activity_main.xml` Layout for Devices in Portrait Orientation

In the two prior apps, you defined the app's GUI in `activity_main.xml`. When working with Fragments, an Actvity's GUI typically displays one or more Fragments' GUIs. In this app, the layout for `MainActivity`—`activity_main.xml`—uses an `<include>` element in the XML to include in `MainActivity`'s layout the GUI defined in `content_main.xml`. The `content_main.xml` layout, in turn, displays `MainActivityFragment` for which the GUI is defined in `fragment_main.xml`. All three layout files were created by the IDE when you created the project in Section 4.4.1.

The `content_main.xml` file defined by the IDE contains a `<fragment>` element as its root layout. At runtime, the `MainActivityFragment`'s GUI will fill the part of the screen occupied by this `<fragment>` element.

Look-and-Feel Observation 4.2

According to the Android design guidelines, 16dp is the recommended space between the edges of a device's touchable screen area and the app's content; however, many apps (such as games) use the full screen.

We work with multiple Fragments in this app's code. To make the code more readable when obtaining references to these Fragments, we changed this `<fragment>` element's **id** property. To do so:

1. Open `content_main.xml` in the **Design** tab.
2. In the **Component Tree** window select `fragment`—the default **id** created by the IDE.
3. In the **Properties** window, set the **id** to `quizFragment`.
4. Save `content_main.xml`.

4.5.2 Designing `fragment_main.xml` Layout

You'll typically define a layout for each of your Fragments, though you will not need to define one for this app's `SettingsActivityFragment`—its GUI will be auto-generated by the capabilities inherited from its superclass `PreferenceFragment`. This section presents the `MainActivityFragment`'s layout (`fragment_main.xml`). Figure 4.18 shows the Main-

ActivityFragment GUI's **id** property values—you should set these **id** values as you add the components to the layout.

Fig. 4.18 | **Flag Quiz** GUI's components labeled with their **id** property values—the components are arranged in a vertical LinearLayout.

Using the techniques you learned in Chapter 3, you'll build the GUI in Fig. 4.18. Recall that it's often easiest to select a particular GUI component in the **Component Tree** window. You'll start with the basic layout and controls, then customize the controls' properties to complete the design.

Step 1: Changing from a RelativeLayout to a LinearLayout

As in the activity_main.xml layouts for the two prior apps, the default layout in fragment_main.xml is a RelativeLayout. Here, you'll change this to a vertical Linear-Layout for this app's design:

1. Open the fragment_main.xml file, and switch to the **Text** tab.

2. In the XML, change RelativeLayout to LinearLayout.

3. Switch back to the **Design** tab.

4. In the **Component Tree** select LinearLayout.

5. In the **Properties** window, set the LinearLayout's **orientation** to vertical.

6. Ensure that **layout:width** and **layout:height** are set to match_parent.

7. Set the LinearLayout's **id** to quizLinearLayout for programmatic access.

By default, the IDE set the layout's **Padding Left** and **Padding Right** properties to a predefined dimension resource named @dimen/activity_horizontal_margin—located in the dimens.xml file of the project's res/values folder. This resource's value is 16dp, so there will be 16dp of padding on the layout's left and right sides. The IDE created this resource when you created the app's project. Similarly, the IDE sets the **Padding Top** and **Padding Bottom** properties to @dimen/activity_vertical_margin—another predefined dimension resource with the value 16dp. So there will be 16dp of padding above and below the layout. Thus, all of MainActivityFragment's GUI will be inset 16dp from the rest of MainActivity's GUI.

Step 2: Adding the questionNumberTextView to the LinearLayout

Drag a **Medium Text** component from the **Palette's Widgets** section onto the quizLinearLayout in the **Component Tree** window, then set its **id** property to questionNumberTextView. Use the **Properties** window to set the following properties:

- **layout:gravity center:** horizontal—Centers the component horizontally within the layout.

- **layout:margin:** @dimen/spacing—Set this only for the **bottom margin** to add 8dp of space below this component. Create this dimension resource using the techniques you learned in Section 2.5.6.

- **text:** @string/question—To set this property, click the **text** property's field, then click the ellipsis (...) button. In the **Resources** dialog's **Project** tab (Fig. 4.19), select the question resource, then click **OK**.

Step 3: Adding the flagImageView to the LinearLayout

Drag an **ImageView** component from the **Palette's Widgets** section onto the quizLinearLayout in the **Component Tree** window, then set its **id** property to flagImageView. Use the **Properties** window to set the following properties:

- **layout:width:** match_parent

- **layout:height:** 0dp—This will let the View's height be determined by the **layout:weight** property.

- **layout:gravity center:** both

- **layout:margin bottom:** @dimen/spacing—Adds 8dp of space below this component.

- **layout:margin left** and **right:** @dimen/activity_horizontal_margin—Adds 16dp of space to the left and right of this component, so the complete flag displays during the flag-shake animation that moves the flag left and right.

- **layout:weight:** 1—Setting the **layout:weight** of this component to 1 (the default is 0 for all components) makes the flagImageView more important than the other components in the quizLinearLayout. When Android lays out the components, they'll use *only the vertical space they need* and the flagImageView will occupy *all*

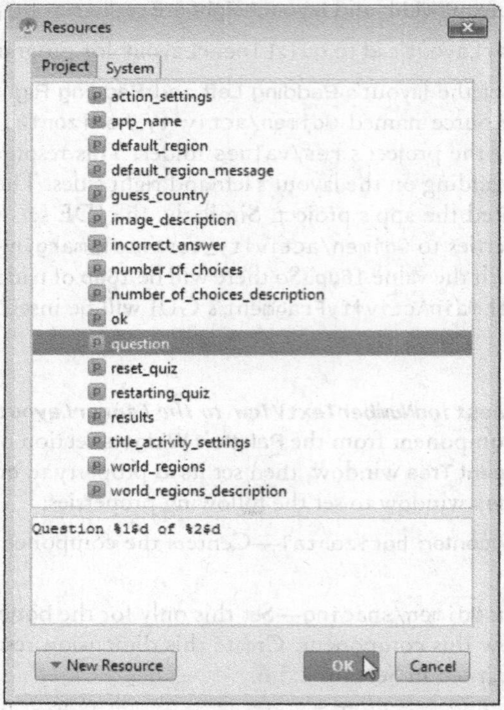

Fig. 4.19 | **Resource Chooser** dialog—selecting the existing `String` resource `question`.

remaining vertical space. Setting `flagImageView`'s **layout:height** to 0dp is recommended by the IDE to help Android lay out the GUI faster at runtime.

- **adjustViewBounds:** `true`—Setting this property to `true` (by checking its checkbox) indicates that the `ImageView` maintains its image's aspect ratio.

- **contentDescription:** `@string/image_description`

- **scaleType:** `fitCenter`—This indicates that the `ImageView` should scale the image to fill either the `ImageView`'s width or height while maintaining the original image's aspect ratio. If the image's width is less than the `ImageView`'s, the image is centered horizontally. Similarly, if the image's height is less than the `ImageView`'s, the image is centered vertically.

Look-and-Feel Observation 4.3

*Recall that it's considered a best practice in Android to ensure that every GUI component can be used with TalkBack. For components that don't have descriptive text, such as `ImageViews`, set the component's **contentDescription** property.*

Step 4: Adding the `guessCountryTextView` to the `LinearLayout`

Drag a **Medium Text** component from the **Palette**'s **Widgets** section onto the quizLinear-Layout in the **Component Tree** window, then set its **id** property to guessCountryTextView. Use the **Properties** window to set the following properties:

- **layout:gravity center:** horizontal
- **text:** @string/guess_country

Step 5: Adding the `Buttons` to the `LinearLayout`

For this app, we add the Buttons to the layout in rows—each row is a horizontal Linear-Layout containing two Buttons. You'll set the properties of the eight Buttons in *Step 7*. Follow these steps to add the eight Buttons to the layout:

1. Drag a **LinearLayout (Horizontal)** from the **Palette**'s **Layouts** section to the qui-zLinearLayout in the **Component Tree** and set its **id** to row1LinearLayout and its **layout:height** to wrap_content.

2. Drag a Button from the **Palette**'s **Widgets** section onto the row1LinearLayout in the **Component Tree**. You do not need to set its **id** because the Buttons are not referenced by their **id**s in this app's Java code.

3. Repeat *Step 2* for the other Button in the first row.

4. Repeat *Steps 1–3* for the three remaining LinearLayouts and set their **id**s to the values shown in Fig. 4.18 to create the last three rows of buttons.

Step 6: Adding the `answerTextView` to the `LinearLayout`

Drag a **Medium Text** component from the **Palette**'s **Widgets** section onto the quizLinear-Layout in the **Component Tree** window, then set its **id** property to answerTextView. Use the **Properties** window to set the following properties:

- **layout:gravity:** Check **bottom** and set **center** to horizontal.
- **gravity:** center_horizontal—This centers the TextView's text when it displays as two or more lines.
- **textSize:** @dimen/answer_size—This changes the text's size to 36sp. Create this dimension resource using the techniques you learned in Section 2.5.6.
- **textStyle:** bold

This TextView's **text** property will be set programmatically. At this point, the **Component Tree** window should appear as shown in Fig. 4.20.

Step 7: Setting the Properties of the `Buttons`

Once you've completed *Step 6*, configure the properties of the Buttons with the values shown in Fig. 4.21—you can select all eight Buttons in the **Component Tree**, then set these properties to configure all the Buttons at the same time:

- Setting each Button's **layout:width** to 0dp and **layout:weight** to 1 enables the Buttons in a given LinearLayout to divide the horizontal space equally.
- Setting each Button's **layout:height** to match_parent sets the Button's height to the LinearLayout's height.

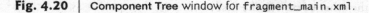

Fig. 4.20 | **Component Tree** window for `fragment_main.xml`.

- Setting each Button's **lines** property to 2 ensures that all of the Buttons are the same height for country names that take up different numbers of lines—if a Button's text is too long, any text that does not fit in two lines is simply truncated.

- Setting the **style** property to @android:style/Widget.Material.Button.Colored causes the Button to take on a colored appearance, based on the colors of the app's theme. The Buttons' color will be the app's accent color, which you specified in Section 4.4.7. To set this property, click the ellipsis (...) to open the **Resources** dialog, then select `Widget.Material.Button.Colored` from the **System** tab and click **OK**.

- Setting the **textColor** property to the @color/button_text_color color state list you defined in Section 4.4.8 ensures that the text changes color based on each Button's enabled/disabled states.

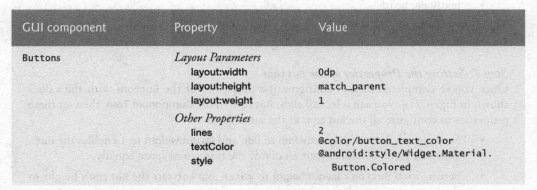

GUI component	Property	Value
Buttons	*Layout Parameters*	
	layout:width	0dp
	layout:height	match_parent
	layout:weight	1
	Other Properties	
	lines	2
	textColor	@color/button_text_color
	style	@android:style/Widget.Material. Button.Colored

Fig. 4.21 | Property values for the Buttons components in `fragment_main.xml`.

4.5.3 Graphical Layout Editor Toolbar

You've now completed the MainActivityFragment's GUI. The layout editor's toolbar (Fig. 4.22) contains various buttons that enable you to preview the design for other screen sizes and orientations. In particular, you can view thumbnail images of many screen sizes and orientations. To do so, first open content_main.xml, then click the virtual device drop-down at the top of the layout editor and select **Preview All Screen Sizes**. Figure 4.23 overviews some of the buttons in the layout editor's toolbar.

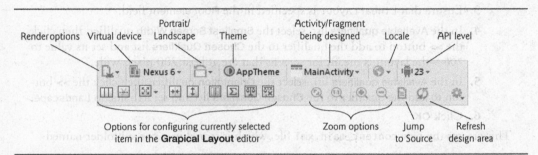

Fig. 4.22 | Canvas configuration options.

Option	Description
Render options	View one design screen at a time or see your design on a variety of screen sizes all at once.
Virtual device	Android runs on a wide variety of devices, so the layout editor comes with many device configurations that represent various screen sizes and resolutions that you can use to design your GUI. In this book, we use the predefined **Nexus 6** and **Nexus 9** screens, depending on the app. In Fig. 4.22, we selected **Nexus 6**.
Portrait/landscape	Toggles the design area between *portrait* and *landscape* orientations.
Theme	Can be used to set the theme for the GUI.
Activity/fragment being designed	Shows the Activity or Fragment class that corresponds to the GUI being designed.
Locale	For *internationalized* apps (Section 2.8), allows you to select a specific localization, so that you can see, for example, what your design looks like with different language strings.
API level	Specifies the target API level for the design. With each new API level, there have typically been new GUI features. The layout editor window shows only features that are available in the selected API level.

Fig. 4.23 | Explanation of the canvas configuration options.

4.5.4 content_main.xml Layout for Tablet Landscape Orientation

As we mentioned previously, MainActivity's default content_main.xml layout displays the MainActivityFragment's GUI. You'll now define MainActivity's layout for tablets in landscape orientation, which will show both the SettingsActivityFragment and the

MainActivityFragment side-by-side. To do so, you'll create a second `content_main.xml` layout that Android will use only on appropriate devices.

Creating `content_main.xml` for Tablets in Landscape Orientation

To create the layout, perform the following steps:

1. Right click the project's `res/layout` folder, and select **New > Layout resource file**.

2. Enter `content_main.xml` in the **File name** field of the **New Resource File** dialog.

3. Ensure that `LinearLayout` is specified in the **Root element** field.

4. In the **Available qualifiers** list, select the **Smallest Screen Width** qualifier, then click the **>>** button to add the qualifier to the **Chosen Qualifiers** list and set its value to 700—the layout is meant for screens that are at least 700 pixels wide.

5. In the **Available qualifiers** list, select the **Orientation** qualifier, then click the **>>** button to add the qualifier to the **Chosen Qualifiers** list and set its value to `Landscape`.

6. Click **OK**.

This creates the new `content_main.xml` file, which is stored in a `res` subfolder named

```
layout-sw700dp-land
```

indicating that the layout should be used only on a device with a minumum screen width (`sw`) of 700dp and only when the device is in landscape (`land`) orientation. Android uses the qualifiers `sw` and `land` to select appropriate resources at runtime.

In Android Studio, the **Project** window does not show the separate `layout` and `layout-sw700dp-land` folders that you'll see if you explore the project's folders on disk. Instead, it combines both layouts into a single node `content_main.xml` (2) node in the **Project** window's `res/layout` folder—(2) indicates that there are two layouts in the node. Expanding this node shows

- `content_main.xml` and
- `content_main.xml` (sw700dp-land).

The layout without qualifiers in parentheses is the default layout. The one with qualifiers is used only if appropriate. After creating the file, Android Studio opens the layout in the layout editor. The **Design** view presents the layout in layout orientation.

Creating the Tablet Layout's GUI

Next, you'll build the tablet layout's GUI:

1. Select `LinearLayout` (`vertical`) in the **Component Tree** window and set the **orientation** property to `horizontal`.

2. Click `<fragment>` in the **Palette**'s **Custom** section. In the **Fragments** dialog, select `SettingsActivityFragment`, and click **OK**. Then click the `LinearLayout` node in the **Component Tree** window. This adds the `<fragment>` to the layout. Set the **id** of the `<fragment>` to `settingsActivityFragment`.

3. Repeat the preceding step, but this time select `MainActivityFragment`. Also, set the **id** of this `<fragment>` to `quizFragment`.

4. Select the `settingsActivityFragment` node in the **Component Tree** window. Set **layout:width** to 0dp, **layout:height** to match_parent and **layout:weight** to 1.

5. Select the quizFragment node in the **Component Tree** window. Set **layout:width** to 0dp, **layout:height** to match_parent and **layout:weight** to 2. MainActivity-Fragment's **layout:weight** is 2 and SettingsActivityFragment's is 1, so the total of the weights is 3 and MainActivityFragment will occupy two-thirds of the layout's horizontal space.

6. Switch to the **Text** tab and add the following two lines to the opening Linear-Layout tag to ensure that the top of the layout appears below the app bar, rather than behind it:

```
xmlns:app="http://schemas.android.com/apk/res-auto"
app:layout_behavior="@string/appbar_scrolling_view_behavior"
```

Selecting a Fragment to Preview in the Layout Editor's **Design View**

The layout editor's **Design** view can show a preview of any fragment(s) displayed in a layout. If you do not specify which fragment to preview, the layout editor displays a **"Rendering Problems"** message. To specify the fragment to preview, right click the fragment—either in **Design** view or in the **Component Tree**—and click **Choose Preview Layout....** Then in the **Resources** dialog, select the name of the fragment layout.

4.6 MainActivity Class

Class MainActivity (Sections 4.6.1—4.6.7) hosts the app's MainActivityFragment when the app is running in portrait orientation, and hosts both the SettingsActivityFragment and MainActivityFragment when the app is running on a tablet in landscape orientation.

4.6.1 package Statement and import Statements

Figure 4.24 shows the MainActivity package statement and import statements. Lines 6–19 import the various Android and Java classes and interfaces that the app uses. We've highlighted the new import statements, and we discuss the corresponding classes and interfaces in Section 4.3 and as they're encountered in Sections 4.6.2—4.6.7.

```
1  // MainActivity.java
2  // Hosts the MainActivityFragment on a phone and both the
3  // MainActivityFragment and SettingsActivityFragment on a tablet
4  package com.deitel.flagquiz;
5
6  import android.content.Intent;
7  import android.content.SharedPreferences;
8  import android.content.SharedPreferences.OnSharedPreferenceChangeListener;
9  import android.content.pm.ActivityInfo;
10 import android.content.res.Configuration;
11 import android.os.Bundle;
12 import android.preference.PreferenceManager;
13 import android.support.v7.app.AppCompatActivity;
14 import android.support.v7.widget.Toolbar;
```

Fig. 4.24 | MainActivity package statement and import statements. (Part 1 of 2.)

```
15    import android.view.Menu;
16    import android.view.MenuItem;
17    import android.widget.Toast;
18
19    import java.util.Set;
20
```

Fig. 4.24 | MainActivity package statement and import statements. (Part 2 of 2.)

4.6.2 Fields

Figure 4.25 shows class MainActivity's fields. Lines 23–24 define constants for the preference keys you created in Section 4.4.11. You'll use these to access the preference values. The boolean variable phoneDevice (line 26) specifies whether the app is running on a phone—if so, the app will allow only portrait orientation. The boolean variable preferencesChanged (line 27) specifies whether the app's preferences have changed—if so, the MainActivity's onStart lifecycle method (Section 4.6.4) will call the MainActivityFragment's methods updateGuessRows (Section 4.7.4) and updateRegions (Section 4.7.5) to reconfigure the quiz, based on the new settings. We set this boolean to true initially so that when the app first executes, the quiz is configured using the default preferences.

```
21    public class MainActivity extends Activity {
22       // keys for reading data from SharedPreferences
23       public static final String CHOICES = "pref_numberOfChoices";
24       public static final String REGIONS = "pref_regionsToInclude";
25
26       private boolean phoneDevice = true; // used to force portrait mode
27       private boolean preferencesChanged = true; // did preferences change?
28
```

Fig. 4.25 | MainActivity declaration and fields.

4.6.3 Overridden Activity Method onCreate

Fig. 4.26 shows the overridden Activity method onCreate—we removed the predefined event handler for the FloatingActionButton, which is not used in this app. Line 33 calls setContentView to set MainActivity's GUI. Recall that activity_main.xml embeds in its layout the contents of the file content_main.xml, and that this app has two versions of that file. When inflating activity_main.xml, Android embeds the default content_main.xml file from the app's res/layout folder unless the app is running on a devices that's at least 700 pixels wide in landscape orientation—in that case, Android uses the version in the res/layout-sw700dp-land folder. Lines 34–35 were generated by the IDE to set the Toolbar defined in MainActivity's layout as the app bar (formerly called the action bar)—again, this is the backward-compatible manner in which an app displays an app bar.

Setting the Default Preference Values and Registering a Change Listener
When you install and launch the app for the first time, line 38 sets the app's *default preferences* by calling PreferenceManager method **setDefaultValues**—this creates and initializes the app's SharedPreferences file using the default values that you specified in preferences.xml. The method requires three arguments:

```
29      // configure the MainActivity
30      @Override
31      protected void onCreate(Bundle savedInstanceState) {
32          super.onCreate(savedInstanceState);
33          setContentView(R.layout.activity_main);
34          Toolbar toolbar = (Toolbar) findViewById(R.id.toolbar);
35          setSupportActionBar(toolbar);
36
37          // set default values in the app's SharedPreferences
38          PreferenceManager.setDefaultValues(this, R.xml.preferences, false);
39
40          // register listener for SharedPreferences changes
41          PreferenceManager.getDefaultSharedPreferences(this).
42              registerOnSharedPreferenceChangeListener(
43                  preferencesChangeListener);
44
45          // determine screen size
46          int screenSize = getResources().getConfiguration().screenLayout &
47              Configuration.SCREENLAYOUT_SIZE_MASK;
48
49          // if device is a tablet, set phoneDevice to false
50          if (screenSize == Configuration.SCREENLAYOUT_SIZE_LARGE ||
51              screenSize == Configuration.SCREENLAYOUT_SIZE_XLARGE)
52              phoneDevice = false; // not a phone-sized device
53
54          // if running on phone-sized device, allow only portrait orientation
55          if (phoneDevice)
56              setRequestedOrientation(
57                  ActivityInfo.SCREEN_ORIENTATION_PORTRAIT);
58      }
59
```

Fig. 4.26 | MainActivity overridden Activity method onCreate.

- The preferences' **Context** (package **android.content**), which provides access to information about the environment in which the app is running and allows you to use various Android services—in this case, the Context is the Activity (this) for which you are setting the default preferences.

- The resource ID for the preferences XML file (R.xml.preferences) that you created in Section 4.4.11.

- A boolean indicating whether the default values should be reset each time method setDefaultValues is called—false indicates that the default preference values should be set only the first time this method is called.

Each time the user changes the app's preferences, MainActivity should call MainActivityFragment's methods updateGuessRows or updateRegions to reconfigure the quiz. MainActivity registers an OnSharedPreferenceChangedListener (lines 41–43) so that it will be notified each time a preference changes. PreferenceManager method **getDefaultSharedPreferences** returns a reference to the SharedPreferences object representing the app's preferences, and SharedPreferences method **registerOnSharedPreferenceChangeListener** registers the listener (defined in Section 4.6.7).

Configuring a Phone Device for Portrait Orientation

Lines 46–52 determine whether the app is running on a tablet or a phone. Inherited method **getResources** returns the app's **Resources** object (package android.content.res) for accessing an app's resources and determining information about its environment. Method **getConfiguration** returns a **Configuration** object (package android.content.res) containing public instance variable screenLayout, which specifies the device's screen-size category. To do so, first you combine the value of screenLayout with Configuration.SCREENLAYOUT_SIZE_MASK using the bitwise AND (&) operator. Then, you compare the result to the constants SCREENLAYOUT_SIZE_LARGE and SCREENLAYOUT_SIZE_XLARGE (lines 50–51). If either is a match, the app is running on a tablet-sized device. Finally, if the device is a phone, lines 56–57 call inherited Activity method **setRequestedOrientation** to force the app to display MainActivity in only portrait orientation.

4.6.4 Overridden Activity Method onStart

Overridden Activity lifecycle method **onStart** (Fig. 4.27) is called in two scenarios:

- When the app first executes, onStart is called after onCreate. We use onStart in this case to ensure that the quiz is configured correctly based on the app's default preferences when the app is installed and executes for the first time or based on the user's updated preferences when the app is launched subsequently.

- When the app is running in portrait orientation and the user opens the SettingsActivity, the MainActivity is *stopped* while the SettingsActivity is displayed. When the user returns to the MainActivity, onStart is called again. We use onStart in this case to ensure that the quiz is reconfigured properly if the user made any preference changes.

In both cases, if preferencesChanged is true, onStart calls MainActivityFragment's updateGuessRows (Section 4.7.4) and updateRegions (Section 4.7.5) methods to reconfigure the quiz. To get a reference to the MainActivityFragment so we can call its methods, lines 68–70 use inherited AppCompatActivity method getSupportFragmentManager to get the FragmentManager, then call its findFragmentById method. Next, lines 71–74 call MainActivityFragment's updateGuessRows and updateRegions methods, passing the app's SharedPreferences object as an argument so those methods can load the current preferences. Line 75 resets the quiz and line 76 sets preferencesChanged back to false.

```
60      // called after onCreate completes execution
61      @Override
62      protected void onStart() {
63         super.onStart();
64
65         if (preferencesChanged) {
66            // now that the default preferences have been set,
67            // initialize MainActivityFragment and start the quiz
68            MainActivityFragment quizFragment = (MainActivityFragment)
69               getSupportFragmentManager().findFragmentById(
70                  R.id.quizFragment);
```

Fig. 4.27 | MainActivity overridden Activity method onStart. (Part 1 of 2.)

```
71            quizFragment.updateGuessRows(
72               PreferenceManager.getDefaultSharedPreferences(this));
73            quizFragment.updateRegions(
74               PreferenceManager.getDefaultSharedPreferences(this));
75            quizFragment.resetQuiz();
76            preferencesChanged = false;
77         }
78      }
79
```

Fig. 4.27 | MainActivity overridden Activity method onStart. (Part 2 of 2.)

4.6.5 Overridden Activity Method onCreateOptionsMenu

Overridden Activity method onCreateOptionsMenu (Fig. 4.28) initializes the Activity's options menu—this method and method onOptionsItemSelected (Section 4.6.6) were autogenerated by Android Studio's **Blank Activity** template. The system passes in the Menu object where the options will appear. In this app, we want to show the menu only when the app is running in portrait orientation, so we modified this method to check the device's orientation. Line 84 uses the Activity's Resources object (returned by inherited method **getResources**) to obtain a Configuration object (returned by method **getConfiguration**) that represents the device's current configuration. This object's public instance variable orientation contains either Configuration.ORIENTATION_PORTRAIT or Configuration.ORIENTATION_LANDSCAPE. If the device is in portrait orientation (line 87), line 89 creates the menu from menu_main.xml—the default menu resource that the IDE defined when you created the project. Inherited Activity method **getMenuInflater** returns a **MenuInflater** on which we call **inflate** with two arguments—the resource ID of the menu resource that populates the menu and the Menu object in which the menu items will be placed. Returning true from onCreateOptionsMenu indicates that the menu should be displayed.

```
80      // show menu if app is running on a phone or a portrait-oriented tablet
81      @Override
82      public boolean onCreateOptionsMenu(Menu menu) {
83         // get the device's current orientation
84         int orientation = getResources().getConfiguration().orientation;
85
86         // display the app's menu only in portrait orientation
87         if (orientation == Configuration.ORIENTATION_PORTRAIT) {
88            // inflate the menu
89            getMenuInflater().inflate(R.menu.menu_main, menu);
90            return true;
91         }
92         else
93            return false;
94      }
95
```

Fig. 4.28 | MainActivity overridden Activity method onCreateOptionsMenu.

4.6.6 Overridden Activity Method onOptionsItemSelected

Method onOptionsItemSelected (Fig. 4.29) is called when a menu item is selected. In this app, the default menu provided by the IDE when you created the project contains only the **Settings** menu item, so if this method is called, the user selected **Settings**. Line 99 creates an explicit Intent for launching the SettingsActivity. The Intent constructor used here receives the Context from which the Activity will be launched and the class representing the Activity to launch (SettingsActivity.class). We then pass this Intent to the inherited Activity method startActivity to launch the Activity (line 100).

```
96      // displays the SettingsActivity when running on a phone
97      @Override
98      public boolean onOptionsItemSelected(MenuItem item) {
99          Intent preferencesIntent = new Intent(this, SettingsActivity.class);
100         startActivity(preferencesIntent);
101         return super.onOptionsItemSelected(item);
102     }
103
```

Fig. 4.29 | MainActivity overridden Activity method onOptionsItemSelected.

4.6.7 Anonymous Inner Class That Implements OnSharedPreferenceChangeListener

The preferencesChangeListener objec (Fig. 4.30) is an anonymous-inner-class object that implements the OnSharedPreferenceChangeListener interface. This object was registered in method onCreate to listen for changes to the app's SharedPreferences. When a change occurs, method onSharedPreferenceChanged sets preferencesChanged to true (line 111), then gets a reference to the MainActivityFragment (lines 113–115) so that the quiz can be reset with the new preferences. If the CHOICES preference changed, lines 118–119 call the MainActivityFragment's updateGuessRows and resetQuiz methods.

```
104     // listener for changes to the app's SharedPreferences
105     private OnSharedPreferenceChangeListener preferencesChangeListener =
106         new OnSharedPreferenceChangeListener() {
107         // called when the user changes the app's preferences
108         @Override
109         public void onSharedPreferenceChanged(
110             SharedPreferences sharedPreferences, String key) {
111             preferencesChanged = true; // user changed app settings
112
113             MainActivityFragment quizFragment = (MainActivityFragment)
114                 getSupportFragmentManager().findFragmentById(
115                     R.id.quizFragment);
116
117             if (key.equals(CHOICES)) { // # of choices to display changed
118                 quizFragment.updateGuessRows(sharedPreferences);
```

Fig. 4.30 | Anonymous Inner class that implements OnSharedPreferenceChangeListener. (Part I of 2.)

```
119                 quizFragment.resetQuiz();
120             }
121             else if (key.equals(REGIONS)) { // regions to include changed
122                 Set<String> regions =
123                     sharedPreferences.getStringSet(REGIONS, null);
124
125                 if (regions != null && regions.size() > 0) {
126                     quizFragment.updateRegions(sharedPreferences);
127                     quizFragment.resetQuiz();
128                 }
129                 else {
130                     // must select one region--set North America as default
131                     SharedPreferences.Editor editor =
132                         sharedPreferences.edit();
133                     regions.add(getString(R.string.default_region));
134                     editor.putStringSet(REGIONS, regions);
135                     editor.apply();
136
137                     Toast.makeText(MainActivity.this,
138                         R.string.default_region_message,
139                         Toast.LENGTH_SHORT).show();
140                 }
141             }
142
143             Toast.makeText(MainActivity.this,
144                 R.string.restarting_quiz,
145                 Toast.LENGTH_SHORT).show();
146         }
147     };
148 }
```

Fig. 4.30 | Anonymous Inner class that implements OnSharedPreferenceChangeListener. (Part 2 of 2.)

If the REGIONS preference changed, lines 122–123 get the Set<String> containing the enabled regions. SharedPreferences method **getStringSet** returns a Set<String> for the specified key. The quiz must have at least one region enabled, so if the Set<String> is not empty, lines 126–127 call the MainActivityFragment's updateRegions and resetQuiz methods.

If the Set<String> is empty, lines 131–135 update the REGIONS preference with North America set as the default region. To obtain the default region's name, line 133 calls Activity's inherited method **getString**, which returns the String resource for the specified resource ID (R.string.default_region).

To change a SharedPreferences object's contents, first call its **edit** method to obtain a SharedPreferences.Editor object (lines 131–132), which can add key–value pairs to, remove key–value pairs from, and modify the value associated with a particular key in a SharedPreferences file. Line 134 calls SharedPreferences.Editor method **putStringSet** to store the contents of regions (the Set<String>). Line 135 *commits* (saves) the changes by calling SharedPreferences.Editor method **apply**, which immediately makes the changes to the in-memory representation of the SharedPreferences, and asynchronously writes the changes to the file in the background. There is also a **commit** method that writes the writes the changes to the file synchronously (immediately).

Lines 137–139 use a Toast to indicate that the default region was set. Toast method **makeText** receives as arguments the Context on which the Toast is displayed, the message to display and the duration for which the Toast will be displayed. Toast method show displays the Toast. Regardless of which preference changed, lines 143–145 display a Toast indicating that the quiz will be reset with the new preferences. Figure 4.31 shows the Toast that appears after the user changes the app's preferences.

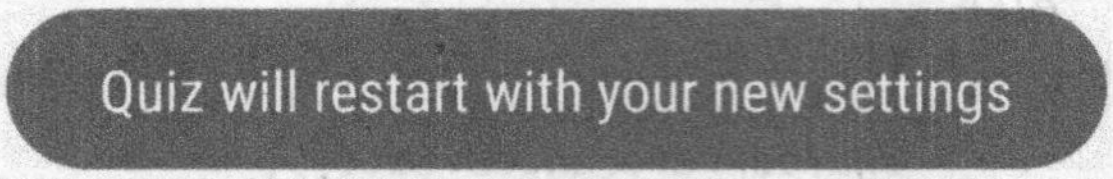

Quiz will restart with your new settings

Fig. 4.31 | Toast displayed after a preference is changed.

4.7 MainActivityFragment Class

Class MainActivityFragment (Figs. 4.32–4.42)—a subclass of the Android Support Library's Fragment class (package android.support.v4.app)—builds the **Flag Quiz**'s GUI and implements the quiz's logic.

4.7.1 package and import Statements

Figure 4.32 shows the MainActivityFragment package statement and import statements. Lines 5–36 import the various Java and Android classes and interfaces that the app uses. We've highlighted the key import statements, and we discuss the corresponding classes and interfaces in Section 4.3 and as they're encountered in Sections 4.7.2—4.7.11.

```
 1   // MainActivityFragment.java
 2   // Contains the Flag Quiz logic
 3   package com.deitel.flagquiz;
 4
 5   import java.io.IOException;
 6   import java.io.InputStream;
 7   import java.security.SecureRandom;
 8   import java.util.ArrayList;
 9   import java.util.Collections;
10   import java.util.List;
11   import java.util.Set;
12
13   import android.animation.Animator;
14   import android.animation.AnimatorListenerAdapter;
15   import android.app.AlertDialog;
16   import android.app.Dialog;
17   import android.content.DialogInterface;
18   import android.content.SharedPreferences;
19   import android.content.res.AssetManager;
20   import android.graphics.drawable.Drawable;
```

Fig. 4.32 | MainActivityFragment package statement, import statements. (Part 1 of 2.)

```
21    import android.os.Bundle;
22    import android.support.v4.app.DialogFragment;
23    import android.support.v4.app.Fragment;
24    import android.os.Handler;
25    import android.util.Log;
26    import android.view.LayoutInflater;
27    import android.view.View;
28    import android.view.View.OnClickListener;
29    import android.view.ViewAnimationUtils;
30    import android.view.ViewGroup;
31    import android.view.animation.Animation;
32    import android.view.animation.AnimationUtils;
33    import android.widget.Button;
34    import android.widget.ImageView;
35    import android.widget.LinearLayout;
36    import android.widget.TextView;
37
```

Fig. 4.32 | MainActivityFragment package statement, import statements. (Part 2 of 2.)

4.7.2 Fields

Figure 4.33 lists class MainActivityFragment's static and instance variables. The constant TAG (line 40) is used when we log error messages using class Log (Fig. 4.38) to distinguish this Activity's error messages from others that are being written to the device's log. The constant FLAGS_IN_QUIZ (line 42) represents the number of flags in the quiz.

```
38    public class MainActivityFragment extends Fragment {
39       // String used when logging error messages
40       private static final String TAG = "FlagQuiz Activity";
41
42       private static final int FLAGS_IN_QUIZ = 10;
43
44       private List<String> fileNameList; // flag file names
45       private List<String> quizCountriesList; // countries in current quiz
46       private Set<String> regionsSet; // world regions in current quiz
47       private String correctAnswer; // correct country for the current flag
48       private int totalGuesses; // number of guesses made
49       private int correctAnswers; // number of correct guesses
50       private int guessRows; // number of rows displaying guess Buttons
51       private SecureRandom random; // used to randomize the quiz
52       private Handler handler; // used to delay loading next flag
53       private Animation shakeAnimation; // animation for incorrect guess
54
55       private LinearLayout quizLinearLayout; // layout that contains the quiz
56       private TextView questionNumberTextView; // shows current question #
57       private ImageView flagImageView; // displays a flag
58       private LinearLayout[] guessLinearLayouts; // rows of answer Buttons
59       private TextView answerTextView; // displays correct answer
60
```

Fig. 4.33 | MainActivityFragment fields.

Good Programming Practice 4.1

For readability and modifiability, use String *constants to represent filenames* String *literals (such as those used as the names of files or to log error messages) that do not need to be localized, and thus are not defined in* strings.xml.

Variable fileNameList (line 44) holds the flag-image file names for the currently enabled geographic regions. Variable quizCountriesList (line 45) holds the flag file names for the countries used in the current quiz. Variable regionsSet (line 46) stores the geographic regions that are enabled.

Variable correctAnswer (line 47) holds the flag file name for the current flag's correct answer. Variable totalGuesses (line 48) stores the total number of correct and incorrect guesses the player has made so far. Variable correctAnswers (line 49) is the number of correct guesses so far; this will eventually be equal to FLAGS_IN_QUIZ if the user completes the quiz. Variable guessRows (line 50) is the number of two-Button LinearLayouts displaying the flag answer choices—this is controlled by the app's settings (Section 4.7.4).

Variable random (line 51) is the random-number generator used to randomly pick the flags to include in the quiz and which Button in the two-Button LinearLayouts represents the correct answer. When the user selects a correct answer and the quiz is not over, we use the Handler object handler (line 52) to load the next flag after a short delay.

The Animation shakeAnimation (line 53) holds the dynamically inflated *shake animation* that's applied to the flag image when an incorrect guess is made. Lines 55–59 contain variables that we use to manipulate various GUI components programmatically.

4.7.3 Overridden Fragment Method onCreateView

MainActivityFragment's onCreateView method (Fig. 4.34) inflates the GUI and initializes most of the MainActivityFragment's instance variables—guessRows and regionsSet are initialized when the MainActivity calls MainActivityFragment's updateGuessRows and updateRegions methods. After calling the superclass's onCreateView method (line 65), we inflate the MainActivityFragment's GUI (line 66–67) using the LayoutInflater that method onCreateView receives as an argument. The LayoutInflater's **inflate** method receives three arguments:

- The layout resource ID indicating the layout to inflate.

- The ViewGroup (layout object) in which the Fragment will be displayed, which is received as onCreateView's second argument.

- A boolean indicating whether or not the inflated GUI needs to be attached to the ViewGroup in the second argument. In a fragment's onCreateView method, this should always be false—the system automatically attaches a fragment to the appropriate host Activity's ViewGroup. Passing true here would cause an exception, because the fragment's GUI is already attached.

Method inflate returns a reference to a View that contains the inflated GUI. We store that in local variable view so that it can be returned by onCreateView after the MainActivityFragment's other instance variables are initialized. [*Note:* We removed the autogenerated, empty, no-argument constructor from this class (which appeared before method onCreateView in the class definition created by the IDE), as the compiler provides a default constructor for any class without constructors.]

```
61   // configures the MainActivityFragment when its View is created
62   @Override
63   public View onCreateView(LayoutInflater inflater, ViewGroup container,
64      Bundle savedInstanceState) {
65      super.onCreateView(inflater, container, savedInstanceState);
66      View view =
67         inflater.inflate(R.layout.fragment_main, container, false);
68
69      fileNameList = new ArrayList<>();          // diamond operator
70      quizCountriesList = new ArrayList<>();
71      random = new SecureRandom();
72      handler = new Handler();
73
74      // load the shake animation that's used for incorrect answers
75      shakeAnimation = AnimationUtils.loadAnimation(getActivity(),
76         R.anim.incorrect_shake);
77      shakeAnimation.setRepeatCount(3); // animation repeats 3 times
78
79      // get references to GUI components
80      quizLinearLayout =
81         (LinearLayout) view.findViewById(R.id.quizLinearLayout);
82      questionNumberTextView =
83         (TextView) view.findViewById(R.id.questionNumberTextView);
84      flagImageView = (ImageView) view.findViewById(R.id.flagImageView);
85      guessLinearLayouts = new LinearLayout[4];
86      guessLinearLayouts[0] =
87         (LinearLayout) view.findViewById(R.id.row1LinearLayout);
88      guessLinearLayouts[1] =
89         (LinearLayout) view.findViewById(R.id.row2LinearLayout);
90      guessLinearLayouts[2] =
91         (LinearLayout) view.findViewById(R.id.row3LinearLayout);
92      guessLinearLayouts[3] =
93         (LinearLayout) view.findViewById(R.id.row4LinearLayout);
94      answerTextView = (TextView) view.findViewById(R.id.answerTextView);
95
96      // configure listeners for the guess Buttons
97      for (LinearLayout row : guessLinearLayouts) {
98         for (int column = 0; column < row.getChildCount(); column++) {
99            Button button = (Button) row.getChildAt(column);
100           button.setOnClickListener(guessButtonListener);
101        }
102     }
103
104     // set questionNumberTextView's text
105     questionNumberTextView.setText(
106        getString(R.string.question, 1, FLAGS_IN_QUIZ));
107     return view; // return the fragment's view for display
108  }
109
```

Fig. 4.34 | MainActivityFragment overridden Fragment method onCreateView.

Lines 69–70 create ArrayList<String> objects that will store the flag-image file names for the currently enabled geographical regions and the names of the countries in the current quiz, respectively. Line 71 creates the SecureRandom object for randomizing the quiz's flags and guess Buttons. Line 72 creates the Handler object handler, which we'll use to delay by two seconds the appearance of the next flag after the user correctly guesses the current flag.

Lines 75–76 dynamically load the *shake animation* that will be applied to the flag when an incorrect guess is made. AnimationUtils static method loadAnimation loads the animation from the XML file represented by the constant R.anim.incorrect_shake. The first argument indicates the Context containing the resources that will be animated— inherited Fragment method getActivity returns the Activity that hosts this Fragment. Activity is an indirect subclass of Context. Line 77 specifies the number of times the animation should repeat with Animation method setRepeatCount.

Lines 80–94 get references to various GUI components that we'll programmatically manipulate. Lines 97–102 get each guess Button from the four guessLinearLayouts and register guessButtonListener (Section 4.7.10) as the **OnClickListener**—we implement this interface to handle the event raised when the user touches any of the guess Buttons.

Lines 105–106 set the text in questionNumberTextView to the String returned by calling an overloaded version of Fragment's inherited method getString. The first argument to format is the String resource R.string.question, which represents the format String

```
Question %1$d of %2$d
```

This String contains placeholders for two integer values (as described in Section 4.4.5). The remaining arguments are the values to insert in the format String. Line 107 returns the MainActivityFragment's GUI.

4.7.4 Method updateGuessRows

Method updateGuessRows (Fig. 4.35) is called from the app's MainActivity when the app is launched and each time the user changes the number of guess Buttons to display with each flag. Lines 113–114 use the method's SharedPreferences argument to get the String for the key MainActivity.CHOICES—a constant containing the name of the preference in which the SettingsActivityFragment stores the number of guess Buttons to display. Line 115 converts the preference's value to an int and divides it by 2 to determine the value for guessRows, which indicates how many of the guessLinearLayouts should be displayed— each with two guess Buttons. Next, lines 118–119 hide all of the guessLinearLayouts, so that lines 122–123 can show the appropriate guessLinearLayouts based on the value of guessRows. The constant View.GONE (line 119) indicates that Android should not consider the sizes of the specified components when laying out the rest of the components in the layout. There is also the constant View.INVISIBLE, which simply hides the component, and any space allocated to the component remains empty on the screen.

```
110    // update guessRows based on value in SharedPreferences
111    public void updateGuessRows(SharedPreferences sharedPreferences) {
112       // get the number of guess buttons that should be displayed
113       String choices =
114          sharedPreferences.getString(MainActivity.CHOICES, null);
```

Fig. 4.35 | MainActivityFragment method updateGuessRows. (Part 1 of 2.)

```
115            guessRows = Integer.parseInt(choices) / 2;
116
117            // hide all guess button LinearLayouts
118            for (LinearLayout layout : guessLinearLayouts)
119                layout.setVisibility(View.GONE);
120
121            // display appropriate guess button LinearLayouts
122            for (int row = 0; row < guessRows; row++)
123                guessLinearLayouts[row].setVisibility(View.VISIBLE);
124        }
125
```

Fig. 4.35 | MainActivityFragment method updateGuessRows. (Part 2 of 2.)

4.7.5 Method updateRegions

Method updateRegions (Fig. 4.36) is called from the app's MainActivity when the app is launched and each time the user changes the world regions that should be included in the quiz. Lines 128–129 use the method's SharedPreferences argument to get the names of all of the enabled regions as a Set<String>. MainActivity.REGIONS is a constant containing the name of the preference in which the SettingsActivityFragment stores the enabled world regions.

```
126        // update world regions for quiz based on values in SharedPreferences
127        public void updateRegions(SharedPreferences sharedPreferences) {
128            regionsSet =
129                sharedPreferences.getStringSet(MainActivity.REGIONS, null);
130        }
131
```

Fig. 4.36 | MainActivityFragment method updateRegions.

4.7.6 Method resetQuiz

Method resetQuiz (Fig. 4.37) sets up and starts a quiz. Recall that the images for the game are stored in the app's assets folder. To access this folder's contents, the method gets the app's AssetManager (line 135) by calling the parent Activity's **getAssets** method. Next, line 136 clears the fileNameList to prepare to load image file names for only the enabled geographical regions. Lines 140–146 iterate through all the enabled world regions. For each, we use the AssetManager's list method (line 142) to get an array of the flag-image file names, which we store in the String array paths. Lines 144–145 remove the .png extension from each file name and place the names in the fileNameList. Asset-Manager's list method throws IOExceptions, which are *checked* exceptions (so you must catch or declare the exception). If an exception occurs because the app is unable to access the assets folder, lines 148–150 catch the exception and *log* it for debugging purposes with Android's built-in logging mechanism. Log static method **e** is used to log error messages. You can see the complete list of Log methods at

http://developer.android.com/reference/android/util/Log.html

```
132    // set up and start the next quiz
133    public void resetQuiz() {
134       // use AssetManager to get image file names for enabled regions
135       AssetManager assets = getActivity().getAssets();
136       fileNameList.clear(); // empty list of image file names
137
138       try {
139          // loop through each region
140          for (String region : regionsSet) {
141             // get a list of all flag image files in this region
142             String[] paths = assets.list(region);
143
144             for (String path : paths)
145                fileNameList.add(path.replace(".png", ""));
146          }
147       }
148       catch (IOException exception) {
149          Log.e(TAG, "Error loading image file names", exception);
150       }
151
152       correctAnswers = 0; // reset the number of correct answers made
153       totalGuesses = 0; // reset the total number of guesses the user made
154       quizCountriesList.clear(); // clear prior list of quiz countries
155
156       int flagCounter = 1;
157       int numberOfFlags = fileNameList.size();
158
159       // add FLAGS_IN_QUIZ random file names to the quizCountriesList
160       while (flagCounter <= FLAGS_IN_QUIZ) {
161          int randomIndex = random.nextInt(numberOfFlags);
162
163          // get the random file name
164          String filename = fileNameList.get(randomIndex);
165
166          // if the region is enabled and it hasn't already been chosen
167          if (!quizCountriesList.contains(filename)) {
168             quizCountriesList.add(filename); // add the file to the list
169             ++flagCounter;
170          }
171       }
172
173       loadNextFlag(); // start the quiz by loading the first flag
174    }
175
```

Fig. 4.37 | MainActivityFragment method resetQuiz.

Next, lines 152–154 reset the counters for the number of correct guesses the user has made (correctAnswers) and the total number of guesses the user has made (total-Guesses) to 0 and clear the quizCountriesList.

Lines 160–171 add 10 (FLAGS_IN_QUIZ) randomly selected file names to the quiz-CountriesList. We get the total number of flags, then randomly generate the index in the range 0 to one less than the number of flags. We use this index to select one image file name from fileNameList. If the quizCountriesList does not already contain that file name, we add it to quizCountriesList and increment the flagCounter. We repeat this process until 10 (FLAGS_IN_QUIZ) unique file names have been selected. Then line 173 calls loadNextFlag (Fig. 4.38) to load the quiz's first flag.

4.7.7 Method loadNextFlag

Method loadNextFlag (Fig. 4.38) loads and displays the next flag and the corresponding set of answer Buttons. The image file names in quizCountriesList have the format

   regionName-countryName

without the .png extension. If a *regionName* or *countryName* contains multiple words, they're separated by underscores (_).

```
176     // after the user guesses a correct flag, load the next flag
177     private void loadNextFlag() {
178        // get file name of the next flag and remove it from the list
179        String nextImage = quizCountriesList.remove(0);
180        correctAnswer = nextImage; // update the correct answer
181        answerTextView.setText(""); // clear answerTextView
182
183        // display current question number
184        questionNumberTextView.setText(getString(
185           R.string.question, (correctAnswers + 1), FLAGS_IN_QUIZ));
186
187        // extract the region from the next image's name
188        String region = nextImage.substring(0, nextImage.indexOf('-'));
189
190        // use AssetManager to load next image from assets folder
191        AssetManager assets = getActivity().getAssets();
192
193        // get an InputStream to the asset representing the next flag
194        // and try to use the InputStream
195        try (InputStream stream =
196           assets.open(region + "/" + nextImage + ".png")) {
197           // load the asset as a Drawable and display on the flagImageView
198           Drawable flag = Drawable.createFromStream(stream, nextImage);
199           flagImageView.setImageDrawable(flag);
200
201           animate(false); // animate the flag onto the screen
202        }
203        catch (IOException exception) {
204           Log.e(TAG, "Error loading " + nextImage, exception);
205        }
206
207        Collections.shuffle(fileNameList); // shuffle file names
208
209        // put the correct answer at the end of fileNameList
210        int correct = fileNameList.indexOf(correctAnswer);
211        fileNameList.add(fileNameList.remove(correct));
212
```

Fig. 4.38 | MainActivityFragment method loadNextFlag. (Part 1 of 2.)

```
213        // add 2, 4, 6 or 8 guess Buttons based on the value of guessRows
214        for (int row = 0; row < guessRows; row++) {
215            // place Buttons in currentTableRow
216            for (int column = 0;
217                column < guessLinearLayouts[row].getChildCount();
218                column++) {
219                // get reference to Button to configure
220                Button newGuessButton =
221                    (Button) guessLinearLayouts[row].getChildAt(column);
222                newGuessButton.setEnabled(true);
223
224                // get country name and set it as newGuessButton's text
225                String filename = fileNameList.get((row * 2) + column);
226                newGuessButton.setText(getCountryName(filename));
227            }
228        }
229
230        // randomly replace one Button with the correct answer
231        int row = random.nextInt(guessRows); // pick random row
232        int column = random.nextInt(2); // pick random column
233        LinearLayout randomRow = guessLinearLayouts[row]; // get the row
234        String countryName = getCountryName(correctAnswer);
235        ((Button) randomRow.getChildAt(column)).setText(countryName);
236    }
237
```

Fig. 4.38 | MainActivityFragment method loadNextFlag. (Part 2 of 2.)

Line 179 removes the first name from quizCountriesList and stores it in nextImage. We also save this in correctAnswer so it can be used later to determine whether the user made a correct guess. Next, we clear the answerTextView and display the current question number in the questionNumberTextView (lines 184–185) using the formatted String resource R.string.question.

Line 188 extracts from nextImage the region to be used as the assets subfolder name from which we'll load the image. Next we get the AssetManager, then use it in the *try-with-resources* statement to open an InputStream (package java.io) to read bytes from the flag image's file. We use that stream as an argument to class **Drawable**'s static method **createFromStream**, which creates a Drawable object (package android.graphics.drawable). The Drawable is set as flagImageView's item to display by calling its **setImage-Drawable** method. If an exception occurs, we log it for debugging purposes (line 204). Next, we call the animate method with false to animate the next flag and answer Buttons onto the screen (line 201).

Next, line 207 shuffles the fileNameList, and lines 210–211 locate the correctAnswer and move it to the end of the fileNameList—later we'll insert this answer randomly into the one of the guess Buttons.

Lines 214–228 iterate through the Buttons in the guessLinearLayouts for the current number of guessRows. For each Button:

- lines 220–221 get a reference to the next Button

- line 222 enables the Button

- line 225 gets the flag file name from the fileNameList
- line 226 sets Button's text with the country name that method getCountryName (Section 4.7.8) returns.

Lines 231–235 pick a random row (based on the current number of guessRows) and column, then set the text of the corresponding Button.

4.7.8 Method getCountryName

Method getCountryName (Fig. 4.39) parses the country name from the image file name. First, we get a substring starting from the dash (-) that separates the region from the country name. Then we call String method replace to replace the underscores (_) with spaces.

```
238     // parses the country flag file name and returns the country name
239     private String getCountryName(String name) {
240         return name.substring(name.indexOf('-') + 1).replace('_', ' ');
241     }
242
```

Fig. 4.39 | MainActivityFragment method getCountryName.

4.7.9 Method animate

Method animate (Fig. 4.40) executes the *circular reveal* animation on the entire layout (quizLinearLayout) of the quiz to transition between questions. Lines 246–247 return immediately for the first question to allow the first question to just appear rather than animate onto the screen. Lines 250–253 calculate the screen coordinates of the center of the quiz UI. Lines 256–257 calculate the maximum radius of the circle in the animation (the minimum radius is always 0). The animate method accepts one parameter, animateOut, and can be used in two ways. Line 262 uses animateOut to determine whether the animation will show or hide the quiz.

```
243     // animates the entire quizLinearLayout on or off screen
244     private void animate(boolean animateOut) {
245         // prevent animation into the the UI for the first flag
246         if (correctAnswers == 0)
247             return;
248
249         // calculate center x and center y
250         int centerX = (quizLinearLayout.getLeft() +
251             quizLinearLayout.getRight()) / 2;
252         int centerY = (quizLinearLayout.getTop() +
253             quizLinearLayout.getBottom()) / 2;
254
255         // calculate animation radius
256         int radius = Math.max(quizLinearLayout.getWidth(),
257             quizLinearLayout.getHeight());
258
```

Fig. 4.40 | MainActivityFragment method animate. (Part 1 of 2.)

```
259            Animator animator;
260
261            // if the quizLinearLayout should animate out rather than in
262            if (animateOut) {
263                // create circular reveal animation
264                animator = ViewAnimationUtils.createCircularReveal(
265                    quizLinearLayout, centerX, centerY, radius, 0);
266                animator.addListener(
267                    new AnimatorListenerAdapter() {
268                        // called when the animation finishes
269                        @Override
270                        public void onAnimationEnd(Animator animation) {
271                            loadNextFlag();
272                        }
273                    }
274                );
275            }
276            else { // if the quizLinearLayout should animate in
277                animator = ViewAnimationUtils.createCircularReveal(
278                    quizLinearLayout, centerX, centerY, 0, radius);
279            }
280
281            animator.setDuration(500); // set animation duration to 500 ms
282            animator.start(); // start the animation
283        }
284
```

Fig. 4.40 | `MainActivityFragment` method animate. (Part 2 of 2.)

If animate is called with the value true, the method will animate the `quizLinear-Layout` off the screen (lines 264–274). Lines 264–265 create a circular-reveal Animator object by calling `ViewAnimationUtils` method `createCircularReveal`. This method takes five parameters:

- The first specifies the `View` on which to apply the animation (`quizLinearLayout`).

- The second and third provide the *x*- and *y*-coordinates of the animation circle's center.

- The last two determine the starting and ending radius of the animation's circle.

Because this animates the `quizLinearLayout` off screen, its starting radius is the calculated radius and its ending radius is 0. Lines 266–274 create and associate an **AnimatorListenerAdapter** with the Animator. The AnimatorListenerAdapter's **onAnimationEnd** (lines 269–272) method is called when the animation finishes and loads the next flag (line 271).

If animate is called with the value false, the method will animate the `quizLinear-Layout` onto the screen at the start of the next question. Lines 277–278 create the Animator by calling the `createCircularReveal` method, but this time, we specify 0 for the starting radius and the calculated radius for the ending radius. This causes the `quizLinearLayout` to animate onto the screen rather than off the screen.

Line 281 calls Animator's `setDuration` method to specify a duration of 500 milliseconds for the animation. Finally, line 282 starts the animation.

4.7.10 Anonymous Inner Class That Implements OnClickListener

In Fig. 4.34, lines 97–102 registered guessButtonListener (Fig. 4.41) as the event-handling object for each guess Button. Instance variable guessButtonListener refers to an anonymous-inner-class object that implements interface OnClickListener to respond to Button events. The method receives the clicked Button as parameter v. We get the Button's text (line 290) and the parsed country name (line 291), then increment total-Guesses. If the guess is correct (line 294), we increment correctAnswers. Next, we set the answerTextView's text to the country name and change its color to the color represented by the constant R.color.correct_answer (green), and we call our utility method disableButtons (Section 4.7.11) to disable all the answer Buttons.

```
285    // called when a guess Button is touched
286    private OnClickListener guessButtonListener = new OnClickListener() {
287       @Override
288       public void onClick(View v) {
289          Button guessButton = ((Button) v);
290          String guess = guessButton.getText().toString();
291          String answer = getCountryName(correctAnswer);
292          ++totalGuesses; // increment number of guesses the user has made
293
294          if (guess.equals(answer)) { // if the guess is correct
295             ++correctAnswers; // increment the number of correct answers
296
297             // display correct answer in green text
298             answerTextView.setText(answer + "!");
299             answerTextView.setTextColor(
300                getResources().getColor(R.color.correct_answer,
301                   getContext().getTheme()));
302
303             disableButtons(); // disable all guess Buttons
304
305             // if the user has correctly identified FLAGS_IN_QUIZ flags
306             if (correctAnswers == FLAGS_IN_QUIZ) {
307                // DialogFragment to display quiz stats and start new quiz
308                DialogFragment quizResults =
309                   new DialogFragment() {
310                      // create an AlertDialog and return it
311                      @Override
312                      public Dialog onCreateDialog(Bundle bundle) {
313                         AlertDialog.Builder builder =
314                            new AlertDialog.Builder(getActivity());
315                         builder.setMessage(
316                            getString(R.string.results,
317                               totalGuesses,
318                               (1000 / (double) totalGuesses)));
319
320                         // "Reset Quiz" Button
321                         builder.setPositiveButton(R.string.reset_quiz,
322                            new DialogInterface.OnClickListener() {
```

Fig. 4.41 | Anonymous inner class that implements OnClickListener. (Part 1 of 2.)

```
323                            public void onClick(DialogInterface dialog,
324                               int id) {
325                               resetQuiz();
326                            }
327                         }
328                      );
329
330                   return builder.create(); // return the AlertDialog
331                }
332             };
333
334             // use FragmentManager to display the DialogFragment
335             quizResults.setCancelable(false);
336             quizResults.show(getFragmentManager(), "quiz results");
337          }
338          else { // answer is correct but quiz is not over
339             // load the next flag after a 2-second delay
340             handler.postDelayed(
341                new Runnable() {
342                   @Override
343                   public void run() {
344                      animate(true); // animate the flag off the screen
345                   }
346                }, 2000); // 2000 milliseconds for 2-second delay
347          }
348       }
349       else { // answer was incorrect
350          flagImageView.startAnimation(shakeAnimation); // play shake
351
352          // display "Incorrect!" in red
353          answerTextView.setText(R.string.incorrect_answer);
354          answerTextView.setTextColor(getResources().getColor(
355             R.color.incorrect_answer, getContext().getTheme()));
356          guessButton.setEnabled(false); // disable incorrect answer
357       }
358    }
359 };
360
```

Fig. 4.41 | Anonymous inner class that implements OnClickListener. (Part 2 of 2.)

If correctAnswers is FLAGS_IN_QUIZ (line 306), the quiz is over. Lines 308–332 create a new anonymous inner class that extends DialogFragment (package android.support.v4.app) and will be used to display the quiz results. The DialogFragment's **onCreateDialog** method uses an AlertDialog.Builder (discussed momentarily) to configure and create an AlertDialog for showing the quiz results, then returns it. When the user touches this dialog's **Reset Quiz** Button, method resetQuiz is called to start a new game (line 325). Line 335 indicates that the dialog is not cancelable—the user must interact with the dialog, because touching outside the dialog or touching the back button will not return the user to the quiz. To display the DialogFragment, line 336 calls its **show** method, passing as arguments the FragmentManager returned by getFragmentManager and a String. The second argument can be used with FragmentManager method **getFragment-**

ByTag to get a reference to the `DialogFragment` at a later time—we don't use this capability in this app.

If `correctAnswers` is less than `FLAGS_IN_QUIZ`, then lines 340–346 call the `postDelayed` method of `Handler` object `handler`. The first argument defines an anonymous inner class that implements the `Runnable` interface—this represents the task to perform, `animate(true)`, which animates the flags and answer `Button`s off the screen and starts the transition to the next question, some number of milliseconds into the future. The second argument is the delay in milliseconds (2000). If the guess is incorrect, line 350 invokes `flagImageView`'s `startAnimation` method to play the `shakeAnimation` that was loaded in method `onCreateView`. We also set the text on `answerTextView` to display `"Incorrect!"` in red (lines 353–355), then disable the `guessButton` that corresponds to the incorrect answer.

> ### Look-and-Feel Observation 4.4
> *You can set an `AlertDialog`'s title (which appears above the dialog's message) with `AlertDialog.Builder` method `setTitle`. According to the Android design guidelines for dialogs (http://developer.android.com/design/building-blocks/dialogs.html), most dialogs do not need titles. A dialog should display a title for "a high-risk operation involving potential loss of data, connectivity, extra charges, and so on." Also, dialogs that display lists of options use the title to specify the dialog's purpose.*

Creating and Configuring the `AlertDialog`

Lines 313–329 use an `AlertDialog.Builder` to create and configure an `AlertDialog`. Lines 313–314 create the `AlertDialog.Builder`, passing the fragment's `Activity` as the `Context` argument—the dialog will be displayed in the context of the `Activity` that hosts the `MainActivityFragment`. Next, lines 315–318 set the dialog's message to a formatted `String` showing the quiz results—the resource `R.string.results` contains placeholders for the total number of guesses and the percentage of the total guesses that were correct.

In this `AlertDialog`, we need only one button that allows the user to acknowledge the message and reset the quiz. We specify this as the dialog's *positive* `Button` (lines 321–328)—touching this `Button` indicates that the user acknowledges the message displayed in the dialog and dismisses the dialog. Method `setPositiveButton` receives the `Button`'s label (specified with the `String` resource `R.string.reset_quiz`) and a reference to the `Button`'s event handler. If the app does not need to respond to the event, you can specify `null` for the event handler. In this case, we provide an object of an anonymous inner class that implements interface `DialogInterface.OnClickListener`. You override this interface's `onClick` method to respond to the event when the user touches the corresponding `Button` in the dialog.

4.7.11 Method `disableButtons`

Method `disableButtons` (Fig. 4.42) iterates through the guess `Button`s and disables them. This method is called when the user makes a correct guess.

```
361    // utility method that disables all answer Buttons
362    private void disableButtons() {
363        for (int row = 0; row < guessRows; row++) {
```

Fig. 4.42 | MainActivityFragment method `disableButtons`. (Part 1 of 2.)

```
364            LinearLayout guessRow = guessLinearLayouts[row];
365            for (int i = 0; i < guessRow.getChildCount(); i++)
366                guessRow.getChildAt(i).setEnabled(false);
367        }
368    }
369 }
```

Fig. 4.42 | MainActivityFragment method disableButtons. (Part 2 of 2.)

4.8 SettingsActivity Class

Class SettingsActivity (Fig. 4.43) hosts the SettingsActivityFragment when the app is running in portrait orientation. Overridden method onCreate (lines 11–18) calls method setContentView to inflate the GUI defined by activity_settings.xml (represented by the resource R.layout.activity_settings), then displays the Toolbar defined in SettingsActivity's layout. Line 17 displays on the app bar an *up button* that the user can touch to return to the parent MainActivity. The IDE added this line when you added the SettingsActivity to the project and specified its hierarchical parent (Section 4.4.12). We removed from the class the remaining autogenerated code that's not used in this app. You can also remove the unused menu resource menu_settings.xml.

```
1  // SettingsActivity.java
2  // Activity to display SettingsActivityFragment on a phone
3  package com.deitel.flagquiz;
4
5  import android.os.Bundle;
6  import android.support.v7.app.AppCompatActivity;
7  import android.support.v7.widget.Toolbar;
8
9  public class SettingsActivity extends AppCompatActivity {
10     // inflates the GUI, displays Toolbar and adds "up" button
11     @Override
12     protected void onCreate(Bundle savedInstanceState) {
13         super.onCreate(savedInstanceState);
14         setContentView(R.layout.activity_settings);
15         Toolbar toolbar = (Toolbar) findViewById(R.id.toolbar);
16         setSupportActionBar(toolbar);
17         getSupportActionBar().setDisplayHomeAsUpEnabled(true);
18     }
19 }
```

Fig. 4.43 | SettingsActivity displays the SettingsActivityFragment on a phone device and on a tablet device in portrait orientation.

4.9 SettingsActivityFragment Class

Class SettingsActivityFragment (Fig. 4.44) inherits from PreferenceFragment (package android.preference). When the SettingsActivityFragment is created, method onCreate (lines 10–14) builds the preferences GUI by calling inherited PreferenceFragment method **addPreferencesFromResource** to build the preferences GUI from the preferences.xml (Section 4.4.11). As the user interacts with the preferences GUI, the preferences are automatically stored into a SharedPreferences file on the device. If the file does not exist, it will be created; otherwise, it will be updated. We removed the other unused autogenerated code from this class.

```java
 1  // SettingsActivityFragment.java
 2  // Subclass of PreferenceFragment for managing app settings
 3  package com.deitel.flagquiz;
 4
 5  import android.os.Bundle;
 6  import android.preference.PreferenceFragment;
 7
 8  public class SettingsActivityFragment extends PreferenceFragment {
 9      // creates preferences GUI from preferences.xml file in res/xml
10      @Override
11      public void onCreate(Bundle bundle) {
12          super.onCreate(bundle);
13          addPreferencesFromResource(R.xml.preferences); // load from XML
14      }
15  }
```

Fig. 4.44 | SettingsActivityFragment subclass of PreferenceFragment displays the app's preferences.

4.10 AndroidManifest.xml

Figure 4.45 shows the **Flag Quiz** app's autogenerated manifest. Each Activity in an app must be declared in AndroidManifest.xml; otherwise, Android will not know that the Activity exists and will not be able to launch it. When you created the app, the IDE declared MainActivity in AndroidManifest.xml (lines 11–21). The notation

```
.MainActivity
```

in line 12 indicates that the class is in the package specified in line 2 and is shorthand for

```
com.deitel.flagquiz.MainActivity
```

We added line 14, which we'll discuss momentarily.

```xml
 1  <?xml version="1.0" encoding="utf-8"?>
 2  <manifest package="com.deitel.flagquiz"
 3      xmlns:android="http://schemas.android.com/apk/res/android">
 4
 5      <application
 6          android:allowBackup="true"
 7          android:icon="@mipmap/ic_launcher"
 8          android:label="@string/app_name"
 9          android:supportsRtl="true"
10          android:theme="@style/AppTheme">
11          <activity
12              android:name=".MainActivity"
13              android:label="@string/app_name"
```

Fig. 4.45 | AndroidManifest.xml with SettingsActivity declared. (Part 1 of 2.)

```
14              android:launchMode="singleTop"
15              android:theme="@style/AppTheme.NoActionBar">
16          <intent-filter>
17              <action android:name="android.intent.action.MAIN"/>
18
19              <category android:name="android.intent.category.LAUNCHER"/>
20          </intent-filter>
21      </activity>
22      <activity
23          android:name=".SettingsActivity"
24          android:label="@string/title_activity_settings"
25          android:parentActivityName=".MainActivity"
26          android:theme="@style/AppTheme.NoActionBar">
27          <meta-data
28              android:name="android.support.PARENT_ACTIVITY"
29              android:value="com.deitel.flagquiz.MainActivity">
30      </activity>
31  </application>
32
33  </manifest>
```

Fig. 4.45 | AndroidManifest.xml with SettingsActivity declared. (Part 2 of 2.)

When you added the SettingsActivity to the project (Section 4.4.1), the IDE added SettingsActivity to the manifest file automatically (lines 22–30). If you were to create a new Activity without using the IDE's tools, you'd have to declare the new Activity by inserting an <activity> element like the one in lines 22–30. For complete manifest file details, visit

http://developer.android.com/guide/topics/manifest/manifest-intro.html

Launch Mode
Line 14 specifies MainActivity's launchMode. By default each Activity you create uses the "standard" launch mode. In this mode, when Android receives an Intent to launch the Activity, Android creates a new instance of that Activity.

Recall from Section 4.4.12 that you specified SettingsActivity's hierarchical parent. Again, this enables Android to define on the app bar an *up button* that a user can touch to navigate back to the specified parent Activity. When the user touches this button and the parent Activity uses "standard" launch mode, Android uses an Intent to launch the parent Activity. This results in a new instance of MainActivity. This also causes the **Flag Quiz** app to crash in MainActivity's OnSharedPreferenceChangeListener (Section 4.6.7) when it tries to update a quizFragment that no longer exists—it was defined in a different MainActivity instance.

Line 14 fixes this problem by changing MainActivity's launchMode to "singleTop". With this launch mode, when the user touches the *up button*, Android brings the *existing* MainActivity to the foreground, rather than creating a new MainActivity object. For more information on the <activity> element's lauchMode values, visit

https://developer.android.com/guide/topics/manifest/activity-element.html#lmode

4.11 Wrap-Up

In this chapter, you built a **Flag Quiz** app that tests a user's ability to correctly identify country flags. A key feature of this chapter was using Fragments to create portions of an Activity's GUI. You used two activities to display the MainActivityFragment and the SettingsActivityFragment when the app was running in portrait orientation. You used one Activity to display both Fragments when the app was running on a tablet in landscape orientation—thus, making better use of the available screen real estate. You used a subclass of PreferenceFragment to automatically maintain and persist the app's settings and a subclass of DialogFragment to display an AlertDialog to the user. We discussed portions of a Fragment's lifecycle and showed how to use the FragmentManager to obtain a reference to a Fragment so that you could interact with it programmatically.

In portrait orientation, you provided an icon for the MainActivity's **Settings** menu item. This appeared on the app bar, so the user could touch it to display the SettingsActivity containing the SettingsActivityFragment. To launch the SettingsActivity, you used an explicit Intent. You saw how to obtain preferences from the app's SharedPreferences file and how to edit that file using a SharedPreferences.Editor.

We showed how to use a Configuration object to determine whether the app was running on a tablet in landscape orientation. We demonstrated how to manage a large number of image resources using subfolders in the app's assets folder and how to access those resources via an AssetManager. You created a Drawable from an image's bytes by reading them from an InputStream, then displayed the Drawable in an ImageView.

You learned about additional subfolders of the app's res folder—menu for storing menu resource files, anim for storing animation resource files and xml for storing XML data files. We discussed how to use qualifiers to create a folder for storing a layout that should be used only on large devices in landscape orientation. We also demonstrated how to use a color state list resource to ensure that the text in the Buttons is readable for both the *enabled* and *disabled* states.

You used Toasts to display minor error messages or informational messages that appear on the screen briefly. To display the next flag in the quiz after a short delay, you used a Handler, which executes a Runnable after a specified number of milliseconds. You learned that a Handler's Runnable executes in the thread that created the Handler (the GUI thread in this app).

We defined an Animation in XML and applied it to the app's ImageView when the user guessed incorrectly to provide visual feedback to the user. We also used ViewAnimationUtils to create a circular reveal Animator for transitioning between questions. You learned how to log exceptions for debugging purposes with Android's built-in logging mechanism and class Log. You also used various classes and interfaces from the java.util package, including List, ArrayList, Collections and Set.

Finally, we presented the app's AndroidManifest.xml file. We discussed the autogenerated <activity> elements. We also changed the MainActivity's launchMode to "singleTop" so that the app used one instance of MainActivity, rather than creating a new one each time the user touches the *up button* on the app bar.

In Chapter 5, we present the **Doodlz** app, which uses Android's graphics capabilities to turn a device's screen into a *virtual canvas*. You'll also learn about Android's immersive mode and printing capabilities.

Self-Review Exercises

4.1 Fill in the blanks in each of the following statements:

a) To access the app's assets folder's contents, a method should get the app's AssetManager by calling method _____ (inherited indirectly from class ContextWrapper).

b) Files in the assets folders are accessed via a(n) _____ (package android.content.res), which can provide a list of all of the file names in a specified subfolder of assets and can be used to access each asset.

c) A(n) _____ animation moves a View within its parent.

d) By default, animations in an animation set are applied in parallel, but you can use the _____ attribute to specify the number of milliseconds into the future at which an animation should begin. This can be used to sequence the animations in a set.

4.2 State whether each of the following is *true* or *false*. If *false*, explain why.

a) AnimationUtils static method loadAnimation loads an animation from an XML file that specifies the animation's options.

b) Android does not provide a logging mechanism for debugging purposes.

c) ImageView's adjustViewBounds property specifies whether or not the ImageView maintains the aspect ratio of its Drawable.

d) You load color and String array resources from the colors.xml and strings.xml files into memory by using the Activity's Resources object.

e) Use activities to create reusable components and make better use of the screen real estate in a tablet app.

Answers to Self-Review Exercises

4.1 a) getAssets. b) AssetManager. c) translate. d) android:startOffset.

4.2 a) True. b) False. When exceptions occur, you can log them for debugging purposes with the built-in Log class's methods. c) True. d) True. e) False. Use Fragments to create reusable components and make better use of the screen real estate in a tablet app.

Exercises

4.3 Fill in the blanks in each of the following statements:

a) When the user selects an item from a Menu or touches a menu item displayed on the app bar, Activity method _____ is called to respond to the selection.

b) To delay an action, we use a(n) _____ (package android.os) object to execute a Runnable after a specified delay.

c) You can specify the number of times an animation should repeat with Animation method _____ and perform the animation by calling View method startAnimation (with the Animation as an argument) on the ImageView.

d) A(n) _____ is a collection of animations which make up a larger animation.

e) Android supports _____ animations which allow you to animate any property of any object.

f) For the android:fromXDelta attribute, specifying the value -5%p indicates that the View should move to the _____ by 5% of the parent's width (p indicates "percent").

g) A(n) _____ briefly displays a message to the user.

h) A(n) _____ resource file defines a color resource that changes colors based on a View's state.

i) Android Studio's _____ is used to add material design icons to a project.

j) We implement interface _____ to handle the events that occur when the user touches a button on an AlertDialog.

4.4 State whether each of the following is *true* or *false*. If *false*, explain why.
  a) The base class of all fragments is BaseFragment (package android.app).
  b) Like an Activity, each Fragment has a life cycle.
  c) Fragments can be executed independently of a parent Activity.

Project Exercises

4.5 *(Enhanced Flag Quiz App)* Make the following enhancements to the Flag Quiz app:
  a) Count the number of questions that were answered correctly on the first try. After all the questions have been answered, display a message describes how well the user performed on first guesses.
  b) Keep track of the score as the user proceeds through the app. Give the user the most points for answering correctly on the first guess, fewer points for answering correctly on the next guess, etc.
  c) Investigate class SharedPreferences, then store the top five high scores in the Shared-Preferences file that also stores this app's settings.
  d) Add multiplayer functionality.
  e) If the user guesses the correct flag, include a "bonus question" asking the user to name the capital of the country. If the user answers correctly on the first guess, add 10 bonus points to the score; otherwise, simply display the correct answer, then allow the user to proceed to the next flag.

4.6 *(Road Sign Quiz App)* Create an app that tests the user's knowledge of road signs. Display a random sign image and ask the user to select the sign's name. Visit http://mutcd.fhwa.dot.gov/ser-shs_millennium.htm for traffic sign images and information.

4.7 *(U.S. State Quiz App)* Using the techniques you learned in this chapter, create an app that displays an outline of a U.S. state and asks the user to identify the state. If the user guesses the correct state, include a "bonus question" asking the user to name the state's capital. If the user answers correctly, add 10 bonus points to the score; otherwise, simply display the correct answer, then allow the user to proceed to the next state. Keep score as described in Exercise 4.5(c).

4.8 *(Country Quiz App)* Using the techniques you learned in this chapter, create an app that displays an outline of a country and asks the user to identify its name. If the user guesses the correct country, include a "bonus question" asking the user to name the country's capital. If the user answers correctly, add 10 bonus points to the score; otherwise, simply display the correct answer, then allow the user to proceed to the next country. Keep score as described in Exercise 4.5(c).

4.9 *(Android Programming Quiz App)* Using the Android knowledge you've gained thus far, create a multiple-choice Android programming quiz *using original questions that you create*. Add multiplayer capabilities so you can compete against your classmates.

4.10 *(Movie Trivia Quiz App)* Create a movie trivia quiz app.

4.11 *(Sports Trivia Quiz App)* Create a sports trivia quiz app.

4.12 *(Custom Quiz App)* Create an app that allows the user to create a customized true/false or multiple-choice quiz. This is a great study aid. The user can input questions on any subject and include answers, then use it to study for a test or final exam.

4.13 *(Lottery Number Picker App)* Create an app that randomly picks lottery numbers. Ask the user how many numbers to pick and the maximum valid number in the lottery (set a maximum value of 99). Provide five possible lottery-number combinations to choose from. Include a feature that allows the user to easily pick from a list of five popular lottery games. Find five of the most popular lottery games in your area and research how many numbers must be picked for a lottery ticket and the highest valid number. Allow the user to tap the name of the lottery game to pick random numbers for that game.

4.14 *(Craps Game App)* Create an app that simulates playing the dice game of craps. In this game, a player rolls two dice. Each die has six faces—we've provided die images with the book's examples. Each face contains one, two, three, four, five or six spots. After the dice have come to rest, the sum of the spots on the two top faces is calculated. If the sum is 7 or 11 on the first throw, the player wins. If the sum is 2, 3 or 12 on the first throw (called "craps"), the player loses (the "house" wins). If the sum is 4, 5, 6, 8, 9 or 10 on the first throw, that sum becomes the player's "point." To win, a player must continue rolling the dice until the point value is rolled. The player loses by rolling a 7 before rolling the point.

4.15 *(Craps Game App Modification)* Modify the craps app to allow wagering. Initialize the variable balance to 1000 dollars. Prompt the player to enter a wager. Check that wager is less than or equal to balance, and if it's not, have the user reenter wager until a valid wager is entered. After a correct wager is entered, run one game of craps. If the player wins, increase balance by wager and display the new balance. If the player loses, decrease balance by wager, display the new balance, check whether balance has become zero and, if so, display the message "Sorry. You busted!"

4.16 *(Computer-Assisted Instruction App)* Create an app that will help an elementary school student learn multiplication. Select two positive one-digit integers. The app should then prompt the user with a question, such as

```
How much is 6 times 7?
```

The student then inputs the answer. Next, the app checks the student's answer. If it's correct, display one of the following messages:

```
Very good!
Excellent!
Nice work!
Keep up the good work!
```

and ask another question. If the answer is wrong, display one of the following messages:

```
No. Please try again.
Wrong. Try once more.
Don't give up!
No. Keep trying.
```

and let the student try the same question repeatedly until the student gets it right. Enhance the app to ask addition, subtraction and multiplication questions.

Doodlz App

Objectives

In this chapter you'll:

- Detect when the user touches the screen, moves a finger across the screen and removes a finger from the screen.

- Process multiple touches so the user can draw with multiple fingers at once.

- Use a `SensorManager` and the accelerometer to detect motion events.

- Use a `Paint` object to specify the color and width of a line.

- Use `Path` objects to store each line's data and use a `Canvas` to draw each line into a `Bitmap`.

- Create a menu and display menu items on the app bar.

- Use the printing framework and the Android Support Library's `PrintHelper` class to enable the user to print a drawing.

- Use Android 6.0's new permissions model to request permission for saving an image to external storage.

- Add libraries to an app with the Gradle build system.

5.1 Introduction

The **Doodlz** app enables you to paint by dragging one or more fingers across the screen (Fig. 5.1). The app provides options for setting the drawing color and line width. Additional options allow you to

- clear the screen
- save the current drawing on your device, and
- print the current drawing.

Depending on your device's screen size, some or all of the app's options are displayed as icons directly on the app bar—any that do not fit are displayed as text in the overflow options menu (⋮) that appears on the app bar.

Fig. 5.1 | **Doodlz** app with a finished drawing.

This app introduces Android 6.0's new permissions mechanism. For example, Android requires the user's permission to allow an app to save files (like this app's drawings) on a device. In Android 6.0, rather than prompting the user at installation time with a complete list of permissions the app requires, the app requests each permission individually, only when the permission is required to perform a given task for the first time. In this app, Android prompts for permission the first time the user attempts to save a drawing.

First, you'll test-drive the app. Then we'll overview the technologies used to build it. Next, you'll design the app's GUI. Finally, we'll walk through the app's complete source code, emphasizing the app's new features.

5.2 Test-Driving the Doodlz App in an Android Virtual Device (AVD)

Opening and Running the App

Open Android Studio and open the **Doodlz** app from the Doodlz folder in the book's examples folder, then execute the app in the AVD or on a device. This builds the project and runs the app.

Understanding the App's Options

Figure 5.2(a) and (b) show the app bar and overflow options menu on the Nexus 6 AVD, and Fig. 5.2(c) shows the app bar on the Nexus 9 AVD.

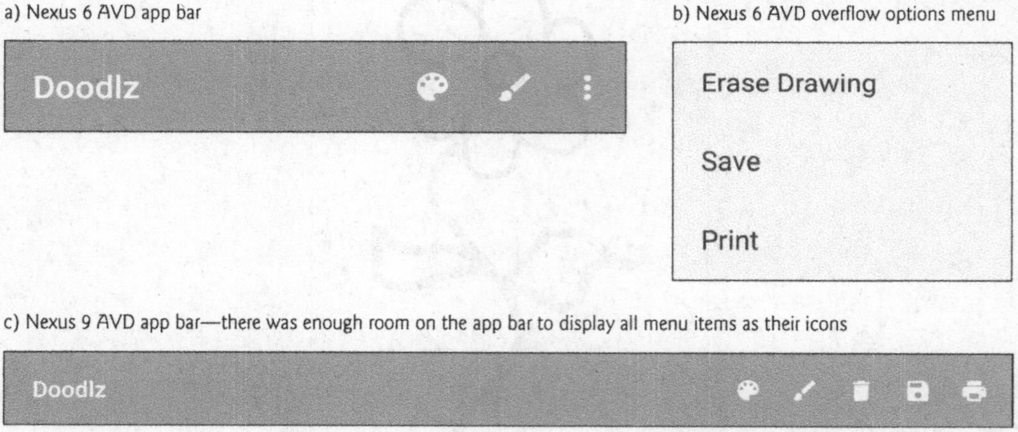

a) Nexus 6 AVD app bar

b) Nexus 6 AVD overflow options menu

Doodlz

Erase Drawing

Save

Print

c) Nexus 9 AVD app bar—there was enough room on the app bar to display all menu items as their icons

Doodlz

Fig. 5.2 | **Doodlz** app bar and overflow menu.

This app has the following menu items:

- **Color** (🎨)—Displays a dialog for changing the line color.

- **Line Width** (✏️)—Displays a dialog for changing the thickness of the line that will be drawn as you drag your finger(s) on the screen.

- **Erase Image** (🗑)—First confirms whether you wish to erase the entire image, then clears the drawing area if you do not cancel the action.

- **Save** (💾)—Saves the image on the device. You can view the image via the Google **Photos** app by opening that app's menu and touching **Device Folders** to see thumbnails of your stored images.[1]

---

1.   On some devices you might need to take a picture with the device's camera app before you'll be able to save properly from the **Doodlz** app.

- **Print (🖶)**—Displays a GUI for selecting an available printer so you can print your image or save it as a PDF document (the default).

You'll explore each of these options momentarily.

Look-and-Feel Observation 5.1

When a menu item is displayed on the app bar, if the menu item has an icon, that icon is displayed; otherwise, the menu item's text is displayed in small capital letters. Any menu items in this app that cannot fit on the app bar are accessible in the drop-down options menu (⋮), which displays the menu items using their text labels.

Changing the Brush Color to Red

To change the brush color, touch 🎨 on the app bar—or select **Color** from the options menu if the icon is not displayed on the app bar. This displays the **Choose Color** dialog (Fig. 5.3).

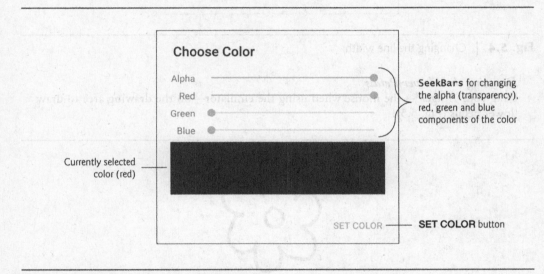

Fig. 5.3 | Changing the drawing color to red.

Colors are defined using the *ARGB color scheme* in which the *alpha* (i.e., *transparency*), red, green and blue components, respectively, are specified by integers in the range 0–255. For alpha, 0 means *completely transparent* and 255 means *completely opaque*. For red, green and blue, 0 means *none* of that color and 255 means the *maximum amount* of that color. The GUI consists of **Alpha**, **Red**, **Green** and **Blue** SeekBars that allow you to select the amount of alpha, red, green and blue, respectively, in the drawing color. You drag the SeekBars to change the color. As you do, the app displays the new color below the Seek-Bars. Select a red color now by dragging the **Red** SeekBar to the right as in Fig. 5.3. Touch the **SET COLOR** button to set this color as the drawing color and dismiss the dialog. If you do not wish to change the color, you can simply touch outside the dialog to dismiss it. You can erase by changing the drawing color to white (i.e., moving all four SeekBars' thumbs to the far right).

Changing the Line Width

To change the line width, touch ✐ on the app bar—or select **Line Width** from the options menu if the icon is not displayed on the app bar. This displays the **Choose Line Width** dialog. Drag the SeekBar for the line width to the right to thicken the line (Fig. 5.4). Touch the **SET LINE WIDTH** button to return to the drawing area.

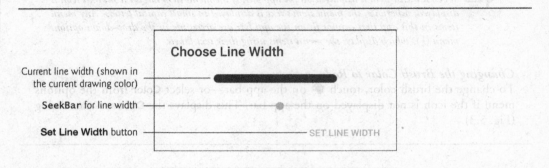

Fig. 5.4 | Changing the line width.

Drawing the Flower Petals

Drag your "finger"—the mouse when using the emulator—on the drawing area to draw flower petals (Fig. 5.5).

Fig. 5.5 | Drawing the flower petals.

Changing the Brush Color to Dark Green

Touch ❀ or select the **Color** menu item to display the **Choose Color** dialog. Select a dark green color by dragging the **Green** SeekBar to the right and ensuring that the **Red** and **Blue** SeekBars are at the far left (Fig. 5.6(a)).

Changing the Line Width and Drawing the Stem and Leaves

Touch ✐ or select the **Line Width** menu item to display the **Choose Line Width** dialog. Drag the SeekBar for the line width to the right to thicken the line (Fig. 5.6(b)). Draw the flower stem and leaves. Repeat *Steps 9* and *10* for a lighter green color and thinner line, then draw the grass (Fig. 5.7).

a) Selecting dark green as the drawing color

b) Selecting a thicker line

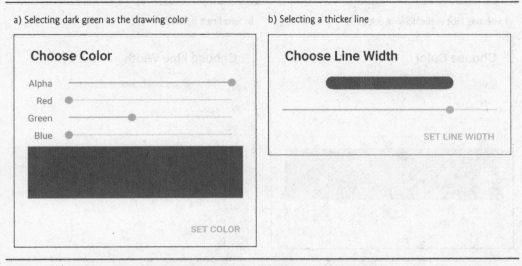

Fig. 5.6 | Changing the color to dark green and making the line thicker.

Fig. 5.7 | Drawing the stem and grass.

Finishing the Drawing

Next, change the drawing color to a semitransparent blue (Fig. 5.8(a)) and select a narrower line (Fig. 5.8(b)). Then draw the raindrops (Fig. 5.9).

a) Selecting blue as the drawing color

b) Selecting a thinner line

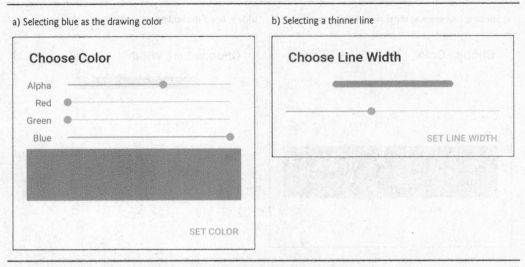

Choose Color

Alpha

Red

Green

Blue

SET COLOR

Choose Line Width

SET LINE WIDTH

Fig. 5.8 | Changing the line color to blue and narrowing the line.

Fig. 5.9 | Drawing the rain in the new line color and line width.

Saving the Image

You can save your image to the device and view it using the **Photos** app. To do so, touch 💾 on the app bar—or select **Save** from the options menu if the icon is not displayed on the app bar. You can then view this image and others stored on the device by opening the **Photos** app.

Printing the Image
To print the image, touch 🖶 on the app bar—or select **Print** from the options menu if the icon is not displayed on the app bar. This displays a dialog of printing options. By default, you can save the image as a PDF document. To choose a printer, tap **Save as PDF** and select from the list of available printers. If no printers appear in the list, you need to configure Google Cloud Print for your printer. For information on this, visit

```
http://www.google.com/cloudprint/learn/
```

5.3 Technologies Overview

This section presents the new technologies that we use in the **Doodlz** app.

5.3.1 Activity and Fragment Lifecycle Methods

A Fragment's lifecycle is tied to that of its parent Activity. There are six Activity lifecycle methods that have corresponding Fragment lifecycle methods—onCreate, onStart, onResume, onPause, onStop and onDestroy. When the system calls these methods on an Activity, it will also call the corresponding methods (and potentially other Fragment lifecycle methods) on all of the Activity's attached Fragments.

This app uses Fragment lifecycle methods onResume and onPause. An Activity's **onResume** method is called when a Fragment is on the screen and ready for the user to interact with it. When an Activity hosts Fragments and the Activity is resumed, all of its Fragments' onResume methods are called. In this app, MainActivityFragment overrides onResume to enable listening for the accelerometer events so the user can shake the device to erase a drawing (Section 5.7.3).

An Activity's **onPause** method is called when *another* Activity receives the focus, which pauses the one that loses the focus and sends it to the background. When an Activity hosts Fragments and the Activity is paused, all of its Fragments' **onPause** methods are called. In this app, MainActivityFragment overrides onPause to suspend listening for the shake-to-erase accelerometer events (Section 5.7.4).

 Performance Tip 5.1
When an app is paused, it should remove listeners for sensor events so these events are not delivered to the app when it's not on the screen. This saves battery.

We discuss other Activity and Fragment lifecycle methods as we need them. For more information on the complete Activity lifecycle, visit

```
http://developer.android.com/reference/android/app/Activity.html
    #ActivityLifecycle
```

and for more information on the complete Fragment lifecycle, visit

```
http://developer.android.com/guide/components/fragments.html
    #Lifecycle
```

5.3.2 Custom Views

You can create a *custom view* by extending class View or one of its subclasses, as we do with class DoodleView (Section 5.8), which extends View. To add a custom component to a layout's XML file, you must provide its *fully qualified name* (i.e., its package and class name), so the custom View's class must exist before you add it to the layout. We demonstrate how to create the DoodleView class and add it to a layout in Section 5.5.2.

5.3.3 Using SensorManager to Listen for Accelerometer Events

In this app, you can shake the device to erase a drawing. Most devices have an **accelerometer** for detecting device movement. Other currently supported sensors include gravity, gyroscope, light, linear acceleration, magnetic field, orientation, pressure, proximity, rotation vector and temperature. You'll use class **Sensor's** sensor-type constants to specify the sensors for which your app should receive data. The list of Sensor constants can be found at

```
http://developer.android.com/reference/android/hardware/Sensor.html
```

We'll discuss the accelerometer and sensor event handling in Section 5.7. For a complete discussion of Android's other sensors, see the *Sensors Overview* at

```
http://developer.android.com/guide/topics/sensors/
    sensors_overview.html
```

5.3.4 Custom DialogFragments

Several previous apps have used AlertDialogs in DialogFragments to display information to the user or to ask questions and receive responses from the user in the form of Button clicks. The AlertDialogs you've used so far were created using anonymous inner classes that extended DialogFragment and displayed only text and buttons. AlertDialogs may also contain custom Views. In this app, you'll define three subclasses of DialogFragment:

- ColorDialogFragment (Section 5.9) displays an AlertDialog with a custom View containing GUI components for previewing and selecting a new ARGB drawing color.

- LineWidthDialogFragment (Section 5.10) displays an AlertDialog with a custom View containing a GUI for previewing and selecting the line thickness.

- EraseImageDialogFragment (Section 5.11) displays a standard AlertDialog asking the user to confirm whether the entire image should be erased.

For the ColorDialogFragment and EraseImageDialogFragment, you'll inflate the custom View from a layout resource file. In each of the three DialogFragment subclasses, you'll also override the following Fragment lifecycle methods:

- **onAttach**—The *first* Fragment lifecycle method called when a Fragment is attached to a parent Activity.

- **onDetach**—The *last* Fragment lifecycle method called when a Fragment is about to be detached from a parent Activity.

Preventing Multiple Dialogs from Appearing at the Same Time
It's possible that the event handler for the shake event could try to display the confirmation dialog for erasing an image when another dialog is already on the screen. To prevent this,

you'll use onAttach and onDetach to set the value of a boolean that indicates whether a dialog is on the screen. When this boolean's value is true, we will not allow the event handler for the shake event to display a dialog.

5.3.5 Drawing with Canvas, Paint and Bitmap

You can use methods of class **Canvas** to draw text, lines and circles. Canvas methods draw on a View's **Bitmap** (both from package android.graphics). You can associate a Canvas with a Bitmap, then use the Canvas to draw on the Bitmap, which can then be displayed on the screen (Section 5.8). A Bitmap also can be saved into a file—we'll use this capability to store drawings in the device's gallery when you touch the **Save** option. Each drawing method in class Canvas uses an object of class **Paint** (package android.graphics) to specify drawing characteristics, including color, line thickness, font size and more. These capabilities are presented with the onDraw method in the DoodleView class (Section 5.8.6). For more details on the drawing characteristics you can specify with a Paint object, visit

> http://developer.android.com/reference/android/graphics/Paint.html

5.3.6 Processing Multiple Touch Events and Storing Lines in Paths

You can drag one or more fingers across the screen to draw. The app stores the information for each *individual* finger as a **Path** object (package android.graphics) that represents line segments and curves. You process *touch events* by overriding the View method **onTouchEvent** (Section 5.8.7). This method receives a **MotionEvent** (package android.view) that contains the type of touch event that occurred and the ID of the finger (known as a *pointer*) that generated the event. We use the IDs to distinguish the different fingers and add information to the corresponding Path objects. We use the type of the touch event to determine whether the user has *touched* the screen, *dragged* across the screen or *lifted a finger* from the screen.

In addition to standard touch-event handling, Android 6.0 provides enhanced support for using a Bluetooth stylus with apps, including access to pressure data and which stylus button the user presses. In this app, for example, you could use a stylus button to specify an erase mode, or you could use the stylus' pressure data to change the stroke thickness dynamically as the user draws. For more information, visit

> https://developer.android.com/about/versions/marshmallow/android-
> 6.0.html#bluetooth-stylus

5.3.7 Saving to the Device

The app's **Save** option allows you to save a drawing to the device. You can view the image in the **Photos** app by selecting **Device Folders** from the app's menu to see thumbnails of the stored images—touch a thumbnail to view the full-size image. A **ContentResolver** (package android.content) enables the app to read data from and store data on a device. You'll use a ContentResolver (Section 5.8.11) and the method **insertImage** of class MediaStore.Images.Media to save an image into the device's **Photos** app. The **MediaStore** manages media files (images, audio and video) stored on a device.

5.3.8 Printing and the Android Support Library's `PrintHelper` Class

In this app, we use class `PrintHelper` (Section 5.8.12) from Android's printing framework to print the current drawing. Class `PrintHelper` provides a user interface for selecting a printer, has a method for determining whether a given device supports printing and provides a method for printing a `Bitmap`. `PrintHelper` is part of the *Android Support Library*, which provides new Android features for use in current and older Android versions. The support library also includes additional convenience features, like class `PrintHelper`, that support specific Android versions.

5.3.9 New Android 6.0 (Marshmallow) Permissions Model

Android requires the permission **android.permission.WRITE_EXTERNAL_PERMISSION** before an app can write to external storage. For **Doodlz**, we need this permission to save the image that the user draws.

Android 6.0 (Marshmallow) has a new permissions model that's designed for a better user experience. Before Android 6.0, a user was required *at installation time* to grant in advance all permissions that an app would ever need—this caused many people not to install certain apps. With the new model, the app is installed without asking for *any* permissions. Instead, the user is asked to grant a permission only the first time the corresponding feature is used.

Once the user grants a permission, the app has that permission until:

* the app is reinstalled or
* the user changes the app's permissions via the Android **Settings** app.

You'll learn how to implement the new permissions model in Sections 5.7.8—5.7.9.

5.3.10 Adding Dependencies Using the Gradle Build System

Android Studio uses the **Gradle build system** to compile your code into an APK file—the installable app. Gradle also handles project dependencies, such as including in the build process any libraries used by the app. For **Doodlz**, you'll add a support library dependency to your project so you can use the `PrintHelper` class for printing an image (Section 5.4.2).

5.4 Creating the Project and Resources

In this section, you'll create the project, import material design icons for the app's menu items and edit the various resources used by the GUI and the app's Java code.

5.4.1 Creating the Project

Create a new **Blank Activity** project. Specify the following values in the **Create New Project** dialog's **New Project** step:

* **Application name:** Doodlz
* **Company Domain:** deitel.com (or specify your own domain name)

For the remaining steps in the **Create New Project** dialog, use the same settings as in Section 4.4.1. This creates a `MainActivity` that hosts a `Fragment`. The `Fragment` will define the app's drawing area and respond to the user's touches. Follow the steps in Section 2.5.2 to add an app icon to your project.

Once the project is open in Android Studio, in the layout editor, select **Nexus 6** from the virtual-device drop-down list (Fig. 2.11). Also, delete the **Hello world!** TextView in fragment_main.xml and the FloatingActionButton in activity_main.xml.

Use the **Theme Editor** (Section 3.5.2) to specify **Material Blue 500** as the app's primary color, **Material Blue 700** as the dark primary color and **Light blue accent 400** as the accent color. Also, follow the steps in Section 4.4.3 to configure the project for Java SE 7 support.

5.4.2 Gradle: Adding a Support Library to the Project

This app requires the Android Support Library to use the PrintHelper class. To add the support library as a project dependency, follow these steps:

1. Right click the app folder, then select **Open Module Settings**.

2. In the **Project Structure** window that appears, open the **Dependencies** tab.

3. Click the **Add** button (+), then select **Library dependency** to open the **Choose Library Dependency** dialog.

4. Select **support-v4 (com.android.support:support-v4:23.1.0)** from the list, then click **OK**. The dependency will appear in the list in the **Dependencies** tab.

5. Click **OK**. The IDE will display **Gradle project sync in progress...** while the project is being configured to use the Android Support Library.

For more on when to use and how to set up the Android Support Library, visit

```
http://developer.android.com/tools/support-library
http://developer.android.com/tools/support-library/setup.html
```

5.4.3 strings.xml

You created String resources in earlier chapters, so we show only a table of the String resource names and corresponding values here (Fig. 5.10). Double click strings.xml in the res/values folder, then click the **Open editor** link to display the **Translations Editor** for creating these String resources.

 Look-and-Feel Observation 5.2

For languages that support uppercase letters, Google's material design specification indicates that a Button's text should use all capital letters (e.g., CANCEL or SET COLOR).

Key	Default Value
button_erase	Erase Image
button_set_color	Set Color
button_set_line_width	Set Line Width
line_imageview_description	This displays the line thickness

Fig. 5.10 | String resources used in the **Doodlz** app. (Part 1 of 2.)

Key	Default Value
label_alpha	Alpha
label_red	Red
label_green	Green
label_blue	Blue
menuitem_color	Color
menuitem_delete	Erase Drawing
menuitem_line_width	Line Width
menuitem_save	Save
menuitem_print	Print
message_erase	Erase the drawing?
message_error_saving	There was an error saving the image
message_saved	Your saved painting can be viewed in the Photos app by selecting Device Folders from that app\'s menu [*Note:* \' is the single-quote (') escape sequence—without the \, the IDE issues the warning "Apostrophe not preceded by \".]
message_error_printing	Your device does not support printing
permission_explanation	To save an image, the app requires permission to write to external storage
title_color_dialog	Choose Color
title_line_width_dialog	Choose Line Width

Fig. 5.10 | String resources used in the **Doodlz** app. (Part 2 of 2.)

5.4.4 Importing the Material Design Icons for the App's Menu Items

This app's menu specifies icons for each menu item. Menus items that fit on the app bar (which depends on the device) display the corresponding icon. Use the techniques you learned in Section 4.4.9 to import the following material design vector icons:

- 🎨 (ic_palette_24dp)
- 🖌 (ic_brush_24dp)
- 🗑 (ic_delete_24dp)
- 💾 (ic_save_24dp)
- 🖨 (ic_print_24dp)

The names in parentheses are the names that are displayed as tooltips in the **Vector Asset Studio** dialog when you hover over an image. For each image, open its XML file and change the fillColor to

        @android:color/white

so that the icons are displayed in white against the app's blue app bar.

5.4.5 MainActivityFragment Menu

In Chapter 4, you edited the default menu provided by the IDE to display the **Flag Quiz** app's **Settings** menu item. In this app, you'll define your own menu for the `MainActivityFragment`. You will not use `MainActivity`'s default menu in this app, so you can delete the `menu_main.xml` file in your project's `res/menu` folder. You should also remove the methods `onCreateOptionsMenu` and `onOptionsItemSelected` from class `MainActivity`, as these will not be used.

Menus for Different Android Versions

Keep in mind that the printing capability is not available in versions prior to Android 4.4. If you are developing an app with menus for multiple versions of Android, you may want to create multiple menu resources by using the resource qualifiers discussed in earlier apps. For example, you could create a menu resource for Android versions prior to 4.4 and a separate one for Android versions 4.4 and higher. In the menu resource for pre-Android-4.4, you can omit menu options that are unavailable in earlier Android versions. For more information on creating menu resources, visit

```
http://developer.android.com/guide/topics/ui/menus.html
```

Creating the Menu

To create the menu resource, follow these steps:

1. Right click the `res/menu` folder and select **New > Menu resource file** to open the **New Resource File** dialog.

2. Enter `doodle_fragment_menu.xml` in the **File name** field, and click **OK**. The IDE opens the file in the editor where it displays the file's XML. You must edit the XML directly to add menu items to the menu resource.

3. In this menu, we'll use each menu item's `showAsAction` property to specify that the menu item should be displayed on the app bar if there is room. When working with the Android Support Libraries to provide a backward-compatible app bar, you must use the `showAsAction` attribute from the XML namespace app, rather than the XML namespace android. Edit the `<menu>` element's opening tag to include the app XML namespace

```
xmlns:app="http://schemas.android.com/apk/res-auto"
```

4. Add the code for the first menu item in Fig. 5.11 to the XML file. The id of the menu item is `@+id/color`, its `title` property is `@string/menuitem_color`, its `icon` property is `@drawable/ic_palette_24dp` and its `showAsAction` property is `ifRoom`. The value `ifRoom` indicates that Android should display the menu item on the app bar if there's room available; otherwise, the menu item will appear as a text menu item in the overflow options menu at the right side of the app bar. Other `showAsAction` values can be found at

```
http://developer.android.com/guide/topics/resources/menu-
    resource.html
```

```
1    <item
2        android:id="@+id/color"
3        android:title="@string/menuitem_color"
4        android:icon="@drawable/ic_palette_24dp"
5        app:showAsAction="ifRoom">
6    </item>
```

Fig. 5.11 | An <item> element representing a menu item.

5. Repeat *Step 3* for each of the IDs and titles in Fig. 5.12 to create the menu items for **Line Width**, **Delete**, **Save** and **Print**, then save and close the menu's file. The completed XML for the menu is shown in Fig. 5.13.

Id	Title
@+id/line_width	@string/menuitem_line_width
@+id/delete_drawing	@string/menuitem_delete
@+id/save	@string/menuitem_save
@+id/print	@string/menuitem_print

Fig. 5.12 | Additional menu items for the MainActivityFragment.

```
1    <?xml version="1.0" encoding="utf-8"?>
2    <menu xmlns:android="http://schemas.android.com/apk/res/android"
3        xmlns:app="http://schemas.android.com/apk/res-auto">
4        <item
5            android:id="@+id/color"
6            android:title="@string/menuitem_color"
7            android:icon="@drawable/ic_palette_24dp"
8            app:showAsAction="ifRoom">
9        </item>
10
11       <item
12           android:id="@+id/line_width"
13           android:title="@string/menuitem_line_width"
14           android:icon="@drawable/ic_brush_24dp"
15           app:showAsAction="ifRoom">
16       </item>
17
18       <item
19           android:id="@+id/delete_drawing"
20           android:title="@string/menuitem_delete"
21           android:icon="@drawable/ic_delete_24dp"
22           app:showAsAction="ifRoom">
23       </item>
24
```

Fig. 5.13 | doodle_fragment_menu.xml. (Part 1 of 2.)

```
25      <item
26          android:id="@+id/save"
27          android:title="@string/menuitem_save"
28          android:icon="@drawable/ic_save_24dp"
29          app:showAsAction="ifRoom">
30      </item>
31
32      <item
33          android:id="@+id/print"
34          android:title="@string/menuitem_print"
35          android:icon="@drawable/ic_print_24dp"
36          app:showAsAction="ifRoom">
37      </item>
38  </menu>
```

Fig. 5.13 | doodle_fragment_menu.xml. (Part 2 of 2.)

5.4.6 Adding a Permission to AndroidManifest.xml

In addition to using Android 6.0's new permissions model in which the app asks the user to grant permissions dynamically, each app also must specify any permissions it uses in the AndroidManifest.xml file. To do so:

1. Expand the project's manifests folder and open AndroidManifest.xml.

2. Inside the <manifest> element and before the <application> element, add

```
<uses-permission
    android:name="android.permission.WRITE_EXTERNAL_STORAGE" />
```

5.5 Building the App's GUI

In this section, you'll create the app's GUI and create the classes for the app's dialogs.

5.5.1 content_main.xml Layout for MainActivity

The content_main.xml layout for this app's MainActivity contains only the MainActivityFragment, which was created automatically when you created the project. For more readable code, we changed the fragment's id property:

1. Open content_main.xml in the layout editor's **Design** view.

2. Select the fragment in the **Component Tree**, then change the Fragment's id to doodleFragment in the **Properties** window and save the layout.

5.5.2 fragment_main.xml Layout for MainActivityFragment

The fragment_main.xml layout for the MainActivityFragment needs to display only a DoodleView. The layout file was created with a RelativeLayout automatically when you created the project. To change the root element of the layout from a RelativeLayout to a DoodleView, you must first create class DoodleView (a subclass of View), so you can select it when placing the custom view in the layout:

1. Expand the java folder in the **Project** window.

2. Right click the com.deitel.doodlz node, then select **New > Java Class**.

3. In the **Create New Class** dialog that appears, enter DoodleView in the **Name** field, then click **OK**. The file will open in the editor automatically.

4. In DoodleView.java, indicate that class DoodleView is a subclass of View by adding extends View to the class's definition. If the IDE does not add an import for android.view.View, place the cursor immediately following extends View. Next, click the red bulb (💡) that appears above the beginning of class Doodle-View's definition and select **Import Class**.

5. The IDE will display an error indicating that you have not defined a constructor for the new class. To fix this, place the cursor immediately following extends View. Click the red bulb (💡) that appears above the beginning of class Doodle-View's definition and select **Create constructor matching super**. In the **Choose Super Class Constructors** dialog, choose the two-argument constructor, then click **OK**. The IDE will add the constructor to the class. You'll add code to this constructor in Section 5.8.3. The two-argument constructor is called by Android when inflating the DoodleView from a layout—the second argument specifies the View properties set in the layout XML file. You can learn more about class View's constructors at

   http://developer.android.com/reference/android/view/
   View.html#View(android.content.Context)

6. Switch back to fragment_main.xml in the layout editor and click the **Text** tab.

7. Change RelativeLayout to com.deitel.doodlz.DoodleView.

8. Remove the properties for top, right, bottom and left padding—the DoodleView should occupy the entire screen.

9. In **Design** view, select **CustomView - com.deitel.doodlz.DoodleView** in the **Component Tree** window, then set the **id** to doodleView.

10. Save and close fragment_main.xml.

5.5.3 fragment_color.xml Layout for ColorDialogFragment

The fragment_color.xml layout for the ColorDialogFragment contains a two-column GridLayout that displays a GUI for selecting and previewing a new drawing color. In this section, you'll create ColorDialogFragment's layout and the ColorDialogFragment class. To add the fragment_color.xml layout:

1. Expand the project's res/layout node in the **Project** window.

2. Right click the layout folder and select **New > Layout resource file** to display the **New Resource File** dialog.

3. In the dialog's **File name** field, enter fragment_color.xml

4. In the **Root element** field, enter GridLayout, then click **OK**.

5. In the **Component Tree** window, select the **GridLayout**.

6. In the **Properties** window, change the **id** value to colorDialogGridLayout and the **columnCount** to 2.

7. Using the layout editor's **Palette**, drag **Plain TextViews** and **SeekBars** onto the colorDialogGridLayout node in the **Component Tree** window. Drag the items in the order they're listed in Fig. 5.14 and set each item's **id** as shown in the figure. We'll show you how to add the colorView next.

Fig. 5.14 | Component Tree view for fragment_color.xml.

Adding the colorView to the Layout

The colorView does not need its own class—we'll programmatically use methods of class View to change the color displayed in colorView. Android Studio does not provide a drag-and-drop way to add an object of class View to a layout, so you'll need to edit the layout's XML directly to add the colorView. To do so:

1. Click the **Text** tab at the bottom of the layout editor to switch from the **Design** view to the layout's XML text.

2. Add the code in Fig. 5.15 immediately before closing </GridLayout> tag.

```
1    <View
2        android:layout_width="wrap_content"
3        android:layout_height="@dimen/color_view_height"
4        android:id="@+id/colorView"
5        android:layout_column="0"
6        android:layout_columnSpan="2"
7        android:layout_gravity="fill_horizontal"/>
```

Fig. 5.15 | fragment_color.xml.

3. Switch back to the layout editor's **Design** tab.

4. Configure the GUI component properties with the values shown in Fig. 5.16. For the dimension value color_view_height, recall that in the **Resources** dialog, you can click **New Resource** and select **New Dimension Value...** to open the **New Dimension Value Resource** dialog. Specify 80dp for the color_view_height.

5. Save and close fragment_color.xml.

GUI component	Property	Value
colorDialogGridLayout	columnCount	2
	orientation	vertical
	useDefaultMargins	true
	padding top	@dimen/activity_vertical_margin
	padding bottom	@dimen/activity_vertical_margin
	padding left	@dimen/activity_horizontal_margin
	padding right	@dimen/activity_horizontal_margin
alphaTextView	*Layout Parameters*	
	layout:column	0
	layout:gravity	right, center_vertical
	layout:row	0
	Other Properties	
	text	@string/label_alpha
alphaSeekBar	*Layout Parameters*	
	layout:column	1
	layout:gravity	fill_horizontal
	layout:row	0
	Other Properties	
	max	255
redTextView	*Layout Parameters*	
	layout:column	0
	layout:gravity	right, center_vertical
	layout:row	1
	Other Properties	
	text	@string/label_red
redSeekBar	*Layout Parameters*	
	layout:column	1
	layout:gravity	fill_horizontal
	layout:row	1
	Other Properties	
	max	255
greenTextView	*Layout Parameters*	
	layout:column	0
	layout:gravity	right, center_vertical
	layout:row	2
	Other Properties	
	text	@string/label_green
greenSeekBar	*Layout Parameters*	
	layout:column	1
	layout:gravity	fill_horizontal
	layout:row	2
	Other Properties	
	max	255

Fig. 5.16 | Property values for the GUI components in `fragment_color.xml`. (Part 1 of 2.)

GUI component	Property	Value
blueTextView	*Layout Parameters*	
	layout:column	0
	layout:gravity	right, center_vertical
	layout:row	3
	Other Properties	
	text	@string/label_blue
blueSeekBar	*Layout Parameters*	
	layout:column	1
	layout:gravity	fill_horizontal
	layout:row	3
	Other Properties	
	max	255
colorView	*Layout Parameters*	
	layout:height	@dimen/color_view_height
	layout:column	0
	layout:columnSpan	2
	layout:gravity	fill_horizontal

Fig. 5.16 | Property values for the GUI components in fragment_color.xml. (Part 2 of 2.)

Adding Class ColorDialogFragment to the Project

To add class ColorDialogFragment to the project:

1. In the project's java folder, right click the upper package com.deitel.doodlz and select **New > Java Class** to display the **Create New Class** dialog.

2. In the **Name** field, enter ColorDialogFragment.

3. Click **OK** to create the class. You'll create the code for this class in Section 5.9.

5.5.4 fragment_line_width.xml Layout for LineWidthDialogFragment

The fragment_line_width.xml layout for the LineWidthDialogFragment contains a GridLayout that displays a GUI for selecting and previewing a new line thickness. In this section, you'll create LineWidthDialogFragment's layout and the LineWidthDialogFragment class. To add the fragment_line_width.xml layout:

1. Expand the project's res/layout node in the **Project** window.

2. Right click the layout folder and select **New > Layout resource file** to display the **New Resource File** dialog.

3. In the dialog's **File name** field, enter fragment_line_width.xml

4. In the **Root element** field, enter GridLayout, then click **OK**.

5. In the **Component Tree** window, select the **GridLayout**, and change its **id** value to lineWidthDialogGridLayout.

6. Using the layout editor's **Palette**, drag an **ImageView** and a **SeekBar** onto the `lineWidthDialogGridLayout` node in the **Component Tree** window so that the window appears as shown in Fig. 5.17. Set each item's **id** as shown in the figure.

Fig. 5.17 | **Component Tree** view for `fragment_line_width.xml`.

7. Configure the GUI component properties with the values shown in Fig. 5.18. Give the dimension value `line_imageview_height` a value of 50dp.

8. Save and close `fragment_line_width.xml`.

GUI component	Property	Value
`lineWidthDialog-GridLayout`	column Count	1
	orientation	`vertical`
	useDefaultMargins	`true`
	padding top	`@dimen/activity_vertical_margin`
	padding bottom	`@dimen/activity_vertical_margin`
	padding left	`@dimen/activity_horizontal_margin`
	padding right	`@dimen/activity_horizontal_margin`
`widthImageView`	*Layout Parameters*	
	layout:height	`@dimen/line_imageview_height`
	layout:gravity	`fill_horizontal`
	Other Properties	
	contentDescription	`@string/line_imageview_description`
`widthSeekBar`	*Layout Parameters*	
	layout:gravity	`fill_horizontal`
	Other Properties	
	max	50

Fig. 5.18 | Property values for the GUI components in `fragment_line_width.xml`.

Adding Class *LineWidthDialogFragment to the Project*
To add class `LineWidthDialogFragment` to the project:

1. In the project's java folder, right click the upper package `com.deitel.doodlz` and select **New > Java Class** to display the **Create New Class** dialog.

2. In the **Name** field, enter `LineWidthDialogFragment`.

3. Click **OK** to create the class.

5.5.5 Adding Class EraseImageDialogFragment

The EraseImageDialogFragment does not require a layout resource, as it will display a simple AlertDialog containing text. To add class EraseImageDialogFragment to the project:

1. In the project's java folder, right click the upper package com.deitel.doodlz and select **New > Java Class** to display the **Create New Class** dialog.

2. In the **Name** field, enter EraseImageDialogFragment.

3. Click **OK** to create the class.

5.6 MainActivity Class

This app consists of six classes:

- MainActivity (discussed below)—This is the parent Activity for the app's Fragments.

- MainActivityFragment (Section 5.7)—Manages the DoodleView and accelerometer event handling.

- DoodleView (Section 5.8)—Provides the drawing, saving and printing capabilities.

- ColorDialogFragment (Section 5.9)—A DialogFragment that's displayed when the user chooses the option to set the drawing color.

- LineWidthDialogFragment (Section 5.10)—A DialogFragment that's displayed when the user chooses the option to set the line width.

- EraseImageDialogFragment (Section 5.11)—A DialogFragment that's displayed when the user chooses the option to erase, or shakes the device to erase, the current drawing.

Class MainActivity's onCreate method (Fig. 5.19) inflates the GUI (line 16) and configures its app bar (lines 17–18), then uses the techniques you learned in Section 4.6.3 to determine the device's size and set MainActivity's orientation. If this app is running on an extra-large device (line 26), we set the orientation to landscape (lines 27–28); otherwise, we set it to portrait (lines 30–31). We removed the other autogenerated methods in class MainActivity, as they're not used in this app.

```
1   // MainActivity.java
2   // Sets MainActivity's layout
3   package com.deitel.doodlz;
4
5   import android.content.pm.ActivityInfo;
6   import android.content.res.Configuration;
7   import android.os.Bundle;
8   import android.support.v7.app.AppCompatActivity;
9   import android.support.v7.widget.Toolbar;
```

Fig. 5.19 | MainActivity class. (Part 1 of 2.)

```
10
11   public class MainActivity extends AppCompatActivity {
12       // configures the screen orientation for this app
13       @Override
14       protected void onCreate(Bundle savedInstanceState) {
15           super.onCreate(savedInstanceState);
16           setContentView(R.layout.activity_main);
17           Toolbar toolbar = (Toolbar) findViewById(R.id.toolbar);
18           setSupportActionBar(toolbar);
19
20           // determine screen size
21           int screenSize =
22               getResources().getConfiguration().screenLayout &
23                   Configuration.SCREENLAYOUT_SIZE_MASK;
24
25           // use landscape for extra large tablets; otherwise, use portrait
26           if (screenSize == Configuration.SCREENLAYOUT_SIZE_XLARGE)
27               setRequestedOrientation(
28                   ActivityInfo.SCREEN_ORIENTATION_LANDSCAPE);
29           else
30               setRequestedOrientation(
31                   ActivityInfo.SCREEN_ORIENTATION_PORTRAIT);
32       }
33   }
```

Fig. 5.19 | MainActivity class. (Part 2 of 2.)

5.7 MainActivityFragment Class

MainActivityFragment (Sections 5.7.1—5.7.10) displays the DoodleView (Section 5.8), manages the menu options displayed on the app bar and in the options menu, and manages the sensor event handling for the app's *shake-to-erase* feature.

5.7.1 package Statement, import Statements and Fields

Section 5.3 discussed the key new classes and interfaces used by MainActivityFragment. We've highlighted these classes and interfaces in Fig. 5.20. DoodleView variable doodle-View (line 24) represents the drawing area. Accelerometer information is delivered to the app as float values. The float variables in lines 25–27 are used to calculate changes in the device's acceleration to determine when a *shake event* occurs (so we can ask whether the user would like to erase the drawing). Line 28 defines a boolean variable with the default value false that will be used throughout this class to specify when there's a dialog displayed on the screen. We use this to prevent multiple dialogs from being displayed simultaneously—for example, if the **Choose Color** dialog is displayed and the user accidentally shakes the device, the dialog for erasing the image should *not* be displayed. The constant in line 31 is used to ensure that small device movements (which happen frequently) are *not* interpreted as shakes—we picked this constant via trial and error by shaking the app on several different types of devices. The constant in line 35 is used to identify the request for the permission needed to save the user's drawing.

```
1    // MainActivityFragment.java
2    // Fragment in which the DoodleView is displayed
3    package com.deitel.doodlz;
4
5    import android.Manifest;
6    import android.app.AlertDialog;
7    import android.content.Context;
8    import android.content.DialogInterface;
9    import android.content.pm.PackageManager;
10   import android.hardware.Sensor;
11   import android.hardware.SensorEvent;
12   import android.hardware.SensorEventListener;
13   import android.hardware.SensorManager;
14   import android.os.Bundle;
15   import android.support.v4.app.Fragment;
16   import android.view.LayoutInflater;
17   import android.view.Menu;
18   import android.view.MenuInflater;
19   import android.view.MenuItem;
20   import android.view.View;
21   import android.view.ViewGroup;
22
23   public class MainActivityFragment extends Fragment {
24      private DoodleView doodleView; // handles touch events and draws
25      private float acceleration;
26      private float currentAcceleration;
27      private float lastAcceleration;
28      private boolean dialogOnScreen = false;
29
30      // value used to determine whether user shook the device to erase
31      private static final int ACCELERATION_THRESHOLD = 100000;
32
33      // used to identify the request for using external storage, which
34      // the save image feature needs
35      private static final int SAVE_IMAGE_PERMISSION_REQUEST_CODE = 1;
36
```

Fig. 5.20 | MainActivityFragment class package statement, import statements and fields.

5.7.2 Overridden Fragment Method onCreateView

Method onCreateView (Fig. 5.21) inflates MainActivityFragment's GUI and initializes the instance variables. A Fragment can place items in the app's app bar and options menu. To do so, the Fragment must call its setHasOptionsMenu method with the argument true. If the parent Activity also has options menu items, then the Activity's and the Fragment's items will be placed on the app bar or in the options menu (based on their settings).

```
37      // called when Fragment's view needs to be created
38      @Override
39      public View onCreateView(LayoutInflater inflater, ViewGroup container,
40         Bundle savedInstanceState) {
```

Fig. 5.21 | Overriding Fragment method onCreateView. (Part 1 of 2.)

```
41    super.onCreateView(inflater, container, savedInstanceState);
42    View view =
43       inflater.inflate(R.layout.fragment_main, container, false);
44
45    setHasOptionsMenu(true); // this fragment has menu items to display
46
47    // get reference to the DoodleView
48    doodleView = (DoodleView) view.findViewById(R.id.doodleView);
49
50    // initialize acceleration values
51    acceleration = 0.00f;
52    currentAcceleration = SensorManager.GRAVITY_EARTH;
53    lastAcceleration = SensorManager.GRAVITY_EARTH;
54    return view;
55  }
56
```

Fig. 5.21 | Overriding Fragment method onCreateView. (Part 2 of 2.)

Line 48 gets a reference to the DoodleView, then lines 51–53 initialize the instance variables that help calculate acceleration changes to determine whether the user shook the device. We initially set variables currentAcceleration and lastAcceleration to SensorManager's GRAVITY_EARTH constant, which represents the acceleration due to Earth's gravity. SensorManager also provides constants for other planets in the solar system, for the moon and for other entertaining values, which you can see at

> http://developer.android.com/reference/android/hardware/
> SensorManager.html

5.7.3 Methods onResume and enableAccelerometerListening

Accelerometer listening should be enabled only when the MainActivityFragment is visible. For this reason, we override Fragment lifecycle method onResume (Fig. 5.22, lines 58–62), which is called when the Fragment is on the screen and ready for the user to interact with it. Method onResume calls method enableAccelerometerListening (lines 65–75) to begin listening for accelerometer events. A SensorManager is used to register listeners for accelerometer events.

Method enableAccelerometerListening first uses Activity's getSystemService method to retrieve the system's SensorManager service, which enables the app to interact with the device's sensors. Lines 72–74 then register to receive accelerometer events using SensorManager's registerListener method, which receives three arguments:

- The SensorEventListener that responds to the events (defined in Section 5.7.5).
- A Sensor object representing the type of sensor data the app wishes to receive— this is retrieved by calling SensorManager's **getDefaultSensor** method and passing a Sensor-type constant (Sensor.TYPE_ACCELEROMETER in this app).
- The rate at which Android delivers sensor events— SENSOR_DELAY_NORMAL indicates the default rate. A faster rate can be used to get more accurate data, but this is also more CPU and battery intensive.

```
57     // start listening for sensor events
58     @Override
59     public void onResume() {
60         super.onResume();
61         enableAccelerometerListening(); // listen for shake event
62     }
63
64     // enable listening for accelerometer events
65     private void enableAccelerometerListening() {
66         // get the SensorManager
67         SensorManager sensorManager =
68             (SensorManager) getActivity().getSystemService(
69                 Context.SENSOR_SERVICE);
70
71         // register to listen for accelerometer events
72         sensorManager.registerListener(sensorEventListener,
73             sensorManager.getDefaultSensor(Sensor.TYPE_ACCELEROMETER),
74             SensorManager.SENSOR_DELAY_NORMAL);
75     }
76
```

Fig. 5.22 | Methods onResume and enableAccelerometerListening.

5.7.4 Methods onPause and disableAccelerometerListening

To ensure that accelerometer listening is disabled when the MainActivityFragment is not on the screen, we override Fragment lifecycle method onPause (Fig. 5.23, lines 78–82), which calls method disableAccelerometerListening (lines 85–94). Method disable-AccelerometerListening uses class SensorManager's **unregisterListener** method to stop listening for accelerometer events.

```
77     // stop listening for accelerometer events
78     @Override
79     public void onPause() {
80         super.onPause();
81         disableAccelerometerListening(); // stop listening for shake
82     }
83
84     // disable listening for accelerometer events
85     private void disableAccelerometerListening() {
86         // get the SensorManager
87         SensorManager sensorManager =
88             (SensorManager) getActivity().getSystemService(
89                 Context.SENSOR_SERVICE);
90
91         // stop listening for accelerometer events
92         sensorManager.unregisterListener(sensorEventListener,
93             sensorManager.getDefaultSensor(Sensor.TYPE_ACCELEROMETER));
94     }
95
```

Fig. 5.23 | Methods onPause and disableAccelerometerListening.

5.7.5 Anonymous Inner Class for Processing Accelerometer Events

Figure 5.24 overrides SensorEventListener method **onSensorChanged** (lines 100–123) to process accelerometer events. If the user moves the device, this method determines whether the movement was enough to be considered a shake. If so, line 121 calls method confirmErase (Section 5.7.6) to display an EraseImageDialogFragment (Section 5.11) and confirm whether the user really wants to erase the image. Interface SensorEventListener also contains method onAccuracyChanged (line 127)—we don't use this method in this app, so we provide an empty body because the method is required by the interface.

```
96     // event handler for accelerometer events
97     private final SensorEventListener sensorEventListener =
98        new SensorEventListener() {
99           // use accelerometer to determine whether user shook device
100          @Override
101          public void onSensorChanged(SensorEvent event) {
102             // ensure that other dialogs are not displayed
103             if (!dialogOnScreen) {
104                // get x, y, and z values for the SensorEvent
105                float x = event.values[0];
106                float y = event.values[1];
107                float z = event.values[2];
108
109                // save previous acceleration value
110                lastAcceleration = currentAcceleration;
111
112                // calculate the current acceleration
113                currentAcceleration = x * x + y * y + z * z;
114
115                // calculate the change in acceleration
116                acceleration = currentAcceleration *
117                   (currentAcceleration - lastAcceleration);
118
119                // if the acceleration is above a certain threshold
120                if (acceleration > ACCELERATION_THRESHOLD)
121                   confirmErase();
122             }
123          }
124
125          // required method of interface SensorEventListener
126          @Override
127          public void onAccuracyChanged(Sensor sensor, int accuracy) {}
128       };
129
```

Fig. 5.24 | Anonymous inner class that implements interface SensorEventListener to process accelerometer events.

The user can shake the device even when dialogs are already displayed on the screen. For this reason, onSensorChanged first checks whether a dialog is displayed (line 103). This test ensures that no other dialogs are displayed; otherwise, onSensorChanged simply returns. This is important because the sensor events occur in a different thread of execution. Without this test, we'd be able to display the confirmation dialog for erasing the image when another dialog is on the screen.

The **SensorEvent** parameter contains information about the sensor change that occurred. For accelerometer events, this parameter's values array contains three elements representing the acceleration (in *meters/second*^{2}) in the *x* (left/right), *y* (up/down) and *z* (forward/backward) directions. A description and diagram of the coordinate system used by the SensorEvent API is available at

```
http://developer.android.com/reference/android/hardware/
SensorEvent.html
```

This link also describes the real-world meanings for a SensorEvent's *x, y* and *z* values for each different Sensor.

Lines 105–107 store the acceleration values. It's important to handle sensor events quickly or to copy the event data (as we did here) because the array of sensor values is *reused* for each sensor event. Line 110 stores the last value of currentAcceleration. Line 113 sums the squares of the x, y and z acceleration values and stores them in currentAcceleration. Then, using the currentAcceleration and lastAcceleration values, we calculate a value (acceleration) that can be compared to our ACCELERATION_THRESHOLD constant. If the value is greater than the constant, the user moved the device enough for this app to consider the movement a shake. In this case, we call method confirmErase.

5.7.6 Method confirmErase

Method confirmErase (Fig. 5.25) simply creates an EraseImageDialogFragment (Section 5.11) and uses the DialogFragment method show to display it.

```
130    // confirm whether image should be erased
131    private void confirmErase() {
132       EraseImageDialogFragment fragment = new EraseImageDialogFragment();
133       fragment.show(getFragmentManager(), "erase dialog");
134    }
135
```

Fig. 5.25 | Method confirmErase displays an EraseImageDialogFragment.

5.7.7 Overridden Fragment Methods onCreateOptionsMenu and onOptionsItemSelected

Figure 5.26 overrides Fragment's **onCreateOptionsMenu** method (lines 137–141) to add the options to the method's Menu argument using the method's MenuInflater argument. When the user selects a menu item, Fragment method **onOptionsItemSelected** (lines 144–169) responds to the selection.

We use the MenuItem argument's **getItemID** method (line 147) to get the resource ID of the selected menu item, then take different actions based on the selection. The actions are as follows:

- For R.id.color, lines 149–150 create and show a ColorDialogFragment (Section 5.9) to allow the user to select a new drawing color.

- For R.id.line_width, lines 153–155 create and show a LineWidthDialogFragment (Section 5.10) to allow the user to select a new line width.

- For R.id.delete_drawing, line 158 calls method confirmErase (Section 5.7.6) to display an EraseImageDialogFragment (Section 5.11) and confirm whether the user really wants to erase the image.

- For R.id.save, line 161 calls the saveImage method to save the painting as an image stored in the device's **Photos** after checking for and, if necessary, requesting permission to write to external storage.

- For R.id.print, line 164 calls doodleView's printImage method to allow the user to save the image as a PDF or to print the image.

```
136    // displays the fragment's menu items
137    @Override
138    public void onCreateOptionsMenu(Menu menu, MenuInflater inflater) {
139       super.onCreateOptionsMenu(menu, inflater);
140       inflater.inflate(R.menu.doodle_fragment_menu, menu);
141    }
142
143    // handle choice from options menu
144    @Override
145    public boolean onOptionsItemSelected(MenuItem item) {
146       // switch based on the MenuItem id
147       switch (item.getItemId()) {
148          case R.id.color:
149             ColorDialogFragment colorDialog = new ColorDialogFragment();
150             colorDialog.show(getFragmentManager(), "color dialog");
151             return true; // consume the menu event
152          case R.id.line_width:
153             LineWidthDialogFragment widthDialog =
154                new LineWidthDialogFragment();
155             widthDialog.show(getFragmentManager(), "line width dialog");
156             return true; // consume the menu event
157          case R.id.delete_drawing:
158             confirmErase(); // confirm before erasing image
159             return true; // consume the menu event
160          case R.id.save:
161             saveImage(); // check permission and save current image
162             return true; // consume the menu event
163          case R.id.print:
164             doodleView.printImage(); // print the current images
165             return true; // consume the menu event
166       }
167
168       return super.onOptionsItemSelected(item);
169    }
170
```

Fig. 5.26 | Overridden Fragment methods onCreateOptionsMenu and onOptionsItemSelected.

5.7.8 Method saveImage

Method saveImage (Fig. 5.27) is called by the onOptionsItemSelected method when the user selects the **Save** option in the options menu. The saveImage method implements part of the new Android 6.0 permissions model that first checks whether the app has the required permission before performing a task. If not, the app requests permission from the user before attempting to perform the task.

Lines 176–178 check whether the app does not yet have permission to write to external storage so that it can save the image. If the app does not have the permission android.permission.WRITE_EXTERNAL_STORAGE, lines 181–182 use the built-in **shouldShowRequestPermissionRationale** method to determine whether an explanation of why the app needs this permission should be displayed. The method returns true when it would be helpful to explain to the user why the app requires permission—for example, if the user denied the permission previously. If so, lines 183–203 create and display a dialog with the explanation. When the user clicks the dialog's **OK** button, lines 195–197 request the android.permission.WRITE_EXTERNAL_STORAGE permission using the inherited Fragment method **requestPermissions**. If an explanation is not necessary—for example, if this is the first time the app needs the permission—lines 207–209 immediately request the permission.

```
171        // requests the permission needed for saving the image if
172        // necessary or saves the image if the app already has permission
173        private void saveImage() {
174           // checks if the app does not have permission needed
175           // to save the image
176           if (getContext().checkSelfPermission(
177              Manifest.permission.WRITE_EXTERNAL_STORAGE) !=
178              PackageManager.PERMISSION_GRANTED) {
179
180              // shows an explanation of why permission is needed
181              if (shouldShowRequestPermissionRationale(
182                 Manifest.permission.WRITE_EXTERNAL_STORAGE)) {
183                 AlertDialog.Builder builder =
184                    new AlertDialog.Builder(getActivity());
185
186                 // set Alert Dialog's message
187                 builder.setMessage(R.string.permission_explanation);
188
189                 // add an OK button to the dialog
190                 builder.setPositiveButton(android.R.string.ok,
191                    new DialogInterface.OnClickListener() {
192                       @Override
193                       public void onClick(DialogInterface dialog, int which) {
194                          // request permission
195                          requestPermissions(new String[]{
196                             Manifest.permission.WRITE_EXTERNAL_STORAGE},
197                             SAVE_IMAGE_PERMISSION_REQUEST_CODE);
198                       }
199                    }
200                 );
201
```

Fig. 5.27 | Method saveImage. (Part 1 of 2.)

```
202            // display the dialog
203            builder.create().show();
204         }
205         else {
206            // request permission
207            requestPermissions(
208               new String[]{Manifest.permission.WRITE_EXTERNAL_STORAGE},
209               SAVE_IMAGE_PERMISSION_REQUEST_CODE);
210         }
211      }
212      else { // if app already has permission to write to external storage
213         doodleView.saveImage(); // save the image
214      }
215   }
216
```

Fig. 5.27 | Method saveImage. (Part 2 of 2.)

The requestPermissions method receives a String array of permissions the app is requesting and an integer (SAVE_IMAGE_PERMISSION_REQUEST_CODE) that's used to identify this request for permission. When requestPermissions is called, Android displays a dialog (Fig. 5.28) that allows the user to **DENY** or **ALLOW** the requested permissions. The system invokes the callback method **onRequestPermissionsResult** (Section 5.7.9) to process the user's response. If the app already has the requested permission, line 213 calls the DoodleView's saveImage method to save the image.

Fig. 5.28 | Dialog enabling the user to deny or allow writing to external storage.

5.7.9 Overridden Method onRequestPermissionsResult

Method onRequestPermissionsResult (Fig. 5.29) receives a permission requestCode for the request that was made and passes it to the switch in lines 224–229, which executes appropriate code for the request. This app has only one permission request, so the switch statement has only one case identified by the SAVE_IMAGE_PERMISSION_REQUEST_CODE constant. For apps that require multiple permissions you should specify unique values for each permission when you call method requestPermissions. Line 226 checks whether the user granted the app permission to write to external storage. If so, line 227 calls the DoodleView's saveImage method to save the image.

Software Engineering Observation 5.1

If the user attempts to save the image and denies permission, the next time the user attempts to save, the permission dialog will contain a **Never ask again** *checkbox. If the user checks this and denies permission, then attempts to save in the future, method* onRequestPermission-Result *will be called with* PackageManager.PERMISSION_DENIED *as an argument. A production app should handle this case and tell the user how to change the app's permissions via the* **Settings** *app.*

```
217    // called by the system when the user either grants or denies the
218    // permission for saving an image
219    @Override
220    public void onRequestPermissionsResult(int requestCode,
221       String[] permissions, int[] grantResults) {
222       // switch chooses appropriate action based on which feature
223       // requested permission
224       switch (requestCode) {
225          case SAVE_IMAGE_PERMISSION_REQUEST_CODE:
226             if (grantResults[0] == PackageManager.PERMISSION_GRANTED)
227                doodleView.saveImage(); // save the image
228             return;
229       }
230    }
231
```

Fig. 5.29 | Overridden Fragment method onRequestPermissionsResult.

5.7.10 Methods getDoodleView and setDialogOnScreen

Methods getDoodleView and setDialogOnScreen (Fig. 5.30) are called by methods of the app's DialogFragment subclasses. Method getDoodleView returns a reference to this Fragment's DoodleView so that a DialogFragment can set the drawing color, set the line width or clear the image. Method setDialogOnScreen is called by Fragment lifecycle methods of the app's DialogFragment subclasses to indicate when a dialog is on the screen.

Software Engineering Observation 5.2

This app's Fragments interact with one another directly. We chose this tightly coupled approach for simplicity in this app. Generally, a parent Activity manages an app's Fragment interactions. To pass data to a Fragment, the Activity provides a Bundle of arguments. Each Fragment class typically provides an interface of callback methods that the Activity implements. When the Fragment needs to notify its parent Activity of a state change, the Fragment calls the appropriate callback method. These techniques make Fragments more reusable across activities. We'll demonstrate these techniques in Chapter 9's **Address Book** *app.*

```
232    // returns the DoodleView
233    public DoodleView getDoodleView() {
234       return doodleView;
235    }
```

Fig. 5.30 | Methods getDoodleView and setDialogOnScreen. (Part 1 of 2.)

```
236
237     // indicates whether a dialog is displayed
238     public void setDialogOnScreen(boolean visible) {
239        dialogOnScreen = visible;
240     }
241  }
```

Fig. 5.30 | Methods getDoodleView and setDialogOnScreen. (Part 2 of 2.)

5.8 DoodleView Class

The DoodleView class (Sections 5.8.1—5.8.12) processes the user's touches and draws the corresponding lines.

5.8.1 package Statement and import Statements

Figure 5.31 lists class DoodleView's package statement and import statements. The new classes and interfaces are highlighted here. Many of these were discussed in Section 5.3, and the rest are discussed as we use them throughout class DoodleView.

```
 1     // DoodleView.java
 2     // Main View for the Doodlz app.
 3     package com.deitel.doodlz;
 4
 5     import android.content.Context;
 6     import android.graphics.Bitmap;
 7     import android.graphics.Canvas;
 8     import android.graphics.Color;
 9     import android.graphics.Paint;
10     import android.graphics.Path;
11     import android.graphics.Point;
12     import android.provider.MediaStore;
13     import android.support.v4.print.PrintHelper;
14     import android.util.AttributeSet;
15     import android.view.Gravity;
16     import android.view.MotionEvent;
17     import android.view.View;
18     import android.widget.Toast;
19
20     import java.util.HashMap;
21     import java.util.Map;
22
```

Fig. 5.31 | DooldeView package statement and import statements.

5.8.2 static and Instance Variables

Class DoodleView's static and instance variables (Fig. 5.32) are used to manage the data for the set of lines that the user is currently drawing and to draw those lines. Line 34 creates the pathMap, which maps each finger ID (known as a pointer) to a corresponding Path object for the lines currently being drawn. Line 35 creates the previousPointMap, which maintains the last point for each finger—as each finger moves, we draw a line from its cur-

rent point to its previous point. We discuss the other fields as we use them in class DoodleView.

```
23   // custom View for drawing
24   public class DoodleView extends View {
25      // used to determine whether user moved a finger enough to draw again
26      private static final float TOUCH_TOLERANCE = 10;
27
28      private Bitmap bitmap; // drawing area for displaying or saving
29      private Canvas bitmapCanvas; // used to to draw on the bitmap
30      private final Paint paintScreen; // used to draw bitmap onto screen
31      private final Paint paintLine; // used to draw lines onto bitmap
32
33      // Maps of current Paths being drawn and Points in those Paths
34      private final Map<Integer, Path> pathMap = new HashMap<>();
35      private final Map<Integer, Point> previousPointMap = new HashMap<>();
36
```

Fig. 5.32 | DoodleView static and instance variables.

5.8.3 Constructor

The constructor (Fig. 5.33) initializes several of the class's instance variables—the two
Maps are initialized in their declarations in Fig. 5.32. Line 40 of Fig. 5.33 creates the Paint
object paintScreen that will be used to display the user's drawing on the screen, and line
43 creates the Paint object paintLine that specifies the settings for the line(s) the user is
currently drawing. Lines 44–48 specify the settings for the paintLine object. We pass
true to Paint's **setAntiAlias** method to enable *anti-aliasing* which smooths the edges of
the lines. Next, we set the Paint's style to Paint.Style.STROKE with Paint's **setStyle**
method. The style can be STROKE, FILL or FILL_AND_STROKE for a line, a filled shape without a border and a filled shape with a border, respectively. The default option is
Paint.Style.FILL. We set the line's width using Paint's setStrokeWidth method. This
sets the app's *default line width* to five pixels. We also use Paint's setStrokeCap method
to round the ends of the lines with Paint.Cap.ROUND.

```
37      // DoodleView constructor initializes the DoodleView
38      public DoodleView(Context context, AttributeSet attrs) {
39         super(context, attrs); // pass context to View's constructor
40         paintScreen = new Paint(); // used to display bitmap onto screen
41
42         // set the initial display settings for the painted line
43         paintLine = new Paint();
44         paintLine.setAntiAlias(true); // smooth edges of drawn line
45         paintLine.setColor(Color.BLACK); // default color is black
46         paintLine.setStyle(Paint.Style.STROKE); // solid line
47         paintLine.setStrokeWidth(5); // set the default line width
48         paintLine.setStrokeCap(Paint.Cap.ROUND); // rounded line ends
49      }
50
```

Fig. 5.33 | DoodleView constructor.

5.8.4 Overridden View Method onSizeChanged

The DoodleView's size is not determined until it's inflated and added to the MainActivity's View hierarchy; therefore, we can't determine the size of the drawing Bitmap in on-Create. So, we override View method onSizeChanged (Fig. 5.34), which is called when the DoodleView's size changes—e.g., when it's added to an Activity's View hierarchy or when the user rotates the device. In this app, onSizeChanged is called only when the DoodleView is added to the Doodlz Activity's View hierarchy, because the app always displays in portrait on phones and small tablets, and in landscape on large tablets.

Software Engineering Observation 5.3

In apps that support both portrait and landscape orientations, onSizeChanged is called each time the user rotates the device. In this app, that would result in a new Bitmap each tim the method is called. When replacing a Bitmap, you should call the prior Bitmap's recycle method to release its resources.

```
51   // creates Bitmap and Canvas based on View's size
52   @Override
53   public void onSizeChanged(int w, int h, int oldW, int oldH) {
54       bitmap = Bitmap.createBitmap(getWidth(), getHeight(),
55           Bitmap.Config.ARGB_8888);
56       bitmapCanvas = new Canvas(bitmap);
57       bitmap.eraseColor(Color.WHITE); // erase the Bitmap with white
58   }
59
```

Fig. 5.34 | Overridden View method onSizeChanged.

Bitmap's static **createBitmap** method creates a Bitmap of the specified width and height—here we use the DoodleView's width and height as the Bitmap's dimensions. The last argument to createBitmap is the Bitmap's encoding, which specifies how each pixel in the Bitmap is stored. The constant Bitmap.Config.ARGB_8888 indicates that each pixel's color is stored in four bytes (one byte each for the alpha, red, green and blue values) of the pixel's color. Next, we create a new Canvas that's used to draw shapes directly to the Bitmap. Finally, we use Bitmap's eraseColor method to fill the Bitmap with white pixels—the default Bitmap background is black.

5.8.5 Methods clear, setDrawingColor, getDrawingColor, setLineWidth and getLineWidth

Figure 5.35 defines methods clear (lines 61–66), setDrawingColor (lines 69–71), getDrawingColor (lines 74–76), setLineWidth (lines 79–81) and getLineWidth (lines 84–86), which are called from the MainActivityFragment. Method clear, which we use in the EraseImageDialogFragment, empties the pathMap and previousPointMap, erases the Bitmap by setting all of its pixels to white, then calls the inherited View method **invalidate** to indicate that the View needs to be redrawn. Then, the system automatically determines when the View's onDraw method should be called. Method setDrawingColor changes the current drawing color by setting the color of the Paint object paintLine.

Paint's setColor method receives an int that represents the new color in ARGB format. Method getDrawingColor returns the current color, which we use in the ColorDialog-Fragment. Method setLineWidth sets paintLine's stroke width to the specified number of pixels. Method getLineWidth returns the current stroke width, which we use in the LineWidthDialogFragment.

```
60    // clear the painting
61    public void clear() {
62        pathMap.clear(); // remove all paths
63        previousPointMap.clear(); // remove all previous points
64        bitmap.eraseColor(Color.WHITE); // clear the bitmap
65        invalidate(); // refresh the screen
66    }
67
68    // set the painted line's color
69    public void setDrawingColor(int color) {
70        paintLine.setColor(color);
71    }
72
73    // return the painted line's color
74    public int getDrawingColor() {
75        return paintLine.getColor();
76    }
77
78    // set the painted line's width
79    public void setLineWidth(int width) {
80        paintLine.setStrokeWidth(width);
81    }
82
83    // return the painted line's width
84    public int getLineWidth() {
85        return (int) paintLine.getStrokeWidth();
86    }
87
```

Fig. 5.35 | DoodleView methods clear, setDrawingColor, getDrawingColor, setLineWidth and getLineWidth.

5.8.6 Overridden View Method onDraw

When a View needs to be *redrawn*, its **onDraw** method is called. Figure 5.36 overrides onDraw to display bitmap (the Bitmap that contains the drawing) on the DoodleView by calling the Canvas argument's **drawBitmap** method. The first argument is the Bitmap to draw, the next two arguments are the *x-y* coordinates where the upper-left corner of the Bitmap should be placed on the View and the last argument is the Paint object that specifies the drawing characteristics. Lines 95–96 then loop through and display the Paths that are currently being drawn. For each Integer key in the pathMap, we pass the corresponding Path to Canvas's **drawPath** method to draw the Path using the paintLine object, which defines the line *width* and *color*.

```
88      // perform custom drawing when the DoodleView is refreshed on screen
89      @Override
90      protected void onDraw(Canvas canvas) {
91         // draw the background screen
92         canvas.drawBitmap(bitmap, 0, 0, paintScreen);
93
94         // for each path currently being drawn
95         for (Integer key : pathMap.keySet())
96            canvas.drawPath(pathMap.get(key), paintLine); // draw line
97      }
98
```

Fig. 5.36 | Overridden View method onDraw.

5.8.7 Overridden View Method onTouchEvent

Method onTouchEvent (Fig. 5.37) is called when the View receives a touch event. Android supports *multitouch*—that is, having multiple fingers touching the screen. At any time, the user can touch the screen with more fingers or remove fingers from the screen. For this reason, each finger—known as a *pointer*—has a unique ID that identifies it across touch events. We'll use that ID to locate the corresponding Path objects that represent each line currently being drawn. These Paths are stored in pathMap.

```
99      // handle touch event
100     @Override
101     public boolean onTouchEvent(MotionEvent event) {
102        int action = event.getActionMasked(); // event type
103        int actionIndex = event.getActionIndex(); // pointer (i.e., finger)
104
105        // determine whether touch started, ended or is moving
106        if (action == MotionEvent.ACTION_DOWN ||
107           action == MotionEvent.ACTION_POINTER_DOWN) {
108           touchStarted(event.getX(actionIndex), event.getY(actionIndex),
109              event.getPointerId(actionIndex));
110        }
111        else if (action == MotionEvent.ACTION_UP ||
112           action == MotionEvent.ACTION_POINTER_UP) {
113           touchEnded(event.getPointerId(actionIndex));
114        }
115        else {
116           touchMoved(event);
117        }
118
119        invalidate(); // redraw
120        return true;
121     }
122
```

Fig. 5.37 | Overridden View method onTouchEvent.

MotionEvent's **getActionMasked** method (line 102) returns an int representing the MotionEvent type, which you can use with constants from class MotionEvent to determine how to handle each event. MotionEvent's **getActionIndex** method (line 103) returns an integer index representing which finger caused the event. This index is *not* the finger's unique ID—it's simply the index at which that finger's information is located in this MotionEvent object. To get the finger's unique ID that persists across MotionEvents until the user removes that finger from the screen, we'll use MotionEvent's **getPointerID** method (lines 109 and 113), passing the finger index as an argument.

If the action is MotionEvent.ACTION_DOWN or MotionEvent.ACTION_POINTER_DOWN (lines 106–107), the user *touched the screen with a new finger.* The first finger to touch the screen generates a MotionEvent.ACTION_DOWN event, and all other fingers generate MotionEvent.ACTION_POINTER_DOWN events. For these cases, we call the touchStarted method (Fig. 5.38) to store the initial coordinates of the touch. If the action is Motion-Event.ACTION_UP or MotionEvent.ACTION_POINTER_UP, the user *removed a finger from the screen*, so we call method touchEnded (Fig. 5.40) to draw the completed Path to the bitmap so that we have a permanent record of that Path. For all other touch events, we call method touchMoved (Fig. 5.39) to draw the lines. After the event is processed, line 119 (of Fig. 5.37) calls the inherited View method invalidate to redraw the screen, and line 120 returns true to indicate that the event has been processed.

5.8.8 touchStarted Method

The touchStarted method (Fig. 5.38) is called when a finger *first touches* the screen. The coordinates of the touch and its ID are supplied as arguments. If a Path already exists for the given ID (line 129), we call Path's **reset** method to *clear* any existing points so we can *reuse* the Path for a new stroke. Otherwise, we create a new Path, add it to pathMap, then add a new Point to the previousPointMap. Lines 142–144 call Path's **moveTo** method to set the Path's starting coordinates and specify the new Point's x and y values.

```
123    // called when the user touches the screen
124    private void touchStarted(float x, float y, int lineID) {
125        Path path; // used to store the path for the given touch id
126        Point point; // used to store the last point in path
127
128        // if there is already a path for lineID
129        if (pathMap.containsKey(lineID)) {
130            path = pathMap.get(lineID); // get the Path
131            path.reset(); // resets the Path because a new touch has started
132            point = previousPointMap.get(lineID); // get Path's last point
133        }
134        else {
135            path = new Path();
136            pathMap.put(lineID, path); // add the Path to Map
137            point = new Point(); // create a new Point
138            previousPointMap.put(lineID, point); // add the Point to the Map
139        }
140
141        // move to the coordinates of the touch
142        path.moveTo(x, y);
```

Fig. 5.38 | touchStarted method of class DoodleView. (Part 1 of 2.)

143	`        point.x = (int) x;`
144	`        point.y = (int) y;`
145	`    }`
146	

Fig. 5.38 | touchStarted method of class DoodleView. (Part 2 of 2.)

5.8.9 touchMoved Method

The touchMoved method (Fig. 5.39) is called when the user moves one or more fingers across the screen. The system MotionEvent passed from onTouchEvent contains touch information for multiple moves on the screen if they occur at the same time. MotionEvent method **getPointerCount** (line 150) returns the number of touches this MotionEvent describes. For each, we store the finger's ID (line 152) in pointerID, and store the finger's corresponding index in this MotionEvent (line 153) in pointerIndex. Then we check whether there's a corresponding Path in pathMap (line 156). If so, we use MotionEvent's getX and getY methods to get the last coordinates for this *drag* event for the specified pointerIndex. We get the corresponding Path and last Point for the pointerID from each respective HashMap, then calculate the difference between the last point and the current point—we want to update the Path *only* if the user has moved a distance that's greater than our TOUCH_TOLERANCE constant. We do this because many devices are sensitive enough to generate MotionEvents indicating small movements when the user is attempting to hold a finger motionless on the screen. If the user moved a finger further than the TOUCH_TOLERANCE, we use Path's **quadTo** method (lines 173–174) to add a geometric curve (specifically a *quadratic Bezier curve*) from the previous Point to the new Point. We then update the most recent Point for that finger.

```
147    // called when the user drags along the screen
148    private void touchMoved(MotionEvent event) {
149        // for each of the pointers in the given MotionEvent
150        for (int i = 0; i < event.getPointerCount(); i++) {
151            // get the pointer ID and pointer index
152            int pointerID = event.getPointerId(i);
153            int pointerIndex = event.findPointerIndex(pointerID);
154
155            // if there is a path associated with the pointer
156            if (pathMap.containsKey(pointerID)) {
157                // get the new coordinates for the pointer
158                float newX = event.getX(pointerIndex);
159                float newY = event.getY(pointerIndex);
160
161                // get the path and previous point associated with
162                // this pointer
163                Path path = pathMap.get(pointerID);
164                Point point = previousPointMap.get(pointerID);
165
```

Fig. 5.39 | touchMoved method of class DoodleView. (Part 1 of 2.)

```
166            // calculate how far the user moved from the last update
167            float deltaX = Math.abs(newX - point.x);
168            float deltaY = Math.abs(newY - point.y);
169
170            // if the distance is significant enough to matter
171            if (deltaX >= TOUCH_TOLERANCE || deltaY >= TOUCH_TOLERANCE) {
172               // move the path to the new location
173               path.quadTo(point.x, point.y, (newX + point.x) / 2,
174                  (newY + point.y) / 2);
175
176               // store the new coordinates
177               point.x = (int) newX;
178               point.y = (int) newY;
179            }
180         }
181      }
182   }
183
```

Fig. 5.39 | touchMoved method of class DoodleView. (Part 2 of 2.)

5.8.10 touchEnded Method

The touchEnded method (Fig. 5.40) is called when the user lifts a finger from the screen. The method receives the ID of the finger (lineID) for which the touch just ended as an argument. Line 186 gets the corresponding Path. Line 187 calls the bitmapCanvas's draw-Path method to draw the Path on the Bitmap object named bitmap before we call Path's reset method to clear the Path. Resetting the Path does not erase its corresponding painted line from the screen, because those lines have already been drawn to the bitmap that's displayed to the screen. The lines that are currently being drawn by the user are displayed on top of that bitmap.

```
184   // called when the user finishes a touch
185   private void touchEnded(int lineID) {
186      Path path = pathMap.get(lineID); // get the corresponding Path
187      bitmapCanvas.drawPath(path, paintLine); // draw to bitmapCanvas
188      path.reset(); // reset the Path
189   }
190
```

Fig. 5.40 | touchEnded method of class DoodleView.

5.8.11 Method saveImage

Method saveImage (Fig. 5.41) saves the current drawing. Line 194 creates a filename for the image, then lines 197–199 store the image in the device's **Photos** app by calling class MediaStore.Images.Media's insertImage method. The method receives four arguments:

- a ContentResolver that the method uses to locate where the image should be stored on the device
- the Bitmap to store

- the name of the image
- a description of the image

Method `insertImage` returns a `String` representing the image's location on the device, or null if the image could not be saved. Lines 201–217 check whether the image was saved and display an appropriate `Toast`.

```
191    // save the current image to the Gallery
192    public void saveImage() {
193        // use "Doodlz" followed by current time as the image name
194        final String name = "Doodlz" + System.currentTimeMillis() + ".jpg";
195
196        // insert the image on the device
197        String location = MediaStore.Images.Media.insertImage(
198            getContext().getContentResolver(), bitmap, name,
199            "Doodlz Drawing");
200
201        if (location != null) {
202            // display a message indicating that the image was saved
203            Toast message = Toast.makeText(getContext(),
204                R.string.message_saved,
205                Toast.LENGTH_SHORT);
206            message.setGravity(Gravity.CENTER, message.getXOffset() / 2,
207                message.getYOffset() / 2);
208            message.show();
209        }
210        else {
211            // display a message indicating that there was an error saving
212            Toast message = Toast.makeText(getContext(),
213                R.string.message_error_saving, Toast.LENGTH_SHORT);
214            message.setGravity(Gravity.CENTER, message.getXOffset() / 2,
215                message.getYOffset() / 2);
216            message.show();
217        }
218    }
219
```

Fig. 5.41 | `DoodleView` method `saveImage`.

5.8.12 Method `printImage`

Method `printImage` (Fig. 5.42) uses the Android Support Library's `PrintHelper` class to print the current drawing—this is available only on devices running Android 4.4 or higher. Line 222 first confirms that printing support is available on the device. If so, line 224 creates a `PrintHelper` object. Next, line 227 specifies the image's *scale mode*—`PrintHelper.SCALE_MODE_FIT` indicates that the image should fit within the printable area of the paper. There's also the scale mode `PrintHelper.SCALE_MODE_FILL`, which causes the image to fill the paper, possibly cutting off a portion of the image. Finally, line 228 calls `Print-Helper` method **`printBitmap`**, passing as arguments the print job name (used by the printer to identify the print) and the `Bitmap` containing the image to print. This displays Android's print dialog, which allows the user to choose whether to save the image as a PDF document on the device or to print it to an available printer.

```
220      // print the current image
221      public void printImage() {
222         if (PrintHelper.systemSupportsPrint()) {
223            // use Android Support Library's PrintHelper to print image
224            PrintHelper printHelper = new PrintHelper(getContext());
225
226            // fit image in page bounds and print the image
227            printHelper.setScaleMode(PrintHelper.SCALE_MODE_FIT);
228            printHelper.printBitmap("Doodlz Image", bitmap);
229         }
230         else {
231            // display message indicating that system does not allow printing
232            Toast message = Toast.makeText(getContext(),
233               R.string.message_error_printing, Toast.LENGTH_SHORT);
234            message.setGravity(Gravity.CENTER, message.getXOffset() / 2,
235               message.getYOffset() / 2);
236            message.show();
237         }
238      }
239   }
```

Fig. 5.42 | DoodleView method printImage.

5.9 ColorDialogFragment Class

Class ColorDialogFragment (Figs. 5.43–5.47) extends DialogFragment to create an AlertDialog for setting the drawing color. The class's instance variables (lines 18–23) are used to reference the GUI controls for selecting the new color, displaying a preview of it and storing the color as a 32-bit int value that represents the color's ARGB values.

```
 1   // ColorDialogFragment.java
 2   // Allows user to set the drawing color on the DoodleView
 3   package com.deitel.doodlz;
 4
 5   import android.app.Activity;
 6   import android.app.AlertDialog;
 7   import android.app.Dialog;
 8   import android.content.DialogInterface;
 9   import android.graphics.Color;
10   import android.os.Bundle;
11   import android.support.v4.app.DialogFragment;
12   import android.view.View;
13   import android.widget.SeekBar;
14   import android.widget.SeekBar.OnSeekBarChangeListener;
15
16   // class for the Select Color dialog
17   public class ColorDialogFragment extends DialogFragment {
18      private SeekBar alphaSeekBar;
19      private SeekBar redSeekBar;
```

Fig. 5.43 | ColorDialogFragment's package statement, import statements and instance variables. (Part 1 of 2.)

```
20      private SeekBar greenSeekBar;
21      private SeekBar blueSeekBar;
22      private View colorView;
23      private int color;
24
```

Fig. 5.43 | ColorDialogFragment's package statement, import statements and instance variables. (Part 2 of 2.)

5.9.1 Overridden DialogFragment Method onCreateDialog

Method onCreateDialog (Fig. 5.44) inflates the custom View (lines 31–32) defined by fragment_color.xml containing the GUI for selecting a color, then attaches that View to the AlertDialog by calling AlertDialog.Builder's setView method (line 33). Lines 39–47 get references to the dialog's SeekBars and colorView. Next, lines 50–53 register colorChangedListener (Fig. 5.47) as the listener for the SeekBars' events.

```
25      // create an AlertDialog and return it
26      @Override
27      public Dialog onCreateDialog(Bundle bundle) {
28          // create dialog
29          AlertDialog.Builder builder =
30              new AlertDialog.Builder(getActivity());
31          View colorDialogView = getActivity().getLayoutInflater().inflate(
32              R.layout.fragment_color, null);
33          builder.setView(colorDialogView); // add GUI to dialog
34
35          // set the AlertDialog's message
36          builder.setTitle(R.string.title_color_dialog);
37
38          // get the color SeekBars and set their onChange listeners
39          alphaSeekBar = (SeekBar) colorDialogView.findViewById(
40              R.id.alphaSeekBar);
41          redSeekBar = (SeekBar) colorDialogView.findViewById(
42              R.id.redSeekBar);
43          greenSeekBar = (SeekBar) colorDialogView.findViewById(
44              R.id.greenSeekBar);
45          blueSeekBar = (SeekBar) colorDialogView.findViewById(
46              R.id.blueSeekBar);
47          colorView = colorDialogView.findViewById(R.id.colorView);
48
49          // register SeekBar event listeners
50          alphaSeekBar.setOnSeekBarChangeListener(colorChangedListener);
51          redSeekBar.setOnSeekBarChangeListener(colorChangedListener);
52          greenSeekBar.setOnSeekBarChangeListener(colorChangedListener);
53          blueSeekBar.setOnSeekBarChangeListener(colorChangedListener);
54
55          // use current drawing color to set SeekBar values
56          final DoodleView doodleView = getDoodleFragment().getDoodleView();
57          color = doodleView.getDrawingColor();
```

Fig. 5.44 | Overridden DialogFragment method onCreateDialog. (Part 1 of 2.)

```
58        alphaSeekBar.setProgress(Color.alpha(color));
59        redSeekBar.setProgress(Color.red(color));
60        greenSeekBar.setProgress(Color.green(color));
61        blueSeekBar.setProgress(Color.blue(color));
62
63        // add Set Color Button
64        builder.setPositiveButton(R.string.button_set_color,
65           new DialogInterface.OnClickListener() {
66              public void onClick(DialogInterface dialog, int id) {
67                 doodleView.setDrawingColor(color);
68              }
69           }
70        );
71
72        return builder.create(); // return dialog
73     }
74
```

Fig. 5.44 | Overridden `DialogFragment` method `onCreateDialog`. (Part 2 of 2.)

Line 56 (Fig. 5.44) calls method `getDoodleFragment` (Fig. 5.45) to get a reference to the `DoodleFragment`, then calls the `MainActivityFragment`'s `getDoodleView` method to get the `DoodleView`. Lines 57–61 get the `DoodleView`'s current drawing color, then use it to set each `SeekBar`'s value. `Color`'s static methods **alpha**, **red**, **green** and **blue** extract the ARGB values from the color, and `SeekBar`'s `setProgress` method positions the thumbs. Lines 64–70 configure the `AlertDialog`'s positive button to set the `DoodleView`'s new drawing color. Line 72 returns the `AlertDialog`.

5.9.2 Method getDoodleFragment

Method `getDoodleFragment` (Fig. 5.45) simply uses the `FragmentManager` to get a reference to the `DoodleFragment`.

```
75     // gets a reference to the MainActivityFragment
76     private MainActivityFragment getDoodleFragment() {
77        return (MainActivityFragment) getFragmentManager().findFragmentById(
78           R.id.doodleFragment);
79     }
80
```

Fig. 5.45 | Method getDoodleFragment.

5.9.3 Overridden Fragment Lifecycle Methods onAttach and onDetach

When the `ColorDialogFragment` is added to a parent `Activity`, method `onAttach` (Fig. 5.46, lines 82–89) is called. Line 85 gets a reference to the `MainActivityFragment`. If that reference is not null, line 88 calls `MainActivityFragment`'s `setDialogOnScreen` method to indicate that the **Choose Color** dialog is now displayed. When the `ColorDialogFragment` is removed from a parent `Activity`, method `onDetach` (lines 92–99) is called. Line 98 calls MainActivityFragment's setDialogOnScreen method to indicate that the **Choose Color** dialog is no longer on the screen.

```
81    // tell MainActivityFragment that dialog is now displayed
82    @Override
83    public void onAttach(Activity activity) {
84       super.onAttach(activity);
85       MainActivityFragment fragment = getDoodleFragment();
86
87       if (fragment != null)
88          fragment.setDialogOnScreen(true);
89    }
90
91    // tell MainActivityFragment that dialog is no longer displayed
92    @Override
93    public void onDetach() {
94       super.onDetach();
95       MainActivityFragment fragment = getDoodleFragment();
96
97       if (fragment != null)
98          fragment.setDialogOnScreen(false);
99    }
100
```

Fig. 5.46 | Overridden Fragment lifecycle methods onAttach and onDetach.

5.9.4 Anonymous Inner Class That Responds to the Events of the Alpha, Red, Green and Blue SeekBars

Figure 5.47 defines an anonymous inner class that implements interface OnSeekBarChangeListener to respond to events when the user adjusts the SeekBars in the **Choose Color** Dialog. This was registered as the SeekBars' event handler in Fig. 5.44 (lines 50–53). Method onProgressChanged (Fig. 5.47, lines 105–114) is called when the position of a SeekBar's thumb changes. If the user moved a SeekBar's thumb (line 109), lines 110–112 store the new color. Class Color's **static** method **argb** combines the SeekBars' values into a Color and returns the appropriate color as an int. We then use class View's **setBackgroundColor** method to update the colorView with a color that matches the current state of the SeekBars.

```
101   // OnSeekBarChangeListener for the SeekBars in the color dialog
102   private final OnSeekBarChangeListener colorChangedListener =
103      new OnSeekBarChangeListener() {
104         // display the updated color
105         @Override
106         public void onProgressChanged(SeekBar seekBar, int progress,
107            boolean fromUser) {
108
```

Fig. 5.47 | Anonymous inner class that implements interface OnSeekBarChangeListener to respond to the events of the alpha, red, green and blue SeekBars. (Part 1 of 2.)

```
109                 if (fromUser) // user, not program, changed SeekBar progress
110                     color = Color.argb(alphaSeekBar.getProgress(),
111                         redSeekBar.getProgress(), greenSeekBar.getProgress(),
112                         blueSeekBar.getProgress());
113                 colorView.setBackgroundColor(color);
114             }
115
116             @Override
117             public void onStartTrackingTouch(SeekBar seekBar) {} // required
118
119             @Override
120             public void onStopTrackingTouch(SeekBar seekBar) {} // required
121         };
122 }
```

Fig. 5.47 | Anonymous inner class that implements interface OnSeekBarChangeListener to respond to the events of the alpha, red, green and blue SeekBars. (Part 2 of 2.)

5.10 LineWidthDialogFragment Class

Class LineWidthDialogFragment (Fig. 5.48) extends DialogFragment to create an Alert-Dialog for setting the line width. The class is similar to class ColorDialogFragment, so we discuss only the key differences here. The class's only instance variable is an ImageView (line 21) in which we draw a line showing the current line-width setting.

```
1   // LineWidthDialogFragment.java
2   // Allows user to set the drawing color on the DoodleView
3   package com.deitel.doodlz;
4
5   import android.app.Activity;
6   import android.app.AlertDialog;
7   import android.app.Dialog;
8   import android.content.DialogInterface;
9   import android.graphics.Bitmap;
10  import android.graphics.Canvas;
11  import android.graphics.Paint;
12  import android.os.Bundle;
13  import android.support.v4.app.DialogFragment;
14  import android.view.View;
15  import android.widget.ImageView;
16  import android.widget.SeekBar;
17  import android.widget.SeekBar.OnSeekBarChangeListener;
18
19  // class for the Select Line Width dialog
20  public class LineWidthDialogFragment extends DialogFragment {
21      private ImageView widthImageView;
22
```

Fig. 5.48 | Class LineWidthDialogFragment. (Part 1 of 3.)

```
23     // create an AlertDialog and return it
24     @Override
25     public Dialog onCreateDialog(Bundle bundle) {
26        // create the dialog
27        AlertDialog.Builder builder =
28           new AlertDialog.Builder(getActivity());
29        View lineWidthDialogView =
30           getActivity().getLayoutInflater().inflate(
31              R.layout.fragment_line_width, null);
32        builder.setView(lineWidthDialogView); // add GUI to dialog
33
34        // set the AlertDialog's message
35        builder.setTitle(R.string.title_line_width_dialog);
36
37        // get the ImageView
38        widthImageView = (ImageView) lineWidthDialogView.findViewById(
39           R.id.widthImageView);
40
41        // configure widthSeekBar
42        final DoodleView doodleView = getDoodleFragment().getDoodleView();
43        final SeekBar widthSeekBar = (SeekBar)
44           lineWidthDialogView.findViewById(R.id.widthSeekBar);
45        widthSeekBar.setOnSeekBarChangeListener(lineWidthChanged);
46        widthSeekBar.setProgress(doodleView.getLineWidth());
47
48        // add Set Line Width Button
49        builder.setPositiveButton(R.string.button_set_line_width,
50           new DialogInterface.OnClickListener() {
51              public void onClick(DialogInterface dialog, int id) {
52                 doodleView.setLineWidth(widthSeekBar.getProgress());
53              }
54           }
55        );
56
57        return builder.create(); // return dialog
58     }
59
60     // return a reference to the MainActivityFragment
61     private MainActivityFragment getDoodleFragment() {
62        return (MainActivityFragment) getFragmentManager().findFragmentById(
63           R.id.doodleFragment);
64     }
65
66     // tell MainActivityFragment that dialog is now displayed
67     @Override
68     public void onAttach(Activity activity) {
69        super.onAttach(activity);
70        MainActivityFragment fragment = getDoodleFragment();
71
72        if (fragment != null)
73           fragment.setDialogOnScreen(true);
74     }
```

Fig. 5.48 | Class LineWidthDialogFragment. (Part 2 of 3.)

```
75
76        // tell MainActivityFragment that dialog is no longer displayed
77        @Override
78        public void onDetach() {
79           super.onDetach();
80           MainActivityFragment fragment = getDoodleFragment();
81
82           if (fragment != null)
83              fragment.setDialogOnScreen(false);
84        }
85
86        // OnSeekBarChangeListener for the SeekBar in the width dialog
87        private final OnSeekBarChangeListener lineWidthChanged =
88           new OnSeekBarChangeListener() {
89              final Bitmap bitmap = Bitmap.createBitmap(
90                 400, 100, Bitmap.Config.ARGB_8888);
91              final Canvas canvas = new Canvas(bitmap); // draws into bitmap
92
93              @Override
94              public void onProgressChanged(SeekBar seekBar, int progress,
95                 boolean fromUser) {
96                 // configure a Paint object for the current SeekBar value
97                 Paint p = new Paint();
98                 p.setColor(
99                    getDoodleFragment().getDoodleView().getDrawingColor());
100                p.setStrokeCap(Paint.Cap.ROUND);
101                p.setStrokeWidth(progress);
102
103                // erase the bitmap and redraw the line
104                bitmap.eraseColor(
105                   getResources().getColor(android.R.color.transparent,
106                      getContext().getTheme()));
107                canvas.drawLine(30, 50, 370, 50, p);
108                widthImageView.setImageBitmap(bitmap);
109             }
110
111             @Override
112             public void onStartTrackingTouch(SeekBar seekBar) {} // required
113
114             @Override
115             public void onStopTrackingTouch(SeekBar seekBar) {} // required
116          };
117    }
```

Fig. 5.48 | Class LineWidthDialogFragment. (Part 3 of 3.)

5.10.1 Method onCreateDialog

Method onCreateDialog (lines 24–58) inflates the custom View (lines 29–31) defined by
fragment_line_width.xml that displays the GUI for selecting the line width, then attaches that View to the AlertDialog by calling AlertDialog.Builder's setView method (line
32). Lines 38–39 get a reference to the ImageView in which the sample line will be drawn.
Next, lines 42–46 get a reference to the widthSeekBar, register lineWidthChanged (lines
87–116) as the SeekBar's listener and set the SeekBar's current value to the current line

width. Lines 49–55 define the dialog's positive button to call the DoodleView's setLine-Width method when the user touches the **Set Line Width** button. Line 57 returns the AlertDialog for display.

5.10.2 Anonymous Inner Class That Responds to the Events of the widthSeekBar

Lines 87–116 define the lineWidthChanged OnSeekBarChangeListener that responds to events when the user adjusts the SeekBar in the **Choose Line Width** dialog. Lines 89–90 create a Bitmap on which to display a sample line representing the selected line thickness. Line 91 creates a Canvas for drawing on the Bitmap. Method onProgressChanged (lines 93–109) draws the sample line based on the current drawing color and the SeekBar's value. First, lines 97–101 configure a Paint object for drawing the sample line. Class Paint's **setStrokeCap** method (line 100) specifies the appearance of the line ends—in this case, they're rounded (Paint.Cap.ROUND). Lines 104–106 clear bitmap's background to the predefined Android color android.R.color.transparent with Bitmap method **eraseColor**. We use canvas to draw the sample line. Finally, line 108 displays bitmap in the widthImageView by passing it to ImageView's **setImageBitmap** method.

5.11 EraseImageDialogFragment Class

Class EraseImageDialogFragment (Fig. 5.49) extends DialogFragment to create an AlertDialog that confirms whether the user really wants to erase the entire image. The class is similar to class ColorDialogFragment and LineWidthDialogFragment, so we discuss only method onCreateDialog (lines 15–35) here. The method creates an AlertDialog with **Erase Image** and **Cancel** button. Lines 24–30 configure the **Erase Image** button as the positive button—when the user touches this, line 27 in the button's listener calls the DoodleView's clear method to erase the image. Line 33 configures **Cancel** as the negative button—when the user touches this, the dialog is dismissed. In this case, we use the predefined Android String resource android.R.string.cancel. For other predefined String resources, visit

http://developer.android.com/reference/android/R.string.html

Line 34 returns the AlertDialog.

```
1   // EraseImageDialogFragment.java
2   // Allows user to erase image
3   package com.deitel.doodlz;
4
5   import android.app.Activity;
6   import android.app.AlertDialog;
7   import android.app.Dialog;
8   import android.support.v4.app.DialogFragment;
9   import android.content.DialogInterface;
10  import android.os.Bundle;
11
```

Fig. 5.49 | Class EraseImageDialogFragment. (Part 1 of 2.)

```
12    // class for the Erase Image dialog
13    public class EraseImageDialogFragment extends DialogFragment {
14        // create an AlertDialog and return it
15        @Override
16        public Dialog onCreateDialog(Bundle bundle) {
17            AlertDialog.Builder builder =
18                new AlertDialog.Builder(getActivity());
19
20            // set the AlertDialog's message
21            builder.setMessage(R.string.message_erase);
22
23            // add Erase Button
24            builder.setPositiveButton(R.string.button_erase,
25                new DialogInterface.OnClickListener() {
26                    public void onClick(DialogInterface dialog, int id) {
27                        getDoodleFragment().getDoodleView().clear(); // clear image
28                    }
29                }
30            );
31
32            // add cancel Button
33            builder.setNegativeButton(android.R.string.cancel, null);
34            return builder.create(); // return dialog
35        }
36
37        // gets a reference to the MainActivityFragment
38        private MainActivityFragment getDoodleFragment() {
39            return (MainActivityFragment) getFragmentManager().findFragmentById(
40                R.id.doodleFragment);
41        }
42
43        // tell MainActivityFragment that dialog is now displayed
44        @Override
45        public void onAttach(Activity activity) {
46            super.onAttach(activity);
47            MainActivityFragment fragment = getDoodleFragment();
48
49            if (fragment != null)
50                fragment.setDialogOnScreen(true);
51        }
52
53        // tell MainActivityFragment that dialog is no longer displayed
54        @Override
55        public void onDetach() {
56            super.onDetach();
57            MainActivityFragment fragment = getDoodleFragment();
58
59            if (fragment != null)
60                fragment.setDialogOnScreen(false);
61        }
62 }
```

Fig. 5.49 | Class EraseImageDialogFragment. (Part 2 of 2.)

5.12 Wrap-Up

In this chapter, you built the **Doodlz** app, which enables users to paint by dragging one or more fingers across the screen. You implemented a shake-to-erase feature by using Android's SensorManager to register a SensorEventListener that responds to accelerometer events, and you learned that Android supports many other sensors.

You created subclasses of DialogFragment for displaying custom Views in AlertDialogs. You also overrode the Fragment lifecycle methods onAttach and onDetach, which are called when a Fragment is attached to or detached from a parent Activity, respectively.

We showed how to associate a Canvas with a Bitmap, then use the Canvas to draw into the Bitmap. We demonstrated how to handle multitouch events, so the app could respond to multiple fingers being dragged across the screen at the same time. You stored the information for each individual finger as a Path. You processed the touch events by overriding the View method onTouchEvent, which receives a MotionEvent containing the event type and the ID of the pointer (finger) that generated the event. We used the IDs to distinguish among the fingers and add information to the corresponding Path objects.

You used a ContentResolver and the MediaStore.Images.Media.insertImage method to save an image onto the device. To enable this feature, you used Android 6.0's new permissions model to request permission from the user to save to external storage.

We showed how to use the printing framework to allow users to print their drawings. You used the Android Support Library's PrintHelper class to print a Bitmap. The PrintHelper displayed a user interface for selecting a printer or saving the image into a PDF document. To incorporate Android Support Library features into the app, you used Gradle to specify the app's dependency on features from that library.

In Chapter 6, you'll create a **Cannon Game** using multithreading and frame-by-frame animation. You'll handle touch gestures to fire a cannon. You'll also learn how to create a game loop that updates the display as fast as possible to create smooth animations and to make the game feel like it executes at the same speed regardless of a given device's processor speed.

Self-Review Exercises

5.1 Fill in the blanks in each of the following statements:

a) You use the SensorManager to register the sensor changes that your app should receive and to specify the _____ that will handle those sensor-change events.

b) A Path object (package android.graphics) represents a geometric path consisting of line segments and _____.

c) You use the type of the touch event to determine whether the user has touched the screen, _____ or lifted a finger from the screen.

d) Use class SensorManager's _____ method to stop listening for accelerometer events.

e) Override SensorEventListener method _____ to process accelerometer events.

f) Override Fragment method _____ to respond to the event when a Fragment is attached to a parent Activity.

g) When a View needs to be redrawn, its _____ method is called.

h) MotionEvent's _____ method returns an int representing the MotionEvent type, which you can use with constants from class MotionEvent to determine how to handle each event.

5.2 State whether each of the following is *true* or *false*. If *false*, explain why.
   a) You unregister the accelerometer event handler when the app is sent to the foreground.
   b) Call the inherited View method validate to indicate that the View needs to be redrawn.
   c) If the action is MotionEvent.ACTION_DOWN or MotionEvent.ACTION_POINTER_DOWN, the user touched the screen with the same finger.
   d) Resetting the Path erases its corresponding painted line from the screen, because those lines have already been drawn to the bitmap that's displayed to the screen.
   e) Method MediaStore.Images.Media.saveImage saves a Bitmap into the **Photos** app.

Answers to Self-Review Exercises

5.1 a) SensorEventListener. b) curves. c) dragged across the screen. d) unregisterListener. e) onSensorChanged. f) onAttach. g) onDraw. h) getActionMasked.

5.2 a) False. You unregister the accelerometer event handler when the app is sent to the *background*. b) False. Call the inherited View method invalidate to indicate that the View needs to be redrawn. c) False. If the action is MotionEvent.ACTION_DOWN or MotionEvent.ACTION_POINTER_DOWN, the user touched the screen with a new finger. d) False. Resetting the Path *does not erase* its corresponding painted line from the screen, because those lines have already been drawn to the bitmap that's displayed to the screen. e) False. The method MediaStore.Images.Media.insertImage saves a Bitmap into the device's **Photos** app.

Exercises

5.3 Fill in the blanks in each of the following statements:
   a) Most Android devices have a(n) _____ that allows apps to detect movement.
   b) Override Fragment method _____ to respond to the event when a Fragment is removed from a parent Activity.
   c) The _____ monitors the accelerometer to detect device movement.
   d) SensorManager's _____ constant represents the acceleration due to gravity on earth.
   e) You register to receive accelerometer events with SensorManager method registerListener, which receives: the SensorEventListener that responds to the events, a Sensor representing the type of sensor data the app wishes to receive and _____.
   f) You pass true to Paint's _____ method to enable anti-aliasing which smooths the edges of the lines.
   g) Paint method _____ sets the stroke width to the specified number of pixels.
   h) Android supports _____—that is, having multiple fingers touching the screen.
   i) The Android Support Library's _____ class provides a GUI for selecting a printer and method _____ for printing a Bitmap.
   j) Android Studio uses the _____ to compile your code into an APK file and to handle project dependencies, such as including in the build process any libraries used by the app.
   k) The attribute android:showAsAction defines how a menu item should appear on the app bar. The value _____ specifies that this item should be visible on the app bar if there's room to display the item.

5.4 State whether each of the following is *true* or *false*. If *false*, explain why.
   a) In Android, sensor events are handled in the GUI thread.

b) The alpha component specifies the `Color`'s transparency with 0 representing completely transparent and 100 representing completely opaque.

c) For accelerometer events, the `SensorEvent` parameter `values` array contains three elements representing the acceleration (in meters/second^2) in the x (left/right), y (up/down) and z (forward/backward) directions.

d) Method `onProgressChanged` is called once when the user drags a `SeekBar`'s thumb.

e) To get the finger's unique ID that persists across `MotionEvents` until the user removes that finger from the screen, you use `MotionEvent`'s `getID` method, passing the finger index as an argument.

f) The system `MotionEvent` passed from `onTouchEvent` contains touch information for multiple moves on the screen if they occur at the same time.

g) Prior to Android 6.0, the user was asked to grant some app permissions at installation time and others at execution time.

h) With the new Android 6.0 permissions model, an app is installed without asking the user for any permissions before installation. The user is asked to grant a permission only the first time the corresponding feature is used.

5.5 *(Enhanced Doodlz App)* Make the following enhancements to the **Doodlz** app:

a) Allow the user to select a background color. The erase capability should use the selected background color. Erasing the entire image should return the background to the default white background.

b) Allow the user to select a background image on which to draw. Clearing the entire image should return the background to the default white background. The erase capability should use the default white background color.

c) Use pressure to determine the line thickness. Class `MotionEvent` has methods that allow you to get the pressure of the touch (http://developer.android.com/reference/android/view/MotionEvent.html).

d) Add the ability to draw rectangles and ovals. Options should include whether the shape is filled or hollow. The user should be able to specify the line thickness for each shape's border and the shape's fill color.

5.6 *(Hangman Game App)* Recreate the classic word game Hangman using the Android robot icon rather than a stick figure. (For the Android logo terms of use, visit www.android.com/branding.html). At the start of the game, display a dashed line with one dash representing each letter in the word. As a hint to the user, provide either a category for the word (e.g., sport or landmark) or the word's definition. Ask the user to enter a letter. If the letter is in the word, place it in the location of the corresponding dash. If the letter is not part of the word, draw part of the Android robot on the screen (e.g., the robot's head). For each incorrect answer, draw another part of the Android robot. The game ends when the user completes the word or the entire Android Robot is drawn to the screen.

5.7 *(Fortune Teller App)* The user "asks a question" then shakes the phone to find a fortune (e.g., "probably not," "looks promising," "ask me again later." etc.

5.8 *(Block Breaker Game)* Display several columns of blocks in red, yellow, blue and green. Each column should have blocks of each color randomly placed. Blocks can be removed from the screen only if they are in groups of two or more. A group consists of blocks of the same color that are vertically and/or horizontally adjacent. When the user taps a group of blocks, the group disappears and the blocks above move down to fill the space. The goal is to clear all of the blocks from the screen. More points should be awarded for larger groups of blocks.

5.9 *(Enhanced Block Breaker Game)* Modify the **Block Breaker** game in Exercise 5.8 as follows:

a) Provide a timer—the user wins by clearing the blocks in the alotted time. Add more blocks to the screen the longer it takes the user to clear the screen.

b) Add multiple levels. In each level, the alotted time for clearing the screen decreases.

    c) Provide a continous mode in which as the user clears blocks, a new row of blocks is added. If the space below a given block is empty, the block should drop into that space. In this mode, the game ends when the user cannot remove any more blocks.

    d) Keep track of the high scores in each game mode.

5.10   *(Word Search App)* Create a grid of letters that fills the screen. Hidden in the grid should be at least ten words. The words may be horizontal, vertical or diagonal, and, in each case, forwards, backwards, up or down. Allow the user to highlight the words by dragging a finger across the letters on the screen or tapping each letter of the word. Include a timer. The less time it takes the user to complete the game, the higher the score. Keep track of the high scores.

5.11   *(Fractal App)* Research how to draw fractals and develop an app that draws them. Provide options that allow the user to control the number of levels of the fractal and its colors.

5.12   *(Kaleidascope App)* Create an app that simulates a kaleidoscope. Allow the user to shake the device to redraw the screen.

5.13   *(Game of Snake App)* Research the Game of Snake online and develop an app that allows a user to play the game.

6

Cannon Game App

Objectives

In this chapter you'll:

- Create a simple game app that's easy to code and fun to play.

- Create a custom `SurfaceView` subclass for displaying the game's graphics from a separate thread of execution.

- Draw graphics using `Paint`s and a `Canvas`.

- Override `View`'s `onTouchEvent` method to fire a cannonball when the user touches the screen.

- Perform simple collision detection.

- Add sound to your app using a `SoundPool` and the `AudioManager`.

- Override `Fragment` lifecycle method `onDestroy`.

- Use immersive mode to enable the game to occupy the entire screen, but still allow the user to access the system bars.

6.1 Introduction

The **Cannon Game**[1] app challenges you to destroy nine targets before a ten-second time limit expires (Fig. 6.1). The game consists of four types of visual components—a *cannon*

---

1. We'd like to thank Prof. Hugues Bersini—author of a French-language object-oriented programming book for Éditions Eyrolles, Secteur Informatique—for sharing with us his suggested refactoring of our original **Cannon Game** app. We used this as inspiration for our own refactoring in the latest versions of this app in this book and *iOS® 8 for Programmers: An App-Driven Approach*.

that you control, a *cannonball*, nine *targets* and a *blocker* that defends the targets. You aim and fire the cannon by *touching* the screen—the cannon then aims at the touched point and fires the cannonball in a straight line in that direction.

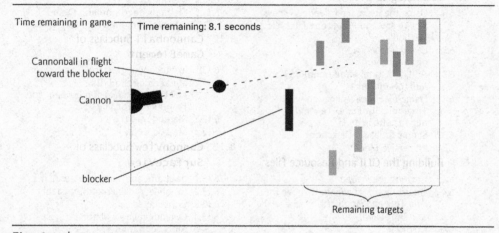

Fig. 6.1 | Completed **Cannon Game** app.

Each time you destroy a target, a three-second time bonus is *added* to your remaining time, and each time you hit the blocker, a two-second time penalty is *subtracted* from your remaining time. You win by destroying all nine target sections before you run out of time—if the timer reaches zero, you lose. At the end of the game, the app displays an AlertDialog indicating whether you won or lost, and shows the number of shots fired and the elapsed time (Fig. 6.2).

a) AlertDialog displayed after user destroys all nine targets

b) AlertDialog displayed when game ends before user destroys all the targets

You win!

Shots fired: 18
Total time: 21.7

RESET GAME

You lose!

Shots fired: 5
Total time: 7.0

RESET GAME

Fig. 6.2 | **Cannon Game** app AlertDialogs showing a win and a loss.

When you fire the cannon, the game plays a *firing sound*. When a cannonball hits a target, a *glass-breaking sound* plays and that target disappears. When the cannonball hits the blocker, a *hit sound* plays and the cannonball bounces back. The blocker cannot be destroyed. Each of the targets and the blocker move *vertically* at different speeds, changing direction when they hit the top or bottom of the screen.

[*Note:* The Android Emulator performs slowly on some computers. For the best experience, you should test this app on an Android device. On a slow emulator, the cannonball will sometimes appear to pass through the blocker or targets.]

6.2 Test-Driving the Cannon Game App

Opening and Running the App

Open Android Studio and open the **Cannon Game** app from the CannonGame folder in the book's examples folder, then execute the app in the AVD or on a device. This builds the project and runs the app.

Playing the Game

Tap the screen to aim and fire the cannon. You can fire a cannonball only if there is not another cannonball on the screen. If you're running on an AVD, the mouse is your "finger." Destroy all of the targets as fast as you can—the game ends if the timer runs out or you destroy all nine targets.

6.3 Technologies Overview

This section presents the new technologies that we use in the **Cannon Game** app in the order they're encountered in the chapter.

6.3.1 Using the Resource Folder res/raw

Media files, such as the sounds used in the **Cannon Game** app, are placed in the app's resource folder **res/raw**. Section 6.4.5 discusses how to create this folder. You'll copy the app's sound files into it.

6.3.2 Activity and Fragment Lifecycle Methods

We introduced Activity and Fragment lifecycle methods in Section 5.3.1. This app uses Fragment lifecycle method onDestroy. When an Activity is shut down, its **onDestroy** method is called, which in turn calls the **onDestroy** methods of all the Fragments hosted by the Activity. We use this method in the MainActivityFragment to release the CannonView's sound resources.

Error-Prevention Tip 6.1

Method onDestroy *is not guaranteed to be called, so it should be used only to release resources, not to save data. The Android documentation recommends that you save data in methods* onPause *or* onSaveInstanceState.

6.3.3 Overriding View Method onTouchEvent

Users interact with this app by touching the device's screen. A touch aligns the cannon to face the touch point on the screen, then fires the cannon. To process simple touch events for the CannonView, you'll override View method **onTouchEvent** (Section 6.13.14), then use constants from class MotionEvent (package android.view) to test which type of event occurred and process it accordingly.

6.3.4 Adding Sound with SoundPool and AudioManager

An app's sound effects are managed with a **SoundPool** (package android.media), which can be used to *load*, *play* and *unload* sounds. Sounds are played using one of Android's audio streams for *alarms*, *music*, *notifications*, *phone rings*, *system sounds*, *phone calls* and more. You'll configure and create a SoundPool object using a **SoundPool.Builder** object. You'll also use an AudioAttributes.Builder object to create an **AudioAttributes** object that will be associated with the SoundPool. We call the AudioAttributes's **setUsage** method to designate the audio as game audio. The Android documentation recommends that games use the *music audio stream* to play sounds, because that stream's volume can be controlled via the device's volume buttons. In addition, we use the Activity's **setVolumeControlStream** method to allow the game's volume to be controlled with the device's volume buttons. The method receives a constant from class **AudioManager** (package android.media), which provides access to the device's volume and phone-ringer controls.

6.3.5 Frame-by-Frame Animation with Threads, SurfaceView and SurfaceHolder

This app *performs its animations manually* by updating the game elements from a separate thread of execution. To do this, we use a subclass of Thread with a run method that directs our custom CannonView to update the positions of the game's elements, then draws them. The run method drives the *frame-by-frame animations*—this is known as the **game loop**.

All updates to an app's user interface must be performed in the GUI thread of execution, because GUI components are not thread safe—updates performed outside the GUI thread can corrupt the GUI. Games, however, often require complex logic that should be performed in separate threads of execution, and those threads often need to draw to the screen. For such cases, Android provides class **SurfaceView**—a subclass of View that provides a dedicated drawing area in which other threads can display graphics on the screen in a thread-safe manner.

Performance Tip 6.1

It's important to minimize the amount of work you do in the GUI thread to ensure that the GUI remains responsive and does not display ANR (Application Not Responding) dialogs.

You manipulate a SurfaceView via an object of class **SurfaceHolder**, which enables you to obtain a Canvas on which you can draw graphics. Class SurfaceHolder also provides methods that give a thread *exclusive access* to the Canvas for drawing—only one thread at a time can draw to a SurfaceView. Each SurfaceView subclass should implement the interface **SurfaceHolder.Callback**, which contains methods that are called when the SurfaceView is *created*, *changed* (e.g., its size or orientation changes) or *destroyed*.

6.3.6 Simple Collision Detection

The CannonView performs simple *collision detection* to determine whether the cannonball has collided with any of the CannonView's edges, with the blocker or with a section of the target. These techniques are presented in Section 6.13.11.

Game-development frameworks typically provide more sophisticated "pixel-perfect" collision-detection capabilities. Many such frameworks are available (free and fee-based) for developing the simplest 2D games to the most complex 3D console-style games (such as games for Sony's PlayStation® and Microsoft's Xbox®). Figure 6.3 lists a few game-development frameworks—there are dozens more. Many support multiple platforms, including Android and iOS. Some require C++ or other programming languages.

Game-development frameworks
AndEngine—`http://www.andengine.org`
Cocos2D—`http://code.google.com/p/cocos2d-android`
GameMaker—`http://www.yoyogames.com/studio`
libgdx—`https://libgdx.badlogicgames.com`
Unity—`http://www.unity3d.com`
Unreal Engine—`http://www.unrealengine.com`

Fig. 6.3 | Game-development frameworks.

6.3.7 Immersive Mode

To immerse users in games, game developers often use full-screen themes, such as

```
Theme.Material.Light.NoActionBar.Fullscreen
```

that display only the bottom system bar. In landscape orientation on phones, that system bar appears at the screen's right edge.

In Android 4.4 (KitKat), Google added support for full-screen *immersive mode* (Section 6.13.16), which enables an app to take advantage of the entire screen. When an app is in immersive mode, the user can swipe down from the top of the screen to display the system bars temporarily. If the user does not interact with the system bars, they disappear after a few seconds.

6.4 Building the GUI and Resource Files

In this section, you'll create the app's resource files, GUI layout files and classes.

6.4.1 Creating the Project

For this app, you'll add a Fragment and its layout manually—much of the autogenerated code in the **Blank Activity** template with a Fragment is not needed in the **Cannon Game**. Create a new project using the **Empty Activity** template. In the **Create New Project** dialog's **New Project** step, specify

- **Application name:** Cannon Game
- **Company Domain:** `deitel.com` (or specify your own domain name)

In the layout editor, select **Nexus 6** from the virtual-device drop-down list (Fig. 2.11). Once again, we'll use this device as the basis for our design. Also, delete the **Hello world!** TextView from `activity_main.xml`. As you've done previously, add an app icon to your project.

Configure the App for Landscape Orientation

The **Cannon** game is designed for only landscape orientation. Follow the steps you performed in Section 3.7 to set the screen orientation, but this time set `android:screenOrientation` to `landscape` rather than `portrait`.

6.4.2 Adjusting the Theme to Remove the App Title and App Bar

As we noted in Section 6.3.7, game developers often use full-screen themes, such as

```
Theme.Material.Light.NoActionBar.Fullscreen
```

that display only the bottom system bar, which in landscape orientation appears at the screen's right edge. The AppCompat themes do not include a full-screen theme by default, but you can modify the app's theme to achieve this. To do so:

1. Open styles.xml.

2. Add the following lines to the <style> element:

```
<item name="windowNoTitle">true</item>
<item name="windowActionBar">false</item>
<item name="android:windowFullscreen">true</item>
```

The first line indicates that the title (usually the app's name) should not be displayed. The second indicates that the app bar should not be displayed. The last line indicates that the app should use the full screen.

6.4.3 strings.xml

You created String resources in earlier chapters, so we show here only a table of the String resource names and corresponding values (Fig. 6.4). Double click strings.xml in the res/values folder, then click the **Open editor** link to display the **Translations Editor** for creating these String resources.

Key	Value
results_format	Shots fired: %1$d\nTotal time: %2$.1f
reset_game	Reset Game
win	You win!
lose	You lose!
time_remaining_format	Time remaining: %.1f seconds

Fig. 6.4 | String resources used in the **Cannon Game** app.

6.4.4 Colors

This app draws targets of alternating colors on the Canvas. For this app, we added the following dark blue and yellow color resources to colors.xml:

```
<color name="dark">#1976D2</color>
<color name="light">#FFE100</color>
```

6.4.5 Adding the Sounds to the App

As we mentioned previously, sound files are stored in the app's res/raw folder. This app uses three sound files—blocker_hit.wav, target_hit.wav and cannon_fire.wav—which are located with the book's examples in the sounds folder. To add these files to your project:

1. Right click the app's `res` folder, then select **New > Android resource directory**, to open the **New Resource Directory** dialog

2. In the **Resource type** drop-down, select raw. The **Directory name** will automatically change to raw.

3. Click **OK** to create the folder.

4. Copy and paste the sound files into the res/raw folder. In the **Copy** dialog that appears, click **OK**.

6.4.6 Adding Class `MainActivityFragment`

Next, you'll add class `MainActivityFragment` to the project:

1. In the **Project** window, right click the **com.deitel.cannongame** node and select **New > Fragment > Fragment (Blank)**.

2. For **Fragment Name** specify `MainActivityFragment` and for **Fragment Layout Name** specify `fragment_main`.

3. Uncheck the checkboxes for **Include fragment factory methods?** and **Include interface callbacks?**

By default, `fragment_main.xml` contains a `FrameLayout` that displays a `TextView`. A **FrameLayout** is designed to display one `View`, but can also be used to layer views. Remove the `TextView`—in this app, the `FrameLayout` will display the `CannonView`.

6.4.7 Editing `activity_main.xml`

In this app, `MainActivity`'s layout displays only `MainActivityFragment`. Edit the layout as follows:

1. Open `activity_main.xml` in the layout editor and switch to the **Text** tab.

2. Change `RelativeLayout` to `fragment` and remove the padding properties so that the `fragment` element will fill the entire screen.

3. Switch to **Design** view, select **fragment** in the **Component Tree**, then set the **id** to fragment.

4. Set the **name** to com.deitel.cannongame.MainActivityFragment—rather than typing this, you can click the ellipsis button to the right of the **name** property's value field, then select the class from the **Fragments** dialog that appears.

Recall that the layout editor's **Design** view can show a preview of a fragment displayed in a particular layout. If you do not specify which fragment to preview in `MainActivity`'s layout, the layout editor displays a **"Rendering Problems"** message. To specify the fragment to preview, right click the fragment—either in **Design** view or in the **Component Tree** and click **Choose Preview Layout....** Then, in the **Resources** dialog, select the name of the fragment layout.

6.4.8 Adding the `CannonView` to `fragment_main.xml`

You'll now add the `CannonView` to `fragment_main.xml`. You first must create `CannonView.java`, so that you can select class `CannonView` when placing a **CustomView** in the layout. Follow these steps to create `CannonView.java` and add the `CannonView` to the layout:

1. Expand the java folder in the Project window.

2. Right click package com.deitel.cannongame's folder, then select **New > Java Class**.

3. In the **Create New Class** dialog that appears, enter CannonView in the **Name** field, then click **OK**. The file will open in the editor automatically.

4. In CannonView.java, indicate that CannonView extends SurfaceView. If the import statement for the android.view.SurfaceView class does not appear, place the cursor at the end of the class name SurfaceView. Click the red bulb menu (💡) that appears above the beginning of the line and select **Import Class**.

5. Place the cursor at the end of SurfaceView if you have not already done so. Click the red bulb menu that appears and select **Create constructor matching super**. Choose the two-argument constructor in the list in the **Choose Super Class Constructors** dialog that appears, then click **OK**. The IDE will add the constructor to the file automatically.

6. Switch back to fragment_main.xml's **Design** view in the layout editor.

7. Click **CustomView** in the **Custom** section of the **Palette**.

8. In the **Views** dialog that appears, select CannonView (com.deitel.cannongame), then click **OK**.

9. Hover over and click the FrameLayout in the **Component Tree**. The view (**Custom-View**)—which is a CannonView—should appear in the **Component Tree** within the FrameLayout.

10. Ensure that **view (CustomView)** is selected in the **Component Tree** window. In the **Properties** window, set **layout:width** and **layout:height** to match_parent.

11. In the **Properties** window, change the id from view to cannonView.

12. Save and close fragment_main.xml.

6.5 Overview of This App's Classes

This app consists of eight classes:

- MainActivity (the Activity subclass; Section 6.6)—Hosts the MainActivityFragment.
- MainActivityFragment (Section 6.7)—Displays the CannonView.
- GameElement (Section 6.8)—The superclass for items that move up and down (Blocker and Target) or across (Cannonball) the screen.
- Blocker (Section 6.9)—Represents a blocker, which makes destroying targets more challenging.
- Target (Section 6.10)—Represents a target that can be destroyed by a cannonball.
- Cannon (Section 6.11)—Represents the cannon, which fires a cannonball each time the user touches the screen.
- Cannonball (Section 6.12)—Represents a cannonball that the cannon fires when the user touches the screen.

- CannonView (Section 6.13)—Contains the game's logic and coordinates the behaviors of the Blocker, Targets, Cannonball and Cannon.

You must create the classes GameElement, Blocker, Target, Cannonball and Cannon. For each class, right click the package folder com.deitel.cannongame in the project's app/ java folder and select **New > Java Class**. In the **Create New Class** dialog, enter the name of the class in the **Name** field and click **OK**.

6.6 MainActivity Subclass of Activity

Class MainActivity (Fig. 6.5) is the host for the **Cannon Game** app's MainActivityFragment. In this app, we override only the Activity method onCreate, which inflates the GUI. We deleted the autogenerated MainActivity methods that managed its menu, because the menu is not used in this app.

```
1   // MainActivity.java
2   // MainActivity displays the MainActivityFragment
3   package com.deitel.cannongame;
4
5   import android.support.v7.app.AppCompatActivity;
6   import android.os.Bundle;
7
8   public class MainActivity extends AppCompatActivity {
9      // called when the app first launches
10     @Override
11     protected void onCreate(Bundle savedInstanceState) {
12        super.onCreate(savedInstanceState);
13        setContentView(R.layout.activity_main);
14     }
15  }
```

Fig. 6.5 | MainActivity class displays the MainActivityFragment.

6.7 MainActivityFragment Subclass of Fragment

Class MainActivityFragment (Fig. 6.6) overrides four Fragment methods:

- onCreateView (lines 17–28)—As you learned in Section 4.3.3, this method is called after a Fragment's onCreate method to build and return a View containing the Fragment's GUI. Lines 22–23 inflate the GUI. Line 26 gets a reference to the MainActivityFragment's CannonView so that we can call its methods.

- onActivityCreated (lines 31–37)—This method is called after the Fragment's host Activity is created. Line 36 calls the Activity's setVolumeControlStream method to allow the game's volume to be controlled by the device's volume buttons. There are seven sound streams identified by AudioManager constants, but the music stream (AudioManager.STREAM_MUSIC) is recommended for sound in games, because this stream's volume can be controlled via the device's buttons.

- onPause (lines 40–44)—When the MainActivity is sent to the *background* (and thus, paused), MainActivityFragment's onPause method executes. Line 43 calls the CannonView's stopGame method (Section 6.13.12) to stop the game loop.

- onDestroy (lines 47–51)—When the MainActivity is destroyed, its onDestroy method calls MainActivityFragment's onDestroy. Line 50 calls the CannonView's releaseResources method to release the sound resources (Section 6.13.12).

```
 1   // MainActivityFragment.java
 2   // MainActivityFragment creates and manages a CannonView
 3   package com.deitel.cannongame;
 4
 5   import android.media.AudioManager;
 6   import android.os.Bundle;
 7   import android.support.v4.app.Fragment;
 8   import android.view.LayoutInflater;
 9   import android.view.View;
10   import android.view.ViewGroup;
11
12   public class MainActivityFragment extends Fragment {
13      private CannonView cannonView; // custom view to display the game
14
15      // called when Fragment's view needs to be created
16      @Override
17      public View onCreateView(LayoutInflater inflater, ViewGroup container,
18         Bundle savedInstanceState) {
19         super.onCreateView(inflater, container, savedInstanceState);
20
21         // inflate the fragment_main.xml layout
22         View view =
23            inflater.inflate(R.layout.fragment_main, container, false);
24
25         // get a reference to the CannonView
26         cannonView = (CannonView) view.findViewById(R.id.cannonView);
27         return view;
28      }
29
30      // set up volume control once Activity is created
31      @Override
32      public void onActivityCreated(Bundle savedInstanceState) {
33         super.onActivityCreated(savedInstanceState);
34
35         // allow volume buttons to set game volume
36         getActivity().setVolumeControlStream(AudioManager.STREAM_MUSIC);
37      }
38
39      // when MainActivity is paused, terminate the game
40      @Override
41      public void onPause() {
42         super.onPause();
43         cannonView.stopGame(); // terminates the game
44      }
45
46      // when MainActivity is paused, MainActivityFragment releases resources
47      @Override
48      public void onDestroy() {
```

Fig. 6.6 | MainActivityFragment creates and manages the CannonView. (Part I of 2.)

```
49          super.onDestroy();
50          cannonView.releaseResources();
51       }
52   }
```

Fig. 6.6 | MainActivityFragment creates and manages the CannonView. (Part 2 of 2.)

6.8 Class GameElement

Class GameElement (Fig. 6.7)—the superclass of the Blocker, Target and Cannonball—contains the common data and functionality of an object that moves in the **Cannon Game** app.

```
1    // GameElement.java
2    // Represents a rectangle-bounded game element
3    package com.deitel.cannongame;
4
5    import android.graphics.Canvas;
6    import android.graphics.Paint;
7    import android.graphics.Rect;
8
9    public class GameElement {
10       protected CannonView view; // the view that contains this GameElement
11       protected Paint paint = new Paint(); // Paint to draw this GameElement
12       protected Rect shape; // the GameElement's rectangular bounds
13       private float velocityY; // the vertical velocity of this GameElement
14       private int soundId; // the sound associated with this GameElement
15
16       // public constructor
17       public GameElement(CannonView view, int color, int soundId, int x,
18          int y, int width, int length, float velocityY) {
19          this.view = view;
20          paint.setColor(color);
21          shape = new Rect(x, y, x + width, y + length); // set bounds
22          this.soundId = soundId;
23          this.velocityY = velocityY;
24       }
25
26       // update GameElement position and check for wall collisions
27       public void update(double interval) {
28          // update vertical position
29          shape.offset(0, (int) (velocityY * interval));
30
31          // if this GameElement collides with the wall, reverse direction
32          if (shape.top < 0 && velocityY < 0 ||
33             shape.bottom > view.getScreenHeight() && velocityY > 0)
34             velocityY *= -1; // reverse this GameElement's velocity
35       }
36
```

Fig. 6.7 | GameElement class represents a rectangle-bounded game element. (Part 1 of 2.)

```
37    // draws this GameElement on the given Canvas
38    public void draw(Canvas canvas) {
39       canvas.drawRect(shape, paint);
40    }
41
42    // plays the sound that corresponds to this type of GameElement
43    public void playSound() {
44       view.playSound(soundId);
45    }
46 }
```

Fig. 6.7 | GameElement class represents a rectangle-bounded game element. (Part 2 of 2.)

6.8.1 Instance Variables and Constructor

The GameElement constructor receives a reference to the CannonView (Section 6.13), which implements the game's logic and draws the game elements. The constructor receives an int representing the GameElement's 32-bit color, and an int representing the ID of a sound that's associated with this GameElement. The CannonView stores all of the sounds in the game and provides an ID for each. The constructor also receives

- ints for the x and y position of the GameElement's upper-left corner
- ints for its width and height, and
- an initial vertical velocity, velocityY, of this GameElement.

Line 20 sets the paint object's color, using the int representation of the color passed to the constructor. Line 21 calculates the GameElement's bounds and stores them in a Rect object that represents a rectangle.

6.8.2 Methods update, draw, and playSound

A GameElement has the following methods:

- update (lines 27–35)—In each iteration of the game loop, this method is called to update the GameElement's position. Line 29 updates the vertical position of shape, based on the vertical velocity (velocityY) and the elapsed time between calls to update, which the method receives as the parameter interval. Lines 32–34 check whether this GameElement is colliding with the top or bottom edge of the screen and, if so, reverse its vertical velocity.

- draw (lines 38–40)—This method is called when a GameElement needs to be redrawn on the screen. The method receives a Canvas and draws this GameElement as a rectangle on the screen—we'll override this method in class Cannonball to draw a circle instead. The GameElement's paint instance variable specifies the rectangle's color, and the GameElement's shape specifies the rectangle's bounds on the screen.

- playSound (lines 43–45)—Every game element has an associated sound that can be played by calling method playSound. This method passes the value of the soundId instance variable to the CannonView's playSound method. Class CannonView loads and maintains references to the game's sounds.

6.9 Blocker Subclass of GameElement

Class Blocker (Fig. 6.8)—a subclass of GameElement—represents the blocker, which makes it more difficult for the player to destroy targets. Class Blocker's missPenalty is subtracted from the remaining game time if the Cannonball collides with the Blocker. The getMissPenalty method (lines 17–19) returns the missPenalty—this method is called from CannonView's testForCollisions method when subtracting the missPenalty from the remaining time (Section 6.13.11). The Blocker constructor (lines 9–14) passes its arguments and the ID for the blocker-hit sound (CannonView.BLOCKER_SOUND_ID) to the superclass constructor (line 11), then initializes missPenalty.

```
1   // Blocker.java
2   // Subclass of GameElement customized for the Blocker
3   package com.deitel.cannongame;
4
5   public class Blocker extends GameElement {
6      private int missPenalty; // the miss penalty for this Blocker
7
8      // constructor
9      public Blocker(CannonView view, int color, int missPenalty, int x,
10        int y, int width, int length, float velocityY) {
11        super(view, color, CannonView.BLOCKER_SOUND_ID, x, y, width, length,
12           velocityY);
13        this.missPenalty = missPenalty;
14     }
15
16     // returns the miss penalty for this Blocker
17     public int getMissPenalty() {
18        return missPenalty;
19     }
20  }
```

Fig. 6.8 | Blocker subclass of GameElement.

6.10 Target Subclass of GameElement

Class Target (Fig. 6.9)—a subclass of GameElement—represents a target that the player can destroy. Class Target's hitPenalty is added to the remaining game time if the Cannonball collides with a Target. The getHitReward method (lines 17–19) returns the hitReward—this method is called from CannonView's testForCollisions method when adding the hitReward to the remaining time (Section 6.13.11). The Target constructor (lines 9–14) passes its arguments and the ID for the target-hit sound (CannonView.TARGET_SOUND_ID) to the super constructor (line 11), then initializes hitReward.

```
1   // Target.java
2   // Subclass of GameElement customized for the Target
3   package com.deitel.cannongame;
4
```

Fig. 6.9 | Target subclass of GameElement. (Part 1 of 2.)

```
 5   public class Target extends GameElement {
 6      private int hitReward; // the hit reward for this target
 7
 8      // constructor
 9      public Target(CannonView view, int color, int hitReward, int x, int y,
10         int width, int length, float velocityY) {
11         super(view, color, CannonView.TARGET_SOUND_ID, x, y, width, length,
12            velocityY);
13         this.hitReward = hitReward;
14      }
15
16      // returns the hit reward for this Target
17      public int getHitReward() {
18         return hitReward;
19      }
20   }
```

Fig. 6.9 | Target subclass of GameElement. (Part 2 of 2.)

6.11 Cannon Class

The Cannon class (Figs. 6.10–6.14) represents the cannon in the **Cannon Game** app. The cannon has a base and a barrel, and it can fire a cannonball.

6.11.1 Instance Variables and Constructor

The Cannon constructor (Fig. 6.10) has four parameters. It receives

- the CannonView that this Cannon is in (view),
- the radius of the Cannon's base (baseRadius),
- the length of the Cannon's barrel (barrelLength) and
- the width of the Cannon's barrel (barrelWidth).

Line 25 sets the width of the Paint object's stroke so that the barrel will be drawn with the given barrelWidth. Line 27 aligns the Cannon's barrel to be initially parallel with the top and bottom edges of the screen. The Cannon class has a Point barrelEnd that's used to draw the barrel, barrelAngle to store the current angle of the barrel, and cannonball to store the Cannonball that was most recently fired if it's still on the screen.

```
 1   // Cannon.java
 2   // Represents Cannon and fires the Cannonball
 3   package com.deitel.cannongame;
 4
 5   import android.graphics.Canvas;
 6   import android.graphics.Color;
 7   import android.graphics.Paint;
 8   import android.graphics.Point;
 9
```

Fig. 6.10 | Cannon instance variables and constructor. (Part 1 of 2.)

```
10   public class Cannon {
11      private int baseRadius; // Cannon base's radius
12      private int barrelLength; // Cannon barrel's length
13      private Point barrelEnd = new Point(); // endpoint of Cannon's barrel
14      private double barrelAngle; // angle of the Cannon's barrel
15      private Cannonball cannonball; // the Cannon's Cannonball
16      private Paint paint = new Paint(); // Paint used to draw the cannon
17      private CannonView view; // view containing the Cannon
18
19      // constructor
20      public Cannon(CannonView view, int baseRadius, int barrelLength,
21         int barrelWidth) {
22         this.view = view;
23         this.baseRadius = baseRadius;
24         this.barrelLength = barrelLength;
25         paint.setStrokeWidth(barrelWidth); // set width of barrel
26         paint.setColor(Color.BLACK); // Cannon's color is Black
27         align(Math.PI / 2); // Cannon barrel facing straight right
28      }
29
```

Fig. 6.10 | Cannon instance variables and constructor. (Part 2 of 2.)

6.11.2 Method align

Method align (Fig. 6.11) aims the cannon. The method receives as an argument the barrel angle in radians. We use the cannonLength and the barrelAngle to determine the *x*- and *y*-coordinate values for the endpoint of the cannon's barrel, barrelEnd—this is used to draw a line from the cannon base's center at the left edge of the screen to the cannon's barrel endpoint. Line 32 stores the barrelAngle so that the ball can be fired at angle later.

```
30      // aligns the Cannon's barrel to the given angle
31      public void align(double barrelAngle) {
32         this.barrelAngle = barrelAngle;
33         barrelEnd.x = (int) (barrelLength * Math.sin(barrelAngle));
34         barrelEnd.y = (int) (-barrelLength * Math.cos(barrelAngle)) +
35            view.getScreenHeight() / 2;
36      }
37
```

Fig. 6.11 | Cannon method align.

6.11.3 Method fireCannonball

The fireCannonball method (Fig. 6.12) fires a Cannonball across the screen at the Cannon's current trajectory (barrelAngle). Lines 41–46 calculate the horizontal and vertical components of the Cannonball's velocity. Lines 49–50 calculate the radius of the Cannonball, which is CannonView.CANNONBALL_RADIUS_PERCENT of the screen height. Lines 53–56 "load the cannon" (that is, construct a new Cannonball and position it inside the Cannon). Finally, we play the Cannonball's firing sound (line 58).

```
38    // creates and fires Cannonball in the direction Cannon points
39    public void fireCannonball() {
40       // calculate the Cannonball velocity's x component
41       int velocityX = (int) (CannonView.CANNONBALL_SPEED_PERCENT *
42          view.getScreenWidth() * Math.sin(barrelAngle));
43
44       // calculate the Cannonball velocity's y component
45       int velocityY = (int) (CannonView.CANNONBALL_SPEED_PERCENT *
46          view.getScreenWidth() * -Math.cos(barrelAngle));
47
48       // calculate the Cannonball's radius
49       int radius = (int) (view.getScreenHeight() *
50          CannonView.CANNONBALL_RADIUS_PERCENT);
51
52       // construct Cannonball and position it in the Cannon
53       cannonball = new Cannonball(view, Color.BLACK,
54          CannonView.CANNON_SOUND_ID, -radius,
55          view.getScreenHeight() / 2 - radius, radius, velocityX,
56          velocityY);
57
58       cannonball.playSound(); // play fire Cannonball sound
59    }
60
```

Fig. 6.12 | Cannon method `fireCannonball`.

6.11.4 Method draw

The draw method (Fig. 6.13) draws the Cannon on the screen. We draw the Cannon in two parts. First we draw the Cannon's barrel, then the Cannon's base.

```
61    // draws the Cannon on the Canvas
62    public void draw(Canvas canvas) {
63       // draw cannon barrel
64       canvas.drawLine(0, view.getScreenHeight() / 2, barrelEnd.x,
65          barrelEnd.y, paint);
66
67       // draw cannon base
68       canvas.drawCircle(0, (int) view.getScreenHeight() / 2,
69          (int) baseRadius, paint);
70    }
71
```

Fig. 6.13 | Cannon method draw.

Drawing the Cannon Barrel with Canvas Method drawLine

We use Canvas's **drawLine method** to display the Cannon barrel (lines 64–65). This method receives five parameters—the first four represent the *x-y* coordinates of the line's start and end, and the last is the Paint object specifying the line's characteristics, such as its thickness. Recall that paint was configured to draw the barrel with the thickness given in the constructor (Fig. 6.10, line 25).

Drawing the Cannon Base with **Canvas** *Method* **drawCircle**

Lines 68–69 use Canvas's drawCircle method to draw the Cannon's half-circle base by drawing a circle that's centered at the left edge of the screen. Because a circle is displayed based on its center point, half of this circle is drawn off the left side of the SurfaceView.

6.11.5 Methods getCannonball and removeCannonball

Figure 6.14 shows the getCannonball and removeCannonball methods. The getCannonball method (lines 73–75) returns the current Cannonball instance, which Cannon stores. A cannonball value of null means that currently no Cannonball exists in the game. The CannonView uses this method to avoid firing a Cannonball if another Cannonball is already on the screen (Section 6.13.8, Fig. 6.26). The removeCannonball method (lines 78–80 of Fig. 6.14) removes the CannnonBall from the game by setting cannonball to null. The CannonView uses this method to remove the Cannonball from the game when it destroys a Target or after it leaves the screen (Section 6.13.11, Fig. 6.29).

```
72      // returns the Cannonball that this Cannon fired
73      public Cannonball getCannonball() {
74          return cannonball;
75      }
76
77      // removes the Cannonball from the game
78      public void removeCannonball() {
79          cannonball = null;
80      }
81  }
```

Fig. 6.14 | CannonView methods getCannonball and removeCannonball.

6.12 Cannonball Subclass of GameElement

The Cannonball subclass of GameElement (Sections 6.12.1—6.12.4) represents a cannonball fired from the cannon.

6.12.1 Instance Variables and Constructor

The Cannonball constructor (Fig. 6.15) receives the cannonball's radius rather than width and height in the GameElement constructor. Lines 15–16 call super with width and height values calculated from the radius. The constructor also receives the horizontal velocity of the Cannonball, velocityX, in addition to its vertical velocity, velocityY. Line 18 initializes onScreen to true because the Cannonball is initially on the screen.

```
1   // Cannonball.java
2   // Represents the Cannonball that the Cannon fires
3   package com.deitel.cannongame;
4
5   import android.graphics.Canvas;
6   import android.graphics.Rect;
```

Fig. 6.15 | Cannonball instance variables and constructor. (Part 1 of 2.)

```
7
8    public class Cannonball extends GameElement {
9       private float velocityX;
10      private boolean onScreen;
11
12      // constructor
13      public Cannonball(CannonView view, int color, int soundId, int x,
14         int y, int radius, float velocityX, float velocityY) {
15         super(view, color, soundId, x, y,
16            2 * radius, 2 * radius, velocityY);
17         this.velocityX = velocityX;
18         onScreen = true;
19      }
20
```

Fig. 6.15 | Cannonball instance variables and constructor. (Part 2 of 2.)

6.12.2 Methods getRadius, collidesWith, isOnScreen, and reverseVelocityX

Method getRadius (Fig. 6.16, lines 22–24) returns the Cannonball's radius by finding half the distance between the shape.right and shape.left bounds of the Cannonball's shape. Method isOnScreen (lines 32–34) returns true if the Cannonball is on the screen.

```
21      // get Cannonball's radius
22      private int getRadius() {
23         return (shape.right - shape.left) / 2;
24      }
25
26      // test whether Cannonball collides with the given GameElement
27      public boolean collidesWith(GameElement element) {
28         return (Rect.intersects(shape, element.shape) && velocityX > 0);
29      }
30
31      // returns true if this Cannonball is on the screen
32      public boolean isOnScreen() {
33         return onScreen;
34      }
35
36      // reverses the Cannonball's horizontal velocity
37      public void reverseVelocityX() {
38         velocityX *= -1;
39      }
40
```

Fig. 6.16 | Cannonball methods getRadius, collidesWith, isOnScreen and reverseVelocityX.

Checking for Collisions with Another GameElement with the collidesWith Method
The collidesWith method (line 27–29) checks whether the cannonball has *collided* with the given GameElement. We perform simple *collision detection*, based on the rectangular

boundary of the Cannonball. Two conditions must be met if the Cannonball is colliding with the GameElement:

- The Cannonball's bounds, which are stored in the shape Rect, must intersect the bounds of the given GameElement's shape. Rect's intersects method is used to check if the bounds of the Cannonball and the given GameElement intersect.
- The Cannonball must be moving horizontally towards the given GameElement. The Cannonball travels from left to right (unless it hits the blocker). If velocityX (the horizontal velocity) is positive, the Cannonball is moving left-to-right toward the given GameElement.

Reversing the Cannonball's Horizontal Velocity with reverseVelocityX

The reverseVelocityX method reverses the horizontal velocity of the Cannonball by multiplying velocityX by -1. If the collidesWith method returns true, CannonView method testForCollisions calls reverseVelocityX to reverse the ball's horizontal velocity, so the cannonball bounces back toward the cannon (Section 6.13.11).

6.12.3 Method update

The update method (Fig. 6.17) first calls the superclass's update method (line 44) to update the Cannonball's vertical velocity and to check for vertical collisions. Line 47 uses Rect's **offset method** to horizontally translate the bounds of this Cannonball. We multiply its horizontal velocity (velocityX) by the amount of time that passed (interval) to determine the translation amount. Lines 50–53 set onScreen to false if the Cannonball hits one of the screen's edges.

```
41    // updates the Cannonball's position
42    @Override
43    public void update(double interval) {
44        super.update(interval); // updates Cannonball's vertical position
45
46        // update horizontal position
47        shape.offset((int) (velocityX * interval), 0);
48
49        // if Cannonball goes off the screen
50        if (shape.top < 0 || shape.left < 0 ||
51            shape.bottom > view.getScreenHeight() ||
52            shape.right > view.getScreenWidth())
53            onScreen = false; // set it to be removed
54    }
55
```

Fig. 6.17 | Overridden GameElement method update.

6.12.4 Method draw

The draw method (Fig. 6.18) overrides GameElement's draw method and uses Canvas's **drawCircle method** to draw the Cannonball in its current position. The first two arguments represent the coordinates of the circle's *center*. The third argument is the circle's *radius*. The last argument is the Paint object specifying the circle's drawing characteristics.

```
56      // draws the Cannonball on the given canvas
57      @Override
58      public void draw(Canvas canvas) {
59          canvas.drawCircle(shape.left + getRadius(),
60              shape.top + getRadius(), getRadius(), paint);
61      }
62   }
```

Fig. 6.18 | Overridden GameElement method draw.

6.13 CannonView Subclass of SurfaceView

Class CannonView (Figs. 6.19–6.33) is a custom subclass of View that implements the **Cannon Game**'s logic and draws game objects on the screen.

6.13.1 package and import Statements

Figure 6.19 lists the package statement and the import statements for class CannonView. Section 6.3 discussed the key new classes and interfaces that class CannonView uses. We've highlighted them in Fig. 6.19.

```
1    // CannonView.java
2    // Displays and controls the Cannon Game
3    package com.deitel.cannongame;
4
5    import android.app.Activity;
6    import android.app.AlertDialog;
7    import android.app.Dialog;
8    import android.app.DialogFragment;
9    import android.content.Context;
10   import android.content.DialogInterface;
11   import android.graphics.Canvas;
12   import android.graphics.Color;
13   import android.graphics.Paint;
14   import android.graphics.Point;
15   import android.media.AudioAttributes;
16   import android.media.SoundPool;
17   import android.os.Build;
18   import android.os.Bundle;
19   import android.util.AttributeSet;
20   import android.util.Log;
21   import android.util.SparseIntArray;
22   import android.view.MotionEvent;
23   import android.view.SurfaceHolder;
24   import android.view.SurfaceView;
25   import android.view.View;
26
27   import java.util.ArrayList;
28   import java.util.Random;
29
```

Fig. 6.19 | CannonView class's package and import statements. (Part 1 of 2.)

```
30    public class CannonView extends SurfaceView
31       implements SurfaceHolder.Callback {
32
```

Fig. 6.19 | CannonView class's package and import statements. (Part 2 of 2.)

6.13.2 Instance Variables and Constants

Figure 6.20 lists the large number of class CannonView's constants and instance variables. We'll explain each as we encounter it in the discussion. Many of the constants are used in calculations that scale the game elements' sizes based on the screen's dimensions.

```
33       private static final String TAG = "CannonView"; // for logging errors
34
35       // constants for game play
36       public static final int MISS_PENALTY = 2; // seconds deducted on a miss
37       public static final int HIT_REWARD = 3; // seconds added on a hit
38
39       // constants for the Cannon
40       public static final double CANNON_BASE_RADIUS_PERCENT = 3.0 / 40;
41       public static final double CANNON_BARREL_WIDTH_PERCENT = 3.0 / 40;
42       public static final double CANNON_BARREL_LENGTH_PERCENT = 1.0 / 10;
43
44       // constants for the Cannonball
45       public static final double CANNONBALL_RADIUS_PERCENT = 3.0 / 80;
46       public static final double CANNONBALL_SPEED_PERCENT = 3.0 / 2;
47
48       // constants for the Targets
49       public static final double TARGET_WIDTH_PERCENT = 1.0 / 40;
50       public static final double TARGET_LENGTH_PERCENT = 3.0 / 20;
51       public static final double TARGET_FIRST_X_PERCENT = 3.0 / 5;
52       public static final double TARGET_SPACING_PERCENT = 1.0 / 60;
53       public static final double TARGET_PIECES = 9;
54       public static final double TARGET_MIN_SPEED_PERCENT = 3.0 / 4;
55       public static final double TARGET_MAX_SPEED_PERCENT = 6.0 / 4;
56
57       // constants for the Blocker
58       public static final double BLOCKER_WIDTH_PERCENT = 1.0 / 40;
59       public static final double BLOCKER_LENGTH_PERCENT = 1.0 / 4;
60       public static final double BLOCKER_X_PERCENT = 1.0 / 2;
61       public static final double BLOCKER_SPEED_PERCENT = 1.0;
62
63       // text size 1/18 of screen width
64       public static final double TEXT_SIZE_PERCENT = 1.0 / 18;
65
66       private CannonThread cannonThread; // controls the game loop
67       private Activity activity; // to display Game Over dialog in GUI thread
68       private boolean dialogIsDisplayed = false;
69
70       // game objects
71       private Cannon cannon;
```

Fig. 6.20 | CannonView class's static and instance variables. (Part 1 of 2.)

```
72      private Blocker blocker;
73      private ArrayList<Target> targets;
74
75      // dimension variables
76      private int screenWidth;
77      private int screenHeight;
78
79      // variables for the game loop and tracking statistics
80      private boolean gameOver; // is the game over?
81      private double timeLeft; // time remaining in seconds
82      private int shotsFired; // shots the user has fired
83      private double totalElapsedTime; // elapsed seconds
84
85      // constants and variables for managing sounds
86      public static final int TARGET_SOUND_ID = 0;
87      public static final int CANNON_SOUND_ID = 1;
88      public static final int BLOCKER_SOUND_ID = 2;
89      private SoundPool soundPool; // plays sound effects
90      private SparseIntArray soundMap; // maps IDs to SoundPool
91
92      // Paint variables used when drawing each item on the screen
93      private Paint textPaint; // Paint used to draw text
94      private Paint backgroundPaint; // Paint used to clear the drawing area
95
```

Fig. 6.20 | CannonView class's static and instance variables. (Part 2 of 2.)

6.13.3 Constructor

Figure 6.21 shows class CannonView's constructor. When a View is inflated, its constructor is called with a Context and an AttributeSet as arguments. The Context is the Activity that displays the MainActivityFragment containing the CannonView, and the **Attribute-Set** (package android.util) contains the CannonView attribute values that are set in the layout's XML document. These arguments are passed to the superclass constructor (line 96) to ensure that the custom View is properly configured with the values of any standard View attributes specified in the XML. Line 99 stores a reference to the MainActivity so we can use it at the end of a game to display an AlertDialog from the GUI thread. Though we chose to store the Activity reference, we can access this at any time by calling the inherited View method getContext.

```
96      // constructor
97      public CannonView(Context context, AttributeSet attrs) {
98          super(context, attrs); // call superclass constructor
99          activity = (Activity) context; // store reference to MainActivity
100
101         // register SurfaceHolder.Callback listener
102         getHolder().addCallback(this);
103
```

Fig. 6.21 | CannonView constructor. (Part 1 of 2.)

```
104      // configure audio attributes for game audio
105      AudioAttributes.Builder attrBuilder = new AudioAttributes.Builder();
106      attrBuilder.setUsage(AudioAttributes.USAGE_GAME);
107
108      // initialize SoundPool to play the app's three sound effects
109      SoundPool.Builder builder = new SoundPool.Builder();
110      builder.setMaxStreams(1);
111      builder.setAudioAttributes(attrBuilder.build());
112      soundPool = builder.build();
113
114      // create Map of sounds and pre-load sounds
115      soundMap = new SparseIntArray(3); // create new SparseIntArray
116      soundMap.put(TARGET_SOUND_ID,
117         soundPool.load(context, R.raw.target_hit, 1));
118      soundMap.put(CANNON_SOUND_ID,
119         soundPool.load(context, R.raw.cannon_fire, 1));
120      soundMap.put(BLOCKER_SOUND_ID,
121         soundPool.load(context, R.raw.blocker_hit, 1));
122
123      textPaint = new Paint();
124      backgroundPaint = new Paint();
125      backgroundPaint.setColor(Color.WHITE);
126   }
127
```

Fig. 6.21 | CannonView constructor. (Part 2 of 2.)

Registering the SurfaceHolder.Callback Listener

Line 102 registers this (i.e., the CannonView) as the SurfaceHolder.Callback that receives method calls when the SurfaceView is *created*, *updated* and *destroyed*. Inherited SurfaceView method **getHolder** returns the SurfaceHolder object for managing the SurfaceView, and SurfaceHolder method **addCallback** stores the object that implements interface SurfaceHolder.Callback.

Configuring the SoundPool and Loading the Sounds

Lines 105–121 configure the sounds that we use in the app. First we create an AudioAttributes.Builder object (line 105) and call the setUsage method (line 106), which receives a constant that represents what the audio will be used for. For this app, we use the AudioAttribute.USAGE_GAME constant, which indicates that the audio is being used as game audio. Next, we create a SoundPool.Builder object (line 109), which will enable us to create the SoundPool that's used to load and play the app's sound effects. Next, we call SoundPool.Builder's setMaxStreams method (line 110), which takes an argument that represents the maximum number of simultaneous sound streams that can play at once. We play only one sound at a time, so we pass 1. Some more complex games might play many sounds at the same time. We then call AudioAttributes.Builder's setAudioAttributes method (line 111) to use the audio attributes with the SoundPool object after creating it.

Line 115 creates a SparseIntArray (soundMap), which maps integer keys to integer values. SparseIntArray is similar to—but more efficient than—a HashMap<Integer, Integer> for small numbers of key–value pairs. In this case, we map the sound keys (defined in Fig. 6.20, lines 86–88) to the loaded sounds' IDs, which are represented by the return values of the SoundPool's **load** method (called in Fig. 6.21, lines 117, 119 and 121). Each sound ID can be used to *play* a sound (and later to return its resources to the system). SoundPool method load receives three arguments—the application's Context, a resource ID representing the sound file to load and the sound's priority. According to the documentation for this method, the last argument is not currently used and should be specified as 1.

*Creating the **Paint** Objects Used to Draw the Background and Timer Text*
Lines 123–124 create the Paint objects that are used when drawing the game's background and **Time remaining** text. The text color defaults to black and line 125 sets the background color to white.

6.13.4 Overriding View Method onSizeChanged

Figure 6.22 overrides class View's **onSizeChanged** method, which is called whenever the View's size changes, including when the View is first added to the View hierarchy as the layout is inflated. This app always displays in landscape mode, so onSizeChanged is called only once when the activity's onCreate method inflates the GUI. The method receives the View's new width and height and its old width and height. The first time this method is called, the old width and height are 0. Lines 138–139 configure the textPaint object, which is used to draw the **Time remaining** text. Line 138 sets the size of the text to be TEXT_SIZE_PERCENT of the height of the screen (screenHeight). We arrived at the value for TEXT_SIZE_PERCENT and the other scaling factors in Fig. 6.20 via trial and error, choosing values that made the game elements look nice on the screen.

```
128    // called when the size of the SurfaceView changes,
129    // such as when it's first added to the View hierarchy
130    @Override
131    protected void onSizeChanged(int w, int h, int oldw, int oldh) {
132        super.onSizeChanged(w, h, oldw, oldh);
133
134        screenWidth = w; // store CannonView's width
135        screenHeight = h; // store CannonView's height
136
137        // configure text properties
138        textPaint.setTextSize((int) (TEXT_SIZE_PERCENT * screenHeight));
139        textPaint.setAntiAlias(true); // smoothes the text
140    }
141
```

Fig. 6.22 | Overriding View method onSizeChanged.

6.13.5 Methods getScreenWidth, getScreenHeight, and playSound

In Fig. 6.23, the methods getScreenWidth and getScreenHeight return the width and height of the screen, which are updated in the onSizeChanged method (Fig. 6.22). Using soundPool's **play** method, the playSound method (lines 153–155) plays the sound in soundMap with the given soundId, which was associated with the sound when soundMap was constructed (Fig. 6.21, lines 113–119). The soundId is used as the soundMap key to locate the sound's ID in the SoundPool. An object of class GameElement can call the play-Sound method to play its sound.

```
142        // get width of the game screen
143        public int getScreenWidth() {
144            return screenWidth;
145        }
146
147        // get height of the game screen
148        public int getScreenHeight() {
149            return screenHeight;
150        }
151
152        // plays a sound with the given soundId in soundMap
153        public void playSound(int soundId) {
154            soundPool.play(soundMap.get(soundId), 1, 1, 1, 0, 1f);
155        }
156
```

Fig. 6.23 | CannonView methods getScreenWidth, getScreenHeight and playSound.

6.13.6 Method newGame

Method newGame (Fig. 6.24) resets the instance variables that are used to control the game. Lines 160–163 create a new Cannon object with

- a base radius of CANNON_BASE_RADIUS_PERCENT of the screen height,

- a barrel length of CANNON_BARREL_LENGTH_PERCENT of the screen width and

- a barrel width of CANNON_BARREL_WIDTH_PERCENT of the screen height.

```
157        // reset all the screen elements and start a new game
158        public void newGame() {
159            // construct a new Cannon
160            cannon = new Cannon(this,
161                (int) (CANNON_BASE_RADIUS_PERCENT * screenHeight),
162                (int) (CANNON_BARREL_LENGTH_PERCENT * screenWidth),
163                (int) (CANNON_BARREL_WIDTH_PERCENT * screenHeight));
164
165            Random random = new Random(); // for determining random velocities
166            targets = new ArrayList<>(); // construct a new Target list
167
168            // initialize targetX for the first Target from the left
169            int targetX = (int) (TARGET_FIRST_X_PERCENT * screenWidth);
170
171            // calculate Y coordinate of Targets
172            int targetY = (int) ((0.5 - TARGET_LENGTH_PERCENT / 2) *
173                screenHeight);
174
```

Fig. 6.24 | CannonView method newGame. (Part 1 of 2.)

```
175      // add TARGET_PIECES Targets to the Target list
176      for (int n = 0; n < TARGET_PIECES; n++) {
177
178         // determine a random velocity between min and max values
179         // for Target n
180         double velocity = screenHeight * (random.nextDouble() *
181            (TARGET_MAX_SPEED_PERCENT - TARGET_MIN_SPEED_PERCENT) +
182            TARGET_MIN_SPEED_PERCENT);
183
184         // alternate Target colors between dark and light
185         int color = (n % 2 == 0) ?
186            getResources().getColor(R.color.dark,
187               getContext().getTheme()) :
188            getResources().getColor(R.color.light,
189               getContext().getTheme());
190
191         velocity *= -1; // reverse the initial velocity for next Target
192
193         // create and add a new Target to the Target list
194         targets.add(new Target(this, color, HIT_REWARD, targetX, targetY,
195            (int) (TARGET_WIDTH_PERCENT * screenWidth),
196            (int) (TARGET_LENGTH_PERCENT * screenHeight),
197            (int) velocity));
198
199         // increase the x coordinate to position the next Target more
200         // to the right
201         targetX += (TARGET_WIDTH_PERCENT + TARGET_SPACING_PERCENT) *
202            screenWidth;
203      }
204
205      // create a new Blocker
206      blocker = new Blocker(this, Color.BLACK, MISS_PENALTY,
207         (int) (BLOCKER_X_PERCENT * screenWidth),
208         (int) ((0.5 - BLOCKER_LENGTH_PERCENT / 2) * screenHeight),
209         (int) (BLOCKER_WIDTH_PERCENT * screenWidth),
210         (int) (BLOCKER_LENGTH_PERCENT * screenHeight),
211         (float) (BLOCKER_SPEED_PERCENT * screenHeight));
212
213      timeLeft = 10; // start the countdown at 10 seconds
214
215      shotsFired = 0; // set the initial number of shots fired
216      totalElapsedTime = 0.0; // set the time elapsed to zero
217
218      if (gameOver) {// start a new game after the last game ended
219         gameOver = false; // the game is not over
220         cannonThread = new CannonThread(getHolder()); // create thread
221         cannonThread.start(); // start the game loop thread
222      }
223
224      hideSystemBars();
225   }
226
```

Fig. 6.24 | CannonView method newGame. (Part 2 of 2.)

Line 165 creates a new Random object that's used to randomize the Target velocities. Line 166 creates a new ArrayList of Targets. Line 169 initializes targetX to the number of pixels from the left that the first Target will be positioned on the screen. The first Target is positioned TARGET_FIRST_X_PERCENT of the way across the screen. Lines 172–173 initialize targetY with a value to vertically center all Targets on the screen. Lines 176–203 construct TARGET_PIECES (9) new Targets and add them to targets. Lines 180–182 set the velocity of the new Target to a random value between the screen height percentages TARGET_MIN_SPEED_PERCENT and TARGET_MAX_SPEED_PERCENT. Lines 185–189 set the color of the new Target to alternate between the R.color.dark and R.color.light colors and alternate between positive and negative vertical velocities. Line 191 reverses the target velocity for each new target so that some targets move up to start and some move down. The new Target is constructed and added to targets (lines 194–197). The Target is given a width of TARGET_WIDTH_PERCENT of the screen width and a height of TARGET_HEIGHT_PERCENT of the screen height. Finally, targetX is incremented to position the next Target.

A new Blocker is constructed and stored in blocker in lines 206–211. The Blocker is positioned BLOCKER_X_PERCENT of the screen width from the left and is vertically centered on the screen to start the game. The Blocker's width is BLOCKER_WIDTH_PERCENT of the screen width and the Blocker's height is BLOCKER_HEIGHT_PERCENT of the screen height. The Blocker's speed is BLOCKER_SPEED_PERCENT of the screen height.

If variable gameOver is true, which occurs only *after* the first game completes, line 219 resets gameOver and lines 220–221 create a new CannonThread and call its start method to begin the *game loop* that controls the game. Line 224 calls method hideSystemBars (Section 6.13.16) to put the app in immersive mode—this hides the system bars and enables the user to display them at any time by swiping down from the top of the screen.

6.13.7 Method updatePositions

Method updatePositions (Fig. 6.25) is called by the CannonThread's run method (Section 6.13.15) to update the on-screen elements' positions and to perform simple *collision detection*. The new locations of the game elements are calculated based on the elapsed time in milliseconds between the previous and current animation frames. This enables the game to update the amount by which each game element moves, based on the device's *refresh rate*. We discuss this in more detail when we cover game loops in Section 6.13.15.

```
227    // called repeatedly by the CannonThread to update game elements
228    private void updatePositions(double elapsedTimeMS) {
229        double interval = elapsedTimeMS / 1000.0; // convert to seconds
230
231        // update cannonball's position if it is on the screen
232        if (cannon.getCannonball() != null)
233            cannon.getCannonball().update(interval);
234
235        blocker.update(interval); // update the blocker's position
236
237        for (GameElement target : targets)
238            target.update(interval); // update the target's position
```

Fig. 6.25 | CannonView method updatePositions. (Part 1 of 2.)

```
239
240        timeLeft -= interval; // subtract from time left
241
242        // if the timer reached zero
243        if (timeLeft <= 0) {
244            timeLeft = 0.0;
245            gameOver = true; // the game is over
246            cannonThread.setRunning(false); // terminate thread
247            showGameOverDialog(R.string.lose); // show the losing dialog
248        }
249
250        // if all pieces have been hit
251        if (targets.isEmpty()) {
252            cannonThread.setRunning(false); // terminate thread
253            showGameOverDialog(R.string.win); // show winning dialog
254            gameOver = true;
255        }
256    }
257
```

Fig. 6.25 | CannonView method updatePositions. (Part 2 of 2.)

Elapsed Time Since the Last Animation Frame

Line 229 converts the elapsed time since the last animation frame from milliseconds to seconds. This value is used to modify the positions of various game elements.

Updating the Cannonball, Blocker and Target Positions

To update the positions of the GameElements, lines 232–238 call the update methods of the Cannonball (if there is one on the screen), the Blocker and all of the remaining Targets. The update method receives the time elapsed since the previous frame so that the positions can be updated by the correct amount for the interval.

Updating the Time Left and Determining Whether Time Ran Out

We decrease timeLeft by the time that has passed since the prior animation frame (line 240). If timeLeft has reached zero, the game is over, so we set timeLeft to 0.0 just in case it was negative; otherwise, sometimes a negative final time would display on the screen. Then we set gameOver to true, terminate the CannonThread by calling its setRunning method with the argument false and call method showGameOverDialog with the String resource ID representing the losing message.

6.13.8 Method alignAndFireCannonball

When the user touches the screen, method onTouchEvent (Section 6.13.14) calls align-AndFireCannonball (Fig. 6.26). Lines 267–272 calculate the angle necessary to aim the cannon at the touch point. Line 275 calls Cannon's align method to aim the cannon with trajectory angle. Finally, if the Cannonball exists and is on the screen, lines 280–281 fire the Cannonball and increment shotsFired.

```
258        // aligns the barrel and fires a Cannonball if a Cannonball is not
259        // already on the screen
260     public void alignAndFireCannonball(MotionEvent event) {
261        // get the location of the touch in this view
262        Point touchPoint = new Point((int) event.getX(),
263           (int) event.getY());
264
265        // compute the touch's distance from center of the screen
266        // on the y-axis
267        double centerMinusY = (screenHeight / 2 - touchPoint.y);
268
269        double angle = 0; // initialize angle to 0
270
271        // calculate the angle the barrel makes with the horizontal
272        angle = Math.atan2(touchPoint.x, centerMinusY);
273
274        // point the barrel at the point where the screen was touched
275        cannon.align(angle);
276
277        // fire Cannonball if there is not already a Cannonball on screen
278        if (cannon.getCannonball() == null ||
279           !cannon.getCannonball().isOnScreen()) {
280           cannon.fireCannonball();
281           ++shotsFired;
282        }
283     }
284
```

Fig. 6.26 | CannonView method alignAndFireCannonball.

6.13.9 Method showGameOverDialog

When the game ends, the showGameOverDialog method (Fig. 6.27) displays a Dialog-Fragment (using the techniques you learned in Section 4.7.10) containing an Alert-Dialog that indicates whether the player won or lost, the number of shots fired and the total time elapsed. The call to method setPositiveButton (lines 301–311) creates a reset button for starting a new game.

```
285        // display an AlertDialog when the game ends
286        private void showGameOverDialog(final int messageId) {
287           // DialogFragment to display game stats and start new game
288           final DialogFragment gameResult =
289              new DialogFragment() {
290                 // create an AlertDialog and return it
291                 @Override
292                 public Dialog onCreateDialog(Bundle bundle) {
293                    // create dialog displaying String resource for messageId
294                    AlertDialog.Builder builder =
295                       new AlertDialog.Builder(getActivity());
296                    builder.setTitle(getResources().getString(messageId));
297
```

Fig. 6.27 | CannonView method showGameOverDialog. (Part I of 2.)

```
298                    // display number of shots fired and total time elapsed
299                    builder.setMessage(getResources().getString(
300                        R.string.results_format, shotsFired, totalElapsedTime));
301                    builder.setPositiveButton(R.string.reset_game,
302                        new DialogInterface.OnClickListener() {
303                            // called when "Reset Game" Button is pressed
304                            @Override
305                            public void onClick(DialogInterface dialog,
306                                int which) {
307                                dialogIsDisplayed = false;
308                                newGame(); // set up and start a new game
309                            }
310                        }
311                    );
312
313                    return builder.create(); // return the AlertDialog
314                }
315            };
316
317            // in GUI thread, use FragmentManager to display the DialogFragment
318            activity.runOnUiThread(
319                new Runnable() {
320                    public void run() {
321                        showSystemBars(); // exit immersive mode
322                        dialogIsDisplayed = true;
323                        gameResult.setCancelable(false); // modal dialog
324                        gameResult.show(activity.getFragmentManager(), "results");
325                    }
326                }
327            );
328        }
329
```

Fig. 6.27 | CannonView method showGameOverDialog. (Part 2 of 2.)

The onClick method of the Button's listener indicates that the dialog is no longer displayed and calls newGame to set up and start a new game. A dialog must be displayed from the GUI thread, so lines 318–327 call Activity method **runOnUiThread** to specify a Runnable that should execute in the GUI thread as soon as possible. The argument is an object of an anonymous inner class that implements Runnable. The Runnable's run method calls method showSystemBars (Section 6.13.16) to remove the app from immersive mode, then indicates that the dialog is displayed and displays it.

6.13.10 Method drawGameElements

The method drawGameElements (Fig. 6.28) draws the Cannon, Cannonball, Blocker and Targets on the SurfaceView using the Canvas that the CannonThread (Section 6.13.15) obtains from the SurfaceView's SurfaceHolder.

Clearing the Canvas with Method drawRect

First, we call Canvas's **drawRect** method (lines 333–334) to clear the Canvas so that the game elements can be displayed in their new positions. The method receives the rectangle's

```
330      // draws the game to the given Canvas
331      public void drawGameElements(Canvas canvas) {
332          // clear the background
333          canvas.drawRect(0, 0, canvas.getWidth(), canvas.getHeight(),
334              backgroundPaint);
335
336          // display time remaining
337          canvas.drawText(getResources().getString(
338              R.string.time_remaining_format, timeLeft), 50, 100, textPaint);
339
340          cannon.draw(canvas); // draw the cannon
341
342          // draw the GameElements
343          if (cannon.getCannonball() != null &&
344              cannon.getCannonball().isOnScreen())
345              cannon.getCannonball().draw(canvas);
346
347          blocker.draw(canvas); // draw the blocker
348
349          // draw all of the Targets
350          for (GameElement target : targets)
351              target.draw(canvas);
352      }
353
```

Fig. 6.28 | CannonView method drawGameElements.

upper-left *x-y* coordinates, width and height, and the Paint object that specifies the drawing characteristics—recall that backgroundPaint sets the drawing color to white.

Displaying the Time Remaining with Canvas Method drawText

Next, we call Canvas's **drawText method** (lines 337–338) to display the time remaining in the game. We pass as arguments the String to be displayed, the *x*- and *y*-coordinates at which to display it and the textPaint (configured in Fig. 6.22, lines 138–139) to describe how the text should be rendered (that is, the text's font size, color and other attributes).

Drawing the Cannon, Cannonball, Blocker and Targets with the draw Method

Lines 339–350 draw the Cannon, the Cannonball (if it is on the screen), the Blocker, and each of the Targets. Each of these elements is drawn by calling its draw method and passing in canvas.

6.13.11 Method testForCollisions

The testForCollisions method (Fig. 6.29) checks whether the Cannonball is colliding with any of the Targets or with the Blocker, and applies certain effects in the game if a collision occurs. Lines 359–360 check whether a Cannonball is on the screen. If so, line 362 calls the Cannonball's collidesWith method to determine whether the Cannonball is colliding with a Target. If ther is a collision, line 363 calls the Target's playSound method to play the target-hit sound, line 366 increments timeLeft by the hit reward associated with the Target, and lines 368–369 remove the Cannonball and Target from the screen. Line 370 decrements n to ensure the target that's now in position n gets tested for a collision. Line 376 destroys the Cannonball associated with Cannon if it's not on the screen. If the Cannonball is still on the screen, lines 380–381 call collidesWith again to determine whether the Cannonball is colliding with the Blocker. If so, line 382 calls the Blocker's playSound method to play the blocker-hit sound, line 385 reverses the cannonball's horizontal velocity by calling class Cannonball's reverseVelocityX method, and line 388 decrements timeLeft by the miss penalty associated with the Blocker.

```
354    // checks if the ball collides with the Blocker or any of the Targets
355    // and handles the collisions
356    public void testForCollisions() {
357        // remove any of the targets that the Cannonball
358        // collides with
359        if (cannon.getCannonball() != null &&
360            cannon.getCannonball().isOnScreen()) {
361            for (int n = 0; n < targets.size(); n++) {
362                if (cannon.getCannonball().collidesWith(targets.get(n))) {
363                    targets.get(n).playSound(); // play Target hit sound
364
365                    // add hit rewards time to remaining time
366                    timeLeft += targets.get(n).getHitReward();
367
368                    cannon.removeCannonball(); // remove Cannonball from game
369                    targets.remove(n); // remove the Target that was hit
370                    --n; // ensures that we don't skip testing new target n
371                    break;
372                }
373            }
374        }
375        else { // remove the Cannonball if it should not be on the screen
376            cannon.removeCannonball();
377        }
378
379        // check if ball collides with blocker
380        if (cannon.getCannonball() != null &&
381            cannon.getCannonball().collidesWith(blocker)) {
382            blocker.playSound(); // play Blocker hit sound
383
384            // reverse ball direction
385            cannon.getCannonball().reverseVelocityX();
386
387            // deduct blocker's miss penalty from remaining time
388            timeLeft -= blocker.getMissPenalty();
389        }
390    }
391
```

Fig. 6.29 | CannonView method testForCollisions.

6.13.12 Methods stopGame and releaseResources

Class MainActivityFragment's onPause and onDestroy methods (Section 6.13) call class CannonView's stopGame and releaseResources methods (Fig. 6.30), respectively. Method stopGame (lines 393–396) is called from the main Activity to stop the game when the

Activity's onPause method is called—for simplicity, we don't store the game's state in this example. Method releaseResources (lines 399–402) calls the SoundPool's **release method** to release the resources associated with the SoundPool.

```
392        // stops the game: called by CannonGameFragment's onPause method
393        public void stopGame() {
394            if (cannonThread != null)
395                cannonThread.setRunning(false); // tell thread to terminate
396        }
397
398        // release resources: called by CannonGame's onDestroy method
399        public void releaseResources() {
400            soundPool.release(); // release all resources used by the SoundPool
401            soundPool = null;
402        }
403
```

Fig. 6.30 | CannonView methods stopGame and releaseResources.

6.13.13 Implementing the SurfaceHolder.Callback Methods

Figure 6.31 implements the **surfaceChanged**, **surfaceCreated** and **surfaceDestroyed** methods of interface SurfaceHolder.Callback. Method surfaceChanged has an empty body in this app because the app is *always* displayed in landscape orientation. This method is called when the SurfaceView's size or orientation changes, and would typically be used to redisplay graphics based on those changes.

```
404        // called when surface changes size
405        @Override
406        public void surfaceChanged(SurfaceHolder holder, int format,
407            int width, int height) { }
408
409        // called when surface is first created
410        @Override
411        public void surfaceCreated(SurfaceHolder holder) {
412            if (!dialogIsDisplayed) {
413                newGame(); // set up and start a new game
414                cannonThread = new CannonThread(holder); // create thread
415                cannonThread.setRunning(true); // start game running
416                cannonThread.start(); // start the game loop thread
417            }
418        }
419
420        // called when the surface is destroyed
421        @Override
422        public void surfaceDestroyed(SurfaceHolder holder) {
423            // ensure that thread terminates properly
424            boolean retry = true;
425            cannonThread.setRunning(false); // terminate cannonThread
426
```

Fig. 6.31 | Implementing the SurfaceHolder.Callback methods. (Part 1 of 2.)

```
427        while (retry) {
428            try {
429                cannonThread.join(); // wait for cannonThread to finish
430                retry = false;
431            }
432            catch (InterruptedException e) {
433                Log.e(TAG, "Thread interrupted", e);
434            }
435        }
436    }
437
```

Fig. 6.31 | Implementing the SurfaceHolder.Callback methods. (Part 2 of 2.)

Method surfaceCreated (lines 410–418) is called when the SurfaceView is created—e.g., when the app first loads or when it resumes from the background. We use surfaceCreated to create and start the CannonThread to begin the game loop. Method surfaceDestroyed (lines 421–436) is called when the SurfaceView is destroyed—e.g., when the app terminates. We use surfaceDestroyed to ensure that the CannonThread terminates properly. First, line 425 calls CannonThread's setRunning method with false as an argument to indicate that the thread should *stop*, then lines 427–435 wait for the thread to *terminate*. This ensures that no attempt is made to draw to the SurfaceView once surfaceDestroyed completes execution.

6.13.14 Overriding View Method onTouchEvent

In this example, we override View method onTouchEvent (Fig. 6.32) to determine when the user touches the screen. The MotionEvent parameter contains information about the event that occurred. Line 442 uses the MotionEvent's getAction method to determine which type of touch event occurred. Then, lines 445–446 determine whether the user touched the screen (MotionEvent.ACTION_DOWN) or dragged a finger across the screen (MotionEvent.ACTION_MOVE). In either case, line 448 calls the cannonView's alignAndFireCannonball method to aim and fire the cannon toward that touch point. Line 451 then returns true to indicate that the touch event was handled.

```
438        // called when the user touches the screen in this activity
439        @Override
440        public boolean onTouchEvent(MotionEvent e) {
441            // get int representing the type of action which caused this event
442            int action = e.getAction();
443
444            // the user touched the screen or dragged along the screen
445            if (action == MotionEvent.ACTION_DOWN ||
446                action == MotionEvent.ACTION_MOVE) {
447                // fire the cannonball toward the touch point
448                alignAndFireCannonball(e);
449            }
450
```

Fig. 6.32 | Overriding View method onTouchEvent. (Part 1 of 2.).

```
451        return true;
452    }
453
```

Fig. 6.32 | Overriding View method onTouchEvent. (Part 2 of 2.).

6.13.15 CannonThread: Using a Thread to Create a Game Loop

Figure 6.33 defines a subclass of Thread which updates the game. The thread maintains a reference to the SurfaceView's SurfaceHolder (line 456) and a boolean indicating whether the thread is *running*.

```
454    // Thread subclass to control the game loop
455    private class CannonThread extends Thread {
456        private SurfaceHolder surfaceHolder; // for manipulating canvas
457        private boolean threadIsRunning = true; // running by default
458
459        // initializes the surface holder
460        public CannonThread(SurfaceHolder holder) {
461            surfaceHolder = holder;
462            setName("CannonThread");
463        }
464
465        // changes running state
466        public void setRunning(boolean running) {
467            threadIsRunning = running;
468        }
469
470        // controls the game loop
471        @Override
472        public void run() {
473            Canvas canvas = null; // used for drawing
474            long previousFrameTime = System.currentTimeMillis();
475
476            while (threadIsRunning) {
477                try {
478                    // get Canvas for exclusive drawing from this thread
479                    canvas = surfaceHolder.lockCanvas(null);
480
481                    // lock the surfaceHolder for drawing
482                    synchronized(surfaceHolder) {
483                        long currentTime = System.currentTimeMillis();
484                        double elapsedTimeMS = currentTime - previousFrameTime;
485                        totalElapsedTime += elapsedTimeMS / 1000.0;
486                        updatePositions(elapsedTimeMS); // update game state
487                        testForCollisions(); // test for GameElement collisions
488                        drawGameElements(canvas); // draw using the canvas
489                        previousFrameTime = currentTime; // update previous time
490                    }
491            }
```

Fig. 6.33 | Nested class CannonThread manages the game loop, updating the game elements every TIME_INTERVAL milliseconds. (Part 1 of 2.)

```
492                finally {
493                    // display canvas's contents on the CannonView
494                    // and enable other threads to use the Canvas
495                    if (canvas != null)
496                        surfaceHolder.unlockCanvasAndPost(canvas);
497                }
498            }
499        }
500    }
```

Fig. 6.33 | Nested class CannonThread manages the game loop, updating the game elements every TIME_INTERVAL milliseconds. (Part 2 of 2.)

The class's run method (lines 471–499) drives the *frame-by-frame animations*—this is known as the *game loop*. Each update of the game elements on the screen is performed, based on the number of milliseconds that have passed since the last update. Line 474 gets the system's current time in milliseconds when the thread begins running. Lines 476–498 loop until threadIsRunning is false.

First we obtain the Canvas for drawing on the SurfaceView by calling SurfaceHolder method **lockCanvas** (line 479). Only one thread at a time can draw to a SurfaceView. To ensure this, you must first *lock* the SurfaceHolder by specifying it as the expression in the parentheses of a synchronized block (line 482). Next, we get the current time in milliseconds, then calculate the elapsed time and add that to the total time so far—this will be used to help display the amount of time left in the game. Line 486 calls method update-Positions to move all the game elements, passing the elapsed time in milliseconds as an argument. This ensures that the game operates at the same speed *regardless of how fast the device is*. If the time between frames is larger (i.e, the device is slower), the game elements will move further when each frame of the animation is displayed. If the time between frames is smaller (i.e, the device is faster), the game elements will move less when each frame of the animation is displayed. Line 487 calls testForCollisions to determine whether the Cannonball collided with the Blocker or a Target:

- If a collision occurs with the Blocker, testForCollisions reverses the Cannonball's velocity.

- If a collision occurs with a Target, testForCollisions removes the Cannonball.

Finally, line 488 calls the drawGameElements method to draw the game elements using the SurfaceView's Canvas, and line 489 stores the currentTime as the previousFrameTime to prepare to calculate the elapsed time between this animation frame and the *next*.

6.13.16 Methods hideSystemBars and showSystemBars

This app uses *immersive mode*—at any time during game play, the user can view the system bars by swiping down from the top of the screen. Immersive mode is available only on devices running Android 4.4 or higher. So, methods hideSystemBars and showSystemBars (Fig. 6.34) first check whether the device's Android version—Build.VERSION_SDK_INT— is greater than or equal to Build.VERSION_CODES_KITKAT—the constant for Android 4.4 (API level 19). If so, both methods use View method **setSystemUiVisibility** to configure the system bars and app bar (though we already hid the app bar by modifying this app's theme). To hide the system bars and app bar and place the UI into immersive mode, you pass to setSystemUiVisibility the constants that are combined via the bitwise OR (|) operator in lines 505–510. To show the system bars and app bar, you pass to setSystemUiVisibility the constants that are combined in lines 517–519. These combinations of View constants ensure that the CannonView is *not* resized each time the system bars and app bar are hidden and redisplayed. Instead, the system bars and app bar *overlay* the Cannon-View—that is, part of the CannonView is temporarily hidden when the system bars are on the screen. For more information on immersive mode, visit

> http://developer.android.com/training/system-ui/immersive.html

```
501     // hide system bars and app bar
502     private void hideSystemBars() {
503        if (Build.VERSION.SDK_INT >= Build.VERSION_CODES.KITKAT)
504           setSystemUiVisibility(
505              View.SYSTEM_UI_FLAG_LAYOUT_STABLE |
506              View.SYSTEM_UI_FLAG_LAYOUT_HIDE_NAVIGATION |
507              View.SYSTEM_UI_FLAG_LAYOUT_FULLSCREEN |
508              View.SYSTEM_UI_FLAG_HIDE_NAVIGATION |
509              View.SYSTEM_UI_FLAG_FULLSCREEN |
510              View.SYSTEM_UI_FLAG_IMMERSIVE);
511     }
512
513     // show system bars and app bar
514     private void showSystemBars() {
515        if (Build.VERSION.SDK_INT >= Build.VERSION_CODES.KITKAT)
516           setSystemUiVisibility(
517              View.SYSTEM_UI_FLAG_LAYOUT_STABLE |
518              View.SYSTEM_UI_FLAG_LAYOUT_HIDE_NAVIGATION |
519              View.SYSTEM_UI_FLAG_LAYOUT_FULLSCREEN);
520     }
521  }
```

Fig. 6.34 | DoodleView methods hideSystemBars and showSystemBars.

6.14 Wrap-Up

In this chapter, you created the **Cannon Game** app, which challenges the player to destroy nine targets before a 10-second time limit expires. The user aims and fires the cannon by touching the screen. To draw on the screen from a separate thread, you created a custom view by extending class SurfaceView. You learned that custom component class names must be fully qualified in the XML layout element that represents the component. We presented additional Fragment lifecycle methods. You learned that method onPause is called when a Fragment is paused and method onDestroy is called when the Fragment is destroyed. You handled touches by overriding View's onTouchEvent method. You added sound effects to the app's res/raw folder and managed them with a SoundPool. You also used the system's AudioManager service to obtain the device's current music volume and use it as the playback volume.

This app manually performs its animations by updating the game elements on a SurfaceView from a separate thread of execution. To do this, you extended class Thread and created a run method that displays graphics by calling methods of class Canvas. You used the SurfaceView's SurfaceHolder to obtain the appropriate Canvas. You also learned how to build a game loop that controls a game, based on the amount of time that has elapsed between animation frames, so that the game will operate at the same overall speed on all devices, regardless of their processor speeds. Finally, you used immersive mode to enable the app to use the entire screen.

In Chapter 7, you'll build the **WeatherViewer** app. You'll use web services to interact with the 16-day weather forecast web service from OpenWeatherMap.org. Like many of today's web services, the OpenWeatherMap.org web service will return the forecast data in JavaScript Object Notation (JSON) format. You'll process the response using the JSONObject and JSONArray classes from the org.json package. You'll then display the daily forecast in a ListView.

Self-Review Exercises

6.1 Fill in the blanks in each of the following statements:
a) You can create a custom view by extending class View or _____.
b) To process simple touch events for an Activity, you can override class Activity's on-TouchEvent method then use constants from class _____ (package android.view) to test which type of event occurred and process it accordingly.
c) Each SurfaceView subclass should implement the interface _____, which contains methods that are called when the SurfaceView is created, changed (e.g., its size or orientation changes) or destroyed.
d) The d in a format specifier indicates that you're formatting a decimal integer and the f in a format specifier indicates that you're formatting a(n) _____ value.
e) Sound files are stored in the app's _____ folder.
f) _____ enables an app to take advantage of the entire screen.

6.2 State whether each of the following is *true* or *false*. If *false*, explain why.
a) The Android documentation recommends that games use the music audio stream to play sounds.
b) In Android, it's important to maximize the amount of work you do in the GUI thread to ensure that the GUI remains responsive and does not display ANR (Application Not Responding) dialogs.
c) A Canvas draws on a View's Bitmap.
d) Format Strings that contain multiple format specifiers must number the format specifiers for localization purposes.
e) There are seven sound streams identified by constants in class AudioManager, but the documentation for class SoundPool recommends using the stream for playing music (AudioManager.STREAM_MUSIC) for sound in games.
f) Custom component class names must be fully qualified in the XML layout element that represents the component.

Answers to Self-Review Exercises

6.1 a) one of its subclasses. b) MotionEvent. c) SurfaceHolder.Callback. d) floating-point. e) res/raw. f) immersive mode.

6.2 a) True. b) False. In Android, it's important to *minimize* the amount of work you do in the GUI thread to ensure that the GUI remains responsive and does not display ANR (Application Not Responding) dialogs. c) True. d) True. e) True. f) True.

Exercises

6.3   Fill in the blanks in each of the following statements:

a) Method _____ is called for the current `Activity` when another activity receives the focus, which sends the current activity to the background.

b) When an `Activity` is shut down, its _____ method is called.

c) `Activity`'s _____ method specifies that an app's volume can be controlled with the device's volume keys and should be the same as the device's music playback volume. The method receives a constant from class `AudioManager` (package `android.media`).

d) Games often require complex logic that should be performed in separate threads of execution and those threads often need to draw to the screen. For such cases, Android provides class _____—a subclass of `View` to which any thread can draw.

e) Method _____ is called for the current `Activity` when another activity receives the focus.

6.4   State whether each of the following is *true* or *false*. If *false*, explain why.

a) Class `SurfaceHolder` also provides methods that give a thread shared access to the `Canvas` for drawing, because only one thread at a time can draw to a `SurfaceView`.

b) A `MotionEvent.ACTION_TOUCH` indicates that the user touched the screen and indicates that the user moved a finger across the screen (`MotionEvent.ACTION_MOVE`).

c) When a `View` is inflated, its constructor is called and passed a `Context` and an `AttributeSet` as arguments.

d) `SoundPool` method `start` receives three arguments—the application's `Context`, a resource ID representing the sound file to load and the sound's priority.

e) When a game loop controls a game based on the amount of time that has elapsed between animation frames, the game will operate at different speeds as appropriate for each device.

6.5   *(Enhanced Cannon Game App)* Modify the **Cannon Game** app as follows:

a) Use images for the cannon base and cannonball.

b) Display a dashed line showing the cannonball's path.

c) Play a sound when the blocker hits the top or bottom of the screen.

d) Play a sound when the target hits the top or bottom of the screen.

e) Enhance the app to have nine levels. In each level, the target should have the same number of target pieces as the level.

f) Keep score. Increase the user's score for each target piece hit by 10 times the current level. Decrease the score by 15 times the current level each time the user hits the blocker. Display the highest score on the screen in the upper-left corner.

g) Save the top five high scores in a `SharedPreferences` file. When the game ends display an `AlertDialog` with the scores shown in descending order. If the user's score is one of the top five, highlight that score by displaying an asterisk (*) next to it.

h) Add an explosion animation each time the cannonball hits one of the target pieces.

i) Add an explosion animation each time the cannonball hits the blocker.

j) When the cannonball hits the blocker, increase the blocker's length by 5%.

k) Make the game more difficult as it progresses by increasing the speed of the target and the blocker.

l) Increase the number of obstacles between the cannon and the target.

m) Add a bonus round that lasts for four seconds. Change the color of the target and add music to indicate that it is a bonus round. If the user hits a piece of the target during those four seconds, give the user 1000 bonus points.

6.6   *(Brick Game App)* Create a game similar to the cannon game that shoots pellets at a stationary brick wall. The goal is to destroy enough of the wall to shoot the moving target behind it. The faster you break through the wall and get the target, the higher your score. Vary the color of the bricks and the number of shots required to destroy each—for example, red bricks can be destroyed in three shots, yellow bricks can be destroyed in six shots, etc. Include multiple layers to the wall and a small moving target (e.g., an icon, animal, etc.). Keep score. Increase difficulty with each round by adding more layers to the wall and increasing the speed of the moving target.

6.7 *(Tablet App: Multiplayer Horse Race with Cannon Game)* One of the most popular carnival or arcade games is the horse race. Each player is assigned a horse. To move the horse, the players must perform a skill—such as shooting a stream of water at a target. Each time a player hits a target, that player's horse moves forward. The goal is to hit the target as many times as possible and as quickly as possible to move the horse toward the finish line and win the race.

Create a multiplayer tablet app that simulates the **Horse Race** game with two players. Instead of a stream of water, use the **Cannon Game** as the skill that will move each horse. Each time a player hits a target piece with the cannonball, move that player's horse one position to the right.

Set the orientation of the screen to landscape. Split the screen into three sections. The first section should run across the entire width of the top of the screen; this will be the race track. Below the race track, include two sections side-by-side. In each of these sections, include separate **Cannon Game**s (use `Fragments` to display separate `CannonView` objects). The two players will need to be sitting side-by-side to play this version of the game.

In the race track, include two horses that start on the left and move right toward a finish line at the right-side of the screen. Number the horses "1" and "2."

Include the many sounds of a traditional horse race. You can find free audios online at websites such as www.audiomicro.com/ or create your own. Before the race, play an audio of the traditional bugle call—the "Call to Post"—that signifies to the horses to take their mark. Include the sound of the shot to start the race, followed by the announcer saying "And they're off!"

6.8 *(Bouncing Ball Game App)* Create a game app in which the user's goal is to prevent a bouncing ball from falling off the bottom of the screen. When the user presses the start button, a ball bounces off the top, left and right sides (the "walls") of the screen. A horizontal bar on the bottom of the screen serves as a paddle to prevent the ball from hitting the bottom of the screen. (The ball can bounce off the paddle, but not the bottom of the screen.) Allow the user to drag the paddle left and right. If the ball hits the paddle, it bounces up, and the game continues. If the ball hits the bottom, the game ends. Decrease the paddle's width every 20 seconds and increase the speed of the ball to make the game more challenging. Consider adding obstacles at random locations.

6.9 *(Digital Clock App)* Create an app that displays a digital clock on the screen. Include alarm-clock functionality.

6.10 *(Analog Clock App)* Create an app that displays an analog clock with hour, minute and second hands that move appropriately as the time changes.

6.11 *(Fireworks Designer App)* Create an app that enables the user to create a customized fireworks display. Create a variety of fireworks demonstrations. Then orchestrate the firing of the fireworks for maximum effect. You might synchronize your fireworks with audios or videos. You could overlay the fireworks on a picture.

6.12 *(Animated Towers of Hanoi App)* Every budding computer scientist must grapple with certain classic problems, and the *Towers of Hanoi* (see Fig. 6.35) is one of the most famous. Legend has it that in a temple in the Far East, priests are attempting to move a stack of disks from one peg to another. The initial stack has 64 disks threaded onto one peg and arranged from bottom to top by decreasing size. The priests are attempting to move the stack from this peg to a second peg under the constraints that exactly one disk is moved at a time and at no time may a larger disk be placed above a smaller disk. A third peg is available for temporarily holding disks. Supposedly, the world will end when the priests complete their task, so there's little incentive for us to facilitate their efforts.

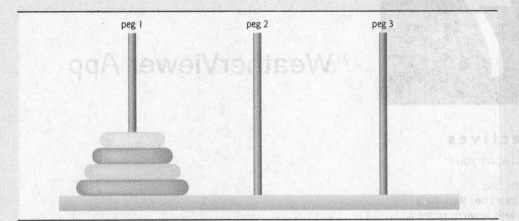

Fig. 6.35 | The Towers of Hanoi for the case with four disks.

Let's assume that the priests are attempting to move the disks from peg 1 to peg 3. We wish to develop an algorithm that will display the precise sequence of peg-to-peg disk transfers.

If we were to approach this problem with conventional methods, we would rapidly find ourselves hopelessly knotted up in managing the disks. Instead, if we attack the problem with recursion in mind, it immediately becomes tractable. Moving n disks can be viewed in terms of moving only $n - 1$ disks (hence the recursion) as follows:

a) Move $n - 1$ disks from peg 1 to peg 2, using peg 3 as a temporary holding area.

b) Move the last disk (the largest) from peg 1 to peg 3.

c) Move the $n - 1$ disks from peg 2 to peg 3, using peg 1 as a temporary holding area.

The process ends when the last task involves moving $n = 1$ disk (i.e., the base case). This task is accomplished by simply moving the disk, without the need for a temporary holding area.

Write an app to solve the Towers of Hanoi problem. Allow the user to enter the number of disks. Use a recursive Tower method with four parameters:

a) the number of disks to be moved,

b) the peg on which these disks are initially threaded,

c) the peg to which this stack of disks is to be moved, and

d) the peg to be used as a temporary holding area.

Your app should display the precise instructions it will take to move the disks from the starting peg to the destination peg and should show animations of the disks moving from peg to peg. For example, to move a stack of three disks from peg 1 to peg 3, your app should display the following series of moves and the corresponding animations:

```
1 --> 3 (This notation means "Move one disk from peg 1 to peg 3.")
1 --> 2
3 --> 2
1 --> 3
2 --> 1
2 --> 3
1 --> 3
```

7

WeatherViewer App

Objectives

In this chapter you'll:

- Use the free OpenWeatherMap.org REST web services to get a 16-day weather forecast for a city specified by the user.

- Use an AsyncTask and an HttpUrlConnection to invoke a REST web service or to download an image in a separate thread and deliver results to the GUI thread.

- Process a JSON response using package org.json classes JSONObjects and JSONArrays.

- Define an ArrayAdapter that specifies the data to display in a ListView.

- Use the ViewHolder pattern to reuse views that scroll off the screen in a ListView, rather than creating new views.

- Use the material design components TextInputLayout, Snackbar and FloatingActionButton from the Android Design Support Library.

7.1 Introduction

The **WeatherViewer** app (Fig. 7.1) uses the free OpenWeatherMap.org REST web services to obtain a specified city's 16-day weather forecast. The app receives the weather data in *JSON (JavaScript Object Notation)* data format. The list of weather data is displayed in a ListView—a view that displays a scrollable list of items. In this app, you'll use a custom list-item format to display:

- a weather-condition icon
- the day of the week with a text description of that day's weather
- the day's low and high temperatures (in °F), and
- the humidity percentage.

The preceding items represent a subset of the returned forecast data. For details of the data returned by the 16-day weather forecast API, visit:

> http://openweathermap.org/forecast16

For a list of all weather data APIs provided by OpenWeatherMap.org, visit:

> http://openweathermap.org/api

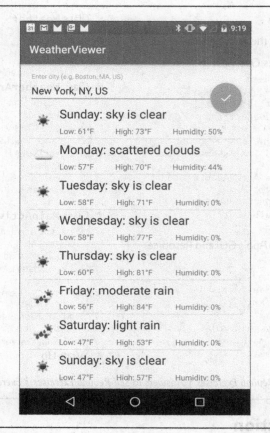

Fig. 7.1 | **Weather Viewer** app displaying the New York, NY, US weather forecast.

7.2 Test-Driving the WeatherViewer App

Opening and Running the App
Open Android Studio and open the **WeatherViewer** app from the WeatherViewer folder in the book's examples folder. Before running this app, you must add your own OpenWeatherMap.org API key. See Section 7.3.1 for information on how to obtain your key and where you should place it in the project. *This is required before you can run the app.* After adding your API key to the project, execute the app in the AVD or on a device.

Viewing a City's 16-Day Weather Forecast
When the app first executes, the EditText at the top of the user interface receives the focus and the virtual keyboard displays so you can enter a city name (Fig. 7.2). You should consider following the city with a comma and the country code. In this case, we entered New York, NY, US to locate the weather for New York, NY in the United States. Once you've entered the city, touch the circular FloatingActionButton containing the done icon (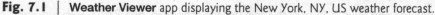) to submit the city to the app, which then requests that city's 16-day weather forecast (shown in Fig. 7.1).

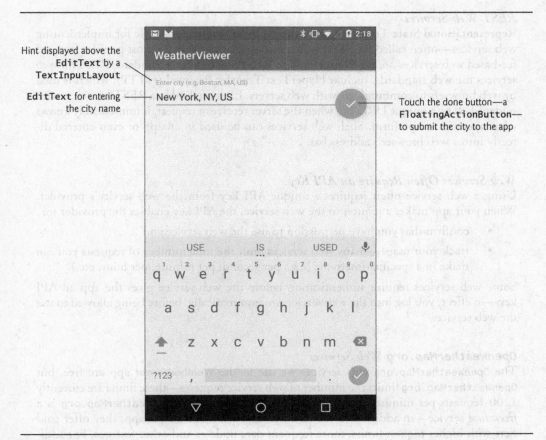

Hint displayed above the
EditText by a
TextInputLayout

EditText for entering
the city name

Touch the done button—a
FloatingActionButton—
to submit the city to the app

Fig. 7.2 | Entering a city.

7.3 Technologies Overview

This section introduces the features you'll use to build the **WeatherViewer** app.

7.3.1 Web Services

This chapter introduces web services, which promote software portability and reusability in applications that operate over the Internet. A **web service** is a software component that can be accessed over a network.

The machine on which a web service resides is the **web service host**. The client—in this case the **WeatherViewer** app—sends a request over a network to the web service host, which processes the request and returns a response over the network to the client. This distributed computing benefits systems in various ways. For example, an app can access data on demand via a web service, rather than storing the data directly on the device. Similarly, an app lacking the processing power to perform specific computations could use a web service to take advantage of another system's superior resources.

REST Web Services

Representational State Transfer (REST) refers to an architectural style for implementing web services—often called **RESTful web services**. Many of today's most popular free and fee-based web services are RESTful. Though REST itself is not a standard, RESTful web services use web standards, such as HyperText Transfer Protocol (HTTP), which is used by web browsers to communicate with web servers. Each method in a RESTful web service is identified by a unique URL. So, when the server receives a request, it immediately knows what operation to perform. Such web services can be used in an app or even entered directly into a web browser's address bar.

Web Services Often Require an API Key

Using a web service often requires a unique **API key** from the web service's provider. When your app makes a request to the web service, the API key enables the provider to:

- confirm that you have permission to use the web service and

- track your usage—many web services limit the total number of requests you can make in a specific timeframe (e.g., per second, per minute, per hour, etc.).

Some web services require authentication before the web service gives the app an API key—in effect, you log into the web service programmatically, before being allowed to use the web service.

OpenWeatherMap.org Web Services

The OpenWeatherMap.org web services we use in the **WeatherViewer** app are free, but OpenWeatherMap.org limits the number of web service requests—these limits are currently 1200 requests-per-minute and 1.7 million requests-per-day. OpenWeatherMap.org is a *freemium* service—in addition to the free tier that you'll use in this app, they offer paid tiers with higher request limits, more frequent data updates and other features. For additional information about the OpenWeatherMap.org web services, visit:

    http://openweathermap.org/api

OpenWeatherMap.org Web Service License

OpenWeatherMap.org uses a creative commons public license for its web services. For the license terms, visit:

    http://creativecommons.org/licenses/by-sa/2.0/

For more information about the license terms, see the Licenses section at

    http://openweathermap.org/terms

Obtaining an OpenWeatherMap.org API Key

Before running this app, you must obtain your own OpenWeatherMap.org API key from

    http://openweathermap.org/register

After registering, copy the hexadecimal API key from the confirmation web page, then replace YOUR_API_KEY in strings.xml with the key.

7.3.2 JavaScript Object Notation (JSON) and the org.json Package

JavaScript Object Notation (JSON) is an alternative to XML for representing data. JSON is a text-based data-interchange format used to represent objects in JavaScript as collections of name/value pairs represented as Strings. JSON is a simple format that makes objects easy to create, read and parse and, because it's much less verbose than XML, allows programs to transmit data efficiently across the Internet. Each JSON object is represented as a list of property names and values contained in curly braces, in the following format:

> {*propertyName1*: *value1*, *propertyName2*: *value2*}

Each property name is a String. Arrays are represented in JSON with square brackets in the following format:

> [*value1*, *value2*, *value3*]

Each array element can be a String, number, JSON object, true, false or null. Figure 7.3 sample JSON returned by OpenWeatherMap.org's daily forecast web service used in this app—this particular sample contains two days of weather data (lines 15–57).

```
 1   {
 2      "city": {
 3         "id": 5128581,
 4         "name": "New York",
 5         "coord": {
 6            "lon": -74.005966,
 7            "lat": 40.714272
 8         },
 9         "country": "US",
10         "population": 0
11      },
12      "cod": "200",
13      "message": 0.0102,
14      "cnt": 2,
15      "list": [{ // you'll use this array of objects to get the daily weather
16         "dt": 1442419200,
17         "temp": {
18            "day": 79.9,
19            "min": 71.74,
20            "max": 82.53,
21            "night": 71.85,
22            "eve": 82.53,
23            "morn": 71.74
24         },
25         "pressure": 1037.39,
26         "humidity": 64,
27         "weather": [{
28            "id": 800,
29            "main": "Clear",
30            "description": "sky is clear",
31            "icon": "01d"
32         }],
```

Fig. 7.3 | Sample JSON from the OpenWeatherMap.org daily forecast web service. (Part I of 2.)

```
33          "speed": 0.92,
34          "deg": 250,
35          "clouds": 0
36       }, { // end of first array element and beginning of second one
37          "dt": 1442505600,
38          "temp": {
39             "day": 79.92,
40             "min": 66.72,
41             "max": 83.1,
42             "night": 70.79,
43             "eve": 81.99,
44             "morn": 66.72
45          },
46          "pressure": 1032.46,
47          "humidity": 62,
48          "weather": [{
49             "id": 800,
50             "main": "Clear",
51             "description": "sky is clear",
52             "icon": "01d"
53          }],
54          "speed": 1.99,
55          "deg": 224,
56          "clouds": 0
57       }] // end of second array element and end of array
58   }
```

Fig. 7.3 | Sample JSON from the `OpenWeatherMap.org` daily forecast web service. (Part 2 of 2.)

There are many properties in the JSON object returned by the daily forecast. We use only the `"list"` property—an array of JSON objects representing the forecasts for up to 16 days (7 by default, unless you specify otherwise). Each `"list"` array element contains many properties of which we use:

- `"dt"`—a `long` integer containing the date/time stamp represented as the number of seconds since January 1, 1970 GMT. We convert this into a day name.

- `"temp"`—a JSON object containing `double` properties representing the day's temperatures. We use only the minimum (`"min"`) and maximum (`"max"`) temperatures, but the web service also returns the average daytime (`"day"`), nighttime (`"night"`), evening (`"eve"`) and morning (`"morn"`) temperatures.

- `"humidity"`—an `int` representing the humidity percentage.

- `"weather"`—a JSON object containing several properties, including a description of the conditions (`"description"`) and the name of an icon that represents the conditions (`"icon"`).

org.json Package

You'll use the following classes from the **`org.json` package** to process the JSON data that the app receives (Section 7.7.6):

- **`JSONObject`**—One of this class's constructors converts a `String` of JSON data into a `JSONObject` containing a `Map<String, Object>` that maps the JSON keys to their corresponding values. You access the JSON properties in your code via JSONObject's *get* methods, which enable you to obtain a JSON key's value as one of the types JSONObject, JSONArray, Object, boolean, double, int, long or String.

- **JSONArray**—This class represents a JSON array and provides methods for accessing its elements. The "list" property in the OpenWeatherMap.org response will be manipulated as a JSONArray.

7.3.3 HttpUrlConnection Invoking a REST Web Service

To invoke the OpenWeatherMap.org daily forecast web service, you'll convert the web service's URL String into a URL object, then use the URL to open an HttpUrlConnection (Section 7.7.5). This will make the HTTP request to the web service. To receive the JSON response, you'll read all the data from the HttpUrlConnection's InputStream and place it in a String. We'll show you how to convert that to a JSONObject for processing.

7.3.4 Using AsyncTask to Perform Network Requests Outside the GUI Thread

You should perform *long-running operations* or operations that *block* execution until they complete (e.g., network, file and database access) *outside* the GUI thread. This helps maintain application responsiveness and avoid *Activity Not Responding (ANR) dialogs* that appear when Android thinks the GUI is not responsive. Recall from Chapter 6, however, that updates to an app's user interface must be performed in the GUI thread, because GUI components are not thread safe.

To perform long-running tasks that result in updates to the GUI, Android provides class **AsyncTask** (package android.os), which performs the long-running operation in one thread and delivers the results to the GUI thread. The details of creating and manipulating threads are handled for you by class AsyncTask, as are communicating the results from the AsyncTask to the GUI thread. We'll use two AsyncTask subclasses in this app—one will invoke the OpenWeatherMap.org web service (Section 7.7.5) and the other will download a weather-condition image (Section 7.6.5).

7.3.5 ListView, ArrayAdapter and the View-Holder Pattern

This app displays the weather data in a ListView (package android.widget)—a scrollable list of items. ListView is a subclass of **AdapterView** (package android.widget), which represents a view that get's its data from a data source via an **Adapter** object (package android.widget). In this app, we use a subclass of **ArrayAdapter** (package android.widget) to create an object that populates the ListView using data from an ArrayList collection object (Section 7.6). When the app updates the ArrayList with weather data, we'll call the ArrayAdapter's **notifyDataSetChanged** method to indicate that the underlying data in the ArrayList has changed. The adapter then notifies the ListView to update its list of displayed items. This is known as **data binding**. Several types of AdapterViews can be bound to data using an Adapter. In Chapter 9, you'll learn how to bind database data to a ListView. For more details on data binding in Android and several tutorials, visit

http://developer.android.com/guide/topics/ui/binding.html

View-Holder Pattern

By default, a `ListView` can display one or two `TextViews`. In this app, you'll customize the `ListView` items to display an `ImageView` and several `TextViews` in a custom layout. Creating custom `ListView` items involves the expensive runtime overhead of creating new objects dynamically. For large lists with complex list-item layouts and for which the user is scrolling rapidly, this overhead can prevent smooth scrolling. To reduce this overhead, as `ListView` items scroll off the screen, Android reuses those list items for the new ones that are scrolling onto the screen. For complex item layouts, you can take advantage of the existing GUI components in the reused list items to increase a `ListView`'s performance.

To do this, we introduce the **view-holder pattern** in which you create a class (typically named `ViewHolder`) containing instance variables for the views that display a `ListView` item's data. When a `ListView` item is created, you also create a `ViewHolder` object and initialize its instance variables with references to the item's nested views. You then store that `ViewHolder` object with the `ListView` item, which is a `View`. Class `View`'s **setTag** method allows you to add any `Object` to a `View`. This `Object` is then available to you via the `View`'s **getTag** method. We'll specify as the tag the `ViewHolder` object that contains references to the `ListView` item's nested views.

As a new item is about to scroll onto the screen, the `ListView` checks whether a reusable view is available. If not, we inflate the new item's view from a layout XML file, then store references to the GUI components in a `ViewHolder` object. Then we'll use `setTag` to set that `ViewHolder` object as the tag for the `ListView` item. If there is a reusable item available, we'll get that item's tag with `getTag`, which will return the existing `ViewHolder` object that was created previously for that `ListView` item. Regardless of how we obtain the `ViewHolder` object, we'll then display data in the `ViewHolder`'s referenced views.

7.3.6 FloatingActionButton

Users touch buttons to initiate actions. With material design in Android 5.0, Google introduced the **floating action button** (Google refers to this as the "FAB") as a button that floats over the app's user interface—that is, it has a higher material-design elevation than the rest of the user interface—and that specifies an important action. For example, a contacts app might use a floating action button containing a + icon to promote the action for adding a new contact. In this app, we use a floating action button containing a done icon (✓) to enable the user to submit a city to the app and obtain that city's forecast. With Android 6.0 and the new Android Design Support Library, Google formalized the floating action button as class **FloatingActionButton** (package android.support.design.widget). In Android Studio 1.4, Google reimplemented the app templates to use material design, and most new template include a `FloatingActionButton` by default.

`FloatingActionButton` is a subclass of `ImageView`, which enables a `FloatingAction-Button` to display an image. The material design guidelines suggest that you position a `FloatingActionButton` at least 16dp from the edges of a phone device and at least 24dp from the edges of a tablet device—the default app templates configure this for you. For more details about how and when you should use a `FloatingActionButton`, visit:

```
https://www.google.com/design/spec/components/buttons-floating-
     action-button.html
```

7.3.7 TextInputLayout

In this app, you'll use an EditText to enable the user to enter the city for which you'd like to obtain a weather forecast. To help the user understand an EditText's purpose, you can provide hint text that's displayed when the EditText is empty. Once the user starts entering text, the hint disappears—possibly causing the user to forget the EditText's purpose.

The Android Design Support Library's TextInputLayout (package android.support.design.widget) solves this problem. In a TextInputLayout, when the EditText receives the focus, the TextInputLayout animates the hint text from it's original size to a smaller size that's displayed above the EditText so that the user can enter data and see the hint (Fig. 7.2). In this app, the EditText receives the focus as the app begins executing, so the TextInputLayout immediately moves the hint above the EditText.

7.3.8 Snackbar

A **Snackbar** (package android.support.design.widget) is a material design component similar in concept to a Toast. In addition to appearing on the screen for a specified time limit, Snackbars are also interactive. Users can swipe them away to dismiss them. A Snackbar also can have an associated action to perform when the user touches the Snackbar. In this app, we'll use a Snackbar to display informational messages.

7.4 Building the App's GUI and Resource Files

In this section, we review the new features in the GUI and resource files for the **Weather Viewer** app.

7.4.1 Creating the Project

Create a new project using the template **Blank Activity**. In the **Create New Project** dialog's **New Project** step, specify:

- **Application name:** WeatherViewer
- **Company Domain:** deitel.com (or specify your own domain name)

For the remaining steps in the **Create New Project** dialog, use the same settings as in Section 2.3. Follow the steps in Section 2.5.2 to add an app icon to your project. Also, follow the steps in Section 4.4.3 to configure Java SE 7 support for the project.

7.4.2 AndroidManifest.xml

The **WeatherViewer** is designed for only portrait orientation. Follow the steps you performed in Section 3.7 to set the android:screenOrientation property to portrait. In addition, add the following Internet-access permission to the <manifest> element before its nested <application> element:

```
<uses-permission android:name="android.permission.INTERNET" />
```

This allows the app to access the Internet, which is required to invoke a web service.

Permissions That Are Automatically Granted in Android 6.0

The new Android 6.0 permissions model (introduced in Chapter 5) automatically grants the Internet permission at installation time, because Internet access is considered a fundamental capability in today's apps. In Android 6.0, the Internet permission and many others that, according to Google, are not "great risk to the user's privacy or security" are granted automatically at installation time—these permissions are grouped into the category **PROTECTION_NORMAL**. For a complete list of such permissions, visit:

> https://developer.android.com/preview/features/runtime-
> permissions.html#best-practices

Android does not ask users to grant such permissions, nor can users revoke such permissions from the app. For this reason, your code does not need to check whether the app has a given PROTECTION_NORMAL permission. You must still request these permissions in AndroidManifest.xml, however, for backward compatibility with earlier Android versions.

7.4.3 strings.xml

Double click strings.xml in the res/values folder, then click the **Open editor** link to display the **Translations Editor** and create the String resources in Fig. 7.4.

Key	Value
api_key	*Use your own OpenWeatherMap.org API key for this resource's value.*
web_service_url	http://api.openweathermap.org/data/2.5/forecast/daily?q=
invalid_url	Invalid URL
weather_condition_image	A graphical representation of the weather conditions
high_temp	High: %s
low_temp	Low: %s
day_description	%1$s: %2$s
humidity	Humidity: %s
hint_text	Enter city (e.g, Boston, MA, US)
read_error	Unable to read weather data
connect_error	Unable to connect to OpenWeatherMap.org

Fig. 7.4 | String resources used in the **WeatherViewer** app.

7.4.4 colors.xml

The Android Studio **Blank Activity** template customizes the app's primary, dark primary and accent colors. In this app, we changed the template's accent color (colorAccent) to a blue shade (hexadecimal value #448AFF) in colors.xml.

7.4.5 activity_main.xml

The Android Studio **Blank Activity** template breaks MainActivity's GUI into two files:

- activity_main.xml defines the activity's Toolbar (the app bar replacement in an AppCompatActivity) and a FloatingActionButton, which is positioned in the bottom-right corner by default.
- content_main.xml defines the rest of MainActivity's GUI and is included in the activity_main.xml file via an <include> element.

Make the following changes to `activity_main.xml` for this app:

1. Add the **id** `coordinatorLayout` to the `CoordinatorLayout`—you'll use this to specify the layout in which a Snackbar will be displayed.

2. Add the material design done (✓) button to the project via the **Vector Asset Studio** (as you did in Section 4.4.9), then specify this new icon for the predefined `FloatingActionButton`'s **src** property.

3. Edit the layout's XML to configure several `FloatingActionButton` properties that are not available via the **Properties** window. Change the `layout_gravity` from `bottom|end` to `top|end` so that the `FloatingActionButton` appears at the top right of the user interface.

4. To move the button to overlap the `EditText`'s right edge, define a new dimension resource named `fab_margin_top` with the value 90dp. Using this dimension resource and the `fab_margin` dimension resource defined by the **Blank Activity** template to define the following `FloatingActionButton` margins:

   ```
   android:layout_marginTop="@dimen/fab_margin_top"
   android:layout_marginEnd="@dimen/fab_margin"
   android:layout_marginBottom="@dimen/fab_margin"
   android:layout_marginStart="@dimen/fab_margin"
   ```

5. Finally, remove the `FloatingActionButton`'s `layout_margin` that was predefined by the **Blank Activity** template.

7.4.6 content_main.xml

This layout is included into `activity_main.xml` and defines `MainActivity`'s primary GUI. Perform the following steps:

1. Remove the default `TextView` defined by the **Blank Activity** template and change the `RelativeLayout` to a vertical `LinearLayout`.

2. Next, insert a `TextInputLayout`. In the layout editor's **Design** view, click **Custom-View** in the **Custom** section. In the dialog that appears, begin typing `TextInput-Layout` to search the list of custom GUI components. Once the IDE highlights `TextInputLayout`, click **OK**, then in the **Component Tree**, click the `LinearLayout` to insert the `TextInputLayout` as a nested layout.

3. To add an `EditText` to the `TextInputLayout`, switch to the layout editor's **Text** view, then change the `TextInputLayout` element's closing `/>` to `>`, position the cursor to the right of the `>`, press *Enter* and type `</`. The IDE will auto-complete the closing tag. Between the `TextInputLayout`'s starting and ending tags, type `<EditText`. The IDE will show an auto-complete window with `EditText` selected. Press *Enter* to insert an `EditText`, then set its `layout_width` to `match_parent` and `layout_height` to `wrap_content`. In **Design** view, set the `EditText`'s **id** to `locationEditText`, check its **singleLine** property's checkbox and set its **hint** property to the `String` resource `hint_text`.

4. To complete the layout, drag a `ListView` onto the `LinearLayout` in the **Component Tree**. Set its **layout:width** to `match_parent`, its **layout:height** to `0dp`, its **layout:weight** to 1 and its **id** to `weatherListView`. Recall that the **layout:height** value

0dp is recommended by the IDE for more efficient rendering when using the **layout:weight** to determine a View's height.

7.4.7 list_item.xml

You'll now add the list_item.xml layout to the project and define the custom layout for displaying weather data in a ListView item (Fig. 7.5). This layout will be inflated by the WeatherArrayAdapter to create the user interface for new ListView items (Section 7.6.4).

Horizontal **LinearLayout** containing an **ImageView** and **GridLayout**

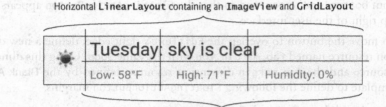

Two row and three column **GridLayout** containing four **TextViews**

Fig. 7.5 | Layout for one day's weather displayed in a ListView item.

Step 1: Creating the Layout File and Customizing the LinearLayout's Orientation
Create the list_item.xml layout file by performing the following steps:

1. Right click the project's layout folder, and select **New > Layout resource file**.

2. Enter list_item.xml in the **File name** field of the **New Resource File** dialog.

3. Ensure that LinearLayout is specified in the **Root element** field, then click **OK**. The list_item.xml file will appear in the layout directory in the **Project** window and will open in the layout editor.

4. Select the LinearLayout and change its orientation to horizontal—this layout will consist of an ImageView and a GridLayout containing the other views.

Step 2: Adding the ImageView for Displaying a Weather-Condition Icon
Perform the following steps to add and configure the ImageView:

1. Drag an ImageView from the **Palette** onto the LinearLayout in the **Component Tree**.

2. Set the **id** to conditionImageView.

3. Set the **layout:width** to 50dp—define the dimension resource image_side_length for this value.

4. Set the **layout:height** to match_parent—the ImageView's height will match the ListView item's height.

5. Set the **contentDescription** to the String resource weather_condition_image that you created in Section 7.4.3.

6. Set the **scaleType** to fitCenter—the icon will fit within the ImageView's bounds and be centered horizontally and vertically.

Step 3: Adding the GridLayout for Displaying the TextViews

Perform the following steps to add and configure the GridLayout:

1. Drag a GridLayout from the **Palette** onto the LinearLayout in the **Component Tree.**

2. Set the **columnCount** to 3 and the **rowCount** to 2.

3. Set the **layout:width** to 0dp—this GridLayout's width will be determined by the **layout:weight.**

4. Set the **layout:height** to match_parent—the GridLayout's height will match the ListView item's height.

5. Set the **layout:weight** to 1—the GridLayout's width will occupy all remaining horizontal space in its parent LinearLayout.

6. Check the **useDefaultMargins** property to add the default spacing between the GridLayout's cells.

Step 4: Adding the TextViews

Perform the following steps to add and configure the four TextViews:

1. Drag a **Large Text** onto the GridLayout in the **Component Tree** and set its **id** to dayTextView, its **layout:column** to 0 and its **layout:columnSpan** to 3.

2. Drag three **Plain TextViews** onto the GridLayout in the **Component Tree** and set their **ids** to lowTextView, hiTextView and humidityTextView, respectively. Set each of these TextViews' **layout:row** to 1 and **layout:columnWeight** to 1. These TextViews will all appear in the GridLayout's second row and, because they all have the same **layout:columnWeight**, the columns will be sized equally.

3. Set lowTextView's **layout:column** to 0, hiTextView's **layout:column** to 1 and humidityTextView's **layout:column** to 2.

This completes the list_item.xml layout. You do not need to change the **text** property of any of the TextViews—their text will be set programmatically.

7.5 Class Weather

This app consists of three classes that are discussed in Sections 7.5—7.7:

- Class Weather (this section) represents one day's weather data. Class MainActivity will convert the JSON weather data into an ArrayList<Weather>.

- Class WeatherArrayAdapter (Section 7.6) defines a custom ArrayAdapter subclass for binding the ArrayList<Weather> to the MainActivity's ListView. ListView items are indexed from 0 and each ListView item's nested views are populated with data from the Weather object at the same index in the ArrayList<Weather>.

- Class MainActivity (Section 7.7) defines the app's user interface and the logic for interacting with the OpenWeatherMap.org daily forecast web service and processing the JSON response.

In this section, we focus on class Weather.

7.5.1 package Statement, import Statements and Instance Variables

Figure 7.6 contains the package statement, import statements and class Weather's instance variables. You'll use classes from the java.text and java.util packages (lines 5–8) to convert the timestamp for each day's weather into that day's name (Monday, Tuesday, etc.). The instance variables are declared final, because they do not need to be modified after they're initialized. We also made them public—recall that Java Strings are immutable, so even though the instance variables are public, their values cannot change.

```java
1   // Weather.java
2   // Maintains one day's weather information
3   package com.deitel.weatherviewer;
4
5   import java.text.NumberFormat;
6   import java.text.SimpleDateFormat;
7   import java.util.Calendar;
8   import java.util.TimeZone;
9
10  class Weather {
11      public final String dayOfWeek;
12      public final String minTemp;
13      public final String maxTemp;
14      public final String humidity;
15      public final String description;
16      public final String iconURL;
17
```

Fig. 7.6 | Weather class package statement, import statements and instance variables.

7.5.2 Constructor

The Weather constructor (Fig. 7.7) initializes the class's instance variables:

- The NumberFormat object creates Strings from numeric values. Lines 22–23 configure the object to round floating-point values to whole numbers.

- Line 25 calls our utility method convertTimeStampToDay (Section 7.5.3) to get the String day name and initialize dayOfWeek.

- Lines 26–27 format the day's minimum and maximum temperature values as whole numbers using the numberFormat object. We append °F to the end of each formatted String, as we'll request Fahrenheit temperatures—the Unicode escape sequence \u00B0 represents the degree symbol (°). The OpenWeatherMap.org APIs also support Kelvin (the default) and Celsius temperature formats.

- Lines 28–29 get a NumberFormat for locale-specific percentage formatting, then use it to format the humidity percentage. The web service returns this percentage as a whole number, so we divide that by 100.0 for formatting—in the U.S. locale, 1.00 is formatted as 100%, 0.5 is formatted as 50%, etc.

- Line 30 initializes the weather condition description.

- Lines 31–32 create a URL String representing the weather condition image for the day's weather—this will be used to download the image.

```
18        // constructor
19        public Weather(long timeStamp, double minTemp, double maxTemp,
20           double humidity, String description, String iconName) {
21           // NumberFormat to format double temperatures rounded to integers
22           NumberFormat numberFormat = NumberFormat.getInstance();
23           numberFormat.setMaximumFractionDigits(0);
24
25           this.dayOfWeek = convertTimeStampToDay(timeStamp);
26           this.minTemp = numberFormat.format(minTemp) + "\u00B0F";
27           this.maxTemp = numberFormat.format(maxTemp) + "\u00B0F";
28           this.humidity =
29              NumberFormat.getPercentInstance().format(humidity / 100.0);
30           this.description = description;
31           this.iconURL =
32              "http://openweathermap.org/img/w/" + iconName + ".png";
33        }
34
```

Fig. 7.7 | Weather class constructor.

7.5.3 Method convertTimeStampToDay

Utility method convertTimeStampToDay (Fig. 7.8) receives as its argument a long value representing the number of seconds since January 1, 1970 GMT—the standard way time is represented on Linux systems (Android is based on Linux). To perform the conversion:

- Line 37 gets a Calendar object for manipulating dates and times, then line 38 calls method setTimeInMillis to set the time using the timestamp argument. The timestamp is in seconds so we multiply by 1000 to convert it to milliseconds.

- Line 39 gets the default TimeZone object, which we use to adjust the time, based on the device's time zone (lines 42–43).

- Line 46 creates a SimpleDateFormat that formats a Date object. The constructor argument "EEEE" formats the Date as just the day name (Monday, Tuesday, etc.). For a complete list of formats, visit:

   http://developer.android.com/reference/java/text/
      SimpleDateFormat.html

- Line 47 formats and returns the day name. Calendar's getTime method returns a Date object containing the time. This Date is passed to the SimpleDateFormat's format method to get the day name.

```
35        // convert timestamp to a day's name (e.g., Monday, Tuesday, ...)
36        private static String convertTimeStampToDay(long timeStamp) {
37           Calendar calendar = Calendar.getInstance(); // create Calendar
38           calendar.setTimeInMillis(timeStamp * 1000); // set time
39           TimeZone tz = TimeZone.getDefault(); // get device's time zone
40
```

Fig. 7.8 | Weather method convertTimeStampToDay. (Part I of 2.)

```
41        // adjust time for device's time zone
42        calendar.add(Calendar.MILLISECOND,
43           tz.getOffset(calendar.getTimeInMillis()));
44
45        // SimpleDateFormat that returns the day's name
46        SimpleDateFormat dateFormatter = new SimpleDateFormat("EEEE");
47        return dateFormatter.format(calendar.getTime());
48     }
49  }
```

Fig. 7.8 | Weather method convertTimeStampToDay. (Part 2 of 2.)

7.6 Class WeatherArrayAdapter

Class WeatherArrayAdapter defines a subclass of ArrayAdapter for binding an Array-List<Weather> to the MainActivity's ListView.

7.6.1 package Statement and import Statements

Figure 7.9 contains WeatherArrayAdapter's package statement and import statements. We'll discuss the imported types as we encounter them.

This app's ListView items require a custom layout. Each item contains an image (the weather-condition icon) and text representing the day, weather description, low temperature, high temperature and humidity. To map weather data to ListView items, we extend class ArrayAdapter (line 23) so that we can override ArrayAdapter method getView to configure a custom layout for each ListView item.

```
1   // WeatherArrayAdapter.java
2   // An ArrayAdapter for displaying a List<Weather>'s elements in a ListView
3   package com.deitel.weatherviewer;
4
5   import android.content.Context;
6   import android.graphics.Bitmap;
7   import android.graphics.BitmapFactory;
8   import android.os.AsyncTask;
9   import android.view.LayoutInflater;
10  import android.view.View;
11  import android.view.ViewGroup;
12  import android.widget.ArrayAdapter;
13  import android.widget.ImageView;
14  import android.widget.TextView;
15
16  import java.io.InputStream;
17  import java.net.HttpURLConnection;
18  import java.net.URL;
19  import java.util.HashMap;
20  import java.util.List;
21  import java.util.Map;
22
23  class WeatherArrayAdapter extends ArrayAdapter<Weather> {
```

Fig. 7.9 | WeatherArrayAdapter class package statement and import statements.

7.6.2 Nested Class ViewHolder

Nested class ViewHolder (Fig. 7.10) defines instance variables that class WeatherArray-Adapter accesses directly when manipulating ViewHolder objects. When a ListView item is created, we'll associate a new ViewHolder object with that item. If there's an existing ListView item that's being reused, we'll simply obtain that item's ViewHolder object.

```
24    // class for reusing views as list items scroll off and onto the screen
25    private static class ViewHolder {
26        ImageView conditionImageView;
27        TextView dayTextView;
28        TextView lowTextView;
29        TextView hiTextView;
30        TextView humidityTextView;
31    }
32
```

Fig. 7.10 | Nested class ViewHolder.

7.6.3 Instance Variable and Constructor

Figure 7.11 defines class WeatherArrayAdapter's instance variable and constructor. We use the instance variable bitmaps (line 34)—a Map<String, Bitmap>—to cache previously loaded weather-condition images, so they do not need to be re-downloaded as the user scrolls through the weather forecast. The cached images will remain in memory until Android terminates the app. The constructor (lines 37–39) simply calls the superclass's three-argument constructor, passing the Context (i.e., the activity in which the ListView is displayed) and the List<Weather> (the List of data to display) as the first and third arguments. The second superclass constructor argument represents a layout resource ID for a layout that contains a TextView in which a ListView item's data is displayed. The argument -1 indicates that we use a custom layout in this app, so we can display more than just one TextView.

```
33    // stores already downloaded Bitmaps for reuse
34    private Map<String, Bitmap> bitmaps = new HashMap<>();
35
36    // constructor to initialize superclass inherited members
37    public WeatherArrayAdapter(Context context, List<Weather> forecast) {
38        super(context, -1, forecast);
39    }
40
```

Fig. 7.11 | WeatherArrayAdapter class instance variable and constructor.

7.6.4 Overridden ArrayAdapter Method getView

Method **getView** (Fig. 7.12) is called to get the View that displays a ListView item's data. Overriding this method enables you to map data to a custom ListView item. The method receives the ListView item's position, the View (convertView) representing that List-View item and that ListView item's parent as arguments. By manipulating convertView, you can customize the ListView item's contents. Line 45 calls the inherited ArrayAdapter method getItem to get from the List<Weather> the Weather object that will be displayed.

Line 47 defines the ViewHolder variable that will be set to a new ViewHolder object or an existing one, depending on whether method getView's convertView argument is null.

```
41   // creates the custom views for the ListView's items
42   @Override
43   public View getView(int position, View convertView, ViewGroup parent) {
44      // get Weather object for this specified ListView position
45      Weather day = getItem(position);
46
47      ViewHolder viewHolder; // object that reference's list item's views
48
49      // check for reusable ViewHolder from a ListView item that scrolled
50      // offscreen; otherwise, create a new ViewHolder
51      if (convertView == null) { // no reusable ViewHolder, so create one
52         viewHolder = new ViewHolder();
53         LayoutInflater inflater = LayoutInflater.from(getContext());
54         convertView =
55            inflater.inflate(R.layout.list_item, parent, false);
56         viewHolder.conditionImageView =
57            (ImageView) convertView.findViewById(R.id.conditionImageView);
58         viewHolder.dayTextView =
59            (TextView) convertView.findViewById(R.id.dayTextView);
60         viewHolder.lowTextView =
61            (TextView) convertView.findViewById(R.id.lowTextView);
62         viewHolder.hiTextView =
63            (TextView) convertView.findViewById(R.id.hiTextView);
64         viewHolder.humidityTextView =
65            (TextView) convertView.findViewById(R.id.humidityTextView);
66         convertView.setTag(viewHolder);
67      }
68      else { // reuse existing ViewHolder stored as the list item's tag
69         viewHolder = (ViewHolder) convertView.getTag();
70      }
71
72      // if weather condition icon already downloaded, use it;
73      // otherwise, download icon in a separate thread
74      if (bitmaps.containsKey(day.iconURL)) {
75         viewHolder.conditionImageView.setImageBitmap(
76            bitmaps.get(day.iconURL));
77      }
78      else {
79         // download and display weather condition image
80         new LoadImageTask(viewHolder.conditionImageView).execute(
81            day.iconURL);
82      }
83
84      // get other data from Weather object and place into views
85      Context context = getContext(); // for loading String resources
86      viewHolder.dayTextView.setText(context.getString(
87         R.string.day_description, day.dayOfWeek, day.description));
88      viewHolder.lowTextView.setText(
89         context.getString(R.string.low_temp, day.minTemp));
```

Fig. 7.12 | Overridden ArrayAdapter method getView. (Part 1 of 2.)

```
90        viewHolder.hiTextView.setText(
91            context.getString(R.string.high_temp, day.maxTemp));
92        viewHolder.humidityTextView.setText(
93            context.getString(R.string.humidity, day.humidity));
94
95        return convertView; // return completed list item to display
96     }
97
```

Fig. 7.12 | Overridden ArrayAdapter method getView. (Part 2 of 2.)

If convertView is null, line 52 creates a new ViewHolder object to store references to a new ListView item's views. Next, line 53 gets the Context's LayoutInflator, which we use in lines 54–55 to inflate the ListView item's layout. The first argument is the layout to inflate (R.layout.list_item), the second is the layout's parent ViewGroup to which the layout's views will be attached and the last argument is a boolean indicating whether the views should be attached automatically. In this case, the third argument is false, because the ListView calls method getView to obtain the item's View, then attaches it to the ListView. Lines 56–65 get references to the views in the newly inflated layout and set the ViewHolder's instance variables. Line 66 sets the new ViewHolder object as the List-View item's tag to store the ViewHolder with the ListView item for future use.

If convertView is not null, the ListView is reusing a ListView item that scrolled off the screen. In this case, line 69 gets the current ListView item's tag, which is the View-Holder that was previously attached to that ListView item.

After creating or getting the ViewHolder, lines 74–93 set the data for the ListItem's views. Lines 74–82 determine if the weather-condition image was previously downloaded, in which case the bitmaps object will contain a key for the Weather object's iconURL. If so, lines 75–76 get the existing Bitmap from bitmaps and set the conditionImageView's image. Otherwise, lines 80–81 create a new LoadImageTask (Section 7.6.5) to download the image in a separate thread. The task's **execute** method receives the iconURL and initiates the task. Lines 86–93 set the Strings for the ListView item's TextViews. Finally, line 95 returns the ListView item's configured View.

Software Engineering Observation 7.1
Every time an AsyncTask is required, you must create a new object of your AsyncTask type—each AsyncTask can be executed only once.

7.6.5 AsyncTask Subclass for Downloading Images in a Separate Thread
Nested class LoadImageTask (Fig. 7.13) extends class AsyncTask and defines how to download a weather-condition image in a separate thread, then return the image to the GUI thread for display in the ListView item's ImageView.

```
98     // AsyncTask to load weather condition icons in a separate thread
99     private class LoadImageTask extends AsyncTask<String, Void, Bitmap> {
100        private ImageView imageView; // displays the thumbnail
```

Fig. 7.13 | AsyncTask subclass for downloading images in a separate thread. (Part I of 2.)

```
101
102        // store ImageView on which to set the downloaded Bitmap
103        public LoadImageTask(ImageView imageView) {
104           this.imageView = imageView;
105        }
106
107        // load image; params[0] is the String URL representing the image
108        @Override
109        protected Bitmap doInBackground(String... params) {
110           Bitmap bitmap = null;
111           HttpURLConnection connection = null;
112
113           try {
114              URL url = new URL(params[0]); // create URL for image
115
116              // open an HttpURLConnection, get its InputStream
117              // and download the image
118              connection = (HttpURLConnection) url.openConnection();
119
120              try (InputStream inputStream = connection.getInputStream()) {
121                 bitmap = BitmapFactory.decodeStream(inputStream);
122                 bitmaps.put(params[0], bitmap); // cache for later use
123              }
124              catch (Exception e) {
125                 e.printStackTrace();
126              }
127           }
128           catch (Exception e) {
129              e.printStackTrace();
130           }
131           finally {
132              connection.disconnect(); // close the HttpURLConnection
133           }
134
135           return bitmap;
136        }
137
138        // set weather condition image in list item
139        @Override
140        protected void onPostExecute(Bitmap bitmap) {
141           imageView.setImageBitmap(bitmap);
142        }
143     }
144  }
```

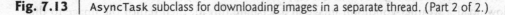

Fig. 7.13 | AsyncTask subclass for downloading images in a separate thread. (Part 2 of 2.)

AsyncTask is a generic type that requires three type parameters:

- The first is the variable-length parameter-list type (String) for AsyncTask's **doInBackground** method, which you *must* overload (lines 108–136). When you call the task's execute method, it creates a thread in which doInBackground performs the task. This app passes the weather-condition icon's URL String as the argument to the AsyncTask's execute method (Fig. 7.12, lines 80–81).

- The second is the variable-length parameter-list type for the AsyncTask's **onProgressUpdate** method. This method executes in the GUI thread and is used to receive *intermediate updates* of the specified type from a long-running task. Overriding this method is optional. We don't use it in this example, so we specify type Void here and ignore this type parameter.

- The third is the type of the task's result (Bitmap), which is passed to AsyncTask's **onPostExecute** method (139–143). This method executes in the GUI thread and enables the ListView item's ImageView to display the AsyncTask's results. The ImageView to update is specified as an argument to class LoadImageTask's constructor (lines 103–105) and stored in the instance variable at line 100.

A key benefit of using an AsyncTask is that it handles the details of creating threads and executing its methods on the appropriate threads for you, so that you do not have to interact with the threading mechanism directly.

Downloading the Weather-Condition Image
Method doInBackground uses an HttpURLConnection to download the weather-condition image. Line 114 converts the URL String that was passed to the AsyncTask's execute method (params[0]) into a URL object. Next, line 118 calls class URL's method openConnection to get an HttpURLConnection—the cast is required, because the method returns a URLConnection. Method openConnection requests the content specified by URL. Line 120 gets the HttpURLConnection's InputStream, which we pass to BitmapFactory method decodeStream to read the image's bytes and return a Bitmap object containing the image (line 121). Line 122 caches the downloaded image in the bitmaps Map for potential reuse and line 132 calls HttpURLConnection's inherited method disconnect to close the connection and release its resources. Line 135 returns the downloaded Bitmap, which is then passed to onPostExecute—in the GUI thread—to display the image.

7.7 Class MainActivity

Class MainActivity defines the app's user interface, the logic for interacting with the OpenWeatherMap.org daily forecast web service and the logic for processing the JSON response from the web service. The nested AsyncTask subclass GetWeatherTask performs the web service request in a separate thread (Section 7.7.5). MainActivity does not require a menu in this app, so we removed the methods onCreateOptionsMenu and onOptionsItemSelected from the autogenerated code.

7.7.1 package Statement and import Statements
Figure 7.14 contains MainActivity's package statement and import statements. We'll discuss the imported types as we encounter them.

```
1   // MainActivity.java
2   // Displays a 16-dayOfWeek weather forecast for the specified city
3   package com.deitel.weatherviewer;
```

Fig. 7.14 | Class MainActivity's package statement and import statements. (Part 1 of 2.)

```
4
5   import android.content.Context;
6   import android.os.AsyncTask;
7   import android.os.Bundle;
8   import android.support.design.widget.FloatingActionButton;
9   import android.support.design.widget.Snackbar;
10  import android.support.v7.app.AppCompatActivity;
11  import android.support.v7.widget.Toolbar;
12  import android.view.View;
13  import android.view.inputmethod.InputMethodManager;
14  import android.widget.EditText;
15  import android.widget.ListView;
16
17  import org.json.JSONArray;
18  import org.json.JSONException;
19  import org.json.JSONObject;
20
21  import java.io.BufferedReader;
22  import java.io.IOException;
23  import java.io.InputStreamReader;
24  import java.net.HttpURLConnection;
25  import java.net.URL;
26  import java.net.URLEncoder;
27  import java.util.ArrayList;
28  import java.util.List;
29
```

Fig. 7.14 | Class MainActivity's package statement and import statements. (Part 2 of 2.)

7.7.2 Instance Variables

Class MainActivity (Fig. 7.15) extends class AppCompatActivity and defines three instance variables:

- weatherList (line 32) is an ArrayList<Weather> that stores the Weather objects—each represents one day in the daily forecast.

- weatherArrayAdapter will refer to a WeatherArrayAdapter object (Section 7.6) that binds the weatherList to the ListView's items.

- weatherListView will refer to MainActivity's ListView.

```
30  public class MainActivity extends AppCompatActivity {
31     // List of Weather objects representing the forecast
32     private List<Weather> weatherList = new ArrayList<>();
33
34     // ArrayAdapter for binding Weather objects to a ListView
35     private WeatherArrayAdapter weatherArrayAdapter;
36     private ListView weatherListView; // displays weather info
37
```

Fig. 7.15 | Class MainActivity's instance variables.

7.7.3 Overridden Activity Method onCreate

Overridden method onCreate (Fig. 7.15) configures MainActivity's GUI. Lines 41–45 were generated by Android Studio when you chose the **Blank Activity** template while creating this project. These lines inflate the GUI, create the app's Toolbar and attach the Toolbar to the activity. Recall that an AppCompatActivity must provide its own Toolbar, because app bars (formerly called action bars) are not supported in early versions of Android.

Lines 48–50 configure the weatherListView's ListAdapter—in this case, an object of the WeatherArrayAdapter subclass of ArrayAdapter. ListView method **setAdapter** connects the WeatherArrayAdapter to the ListView for populating the ListView's items.

```
38      // configure Toolbar, ListView and FAB
39      @Override
40      protected void onCreate(Bundle savedInstanceState) {
41         super.onCreate(savedInstanceState);
42         // autogenerated code to inflate layout and configure Toolbar
43         setContentView(R.layout.activity_main);
44         Toolbar toolbar = (Toolbar) findViewById(R.id.toolbar);
45         setSupportActionBar(toolbar);
46
47         // create ArrayAdapter to bind weatherList to the weatherListView
48         weatherListView = (ListView) findViewById(R.id.weatherListView);
49         weatherArrayAdapter = new WeatherArrayAdapter(this, weatherList);
50         weatherListView.setAdapter(weatherArrayAdapter);
51
52         // configure FAB to hide keyboard and initiate web service request
53         FloatingActionButton fab =
54            (FloatingActionButton) findViewById(R.id.fab);
55         fab.setOnClickListener(new View.OnClickListener() {
56            @Override
57            public void onClick(View view) {
58               // get text from locationEditText and create web service URL
59               EditText locationEditText =
60                  (EditText) findViewById(R.id.locationEditText);
61               URL url = createURL(locationEditText.getText().toString());
62
63               // hide keyboard and initiate a GetWeatherTask to download
64               // weather data from OpenWeatherMap.org in a separate thread
65               if (url != null) {
66                  dismissKeyboard(locationEditText);
67                  GetWeatherTask getLocalWeatherTask = new GetWeatherTask();
68                  getLocalWeatherTask.execute(url);
69               }
70               else {
71                  Snackbar.make(findViewById(R.id.coordinatorLayout),
72                     R.string.invalid_url, Snackbar.LENGTH_LONG).show();
73               }
74            }
75         });
76      }
77
```

Fig. 7.16 | Overridden Activity method onCreate.

Lines 53–75 configure the FloatingActionButton from the **Blank Activity** template. The onClick listener method was autogenerated by Android Studio, but we reimplemented its body for this app. We get a reference to the app's EditText then use it in line 61 to get the user's input. We pass that to method createURL (Section 7.7.4) to create the URL representing the web service request that will return the city's weather forecast.

If the URL is created successfully, line 66 programmatically hides the keyboard by calling method dismissKeyboard (Section 7.7.4). Line 67 then creates a new GetWeatherTask to obtain the weather forecast in a separate thread and line 68 executes the task, passing the URL of the web service request as an argument to AsyncTask method execute. If the URL is not created successfully, lines 71–72 create a Snackbar indicating that the URL was invalid.

7.7.4 Methods dismissKeyboard and createURL

Figure 7.17 contains MainActivity methods dismissKeyboard and createURL. Method dismissKeyboard (lines 79–83) is called to hide the soft keyboard when the user touches the FloatingActionButton to submit a city to the app. Android provides a service for managing the keyboard programmatically. You can obtain a reference to this service (and many other Android services) by calling the inherited Context method **getSystemService** with the appropriate constant—Context.INPUT_METHOD_SERVICE in this case. This method can return objects of many different types, so you must cast its return value to the appropriate type—**InputMethodManager** (package **android.view.inputmethod**). To dismiss the keyboard, call InputMethodManager method **hideSoftInputFromWindow** (line 82).

```
78      // programmatically dismiss keyboard when user touches FAB
79      private void dismissKeyboard(View view) {
80          InputMethodManager imm = (InputMethodManager) getSystemService(
81              Context.INPUT_METHOD_SERVICE);
82          imm.hideSoftInputFromWindow(view.getWindowToken(), 0);
83      }
84
85      // create openweathermap.org web service URL using city
86      private URL createURL(String city) {
87          String apiKey = getString(R.string.api_key);
88          String baseUrl = getString(R.string.web_service_url);
89
90          try {
91              // create URL for specified city and imperial units (Fahrenheit)
92              String urlString = baseUrl + URLEncoder.encode(city, "UTF-8") +
93                  "&units=imperial&cnt=16&APPID=" + apiKey;
94              return new URL(urlString);
95          }
96          catch (Exception e) {
97              e.printStackTrace();
98          }
99
100         return null; // URL was malformed
101     }
102
```

Fig. 7.17 | MainActivity methods dismissKeyboard and createURL.

Method createURL (lines 86–101) assembles the String representation of the URL for the web service request (lines 92–93). Then line 94 attempts to create and return a URL object initialized with the URL String. In line 93, we add parameters to the web service query

```
&units=imperial&cnt=16&APPID=
```

The units parameter can be imperial (for Fahrenheit temperatures), metric (for Celsius) or standard (for Kelvin)—standard is the default if you do not include the units parameter. The cnt parameter specifies how many days should be included in the forecast. The maximum is 16 and the default is 7—providing an invalid number of days results in a seven-day forecast. Finally the APPID parameter is for your OpenWeatherMap.org API key, which we load into the app from the String resource api_key. By default, the forecast is returned in JSON format, but you can add the mode parameter with the value XML or HTML, to receive XML formatted data or a web page, respectively.

7.7.5 AsyncTask Subclass for Invoking a Web Service

Nested AsyncTask subclass GetWeatherTask (Fig. 7.18) performs the web service request and processes the response in a separate thread, then passes the forecast information as a JSONObject to the GUI thread for display.

```
103     // makes the REST web service call to get weather data and
104     // saves the data to a local HTML file
105     private class GetWeatherTask
106         extends AsyncTask<URL, Void, JSONObject> {
107
108         @Override
109         protected JSONObject doInBackground(URL... params) {
110             HttpURLConnection connection = null;
111
112             try {
113                 connection = (HttpURLConnection) params[0].openConnection();
114                 int response = connection.getResponseCode();
115
116                 if (response == HttpURLConnection.HTTP_OK) {
117                     StringBuilder builder = new StringBuilder();
118
119                     try (BufferedReader reader = new BufferedReader(
120                         new InputStreamReader(connection.getInputStream()))) {
121
122                         String line;
123
124                         while ((line = reader.readLine()) != null) {
125                             builder.append(line);
126                         }
127                     }
128                     catch (IOException e) {
129                         Snackbar.make(findViewById(R.id.coordinatorLayout),
130                             R.string.read_error, Snackbar.LENGTH_LONG).show();
131                         e.printStackTrace();
132                     }
```

Fig. 7.18 | AsyncTask subclass for invoking a web service. (Part 1 of 2.)

```
133
134                     return new JSONObject(builder.toString());
135                 }
136             else {
137                 Snackbar.make(findViewById(R.id.coordinatorLayout),
138                     R.string.connect_error, Snackbar.LENGTH_LONG).show();
139             }
140         }
141         catch (Exception e) {
142             Snackbar.make(findViewById(R.id.coordinatorLayout),
143                 R.string.connect_error, Snackbar.LENGTH_LONG).show();
144             e.printStackTrace();
145         }
146         finally {
147             connection.disconnect(); // close the HttpURLConnection
148         }
149
150         return null;
151     }
152
153     // process JSON response and update ListView
154     @Override
155     protected void onPostExecute(JSONObject weather) {
156         convertJSONtoArrayList(weather); // repopulate weatherList
157         weatherArrayAdapter.notifyDataSetChanged(); // rebind to ListView
158         weatherListView.smoothScrollToPosition(0); // scroll to top
159     }
160 }
161
```

Fig. 7.18 | AsyncTask subclass for invoking a web service. (Part 2 of 2.)

For class GetWeatherTask the three generic type parameters are:

- URL for the variable-length parameter-list type of AsyncTask's doInBackground method (lines 108–51)—the URL of the web service request is passed as the only argument to the GetWeatherTask's execute method.

- Void for the variable-length parameter-list type for the onProgressUpdate method—once again, we do not use this method.

- JSONObject for the type of the task's result, which is passed to onPostExecute (154–159) in the GUI thread to display the results.

Line 113 in doInBackground creates the HttpURLConnection that's used to invoke the REST web service. As in Section 7.6.5, simply opening the connection makes the request. Line 114 gets the response code from the web server. If the response code is HttpURLConnection.HTTP_OK, the REST web service was invoked properly and there is a response to process. In this case, lines 119–126 get the HttpURLConnection's InputStream, wrap it in a BufferedReader, read each line of text from the response and append it to a StringBuilder. Then, line 134 converts the JSON String in the StringBuilder to a JSONObject and return it to the GUI thread. Line 147 disconnects the HttpURLConnection.

If there's an error reading the weather data or connecting to the web service, lines 129–130, 137–138 or 142–143 display a Snackbar indicating the problem that occurred.

These problems might occur if the device loses its network access in the middle of a request or if the device does not have network access in the first place—for example, if the device is in airplane mode.

When onPostExecute is called in the GUI thread, line 156 calls method convertJSONtoArrayList (Section 7.7.6) to extract the weather data from the JSONObject and place it in the weatherList. Then line 157 calls the ArrayAdapter's notifyDataSetChanged method, which causes the weatherListView to update itself with the new data. Line 158 calls ListView method **smoothScrollToPosition** to reposition the ListView's first item to the top of the ListView—this ensures that the new weather forecast's first day is shown at the top.

7.7.6 Method convertJSONtoArrayList

In Section 7.3.2, we discussed the JSON returned by the OpenWeatherMap.org daily weather forecast web service. Method convertJSONtoArrayList (Fig. 7.19) extracts this weather data from its JSONObject argument. First, line 164 clears the weatherList of any existing Weather objects. Processing JSON data in a JSONObject or JSONArray can result in JSONExceptions, so lines 168–188 are placed in a try block.

```
162     // create Weather objects from JSONObject containing the forecast
163     private void convertJSONtoArrayList(JSONObject forecast) {
164     weatherList.clear(); // clear old weather data
165
166     try {
167         // get forecast's "list" JSONArray
168         JSONArray list = forecast.getJSONArray("list");
169
170         // convert each element of list to a Weather object
171         for (int i = 0; i < list.length(); ++i) {
172             JSONObject day = list.getJSONObject(i); // get one day's data
173
174             // get the day's temperatures ("temp") JSONObject
175             JSONObject temperatures = day.getJSONObject("temp");
176
177             // get day's "weather" JSONObject for the description and icon
178             JSONObject weather =
179                 day.getJSONArray("weather").getJSONObject(0);
180
181             // add new Weather object to weatherList
182             weatherList.add(new Weather(
183                 day.getLong("dt"), // date/time timestamp
184                 temperatures.getDouble("min"), // minimum temperature
185                 temperatures.getDouble("max"), // maximum temperature
186                 day.getDouble("humidity"), // percent humidity
187                 weather.getString("description"), // weather conditions
188                 weather.getString("icon"))); // icon name
189         }
190     }
```

Fig. 7.19 | MainActivity method convertJSONtoArrayList. (Part 1 of 2.)

```
191      catch (JSONException e) {
192         e.printStackTrace();
193      }
194   }
195 }
```

Fig. 7.19 | MainActivity method convertJSONtoArrayList. (Part 2 of 2.)

Line 168 obtains the "list" JSONArray by calling JSONObject method **getJSONArray** with the name of the array property as an argument. Next, lines 171–189 create a Weather object for every element in the JSONArray. JSONArray method **length** returns the array's number of elements (line 171).

Next, line 172 gets a JSONObject representing one day's forecast from the JSONArray by calling method **getJSONObject**, which receives an index as its argument. Line 175 gets the "temp" JSON object, which contains the day's temperature data. Lines 178–179 get the "weather" JSON array, then get the array's first element which contains the day's weather description and icon.

Lines 182–188 create a Weather object and add it to the weatherList. Line 183 uses JSONObject method **getLong** to get the day's timestamp ("dt"), which the Weather constructor converts to the day name. Lines 184–186 call JSONObject method **getDouble** to get the minimum ("min") and maximum ("max") temperatures from the temperatures object and the "humidity" percentage from the day object. Finally, lines 187–188 use **getString** to get the weather description and the weather-condition icon Strings from the weather object.

7.8 Wrap-Up

In this chapter, you built the **WeatherViewer** app, which used OpenWeatherMap.org web services to obtain a city's 16-day weather forecast and display it in a ListView. We discussed the architectural style for implementing web services known as REST (Representational State Transfer). You learned that apps use web standards, such as HyperText Transfer Protocol (HTTP), to invoke RESTful web services and receive their responses.

The OpenWeatherMap.org web service used in this app returned the forecast as a String in JavaScript Object Notation (JSON) format. You learned that JSON is a text-based format in which objects are represented as collections of name/value pairs. You used the classes JSONObject and JSONArray from the org.json package to process the JSON data.

To invoke the web service, you converted the web service's URL String into a URL object. You then used the URL to open an HttpUrlConnection that invoked the web service via an HTTP request. The app read all the data from the HttpUrlConnection's Input-Stream and placed it in a String, then converted that String to a JSONObject for processing. We demonstrated how to perform long-running operations outside the GUI thread and receive their results in the GUI thread by using AsyncTask objects. This is particularly important for web-service requests, which have indeterminate response times.

You displayed the weather data in a ListView, using a subclass of ArrayAdapter to supply the data for each ListView item. We showed how to improve a ListView's performance via the view-holder pattern by reusing existing ListView items' views as the items scroll off the screen.

Finally, you used several material-design features from the Android Design Support Library's—a TextInputLayout to keep an EditText's hint on the screen even after the user began entering text, a FloatingActionButton to enable the user to submit input and a Snackbar to display an informational message to the user.

In Chapter 8, we build the **Twitter® Searches** app. Many mobile apps display lists of items, just as we did in this app. In Chapter 8, you'll do this by using a RecyclerView that obtains data from an ArrayList<String>. For large data sets, RecyclerView is more efficient than ListView. You'll also store app data as user preferences and learn how to launch the device's web browser to display a web page.

Self-Review Exercises

7.1 Fill in the blanks in each of the following statements:
  a) A(n) _____ is a software component that can be accessed over a network.
  b) _____ refers to an architectural style for implementing web services—often called RESTful web services
  c) Classes from the _____ package process JSON data.
  d) To invoke a REST web service, you can use a URL to open a(n) _____, which makes the HTTP request to the web service.
  e) A(n) _____ (package android.widget) displays a scrollable list of items.
  f) A(n) _____ is a button that floats over the user interface.

7.2 State whether each of the following is *true* or *false*. If *false*, explain why.
  a) Many of today's most popular free and fee-based web services are RESTful.
  b) REST is a standard protocol.
  c) You should perform long-running operations or operations that block execution until they complete (e.g., network, file and database access) outside the GUI thread.
  d) JSON (JavaScript Object Notation)—a simple way to represent JavaScript objects as numbers—is an alternative to XML for passing data between the client and the server.
  e) Arrays are represented in JSON with curly braces in the following format:

  { *value1*, *value2*, *value3* }

  f) Class JSONObject's get methods enable you to obtain a JSON key's value as one of the types JSONObject, JSONArray, Object, boolean, double, int, long or String.

Answers to Self-Review Exercises

7.1 a) web service. b) Representational State Transfer (REST). c) org.json. d) HttpUrlConnection. e) ListView. f) FloatingActionButton.

7.2 a) True. b) False. Though REST itself is not a standard, RESTful web services use web standards, such as HyperText Transfer Protocol (HTTP), which is used by web browsers to communicate with web servers. c) True. d) False. JSON (JavaScript Object Notation)—a simple way to represent JavaScript objects as *strings*—is an alternative to XML for passing data between the client and the server. e) False. Arrays are represented in JSON with *square brackets*. f) True.

Exercises

7.3 Fill in the blanks in each of the following statements:
  a) The machine on which a web service resides is the _____.
  b) Class _____ provides methods for accessing the elements of a JSON array.

   c) To perform long-running tasks that result in updates to the GUI, Android provides class _____ (package android.os), which performs the long-running operation in one thread and delivers the results to the GUI thread.

   d) In the _____ you create a class containing instance variables for the views that display a ListView item's data. When a ListView item is created, you also create an object of this class and initialize its instance variables with references to the item's nested views, then store that object with the ListView item.

   e) Class JSONObject's _____ method returns the String for a given key.

   f) ListView is a subclass of _____, which represents a view that gets its data from a data source via an Adapter object.

7.4 State whether each of the following is *true* or *false*. If *false*, explain why.

   a) To receive a JSON response from a web service invoked by an HttpUrlConnection, you read from the connection's InputStream.

   b) Each object in JSON is represented as a list of property names and values contained in curly braces, in the following format:

$$\{ \text{"propertyName1"} : value1, \text{"propertyName2"}: value2 \}$$

   c) Each value in a JSON array can be a string, a number, a JSON representation of an object, true, false or null.

   d) A ListAdapter populates a ListView using data from an ArrayList collection object.

   e) In an EditTextLayout, when the EditText receives the focus, the layout animates the hint text from it's original size to a smaller size that's displayed above the EditText.

7.5 *(Enhanced Weather Viewer App)* Investigate Android's capabilities for getting a device's last known location

      http://developer.android.com/training/location/retrieve-current.html

and the Android class Geocoder

      http://developer.android.com/reference/android/location/Geocoder.html

When the app first loads, use these capabilities to prepopulate the app's EditText with the user's location and to display the weather for that location.

7.6 *(Enhanced Quiz App)* Modify the Flag Quiz app in Chapter 4 to create your own quiz app that shows videos rather than images. Possible quizzes could include U.S. presidents, world landmarks, movie stars, recording artists, and more. Consider using YouTube web services (https://developers.google.com/youtube/) to obtain videos for display in the app. (Be sure to read the YouTube API terms of service at https://developers.google.com/youtube/terms.)

7.7 *(Word Scramble Game)* Create an app that scrambles the letters of a word or phrase and asks the user to enter the correct word or phrase. Keep track of the user's high score in the app's SharedPreferences. Include levels (three-, four-, five-, six- and seven-letter words). As a hint to the user, provide a definition with each word. Use an online dictionary's web services to select the words and the definitions that are used for hints.

7.8 *(Crossword Puzzle Generator App)* Most people have worked a crossword puzzle, but few have ever attempted to generate one. Create a crossword generator app that use an online dictionary's web services to select the words and the definitions that are used for hints. Display the corresponding hints when the user touches the first square in a word. If the square represents the beginning of both a horizontal and vertical word, show both hints.

Web Services and Mashups

Web services, inexpensive computers, abundant high-speed Internet access, open source software and many other elements have inspired new, exciting, lightweight business models that people can launch with only a small investment. Some types of websites with rich and robust functionality that might have required hundreds of thousands or even millions of dollars to build in the 1990s can now be built for nominal sums. In Chapter 1, we introduced the application-development methodology of mashups, in which you can rapidly develop powerful and intriguing applications by combining (often free) complementary web services and other forms of information feeds. One of the first mashups was www.housingmaps.com, which combined the real estate listings provided by www.craigslist.org with the mapping capabilities of Google Maps—the most widely-used web-service API—to offer maps that showed the locations of apartments for rent in a given area. Figure 1.4 provided a list of several popular web services available from companies including Google, Facebook, eBay, Netflix, Skype and more.

Check out the catalog of web-service APIs at www.programmableweb.com and the apps in Android Market for inspiration. *It's important to read the terms of service for the APIs before building your apps.* Some APIs are free while others may charge fees. There also may be restrictions on the frequency with which your app may query the server.

7.9 *(Mashup)* Use your imagination to create a mashup app using at least two APIs of your choice.

7.10 *(News Aggregator App)* Use web services to create a news aggregator app that gathers news from multiple sources.

7.11 *(Enhanced News Aggregator App)* Enhance the **News Aggregator** app using a maps API. Allow the user to select a region of the world. When the user clicks on a region, display the headlines from the multiple news sources.

7.12 *(Shopping Mashup App)* Create a location-based shopping app using APIs from CityGrid® (www.citygridmedia.com/developer/) or a similar shopping service. Add background music to your app using APIs from a service such as Last.fm (www.last.fm/api) so the user can listen while shopping.

7.13 *(Daily Deals Mashup App)* Create a local daily deals app using Groupon APIs (www.groupon.com/pages/api) or those of a similar service.

7.14 *(Idiomatic Expressions Translator Mashup App)* An idiomatic expression is a common, often strange saying whose meaning cannot be understood from the words in the expression. For example, you might say your favorite sports team is going to "eat [their opponent] for lunch," or "blow [their opponent] out of the water" to indicate that you predict your team will win decisively. Search the web to find popular idiomatic expressions. Create an app that allows the user to enter an idiomatic expression by text or speech, then translate the expression into a foreign language and then back to English. Use a translation API (such as Bing) to perform the translation. Allow the user to select the foreign language. Display the results in English—they may be funny or interesting.

7.15 *(Name That Song App)* Check your favorite music sites to see if they have a web services API. Using a music web services API, create a quiz app (similar to the **Flag Quiz** app in Chapter 5) that plays a song and asks the user to name the song. Other features to include:

    a) Add three lifelines that allow you to call one contact, SMS one contact and e-mail one contact for help answering a question. Once each lifeline is used, disable the capability for that quiz.

    b) Add a timer function so that the user must answer each question within 10 seconds.

    c) Add multiplayer functionality that allows two users to play on the same device.

    d) Add muliplayer functionality to allow users on different devices to compete in the same game.

    e) Keep track of the user's score and display it as a percentage at the bottom of the screen throughout the quiz.

8

Twitter® Searches App

Objectives

In this chapter you'll:

- Use SharedPreferences to store key–value pairs of data associated with an app.

- Use an implicit Intent to open a website in a browser.

- Use an implicit Intent to display an intent chooser containing a list of apps that can share text.

- Display a scrolling list of items in a RecyclerView.

- Use a subclass of RecyclerView.Adapter to specify a RecyclerView's data.

- Use a subclass of RecyclerView.View-Holder to implement the view-holder pattern for a RecyclerView.

- Use a subclass of RecyclerView.Item-Decoration to display lines between a RecyclerView's items.

- Use an AlertDia-log.Builder object to create an AlertDialog that displays a list of options.

8.1 Introduction

Twitter's search mechanism makes it easy to follow trending topics being discussed by Twitter's 300+ million active monthly users[1] (there are over one billion total Twitter accounts[2]). Searches can be fine-tuned using Twitter's *search operators* (Section 8.2), often resulting in lengthy search strings that are time consuming and cumbersome to enter on a mobile device. The **Twitter® Searches** app (Fig. 8.1) allows you to save your favorite search queries with easy-to-remember short tag names (Fig. 8.1(a)) that are displayed as a scrollable list. You can then scroll through your saved searches and simply touch a tag name to quickly view tweets on a given topic (Fig. 8.1(b)). As you'll see, the app also allows you to *share, edit* and *delete* saved searches.

---

1.   https://about.twitter.com/company
2.   http://www.businessinsider.com/twitter-monthly-active-users-2015-7?r=UK&IR=T.

a) App with several saved searches

b) App after the user touches "**Deitel**"

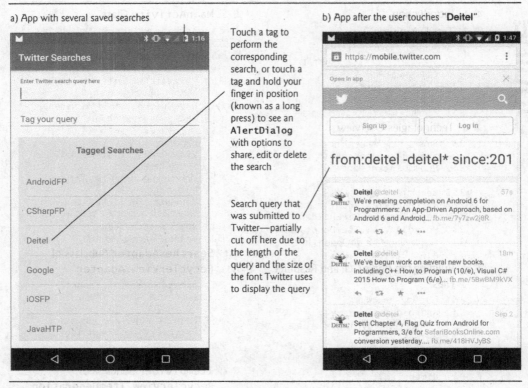

Touch a tag to perform the corresponding search, or touch a tag and hold your finger in position (known as a long press) to see an `AlertDialog` with options to share, edit or delete the search

Search query that was submitted to Twitter—partially cut off here due to the length of the query and the size of the font Twitter uses to display the query

Fig. 8.1 | **Twitter Searches** app.

The app supports both portrait and landscape orientations. In the **Flag Quiz** app, you did this by providing separate layouts for each orientation. In the **Doodlz** app, you did this by programmatically setting the orientation. In this app, we support both orientations by designing a GUI that *dynamically* adjusts, based on the current orientation.

First, you'll test-drive the app. Then we'll overview the technologies we used to build it. Next, we'll design the app's GUI. Finally, we'll walk through the app's complete source code, discussing the new features in more detail.

8.2 Test-Driving the App

Opening and Running the App

Open Android Studio and open the **Twitter Searches** app from the `TwitterSearches` folder in the book's examples folder, then execute the app in the AVD or on a device. This builds the project and runs the app (Fig. 8.2).

8.2.1 Adding a Favorite Search

Touch the top `EditText`, then enter `from:deitel` as the search query—the `from:` operator locates tweets from a specified Twitter account. Figure 8.3 shows several Twitter search

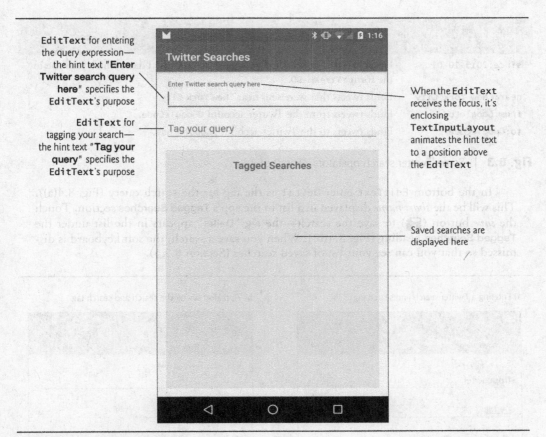

EditText for entering the query expression—the hint text "**Enter Twitter search query here**" specifies the EditText's purpose

EditText for tagging your search—the hint text "**Tag your query**" specifies the EditText's purpose

When the EditText receives the focus, it's enclosing TextInputLayout animates the hint text to a position above the EditText

Saved searches are displayed here

Fig. 8.2 | **Twitter Searches** app when it first executes.

operators—multiple operators can be used to construct more complex queries. A complete list can be found at

        http://bit.ly/TwitterSearchOperators

Example	Finds tweets containing
google android	Implicit *logical and* operator—Finds tweets containing google *and* android.
google OR android	Logical OR operator—Finds tweets containing google *or* android *or both*.
"how to program"	String in quotes("")—Finds tweets containing "how to program".
android ?	? (question mark)—Finds tweets asking questions about android.
google -android	- (minus sign)—Finds tweets containing google but not android.
android :)	:) (happy face)—Finds *positive attitude* tweets containing android.
android :(	:((sad face)—Finds *negative attitude* tweets containing android.

Fig. 8.3 | Some Twitter search operators. (Part 1 of 2.)

Example	Finds tweets containing
`since:2013-10-01`	Finds tweets that occurred *on or after* the specified date, which must be in the form YYYY-MM-DD.
`near:"New York City"`	Finds tweets that were sent near `"New York City"`.
`from:GoogleCode`	Finds tweets from the Twitter account `@GoogleCode`.
`to:GoogleCode`	Finds tweets to the Twitter account `@GoogleCode`.

Fig. 8.3 | Some Twitter search operators. (Part 2 of 2.)

In the bottom `EditText` enter `Deitel` as the tag for the search query (Fig. 8.4(a)). This will be the *short name* displayed in a list in the app's **Tagged Searches** section. Touch the *save* button (💾) to save the search—the tag "**Deitel**" appears in the list under the **Tagged Searches** heading (Fig. 8.4(b)). When you save a search, the soft keyboard is dismissed so that you can see your list of saved searches (Section 8.5.5).

a) Entering a Twitter search and search tag

b) App after saving the search and search tag

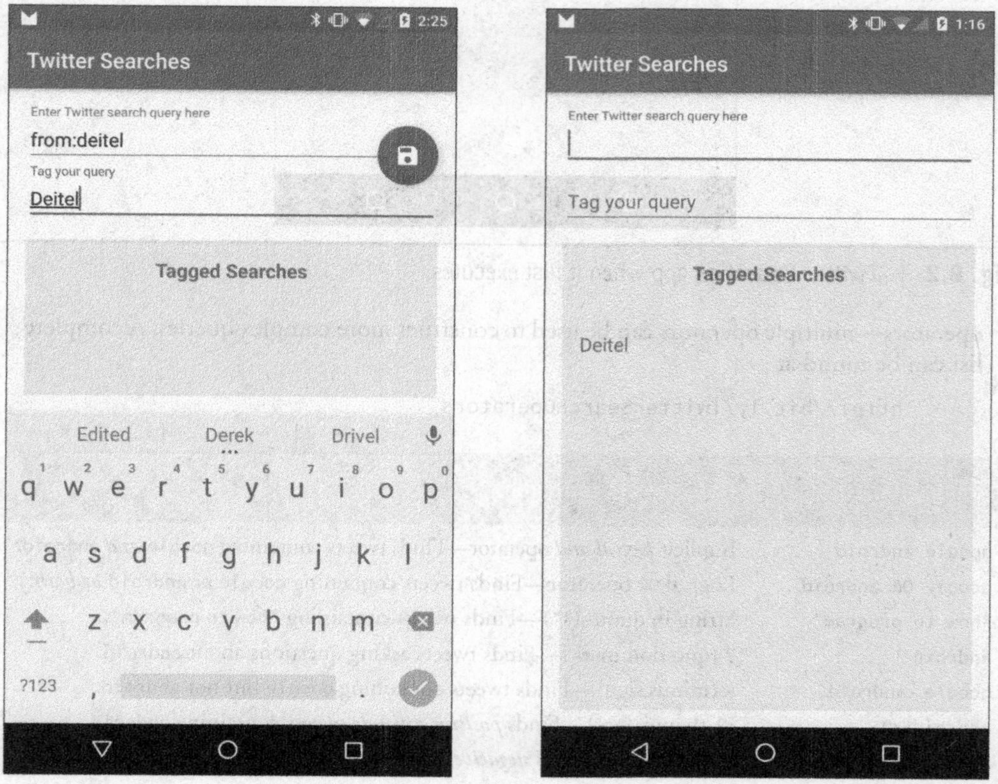

Fig. 8.4 | Entering a Twitter search.

8.2.2 Viewing Twitter Search Results

To view the search results, touch the tag "**Deitel**." This launches the device's web browser and passes a URL that represents the saved search to the Twitter website. Twitter obtains the search query from the URL, then returns the tweets that match the query (if any) as a web page. The web browser then displays the results page (Fig. 8.5). When you're done viewing the results, touch the back button (◀) to return to the **Twitter Searches** app where you can save more searches, and edit, delete and share previously saved searches. For the `"from:deitel"` query, Twitter shows relevant user accounts containing `deitel` in the account name and recent tweets from those accounts.

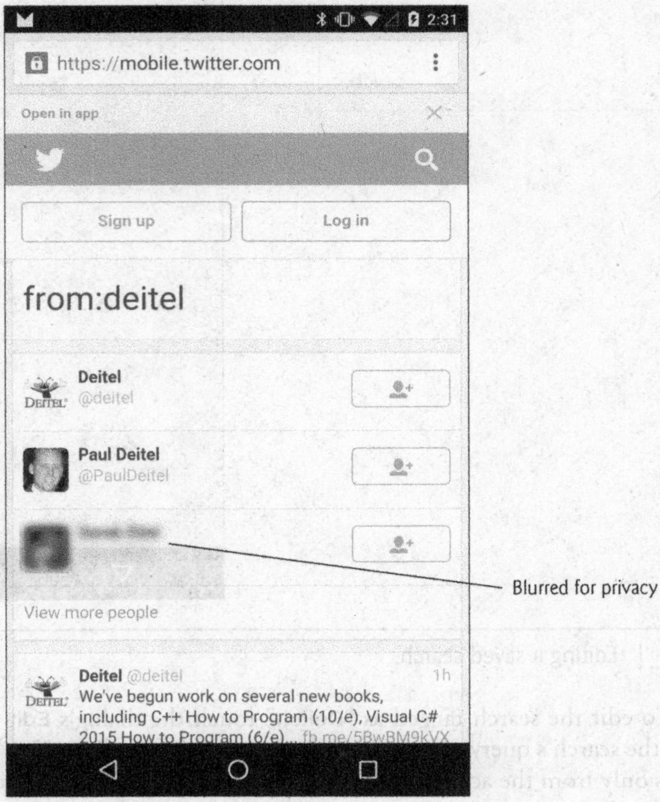

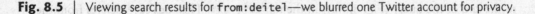

Fig. 8.5 | Viewing search results for `from:deitel`—we blurred one Twitter account for privacy.

8.2.3 Editing a Search

You may also *share*, *edit* or *delete* a search. To see these options, *long press* the search's tag—that is, touch the tag and keep your finger on the screen until the dialog containing **Share**, **Edit** and **Delete** options appears. If you're using an AVD, click and hold the left mouse button on the search tag to perform a long press. When you long press "**Deitel**," the Alert-

Dialog in Fig. 8.6(a) displays the **Share**, **Edit** and **Delete** options for the search tagged as "Deitel." If you don't wish to perform any of these tasks, touch **CANCEL**.

a) Selecting **Edit** to edit an existing search

b) Editing the "**Deitel**" saved search

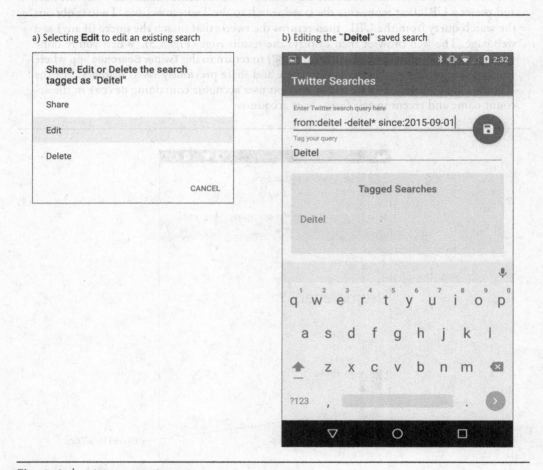

Fig. 8.6 | Editing a saved search.

To edit the search tagged as "**Deitel**," touch the dialog's **Edit** option. The app then loads the search's query and tag into the EditTexts for editing. Let's restrict our search to tweets only from the account @deitel since September 1, 2015. Add a space then

```
-deitel* since:2015-06-01
```

to the end of the query (Fig. 8.6(b)) in the top EditText. The -deitel* deletes from the results tweets from accounts that begin with "deitel" but followed by other characters. The since: operator restricts the search results to tweets that occurred *on or after* the specified date (in the form yyyy-mm-dd). Touch the *save* button (💾) to update the saved search, then view the updated results (Fig. 8.7) by touching **Deitel** in the **Tagged Searches** section of the app. [*Note:* Changing the tag name will create a *new* search, which is useful if you want to create a new query that's based on a previously saved query.]

Fig. 8.7 | Viewing the updated "**Deitel**" search results.

8.2.4 Sharing a Search

Android makes it easy for you to share various types of information from an app via e-mail, instant messaging (SMS), Facebook, Google+, Twitter and more. In this app, you can share a favorite search by *long pressing* the search's tag and selecting **Share** from the **Alert-Dialog** that appears. This displays a so-called **intent chooser** (Fig. 8.8(a)), which can vary, based on the type of content you're sharing and the apps that can handle that content. In this app we're sharing text, and the intent chooser on our phone shows many apps capable of handling text. If no apps can handle the content, the intent chooser will display a message saying so. If only one app can handle the content, that app will launch without you having to select which app to use from the intent chooser. For this test-drive, we touched **Gmail**. Figure 8.8(b) shows the **Gmail** app's **Compose** screen with the from address, e-mail subject and body pre-populated. We blurred the **From** email address for privacy in the screen capture.

a) Intent chooser showing share options

b) Gmail app **Compose** screen for an e-mail containing the "**Deitel**" search

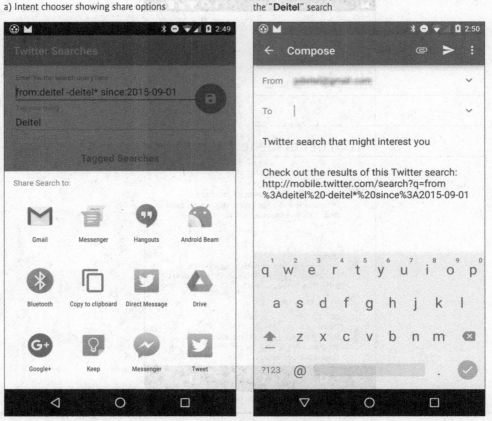

Fig. 8.8 | Sharing a search via e-mail—the Gmail **Compose** window shows your email address by default (blurred for privacy here), positions the cursor in the **To** field so you can enter the recipient's email address and prepopulates the email's subject and content.

8.2.5 Deleting a Search

To delete a search, *long press* the search's tag and select **Delete** from the AlertDialog that appears. The app prompts you to confirm that you'd like to delete the search (Fig. 8.9)—touching **CANCEL** returns you to the main screen *without* deleting the search. Touching **DELETE** deletes the search.

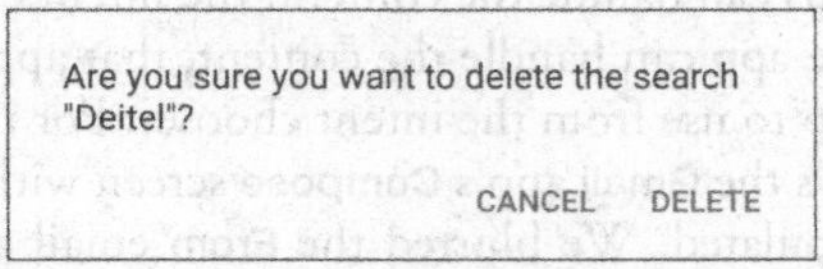

Are you sure you want to delete the search "Deitel"?

CANCEL   DELETE

Fig. 8.9 | AlertDialog confirming a delete.

8.2.6 Scrolling Through Saved Searches

Figure 8.10 shows the app after we've saved several favorite searches—six of which are currently visible. The app allows you to scroll through your favorite searches if there are more than can be displayed on the screen at once. Unlike desktop apps, touch-screen apps do not typically display scrollbars to indicate scrollable areas of the screen. To scroll, simply *drag* or *flick* your finger (or the mouse in an AVD) up or down in the list of **Tagged Searches**. Also, rotate the device to *landscape* orientation to see that the GUI dynamically adjusts.

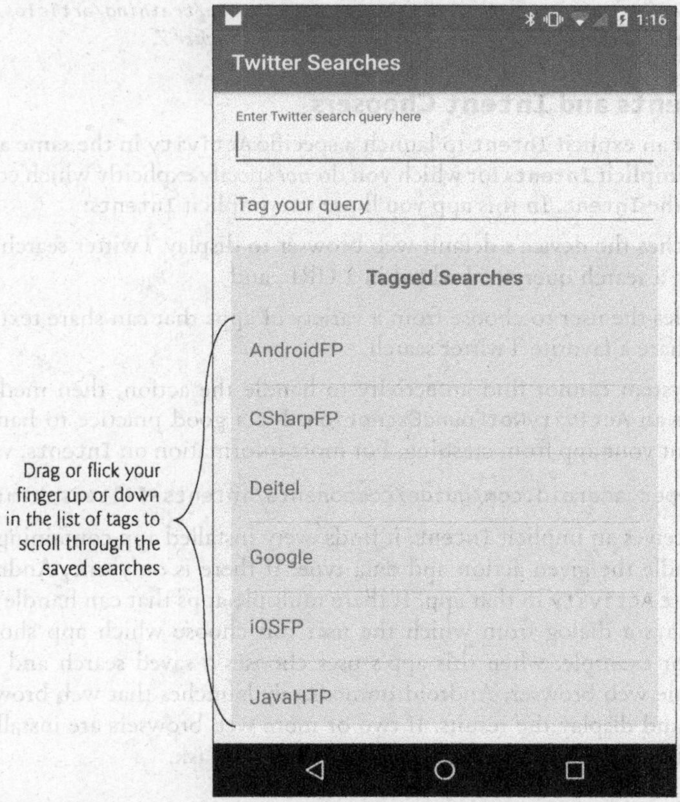

Fig. 8.10 | App with more searches than can be displayed on the screen.

8.3 Technologies Overview

This section introduces the features you'll use to build the **Twitter Searches** app.

8.3.1 Storing Key–Value Data in a SharedPreferences File

Each app can have `SharedPreferences` files containing key–value pairs associated with the app—each key enables you to quickly look up a corresponding value. Chapter 4's **Flag Quiz** app stored the app's preferences in a `SharedPreferences` file on the device. That app's `PreferenceFragment` created the `SharedPreferences` file for you. In this app, you'll create and manage a SharedPreferences file called searches in which you'll store the pairs of tags (the keys) and Twitter search queries (the *values*) that the user creates. Once again, you'll use a SharedPreferences.Editor to make changes to the tag–query pairs.

> **Performance Tip 8.1**
> *This app does not store a lot of data, so we read the saved searches from the device in Main-Activity's onCreate method. Lengthy data access should not be done in the UI thread; otherwise, the app will display an Application Not Responding (ANR) dialog—typically after five seconds of preventing the user from interacting with the app. For information on designing responsive apps, see http://developer.android.com/training/articles/ perf-anr.html and consider using AsyncTasks as shown in Chapter 7.*

8.3.2 Implicit Intents and Intent Choosers

In Chapter 4, you used an explicit Intent to launch a specific Activity in the same app. Android also supports **implicit Intents** for which you do *not* specify explicitly which component should handle the Intent. In this app you'll use two implicit Intents:

- one that launches the device's default web browser to display Twitter search results, based on a search query embedded in a URL, and

- one that enables the user to choose from a variety of apps that can share text, so the user can share a favorite Twitter search.

In either case, if the system cannot find an activity to handle the action, then method startActivity throws an ActivityNotFoundException. It's a good practice to handle this exception to prevent your app from crashing. For more information on Intents, visit

http://developer.android.com/guide/components/intents-filters.html

When Android receives an implicit Intent, it finds every installed app containing an Activity that can handle the given action and data type. If there is only one, Android launches the appropriate Activity in that app. If there multiple apps that can handle the Intent, Android displays a dialog from which the user can choose which app should handle the Intent—for example, when this app's user chooses a saved search and the device contains only one web browser, Android immediately launches that web browser to perform the search and display the results. If two or more web browsers are installed, however, the user must select which browser should perform this task.

8.3.3 RecyclerView

In Chapter 7, you used a ListView to display a weather forecast—a limited set of data. Many mobile apps display extensive lists of information. For example, an e-mail app displays a list of e-mails, an address-book app displays a list of contacts, a news app displays a list of headlines, etc. In each case, the user touches an item in the list to see more information—e.g., the content of the selected e-mail, the details of the selected contact or the text of the selected news story.

RecyclerView vs. ListView

In this app, you'll display the scrollable list of tagged searches using a **RecyclerView** (package **android.support.v7.widget**)—a flexible, customizable view that enables you to control how an app displays a scrolling list of data. RecyclerView was designed as a better

ListView. It provides better separation of the data's presentation from the RecyclerView's capabilities for reusing views (Section 8.3.4), as well as more flexible customization options (Section 8.3.5) for presenting the RecyclerView's items. For example, a ListView's items are always displayed in a vertical list, whereas a RecyclerView has layout managers that can display the items in a vertical list or in a grid. You can even define your own custom layout manager.

RecyclerView *Layout Managers*

For this app, the RecyclerView will use a **LinearLayoutManager**—a subclass of **RecyclerView.LayoutManager**—to specify that the items will appear in a vertical list, and the list items will each display a search's tag as a String in a TextView. You also can design custom layouts for a RecyclerView's items.

8.3.4 RecyclerView.Adapter and RecyclerView.ViewHolder

In Chapter 7, we used a subclass of Adapter to bind data to the ListView. We also introduced the view-holder pattern for reusing views that scroll off-screen. Recall that we created a class called ViewHolder (Section 8.6.2) that maintained references to the views in a ListView item. The Adapter subclass stored a ViewHolder object with each ListView item so that we could reuse the ListView item's views. You're not required to use this pattern, but doing so is recommended to increase the ListView's scrolling performance.

RecyclerView formalizes the view-holder pattern by making it required. You'll create a **RecyclerView.Adapter** subclass to bind the RecyclerView's list items to data in a List (Section 8.6). Each RecyclerView item has a corresponding object of a subclass of class **RecyclerView.ViewHolder** (Section 8.6.2) that maintains references to the item's view(s) for reuse. The RecyclerView and its RecyclerView.Adapter work together to recycle the view(s) for items that scroll off the screen.

8.3.5 RecyclerView.ItemDecoration

Class ListView automatically displays a horizontal line between items, but RecyclerView does not provide any default decorations. To display horizontal lines between the items, you'll define a subclass of **RecyclerView.ItemDecoration** that draws divider lines onto the RecyclerView (Section 8.7).

8.3.6 Displaying a List of Options in an AlertDialog

This app enables the user to long touch a RecyclerView item to display an AlertDialog containing a list of options from which the user can select only one. You'll use an Alert-Dialog.Builder's **setItems** method to specify a String array resource containing names of the option to display and to set the event handler that's called when the user touches one of the options.

8.4 Building the App's GUI and Resource Files

In this section, you'll build the **Twitter Searches** app's GUI and resource files. Recall from Section 8.3.3 that RecyclerView does not define how to render its list items. So you'll also create a layout that defines a list item's GUI. The RecyclerView will inflate this layout as necessary when creating list items.

8.4.1 Creating the Project

Create a new project using the **Blank Activity** template. Fragments are not required for this app, so when you configure the **Blank Activity**, do not check the **Use a Fragment** checkbox. Specify the following values in the **Create New Project** dialog's **New Project** step:

- **Application name:** Twitter Searches
- **Company Domain:** deitel.com (or specify your own domain name)

Follow the steps you used in earlier apps to add an app icon to your project. Delete the **Hello world!** TextView from the content_main.xml, as it's not used. Also, follow the steps in Section 4.4.3 to configure Java SE 7 support for the project.

8.4.2 AndroidManifest.xml

Most users will launch this app so that they can perform an existing saved search. When the first focusable GUI component in an activity is an EditText, Android gives that component the focus when the activity is displayed. When an EditText receives the focus, its corresponding virtual keyboard is displayed unless a hardware keyboard is present. In this app, we want to prevent the soft keyboard from being displayed until the user touches one of the app's EditTexts. To do so, follow the steps in Section 3.7 for setting the window-SoftInputMode option, but set its value to stateAlwaysHidden.

8.4.3 Adding the RecyclerView Library

This app uses new material-design user-interface components from the Android Design Support Library, including the TextInputLayout, FloatingActionButton, and the RecyclerView. Android Studio's new app templates are already configured with Android Design Support Library support for TextInputLayout and FloatingActionButton. To use RecyclerView, however, you must update the app's dependencies to include the RecyclerView library:

1. Right click the project's app folder and select **Open Module Settings** to open the **Project Structure** window.

2. Open the **Dependencies** tab, then click the add icon (+) and select **Library Dependency** to open the **Choose Library Dependency** dialog.

3. Select the **recyclerview-v7** library in the list, then click **OK**. The library will appear in the **Dependencies** tab's list.

4. In the **Project Structure** window, click **OK**.

The IDE updates the project's build.gradle file—the one that appears in the project's **Gradle Scripts** node as **build.gradle (Module: app)**—to specify the new dependency. The Gradle build tool then makes the libraries available for use in your project.

8.4.4 colors.xml

For this app, we changed the app's default accent color (used for the EditTexts, TextInputLayouts and FloatingActionButton) and added a color resource for the background color in the **Tagged Searches** area of the screen. Open colors.xml and replace the hexadecimal value for the colorAccent resource with #FF5722, then add a new color resource named colorTaggedSearches with the value #BBDEFB.

8.4.5 strings.xml

Add the String resources in Fig. 8.11 to strings.xml.

Key	Default Value
query_prompt	Enter Twitter search query here
tag_prompt	Tag your query
save_description	Touch this button to save your tagged search
tagged_searches	Tagged Searches
search_URL	http://mobile.twitter.com/search?q=
share_edit_delete_title	Share, Edit or Delete the search tagged as \"%s\"
cancel	Cancel
share_subject	Twitter search that might interest you
share_message	Check out the results of this Twitter search: %s
share_search	Share Search to:
confirm_message	Are you sure you want to delete the search \"%s\"?
delete	Delete

Fig. 8.11 | String resources used in the **Twitter Searches** app.

8.4.6 arrays.xml

Recall from Chapter 4 that array resources are normally defined in arrays.xml. Follow the steps in Section 4.4.6 to create an arrays.xml file, then add the resource in (Fig. 8.12) to the file.

Array resource name	Values
dialog_items	Share, Edit, Delete

Fig. 8.12 | String array resources defined in arrays.xml.

8.4.7 dimens.xml

Add the dimension resource shown in Fig. 8.13 to the dimens.xml file.

Resource name	Value
fab_margin_top	90dp

Fig. 8.13 | Dimension resources in dimens.xml.

8.4.8 Adding the Save Button Icon

Use Android Studio's **Vector Asset Studio** (Section 4.4.9) to add the material design save icon (📁; located in the **Content** group) to the project—this will be used as the Floating-ActionButton's icon. After adding the vector icon, go to the project's res/drawable folder, open the icon's XML file and change the <path> element's android:fillColor value to

```
"@android:color/white"
```

This will make the icon more visible against the app's accent color, which is applied to the FloatingActionButton by the app's theme.

8.4.9 activity_main.xml

In this section, you'll customize the FloatingActionButton that's built into Android Studio's **Blank Activity** app template. By default, the button contains an email icon and is positioned the bottom-right of MainActivity's layout. You'll replace the email icon with the save icon 📁 that you added in Section 8.4.8 and reposition the button at the layout's top right. Perform the following steps:

1. Open activity_main.xml and, in **Design** view, select the FloatingActionButton in the **Component Tree**.

2. Set the **contentDescription** property to the save_description String resource and set the **src** property to the ic_save_24dp Drawable resource.

At the time of this writing, Android Studio does not display layout properties for components from the Android Design Support Library, so any changes to these properties must be implemented directly in the layout's XML. Switch to **Text** view, then:

3. Change the layout_gravity property's value from "bottom|end" to "top|end" so that the FloatingActionButton's moves to the top of the layout.

4. Change the name of the layout_margin property to layout_marginEnd so it applies only to the FloatingActionButton's right side (or left side for right-to-left languages).

5. Add the following line to the FloatingActionButton's XML element to specify a new value for its top margin—this moves the button down from the top of the layout over the part of the GUI defined by content_main.xml:

```
android:layout_marginTop="@dimen/fab_margin_top"
```

8.4.10 content_main.xml

The RelativeLayout in this app's content_main.xml contains two TextInputLayouts and a LinearLayout that, in turn, contains a TextView and a RecyclerView. Use the layout editor and the **Component Tree** window to form the layout structure shown in Fig. 8.14. As you create the GUI components, set their **ids** as specified in the figure. There are several components in this layout that do not require **ids**, as the app's Java code does not reference them directly.

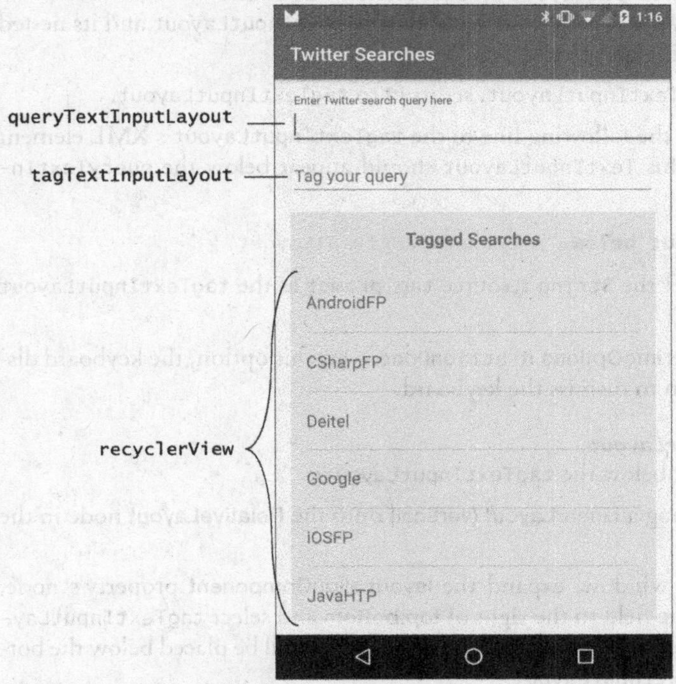

Fig. 8.14 | **Twitter Searches** GUI's components labeled with their **id** property values.

Step 1: Adding the `queryTextInputLayout` and Its Nested `EditText`
Add the queryTextInputLayout and its nested EditText as follows:

1. Insert a TextInputLayout. In the layout editor's **Design** view, click **CustomView** in the **Palette**'s **Custom** section. In the dialog that appears, begin typing TextInputLayout to search the list of custom GUI components. Once the IDE highlights TextInputLayout, click **OK**, then in the **Component Tree**, click the RelativeLayout to insert the TextInputLayout as a nested layout. Select the TextInputLayout and set its id to queryTextInputLayout.

2. To add an EditText to the TextInputLayout, switch to the layout editor's **Text** view, then change the TextInputLayout element's closing /> to >, position the cursor to the right of the >, press *Enter* and type </. The IDE will auto-complete the closing tag. Between the TextInputLayout's starting and ending tags, type <EditText. The IDE will show an auto-complete window with EditText selected. Press *Enter* to insert an EditText, then set its layout_width to match_parent and layout_height to wrap_content.

3. Switch back to **Design** view, then in the **Component Tree**, select the EditText and set its **imeOptions** to actionNext (the keyboard displays a 🔘 button to jump to the next EditText), its **hint** to the String resource query_prompt and check its **singleLine** property's checkbox. To view the **imeOptions** property, you must first click the **Show expert properties** button (🔻) at the top of the **Properties** window.

Step 2: Adding the `tagTextInputLayout` and Its Nested `EditText`

Using the techniques from the previous step, add the `tagTextInputLayout` and its nested `EditText`, with the following changes:

1. After adding the `TextInputLayout`, set its **id** to `tagTextInputLayout`.

2. In **Text** view, add the following line to the `tagTextInputLayout`'s XML element to indicate that this `TextInputLayout` should appear below the `queryTextInputLayout`:

   ```
   android:layout_below="@id/queryTextInputLayout"
   ```

3. In **Design** view, set the `String` resource `tag_prompt` as the `tagTextInputLayout` `EditText`'s **hint**.

4. Set the `EditText`'s **imeOptions** to `actionDone`—for this option, the keyboard displays a ✓ button to dismiss the keyboard.

Step 3: Adding the `LinearLayout`

Next, add a `LinearLayout` below the `tagTextInputLayout`:

1. In **Design** view, drag a **LinearLayout (vertical)** onto the **RelativeLayout** node in the **Component Tree**.

2. In the **Properties** window, expand the **layout:alignComponent** property's node, then click the value field to the right of **top:bottom** and select `tagTextInputLayout`. This indicates that the top of the `LinearLayout` will be placed below the bottom of the `tagTextInputLayout`.

Step 3: Adding the `LinearLayout`'s Nested `TextView` and `RecyclerView`

Finally, add the `LinearLayout`'s nested `TextView` and `RecyclerView`:

1. Drag a **Medium Text** onto the **LinearLayout (vertical)** node in the **Component Tree**, then set its **layout:width** to `match_parent`, its **text** to the `String` resource named `tagged_searches`, its **gravity** to `center_horizontal` and its **textStyle** to `bold`. Also, expand its **padding** property and set **top** and **bottom** to the dimension resource named `activity_vertical_margin`.

2. Next, you'll insert a `RecyclerView`. In the layout editor's **Design** view, click **CustomView** in the **Palette**'s **Custom** section. In the dialog that appears, begin typing `RecyclerView` to search the list of custom GUI components. Once the IDE highlights `RecyclerView`, click **OK**, then in the **Component Tree**, click the `LinearLayout` to insert the `RecyclerView` as a nested view.

3. Select the `RecyclerView` in the **Component Tree**, then set its **id** to `recyclerView`, its **layout:width** to `match_parent`, its **layout:height** to `0dp` and its **layout:weight** to `1`—the `RecyclerView` will fill all remaining vertical space in the `LinearLayout`. Also, expand the `RecyclerView`'s **padding** property and set **left** and **right** to the dimension resource named `activity_horizontal_margin`.

8.4.11 RecyclerView Item's Layout: `list_item.xml`

When populating a `RecyclerView` with data, you must specify each list item's layout. The list items in this app each display the tag name of one saved search. You'll now create a new layout that contains only a TextView with the appropriate formatting. Perform the following steps:

1. In the **Project** window, expand the project's res folder, then right click the layout folder and select **New > Layout resource file** to display the **New Resource File** dialog.

2. In the **File name** field, specify list_item.xml.

3. In the **Root element** field, specify TextView.

4. Click **OK**. The new list_item.xml file will appear in the res/layout folder.

The IDE opens the new layout in the layout editor. Select the TextView in the **Component Tree** window, set its **id** to textView, then set the following properties:

- **layout:width**—match_parent
- **layout:height**—?android:attr/listPreferredItemHeight—This value is a predefined Android resource that represents a list item's preferred height for a touchable view.[3]

> ### Look-and-Feel Observation 8.1
> *The Android design guidelines specify that the minimum recommended size for a touchable item on the screen is 48dp-by-48dp. For more information on GUI sizing and spacing, see https://www.google.com/design/spec/layout/metrics-keylines.html.*

- **gravity**—center_vertical
- **textAppearance**—?android:attr/textAppearanceMedium—This is the predefined theme resource that specifies the font size for medium-sized text.

Other Predefined Android Resources
There are many predefined Android resources like the ones used to set the **height** and **textAppearance** for a list item. You can view the complete list at:

        http://developer.android.com/reference/android/R.attr.html

To use a value in your layouts, specify it in the format

        ?android:attr/*resourceName*

8.5 MainActivity Class
This app consists of three classes:

- Class MainActivity—which we discuss in this section—configures the app's GUI and defines the app's logic.
- Class SearchesAdapter (Section 8.6) is a subclass of RecyclerView.Adapter that defines how to bind the tag names for the user's searches to the RecyclerView's items. Class MainActivity's onCreate method creates an object of class SearchesAdapter as the RecyclerView's adapter.

---

3. At the time of this writing, you must set this directly in the XML due to an Android Studio bug that erroneously appends dp to the end of this property value when you set it via the **Properties** window.

- Class ItemDivider (Section 8.7) is a subclass of RecyclerView.ItemDecoration that the RecyclerView uses to draw a horizontal line between items.

Sections 8.5.1–8.5.10 discuss class MainActivity in detail. This app does not need a menu, so we removed the MainActivity methods onCreateOptionsMenu and onOptions-ItemSelected, and the corresponding menu resource from the project's res/menu folder.

8.5.1 package and import Statements

Figure 8.15 shows MainActivity's package and import statements. We discuss the imported types in Section 8.3 and as we encounter them in class MainActivity.

```
1   // MainActivity.java
2   // Manages your favorite Twitter searches for easy
3   // access and display in the device's web browser
4   package com.deitel.twittersearches;
5
6   import android.app.AlertDialog;
7   import android.content.Context;
8   import android.content.DialogInterface;
9   import android.content.Intent;
10  import android.content.SharedPreferences;
11  import android.net.Uri;
12  import android.os.Bundle;
13  import android.support.design.widget.FloatingActionButton;
14  import android.support.design.widget.TextInputLayout;
15  import android.support.v7.app.AppCompatActivity;
16  import android.support.v7.widget.LinearLayoutManager;
17  import android.support.v7.widget.RecyclerView;
18  import android.support.v7.widget.Toolbar;
19  import android.text.Editable;
20  import android.text.TextWatcher;
21  import android.view.View;
22  import android.view.View.OnClickListener;
23  import android.view.View.OnLongClickListener;
24  import android.view.inputmethod.InputMethodManager;
25  import android.widget.EditText;
26  import android.widget.TextView;
27
28  import java.util.ArrayList;
29  import java.util.Collections;
30  import java.util.List;
31
```

Fig. 8.15 | MainActivity's package and import statements.

8.5.2 MainActivity Fields

As in the **WeatherViewer** app, class MainActivity (Fig. 8.16) extends AppCompatActivity (line 32) so that it can display an app bar and use other AppCompat library features on devices running past or current Android versions. The static String constant SEARCHES (line 34) represents the name of a SharedPreferences file that will store tag–query pairs on the device.

```
32   public class MainActivity extends AppCompatActivity {
33      // name of SharedPreferences XML file that stores the saved searches
34      private static final String SEARCHES = "searches";
35
36      private EditText queryEditText; // where user enters a query
37      private EditText tagEditText; // where user enters a query's tag
38      private FloatingActionButton saveFloatingActionButton; // save search
39      private SharedPreferences savedSearches; // user's favorite searches
40      private List<String> tags; // list of tags for saved searches
41      private SearchesAdapter adapter; // for binding data to RecyclerView
42
```

Fig. 8.16 | MainActivity fields.

Lines 36–41 define MainActivity's instance variables:

- Lines 36–37 declare EditTexts that we'll use to access the queries and tags that the user enters as input.

- Line 38 declares a FloatingActionButton that the user touches to save a search. In the **Blank Activity** app template, this was declared as a local variable in method onCreate (Section 8.5.3)—we renamed it and made it an instance variable, so we can hide the button when the EditTexts are empty and show it when the Edit-Texts both contain input.

- Line 39 declares the SharedPreferences instance variable savedSearches, which we'll use to manipulate the tag–query pairs representing the user's saved searches.

- Line 40 declares the List<String> tags that will store the sorted tag names for the user's searches.

- Line 41 declares the SearchesAdapter instance variable adapter, which will refer to the RecyclerView.Adapter subclass object that provides data to the Recy-clerView.

8.5.3 Overridden Activity Method onCreate

Overridden Activity method onCreate (Fig. 8.17) initializes the Activity's instance variables and configures the GUI components. Lines 52–57 obtain references to the queryEditText and tagEditText and, for each, register a TextWatcher (Section 8.5.4) that's notified when the user enters or removes characters in the EditTexts.

```
43      // configures the GUI and registers event listeners
44      @Override
45      protected void onCreate(Bundle savedInstanceState) {
46         super.onCreate(savedInstanceState);
47         setContentView(R.layout.activity_main);
48         Toolbar toolbar = (Toolbar) findViewById(R.id.toolbar);
49         setSupportActionBar(toolbar);
```

Fig. 8.17 | Overridden Activity method onCreate. (Part 1 of 2.)

```
50
51          // get references to the EditTexts and add TextWatchers to them
52          queryEditText = ((TextInputLayout) findViewById(
53             R.id.queryTextInputLayout)).getEditText();
54          queryEditText.addTextChangedListener(textWatcher);
55          tagEditText = ((TextInputLayout) findViewById(
56             R.id.tagTextInputLayout)).getEditText();
57          tagEditText.addTextChangedListener(textWatcher);
58
59          // get the SharedPreferences containing the user's saved searches
60          savedSearches = getSharedPreferences(SEARCHES, MODE_PRIVATE);
61
62          // store the saved tags in an ArrayList then sort them
63          tags = new ArrayList<>(savedSearches.getAll().keySet());
64          Collections.sort(tags, String.CASE_INSENSITIVE_ORDER);
65
66          // get reference to the RecyclerView to configure it
67          RecyclerView recyclerView =
68             (RecyclerView) findViewById(R.id.recyclerView);
69
70          // use a LinearLayoutManager to display items in a vertical list
71          recyclerView.setLayoutManager(new LinearLayoutManager(this));
72
73          // create RecyclerView.Adapter to bind tags to the RecyclerView
74          adapter = new SearchesAdapter(
75             tags, itemClickListener, itemLongClickListener);
76          recyclerView.setAdapter(adapter);
77
78          // specify a custom ItemDecorator to draw lines between list items
79          recyclerView.addItemDecoration(new ItemDivider(this));
80
81          // register listener to save a new or edited search
82          saveFloatingActionButton =
83             (FloatingActionButton) findViewById(R.id.fab);
84          saveFloatingActionButton.setOnClickListener(saveButtonListener);
85          updateSaveFAB(); // hides button because EditTexts initially empty
86       }
87
```

Fig. 8.17 | Overridden `Activity` method `onCreate`. (Part 2 of 2.)

Getting a SharedPreferences Object
Line 60 uses the method **getSharedPreferences** (inherited indirectly from class `Context`) to get a `SharedPreferences` object that can read existing *tag–query pairs* (if any) from the searches file. The first argument indicates the name of the file that contains the data. The second argument specifies the file's access-level and can be set to:

- **MODE_PRIVATE**—Accessible *only* to this app. In most cases, you'll use this option.
- **MODE_WORLD_READABLE**—Any app on the device can *read* the file.
- **MODE_WORLD_WRITABLE**—Any app on the device can *write* to the file.

These constants can be combined with the bitwise OR operator (|).

*Getting the Keys Stored in the **SharedPreferences** Object*

We'd like to display the search tags alphabetically so the user can easily find a search to perform. First, line 63 gets the Strings representing the keys in the SharedPreferences object and stores them in tags (an ArrayList<String>). SharedPreferences method **getAll** returns all the saved searches as a Map (package java.util)—a collection of key–value pairs. We then call method **keySet** on the Map object to get all the keys as a Set<String> (package java.util)—a collection of unique values. The result is used to initialize tags.

*Sorting the **ArrayList** of Tags*

Line 64 uses **Collections.sort** to sort tags. Since the user could enter tags using mixtures of uppercase and lowercase letters, we perform a *case-insensitive sort* by passing the predefined Comparator<String> object **String.CASE_INSENSITIVE_ORDER** as the second argument to Collections.sort.

*Configuring the **RecyclerView***

Lines 67–79 configure the RecyclerView:

- Lines 67–68 get a reference to the RecyclerView.

- A RecyclerView can arrange its items for display in difference ways. For this app, we use the LinearLayoutManager to display the items in a vertical list. The LinearLayoutManager's constructor receives a Context object, which is the MainActivity in this case. Line 71 creates a LinearLayoutManager calls RecyclerView method setLayoutManager to set the new object as the RecyclerView's layout manager.

- Lines 74–75 create a SearchesAdapter (Section 8.6)—a subclass of RecyclerView.Adapter—that will supply data for display in the RecyclerView. Line 76 calls RecyclerView method setAdapter to specify that the SearchesAdapter will supply the RecyclerView's data.

- Line 79 creates a subclass of RecyclerView.ItemDecoration named ItemDivider (Section 8.7) and passes the object to RecyclerView method addItemDecoration. This enables the RecyclerView to draw a horizontal line decoration between list items.

*Registering a Listener for the **FloatingActionButton***

Lines 82–85 obtain a reference to the saveFloatingActionButton and register its OnClickListener. Instance variable saveButtonListener refers to an *anonymous-inner-class object* that implements interface View.OnClickListener (Section 8.5.5). Line 85 calls method updateSaveFAB (Section 8.5.4), which initially hides the saveFloatingActionButton, because the EditTexts are empty when onCreate is first called—the button displays only when both EditTexts contain input.

8.5.4 TextWatcher Event Handler and Method updateSaveFAB

Figure 8.18 defines an anonymous inner class that implements interface TextWatcher (lines 89–103). The TextWatcher's onTextChanged method calls updateSaveFAB when the contents change in either of the app's EditTexts. Lines 54 and 57 (Fig. 8.17) register the instance variable textWatcher as the listener for the EditTexts events.

```
88      // hide/show saveFloatingActionButton based on EditTexts' contents
89      private final TextWatcher textWatcher = new TextWatcher() {
90         @Override
91         public void beforeTextChanged(CharSequence s, int start, int count,
92            int after) { }
93
94         // hide/show the saveFloatingActionButton after user changes input
95         @Override
96         public void onTextChanged(CharSequence s, int start, int before,
97            int count) {
98            updateSaveFAB();
99         }
100
101        @Override
102        public void afterTextChanged(Editable s) { }
103     };
104
105     // shows or hides the saveFloatingActionButton
106     private void updateSaveFAB() {
107        // check if there is input in both EditTexts
108        if (queryEditText.getText().toString().isEmpty() ||
109           tagEditText.getText().toString().isEmpty())
110           saveFloatingActionButton.hide();
111        else
112           saveFloatingActionButton.show();
113     }
114
```

Fig. 8.18 | TextWatcher event handler and method updateSaveFAB.

The updatedSaveFAB method (Fig. 8.18, lines 106–113) checks whether there's text in both EditTexts (lines 108–109). If either (or both) of the EditTexts is empty, line 110 calls the FloatingActionButton's **hide** method to hide the button, because both the query and tag are required before a tag–query pair can be saved. If both contain text, line 112 calls the FloatingActionButton's **show** method, to display the button so the user can touch it to store a tag–query pair.

8.5.5 saveButton's OnClickListener

Figure 8.19 defines instance variable saveButtonListener, which refers to an anonymous inner class object that implements the interface OnClickListener. Line 84 (Fig. 8.17) registered saveButtonListener as the saveFloatingActionButton's event handler. Lines 119–135 (Fig. 8.19) override interface OnClickListener's onClick method. Lines 121–122 get the Strings from the EditTexts. If the user entered a query and a tag (line 124):

- lines 126–128 hide the soft keyboard
- line 130 calls method addTaggedSearch (Section 8.5.6) to store the tag–query pair
- lines 131–132 clear the two EditTexts, and
- line 133 calls the queryEditText's requestFocus method to position the input cursor in the queryEditText.

```
115        // saveButtonListener save a tag-query pair into SharedPreferences
116        private final OnClickListener saveButtonListener =
117           new OnClickListener() {
118              // add/update search if neither query nor tag is empty
119              @Override
120              public void onClick(View view) {
121                 String query = queryEditText.getText().toString();
122                 String tag = tagEditText.getText().toString();
123
124                 if (!query.isEmpty() && !tag.isEmpty()) {
125                    // hide the virtual keyboard
126                    ((InputMethodManager) getSystemService(
127                       Context.INPUT_METHOD_SERVICE)).hideSoftInputFromWindow(
128                          view.getWindowToken(), 0);
129
130                    addTaggedSearch(tag, query); // add/update the search
131                    queryEditText.setText(""); // clear queryEditText
132                    tagEditText.setText(""); // clear tagEditText
133                    queryEditText.requestFocus(); // queryEditText gets focus
134                 }
135              }
136           };
137
```

Fig. 8.19 | Anonymous inner class that implements the saveButton's OnClickListener to save a new or updated search.

8.5.6 addTaggedSearch Method

The event handler in Fig. 8.19 calls method addTaggedSearch (Fig. 8.20) to add a new search to savedSearches or to modify an existing search.

```
138        // add new search to file, then refresh all buttons
139        private void addTaggedSearch(String tag, String query) {
140           // get a SharedPreferences.Editor to store new tag/query pair
141           SharedPreferences.Editor preferencesEditor = savedSearches.edit();
142           preferencesEditor.putString(tag, query); // store current search
143           preferencesEditor.apply(); // store the updated preferences
144
145           // if tag is new, add to and sort tags, then display updated list
146           if (!tags.contains(tag)) {
147              tags.add(tag); // add new tag
148              Collections.sort(tags, String.CASE_INSENSITIVE_ORDER);
149              adapter.notifyDataSetChanged(); // update tags in RecyclerView
150           }
151        }
152
```

Fig. 8.20 | MainActivity's addTaggedSearch method.

Editing a SharedPreferences Object's Contents

Recall from Section 4.6.7 that to change a SharedPreferences object's contents, you must first call its edit method to obtain a SharedPreferences.Editor object (Fig. 8.20, line 141), which can add key–value pairs to, remove key–value pairs from and modify the value associated with a particular key in a SharedPreferences file. Line 142 calls Shared-Preferences.Editor method **putString** to save the search's tag (the key) and query (the corresponding value)—if the tag already exists in the SharedPreferences this updates the value. Line 143 commits the changes by calling SharedPreferences.Editor method apply to make the changes to the file.

Notifying the RecyclerView.Adapter That Its Data Has Changed

When the user adds a new search, the RecyclerView should be updated to display it. Line 146 determines whether a new tag was added. If so, lines 147–148 add the new search's tag to tags, then sort tags. Line 149 calls the RecyclerView.Adapter's **notifyDataSet-Changed** method to indicate that the underlying data in tags has changed. As with a List-View adapter, the RecyclerView.Adapter then notifies the RecyclerView to update its list of displayed items.

8.5.7 Anonymous Inner Class That Implements View.OnClickListener to Display Search Results

Figure 8.21 defines instance variable itemClickListener, which refers to an anonymous inner-class object that implements interface OnClickListener (a nested interface of class View). Lines 156–168 override the interface's onClick method. The method's argument is the View that the user touched—in this case, the TextView that displays a search tag in the RecyclerView.

```
153    // itemClickListener launches web browser to display search results
154    private final OnClickListener itemClickListener =
155       new OnClickListener() {
156          @Override
157          public void onClick(View view) {
158             // get query string and create a URL representing the search
159             String tag = ((TextView) view).getText().toString();
160             String urlString = getString(R.string.search_URL) +
161                Uri.encode(savedSearches.getString(tag, ""), "UTF-8");
162
163             // create an Intent to launch a web browser
164             Intent webIntent = new Intent(Intent.ACTION_VIEW,
165                Uri.parse(urlString));
166
167             startActivity(webIntent); // show results in web browser
168          }
169       };
170
```

Fig. 8.21 | Anonymous inner class that implements View.OnClickListener to display search results.

Getting String Resources

Line 159 gets the text of the View that the user touched in the RecyclerView—this is the tag for a search. Lines 160–161 create a String containing the Twitter search URL and the query to perform. Line 160 calls Activity's inherited method getString with one argument to get the String resource named search_URL, then we append the query String to it.

Getting *Strings* from a *SharedPreferences* Object

We append the result of line 161 to the search URL to complete the urlString. Shared-Preferences method **getString** returns the query associated with the tag. If the tag does not already exist, the second argument ("" in this case) is returned. Line 161 passes the query to Uri method encode, which *escapes* any special URL characters (such as ?, /, :, etc.) and returns a so-called *URL-encoded* String. Class **Uri** (uniform resource identifier) of package **android.net** enables us to convert a URL into the format required by an Intent that launches the device's web browser.[4] This is important to ensure that the Twitter web server that receives the request can parse the URL properly to obtain the search query.

Creating an *Intent* to Launch the Device's Web Browser

Lines 164–165 create a new Intent, which we'll use to launch the device's web browser and display the search results. In Chapter 4, you used an explicit Intent to launch another activity in the same app. Here you'll use an implicit Intent to launch another app. The first argument of Intent's constructor is a constant describing the action to perform. **Intent.ACTION_VIEW** indicates that we'd like to display a representation of the Intent's data. Many constants are defined in the Intent class describing actions such as *searching*, *choosing*, *sending* and *playing*:

```
http://developer.android.com/reference/android/content/Intent.html
```

The second argument (line 165) is a Uri representing the *data* for which to perform the action. Class Uri's **parse method** converts a String representing a URL (uniform resource locator) to a Uri.

Starting an *Activity* for an *Intent*

Line 167 passes the Intent to the inherited Activity method startActivity, which starts an Activity that can perform the specified *action* for the given *data*. In this case, because we've specified to view a URI, the Intent launches the device's web browser to display the corresponding web page. This page shows the results of the supplied Twitter search.

8.5.8 Anonymous Inner Class That Implements View.OnLongClickListener to Share, Edit or Delete a Search

Figure 8.22 defines instance variable itemLongClickListener, which refers to an anonymous inner-class object that implements interface OnLongClickListener. Lines 175–216 override interface OnLongClickListener's onLongClick method.

---

4. A Uniform Resource Identifier (URI) uniquely identifies a resource on a network. One common type of URI is a Uniform Resource Locator (URL) that identifies items on the Web, such as web pages, image files, web service methods and more.

```
171        // itemLongClickListener displays a dialog allowing the user to share
172        // edit or delete a saved search
173        private final OnLongClickListener itemLongClickListener =
174           new OnLongClickListener() {
175              @Override
176              public boolean onLongClick(View view) {
177                 // get the tag that the user long touched
178                 final String tag = ((TextView) view).getText().toString();
179
180                 // create a new AlertDialog
181                 AlertDialog.Builder builder =
182                    new AlertDialog.Builder(MainActivity.this);
183
184                 // set the AlertDialog's title
185                 builder.setTitle(
186                    getString(R.string.share_edit_delete_title, tag));
187
188                 // set list of items to display and create event handler
189                 builder.setItems(R.array.dialog_items,
190                    new DialogInterface.OnClickListener() {
191                       @Override
192                       public void onClick(DialogInterface dialog, int which) {
193                          switch (which) {
194                             case 0: // share
195                                shareSearch(tag);
196                                break;
197                             case 1: // edit
198                                // set EditTexts to match chosen tag and query
199                                tagEditText.setText(tag);
200                                queryEditText.setText(
201                                   savedSearches.getString(tag, ""));
202                                break;
203                             case 2: // delete
204                                deleteSearch(tag);
205                                break;
206                          }
207                       }
208                    }
209                 );
210
211                 // set the AlertDialog's negative Button
212                 builder.setNegativeButton(getString(R.string.cancel), null);
213
214                 builder.create().show(); // display the AlertDialog
215                 return true;
216              }
217           };
218
```

Fig. 8.22 | Anonymous inner class that implements View.OnLongClickListener.

final *Local Variables for Use in Anonymous Inner Classes*

Line 178 assigns to final local variable tag the text of the item the user *long pressed*—final is required for any local variable or method parameter used in an anonymous inner class.

AlertDialog *That Displays a List of Items*

Lines 181–186 create an AlertDialog.Builder and set the dialog's title to a formatted String (R.string.share_edit_delete_title) in which tag replaces the format specifier. Line 186 calls Activity's inherited method getString that receives multiple arguments— a String resource ID representing a format String and the values that should replace the format specifiers in the format String. In addition to buttons, an AlertDialog can display a list of items. Lines 189–209 use AlertDialog.Builder method setItems to specify that the dialog should display the array of Strings R.array.dialog_items and to define an anonymous inner class object that responds when the user touches any item in the list.

Event Handler *for the Dialog's List of Items*

The anonymous inner class in lines 190–208 determines which item the user selected in the dialog's list and performs the appropriate action. If the user selects **Share**, shareSearch is called (line 195). If the user selects **Edit**, lines 199–201 display the search's query and tag in the EditTexts. If the user selects **Delete**, deleteSearch is called (line 204).

Configuring the Negative Button *and Displaying the Dialog*

Line 212 configures the dialog's negative button. When the negative button's event handler is null, touching the negative button simply dismisses the dialog. Line 214 creates and shows the dialog.

8.5.9 shareSearch Method

Method shareSearch (Fig. 8.23) is called when the user selects to share a search (Fig. 8.22). Lines 222–223 create a String representing the search to share. Lines 226–232 create and configure an Intent that allows the user to send the search URL using an Activity that can handle the **Intent.ACTION_SEND**.

```
219     // allow user to choose an app for sharing URL of a saved search
220     private void shareSearch(String tag) {
221         // create the URL representing the search
222         String urlString = getString(R.string.search_URL) +
223             Uri.encode(savedSearches.getString(tag, ""), "UTF-8");
224
225         // create Intent to share urlString
226         Intent shareIntent = new Intent();
227         shareIntent.setAction(Intent.ACTION_SEND);
228         shareIntent.putExtra(Intent.EXTRA_SUBJECT,
229             getString(R.string.share_subject));
230         shareIntent.putExtra(Intent.EXTRA_TEXT,
231             getString(R.string.share_message, urlString));
232         shareIntent.setType("text/plain");
233
234         // display apps that can share plain text
235         startActivity(Intent.createChooser(shareIntent,
236             getString(R.string.share_search)));
237     }
238
```

Fig. 8.23 | MainActivity's shareSearch method.

*Adding Extras to an **Intent***

An Intent includes a Bundle of *extras*—additional information that's passed to the Activity that handles the Intent. For example, an e-mail Activity can receive *extras* representing the e-mail's subject, CC and BCC addresses, and the body text. Lines 228–231 use Intent method **putExtra** to add to the Intent's Bundle key–value pairs representing the extras. The method's first argument is a String key representing the purpose of the extra and the second argument is the corresponding extra data. Extras may be primitive type values, primitive type arrays, entire Bundle objects and more—see class Intent's documentation for a complete list of the putExtra overloads.

The extra at lines 228–229 specifies an e-mail's subject with the String resource R.string.share_subject. For an Activity that does *not* use a subject (such as sharing on a social network), this extra is ignored. The extra at lines 230–231 represents the text to share—a formatted String in which the urlString is substituted into the String resource R.string.share_message. Line 232 sets the Intent's MIME type to text/plain—such data can be handled by any Activity capable of sending plain text messages.

*Displaying an **Intent** Chooser*

To display the *intent chooser* shown in Fig. 8.8(a), we pass the Intent and a String title to Intent's static **createChooser** method (lines 235–236). The intent chooser's title is specified by the second argument (R.string.share_search). It's important to set this title to remind the user to select an appropriate Activity. You cannot control the apps installed on a user's phone or the Intent filters that can launch those apps, so it's possible that incompatible activities could appear in the chooser. Method createChooser returns an Intent that we pass to startActivity to display the intent chooser.

8.5.10 deleteSearch Method

The deleteSearch method (Fig. 8.24) is called when the user long presses a search tag and selects **Delete** from the dialog displayed by the code in Fig. 8.22. Before deleting the search, the app displays an AlertDialog to confirm the delete operation. Line 243 (Fig. 8.24) sets the dialog's title to a formatted String in which tag replaces the format specifier in the String resource R.string.confirm_message. Line 246 configures the dialog's negative button to dismiss the dialog. Lines 249–264 configure the dialog's positive button to remove the search. Line 252 removes the tag from the tags collection, and lines 255–258 use a SharedPreferences.Editor to remove the search from the app's SharedPreferences. Line 261 then notifies the RecyclerView.Adapter that the underlying data has changed so that the RecyclerView can update its displayed list of items.

```
239    // deletes a search after the user confirms the delete operation
240    private void deleteSearch(final String tag) {
241       // create a new AlertDialog and set its message
242       AlertDialog.Builder confirmBuilder = new AlertDialog.Builder(this);
243       confirmBuilder.setMessage(getString(R.string.confirm_message, tag));
244
245       // configure the negative (CANCEL) Button
246       confirmBuilder.setNegativeButton(getString(R.string.cancel), null);
```

Fig. 8.24 | MainActivity's deleteSearch method. (Part 1 of 2.)

```
247
248        // configure the positive (DELETE) Button
249        confirmBuilder.setPositiveButton(getString(R.string.delete),
250          new DialogInterface.OnClickListener() {
251            public void onClick(DialogInterface dialog, int id) {
252              tags.remove(tag); // remove tag from tags
253
254              // get SharedPreferences.Editor to remove saved search
255              SharedPreferences.Editor preferencesEditor =
256                savedSearches.edit();
257              preferencesEditor.remove(tag); // remove search
258              preferencesEditor.apply(); // save the changes
259
260              // rebind tags to RecyclerView to show updated list
261              adapter.notifyDataSetChanged();
262            }
263          }
264        );
265
266        confirmBuilder.create().show(); // display AlertDialog
267    }
268 }
```

Fig. 8.24 | MainActivity's deleteSearch method. (Part 2 of 2.)

8.6 SearchesAdapter Subclass of RecyclerView.Adapter

This section presents the RecyclerView.Adapter that binds the items in MainActivity's List<String> named tags to the app's RecyclerView.

8.6.1 package Statement, import statements, Instance Variables and Constructor

Figure 8.25 shows the beginning of class SearchesAdapter's definition. The class extends generic class RecyclerView.Adapter, using as its type argument the nested class SearchesAdapter.ViewHolder (defined in Section 8.6.2). The instance variables in lines 17–18 maintain references to the event listeners (defined in class MainActivity) that are registered for each RecyclerView item. The instance variable in line 21 maintains a reference to MainActivity's List<String> that contains the tag names to display.

```
1  // SearchesAdapter.java
2  // Subclass of RecyclerView.Adapter for binding data to RecyclerView items
3  package com.deitel.twittersearches;
4
5  import android.support.v7.widget.RecyclerView;
6  import android.view.LayoutInflater;
7  import android.view.View;
```

Fig. 8.25 | SearchesAdapter package statement, import statements, instance variables and constructor. (Part 1 of 2.)

```
 8    import android.view.ViewGroup;
 9    import android.widget.TextView;
10
11    import java.util.List;
12
13    public class SearchesAdapter
14       extends RecyclerView.Adapter<SearchesAdapter.ViewHolder> {
15
16       // listeners from MainActivity that are registered for each list item
17       private final View.OnClickListener clickListener;
18       private final View.OnLongClickListener longClickListener;
19
20       // List<String> used to obtain RecyclerView items' data
21       private final List<String> tags; // search tags
22
23       // constructor
24       public SearchesAdapter(List<String> tags,
25          View.OnClickListener clickListener,
26          View.OnLongClickListener longClickListener) {
27          this.tags = tags;
28          this.clickListener = clickListener;
29          this.longClickListener = longClickListener;
30       }
31
```

Fig. 8.25 | SearchesAdapter package statement, import statements, instance variables and constructor. (Part 2 of 2.)

8.6.2 Nested ViewHolder Subclass of RecyclerView.ViewHolder

Every item in a RecyclerView must be wrapped in its own RecyclerView.ViewHolder. For this app, we defined a RecyclerView.ViewHolder called ViewHolder (Fig. 8.26). The ViewHolder constructor (line 39–48) receives a View object and listeners for that View's OnClick and OnLongClick events. The View represents an item in the RecyclerView, which is passed to the superclass's constructor (line 42). Line 43 stores a reference to the TextView for the item. Line 46 registers the TextView's OnClickListener, which displays the search results for that TextView's tag. Line 47 registers the TextView's OnLongClick-Listener, which opens the **Share**, **Edit** or **Delete** dialog for that TextView's tag. The constructor is called when the RecyclerView.Adapter creates a new list item method onCreateViewHolder (Section 8.6.3).

```
32    // nested subclass of RecyclerView.ViewHolder used to implement
33    // the view-holder pattern in the context of a RecyclerView--the logic
34    // of recycling views that have scrolled offscreen is handled for you
35    public static class ViewHolder extends RecyclerView.ViewHolder {
36       public final TextView textView;
37
```

Fig. 8.26 | SearchesAdapter nested ViewHolder subclass of RecyclerView.ViewHolder. (Part I of 2.)

```
38              // configures a RecyclerView item's ViewHolder
39              public ViewHolder(View itemView,
40                 View.OnClickListener clickListener,
41                 View.OnLongClickListener longClickListener) {
42                 super(itemView);
43                 textView = (TextView) itemView.findViewById(R.id.textView);
44
45                 // attach listeners to itemView
46                 itemView.setOnClickListener(clickListener);
47                 itemView.setOnLongClickListener(longClickListener);
48              }
49           }
50
```

Fig. 8.26 | SearchesAdapter nested ViewHolder subclass of RecyclerView.ViewHolder. (Part 2 of 2.)

8.6.3 Overridden RecyclerView.Adapter Methods

Figure 8.27 defines the overridden RecyclerView.Adapter methods onCreateViewHolder (lines 52–61), onBindViewHolder (lines 64–67) and getItemCount (lines 70–73).

```
51           // sets up new list item and its ViewHolder
52           @Override
53           public ViewHolder onCreateViewHolder(ViewGroup parent,
54              int viewType) {
55              // inflate the list_item layout
56              View view = LayoutInflater.from(parent.getContext()).inflate(
57                 R.layout.list_item, parent, false);
58
59              // create a ViewHolder for current item
60              return (new ViewHolder(view, clickListener, longClickListener));
61           }
62
63           // sets the text of the list item to display the search tag
64           @Override
65           public void onBindViewHolder(ViewHolder holder, int position) {
66              holder.textView.setText(tags.get(position));
67           }
68
69           // returns the number of items that adapter binds
70           @Override
71           public int getItemCount() {
72              return tags.size();
73           }
74        }
```

Fig. 8.27 | SearchesAdapter overridden RecyclerView.Adapter methods onCreateViewHolder, onBindViewHolder and getItemCount.

Overriding the onCreateViewHolder Method

The RecyclerView calls its RecyclerView.Adapter's onCreateViewHolder method (lines 52–61) to inflate the layout for each RecyclerView item (lines 56–57) and wrap it in an object of the RecyclerView.ViewHolder subclass named ViewHolder (line 60). This new ViewHolder object is then returned to the RecyclerView for display.

Overriding the onBindViewHolder Method

The RecyclerView calls its RecyclerView.Adapter's onBindViewHolder method (lines 64–67) to set the data that's displayed for a particular RecyclerView item. The method receives:

- an object of our custom subclass of RecyclerView.ViewHolder containing the Views in which data will be displayed—in this case, one TextView—and

- an int representing the item's position in the RecyclerView.

Line 66 sets the TextView's text to the String in tags at the given position.

Overriding the getItemCount Method

The RecyclerView calls its RecyclerView.Adapter's getItemCount method (lines 70–73) to obtain the total number of items that that the RecyclerView needs to display—in this case, the number of items in tags (line 72).

8.7 ItemDivider Subclass of RecyclerView.ItemDecoration

A RecyclerView.ItemDecoration object draws *decorations*—such as separators between items—on a RecyclerView. The RecyclerView.ItemDecoration subclass ItemDivider (Fig. 8.28) draws divider lines between list items. Lines 17–18 in the constructor obtain the predefined Android Drawable resource android.R.attr.listDivider, which is the standard Android list-item divider used by default in ListViews.

```
I   // ItemDivider.java
2   // Class that defines dividers displayed between the RecyclerView items;
3   // based on Google's sample implementation at bit.ly/DividerItemDecoration
4   package com.deitel.twittersearches;
5
6   import android.content.Context;
7   import android.graphics.Canvas;
8   import android.graphics.drawable.Drawable;
9   import android.support.v7.widget.RecyclerView;
10  import android.view.View;
11
12  class ItemDivider extends RecyclerView.ItemDecoration {
13     private final Drawable divider;
14
```

Fig. 8.28 | ItemDivider subclass of RecyclerView.ItemDecoration for displaying a horizontal line between items in the RecyclerView. (Part 1 of 2.)

```
15    // constructor loads built-in Android list item divider
16    public ItemDivider(Context context) {
17        int[] attrs = {android.R.attr.listDivider};
18        divider = context.obtainStyledAttributes(attrs).getDrawable(0);
19    }
20
21    // draws the list item dividers onto the RecyclerView
22    @Override
23    public void onDrawOver(Canvas c, RecyclerView parent,
24        RecyclerView.State state) {
25        super.onDrawOver(c, parent, state);
26
27        // calculate left/right x-coordinates for all dividers
28        int left = parent.getPaddingLeft();
29        int right = parent.getWidth() - parent.getPaddingRight();
30
31        // for every item but the last, draw a line below it
32        for (int i = 0; i < parent.getChildCount() - 1; ++i) {
33            View item = parent.getChildAt(i); // get ith list item
34
35            // calculate top/bottom y-coordinates for current divider
36            int top = item.getBottom() + ((RecyclerView.LayoutParams)
37                item.getLayoutParams()).bottomMargin;
38            int bottom = top + divider.getIntrinsicHeight();
39
40            // draw the divider with the calculated bounds
41            divider.setBounds(left, top, right, bottom);
42            divider.draw(c);
43        }
44    }
45 }
```

Fig. 8.28 | `ItemDivider` subclass of `RecyclerView.ItemDecoration` for displaying a horizontal line between items in the `RecyclerView`. (Part 2 of 2.)

Overriding the onDrawOver Method

As the user scrolls through the `RecyclerView`'s items, the `RecyclerView`'s contents are repeatedly redrawn to display the items in their new positions on the screen. As part of this process, the `RecyclerView` calls its `RecyclerView.ItemDecoration`'s `onDrawOver` method (lines 22–44) to draw the decorations on the `RecyclerView`. The method receives:

- a `Canvas` for drawing the decorations on the `RecyclerView`.

- the `RecyclerView` object on which the `Canvas` draws

- the `RecyclerView.State`—an object that stores information passed between various `RecyclerView` components. In this app, we simply pass this value to the superclass's `onDrawOver` method (line 25).

Lines 28–29 calculate the left and right x-coordinates that are used to specify the bound's of the `Drawable` that will be displayed. The left x-coordinate is determined by calling the `RecyclerView`'s `getPaddingLeft` method, which returns the amount of padding between the `RecyclerView`'s left edge and its content. The right x-coordinate is determined by calling the `RecyclerView`'s `getWidth` method and subtracting the result of calling the

RecyclerView's getPaddingRight method, which returns the amount of padding between the RecyclerView's right edge and its content.

Lines 32–43 draw the dividers on the RecyclerView's Canvas by iterating through all but the last item and drawing the dividers below each item. Line 33 gets and stores the current RecyclerView item. Lines 36–37 calculate one divider's top y-coordinate, using the item's bottom y-coordinate plus the item's margin. Line 38 calculates the divider's bottom y-coordinate, using the top y-coordinate plus the divider's height—returned by Drawable method getIntrinsicHeight. Line 41 sets the divider's bounds and line 42 draws it to the Canvas.

8.8 A Note on Fabric: Twitter's New Mobile Development Platform

In Chapter 7, you used REST web services to obtain a weather forecast. Twitter provides extensive REST web services that enable you to integrate Twitter functionality into your apps. Using these web services requires a Twitter developer account and special authentication. The focus of this chapter is not on how to use Twitter's web services. For this reason, the app performs searches as if you enter them directly on the Twitter website in the web browser. The Twitter website then returns the results directly to the device's web browser for display.

Working with the Twitter web services directly using Chapter 7's techniques can be challenging. Twitter recognized this and now offers Fabric—a robust mobile development platform for Android and iOS. Fabric encapsulates the Twitter web services's details in libraries that you incorporate into your projects, making it easier for developers to add Twitter capabilities to their apps. In addition, you can add mobile identity management (called Digits; for user sign-in to websites and apps), advertising-based monetization capabilities (called MoPub) and app crash reporting (called Crashlytics).

To use Fabric, sign up at

```
https://get.fabric.io/
```

and install the Android Studio plug-in. Once installed, click the plug-in's icon on the Android Studio toolbar and the plug-in will walk you through the steps that add the Fabric libraries to your project. The Fabric website also provides documentation and tutorials.

8.9 Wrap-Up

In this chapter, you created the **Twitter Searches** app. You used a SharedPreferences file to store and manipulate key–value pairs representing the user's saved Twitter searches.

We introduced the RecyclerView (from package android.support.v7.widget)—a flexible, customizable view that enables you to control how an app displays a scrolling list of data. You learned that RecyclerViews support different layout managers and arranged this app's RecyclerView items vertically using a LinearLayoutManager—a subclass of RecyclerView.LayoutManager.

We once again used the view-holder pattern for reusing views that scroll off-screen. You learned that RecyclerView formalizes the view–holder pattern, making it required. You created a subclass of RecyclerView.Adapter to bind the RecyclerView's list items to data. You also created a subclass of RecyclerView.ViewHolder to maintain references to each list item's view for reuse. To display decorations between a RecyclerView's items, you defined a subclass of RecyclerView.ItemDecoration to draw divider lines onto the RecyclerView.

You used two implicit Intents for which you did not specify the precise component that should handle each Intent. You used one to launch the device's default web browser to display Twitter search results, based on a search query embedded in a URL, and that displayed an Intent chooser, enabling the user to select from a variety of apps that could share text.

Finally, you displayed an AlertDialog containing a list of options from which the user could select only one. You used an AlertDialog.Builder's setItems method to specify a String array resource containing names of the option to display and to set the event handler that was called when the user touched one of the options.

In Chapter 9, we build the database-driven **Address Book** app, which provides quick and easy access to stored contact information and the ability to add contacts, delete contacts and edit existing contacts. You'll learn how to dynamically swap Fragments in a GUI and provide layouts that optimize screen real estate on phones and tablets.

Self-Review Exercises

8.1 Fill in the blanks in each of the following statements:
  a) _____ are typically used to launch activities—they indicate an action to be performed and the data on which that action is to be performed.
  b) A(n) _____ (package android.support.v7.widget) is a flexible, customizable view that enables you to control how an app displays a scrolling list of data.
  c) Lengthy data access should never be done in the UI thread; otherwise, the app will display a(n) _____ dialog—typically after five seconds of inactivity.
  d) An Intent is a description of an action to be performed with associated _____.
  e) _____ Intents specify an exact Activity class to run in the same app.
  f) Class RecyclerView formalizes the view-holder pattern by requiring you to create a subclass of _____.
  g) _____ is a subclass of RecyclerView.LayoutManager that can be used to display items in a vertical list.

8.2 State whether each of the following is *true* or *false*. If *false*, explain why.
  a) Extensive input/output should be performed on the UI thread; otherwise, this will affect your app's responsiveness.
  b) RecyclerView was designed as a better ListView. It provides better separation of the data's presentation from the RecyclerView's capabilities for reusing views, as well as more flexible customization options for presenting the RecyclerView's items.
  c) An AlertDialog.Builder's setList method receives a String array resource containing names of the options to display as a list in the dialog and an event handler that's called when the user touches one of the options in the list.
  d) Each RecyclerView item has a corresponding object of a subclass of class RecyclerView.ViewHolder that maintains references to the item's view(s) for reuse.

Answers to Self-Review Exercises

8.1 a) Intents. b) RecyclerView. c) Application Not Responding (ANR). d) data. e) Explicit. f) RecyclerView.ViewHolder. g) LinearLayoutManager.

8.2 a) False. Extensive input/output should *not* be performed on the UI thread, since that would affect your app's responsiveness. b) True. c) False. The `AlertDialog.Builder`'s `setItems` method does this. d) True.

Exercises

8.1 Fill in the blanks in each of the following statements:

a) A layout fills the entire client area of the screen if the layout's **Width** and **Height** properties (in the **Layout Parameters** section of the **Properties** window) are each set to _____.

b) _____ object stores key-value pairs.

c) _____ (a `static` method of class `Collections` from package `java.util`) sorts the `List` in its first argument.

d) A(n) _____ is a GUI that shows a list of apps that can handle a specified Intent.

e) A subclass of _____ can be used to display a line between `RecyclerView` items.

8.2 State whether each of the following is *true* or *false*. If *false*, explain why.

a) An `Algorithm` specifies an action to be performed and the data to be acted upon—Android uses `Algorithm`s to launch the appropriate activities.

b) You implement interface `View.OnClickListener` of package `android.view` to specify the code that should execute when the user touches a `Button`.

c) The first argument passed to `Intent`'s constructor is the data to be operated on.

d) An explicit `Intent` allows the system to launch the most appropriate `Activity` based on the type of data.

Project Exercises

8.3 *(Favorite Websites App)* Using the techniques you learned in this chapter, create a **Favorite Websites** app that allows a user to create a list of favorite websites.

8.4 *(Twitter Searches App Enhancement)* Use an `AsyncTask` to modify the **Twitter Searches** app so that it loads and saves the `SharedPreferences` in a separate thread of execution.

8.5 *(Enhanced Twitter Searches App)* Make the following enhancements to the **Twitter Searches** app—some of these require the Twitter web-service APIs:

a) Allow the user to add filters to searches (e.g., include only tweets with videos, images or links). Investigate the Twitter search operators in more detail to determine the filter options.

b) Create an option for following the top five Twitter trends—popular topics being discussed on Twitter.

c) Add the ability to retweet tweets that you find in your searches.

d) Add a feature that suggests people to follow based on the user's favorite Twitter searches.

e) Add translation capabilities to read Tweets in other languages.

f) Share on Facebook.

g) View all replies related to a tweet.

h) Enable the user to reply to a tweet in the search results.

8.6 *(Flickr Searches App)* Investigate Flickr's photo-search web-service API (`https://www.flickr.com/services/api/flickr.photos.search.html`), then reimplement this chapter's **Twitter Searches** app as a **Flickr Searches** app.

8.7 *(Enhanced Flickr Searches App)* Enhance the **Flickr Searches** app from Exercise 8.6 to allow the user to add filters to searches (e.g., include only images containing a specific color, shape, object, etc.).

8.8   *(Twitter App)* Investigate the Twitter Fabric APIs at `https://fabric.io`, then use the APIs in an app that includes some of the following features:

    a)   Post a tweet from within the app to Twitter and Facebook simultaneously.

    b)   Group tweets from favorite twitterers into lists (e.g., friends, colleagues, celebrities).

    c)   Hide specific twitterers from the feed without "unfollowing" them.

    d)   Manage multiple accounts from the same app.

    e)   Color code tweets in the feed from favorite twitterers or tweets that contain specific keywords.

    f)   Geo tag tweets so readers can see the user's location when the tweet was posted.

    g)   Reply to tweets from within the app.

    h)   Retweet from within the app.

    i)   Use the APIs from a URL shortening service to enable the user to shorten URLs to include in tweets.

    j)   Save drafts of tweets to post later.

    k)   Display updates when a favorite posts a new tweet.

8.9   *(Enhanced Flag Quiz App)* Enhance the Flag Quiz app from Chapter 4 so that after the user answers the question correctly, the app provides a link to the Wikipedia for that country, so the user can learn more about the country as they play the game. When the user touches the link, use an `Intent` to launch the device's browser to request and display the web page. In this version of the app, you may want to allow the user to decide when to move to the next flag.

Advanced Project Exercises

8.10   *(Blackjack App)* Create a Blackjack card game app. Two cards each are dealt to the dealer and the player. (We provide card images with the book's examples.) The player's cards are dealt face up. Only the dealer's first card is dealt face up. Each card has a value. A card numbered 2 through 10 is worth its face value. Jacks, queens and kings each count as 10. Aces can count as 1 or 11—whichever value is more beneficial to the player. If the sum of the player's two initial cards is 21 (that is, the player was dealt a card valued at 10 and an ace, which counts as 11 in this situation), the player has "blackjack" and the dealer's face-down card is revealed. If the dealer does not have blackjack, the player immediately wins the game; otherwise, the hand is a "push" (that is, a tie) and no one wins the hand. If the player does not have blackjack, the player can begin taking additional cards one at a time. These cards are dealt face up, and the player decides when to stop taking cards. If the player "busts" (that is, the sum of the player's cards exceeds 21), the game is over, and the player loses. When the player stands (stops taking cards), the dealer's hidden card is revealed. If the dealer's total is 16 or less, the dealer must take another card; otherwise, the dealer must stay. The dealer must continue to take cards until the sum of the dealer's cards is greater than or equal to 17. If the dealer exceeds 21, the player wins. Otherwise, the hand with the higher point total wins. If the dealer and the player have the same point total, the game is a "push," and no one wins. The GUI for this app can be built using `ImageViews`, `TextViews` and `Buttons`.

8.11   *(Enhanced Blackjack App)* Enhance the Blackjack app in Exercise 8.10 as follows:

    a)   Provide a betting mechanism that allows the player to start with $1000 and adds or subtracts from that value based on whether the user wins or loses a hand. If the player wins with a non-blackjack hand, the bet amount is added to the total. If the player wins with blackjack, 1.5 times the bet amount is added to the total. If the player loses the hand, the bet amount is subtracted from the total. The game ends when the user runs out of money.

    b)   Locate images of casino chips and use them to represent the bet amount on the screen.

    c)   Investigate Blackjack rules online and provide capabilities for "doubling down," "surrendering" and other aspects of the game.

    d) Some casinos use variations of the standard Blackjack rules. Provide options that allow the user to choose the rules under which the game should be played.

    e) Some casinos use different numbers of decks of cards. Allow the user to choose how many decks should be used.

    f) Allow the user to save the game's state to continue at a later time.

8.12 *(Other Card Game Apps)* Investigate the rules for any card game of your choice online and implement the game as an app.

8.13 *(Solitaire Card Game App)* Search the web for the rules to various solitaire card games. Choose the version of the game you like then implement it. (We provide card images with the book's examples.)

Address Book App

Objectives

In this chapter you'll:

- Use FragmentTransactions and the back stack to dynamically attach Fragments to and detach Fragments from the GUI.

- Use a RecyclerView to display data from a database.

- Create and open databases with SQLiteOpenHelper.

- Use a ContentProvider and a SQLiteDatabase object to interact with data in a SQLite database.

- Use a ContentResolver to invoke methods of a ContentProvider to perform tasks with a database.

- Use a LoaderManager and Loaders to perform database access asynchronously outside the GUI thread.

- Use Cursors to manipulate database query results.

- Define styles containing common GUI attributes and values, then apply them to multiple GUI components.

Outline

Self-Review Exercises | Answers to Self-Review Exercises | Exercises

9.1 Introduction

The **Address Book** app (Fig. 9.1) provides convenient access to contact information that's stored in a SQLite database on the device. You can:

- scroll through an alphabetical contact list
- view a contact's details by touching a contact's name in the contact list
- add new contacts
- edit or delete existing contacts.

The app provides a separate tablet layout (Fig. 9.2) that always displays the contact list in one third of the screen and uses the screen's remaining two thirds to display either the selected contact's data or the screen for adding and editing a contact.

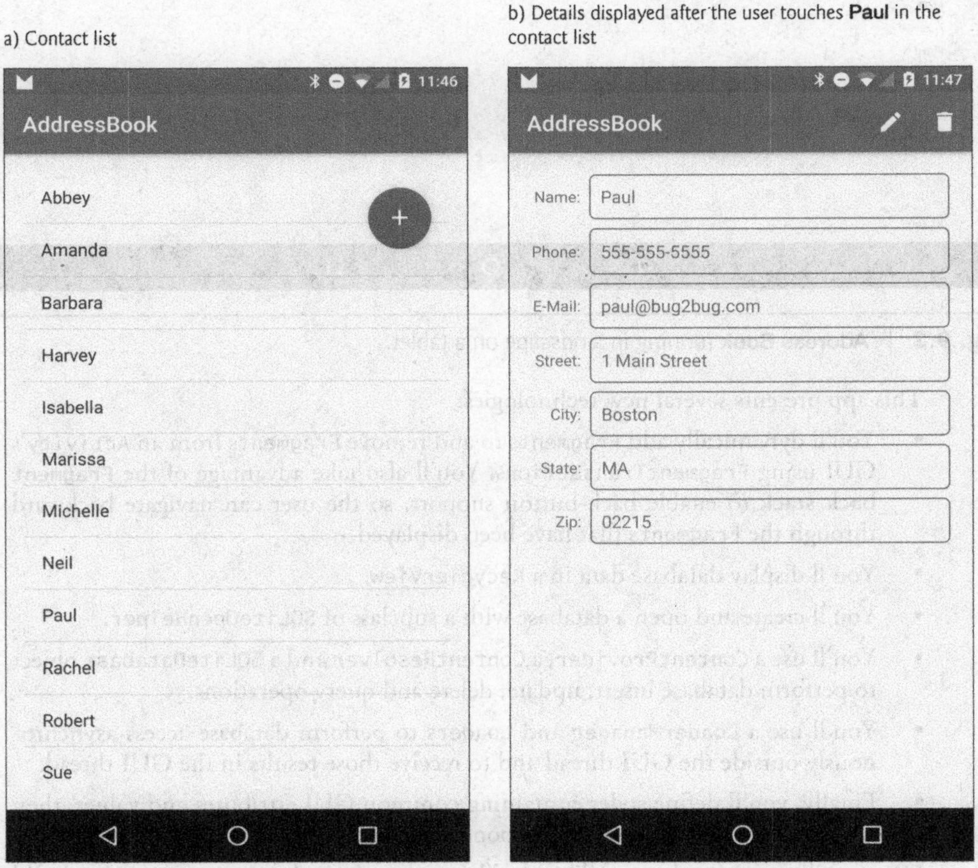

a) Contact list

b) Details displayed after the user touches **Paul** in the contact list

Fig. 9.1 | Contact list and a selected contact's details.

a) In landscape orientation on a phone or tablet, the app bar icons are displayed with their text

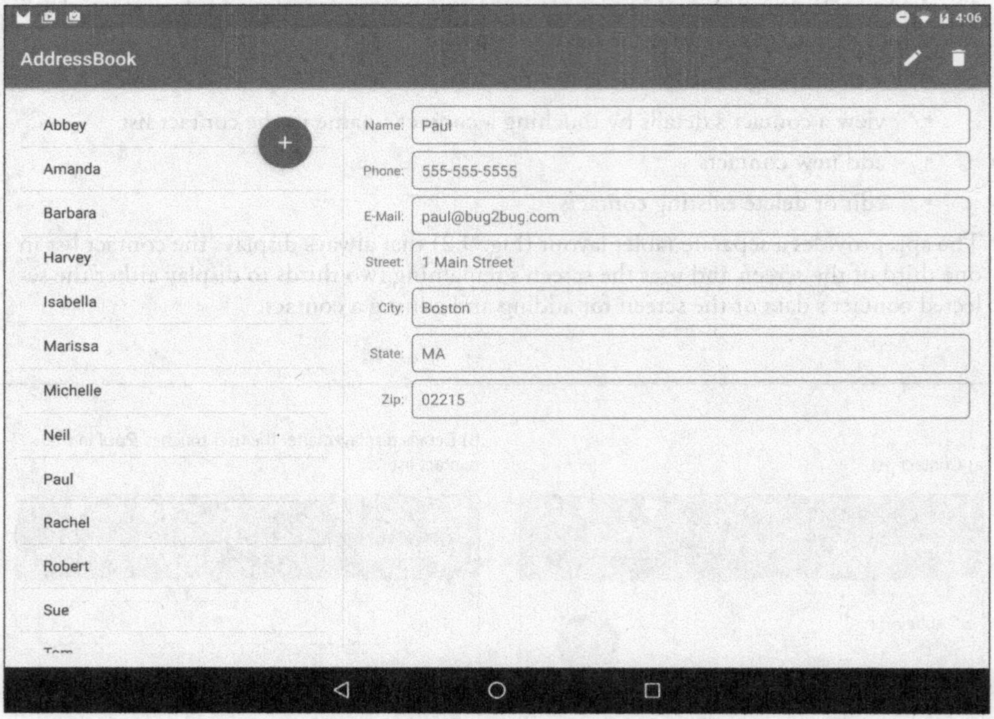

Fig. 9.2 | **Address Book** running in landscape on a tablet.

This app presents several new technologies:

- You'll dynamically add Fragments to and remove Fragments from an Activity's GUI using FragmentTransactions. You'll also take advantage of the **Fragment back stack** to enable back-button support, so the user can navigate backward through the Fragments that have been displayed.

- You'll display database data in a RecyclerView.

- You'll create and open a database with a subclass of SQLiteOpenHelper.

- You'll use a ContentProvider, a ContentResolver and a SQLiteDatabase object to perform database insert, update, delete and query operations.

- You'll use a LoaderManager and Loaders to perform database access asynchronously outside the GUI thread and to receive those results in the GUI thread.

- Finally, you'll define styles containing common GUI attributes and values, then apply them to multiple GUI components.

First, you'll test-drive the app. Then we'll overview the technologies we used to build it. Next, you'll create the app's GUI and resource files. Finally, we'll present and walk through the app's complete source code, discussing the app's new features in more detail.

9.2 Test-Driving the Address Book App

Opening and Running the App

Open Android Studio and open the **Address Book** app from the AddressBook folder in the book's examples folder, then execute the app in the AVD or on a device. This builds the project and runs the app.

9.2.1 Adding a Contact

The first time you run the app, the contact list will be empty. Touch the **+** FloatingActionButton to display the screen for adding a new entry (Fig. 9.3). The app requires each contact to have a name, so the save (🖫) FloatingActionButton appears only when the **Name** EditText is not empty. After adding the contact's information, touch 🖫 to store the contact in the database and return to the app's main screen. If you choose not to add the contact, you can simply touch the device's back button to return to the main screen. Add more contacts if you wish. On a tablet, after adding a contact, the new contact's details are displayed next to the contact list (Fig. 9.2). Notice that on tablets, the contact list is always displayed.

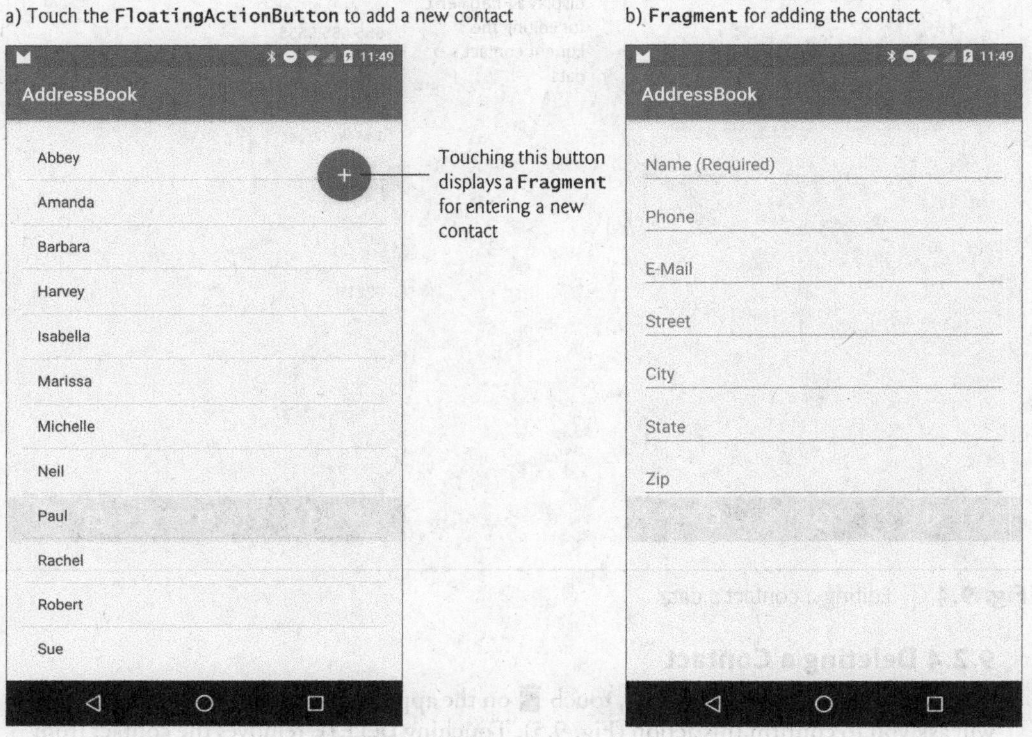

a) Touch the FloatingActionButton to add a new contact

b) **Fragment** for adding the contact

Touching this button displays a **Fragment** for entering a new contact

Fig. 9.3 | Adding a contact to the database.

9.2.2 Viewing a Contact

On a phone or phone AVD, touch the name of the contact you just added to view that contact's details (as you saw in Fig. 9.1). Again, on a tablet, the details are displayed automatically to the right of the contact list (Fig. 9.2).

9.2.3 Editing a Contact

While viewing the contact's details, touch ✏ on the app bar to display a screen of Edit-Texts that are prepopulated with the contact's data (Fig. 9.4). Edit the data as necessary, then touch the FloatingActionButton 💾 to store the updated contact in the database and return to the app's main screen. If you choose not to edit the contact, you can simply touch the device's back button (◁) to return to the prior screen. On a tablet, after editing a contact, the updated contact details are displayed to the right of the contact list.

a) Details for a contact

b) **Fragment** for editing the contact

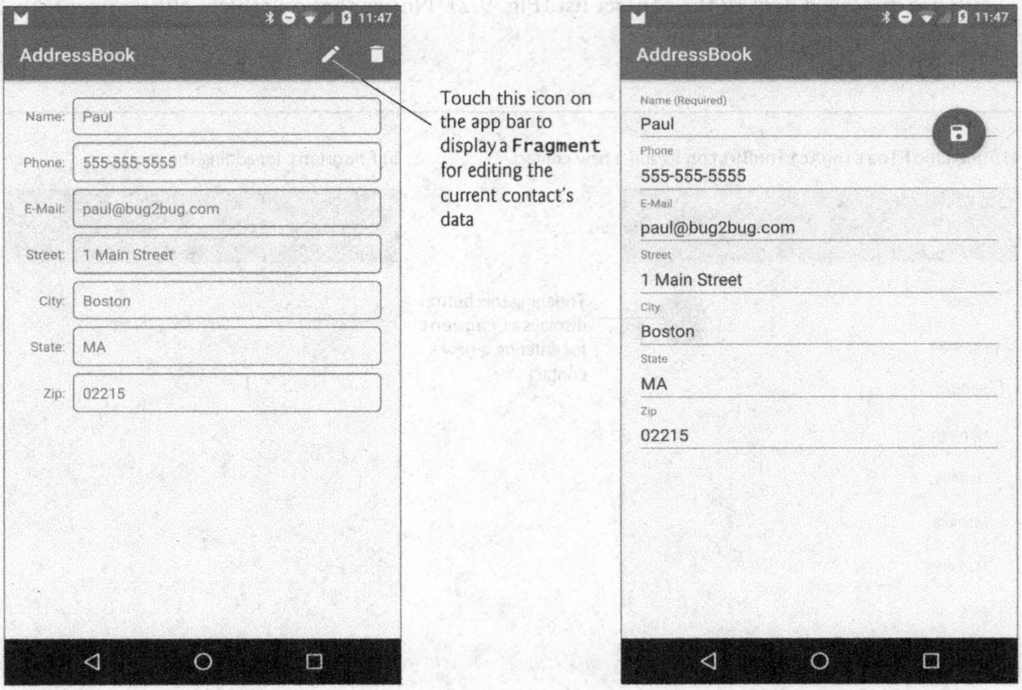

Touch this icon on the app bar to display a **Fragment** for editing the current contact's data

Fig. 9.4 │ Editing a contact's data.

9.2.4 Deleting a Contact

While viewing the contact's details, touch 🗑 on the app bar to delete the contact. A dialog will ask you to confirm this action (Fig. 9.5). Touching **DELETE** removes the contact from the database and the app will display the updated contact list. Touching **CANCEL** retains the contact.

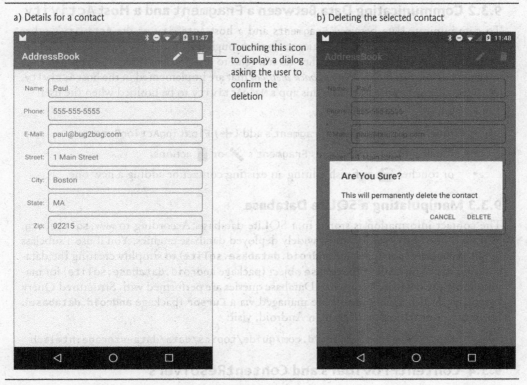

a) Details for a contact

Touching this icon to display a dialog asking the user to confirm the deletion

b) Deleting the selected contact

Fig. 9.5 | Deleting a contact from the database.

9.3 Technologies Overview

This section introduces the features you'll use to build the **Address Book** app.

9.3.1 Displaying Fragments with FragmentTransactions

In earlier apps that used Fragments, you declared each Fragment in an Activity's layout or, for a DialogFragment, called its show method to create it. The **Flag Quiz** app demonstrated how to use multiple activities to host each of the app's Fragments on a phone device, and a single Activity to host multiple Fragments on a tablet device.

In this app, you'll use only one Activity to host all of the app's Fragments. On a phone-sized device, you'll display one Fragment at a time. On a tablet, you'll always display the Fragment containing the contact list and display the Fragments for viewing, adding and editing contacts as they're needed. To do this, you'll use the FragmentManager and **FragmentTransactions** to dynamically display Fragments. In addition, you'll use Android's Fragment **back stack**—a data structure that stores Fragments in last-in-first-out (LIFO) order—to provide automatic support for Android's back button (◁). This enables users to go back to prior Fragments via the back button. For more information on Fragments and FragmentTransactions, visit:

http://developer.android.com/guide/components/fragments.html

9.3.2 Communicating Data Between a Fragment and a Host Activity

To communicate data between Fragments and a host Activity or the Activity's other Fragments, it's considered best practice to do so through the host Activity—this makes the Fragments more reusable, because they do not refer to one another directly. Typically, each Fragment defines an *interface* of *callback methods* that are implemented in the host Activity. We'll use this technique to enable this app's MainActivity to be notified when the user:

- selects a contact to display,
- touches the contact-list Fragment's add (**+**) FloatingActionButton,
- touches the contact details Fragment's 🖉 or 🗑 actions,
- or touches 🖫 to finish editing an existing contact or adding a new one.

9.3.3 Manipulating a SQLite Database

The contact information is stored in a SQLite database. According to www.sqlite.org, SQLite is one of the world's most widely deployed database engines. You'll use a subclass of **SQLiteOpenHelper** (package **android.database.sqlite**) to simplify creating the database and to obtain a **SQLiteDatabase** object (package android.database.sqlite) for manipulating the database's contents. Database queries are performed with Structured Query Language (SQL). Query results are managed via a **Cursor** (package **android.database**). For more information on SQLite in Android, visit:

```
http://developer.android.com/guide/topics/data/data-storage.html#db
```

9.3.4 ContentProviders and ContentResolvers

A **ContentProvider** (package **android.provider**) exposes an app's data for use in that app or in other apps. Android provides various built-in ContentProviders. For example, your apps can interact with data from the Android **Contacts** and **Calendar** apps. There are also ContentProviders for various telephony features, the media store (e.g., for images/video) and the user dictionary (used with Android's predictive text-input capabilities).

In addition to exposing data to other apps, ContentProviders also enable your app to provide custom search suggestions when a user performs searches on a device and are used to support copy-and-paste operations between apps.

In this app, we use a ContentProvider to help access the database asynchronously outside the GUI thread—this is required when working with Loaders and the LoaderManager (introduced in Section 9.3.5). You'll define a subclass of ContentProvider that specifies how to:

- query the database to locate a specific contact or all the contacts
- insert a new contact into the database
- update an existing contact in the database, and
- delete an existing contact from the database.

The ContentProvider will use a subclass of SQLiteOpenHelper to create the database and to obtain SQLiteDatabase objects to perform the preceding tasks. When changes are made to the database, the ContentProvider will notify listeners of those changes so data can be updated in the GUI.

Uris

The ContentProvider will define Uris that help determine the tasks to perform. For example, in this app the ContentProvider's query method is used for two different queries—one that returns a Cursor for a single contact and one that returns a Cursor for the names of all contacts in the database.

ContentResolver

To invoke the ContentProvider's query, insert, update and delete capabilities, we'll use the corresponding methods of the Activity's built-in **ContentResolver** (package **android.content**). The ContentProvider and ContentResolver handle communication for you—including between apps if your ContentProvider exposes its data to other apps. As you'll see, the ContentResolver's methods receive as their first argument a Uri that specifies the ContentProvider to access. Each ContentResolver method invokes the corresponding method of the ContentProvider, which uses the Uri to help determine the task to perform. For more information on ContentProviders and ContentResolvers, see:

> http://developer.android.com/guide/topics/providers/content-
> providers.html

9.3.5 Loader and LoaderManager—Asynchronous Database Access

As we've stated previously, long-running operations or operations that block execution until they complete (e.g., file and database access) should be performed outside the GUI thread. This helps maintain application responsiveness and avoid Activity Not Responding (ANR) dialogs that appear when Android determines that the GUI is not responsive. Loaders and the LoaderManager help you perform asynchronous data access from any Activity or Fragment.

Loaders

A **Loader** (package android.content) performs asynchronous data access. When interacting with a ContentProvider to load and manipulate data, you'll typically use a **CursorLoader**—a subclass of AsyncTaskLoader that uses an AsyncTask to perform the data access in a separate thread. Loaders also:

- Watch for changes to the corresponding data source and make the updated data available to the corresponding Activity or Fragment.

- Reconnect to the last Loader's Cursor, rather than perform a new query, when a configuration change occurs.

LoaderManager and LoaderManager.LoaderCallbacks

An Activity's or Fragment's Loaders are created and managed by its **LoaderManager** (package android.app), which ties each Loader's lifecycle to its Activity's or Fragment's lifecycle. In addition, a LoaderManager invokes methods of the **LoaderManager.LoaderCallbacks** interface to notify an Activity or Fragment when a Loader

- should be created,
- finishes loading its data, or
- is reset and the data is no longer available.

You'll use Loaders and LoaderManagers in several of this app's Fragment subclasses. For more information about Loaders and LoaderManagers, see:

http://developer.android.com/guide/components/loaders.html

9.3.6 Defining Styles and Applying Them to GUI Components

You can define common GUI component attribute–value pairs as **style** resources (Section 9.4.5). You can then apply the styles to all components that share those values (Section 9.4.9) by using the **style attribute**. Any subsequent changes you make to a style are automatically applied to all GUI components that use it. We use this to style the TextViews that display a contact's information. For more information on styles, visit:

http://developer.android.com/guide/topics/ui/themes.html

9.3.7 Specifying a TextView Background

By default TextViews do not have a border. To define one, you can specify a Drawable as the value for the TextView's android:background attribute. The Drawable could be an image, but in this app you'll define a Drawable as a shape in a resource file (Section 9.4.6). Like an image, the resource file for such a Drawable is defined in one (or more) of the app's drawable folders. For more information on drawable resources, visit:

http://developer.android.com/guide/topics/resources/drawable-resource.html

9.4 Building the GUI and Resource Files

In this section, you'll create the **Address Book** app's additional Java source-code files, resource files and GUI layout files.

9.4.1 Creating the Project

Create a new project using the **Blank Activity** template. When configuring the project, check the **Use a Fragment** checkbox. Specify the following values in the **Create New Project** dialog's **New Project** step:

- **Application name:** Address Book
- **Company Domain:** deitel.com (or specify your own domain name)

Follow the steps you used in earlier apps to add an app icon to your project. Follow the steps in Section 4.4.3 to configure Java SE 7 support for the project. Follow the steps in Section 8.4.3 to add the RecyclerView library to this project. In colors.xml, change the colorAccent color's value to #FF4081.

9.4.2 Creating the App's Classes

When you create this project, Android Studio defines the classes MainActivity and MainActivityFragment for you. In this app, we renamed MainActivityFragment as ContactsFragment. To do so:

1. Open class MainActivityFragment in the editor.

2. Right click the class name and select **Refactor > Rename....** The IDE highlights the class name for editing.

3. Type ContactsFragment and press *Enter*. The IDE renames the class and its constructor, and changes class's file name.

Package *com.deitel.addressbook*

This app consists of seven additional classes that you must add to the project (**File > New > Java Class**). The additional classes in package com.deitel.addressbook are:

- Class ContactsAdapter is a subclass of RecyclerView.Adapter that supplies data to the ContactsFragment's RecyclerView.

- Class AddEditFragment is a subclass of Fragment that provides a GUI for adding a new contact or editing an existing one.

- Class DetailFragment is a subclass of Fragment that displays one contact's data and provides menu items for editing and deleting that contact.

- Class ItemDivider is a subclass of RecyclerView.ItemDecoration that the ContactsFragment's RecyclerView uses to draw a horizontal line between items. This class is identical to the one in Section 8.7, so you can simply copy this class from the **Twitter Searches** app's project and paste it into the **app > java > com.deitel.addressbook** node in the **Project** window.

Package *com.deitel.addressbook.data*

This class also defines a nested package named com.deitel.addressbook.data that contains the classes used to manipulate this app's database. To create the package:

1. In the **Project** window, right click the package com.deitel.addressbook and select **New > Package**.

2. Type data as the new package name to create the com.deitel.addressbook.data package.

Next add the following classes to the com.deitel.addressbook.data package:

- Class DatabaseDescription describes the database's contacts table.

- Class AddressBookDatabaseHelper is a subclass of SQLiteOpenHelper that creates the database and is used to access the database.

- Class AddressBookContentProvider is a subclass of ContentProvider that defines how to manipulate the database. To create this class, use **New > Other > Content Provider**. For **URI authorities** specify com.deitel.addressbook.data and uncheck the **Exported** checkbox, then click **Finish**. Unchecking **Exported** indicates that this ContentProvider is for use only in this app. The IDE defines a subclass of ContentProvider and overrides its required methods. In addition, the IDE declares the ContentProvider AndroidManifest.xml as a <provider> element nested in the <application> element. This is *required* to register the ContentProvider with the Android operating system—not only for use in this app, but for use in other apps (when the ContentProvider is exported).

We overview all of the classes in Section 9.5 and discuss their details in Sections 9.6–9.13.

9.4.3 Add the App's Icons

Use Android Studio's **Vector Asset Studio** (Section 4.4.9) to add the material design save (🖫), add (＋), edit (✏) and delete (🗑) icons to the project—this will be used as the FloatingActionButton's icon. After adding the vector icons, go to the project's res/ drawable folder, open each icon's XML file and change the <path> element's android:fillColor to

```
"@android:color/white"
```

9.4.4 strings.xml

Figure 9.6 shows this app's String resource names and corresponding values. Double click strings.xml in the res/values folder to display the resource editor for creating these String resources.

Resource name	Value
menuitem_edit	Edit
menuitem_delete	Delete
hint_name_required	Name (Required)
hint_email	E-Mail
hint_phone	Phone
hint_street	Street
hint_city	City
hint_state	State
hint_zip	Zip
label_name	Name:
label_email	E-Mail:
label_phone	Phone:
label_street	Street:
label_city	City:
label_state	State:
label_zip	Zip:
confirm_title	Are You Sure?
confirm_message	This will permanently delete the contact
button_cancel	Cancel
button_delete	Delete
contact_added	Contact added successfully
contact_not_added	Contact was not added due to an error
contact_updated	Contact updated
contact_not_updated	Contact was not updated due to an error

Fig. 9.6 | String resources used in the **Address Book** app. (Part I of 2.)

Resource name	Value
invalid_query_uri	Invalid query Uri:
invalid_insert_uri	Invalid insert Uri:
invalid_update_uri	Invalid update Uri:
invalid_delete_uri	Invalid delete Uri:
insert_failed	Insert failed: s

Fig. 9.6 | String resources used in the **Address Book** app. (Part 2 of 2.)

9.4.5 styles.xml

In this section, you'll define the styles for the DetailFragment's TextViews that display a contact's information (Section 9.4.9). Like other resources, style resources are placed in the app's res/values folder. When you create a project, the IDE creates a styles.xml file containing predefined styles. Each new style you create specifies a name that's used to apply that style to GUI components and one or more items specifying property values to apply. To create the new styles, in the app's res/values folder, open the styles.xml file then add the code in Fig. 9.7 before the file's closing </resources> tag. When you're done, save and close styles.xml.

```
1   <style name="ContactLabelTextView">
2       <item name="android:layout_width">wrap_content</item>
3       <item name="android:layout_height">wrap_content</item>
4       <item name="android:layout_gravity">right|center_vertical</item>
5   </style>
6
7   <style name="ContactTextView">
8       <item name="android:layout_width">wrap_content</item>
9       <item name="android:layout_height">wrap_content</item>
10      <item name="android:layout_gravity">fill_horizontal</item>
11      <item name="android:textSize">16sp</item>
12      <item name="android:background">@drawable/textview_border</item>
13  </style>
```

Fig. 9.7 | New styles for formatting the DetailFragment's TextViews.

Lines 1–5 define a new style named ContactLabelTextView that defines values for the layout properties layout_width, layout_height and layout_gravity. You'll apply this style to the DetailFragment's TextViews displayed to the left of each piece of a contact's information. Each new style consists of a style element containing item elements. The style's name is used to apply it. An item element's name specifies the property to set and its value is assigned to that property when the style is applied to a view. Lines 7–13 define another new style named ContactTextView that will be applied to the DetailFragment's TextViews that display the contact's information. Line 12 sets the property android:background to the drawable resource defined in Section 9.4.6.

9.4.6 `textview_border.xml`

The `style` `ContactTextView` that you created in the preceding section defines the appearance of the `TextViews` that are used to display a contact's details. You specified a `Drawable` (i.e., an image or graphic) named `@drawable/textview_border` as the value for the `TextView`'s `android:background` attribute. In this section, you'll define that `Drawable` in the app's `res/drawable` folder. To define the `Drawable`:

1. Right click the `res/drawable` folder and select **New > Drawable resource file**.

2. Specify `textview_border.xml` as the **File name** and click **OK**.

3. Replace the file's contents with the XML code in Fig. 9.8.

```
I   <?xml version="1.0" encoding="utf-8"?>
2   <shape xmlns:android="http://schemas.android.com/apk/res/android"
3       android:shape="rectangle">
4       <corners android:radius="5dp"/>
5       <stroke android:width="1dp" android:color="#555"/>
6       <padding android:top="10dp" android:left="10dp" android:bottom="10dp"
7           android:right="10dp"/>
8   </shape>
```

Fig. 9.8 | XML representation of a `Drawable` that's used to place a border on a `TextView`.

The **shape** element's `android:shape` attribute (line 3) can have the value `"rectangle"` (used in this example), `"oval"`, `"line"` or `"ring"`. The **corners** element (line 4) specifies the rectangle's corner radius, which rounds the corners. The **stroke** element (line 5) defines the rectangle's line width and line color. The **padding** element (lines 6–7) specifies the spacing around the content in the element to which this `Drawable` is applied. You must specify the top, left, bottom and right padding amounts separately. The complete details of defining shapes can be viewed at:

> http://developer.android.com/guide/topics/resources/drawable-resource.html#Shape

9.4.7 MainActivity's Layout

By default, `MainActivity`'s layout contains a `FloatingActionButton` and includes the layout file `content_main.xml`. In this app, we provide `FloatingActionButtons` as needed in the app's Fragments. For this reason, open `activity_main.xml` in the `res/layout` folder and remove the predefined `FloatingActionButton`. Also, set the `CoordinatorLayout`'s `id` to `coordinatorLayout`—we use this when displaying `SnackBars`. Remove the code that configures the `FloatingActionButton` from `MainActivity`'s `onCreate` method.

Phone Layout: content_main.xml
In this app, you'll provide two `content_main.xml` layouts to be included into `MainActivity`—one for phone-sized devices and one for tablet-sized devices. For the phone layout, open `content_main.xml` in the `res/layout` folder and replace its contents with the XML in Fig. 9.9. `MainActivity` dynamically displays the app's Fragments in the `FrameLayout` named `fragmentContainer`. This layout fills the available space in `MainActivity`'s layout with 16dp padding on all sides. The `app:layout_behavior` property (line 20) is used by

activity_main.xml's CoordinatorLayout to manage interactions between its views. Setting this property ensures that the contents of the FrameLayout scroll below the Toolbar defined in activity_main.xml.

```
9    <FrameLayout
10       android:id="@+id/fragmentContainer"
11       xmlns:android="http://schemas.android.com/apk/res/android"
12       xmlns:app="http://schemas.android.com/apk/res-auto"
13       xmlns:tools="http://schemas.android.com/tools"
14       android:layout_width="match_parent"
15       android:layout_height="match_parent"
16       android:paddingBottom="@dimen/activity_vertical_margin"
17       android:paddingLeft="@dimen/activity_horizontal_margin"
18       android:paddingRight="@dimen/activity_horizontal_margin"
19       android:paddingTop="@dimen/activity_vertical_margin"
20       app:layout_behavior="@string/appbar_scrolling_view_behavior"
21       tools:context=".MainActivity"/>
```

Fig. 9.9 | content_main.xml used on a phone device.

Tablet Layout: *content_main.xml for Large Devices*

Create the new tablet layout content_main.xml (as in Section 4.5.4). This layout should use a horizontal LinearLayout containing a ContactsFragment and an empty FrameLayout as shown in Fig. 9.10. Create the divider_margin resource (16dp) used in lines 24 and 32. This LinearLayout uses several properties that we have not discussed previously:

- divider (line 9)—This property specifies a drawable resource that's used to separate items in the LinearLayout. In this case, we use the predefined Android drawable theme resource ?android:listDivider. The ?android: indicates that the LinearLayout should use the list divider defined in the current theme.

- showDividers (line 15)—This property is used with the divider property to specify where the dividers appear—in this case, middle indicates that the dividers should appear only between the LinearLayout's elements. You can also display a divider before the first item in the layout (beginning) and after the last item (end), and you can combine these values using |.

- weightSum (line 16)—This helps allocate the horizontal space between the ContactsFragment and FrameLayout. Setting weightSum to 3, then setting the ContactsFragment's and FrameLayout's layout_weights to 1 and 2, respectively, indicates that the ContactsFragment should occupy one-third of the LinearLayout's width and the FrameLayout should occupy the remaining two-thirds.

```
1    <?xml version="1.0" encoding="utf-8"?>
2    <LinearLayout
3       xmlns:android="http://schemas.android.com/apk/res/android"
4       xmlns:app="http://schemas.android.com/apk/res-auto"
5       xmlns:tools="http://schemas.android.com/tools"
6       android:layout_width="match_parent"
```

Fig. 9.10 | content_main.xml used on a tablet device. (Part 1 of 2.)

```
 7       android:layout_height="match_parent"
 8       android:baselineAligned="false"
 9       android:divider="?android:listDivider"
10       android:orientation="horizontal"
11       android:paddingBottom="@dimen/activity_vertical_margin"
12       android:paddingLeft="@dimen/activity_horizontal_margin"
13       android:paddingRight="@dimen/activity_horizontal_margin"
14       android:paddingTop="@dimen/activity_vertical_margin"
15       android:showDividers="middle"
16       android:weightSum="3"
17       app:layout_behavior="@string/appbar_scrolling_view_behavior">
18
19       <fragment
20          android:id="@+id/contactsFragment"
21          android:name="com.deitel.addressbook.ContactsFragment"
22          android:layout_width="0dp"
23          android:layout_height="match_parent"
24          android:layout_marginEnd="@dimen/divider_margin"
25          android:layout_weight="1"
26          tools:layout="@layout/fragment_contacts"/>
27
28       <FrameLayout
29          android:id="@+id/rightPaneContainer"
30          android:layout_width="0dp"
31          android:layout_height="match_parent"
32          android:layout_marginStart="@dimen/divider_margin"
33          android:layout_weight="2"/>
34    </LinearLayout>
```

Fig. 9.10 | content_main.xml used on a tablet device. (Part 2 of 2.)

9.4.8 ContactsFragment's Layout

In addition to renaming class MainActivityFragment as ContactsFragment, we renamed the corresponding layout file as fragment_contacts.xml. We then removed the default TextView, changed the default layout from a RelativeLayout to a FrameLayout and removed the layout's padding properties. Next, we added a RecyclerView named recyclerView and a FloatingActionButton named addButton. The layout's final XML is shown in Fig. 9.11. Ensure that you set the RecyclerView and a FloatingActionButton properties as shown.

```
 1    <FrameLayout
 2       xmlns:android="http://schemas.android.com/apk/res/android"
 3       android:layout_width="match_parent"
 4       android:layout_height="match_parent">
 5
 6       <android.support.v7.widget.RecyclerView
 7          android:id="@+id/recyclerView"
 8          android:layout_width="match_parent"
 9          android:layout_height="match_parent"/>
10
```

Fig. 9.11 | fragment_contacts.xml layout. (Part 1 of 2.)

```
11      <android.support.design.widget.FloatingActionButton
12          android:id="@+id/addButton"
13          android:layout_width="wrap_content"
14          android:layout_height="wrap_content"
15          android:layout_gravity="top|end"
16          android:layout_margin="@dimen/fab_margin"
17          android:src="@drawable/ic_add_24dp"/>
18   </FrameLayout>
```

Fig. 9.11 | `fragment_contacts.xml` layout. (Part 2 of 2.)

9.4.9 DetailFragment's Layout

When the user touches a contact in the `MainActivity`, the app displays the `DetailFragment` (Fig. 9.12). This `Fragment`'s layout (`fragment_details.xml`) consists of a `ScrollView` containing a vertical `GridLayout` with two columns of `TextView`s. A **ScrollView** is a **ViewGroup** that provides scrolling functionality for a view with content too large to display on the screen. We use a `ScrollView` here to ensure that the user can scroll through a contact's details if a device does not have enough vertical space to show all the `TextView`s in Fig. 9.12. For this fragment, create a new `fragment_details.xml` layout resource file and specify a `ScrollView` as the **Root Element**. After creating the file add a `GridLayout` to the `ScrollView`.

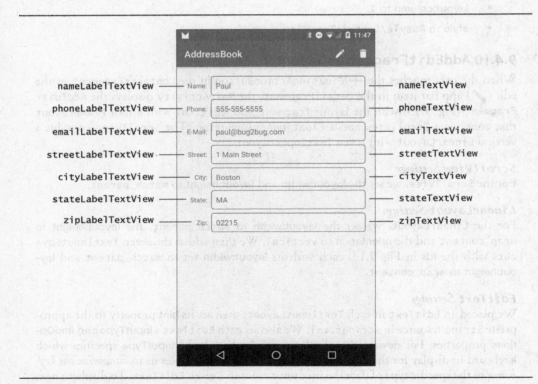

Fig. 9.12 | `DetailFragment`'s GUI components labeled with their `id` property values.

GridLayout Settings

For the GridLayout, we set the layout:width to match_parent, layout:height to wrap_content, columnCount to 2 and useDefaultMargins to true. The layout:height value enables the parent ScrollView to determine the GridLayout's actual height and decide whether to provide scrolling. Add TextViews to the GridLayout as shown in Fig. 9.12.

Left Column TextView Settings

For each TextView in the left column set the TextView's **id** property as specified in Fig. 9.12 and set:

- layout:row to a value from 0–6 depending on the row.
- layout:column to 0.
- text to the appropriate String resource from strings.xml.
- style to @style/ContactLabelTextView—style resources are specified using the syntax @style/*styleName*.

Right Column TextView Settings

For each TextView in the right column set the TextView's **id** property as specified in Fig. 9.12 and set:

- layout:row to a value from 0–6 depending on the row.
- layout:column to 1.
- style to @style/ContactTextView.

9.4.10 AddEditFragment's Layout

When the user touches the ✚ FloatingActionButton in the ContactsFragment or the edit (✐) app bar item in the DetailFragment, the MainActivity displays the AddEdit-Fragment (Fig. 9.13) with the layout fragment_add_edit.xml with a root FrameLayout that contains a ScrollView and a FloatingActionButton. The ScrollView contains a vertical LinearLayout with seven TextInputLayouts.

ScrollView Settings

For the ScrollView, we set the layout:width and layout:height to match_parent.

LinearLayout Settings

For the LinearLayout, we set the layout:width to match_parent, the layout:height to wrap_content and the orientation to vertical. We then added the seven TextInputLayouts with the ids in Fig. 9.13, each with its layout:width set to match_parent and layout:height to wrap_content.

EditText Settings

We placed an EditText in each TextInputLayout, then set its **hint** property to the appropriate String resource in strings.xml. We also set each EditText's **inputType** and **imeOptions** properties. For devices that display a soft keyboard, the **inputType** specifies which keyboard to display for the corresponding EditText. This enables us to *customize the keyboard* to the specific type of data the user must enter in a given EditText. To display a next button (⊙) on the soft keyboards for the EditTexts in the nameTextInputLayout,

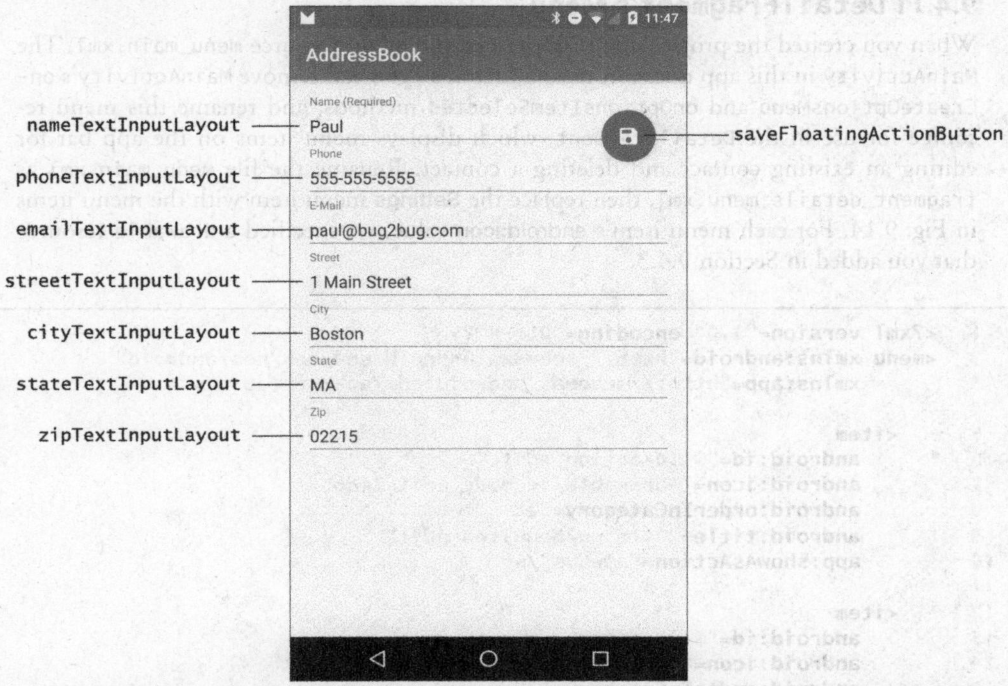

Fig. 9.13 | AddEditFragment's GUI components labeled with their id property values. This GUI's root component is a ScrollView that contains a vertical GridLayout.

phoneTextInputLayout, emailTextInputLayout, streetTextInputLayout, cityText-InputLayout and stateTextInputLayout, we set the **imeOptions** property to actionNext. When one of these EditTexts has the focus, touching ⊙ transfers the focus to the next EditText in the layout. If the EditText in the zipTextInputLayout has the focus, you can hide the soft keyboard by touching the keyboard's ⊘ Button—for this EditText, set the **imeOptions** property to actionDone.

Set the EditTexts' **inputType** properties to display appropriate keyboards as follows:

- nameTextInputLayout's EditText: check textPersonName and textCapWords—for entering names and starts each word with a capital letter.
- phoneTextInputLayout's EditText: check phone—for entering phone numbers.
- emailTextInputLayout's EditText: check textEmailAddress—for entering an e-mail address.
- streetTextInputLayout's EditText: check textPostalAddress and textCap-Words—for entering an address and starts each word with a capital letter.
- cityTextInputLayout's EditText: check textPostalAddress and textCapWords.
- stateTextInputLayout's EditText: check textPostalAddress and textCap-Characters—ensures that state abbreviations are displayed in capital letters.
- zipTextInputLayout's EditText: check number—for entering numbers.

9.4.11 DetailFragment's Menu

When you created the project, the IDE defined the menu resource menu_main.xml. The MainActivity in this app does not need a menu, so you can remove MainActivity's on-CreateOptionsMenu and onOptionsItemSelected methods, and rename this menu resource for use in the DetailFragment, which displays menu items on the app bar for editing an existing contact and deleting a contact. Rename the file menu_main.xml as fragment_details_menu.xml, then replace the **Settings** menu item with the menu items in Fig. 9.14. For each menu item's **android:icon** value, we specified a drawable resource that you added in Section 9.4.3.

```
 1    <?xml version="1.0" encoding="utf-8"?>
 2    <menu xmlns:android="http://schemas.android.com/apk/res/android"
 3          xmlns:app="http://schemas.android.com/apk/res-auto">
 4
 5       <item
 6          android:id="@+id/action_edit"
 7          android:icon="@drawable/ic_mode_edit_24dp"
 8          android:orderInCategory="1"
 9          android:title="@string/menuitem_edit"
10          app:showAsAction="always"/>
11
12       <item
13          android:id="@+id/action_delete"
14          android:icon="@drawable/ic_delete_24dp"
15          android:orderInCategory="2"
16          android:title="@string/menuitem_delete"
17          app:showAsAction="always"/>
18    </menu>
```

Fig. 9.14 | Menu resource file fragment_details_menu.xml.

9.5 Overview of This Chapter's Classes

This app consists of nine classes in two packages. Due to the size of this app we overview the classes and their purposes here.

com.deitel.addressbook.data *Package*

This package contains the three classes that define this app's SQLite database access:

- DatabaseDescription (Section 9.6)—This class contains public static fields that are used with the app's ContentProvider and ContentResolver. The nested Contact class defines static fields for the name of a database table, the Uri used to access that table via the ContentProvider and the names of the database table's columns, and a static method for creating a Uri that references a specific contact in the database.

- AddressBookDatabaseHelper (Section 9.7)—A subclass of SQLiteOpenHelper. that creates the database and enables AddressBookContentProvider to access it.

- AddressBookContentProvider (Section 9.8)—A ContentProvider subclass that defines query, insert, update and delete operations on the database.

com.deitel.addressbook *Package*

This package contains the classes that define this app's MainActivity, Fragments and the adapter that's used to display database contents in a RecyclerView:

- MainActivity (Section 9.9)—This class manages the app's Fragments and implements their callback interface methods to respond when a contact is selected, a new contact is added, or an existing contact is updated or deleted.

- ContactsFragment (Section 9.10)—This class manages the contact-list RecyclerView and the FloatingActionButton for adding contacts. On a phone, this is the first Fragment presented by MainActivity. On a tablet, MainActivity always displays this Fragment. ContactsFragment's nested interface defines callback methods implemented by MainActivity so that it can respond when a contact is selected or added.

- ContactsAdapter (Section 9.11)—This subclass of RecyclerView.Adapter is used by ContactsFragment's RecyclerView to bind the sorted list of contact names to the RecyclerView. RecyclerView.Adapter was introduced in Sections 8.3.4 and 8.6.3, so we discuss only the database-specific operations in this class.

- AddEditFragment (Section 9.12)—This class manages the TextInputLayouts and a FloatingActionButton for adding a new contact or editing and existing one. AddEditFragment's nested interface defines a callback method implemented by MainActivity so that it can respond when a new or updated contact is saved.

- DetailFragment (Section 9.13)—This class manages the styled TextViews that display a selected contact's details and the app bar items that enable the user to edit or delete the currently displayed contact. DetailFragment's nested interface defines callback methods implemented by MainActivity so that it can respond when a contact is deleted or when the user touches the app bar item to edit a contact.

- ItemDivider—This class defines the divider that's displayed between items in the ContactsFragment's RecyclerView. We do not present the class in the chapter, because it's identical to the one presented in Section 8.7.

9.6 DatabaseDescription Class

Class DatabaseDescription contains static fields that are used with the app's ContentProvider and ContentResolver, and a nested Contact class that describes the database's only table and its columns.

9.6.1 static Fields

Class DatabaseDescription defines two static fields (Fig. 9.15; lines 12–17) that together are used to define the ContentProvider's **authority**—the name that's supplied to a ContentResolver to locate a ContentProvider. The authority is typically the package name of the ContentProvider subclass. Each Uri that's used to access a specific ContentProvider begins with "content://" followed by the authority—this is the ContentProvider's base Uri. Line 17 uses Uri method parse to create the base Uri.

```
 1   // DatabaseDescription.java
 2   // Describes the table name and column names for this app's database,
 3   // and other information required by the ContentProvider
 4   package com.deitel.addressbook.data;
 5
 6   import android.content.ContentUris;
 7   import android.net.Uri;
 8   import android.provider.BaseColumns;
 9
10   public class DatabaseDescription {
11      // ContentProvider's name: typically the package name
12      public static final String AUTHORITY =
13         "com.deitel.addressbook.data";
14
15      // base URI used to interact with the ContentProvider
16      private static final Uri BASE_CONTENT_URI =
17         Uri.parse("content://" + AUTHORITY);
18
```

Fig. 9.15 | DatabaseDescription class declaration and static fields.

9.6.2 Nested Class Contact

The nested class Contact (Fig. 9.16) defines the database's table name (line 21), the table's Uri for accessing the table via the ContentProvider (lines 24–25) and the table's column names (lines 28–34). The table name and column names will be used by the AddressBook-DatabaseHelper class (Section 9.7) to create the database. Method buildContactUri creates a Uri for a specific contact in the database table (lines 37–39). Class ContentUris (package android.content) contains static utility methods for manipulating "content://" Uris. Method withAppendedId appends a forward slash (/) and a record ID to the end of the Uri in its first argument. For every database table, you'd typically have a class similar to class Contact.

```
19      // nested class defines contents of the contacts table
20      public static final class Contact implements BaseColumns {
21         public static final String TABLE_NAME = "contacts"; // table's name
22
23         // Uri for the contacts table
24         public static final Uri CONTENT_URI =
25            BASE_CONTENT_URI.buildUpon().appendPath(TABLE_NAME).build();
26
27         // column names for contacts table's columns
28         public static final String COLUMN_NAME = "name";
29         public static final String COLUMN_PHONE = "phone";
30         public static final String COLUMN_EMAIL = "email";
31         public static final String COLUMN_STREET = "street";
32         public static final String COLUMN_CITY = "city";
33         public static final String COLUMN_STATE = "state";
34         public static final String COLUMN_ZIP = "zip";
35
```

Fig. 9.16 | DatabaseDescription nested class Contact. (Part I of 2.)

```
36        // creates a Uri for a specific contact
37        public static Uri buildContactUri(long id) {
38            return ContentUris.withAppendedId(CONTENT_URI, id);
39        }
40    }
41 }
```

Fig. 9.16 | DatabaseDescription nested class Contact. (Part 2 of 2.)

In a database table, each row typically has a primary key that uniquely identifies the row. When working with ListViews and Cursors, this column's name must be "_id"—Android also uses this for the ID column in SQLite database tables. This name is not required for RecyclerViews, but we use it here due to the similarities between ListViews and RecyclerViews, and because we're using Cursors and a SQLite database. Rather than defining this constant directly in class Contact, we implement interface BaseColumns (package android.provider; line 20), which defines the constant _ID with the value "_id".

9.7 AddressBookDatabaseHelper Class

The AddressBookDatabaseHelper class (Fig. 9.17) extends abstract class SQLiteOpen-Helper, which helps apps create databases and manage database version changes.

```
 1   // AddressBookDatabaseHelper.java
 2   // SQLiteOpenHelper subclass that defines the app's database
 3   package com.deitel.addressbook.data;
 4
 5   import android.content.Context;
 6   import android.database.sqlite.SQLiteDatabase;
 7   import android.database.sqlite.SQLiteOpenHelper;
 8
 9   import com.deitel.addressbook.data.DatabaseDescription.Contact;
10
11   class AddressBookDatabaseHelper extends SQLiteOpenHelper {
12       private static final String DATABASE_NAME = "AddressBook.db";
13       private static final int DATABASE_VERSION = 1;
14
15       // constructor
16       public AddressBookDatabaseHelper(Context context) {
17           super(context, DATABASE_NAME, null, DATABASE_VERSION);
18       }
19
20       // creates the contacts table when the database is created
21       @Override
22       public void onCreate(SQLiteDatabase db) {
23           // SQL for creating the contacts table
24           final String CREATE_CONTACTS_TABLE =
25               "CREATE TABLE " + Contact.TABLE_NAME + "(" +
```

Fig. 9.17 | AddressBookDatabaseHelper subclass of SQLiteOpenHelper defines the app's database. (Part 1 of 2.)

```
26              Contact._ID + " integer primary key, " +
27              Contact.COLUMN_NAME + " TEXT, " +
28              Contact.COLUMN_PHONE + " TEXT, " +
29              Contact.COLUMN_EMAIL + " TEXT, " +
30              Contact.COLUMN_STREET + " TEXT, " +
31              Contact.COLUMN_CITY + " TEXT, " +
32              Contact.COLUMN_STATE + " TEXT, " +
33              Contact.COLUMN_ZIP + " TEXT);";
34          db.execSQL(CREATE_CONTACTS_TABLE); // create the contacts table
35      }
36
37      // normally defines how to upgrade the database when the schema changes
38      @Override
39      public void onUpgrade(SQLiteDatabase db, int oldVersion,
40          int newVersion) { }
41  }
```

Fig. 9.17 | AddressBookDatabaseHelper subclass of SQLiteOpenHelper defines the app's database. (Part 2 of 2.)

Constructor

The constructor (lines 16–18) simply calls the superclass constructor, which requires four arguments:

- the Context in which the database is being created or opened,
- the database name—this can be null if you wish to use an in-memory database,
- the CursorFactory to use—null indicates that you wish to use the default SQLite CursorFactory (typically for most apps) and
- the database version number (starting from 1).

Overridden Methods

You must override this class's abstract methods onCreate and onUpgrade. If the database does not yet exist, the DatabaseOpenHelper's **onCreate method** will be called to create it. If you supply a newer version number than the database version currently stored on the device, the DatabaseOpenHelper's **onUpgrade method** will be called to upgrade the database to the new version (perhaps to add tables or to add columns to an existing table).

The onCreate method (lines 22–35) specifies the table to create with the SQL CREATE TABLE command, which is defined as a String (lines 24–33) that's constructed using constants from class Contact (Section 9.6.2). In this case, the contacts table contains an integer primary key field (Contact._ID), and text fields for all the other columns. Line 34 uses SQLiteDatabase's **execSQL** method to execute the CREATE TABLE command.

Since we don't need to upgrade the database, we simply override method onUpgrade with an empty body. Class SQLiteOpenHelper also provides the **onDowngrade method** that can be used to downgrade a database when the currently stored version has a higher version number than the one requested in the call to class SQLiteOpenHelper's constructor. Downgrading might be used to revert the database back to a prior version with fewer columns in a table or fewer tables in the database—perhaps to fix a bug in the app.

9.8 AddressBookContentProvider Class

The AddressBookContentProvider subclass of ContentProvider defines how to perform query, insert, update and delete operations on this app's database.

> **Error-Prevention Tip 9.1**
>
> *ContentProviders can be invoked from multiple threads in one process and multiple processes, so it's important to note that ContentProviders do not provide any synchronization by default. However, SQLite does synchronize access to the database, so in this app it's unnecessary to provide your own synchronization mechanisms.*

9.8.1 AddressBookContentProvider Fields

Class AddressBookContentProvider (Fig. 9.18) defines several fields:

- Instance variable dbHelper (line 17) is a reference to an AddressBookDatabaseHelper object that creates the database and enables this ContentProvider to get readable and writable access to the database.

- Class variable uriMatcher (lines 20–21) is an object of class **UriMatcher** (package android.content). A ContentProvider uses a UriMatcher to help determine which operation to perform in its query, insert, update and delete methods.

- The UriMatcher returns the integer constants ONE_CONTACT and CONTACTS (lines 24–25)—the ContentProvider uses these constants in switch statements in its query, insert, update and delete methods.

```
I   // AddressBookContentProvider.java
2   // ContentProvider subclass for manipulating the app's database
3   package com.deitel.addressbook.data;
4
5   import android.content.ContentProvider;
6   import android.content.ContentValues;
7   import android.content.UriMatcher;
8   import android.database.Cursor;
9   import android.database.SQLException;
10  import android.database.sqlite.SQLiteQueryBuilder;
11  import android.net.Uri;
12
13  import com.deitel.addressbook.data.DatabaseDescription.Contact;
14
15  public class AddressBookContentProvider extends ContentProvider {
16     // used to access the database
17     private AddressBookDatabaseHelper dbHelper;
18
19     // UriMatcher helps ContentProvider determine operation to perform
20     private static final UriMatcher uriMatcher =
21        new UriMatcher(UriMatcher.NO_MATCH);
22
23     // constants used with UriMatcher to determine operation to perform
24     private static final int ONE_CONTACT = 1; // manipulate one contact
25     private static final int CONTACTS = 2; // manipulate contacts table
```

Fig. 9.18 | AddressBookContentProvider fields. (Part 1 of 2.)

```
26
27      // static block to configure this ContentProvider's UriMatcher
28      static {
29         // Uri for Contact with the specified id (#)
30         uriMatcher.addURI(DatabaseDescription.AUTHORITY,
31            Contact.TABLE_NAME + "/#", ONE_CONTACT);
32
33         // Uri for Contacts table
34         uriMatcher.addURI(DatabaseDescription.AUTHORITY,
35            Contact.TABLE_NAME, CONTACTS);
36      }
37
```

Fig. 9.18 | AddressBookContentProvider fields. (Part 2 of 2.)

Lines 28–36 define a static block that adds Uris to the static UriMatcher—this block executes once when class AddressBookContentProvider is loaded into memory. UriMatcher method addUri takes three arguments:

- a String representing the ContentProvider's authority (DatabaseDescription.AUTHORITY in this app)

- a String representing a path—each Uri used to invoke the ContentProvider contains "content://" followed by the authority and a path that the Content-Provider uses to determine the task to perform

- an int code that the UriMatcher returns when a Uri supplied to to the Content-Provider matches a Uri stored in the UriMatcher.

Lines 30–31 add a Uri of the form:

        content://com.deitel.addressbook.data/contacts/#

where # is a **wildcard** that matches a string of numeric characters—in this case, the unique primary-key value for one contact in the contacts table. There is also a * wildcard that matches any number of characters. When a Uri matches this format, the UriMatcher returns the constant ONE_CONTACT.

Lines 34–35 add a Uri of the form:

        content://com.deitel.addressbook.data/contacts

which represents the entire contacts table. When a Uri matches this format, the Uri-Matcher returns the constant CONTACTS. As we discuss the rest of class AddressBookContentProvider, you'll see how the UriMatcher and the constants ONE_CONTACT and CONTACTS are used.

9.8.2 Overridden Methods onCreate and getType

As you'll see, you use a ContentResolver to invoke a ContentProvider's methods. When Android receives a request from a ContentResolver, it automatically creates the corresponding ContentProvider object—or uses an existing one, if it was created previously. When a ContentProvider is created, Android calls its **onCreate** method to configure the ContentProvider (Fig. 9.19, lines 39–44). Line 42 creates the AddressBookDatabase-

Helper object that enables the provider to access the database. The first time the provider is invoked to write to the database, the AddressBookDatabaseHelper object's onCreate method will be called to create the database (Fig. 9.17, lines 22–35).

```
38      // called when the AddressBookContentProvider is created
39      @Override
40      public boolean onCreate() {
41          // create the AddressBookDatabaseHelper
42          dbHelper = new AddressBookDatabaseHelper(getContext());
43          return true; // ContentProvider successfully created
44      }
45
46      // required method: Not used in this app, so we return null
47      @Override
48      public String getType(Uri uri) {
49          return null;
50      }
51
```

Fig. 9.19 | Overridden ContentProvider methods onCreate and getType.

Method **getType** (Fig. 9.19, lines 47–50) is a required ContentProvider method that simply returns null in this app. This method typically is used when creating and starting Intents for Uris with specific MIME types. Android can use MIME types to determine appropriate activities to handle the Intents.

9.8.3 Overridden Method query

The overridden ContentProvider method **query** (Fig. 9.20) retrieves data from the provider's data source—in this case, the database. The method returns a Cursor that's used to interact with the results. Method query receives five arguments:

- uri—A Uri representing the data to retrieve.
- projection—A String array representing the specific columns to retrieve. If this argument is null, all columns will be included in the result.
- selection—A String containing the selection criteria. This is the SQL WHERE clause, specified *without* the WHERE keyword. If this argument is null, all rows will be included in the result.
- selectionArgs—A String array containing the arguments used to replace any argument placeholders (?) in the selection String.
- sortOrder—A String representing the sort order. This is the SQL ORDER BY clause, specified *without* the ORDER BY keywords. If this argument is null, the provider determines this sort order—the order in which results are returned to the app is not guaranteed unless you provide an appropriate sort order.

SQLiteQueryBuilder
Line 58 creates a **SQLiteQueryBuilder** (package android.database.sqlite) for building SQL queries that are submitted to a SQLite database. Line 59 uses method **setTables** to specify that the query will select data from the database's contacts table. This method's

```
52    // query the database
53    @Override
54    public Cursor query(Uri uri, String[] projection,
55       String selection, String[] selectionArgs, String sortOrder) {
56
57       // create SQLiteQueryBuilder for querying contacts table
58       SQLiteQueryBuilder queryBuilder = new SQLiteQueryBuilder();
59       queryBuilder.setTables(Contact.TABLE_NAME);
60
61       switch (uriMatcher.match(uri)) {
62          case ONE_CONTACT: // contact with specified id will be selected
63             queryBuilder.appendWhere(
64                Contact._ID + "=" + uri.getLastPathSegment());
65             break;
66          case CONTACTS: // all contacts will be selected
67             break;
68          default:
69             throw new UnsupportedOperationException(
70                getContext().getString(R.string.invalid_query_uri) + uri);
71       }
72
73       // execute the query to select one or all contacts
74       Cursor cursor = queryBuilder.query(dbHelper.getReadableDatabase(),
75          projection, selection, selectionArgs, null, null, sortOrder);
76
77       // configure to watch for content changes
78       cursor.setNotificationUri(getContext().getContentResolver(), uri);
79       return cursor;
80    }
81
```

Fig. 9.20 | Overridden ContentProvider method query.

String argument can be used to perform table join operations by specifying multiple tables in a comma separated list or as an appropriate SQL JOIN clause.

Using the UriMatcher to Determine the Operation to Perform
In this app, there are two queries:

- select a specific contact from the database to display or edit its details, and

- select all contacts in the database to display their names in the ContactsFragment's RecyclerView.

Lines 61–71 use UriMatcher method **match** to determine which query operation to perform. This method returns one of the constants that was registered with the UriMatcher (Section 9.8.1). If the constant returned is ONE_CONTACT, only the contact with the ID specified in the Uri should be selected. In this case, lines 63–64 use the SQLiteQueryBuilder's **appendWhere** method to add a WHERE clause containing the contact's ID to the query. Uri method **getLastPathSegment** returns the last segment in the Uri—for example, the contact ID 5 in the following Uri

```
content://com.deitel.addressbook.data/contacts/5
```

If the constant returned is CONTACTS, the switch terminates without adding anything to the query—in this case, all contacts will be selected because there is no WHERE clause. For any Uri that is not a match, lines 69–70 throw an UnsupportedOperationException indicating that the Uri was invalid.

Querying the Database

Lines 74–75 use the SQLiteQueryBuilder's **query** method to perform the database query and get a Cursor representing the results. The method's arguments are similar to those received by the ContentProvider's query method:

- A SQLiteDatabase to query—the AddressBookDatabaseHelper's **getReadable-Database** method returns a read-only SQLiteDatabase object.

- projection—A String array representing the specific columns to retrieve. If this argument is null, all columns will be included in the result.

- selection—A String containing the selection criteria. This is the SQL WHERE clause, specified *without* the WHERE keyword. If this argument is null, all rows will be included in the result.

- selectionArgs—A String array containing the arguments used to replace any argument placeholders (?) in the selection String.

- groupBy—A String containing the grouping criteria. This is the SQL GROUP BY clause, specified *without* the GROUP BY keywords. If this argument is null, no grouping is performed.

- having—When using groupBy, this argument is a String indicating which groups to include in the results. This is the SQL HAVING clause, specified *without* the HAVING keyword. If this argument is null, all groups specified by the groupBy argument will be included in the results.

- sortOrder—A String representing the sort order. This is the SQL ORDER BY clause, specified *without* the ORDER BY keywords. If this argument is null, the provider determines this sort order.

Registering the Cursor to Watch for Content Changes

Line 78 calls the Cursor's **setNotificationUri** method to indicate that the Cursor should be updated if the data it refers to changes. This first argument is the ContentResolver that invoked the ContentProvider and the second is the Uri used to invoke the ContentProvider. Line 79 returns the Cursor containing the query results.

9.8.4 Overridden Method insert

The overridden ContentProvider method **insert** (Fig. 9.21) adds a new record to the contacts table. Method insert receives two arguments:

- uri—A Uri representing the table in which the data will be inserted.

- values—A **ContentValues** object containing key–value pairs in which the column names are the keys and each key's value is the data to insert in that column.

Lines 87–108 check whether the Uri is for the contacts table—if not, the Uri is invalid for the insert operation and lines 106–107 throw an UnsupportedOperation-

```
82      // insert a new contact in the database
83      @Override
84      public Uri insert(Uri uri, ContentValues values) {
85          Uri newContactUri = null;
86
87          switch (uriMatcher.match(uri)) {
88              case CONTACTS:
89                  // insert the new contact--success yields new contact's row id
90                  long rowId = dbHelper.getWritableDatabase().insert(
91                      Contact.TABLE_NAME, null, values);
92
93                  // if the contact was inserted, create an appropriate Uri;
94                  // otherwise, throw an exception
95                  if (rowId > 0) { // SQLite row IDs start at 1
96                      newContactUri = Contact.buildContactUri(rowId);
97
98                      // notify observers that the database changed
99                      getContext().getContentResolver().notifyChange(uri, null);
100                 }
101                 else
102                     throw new SQLException(
103                         getContext().getString(R.string.insert_failed) + uri);
104                 break;
105             default:
106                 throw new UnsupportedOperationException(
107                     getContext().getString(R.string.invalid_insert_uri) + uri);
108         }
109
110         return newContactUri;
111     }
112
```

Fig. 9.21 | Overridden ContentProvider method insert.

Exception. If the Uri is a match, lines 90–91 insert the new contact in the database. First, we use the AddressBookDatabaseHelper's **getWritableDatabase** method to get a SQLite-DatabaseObject for modifying data in the database.

SQLiteDatabase's **insert** method (lines 90–91) inserts the values from the third argument's ContentValues object into the table specified as the first argument—the contacts table in this case. The second parameter of this method, which is not used in this app, is named nullColumnHack and is needed because *SQLite does not support inserting a completely empty row into a table*—this would be the equivalent of passing an empty ContentValues object to insert. Instead of making it illegal to pass an empty ContentValues to the method, the nullColumnHack parameter is used to identify a column that accepts NULL values.

Method insert returns the new contact's unique ID if the insert operation is successful or -1 otherwise. Line 95 checks whether the rowID is greater than 0 (rows are indexed from 1 in SQLite). If so, line 96 creates a Uri representing the new contact and line 99 notifies the ContentResolver that the database changed, so the ContentResolver's client code can respond to the database changes. If the rowID is not greater than 0, the database operation failed and lines 102–103 throws a SQLException.

9.8.5 Overridden Method update

The overridden ContentProvider method **update** (Fig. 9.22) updates an existing record. Method update receives four arguments:

- uri—A Uri representing the rows to update.

- values—A ContentValues object containig the columns to update and their corresponding values.

- selection—A String containing the selection criteria. This is the SQL WHERE clause, specified *without* the WHERE keyword. If this argument is null, all rows will be included in the result.

- selectionArgs—A String array containing the arguments used to replace any argument placeholders (?) in the selection String.

```
113    // update an existing contact in the database
114    @Override
115    public int update(Uri uri, ContentValues values,
116       String selection, String[] selectionArgs) {
117       int numberOfRowsUpdated; // 1 if update successful; 0 otherwise
118
119       switch (uriMatcher.match(uri)) {
120          case ONE_CONTACT:
121             // get from the uri the id of contact to update
122             String id = uri.getLastPathSegment();
123
124             // update the contact
125             numberOfRowsUpdated = dbHelper.getWritableDatabase().update(
126                Contact.TABLE_NAME, values, Contact._ID + "=" + id,
127                selectionArgs);
128             break;
129          default:
130             throw new UnsupportedOperationException(
131                getContext().getString(R.string.invalid_update_uri) + uri);
132       }
133
134       // if changes were made, notify observers that the database changed
135       if (numberOfRowsUpdated != 0) {
136          getContext().getContentResolver().notifyChange(uri, null);
137       }
138
139       return numberOfRowsUpdated;
140    }
141
```

Fig. 9.22 | Overridden ContentProvider method update.

Updates in this app are performed only on a specific contact, so lines 119–132 check only for a ONE_CONTACT Uri. Line 122 gets the Uri argument's last path segement, which is the contact's unique ID. Lines 125–127 get a writeable SQLiteDatabase object then call its **update method** to update the specified contact with the values from the Content-Values argument. The update method's arguments are:

- the String name of the table to update
- the ContentValues object containing the columns to update and their new values
- the String representing the SQL WHERE clause that specifies the rows to update
- a String array containing any arguments that should replace ? placeholders in the WHERE clause.

If the operation is successful, method update returns an integer indicating the number of modified rows; otherwise, update returns 0. Line 136 notifies the ContentResolver that the database changed, so the ContentResolver's client code can respond to the changes. Line 139 returns the number of modified rows.

9.8.6 Overridden Method delete

The overridden ContentProvider method **delete** (Fig. 9.23) removes an existing record. Method delete receives three arguments:

- uri—A Uri representing the row(s) to delete.
- selection—A String containing the WHERE clause specifying the rows to delete.
- selectionArgs—A String array containing the arguments used to replace any argument placeholders (?) in the selection String.

```
142     // delete an existing contact from the database
143     @Override
144     public int delete(Uri uri, String selection, String[] selectionArgs) {
145        int numberOfRowsDeleted;
146
147        switch (uriMatcher.match(uri)) {
148           case ONE_CONTACT:
149              // get from the uri the id of contact to update
150              String id = uri.getLastPathSegment();
151
152              // delete the contact
153              numberOfRowsDeleted = dbHelper.getWritableDatabase().delete(
154                 Contact.TABLE_NAME, Contact._ID + "=" + id, selectionArgs);
155              break;
156           default:
157              throw new UnsupportedOperationException(
158                 getContext().getString(R.string.invalid_delete_uri) + uri);
159        }
160
161        // notify observers that the database changed
162        if (numberOfRowsDeleted != 0) {
163           getContext().getContentResolver().notifyChange(uri, null);
164        }
165
166        return numberOfRowsDeleted;
167     }
168  }
```

Fig. 9.23 | Overridden ContentProvider method delete.

Deletions in this app are performed only on a specific contact, so lines 147–159 check for a ONE_CONTACT Uri—any other Uri represents an unsupported operation. Line 150 gets the Uri argument's last path segment, which is the contact's unique ID. Lines 153–154 get a writeable SQLiteDatabase object then call its **delete method** to remove the specified contact. The three arguments are the database table from which to delete the record, the WHERE clause and, if the WHERE clause has arguments, a String array of values to substitute into the WHERE clause. The method returns the number of rows deleted. Line 163 notifies the ContentResolver that the database changed, so the ContentResolver's client code can respond to the changes. Line 166 returns the number of deleted rows.

9.9 MainActivity Class

Class MainActivity manages the app's fragments and coordinates the interactions between them. On phones, MainActivity displays one Fragment at a time, starting with the ContactsFragment. On tablets, MainActivity always displays the ContactsFragment at the left of the layout and, depending on the context, displays either the DetailFragment or the AddEditFragment in the right two-thirds of the layout.

9.9.1 Superclass, Implemented Interfaces and Fields

Class MainActivity (Fig. 9.24) uses class FragmentTransaction from the v4 support library to add and remove the app's Fragments. MainActivity implements three interfaces:

- ContactsFragment.ContactsFragmentListener (Section 9.10.2) contains callback methods that the ContactsFragment uses to tell the MainActivity when the user selects a contact in the contact list or adds a new contact.

- DetailFragment.DetailFragmentListener (Section 9.13.2) contains callback methods that the DetailFragment uses to tell the MainActivity when the user deletes a contact or wishes to edit an existing contact.

- AddEditFragment.AddEditFragmentListener (Section 9.12.2) contains a callback method that the AddEditFragment uses to tell the MainActivity when the user saves a new contact or saves changes to an existing contact.

The constant CONTACT_URI (line 17) is used as a key in a key–value pair that's passed between the MainActivity and its Fragments. The instance variable ContactsFragment (line 19) is used to tell the ContactsFragment to update the displayed list of contacts after a contact is added or deleted.

```
1   // MainActivity.java
2   // Hosts the app's fragments and handles communication between them
3   package com.deitel.addressbook;
4
5   import android.net.Uri;
6   import android.os.Bundle;
7   import android.support.v4.app.FragmentTransaction;
8   import android.support.v7.app.AppCompatActivity;
9   import android.support.v7.widget.Toolbar;
```

Fig. 9.24 | MainActivity's superclass, implemented interfaces and fields. (Part 1 of 2.)

```
10
11   public class MainActivity extends AppCompatActivity
12      implements ContactsFragment.ContactsFragmentListener,
13      DetailFragment.DetailFragmentListener,
14      AddEditFragment.AddEditFragmentListener {
15
16      // key for storing a contact's Uri in a Bundle passed to a fragment
17      public static final String CONTACT_URI = "contact_uri";
18
19      private ContactsFragment contactsFragment; // displays contact list
20
```

Fig. 9.24 | MainActivity's superclass, implemented interfaces and fields, (Part 2 of 2.)

9.9.2 Overridden Method onCreate

Overridden Activity method onCreate (Fig. 9.25) inflates MainActivity's GUI and, if the app is running on a phone-sized device, creates and displays a ContactsFragment. If the Activity is being restored after being shut down or recreated from a configuration change, savedInstanceState will not be null. In this case, lines 43–45 simply get a reference to the existing ContactsFragment—on a phone, it would have been saved by Android and on a tablet, it's part of the MainActivity's layout that was inflated in line 25.

```
21      // display ContactsFragment when MainActivity first loads
22      @Override
23      protected void onCreate(Bundle savedInstanceState) {
24         super.onCreate(savedInstanceState);
25         setContentView(R.layout.activity_main);
26         Toolbar toolbar = (Toolbar) findViewById(R.id.toolbar);
27         setSupportActionBar(toolbar);
28
29         // if layout contains fragmentContainer, the phone layout is in use;
30         // create and display a ContactsFragment
31         if (savedInstanceState != null &&
32            findViewById(R.id.fragmentContainer) != null) {
33            // create ContactsFragment
34            contactsFragment = new ContactsFragment();
35
36            // add the fragment to the FrameLayout
37            FragmentTransaction transaction =
38               getSupportFragmentManager().beginTransaction();
39            transaction.add(R.id.fragmentContainer, contactsFragment);
40            transaction.commit(); // display ContactsFragment
41         }
42         else {
43            contactsFragment =
44               (ContactsFragment) getSupportFragmentManager().
45                  findFragmentById(R.id.contactsFragment);
46         }
47      }
48
```

Fig. 9.25 | Overridden Activity method onCreate.

If the R.id.fragmentContainer exists in MainActivity's layout (line 32), then the app is running on a phone. In this case, line 34 creates the ContactsFragment, then lines 37–40 use a FragmentTransaction to add the ContactsFragment to the user interface. Lines 37–38 call FragmentManager's **beginTransaction** method to obtain a FragmentTransaction. Next, line 39 calls FragmentTransaction method **add** to specify that, when the FragmentTransaction completes, the ContactsFragment should be attached to the View with the ID specified as the first argument. Finally, line 40 uses FragmentTransaction method **commit** to finalize the transaction and display the ContactsFragment.

9.9.3 ContactsFragment.ContactsFragmentListener Methods

Figure 9.26 contains MainActivity's implementations of the callback methods in the interface ContactsFragment.ContactsFragmentListener. Method onContactSelected (lines 50–60) is called by the ContactsFragment to notify the MainActivity when the user selects a contact to display. If the app is running on a phone (line 52), line 53 calls method displayContact (Section 9.9.4), which replaces the ContactsFragment in the fragmentContainer (defined in Section 9.4.7) with the DetailFragment that shows the contact's information. On a tablet, line 56 calls the FragmentManager's **popBackStack** method to *pop* (remove) the top Fragment on the back stack (if there is one), then line 58 calls displayContact, which replaces the contents of the rightPaneContainer (defined in Section 9.4.7) with the DetailFragment that shows the contact's information.

```
49      // display DetailFragment for selected contact
50      @Override
51      public void onContactSelected(Uri contactUri) {
52          if (findViewById(R.id.fragmentContainer) != null) // phone
53              displayContact(contactUri, R.id.fragmentContainer);
54          else { // tablet
55              // removes top of back stack
56              getSupportFragmentManager().popBackStack();
57
58              displayContact(contactUri, R.id.rightPaneContainer);
59          }
60      }
61
62      // display AddEditFragment to add a new contact
63      @Override
64      public void onAddContact() {
65          if (findViewById(R.id.fragmentContainer) != null) // phone
66              displayAddEditFragment(R.id.fragmentContainer, null);
67          else // tablet
68              displayAddEditFragment(R.id.rightPaneContainer, null);
69      }
70
```

Fig. 9.26 | ContactsFragment.ContactsFragmentListener methods.

Method onAddContact (lines 63–69) is called by the ContactsFragment to notify the MainActivity when the user chooses to add a new contact. If the layout contains the fragmentContainer, line 66 calls displayAddEditFragment (Section 9.9.5) to display the Add-

EditFragment in the fragmentContainer; otherwise, line 68 displays the Fragment in the rightPaneContainer. The second argument to displayAddEditFragment is a Bundle that the AddEditFragment uses to determine whether a new contact is being added or an existing contact is being edited—null indicates that a new contact is being added; otherwise, the bundle includes the existing contact's Uri.

9.9.4 Method displayContact

Method displayContact (Fig. 9.27) creates the DetailFragment that displays the selected contact. You can pass arguments to a Fragment by placing them in a Bundle of key–value pairs—we do this to pass the selected contact's Uri so that the DetailFragment knows which contact to get from the ContentProvider. Line 76 creates the Bundle. Line 77 calls its **putParcelable** method to store a key–value pair containing the CONTACT_URI (a String) as the key and the contactUri (a Uri) as the value. Class Uri implements the Parcelable interface, so a Uri can be stored in a Bundle as a Parcel object. Line 78 passes the Bundle to the Fragment's **setArguments** method—the Fragment can then extract the information from the Bundle (as you'll see in Section 9.13).

```
71   // display a contact
72   private void displayContact(Uri contactUri, int viewID) {
73       DetailFragment detailFragment = new DetailFragment();
74
75       // specify contact's Uri as an argument to the DetailFragment
76       Bundle arguments = new Bundle();
77       arguments.putParcelable(CONTACT_URI, contactUri);
78       detailFragment.setArguments(arguments);
79
80       // use a FragmentTransaction to display the DetailFragment
81       FragmentTransaction transaction =
82           getSupportFragmentManager().beginTransaction();
83       transaction.replace(viewID, detailFragment);
84       transaction.addToBackStack(null);
85       transaction.commit(); // causes DetailFragment to display
86   }
87
```

Fig. 9.27 | Method displayContact.

Lines 81–82 get a FragmentTransaction, then line 83 calls FragmentTransaction method **replace** to specify that, when the FragmentTransaction completes, the DetailFragment should replace the contents of the View with the ID specified as the first argument. Line 84 calls FragmentTransaction method **addToBackStack** to *push* (add) the DetailFragment onto the back stack. This allows the user to touch the back button to pop the Fragment from the back stack and allows MainActivity to programmatically pop the Fragment from the back stack. Method addToBackStack's argument is an optional name for a *back state*. This can be used to pop multiple Fragments from the back stack to return to a prior state after multiple Fragments have been added to the back stack. By default, only the topmost Fragment is popped.

9.9.5 Method displayAddEditFragment

Method displayAddEditFragment (Fig. 9.28) receives a View's resource ID specifying where to attach the AddEditFragment and a Uri representing a contact to edit. If the second argument is null, a new contact is being added. Line 90 creates the AddEditFragment. If the contactUri argument is not null, line 95 puts it into the Bundle that's used to supply the Fragment's arguments. Lines 100–104 then create the FragmentTransaction, replace the contents of the View with the specified resource ID, add the Fragment to the back stack and commit the transaction.

```
88      // display fragment for adding a new or editing an existing contact
89      private void displayAddEditFragment(int viewID, Uri contactUri) {
90          AddEditFragment addEditFragment = new AddEditFragment();
91
92          // if editing existing contact, provide contactUri as an argument
93          if (contactUri != null) {
94              Bundle arguments = new Bundle();
95              arguments.putParcelable(CONTACT_URI, contactUri);
96              addEditFragment.setArguments(arguments);
97          }
98
99          // use a FragmentTransaction to display the AddEditFragment
100         FragmentTransaction transaction =
101             getSupportFragmentManager().beginTransaction();
102         transaction.replace(viewID, addEditFragment);
103         transaction.addToBackStack(null);
104         transaction.commit(); // causes AddEditFragment to display
105     }
106
```

Fig. 9.28 | Method displayAddEditFragment.

9.9.6 DetailFragment.DetailFragmentListener Methods

Figure 9.29 contains MainActivity's implementations of the callback methods in the interface DetailFragment.DetailFragmentListener. Method onContactDeleted (lines 108–113) is called by the DetailFragment to notify the MainActivity when the user deletes a contact. In this case, line 111 pops the DetailFragment from the back stack so that the now deleted contact's information is no longer displayed. Line 112 calls the ContactsFragment's updateContactList method to refresh the contacts list.

```
107     // return to contact list when displayed contact deleted
108     @Override
109     public void onContactDeleted() {
110         // removes top of back stack
111         getSupportFragmentManager().popBackStack();
112         contactsFragment.updateContactList(); // refresh contacts
113     }
114
```

Fig. 9.29 | DetailFragment.DetailFragmentListener methods. (Part 1 of 2.)

```
115    // display the AddEditFragment to edit an existing contact
116    @Override
117    public void onEditContact(Uri contactUri) {
118        if (findViewById(R.id.fragmentContainer) != null) // phone
119            displayAddEditFragment(R.id.fragmentContainer, contactUri);
120        else // tablet
121            displayAddEditFragment(R.id.rightPaneContainer, contactUri);
122    }
123
```

Fig. 9.29 | DetailFragment.DetailFragmentListener methods. (Part 2 of 2.)

Method onEditContact (lines 116–122) is called by the DetailFragment to notify the MainActivity when the user touches the app bar item to edit a contact. The Detail-Fragment passes a Uri representing the contact to edit so that it can be displayed in the AddEditFragment's EditTexts for editing. If the layout contains the fragmentContainer, line 119 calls displayAddEditFragment (Section 9.9.5) to display the AddEditFragment in the fragmentContainer; otherwise, line 121 displays the AddEditFragment in the rightPaneContainer.

9.9.7 AddEditFragment.AddEditFragmentListener Method

Method onAddEditCompleted (Fig. 9.30) from the AddEditFragment.AddEditFragment-Listener interface is called by the AddEditFragment to notify the MainActivity when the user saves a new contact or saves changes to an existing one. Line 128 pops the AddEdit-Fragment from the back stack and line 129 updates the ContactsFragment's contact list. If the app is running on a tablet (line 131), line 133 pops the back stack again to remove the DetailFragment (if there is one). Then line 136 displays the new or updated contact's details in the rightPaneContainer.

```
124    // update GUI after new contact or updated contact saved
125    @Override
126    public void onAddEditCompleted(Uri contactUri) {
127        // removes top of back stack
128        getSupportFragmentManager().popBackStack();
129        contactsFragment.updateContactList(); // refresh contacts
130
131        if (findViewById(R.id.fragmentContainer) == null) { // tablet
132            // removes top of back stack
133            getSupportFragmentManager().popBackStack();
134
135            // on tablet, display contact that was just added or edited
136            displayContact(contactUri, R.id.rightPaneContainer);
137        }
138    }
139 }
```

Fig. 9.30 | AddEditFragment.AddEditFragmentListener method.

9.10 ContactsFragment Class

Class ContactsFragment displays the contact list in a RecyclerView and provides a FloatingActionButton that the user can touch to add a new contact.

9.10.1 Superclass and Implemented Interface

Figure 9.31 lists ContactsFragment's package statement and import statements and the beginning of its class definition. The ContactsFragment uses a LoaderManager and a Loader to query the AddressBookContentProvider and receive a Cursor that the ContactsAdapter (Section 9.11) uses to supply data to the RecyclerView. ContactsFragment implements interface LoaderManager.LoaderCallbacks<Cursor> (line 23) so that it can respond to method calls from the LoaderManager to create the Loader and process the results returned by the AddressBookContentProvider.

```
1   // ContactsFragment.java
2   // Fragment subclass that displays the alphabetical list of contact names
3   package com.deitel.addressbook;
4
5   import android.content.Context;
6   import android.database.Cursor;
7   import android.net.Uri;
8   import android.os.Bundle;
9   import android.support.design.widget.FloatingActionButton;
10  import android.support.v4.app.Fragment;
11  import android.support.v4.app.LoaderManager;
12  import android.support.v4.content.CursorLoader;
13  import android.support.v4.content.Loader;
14  import android.support.v7.widget.LinearLayoutManager;
15  import android.support.v7.widget.RecyclerView;
16  import android.view.LayoutInflater;
17  import android.view.View;
18  import android.view.ViewGroup;
19
20  import com.deitel.addressbook.data.DatabaseDescription.Contact;
21
22  public class ContactsFragment extends Fragment
23      implements LoaderManager.LoaderCallbacks<Cursor> {
24
```

Fig. 9.31 | ContactsFragment superclass and implemented interface.

9.10.2 ContactsFragmentListener

Figure 9.32 defines the nested interface ContactsFragmentListener, which contains the callback methods that MainActivity implements to be notified when the user selects a contact (line 28) and when the user touches the FloatingActionButton to add a new contact (line 31).

```
25        // callback method implemented by MainActivity
26     public interface ContactsFragmentListener {
27        // called when contact selected
28        void onContactSelected(Uri contactUri);
29
30        // called when add button is pressed
31        void onAddContact();
32     }
33
```

Fig. 9.32 | Nested interface ContactsFragmentListener.

9.10.3 Fields

Figure 9.33 shows class ContactsFragment's fields. Line 34 declares a constant that's used to identify the Loader when processing the results returned from the AddressBookContentProvider. In this case, we have only one Loader—if a class uses more than one Loader, each should have a constant with a unique integer value so that you can identify which Loader to manipulate in the LoaderManager.LoaderCallbacks<Cursor> callback methods. The instance variable listener (line 37) will refer to the object that implements the interface (MainActivity). Instance variable contactsAdapter (line 39) will refer to the ContactsAdapter that binds data to the RecyclerView.

```
34     private static final int CONTACTS_LOADER = 0; // identifies Loader
35
36     // used to inform the MainActivity when a contact is selected
37     private ContactsFragmentListener listener;
38
39     private ContactsAdapter contactsAdapter; // adapter for recyclerView
40
```

Fig. 9.33 | ContactsFragment fields.

9.10.4 Overridden Fragment Method onCreateView

Overridden Fragment method onCreateView (Fig. 9.34) inflates and configures the Fragment's GUI. Most of this method's code has been presented in prior chapters, so we focus only on the new features here. Line 47 indicates that the ContactsFragment has menu items that should be displayed on the Activity's app bar (or in its options menu). Lines 56–74 configure the RecyclerView. Lines 60–67 create the ContactsAdapter that populates the RecyclerView. The argument to the constructor is an implementation of the ContactsAdapter.ContactClickListener interface (Section 9.11) specifying that when the user touches a contact, the ContactsFragmentListener's onContactSelected should be called with the Uri of the contact to display in a DetailFragment.

```
41      // configures this fragment's GUI
42      @Override
43      public View onCreateView(
44          LayoutInflater inflater, ViewGroup container,
45          Bundle savedInstanceState) {
46          super.onCreateView(inflater, container, savedInstanceState);
47          setHasOptionsMenu(true); // fragment has menu items to display
48
49          // inflate GUI and get reference to the RecyclerView
50          View view = inflater.inflate(
51              R.layout.fragment_contacts, container, false);
52          RecyclerView recyclerView =
53              (RecyclerView) view.findViewById(R.id.recyclerView);
54
55          // recyclerView should display items in a vertical list
56          recyclerView.setLayoutManager(
57              new LinearLayoutManager(getActivity().getBaseContext()));
58
59          // create recyclerView's adapter and item click listener
60          contactsAdapter = new ContactsAdapter(
61              new ContactsAdapter.ContactClickListener() {
62                  @Override
63                  public void onClick(Uri contactUri) {
64                      listener.onContactSelected(contactUri);
65                  }
66              }
67          );
68          recyclerView.setAdapter(contactsAdapter); // set the adapter
69
70          // attach a custom ItemDecorator to draw dividers between list items
71          recyclerView.addItemDecoration(new ItemDivider(getContext()));
72
73          // improves performance if RecyclerView's layout size never changes
74          recyclerView.setHasFixedSize(true);
75
76          // get the FloatingActionButton and configure its listener
77          FloatingActionButton addButton =
78              (FloatingActionButton) view.findViewById(R.id.addButton);
79          addButton.setOnClickListener(
80              new View.OnClickListener() {
81                  // displays the AddEditFragment when FAB is touched
82                  @Override
83                  public void onClick(View view) {
84                      listener.onAddContact();
85                  }
86              }
87          );
88
89          return view;
90      }
91
```

Fig. 9.34 | Overridden Fragment method onCreateView.

9.10.5 Overridden Fragment Methods onAttach and onDetach

Class ContactsFragment overrides Fragment lifecycle methods onAttach and onDetach (Fig. 9.35) to set instance variable listener. In this app, listener refers to the host Activity (line 96) when the ContactsFragment is attached and is set to null (line 103) when the ContactsFragment is detached.

```
92      // set ContactsFragmentListener when fragment attached
93      @Override
94      public void onAttach(Context context) {
95          super.onAttach(context);
96          listener = (ContactsFragmentListener) context;
97      }
98
99      // remove ContactsFragmentListener when Fragment detached
100     @Override
101     public void onDetach() {
102         super.onDetach();
103         listener = null;
104     }
105
```

Fig. 9.35 | Overridden Fragment methods onAttach and onDetach.

9.10.6 Overridden Fragment Method onActivityCreated

Fragment lifecycle method **onActivityCreated** (Fig. 9.36) is called after a Fragment's host Activity has been created and the Fragment's onCreateView method completes execution—at this point, the Fragment's GUI is part of the Activity's view hierarchy. We use this method to tell the LoaderManager to initialize a Loader—doing this after the view hierarchy exists is important because the RecyclerView must exist before we can display the loaded data. Line 110 uses Fragment method **getLoaderManager** to obtain the Fragment's LoaderManager object. Next we call LoaderManager's initLoader method, which receives three arguments:

- the integer ID used to identify the Loader
- a Bundle containing arguments for the Loader's constructor, or null if there are no arguments
- a reference to the implementation of the interface LoaderManager.LoaderCallbacks<Cursor> (this represents the ContactsAdapter)—you'll see the implementations of this interface's methods onCreateLoader, onLoadFinished and onLoaderReset in Section 9.10.8.

If there is not already an active Loader with the specified ID, the initLoader method asynchronously calls the onCreateLoader method to create and start a Loader for that ID. If there is an active Loader, the initLoader method immediately calls the onLoadFinished method.

```
106    // initialize a Loader when this fragment's activity is created
107    @Override
108    public void onActivityCreated(Bundle savedInstanceState) {
109       super.onActivityCreated(savedInstanceState);
110       getLoaderManager().initLoader(CONTACTS_LOADER, null, this);
111    }
112
```

Fig. 9.36 | Overridden Fragment method onActivityCreated.

9.10.7 Method updateContactList

ContactsFragment method updateContactList (Fig. 9.37) simply notifies the Contacts-Adapter when the data changes. This method is called when new contacts are added and when existing contacts are updated or deleted.

```
113    // called from MainActivity when other Fragment's update database
114    public void updateContactList() {
115       contactsAdapter.notifyDataSetChanged();
116    }
117
```

Fig. 9.37 | ContactsFragment method updateContactList.

9.10.8 LoaderManager.LoaderCallbacks<Cursor> Methods

Figure 9.38 presents class ContactsFragment's implementations of the callback methods in interface LoaderManager.LoaderCallbacks<Cursor>.

```
118    // called by LoaderManager to create a Loader
119    @Override
120    public Loader<Cursor> onCreateLoader(int id, Bundle args) {
121       // create an appropriate CursorLoader based on the id argument;
122       // only one Loader in this fragment, so the switch is unnecessary
123       switch (id) {
124          case CONTACTS_LOADER:
125             return new CursorLoader(getActivity(),
126                Contact.CONTENT_URI, // Uri of contacts table
127                null, // null projection returns all columns
128                null, // null selection returns all rows
129                null, // no selection arguments
130                Contact.COLUMN_NAME + " COLLATE NOCASE ASC"); // sort order
131          default:
132             return null;
133       }
134    }
135
```

Fig. 9.38 | LoaderManager.LoaderCallbacks<Cursor> methods. (Part 1 of 2.)

```
136     // called by LoaderManager when loading completes
137     @Override
138     public void onLoadFinished(Loader<Cursor> loader, Cursor data) {
139         contactsAdapter.swapCursor(data);
140     }
141
142     // called by LoaderManager when the Loader is being reset
143     @Override
144     public void onLoaderReset(Loader<Cursor> loader) {
145         contactsAdapter.swapCursor(null);
146     }
147 }
```

Fig. 9.38 | `LoaderManager.LoaderCallbacks<Cursor>` methods. (Part 2 of 2.)

Method onCreateLoader

The `LoaderManager` calls method **onCreateLoader** (lines 119–134) to create and return a new Loader for the specified ID, which the LoaderManager manages in the context of the Fragment's or Activity's lifecycle. Lines 123–133 determine the Loader to create, based on the ID received as onCreateLoader's first argument.

> **Good Programming Practice 9.1**
> *For the ContactsFragment, we need only one Loader, so the switch statement is unnecessary, but we included it here as a good practice.*

Lines 125–130 create and return a CursorLoader that queries the AddressBookContentProvider to get the list of contacts, then makes the results available as a Cursor. The CursorLoader constructor receives the Context in which the Loader's lifecycle is managed and uri, projection, selection, selectionArgs and sortOrder arguments that have the same meaning as those in the ContentProvider's query method (Section 9.8.3). In this case, we specified null for the projection, selection and selectionArgs arguments and indicated that the contacts should be sorted by name in a case insensitive manner.

Method onLoadFinished

Method **onLoadFinished** (lines 137–140) is called by the LoaderManager after a Loader finishes loading its data, so you can process the results in the Cursor argument. In this case, we call the ContactsAdapter's swapCursor method with the Cursor as an argument, so the ContactsAdapter can refresh the RecyclerView based on the new Cursor contents.

Method onLoaderReset

Method **onLoaderReset** (lines 143–146) is called by the LoaderManager when a Loader is reset and its data is no longer available. At this point, the app should immediately disconnect from the data. In this case, we call the ContactsAdapter's swapCursor method with the argument null to indicate that there is no data to bind to the RecyclerView.

9.11 ContactsAdapter Class

In Section 8.6, we discussed how to create a RecyclerView.Adapter that's used to bind data to a RecyclerView. Here we highlight only the new code that helps the ContactsAdapter (Fig. 9.39) to populate the RecyclerView with contact names from a Cursor.

```java
1   // ContactsAdapter.java
2   // Subclass of RecyclerView.Adapter that binds contacts to RecyclerView
3   package com.deitel.addressbook;
4
5   import android.database.Cursor;
6   import android.net.Uri;
7   import android.support.v7.widget.RecyclerView;
8   import android.view.LayoutInflater;
9   import android.view.View;
10  import android.view.ViewGroup;
11  import android.widget.TextView;
12
13  import com.deitel.addressbook.data.DatabaseDescription.Contact;
14
15  public class ContactsAdapter
16     extends RecyclerView.Adapter<ContactsAdapter.ViewHolder> {
17
18     // interface implemented by ContactsFragment to respond
19     // when the user touches an item in the RecyclerView
20     public interface ContactClickListener {
21        void onClick(Uri contactUri);
22     }
23
24     // nested subclass of RecyclerView.ViewHolder used to implement
25     // the view-holder pattern in the context of a RecyclerView
26     public class ViewHolder extends RecyclerView.ViewHolder {
27        public final TextView textView;
28        private long rowID;
29
30        // configures a RecyclerView item's ViewHolder
31        public ViewHolder(View itemView) {
32           super(itemView);
33           textView = (TextView) itemView.findViewById(android.R.id.text1);
34
35           // attach listener to itemView
36           itemView.setOnClickListener(
37              new View.OnClickListener() {
38                 // executes when the contact in this ViewHolder is clicked
39                 @Override
40                 public void onClick(View view) {
41                    clickListener.onClick(Contact.buildContactUri(rowID));
42                 }
43              }
44           );
45        }
46
47        // set the database row ID for the contact in this ViewHolder
48        public void setRowID(long rowID) {
49           this.rowID = rowID;
50        }
51     }
```

Fig. 9.39 | Subclass of RecyclerView.Adapter that binds contacts to RecyclerView. (Part 1 of 2.)

```
52
53      // ContactsAdapter instance variables
54      private Cursor cursor = null;
55      private final ContactClickListener clickListener;
56
57      // constructor
58      public ContactsAdapter(ContactClickListener clickListener) {
59         this.clickListener = clickListener;
60      }
61
62      // sets up new list item and its ViewHolder
63      @Override
64      public ViewHolder onCreateViewHolder(ViewGroup parent, int viewType) {
65         // inflate the android.R.layout.simple_list_item_1 layout
66         View view = LayoutInflater.from(parent.getContext()).inflate(
67            android.R.layout.simple_list_item_1, parent, false);
68         return new ViewHolder(view); // return current item's ViewHolder
69      }
70
71      // sets the text of the list item to display the search tag
72      @Override
73      public void onBindViewHolder(ViewHolder holder, int position) {
74         cursor.moveToPosition(position);
75         holder.setRowID(cursor.getLong(cursor.getColumnIndex(Contact._ID)));
76         holder.textView.setText(cursor.getString(cursor.getColumnIndex(
77            Contact.COLUMN_NAME)));
78      }
79
80      // returns the number of items that adapter binds
81      @Override
82      public int getItemCount() {
83         return (cursor != null) ? cursor.getCount() : 0;
84      }
85
86      // swap this adapter's current Cursor for a new one
87      public void swapCursor(Cursor cursor) {
88         this.cursor = cursor;
89         notifyDataSetChanged();
90      }
91   }
```

Fig. 9.39 | Subclass of `RecyclerView.Adapter` that binds contacts to `RecyclerView`. (Part 2 of 2.)

Nested Interface ContactClickListener

Lines 20–22 define the nested interface `ContactClickListener` that class `ContactsFragment` implements to be notified when the user touches a contact in the `RecyclerView`. Each item in the `RecyclerView` has a click listener that calls the `ContactClickListener`'s `onClick` method and passes the selected contact's `Uri`. The `ContactsFragment` then notifies the `MainActivity` that a contact was selected, so the `MainActivity` can display the contact in a `DetailFragment`.

Nested Class *ViewHolder*

Class ViewHolder (lines 26–51) maintains a reference to a RecyclerView item's TextView and the database's rowID for the corresponding contact. The rowID is necessary because we sort the contacts before displaying them, so each contact's position number in the RecyclerView most likely does not match the contact's row ID in the database. ViewHolder's constructor stores a reference to the RecyclerView item's TextView and sets its View.On-ClickListener, which passes the contact's URI to the adapter's ContactClickListener.

Overridden *RecyclerView.Adapter* Method *onCreateViewHolder*

Method onCreateViewHolder (lines 63–69) inflates the GUI for a ViewHolder object. In this case we used the predefined layout android.R.layout.simple_list_item_1, which defines a layout containing one TextView named text1.

Overridden *RecyclerView.Adapter* Method *onBindViewHolder*

Method onBindViewHolder (lines 72–78) uses Cursor method **moveToPosition** to move to the contact that corresponds to the current RecyclerView item's position. Line 75 sets the ViewHolder's rowID. To get this value, we use Cursor method **getColumnIndex** to look up the column number of the Contact._ID column. We then pass that number to Cursor method **getLong** to get the contact's row ID. Lines 76–77 set the text for the ViewHolder's textView, using a similar process—in this case, look up the column number for the Contact.COLUMN_NAME column, then call Cursor method **getString** to get the contact's name.

Overridden *RecyclerView.Adapter* Method *getItemCount*

Method getItemCount (lines 81–84) returns the total number of rows in the Cursor or 0 if Cursor is null.

Method *swapCursor*

Method swapCursor (lines 87–90) replaces the adapter's current Cursor and notifies the adapter that its data changed. This method is called from the ContactsFragment's on-LoadFinished and onLoaderReset methods.

9.12 AddEditFragment Class

The AddEditFragment class provides a GUI for adding new contacts or editing existing ones. Many of the programming concepts used in this class have been presented earlier in this chapter or in prior chapters, so we focus here only on the new features.

9.12.1 Superclass and Implemented Interface

Figure 9.40 lists the package statement, import statements and the beginning of the AddEditFragment class definition. The class extends Fragment and implements the Loader-Manager.LoaderCallbacks<Cursor> interface to respond to LoaderManager events.

```
1   // AddEditFragment.java
2   // Fragment for adding a new contact or editing an existing one
3   package com.deitel.addressbook;
```

Fig. 9.40 | AddEditFragment package statement and import statements. (Part 1 of 2.)

```
4
5    import android.content.ContentValues;
6    import android.content.Context;
7    import android.database.Cursor;
8    import android.net.Uri;
9    import android.os.Bundle;
10   import android.support.design.widget.CoordinatorLayout;
11   import android.support.design.widget.FloatingActionButton;
12   import android.support.design.widget.Snackbar;
13   import android.support.design.widget.TextInputLayout;
14   import android.support.v4.app.Fragment;
15   import android.support.v4.app.LoaderManager;
16   import android.support.v4.content.CursorLoader;
17   import android.support.v4.content.Loader;
18   import android.text.Editable;
19   import android.text.TextWatcher;
20   import android.view.LayoutInflater;
21   import android.view.View;
22   import android.view.ViewGroup;
23   import android.view.inputmethod.InputMethodManager;
24
25   import com.deitel.addressbook.data.DatabaseDescription.Contact;
26
27   public class AddEditFragment extends Fragment
28      implements LoaderManager.LoaderCallbacks<Cursor> {
29
```

Fig. 9.40 | AddEditFragment package statement and import statements. (Part 2 of 2.)

9.12.2 AddEditFragmentListener

Figure 9.41 declares the nested interface AddEditFragmentListener containing the callback method onAddEditCompleted. MainActivity implements this interface to be notified when the user saves a new contact or saves changes to an existing one.

```
30      // defines callback method implemented by MainActivity
31      public interface AddEditFragmentListener {
32         // called when contact is saved
33         void onAddEditCompleted(Uri contactUri);
34      }
35
```

Fig. 9.41 | Nested interface AddEditFragmentListener.

9.12.3 Fields

Figure 9.42 lists the class's fields:

- The constant CONTACT_LOADER (line 37) identifies the Loader that queries the AddressBookContentProvider to retrieve one contact for editing.

- The instance variable listener (line 39) refers to the AddEditFragmentListener (MainActivity) that's notified when the user saves a new or updated contact.

- The instance variable contactUri (line 40) represents the contact to edit.
- The instance variable addingNewContact (line 41) specifies whether a new contact is being added (true) or an existing contact is being edited (false).
- The instance variables at lines 44–53 refer to the Fragment's TextInputLayouts, FloatingActionButton and CoordinatorLayout.

```
36      // constant used to identify the Loader
37      private static final int CONTACT_LOADER = 0;
38
39      private AddEditFragmentListener listener; // MainActivity
40      private Uri contactUri; // Uri of selected contact
41      private boolean addingNewContact = true; // adding (true) or editing
42
43      // EditTexts for contact information
44      private TextInputLayout nameTextInputLayout;
45      private TextInputLayout phoneTextInputLayout;
46      private TextInputLayout emailTextInputLayout;
47      private TextInputLayout streetTextInputLayout;
48      private TextInputLayout cityTextInputLayout;
49      private TextInputLayout stateTextInputLayout;
50      private TextInputLayout zipTextInputLayout;
51      private FloatingActionButton saveContactFAB;
52
53      private CoordinatorLayout coordinatorLayout; // used with SnackBars
54
```

Fig. 9.42 | AddEditFragment fields.

9.12.4 Overridden Fragment Methods onAttach, onDetach and onCreateView

Figure 9.43 contains the overridden Fragment methods onAttach, onDetach and onCreateView. Methods onAttach and onDetach set instance variable listener to refer to the host Activity when the AddEditFragment is attached and to set listener to null when the AddEditFragment is detached.

```
55      // set AddEditFragmentListener when Fragment attached
56      @Override
57      public void onAttach(Context context) {
58          super.onAttach(context);
59          listener = (AddEditFragmentListener) context;
60      }
61
62      // remove AddEditFragmentListener when Fragment detached
63      @Override
64      public void onDetach() {
65          super.onDetach();
66          listener = null;
67      }
```

Fig. 9.43 | Overridden Fragment Methods onAttach, onDetach and onCreateView. (Part 1 of 2.)

```
68
69     // called when Fragment's view needs to be created
70     @Override
71     public View onCreateView(
72        LayoutInflater inflater, ViewGroup container,
73        Bundle savedInstanceState) {
74        super.onCreateView(inflater, container, savedInstanceState);
75        setHasOptionsMenu(true); // fragment has menu items to display
76
77        // inflate GUI and get references to EditTexts
78        View view =
79           inflater.inflate(R.layout.fragment_add_edit, container, false);
80        nameTextInputLayout =
81           (TextInputLayout) view.findViewById(R.id.nameTextInputLayout);
82        nameTextInputLayout.getEditText().addTextChangedListener(
83           nameChangedListener);
84        phoneTextInputLayout =
85           (TextInputLayout) view.findViewById(R.id.phoneTextInputLayout);
86        emailTextInputLayout =
87           (TextInputLayout) view.findViewById(R.id.emailTextInputLayout);
88        streetTextInputLayout =
89           (TextInputLayout) view.findViewById(R.id.streetTextInputLayout);
90        cityTextInputLayout =
91           (TextInputLayout) view.findViewById(R.id.cityTextInputLayout);
92        stateTextInputLayout =
93           (TextInputLayout) view.findViewById(R.id.stateTextInputLayout);
94        zipTextInputLayout =
95           (TextInputLayout) view.findViewById(R.id.zipTextInputLayout);
96
97        // set FloatingActionButton's event listener
98        saveContactFAB = (FloatingActionButton) view.findViewById(
99           R.id.saveFloatingActionButton);
100       saveContactFAB.setOnClickListener(saveContactButtonClicked);
101       updateSaveButtonFAB();
102
103       // used to display SnackBars with brief messages
104       coordinatorLayout = (CoordinatorLayout) getActivity().findViewById(
105          R.id.coordinatorLayout);
106
107       Bundle arguments = getArguments(); // null if creating new contact
108
109       if (arguments != null) {
110          addingNewContact = false;
111          contactUri = arguments.getParcelable(MainActivity.CONTACT_URI);
112       }
113
114       // if editing an existing contact, create Loader to get the contact
115       if (contactUri != null)
116          getLoaderManager().initLoader(CONTACT_LOADER, null, this);
117
118       return view;
119    }
120
```

Fig. 9.43 | Overridden Fragment Methods onAttach, onDetach and onCreateView. (Part 2 of 2.)

Method onCreateView inflates the GUI and gets references to the Fragment's Text-InputLayouts and configures the FloatingActionButton. Next, we use Fragment method getArguments to get the Bundle of arguments (line 107). When we launch the AddEdit-Fragment from the MainActivity, we pass null for the Bundle argument, because the user is adding a new contact's information. In this case, getArguments returns null. If getArguments returns a Bundle (line 109), then the user is editing an existing contact. Line 111 reads the contact's Uri from the Bundle by calling method getParcelable. If contactUri is not null, line 116 uses the Fragment's LoaderManager to initialize a Loader that the AddEditFragment will use to get the data for the contact being edited.

9.12.5 TextWatcher nameChangedListener and Method updateSaveButtonFAB

Figure 9.44 shows the TextWatcher nameChangedListener and method updatedSave-ButtonFAB. The listener calls method updatedSaveButtonFAB when the user edits the text in the nameTextInputLayout's EditText. The name must be non-empty in this app, so method updatedSaveButtonFAB displays the FloatingActionButton only when the nameTextInputLayout's EditText is not empty.

```
121    // detects when the text in the nameTextInputLayout's EditText changes
122    // to hide or show saveButtonFAB
123    private final TextWatcher nameChangedListener = new TextWatcher() {
124       @Override
125       public void beforeTextChanged(CharSequence s, int start, int count,
126          int after) {}
127
128       // called when the text in nameTextInputLayout changes
129       @Override
130       public void onTextChanged(CharSequence s, int start, int before,
131          int count) {
132          updateSaveButtonFAB();
133       }
134
135       @Override
136       public void afterTextChanged(Editable s) { }
137    };
138
139    // shows saveButtonFAB only if the name is not empty
140    private void updateSaveButtonFAB() {
141       String input =
142          nameTextInputLayout.getEditText().getText().toString();
143
144       // if there is a name for the contact, show the FloatingActionButton
145       if (input.trim().length() != 0)
146          saveContactFAB.show();
147       else
148          saveContactFAB.hide();
149    }
150
```

Fig. 9.44 | TextWatcher nameChangedListener and method updateSaveButtonFAB.

9.12.6 View.OnClickListener saveContactButtonClicked and Method saveContact

When the user touches this Fragment's FloatingActionButton, the saveContactButton-Clicked listener (Fig. 9.45, lines 152–162) executes. Method onClick hides the keyboard (lines 157–159), then calls method saveContact.

```
151    // responds to event generated when user saves a contact
152    private final View.OnClickListener saveContactButtonClicked =
153       new View.OnClickListener() {
154          @Override
155          public void onClick(View v) {
156             // hide the virtual keyboard
157             ((InputMethodManager) getActivity().getSystemService(
158                Context.INPUT_METHOD_SERVICE)).hideSoftInputFromWindow(
159                getView().getWindowToken(), 0);
160             saveContact(); // save contact to the database
161          }
162       };
163
164    // saves contact information to the database
165    private void saveContact() {
166       // create ContentValues object containing contact's key-value pairs
167       ContentValues contentValues = new ContentValues();
168       contentValues.put(Contact.COLUMN_NAME,
169          nameTextInputLayout.getEditText().getText().toString());
170       contentValues.put(Contact.COLUMN_PHONE,
171          phoneTextInputLayout.getEditText().getText().toString());
172       contentValues.put(Contact.COLUMN_EMAIL,
173          emailTextInputLayout.getEditText().getText().toString());
174       contentValues.put(Contact.COLUMN_STREET,
175          streetTextInputLayout.getEditText().getText().toString());
176       contentValues.put(Contact.COLUMN_CITY,
177          cityTextInputLayout.getEditText().getText().toString());
178       contentValues.put(Contact.COLUMN_STATE,
179          stateTextInputLayout.getEditText().getText().toString());
180       contentValues.put(Contact.COLUMN_ZIP,
181          zipTextInputLayout.getEditText().getText().toString());
182
183       if (addingNewContact) {
184          // use Activity's ContentResolver to invoke
185          // insert on the AddressBookContentProvider
186          Uri newContactUri = getActivity().getContentResolver().insert(
187             Contact.CONTENT_URI, contentValues);
188
189          if (newContactUri != null) {
190             Snackbar.make(coordinatorLayout,
191                R.string.contact_added, Snackbar.LENGTH_LONG).show();
192             listener.onAddEditCompleted(newContactUri);
193          }
```

Fig. 9.45 | View.OnClickListener saveContactButtonClicked and method saveContact. (Part 1 of 2.)

```
194          else {
195              Snackbar.make(coordinatorLayout,
196                  R.string.contact_not_added, Snackbar.LENGTH_LONG).show();
197          }
198      }
199      else {
200          // use Activity's ContentResolver to invoke
201          // insert on the AddressBookContentProvider
202          int updatedRows = getActivity().getContentResolver().update(
203              contactUri, contentValues, null, null);
204
205          if (updatedRows > 0) {
206              listener.onAddEditCompleted(contactUri);
207              Snackbar.make(coordinatorLayout,
208                  R.string.contact_updated, Snackbar.LENGTH_LONG).show();
209          }
210          else {
211              Snackbar.make(coordinatorLayout,
212                  R.string.contact_not_updated, Snackbar.LENGTH_LONG).show();
213          }
214      }
215  }
216
```

Fig. 9.45 | View.OnClickListener saveContactButtonClicked and method saveContact. (Part 2 of 2.)

The saveContact method (lines 165–215) creates a ContentValues object (line 167) and adds to it key–value pairs representing the column names and values to be inserted into or updated in the database (lines 168–181). If the user is adding a new contact (lines 183–198), lines 186–187 use ContentResolver method **insert** to invoke insert on the AddressBookContentProvider and place the new contact into the database. If the insert is successful, the returned Uri is non-null and lines 190–192 display a SnackBar indicating that the contact was added, then notify the AddEditFragmentListener with the contact that was added. Recall that when the app is running on a tablet, this results in the contact's data being displayed in a DetailFragment next to the ContactsFragment. If the insert is not successful, lines 195–196 display an appropriate SnackBar.

If the user is editing an existing contact (lines 199–214), lines 202–203 use Content-Resolver method **update** to invoke update on the AddressBookContentProvider and store the edited contact's data. If the update is successful, the returned integer is greater than 0 (indicating the specific number of rows updated) and lines 206–208 notify the Add-EditFragmentListener with the contact that was edited, then display an appropriate message. If the updated is not successful, lines 211–212 display an appropriate SnackBar.

9.12.7 LoaderManager.LoaderCallbacks<Cursor> Methods

Figure 9.46 presents the AddEditFragment's implementations of the methods in interface LoaderManager.LoaderCallbacks<Cursor>. These methods are used in class AddEdit-Fragment only when the user is editing an existing contact. Method onCreateLoader (lines 219–233) creates a CursorLoader for the specific contact being edited. Method on-

LoadFinished (lines 236–267) checks whether the cursor is non-null and, if so, calls cursor method **moveToFirst**. If this method returns true, then a contact matching the contactUri was found in the database and lines 241–263 get the contact's information from the Cursor and display it in the GUI. Method onLoaderReset is not needed in AddEditFragment, so it does nothing.

```
217    // called by LoaderManager to create a Loader
218    @Override
219    public Loader<Cursor> onCreateLoader(int id, Bundle args) {
220        // create an appropriate CursorLoader based on the id argument;
221        // only one Loader in this fragment, so the switch is unnecessary
222        switch (id) {
223            case CONTACT_LOADER:
224                return new CursorLoader(getActivity(),
225                    contactUri, // Uri of contact to display
226                    null, // null projection returns all columns
227                    null, // null selection returns all rows
228                    null, // no selection arguments
229                    null); // sort order
230            default:
231                return null;
232        }
233    }
234
235    // called by LoaderManager when loading completes
236    @Override
237    public void onLoadFinished(Loader<Cursor> loader, Cursor data) {
238        // if the contact exists in the database, display its data
239        if (data != null && data.moveToFirst()) {
240            // get the column index for each data item
241            int nameIndex = data.getColumnIndex(Contact.COLUMN_NAME);
242            int phoneIndex = data.getColumnIndex(Contact.COLUMN_PHONE);
243            int emailIndex = data.getColumnIndex(Contact.COLUMN_EMAIL);
244            int streetIndex = data.getColumnIndex(Contact.COLUMN_STREET);
245            int cityIndex = data.getColumnIndex(Contact.COLUMN_CITY);
246            int stateIndex = data.getColumnIndex(Contact.COLUMN_STATE);
247            int zipIndex = data.getColumnIndex(Contact.COLUMN_ZIP);
248
249            // fill EditTexts with the retrieved data
250            nameTextInputLayout.getEditText().setText(
251                data.getString(nameIndex));
252            phoneTextInputLayout.getEditText().setText(
253                data.getString(phoneIndex));
254            emailTextInputLayout.getEditText().setText(
255                data.getString(emailIndex));
256            streetTextInputLayout.getEditText().setText(
257                data.getString(streetIndex));
258            cityTextInputLayout.getEditText().setText(
259                data.getString(cityIndex));
260            stateTextInputLayout.getEditText().setText(
261                data.getString(stateIndex));
```

Fig. 9.46 | LoaderManager.LoaderCallbacks<Cursor> methods. (Part I of 2.)

```
262        zipTextInputLayout.getEditText().setText(
263            data.getString(zipIndex));
264
265        updateSaveButtonFAB();
266     }
267   }
268
269   // called by LoaderManager when the Loader is being reset
270   @Override
271   public void onLoaderReset(Loader<Cursor> loader) { }
272 }
```

Fig. 9.46 | LoaderManager.LoaderCallbacks<Cursor> methods. (Part 2 of 2.)

9.13 DetailFragment Class

The DetailFragment class displays one contact's information and provides menu items on the app bar that enable the user to edit or delete that contact.

9.13.1 Superclass and Implemented Interface

Figure 9.47 lists the package statement, import statements and the beginning of the DetailFragment class definition. The class extends Fragment and implements the LoaderManager.LoaderCallbacks<Cursor> interface to respond to LoaderManager events.

```
1   // DetailFragment.java
2   // Fragment subclass that displays one contact's details
3   package com.deitel.addressbook;
4
5   import android.app.AlertDialog;
6   import android.app.Dialog;
7   import android.content.Context;
8   import android.content.DialogInterface;
9   import android.database.Cursor;
10  import android.net.Uri;
11  import android.os.Bundle;
12  import android.support.v4.app.DialogFragment;
13  import android.support.v4.app.Fragment;
14  import android.support.v4.app.LoaderManager;
15  import android.support.v4.content.CursorLoader;
16  import android.support.v4.content.Loader;
17  import android.view.LayoutInflater;
18  import android.view.Menu;
19  import android.view.MenuInflater;
20  import android.view.MenuItem;
21  import android.view.View;
22  import android.view.ViewGroup;
23  import android.widget.TextView;
24
```

Fig. 9.47 | package statement, import statements, superclass and implemented interface. (Part 1 of 2.)

```
25  import com.deitel.addressbook.data.DatabaseDescription.Contact;
26
27  public class DetailFragment extends Fragment
28     implements LoaderManager.LoaderCallbacks<Cursor> {
29
```

Fig. 9.47 | package statement, import statements, superclass and implemented interface. (Part 2 of 2.)

9.13.2 DetailFragmentListener

Figure 9.48 declares the nested interface DetailFragmentListener containing the callback methods that MainActivity implements to be notified when the user deletes a contact (line 32) and when the user touches the edit menu item to edit a contact (line 35).

```
30     // callback methods implemented by MainActivity
31     public interface DetailFragmentListener {
32        void onContactDeleted(); // called when a contact is deleted
33
34        // pass Uri of contact to edit to the DetailFragmentListener
35        void onEditContact(Uri contactUri);
36     }
37
```

Fig. 9.48 | Nested interface DetailFragmentListener.

9.13.3 Fields

Figure 9.49 shows the class's fields:

- The constant CONTACT_LOADER (line 38) identifies the Loader that queries the AddressBookContentProvider to retrieve one contact to display.

- The instance variable listener (line 40) refers to the DetailFragmentListener (MainActivity) that's notified when the user deletes a contact or initiates editing of a contact.

- The instance variable contactUri (line 41) represents the contact to display.

- The instance variables at lines 43–49 refer to the Fragment's TextViews.

```
38     private static final int CONTACT_LOADER = 0; // identifies the Loader
39
40     private DetailFragmentListener listener; // MainActivity
41     private Uri contactUri; // Uri of selected contact
42
43     private TextView nameTextView; // displays contact's name
44     private TextView phoneTextView; // displays contact's phone
45     private TextView emailTextView; // displays contact's email
46     private TextView streetTextView; // displays contact's street
47     private TextView cityTextView; // displays contact's city
```

Fig. 9.49 | DetailFragment fields. (Part I of 2.)

```
48        private TextView stateTextView; // displays contact's state
49        private TextView zipTextView; // displays contact's zip
50
```

Fig. 9.49 | DetailFragment fields. (Part 2 of 2.)

9.13.4 Overridden Methods onAttach, onDetach and onCreateView

Figure 9.50 contains overridden Fragment methods onAttach, onDetach and onCreateView. Methods onAttach and onDetach set instance variable listener to refer to the host Activity when the DetailFragment is attached and to set listener to null when the DetailFragment is detached. The onCreateView method (lines 66–95) obtains the selected contact's Uri (lines 74–77). Lines 80–90 inflate the GUI and get references to the TextViews. Line 93 uses the Fragment's LoaderManager to initialize a Loader that the DetailFragment will use to get the data for the contact to display.

```
51        // set DetailFragmentListener when fragment attached
52        @Override
53        public void onAttach(Context context) {
54            super.onAttach(context);
55            listener = (DetailFragmentListener) context;
56        }
57
58        // remove DetailFragmentListener when fragment detached
59        @Override
60        public void onDetach() {
61            super.onDetach();
62            listener = null;
63        }
64
65        // called when DetailFragmentListener's view needs to be created
66        @Override
67        public View onCreateView(
68            LayoutInflater inflater, ViewGroup container,
69            Bundle savedInstanceState) {
70            super.onCreateView(inflater, container, savedInstanceState);
71            setHasOptionsMenu(true); // this fragment has menu items to display
72
73            // get Bundle of arguments then extract the contact's Uri
74            Bundle arguments = getArguments();
75
76            if (arguments != null)
77                contactUri = arguments.getParcelable(MainActivity.CONTACT_URI);
78
79            // inflate DetailFragment's layout
80            View view =
81                inflater.inflate(R.layout.fragment_detail, container, false);
82
83            // get the EditTexts
84            nameTextView = (TextView) view.findViewById(R.id.nameTextView);
```

Fig. 9.50 | Overridden methods onAttach, onDetach and onCreateView. (Part 1 of 2.)

```
85          phoneTextView = (TextView) view.findViewById(R.id.phoneTextView);
86          emailTextView = (TextView) view.findViewById(R.id.emailTextView);
87          streetTextView = (TextView) view.findViewById(R.id.streetTextView);
88          cityTextView = (TextView) view.findViewById(R.id.cityTextView);
89          stateTextView = (TextView) view.findViewById(R.id.stateTextView);
90          zipTextView = (TextView) view.findViewById(R.id.zipTextView);
91
92          // load the contact
93          getLoaderManager().initLoader(CONTACT_LOADER, null, this);
94          return view;
95      }
96
```

Fig. 9.50 | Overridden methods onAttach, onDetach and onCreateView. (Part 2 of 2.)

9.13.5 Overridden Methods onCreateOptionsMenu and onOptionsItemSelected

The DetailFragment displays in the app bar options for editing the current contact and for deleting it. Method onCreateOptionsMenu (Fig. 9.51, lines 98–102) inflates the menu resource file fragment_details_menu.xml. Method onOptionsItemSelected (lines 105–117) uses the selected MenuItem's resource ID to determine which one was selected. If the user touched the edit option (✏), line 109 calls the DetailFragmentListener's onEditContact method with the contactUri—MainActivity passes this to the AddEditFragment. If the user touched the delete option (🗑), line 112 calls method deleteContact (Fig. 9.52).

```
97      // display this fragment's menu items
98      @Override
99      public void onCreateOptionsMenu(Menu menu, MenuInflater inflater) {
100         super.onCreateOptionsMenu(menu, inflater);
101         inflater.inflate(R.menu.fragment_details_menu, menu);
102     }
103
104     // handle menu item selections
105     @Override
106     public boolean onOptionsItemSelected(MenuItem item) {
107         switch (item.getItemId()) {
108             case R.id.action_edit:
109                 listener.onEditContact(contactUri); // pass Uri to listener
110                 return true;
111             case R.id.action_delete:
112                 deleteContact();
113                 return true;
114         }
115
116         return super.onOptionsItemSelected(item);
117     }
118
```

Fig. 9.51 | Overridden methods onCreateOptionsMenu and onOptionsItemSelected.

9.13.6 Method deleteContact and DialogFragment confirmDelete

Method deleteContact (Fig. 9.52, lines 120–123) displays a DialogFragment (lines 126–157) asking the user to confirm that the currently displayed contact should be deleted. If the user touches **DELETE** in the dialog, lines 147–148 call ContentResolver method **delete** (lines 147–148) to invoke the AddressBookContentProvider's delete method and remove the contact from the database. Method delete receives the Uri of the content to delete, a String representing the WHERE clause that determines what to delete and a String array of arguments to insert in the WHERE clause. In this case, the last two arguments are null, because the row ID of the contact to delete is embedded in the Uri—this row ID is extracted from the Uri by the AddressBookContentProvider's delete method. Line 149 calls the listener's onContactDeleted method so that MainActivity can remove the DetailFragment from the screen.

```
119      // delete a contact
120      private void deleteContact() {
121         // use FragmentManager to display the confirmDelete DialogFragment
122         confirmDelete.show(getFragmentManager(), "confirm delete");
123      }
124
125      // DialogFragment to confirm deletion of contact
126      private final DialogFragment confirmDelete =
127         new DialogFragment() {
128            // create an AlertDialog and return it
129            @Override
130            public Dialog onCreateDialog(Bundle bundle) {
131               // create a new AlertDialog Builder
132               AlertDialog.Builder builder =
133                  new AlertDialog.Builder(getActivity());
134
135               builder.setTitle(R.string.confirm_title);
136               builder.setMessage(R.string.confirm_message);
137
138               // provide an OK button that simply dismisses the dialog
139               builder.setPositiveButton(R.string.button_delete,
140                  new DialogInterface.OnClickListener() {
141                     @Override
142                     public void onClick(
143                        DialogInterface dialog, int button) {
144
145                        // use Activity's ContentResolver to invoke
146                        // delete on the AddressBookContentProvider
147                        getActivity().getContentResolver().delete(
148                           contactUri, null, null);
149                        listener.onContactDeleted(); // notify listener
150                     }
151                  }
152               );
153
```

Fig. 9.52 | Method deleteContact and DialogFragment confirmDelete. (Part 1 of 2.)

```
154                 builder.setNegativeButton(R.string.button_cancel, null);
155                 return builder.create(); // return the AlertDialog
156              }
157         };
158
```

Fig. 9.52 | Method deleteContact and DialogFragment confirmDelete. (Part 2 of 2.)

9.13.7 LoaderManager.LoaderCallback<Cursor> Methods

Figure 9.53 presents the DetailFragment's implementations of the methods in interface LoaderManager.LoaderCallbacks<Cursor>. Method onCreateLoader (lines 160–181) creates a CursorLoader for the specific contact being displayed. Method onLoadFinished (lines 184–206) checks whether the cursor is non-null and, if so, calls cursor method moveToFirst. If this method returns true, then a contact matching the contactUri was found in the database and lines 189–204 get the contact's information from the Cursor and display it in the GUI. Method onLoaderReset is not needed in DetailFragment, so it does nothing.

```
159    // called by LoaderManager to create a Loader
160    @Override
161    public Loader<Cursor> onCreateLoader(int id, Bundle args) {
162        // create an appropriate CursorLoader based on the id argument;
163        // only one Loader in this fragment, so the switch is unnecessary
164        CursorLoader cursorLoader;
165
166        switch (id) {
167            case CONTACT_LOADER:
168                cursorLoader = new CursorLoader(getActivity(),
169                    contactUri, // Uri of contact to display
170                    null, // null projection returns all columns
171                    null, // null selection returns all rows
172                    null, // no selection arguments
173                    null); // sort order
174                break;
175            default:
176                cursorLoader = null;
177                break;
178        }
179
180        return cursorLoader;
181    }
182
183    // called by LoaderManager when loading completes
184    @Override
185    public void onLoadFinished(Loader<Cursor> loader, Cursor data) {
186        // if the contact exists in the database, display its data
187        if (data != null && data.moveToFirst()) {
188            // get the column index for each data item
189            int nameIndex = data.getColumnIndex(Contact.COLUMN_NAME);
```

Fig. 9.53 | LoaderManager.LoaderCallback<Cursor> methods. (Part 1 of 2.)

```
190        int phoneIndex = data.getColumnIndex(Contact.COLUMN_PHONE);
191        int emailIndex = data.getColumnIndex(Contact.COLUMN_EMAIL);
192        int streetIndex = data.getColumnIndex(Contact.COLUMN_STREET);
193        int cityIndex = data.getColumnIndex(Contact.COLUMN_CITY);
194        int stateIndex = data.getColumnIndex(Contact.COLUMN_STATE);
195        int zipIndex = data.getColumnIndex(Contact.COLUMN_ZIP);
196
197        // fill TextViews with the retrieved data
198        nameTextView.setText(data.getString(nameIndex));
199        phoneTextView.setText(data.getString(phoneIndex));
200        emailTextView.setText(data.getString(emailIndex));
201        streetTextView.setText(data.getString(streetIndex));
202        cityTextView.setText(data.getString(cityIndex));
203        stateTextView.setText(data.getString(stateIndex));
204        zipTextView.setText(data.getString(zipIndex));
205      }
206   }
207
208   // called by LoaderManager when the Loader is being reset
209   @Override
210   public void onLoaderReset(Loader<Cursor> loader) { }
211 }
```

Fig. 9.53 | LoaderManager.LoaderCallback<Cursor> methods. (Part 2 of 2.)

9.14 Wrap-Up

In this chapter, you created an **Address Book** app for adding, viewing, editing and deleting contact information that's stored in a SQLite database.

You used one activity to host all of the app's Fragments. On a phone-sized device, you displayed one Fragment at a time. On a tablet, the activity displayed the Fragment containing the contact list, and you replaced that with Fragments for viewing, adding and editing contacts as necessary. You used the FragmentManager and FragmentTransactions to dynamically display Fragments. You used Android's Fragment back stack to provide automatic support for Android's back button. To communicate data between Fragments and the host activity, you defined in each Fragment subclass a nested interface of callback methods that the host activity implemented.

You used a subclass of SQLiteOpenHelper to simplify creating the database and to obtain a SQLiteDatabase object for manipulating the database's contents. You also managed database query results via a Cursor (package android.database).

To access the database asynchronously outside the GUI thread, you defined a subclass of ContentProvider that specified how to query, insert, update and delete data. When changes were made to the SQLite database, the ContentProvider notified listeners so data could be updated in the GUI. The ContentProvider defined Uris that it used to determine the tasks to perform.

To invoke the ContentProvider's query, insert, update and delete capabilities, we invoked the corresponding methods of the activity's built-in ContentResolver. You saw that the ContentProvider and ContentResolver handle communication for you. The ContentResolver's methods received as their first argument a Uri that specified the ContentProvider to access. Each ContentResolver method invoked the corresponding method of the ContentProvider, which in turn used the Uri to help determine the task to perform.

As we've stated previously, long-running operations or operations that block execution until they complete (e.g., file and database access) should be performed outside the GUI thread. You used a CursorLoader to perform asynchronous data access. You learned that Loaders are created and managed by an Activity's or Fragment's LoaderManager, which ties each Loader's lifecycle to that of its Activity or Fragment. You implmeneted interface LoaderManager.LoaderCallbacks to respond to Loader events indicating when a Loader should be created, finishes loading its data, or is reset and the data is no longer available.

You defined common GUI component attribute–value pairs as a style resource, then applied the style to the TextViews that display a contact's information. You also defined a border for a TextView by specifying a Drawable for the TextView's background. The Drawable could be an image, but in this app you defined the Drawable as a shape in a resource file.

In Chapter 10, we discuss the business side of Android app development. You'll see how to prepare your app for submission to Google Play, including making icons. We'll discuss how to test your apps on devices and publish them on Google Play. We discuss the characteristics of great apps and the Android design guidelines to follow. We provide tips for pricing and marketing your app. We also review the benefits of offering your app for free to drive sales of other products, such as a more feature-rich version of the app or premium content. We show how to use Google Play to track app sales, payments and more.

Self-Review Exercises

9.1 Fill in the blanks in each of the following statements:

a) SQLite database query results are managed via a(n) _____ (package android.database).

b) A(n) _____ exposes an app's data for use in that app or in other apps.

c) Fragment method _____ returns the Bundle of arguments to the Fragment.

d) The Cursor returned by method query contains all the table rows that match the method's arguments—the so-called _____.

e) A FragmentTransaction (package android.app) obtained from the _____ allows an Activity to add, remove and transition between Fragments.

f) _____ and the _____ help you perform asynchronous data access from any Activity or Fragment.

9.2 State whether each of the following is *true* or *false*. If *false*, explain why.

a) It's good practice to release resources like database connections when they are not being used so that other activities can use the resources.

b) It's considered good practice to ensure that Cursor method moveToFirst returns false before attempting to get data from the Cursor.

c) A ContentProvider defines Uris that help determine the task to perform when the ContentProvider receives a request.

d) An Activity's or Fragment's LoaderManagers are tied to the Activity's or Fragment's lifecycle.

e) To invoke a ContentProvider's query, insert, update and delete capabilities, you use the corresponding methods of a ContentResolver.

f) You must coordinate comminication between a ContentProvider and ContentResolver.

Answers to Self-Review Exercises

9.1   a) `Cursor`. b) `ContentProvider`. c) `getArguments`. d) result set. e) `FragmentManager`. f) Loaders, `LoaderManager`.

9.2   a) True. b) False. It's considered good practice to ensure that `Cursor` method `moveToFirst` returns true before attempting to get data from the `Cursor`. c) True. d) False. An `Activity`'s or `Fragment`'s `Loaders` are created and managed by its `LoaderManager` (package `android.app`), which ties each `Loader`'s lifecycle to its `Activity`'s or `Fragment`'s lifecycle. e) True. f) False. A `ContentProvider` and `ContentResolver` handle communication for you—including between apps if your `ContentProvider` exposes its data to other apps.

Exercises

9.3   *(Flag Quiz App Modification)* Revise the **Flag Quiz** app to use one `Activity`, dynamic Fragments and `FragmentTransactions` as you did in the **Address Book** app.

9.4   *(Movie Collection App)* Using the techniques you learned in this chapter, create an app that allows you to enter information about your movie collection. Provide fields for the title, year, director and any other fields you'd like to track. The app should provide similar activities to the **Address Book** app for viewing the list of movies (in alphabetical order), adding and/or updating the information for a movie and viewing the details of a movie.

9.5   *(Recipe App)* Using the techniques you learned in this chapter, create a cooking recipe app. Provide fields for the recipe name, category (e.g., appetizer, entree, desert, salad, side dish), a list of the ingredients and instructions for preparing the dish. The app should provide similar activities to the **Address Book** app for viewing the list of recipes (in alphabetical order), adding and/or updating a recipe and viewing the details of a recipe.

9.6   *(Shopping List App)* Create an app that allows the user to enter and edit a shopping list. Include a favorites feature that allows the user to easily add items purchased frequently. Include an optional feature to input a price for each item and a quantity so the user can track the total cost of all of the items on the list.

9.7   *(Expense Tracker App)* Create an app that allows the user to keep track of personal expenses. Provide categories for classifying each expense (e.g., monthly expenses, travel, entertainment, necessities). Provide an option for tagging recurring expenses that automatically adds the expense to a calendar at the proper frequency (daily, weekly, monthly or yearly). Optional: Investigate Android's status-bar notifications mechanism at `developer.android.com/guide/topics/ui/notifiers/index.html`. Provide notifications to remind the user when a bill is due.

9.8   *(Cooking with Healthier Ingredients App)* Obesity in the United States is increasing at an alarming rate. Check the map at `http://stateofobesity.org/adult-obesity/`, which shows adult obesity trends in the United States since 1990. As obesity increases, so do occurrences of related problems (e.g., heart disease, high blood pressure, high cholesterol, type 2 diabetes). Create an app that helps users choose healthier ingredients when cooking, and helps those allergic to certain foods (e.g., nuts, gluten) find substitutes. The app should allow the user to enter a recipe, then should suggest healthier replacements for some of the ingredients. For simplicity, your app should assume the recipe has no abbreviations for measures such as teaspoons, cups, and tablespoons, and uses numerical digits for quantities (e.g., 1 egg, 2 cups) rather than spelling them out (one egg, two cups). Some common substitutions are shown in Fig. 9.54. Your app should display a warning such as, "Always consult your physician before making significant changes to your diet."

Ingredient	Substitution
1 cup sour cream	1 cup yogurt
1 cup milk	1/2 cup evaporated milk and 1/2 cup water
1 teaspoon lemon juice	1/2 teaspoon vinegar
1 cup sugar	1/2 cup honey, 1 cup molasses or 1/4 cup agave nectar
1 cup butter	1 cup margarine or yogurt
1 cup flour	1 cup rye or rice flour
1 cup mayonnaise	1 cup cottage cheese or 1/8 cup mayonnaise and 7/8 cup yogurt
1 egg	2 tablespoons cornstarch, arrowroot flour or potato starch or 2 egg whites or 1/2 large banana (mashed)
1 cup milk	1 cup soy milk
1/4 cup oil	1/4 cup applesauce
white bread	whole-grain bread
1 cup sour cream	1 cup yogurt

Fig. 9.54 | Common ingredient substitutions.

The app should take into consideration that replacements are not always one-for-one. For example, if a cake recipe calls for three eggs, it might reasonably use six egg whites instead. Conversion data for measurements and substitutes can be obtained at websites such as:

```
http://chinesefood.about.com/od/recipeconversionfaqs/f/usmetricrecipes.htm
http://www.pioneerthinking.com/eggsub.html
http://www.gourmetsleuth.com/conversions.htm
```

Your app should consider the user's health concerns, such as high cholesterol, high blood pressure, weight loss, gluten allergy, and so on. For high cholesterol, the app should suggest substitutes for eggs and dairy products; if the user wishes to lose weight, low-calorie substitutes for ingredients such as sugar should be suggested.

Google Play and App Business Issues

Objectives

In this chapter you'll be introduced to:

- Preparing your apps for publication.
- Pricing your apps and the benefits of free vs. paid apps.
- Monetizing your apps with in-app advertising.
- Selling virtual goods using in-app billing.
- Registering for Google Play.
- Setting up a merchant account.
- Uploading your apps to Google Play.
- Launching Google Play from within an app.
- Other Android app marketplaces.
- Other popular mobile app platforms to which you can port your apps to broaden your market.
- Marketing your apps.

10.1 Introduction

In Chapters 2–9, we developed a variety of complete working Android apps. Once you've developed and tested your own apps, both in the emulator and on Android devices, the next step is to submit them to Google Play—and/or other app marketplaces—for distribution to a worldwide audience. In this chapter, we'll discuss

- registering for Google Play and setting up a Google Payments merchant account so that you can sell your apps
- preparing your apps for publication and
- uploading them to Google Play.

In a few cases, we'll refer you to the Android documentation instead of showing the steps in the book, because the steps are likely to change. We'll tell you about additional Android app marketplaces where you can distribute your apps. We'll discuss whether you should offer your apps for free or for a fee, and mention key means for monetizing apps, including in-app advertising, in-app billing and selling virtual goods. We'll provide resources for marketing your apps, and mention other app platforms to which you may port your Android apps to broaden your marketplace.

10.2 Preparing Your Apps for Publication

Google provides various documents to help you get ready to release your app. The *Preparing for Release* document

```
http://developer.android.com/tools/publishing/preparing.html
```

summarizes what you need to do, including:

- getting a *cryptographic key* for *digitally signing* your app
- creating an application *icon*
- including an *End User License Agreement* with your app (optional)
- *versioning* your app (e.g., 1.0, 1.1, 2.0, 2.3, 3.0)
- *compiling* your app for release and
- *testing* the release version of your app on Android devices

```
http://developer.android.com/tools/testing/what_to_test.html
```

Before publishing your app, you should also read the *Core App Quality* document

```
http://developer.android.com/distribute/essentials/quality/
    core.html
```

which provides quality guidelines for all apps, the *Tablet App Quality* document

```
http://developer.android.com/distribute/essentials/quality/
    tablets.html
```

which provides guidelines specifically for tablet apps, the *Launch Checklist* for publishing apps on the Google Play store

```
http://developer.android.com/distribute/tools/launch-checklist.html
```

and the *Localization Checklist* for apps that will be sold in various worldwide markets

```
http://developer.android.com/distribute/tools/localization-
    checklist.html
```

The remainder of this section discusses in more detail some of the items you'll need and other considerations before you publish an app.

10.2.1 Testing Your App

You should test your app thoroughly on a variety of devices. The app might work perfectly using the emulator on your computer, but problems could arise when running it on particular Android devices. Google's Cloud Test Lab[1]

```
https://developers.google.com/cloud-test-lab
```

helps you test your app across a wide range of devices.

10.2.2 End User License Agreement

You have the option to include an **End User License Agreement (EULA)** with your app. An EULA is an agreement through which you license your software to the user. It typically stipulates terms of use, limitations on redistribution and reverse engineering, product liability, compliance with applicable laws and more. You might want to consult an attorney when drafting an EULA for your app. To view a sample EULA, see

```
http://www.rocketlawyer.com/document/end-user-license-agreement.rl
```

---

1. Not yet available at the time of this writing.

10.2.3 Icons and Labels

Design an icon for your app and provide a text label (a name) that will appear in Google Play and on the user's device. The icon could be your company logo, an image from the app or a custom image. Google's material design documentation provides all the details to consider for your app icons:

```
https://www.google.com/design/spec/style/icons.html
```

Product icons should be 48-by-48 dp with a 1-dp border. Android scales this to the required size for various screen sizes and densities. For this reason, the guidelines recommend that you design the icon at 192-by-192 dp with a 4-dp edge—larger images that are scaled down to smaller sizes look better than smaller images scaled to larger sizes.

Google Play also displays a high-resolution app icon. This icon should be:

- 512-by-512 pixels
- 32-bit PNG
- 1 MB maximum

Since the app icon is the most important brand asset, having one that's high quality is important. Consider hiring an experienced graphic designer to help you create a compelling, professional icon. Figure 10.1 lists some design sites and firms that offer free, professionally designed icons and paid custom icon design services. Once you've created the icon, you can add it to your project using Android Studio's **Asset Studio** (as you did in Section 4.4.9), which will produce icons at various scaled sizes based on your original icon.

Company	URL	Services
glyphlab	http://www.glyphlab.com/icon_design/	Designs custom icons.
Iconiza	http://www.iconiza.com	Designs custom icons for a flat fee and sells stock icons.
The Iconfactory	http://iconfactory.com/home	Custom and stock icons.
Rosetta®	http://icondesign.rosetta.com/	Designs custom icons for a fee.
The Noun Project	https://thenounproject.com/	Thousands of icons from many artists.
Elance®	http://www.elance.com	Search for freelance icon designers.

Fig. 10.1 | Some custom app icon design firms.

10.2.4 Versioning Your App

It's important to include a *version name* (shown to the users) and a *version code* (an integer version number used internally by Google Play) for your app, and to consider your strategy for numbering updates. For example, the first version name of your app might be 1.0, minor updates might be 1.1 and 1.2, and the next major update might be 2.0. The version code is an integer that typically starts at 1 and is incremented by 1 for each new version of your app that you post. For additional guidelines, see *Versioning Your Applications* at

```
http://developer.android.com/tools/publishing/versioning.html
```

10.2.5 Licensing to Control Access to Paid Apps

The Google Play *licensing service* allows you to create licensing policies to control access to your paid apps. For example, you might use a licensing policy to limit how many simultaneous device installs are allowed. To learn more about the licensing service, visit

> http://developer.android.com/google/play/licensing/index.html

10.2.6 Obfuscating Your Code

You should "obfuscate" any apps you upload to Google Play to discourage reverse engineering of your code and further protect your apps. The free **ProGuard** tool—which runs when you build your app in *release mode*—shrinks the size of your .apk file (the Android app package file that contains your app for installation) and optimizes and obfuscates the code "by removing unused code and renaming classes, fields, and methods with semantically obscure names."[2] To learn how to set up and use the ProGuard tool, go to

> http://developer.android.com/tools/help/proguard.html

10.2.7 Getting a Private Key for Digitally Signing Your App

Before uploading your app to a device, Google Play or other app marketplaces, you must *digitally sign* the .apk file using a **digital certificate** that identifies you as the app's author. A digital certificate includes your name or company name, contact information, and more. It can be self-signed using a **private key** (i.e., a secure password used to *encrypt* the certificate); you do not need to purchase a certificate from a third-party certificate authority (though it's an option). Android Studio automatically digitally signs your app when you execute it in an emulator or on a device for *debugging* purposes. That digital certificate is *not* valid for use with Google Play. For detailed instructions on digitally signing your apps, see *Signing Your Applications* at

> http://developer.android.com/tools/publishing/app-signing.html

10.2.8 Featured Image and Screenshots

The Google Play store shows promotional graphics and screenshots in your app listing— these provide potential buyers with their first impressions of your app.

Featured Image
The featured image is used by Google Play to promote an app on phones, tablets and via the Google Play website. The following Android Developers Blog post discusses the featured image's importance and its requirements:

> http://android-developers.blogspot.com/2011/10/android-market-
> featured-image.html

Screenshots and Using the Android Device Manager's Screen Capture Tool
You may upload a maximum of eight screenshots for each device on which your app runs—smartphone, small tablet, large tablet, Android TV and Android Wear. These

---

2. http://developer.android.com/tools/help/proguard.html.

screenshots provide a preview of your app, since users can't test it before downloading it—although they can return an app for a refund within two hours after purchasing it. Choose attractive screenshots that show the app's functionality. Figure 10.2 describes the image requirements.

Specification	Description
Size	Minimum width or height of 320 pixels and maximum of 3,840 pixels—the maximum dimension may not be more than twice the minimum.
Format	24-bit PNG or JPEG format with no alpha (transparency) effects.

Fig. 10.2 | Screenshot specifications.

You can use the Android Device Monitor to capture device screenshots—this tool is installed with Android Studio and also helps you debug your apps that are running on emulators and devices. To obtain screenshots:

1. Run your app on an emulator or device.

2. In Android Studio, select **Tools > Android > Android Device Monitor** to open the Android Device Monitor.

3. In the **Devices** tab (Fig. 10.3), select the device from which you'd like to obtain a screen capture.

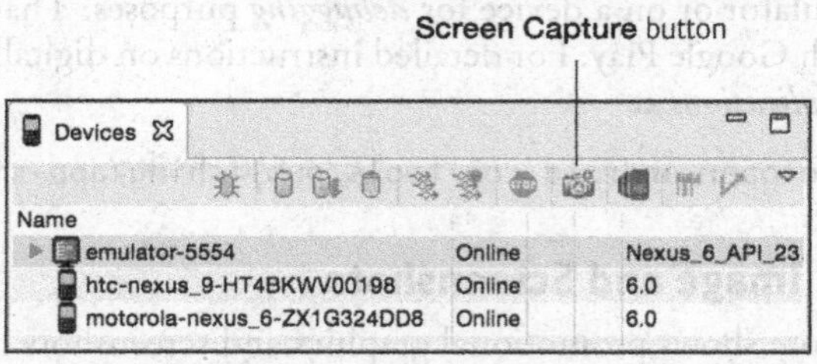

Fig. 10.3 | **Devices** window in the DDMS perspective.

4. Click the **Screen Capture** button to display the **Device Screen Capture** window.

5. After you've ensured that the screen is showing what you'd like to capture, click the **Save** button to save the image.

6. If you wish to change what's on your device's screen before saving an image, make the change on the device (or AVD), then press the **Refresh** button in the **Device Screen Capture** window to recapture the device's screen. You can also click **Rotate** to capture an image in landscape orientation.

For more information on the images you can include with your app listing, visit

```
https://support.google.com/googleplay/android-developer/answer/
  1078870
```

10.2.9 Promotional App Video

Google Play also allows you to include a URL for a short promotional video that's hosted on YouTube. To use this feature, you must sign up for a YouTube account and upload your video to the site. Figure 10.4 lists several promo video examples. Some videos show a person holding a device and interacting with the app. Others use screen captures. Figure 10.5 lists several video creation tools and services (some free, some paid). In additon, Android Studio provides a **Screen Record** tool in the **Android Monitor** window.

App	URL
Pac-Man 256	https://youtu.be/RF0GfRvm-yg
Angry Birds 2	https://youtu.be/jOUEjknadEY
Real Estate and Homes by Trulia®	https://youtu.be/BJDPKBNuqzE
Essential Anatomy 3	https://youtu.be/xmBqxb0aZr8

Fig. 10.4 | Examples of promotional videos for apps in Google Play.

Tools and services	URL
Animoto	http://animoto.com
Apptamin	http://www.apptamin.com
CamStudio™	http://camstudio.org
Jing	http://www.techsmith.com/jing.html
Camtasia Studio®	http://www.techsmith.com/camtasia.html
TurboDemo™	http://www.turbodemo.com/eng/index.php

Fig. 10.5 | Tools and services for creating promotional videos.

10.3 Pricing Your App: Free or Fee

You set the prices for your apps that are distributed through Google Play. Many developers offer their apps for free as a marketing, publicity and branding tool, earning revenue through increased sales of products and services, sales of more feature-rich versions of the same apps and sales of additional content through the apps using *in-app purchase* or *in-app advertising*. Figure 10.6 lists various ways to monetize your apps. The Google Play-specific ways to monetize your apps are listed at

> http://developer.android.com/distribute/monetize/index.html

Ways to monetize an app
• Sell the app in Google Play.
• Sell the app in other Android app marketplaces.

Fig. 10.6 | Ways to monetize an app. (Part 1 of 2.)

Ways to monetize an app
• Sell paid upgrades.
• Sell virtual goods (Section 10.5).
• Sell an app to a company that brands it as their own.
• Use mobile advertising services for in-app ads (Section 10.4).
• Sell in-app advertising space directly to your customers.
• Use it to drive sales of a more feature-rich version of the app.

Fig. 10.6 | Ways to monetize an app. (Part 2 of 2.)

10.3.1 Paid Apps

The average price for apps varies widely by category. For example, according to the app discovery site AppBrain (http://www.appbrain.com), the average price for puzzle-game apps is $1.51 and for business apps is $8.44.[3] Although these prices may seem low, keep in mind that successful apps could sell tens of thousands, hundreds of thousands or even millions of copies.

When setting a price for your app, start by researching your competition. How much do they charge? Do their apps have similar functionality? Is yours more feature-rich? Will offering your app at a lower price than the competition attract users? Is your goal to recoup development costs and generate additional revenue?

If you change your strategy, you can eventually offer your paid app for free. However it's not currently possible to change your free apps to paid.

Financial transactions for paid apps in Google Play are handled by Google Wallet

```
http://google.com/wallet
```

though customers of some mobile carriers (such as AT&T, Sprint and T-Mobile) can opt to use carrier billing to charge paid apps to their wireless bill. Your earnings are paid to your Google Payments merchant account monthly.[4] You're responsible for paying taxes on the revenue you earn through Google Play.

10.3.2 Free Apps

More than 90% of the apps users download are free, and that percentage has been increasing for several years.[5] Given that users are more likely to download an app if it's free, consider offering a free "lite" version of your app to encourage users to try it. For example, if your app is a game, you might offer a free version with just the first few levels. When the user has finished playing the free levels, the app would offer an option to buy through Google Play your more robust app with numerous game levels. Or, your app would display a message that the user can purchase additional levels from within the app for a more

---

3. http://www.appbrain.com/stats/android-market-app-categories.
4. http://support.google.com/googleplay/android-developer/answer/
   137997?hl=en&ref_topic=15867.
5. http://www.statista.com/topics/1002/mobile-app-usage/.

seamless upgrade (see Section 10.5). Many companies use free apps to build brand awareness and drive sales of other products and services (Fig. 10.7).

Free app	Functionality
Amazon® Mobile	Browse and purchase items on Amazon.
Bank of America	Locate ATMs and bank branches in your area, check balances and pay bills.
Best Buy®	Browse and purchase items.
CNN	Get the latest world news, receive breaking news alerts and watch live video.
Epicurious Recipe	View thousands of recipes from several Condé Nast magazines, including *Gourmet* and *Bon Appetit*.
ESPN® ScoreCenter	Set up personalized scoreboards to track your favorite college and professional sports teams.
NFL Mobile	Get the latest NFL news and updates, live programming, NFL Replay and more.
UPS® Mobile	Track shipments, find drop-off locations, get estimated shipping costs and more.
NYTimes	Read articles from *The New York Times*, free of charge.
Pocket Agent™	State Farm Insurance's app enables you contact an agent, file claims, find local repair centers, check your State Farm bank and mutual fund accounts and more.
Progressive® Insurance	Report a claim and submit photos from the scene of a car accident, find a local agent, get car safety information when you're shopping for a new car and more.
USA Today®	Read articles from *USA Today* and get the latest sports scores.
Wells Fargo® Mobile	Locate ATMs and bank branches in your area, check balances, make transfers and pay bills.
Women's Health Workouts Lite	View numerous workouts from one of the leading women's magazines.

Fig. 10.7 | Companies using free Android apps to build brand awareness.

10.4 Monetizing Apps with In-App Advertising

Many developers offer free apps monetized with **in-app advertising**—often banner ads similar to those you find on websites. Mobile advertising networks such as AdMob

        http://www.google.com/admob/

and Google AdSense for Mobile

        http://www.google.com/adsense/start/

aggregate advertisers for you and serve relevant ads to your app (see Section 10.13). You earn advertising revenue based on the number of click-throughs. The top 100 free apps might earn a few hundred dollars to a few thousand dollars per day. In-app advertising does not generate significant revenue for most apps, so if your goal is to recoup development costs and generate profits, you should consider charging a fee for your app.

10.5 Monetizing Apps: Using In-App Billing to Sell Virtual Goods

Google Play's **in-app billing** service

```
http://developer.android.com/google/play/billing/index.html
```

enables you to sell **virtual goods** (e.g., digital content) through apps on devices running Android 2.3 or higher (Fig. 10.8). The in-app billing service is available only for apps purchased through Google Play; it may *not* be used in apps sold through third-party app stores. To use in-app billing, you'll need a Google Play publisher account (see Section 10.6) and a Google Payments merchant account (see Section 10.7). Google pays you 70% of the revenue for all in-app purchases made through your apps.

Virtual goods		
Magazine e-subscriptions	Localized guides	Avatars
Virtual apparel	Additional game levels	Game scenery
Add-on features	Ringtones	Icons
E-cards	E-gifts	Virtual currency
Wallpapers	Images	Virtual pets
Audios	Videos	E-books and more

Fig. 10.8 | Virtual goods.

Selling virtual goods can generate higher revenue *per user* than in-app advertising.[6] Some apps that have been particularly successful selling virtual goods include Angry Birds, DragonVale, Zynga Poker, Bejeweled Blitz, NYTimes and Candy Crush Saga. Virtual goods are particularly popular in mobile games.

To implement in-app billing, follow the steps at

```
http://developer.android.com/google/play/billing/
    billing_integrate.html
```

For additional information about in-app billing, including subscriptions, sample apps, security best practices, testing and more, visit

```
http://developer.android.com/google/play/billing/
    billing_overview.html
```

You also can take the free *Selling In-app Products* training class at

```
http://developer.android.com/training/in-app-billing/index.html
```

---

6. http://www.businessinsider.com/its-morning-in-venture-capital-2012-5?utm_source=readme&utm_medium=rightrail&utm_term=&utm_content=6&utm_campaign=recirc.

In-App Purchase for Apps Sold Through Other App Marketplaces

If you choose to sell your apps through other marketplaces (see Section 10.11), several third-party mobile payment providers can enable you to build *in-app purchase* into your apps using APIs from mobile payment providers (Fig. 10.9)—you cannot use Google Play's in-app billing. Start by building the additional *locked functionality* (e.g., game levels, avatars) into your app. When the user opts to make a purchase, the in-app purchasing tool handles the financial transaction and returns a message to the app verifying payment. The app then unlocks the additional functionality.

Provider	URL	Description
PayPal Mobile Payments Library	`https://developer.paypal.com/webapps/developer/docs/classic/mobile/gs_MPL/`	Users click the **Pay with PayPal** button, log into their PayPal account, then click **Pay**.
Amazon In-App Purchasing	`https://developer.amazon.com/appsandservices/apis/earn/in-app-purchasing`	In-app purchase for apps sold through the Amazon App Store for Android.
Samsung In-App Purchase	`http://developer.samsung.com/in-app-purchase`	In-app purchase for apps designed specifically for Samsung devices.
Boku	`http://www.boku.com`	Users click **Pay by Mobile**, enter their mobile phone number, then complete the transaction by replying to a text message sent to their phone.

Fig. 10.9 | Mobile payment providers for in-app purchase.

10.6 Registering at Google Play

To publish your apps on Google Play, you must register for an account at

    http://play.google.com/apps/publish

There's a one-time $25 registration fee. Unlike other popular mobile platforms, *Google Play has no approval process for uploading apps*, though there is some automated malware testing. You must, however, adhere to the *Google Play Developer Program Policies*. If your app is in violation of these policies, it can be removed at any time; serious or repeated violations may result in account termination (Fig. 10.10).

Violations of the *Google Play Content Policy for Developers*	
• Infringing on others' intellectual property rights (e.g., trademarks, patents and copyrights). • Illegal activities.	• Invading personal privacy. • Interfering with the services of other parties. • Harming the user's device or personal data. • Gambling.

Fig. 10.10 | Some violations of the *Google Play Content Policy for Developers* (`http://play.google.com/about/developer-content-policy.html#showlanguages`). (Part 1 of 2.)

> ### Violations of the *Google Play Content Policy for Developers*
>
> - Creating a "spammy" user experience (e.g., misleading the user about the app's purpose).
> - Adversely impacting a user's service charges or a wireless carrier's network.
> - Impersonation or deception.
>
> - Promoting hate or violence.
> - Providing pornographic or obscene content, or anything unsuitable for children under age 18.
> - Ads in system-level notifications and widgets.

Fig. 10.10 | Some violations of the *Google Play Content Policy for Developers* (http:// play.google.com/about/developer-content-policy.html#showlanguages). (Part 2 of 2.)

10.7 Setting Up a Google Payments Merchant Account

To sell your apps on Google Play, you'll need a **Google Payments merchant account**, available to Google Play developers in over 150 countries.[7] Once you've registered and logged into Google Play at

> http://play.google.com/apps/publish/

click the **set up a merchant account** link and provide

- information by which Google can contact you and
- customer-support contact information where users can contact you.

10.8 Uploading Your Apps to Google Play

Once you've prepared your files and you're ready to upload your app, review the steps in the *Launch Checklist* at:

> http://developer.android.com/distribute/tools/launch-checklist.html

Then log into Google Play at http://play.google.com/apps/publish (Section 10.6) and click the **Publish an Android App on Google Play** button to begin the upload process. You will be asked to upload the following assets:

1. *App .apk file* that includes the app's code files, assets, resources and the manifest file.
2. At least *two screenshots* of your app to be included in Google Play. You may include screenshots for an Android phone, 7" tablet, 10" tablet, Android TV and Android Wear.
3. *High-resolution app icon* (512-by-512 pixels) to be included in Google Play.
4. *Feature graphic* is used by the Google Play Editorial team to promote apps and on your app's product page. This image must be 1024 pixels wide by 500 pixels tall in JPEG format or 24-bit PNG format with no alpha (transparency).
5. *Promotional graphic* (optional) for Google Play to be used by Google if they decide to promote your app (for examples, check out some of the graphics for fea-

---

7. http://support.google.com/googleplay/android-developer/answer/150324?hl=en&ref_topic=15867.

tured apps on Google Play). The graphic must be 180 pixels wide by 120 pixels tall in JPEG format or 24-bit PNG format with no alpha (transparency).

6. *Promotional video* (optional) to be included in Google Play. You may include a URL for a promotional video for your app (e.g., a YouTube link to a video that demonstrates how your app works).

In addition to app assets, you will be asked to provide the following additional listing details for Google Play:

1. *Language.* By default, your app will be listed in English. If you'd like to list it in additional languages, select them from the list provided (Fig. 10.11).

Language			
Afrikaans	English (UK)	Khmer	Romansh
Amharic	Estonian	Korean (South)	Russian
Arabic	Filipino	Kyrgyz	Serbian
Armenian	Finnish	Lao	Sinhala
Azerbaijani	French	Latvian	Slovak
Basque	French (Canada)	Lithuanian	Slovenian
Belarusian	Galician	Macedonian	Spanish (Latin America)
Bengali	Georgian	Malay	Spanish (Spain)
Bulgarian	German	Malayalam	Spanish (US)
Burmese	Greek	Marathi	Swahili
Catalan	Hebrew	Mongolian	Swedish
Chinese (Simplified)	Hindi	Nepali	Tamil
Chinese (Traditional)	Hungarian	Norwegian	Telugu
Croatian	Icelandic	Persian	Thai
Czech	Indonesian	Polish	Turkish
Danish	Italian	Portuguese (Brazil)	Ukrainian
Dutch	Japanese	Portuguese (Portugal)	Vietnamese
English	Kannada	Romanian	Zulu

Fig. 10.11 | Languages for listing apps in Google Play.

2. *Title.* The title of your app as it will appear in Google Play (30 characters maximum). It does *not* need to be unique among all Android apps.

3. *Short description.* A short description of your app (80 characters maximum).

4. *Description.* A description of your app and its features (4,000 characters maximum). It's recommended that you use the last portion of the description to explain why the app requires each permission and how it's used.

5. *Recent changes.* A walkthrough of any changes specific to the latest version of your app (500 characters maximum).

6. *Promo text.* The promotional text for marketing your app (80 characters max).

7. *Application type.* Choose **Applications** or **Games**.

8. *Category.* Select the category that best suits your game or app.

9. *Price.* To sell your app for a fee, you'll need to set up a merchant account.

10. *Content rating.* You may select **High Maturity**, **Medium Maturity**, **Low Maturity** or **Everyone**. For more information, see *Rating your application content for Google Play* at

```
http://support.google.com/googleplay/android-developer/answer/
188189
```

11. *Locations.* By default, the app will be listed in all current and future Google Play countries. If you do not want your app to be available in all these countries, you may pick and choose specific ones where you'd like your app to be listed.

12. *Website.* A **Visit Developer's Website** link will be included in your app's listing in Google Play. Provide a direct link to the page on your website where users interested in downloading your app can find more information, including marketing copy, feature listings, additional screenshots, instructions, etc.

13. *E-mail.* Your e-mail address will also be included in Google Play, so that customers can contact you with questions, report errors, etc.

14. *Phone number.* Sometimes your phone number is included in Google Play. Therefore it's recommended that you leave this field blank unless you provide phone support. You may want to provide a customer-service phone number on your website.

15. *Privacy policy.* A link to your privacy policy.

In addition, if you sell in-app products or use any Google services, you must add your in-app products and specify the services you use. For information on adding in-app products, visit

```
http://developer.android.com/google/play/billing/billing_admin.html
```

10.9 Launching Play Store from Within Your App

To drive additional sales of your apps, you can launch the **Play Store** app (Google Play) from within your app (typically by including a button) so that the user can download other apps you've published or purchase a related app with functionality beyond that of the previously downloaded "lite" version. You also can launch the **Play Store** app to enable users to download the latest updates.

There are two ways to launch the **Play Store** app. First, you can bring up Google Play search results for apps with a specific developer name, package name or string of characters. For example, if you want to encourage users to download other apps you've published, you could include a button in your app that, when touched, launches the **Play Store** app and initiates a search for apps containing your name or company name. The second option is to bring the user to the details page in the **Play Store** app for a specific app. To learn about launching **Play Store** from within an app, see *Linking Your Products* at

```
http://developer.android.com/distribute/tools/promote/linking.html
```

10.10 Managing Your Apps in Google Play

The *Google Play Developer Console* allows you to manage your account and your apps, check users' star ratings for your apps (1 to 5 stars), respond to users' comments, track the overall number of installs of each app and the number of active installs (installs minus uninstalls). You can view installation trends and the distribution of app downloads across Android versions, devices, and more. Crash reports list any crash and freeze information from users. If you've made upgrades to your app, you can easily publish the new version. You can remove the app from Google Play, but users who downloaded it previously may keep it on their devices. Users who uninstalled the app will be able to reinstall it even after it's been removed (it will remain on Google's servers unless it's removed for violating the Terms of Service).

10.11 Other Android App Marketplaces

You may choose to make your apps available through other Android app marketplaces (Fig. 10.12), or through your own website using services such as AndroidLicenser (`http://www.androidlicenser.com`). To learn more about releasing your app through a website see

```
http://developer.android.com/tools/publishing/
    publishing_overview.html
```

Marketplace	URL
Amazon Appstore	`https://developer.amazon.com/public/solutions/platforms/android`
Opera Mobile Store	`http://android.oms.apps.opera.com/en_us/`
Moborobo	`http://www.moborobo.com`
Appitalism®	`http://www.appitalism.com/index.html`
GetJar	`http://www.getjar.com`
SlideMe	`http://www.slideme.org`
AndroidPIT	`http://www.androidpit.com`

Fig. 10.12 | Other Android app marketplaces.

10.12 Other Mobile App Platforms and Porting Your Apps

According to `statista.com`, users will download approximately 225 billion apps in 2016 and almost 270 billion in 2017.[8] By porting your Android apps to other mobile app platforms (Fig. 10.13), especially to iOS (for iPhone, iPad and iPod Touch devices), you could reach an even bigger audience. There are various tools to help you port your apps. For example, Microsoft provides tools that iOS and Android developers can use to port apps to Windows, and similar tools exist for porting Android apps to iOS and vice versa.[9] Various cross-platform app-development tools are also available (Fig. 10.14).

---

8. `http://www.statista.com/statistics/266488/forecast-of-mobile-app-downloads/`.
9. `http://www.wired.com/2015/04/microsoft-unveils-tools-moving-android-ios-apps-onto-windows/`.

Platform	URL
Android	http://developer.android.com
iOS (Apple)	http://developer.apple.com/ios
Windows	https://dev.windows.com/en-us/windows-apps

Fig. 10.13 | Popular mobile app platforms.

Tool	Website
Appcelerator Titanium	http://www.appcelerator.com/product/
PhoneGap	http://phonegap.com/
Sencha	https://www.sencha.com/
Visual Studio	https://www.visualstudio.com/en-us/features/mobile-app-development-vs.aspx
Xamarin	https://xamarin.com/

Fig. 10.14 | Several tools for developing cross-platform mobile apps—there are many more.

10.13 Marketing Your Apps

Once your app has been published, you'll want to market it to your audience.[10] *Viral marketing* through social media sites such as Facebook, Twitter, Google+ and YouTube can help you get your message out. These sites have tremendous visibility. According to a Pew Research Center study, 71% of adults on the Internet use social networks.[11] Figure 10.15 lists some of the most popular social media sites. Also, e-mail and electronic newsletters are still effective and often inexpensive marketing tools.

Name	URL	Description
Facebook	http://www.facebook.com	Social networking
Instagram	https://instagram.com/	Photo and video sharing
Twitter	http://www.twitter.com	Microblogging, social networking
Google+	http://plus.google.com	Social networking
Vine	http://vine.co	Social video sharing
Tumblr	http://www.tumblr.com	Blogging
Groupon	http://www.groupon.com	Daily deals

Fig. 10.15 | Popular social media sites. (Part 1 of 2.)

10. There are many books about mobile app marketing. Check out the latest ones at http://amzn.to/1ZgpYxZ.
11. http://bits.blogs.nytimes.com/2015/01/09/americans-use-more-online-social-networks/?_r=0.

Name	URL	Description
Foursquare	http://www.foursquare.com	Check-in
Snapchat	http://www.snapchat.com	Video messaging
Pinterest	http://www.pinterest.com	Online pinboard
YouTube	http://www.youtube.com	Video sharing
LinkedIn	http://www.linkedin.com	Social networking for business
Flickr	http://www.flickr.com	Photo sharing

Fig. 10.15 | Popular social media sites. (Part 2 of 2.)

Facebook

Facebook, the premier social networking site, has nearly 1.5 billion active users[12] with almost one billion active daily.[13] It's an excellent resource for *viral marketing*. Start by setting up an official Facebook page for your app or business. Use the page to post app information, news, updates, reviews, tips, videos, screenshots, high scores for games, user feedback and links to Google Play, where users can download your app. For example, we post news and updates about Deitel publications on our Facebook page at http://www.facebook.com/DeitelFan.

Next, you need to spread the word. Encourage your co-workers and friends to "like" your Facebook page and ask their friends to do so as well. As people interact with your page, stories will appear in their friends' news feeds, building awareness to a growing audience.

Twitter

Twitter is a microblogging, social networking site with approximately 1 billion users and 316 million monthly active users.[14] You post tweets—messages of 140 characters or less. Twitter then distributes your tweets to all of your followers (at the time of this writing, one famous pop star had over 40 million followers). Many people use Twitter to track news and trends. Tweet about your app—include announcements about new releases, tips, facts, comments from users, etc. Also, encourage your colleagues and friends to tweet about your app. Use a *hashtag* (#) to reference your app. For example, when tweeting about *Android How to Program* on our @deitel Twitter feed, we use the hashtag #AndroidHTP. Others may use this hashtag as well to write comments about the book. This enables you to easily search tweets for related messages.

Viral Video

Viral video—shared on video sites (e.g., YouTube), on social networking sites (e.g., Facebook, Instagram, Twitter, Google+), through e-mail, etc.—is another great way to spread the word about your app. If you create a compelling video, perhaps one that's humorous or even outrageous, it may quickly rise in popularity and may be tagged by users across multiple social networks.

---

12. http://www.statista.com/statistics/272014/global-social-networks-ranked-by-number-of-users/.
13. http://expandedramblings.com/index.php/by-the-numbers-17-amazing-facebook-stats/.
14. http://www.statisticbrain.com/twitter-statistics/.

E-Mail Newsletters

If you have an e-mail newsletter, use it to promote your app. Include links to Google Play, where users can download the app. Also include links to your social networking pages, where users can stay up-to-date with the latest news about your app.

App Reviews

Contact influential bloggers and app review sites (Fig. 10.16) and tell them about your app. Provide them with a promotional code to download your app for free (see Section 10.3). Influential bloggers and reviewers receive many requests, so keep yours concise and informative. Many app reviewers post video app reviews on YouTube and other sites (Fig. 10.17).

Android app review site	URL
Appolicious™	http://www.androidapps.com
AppBrain	http://www.appbrain.com
AppZoom	http://www.appzoom.com
Appstorm	http://android.appstorm.net
Best Android Apps Review	http://www.bestandroidappsreview.com
Android App Review Source	http://www.androidappreviewsource.com
Androinica	http://www.androinica.com
AndroidLib	http://www.androlib.com
Android and Me	http://www.androidandme.com
AndroidGuys	http://www.androidguys.com/category/reviews
Android Police	http://www.androidpolice.com
AndroidPIT	http://www.androidpit.com
Phandroid	http://phandroid.com

Fig. 10.16 | Android app review sites.

Android app review video site	URL
State of Tech	http://http://stateoftech.net/
Crazy Mike's Apps	http://crazymikesapps.com
Appolicious™	http://www.appvee.com/?device_filter=android
Life of Android™	http://www.lifeofandroid.com/video/

Fig. 10.17 | Android app review video sites.

Internet Public Relations

The public relations industry uses media outlets to help companies get their message out to consumers. Public relations practitioners incorporate blogs, tweets, podcasts, RSS feeds and social media into their PR campaigns. Figure 10.18 lists some free and fee-based Internet public relations resources, including press-release distribution sites, press-release writing services and more.

Internet public relations resource	URL	Description
Free Services		
PRWeb®	http://www.prweb.com	Online press-release distribution service with *free* and *fee-based* services.
ClickPress™	http://www.clickpress.com	Submit news stories for approval (*free* of charge). If approved, they'll be available on the ClickPress site and to news search engines. For a *fee*, ClickPress will distribute your press releases globally to top financial newswires.
PRLog	http://www.prlog.org/pub/	*Free* press-release submission and distribution.
Newswire	http://www.newswire.com	*Free* and *fee-based* press-release submission and distribution.
openPR®	http://www.openpr.com	*Free* press-release publication.
Fee-Based Services		
PR Leap	http://www.prleap.com	Online press-release distribution service.
Marketwired	http://www.marketwired.com	Press-release distribution service allows you to target your audience by geography, industry, etc.
Mobility PR	http://www.mobilitypr.com	Public relations services for companies in the mobile industry.
eReleases	http://www.ereleases.com	Press-release distribution and services including press-release writing, proofreading and editing. Check out the tips for writing effective press releases.

Fig. 10.18 | Internet public relations resources.

Mobile Advertising Networks

Purchasing advertising spots (e.g., in other apps, online, in newspapers and magazines or on radio and television) is another way to market your app. Mobile advertising networks (Fig. 10.19) specialize in advertising Android (and other) mobile apps on mobile platforms. Many of these networks can target audiences by location, wireless carrier, platform (e.g., Android, iOS, Windows, BlackBerry) and more. Most apps don't make much money, so be careful how much you spend on advertising.

Mobile ad networks	URL
AdMob (by Google)	http://www.google.com/admob/
Medialets	http://www.medialets.com
Tapjoy®	http://www.tapjoy.com
Millennial Media®	http://www.millennialmedia.com/
Smaato®	http://www.smaato.com
mMedia™	http://mmedia.com
InMobi™	http://www.inmobi.com

Fig. 10.19 | Mobile advertising networks.

You also can use mobile advertising networks to monetize your free apps by including ads (e.g., banners, videos) in your apps. The average eCPM (effective cost per 1,000 impressions) for ads in Android apps varies by network, device, world region, etc. Most ads on Android pay are based on the *click-through rate* (*CTR*) of the ads rather than the number of impressions generated. Like eCPM, CTRs vary based on the app, the device, targeting of the ads by the ad network and more. If your app has a lot of users and the CTRs of the ads in your apps are high, you may earn substantial advertising revenue. Also, your ad network may serve you higher-paying ads, thus increasing your earnings.

10.14 Wrap-Up

In this chapter, we walked through the process of registering for Google Play and setting up a Google Wallet account so you can sell your apps. We discussed how to prepare apps for submission to Google Play, including testing them on the emulator and on Android devices, and the various resources you'll need to submit your app to Google Play. We walked through the steps for uploading your apps to Google Play. We showed you alternative Android app marketplaces. We provided tips for pricing your apps, and resources for monetizing them with in-app advertising and in-app sales of virtual goods. And we included resources for marketing your apps, once they're available through Google Play.

Staying in Contact with the Authors and Deitel & Associates, Inc.

We hope you enjoyed reading *Android How to Program, 3/e* as much as we enjoyed writing it. We'd appreciate your feedback. Please send your questions, comments and suggestions to deitel@deitel.com. To stay up-to-date with the latest news about *Android How to Program*, and Deitel publications and corporate training, sign up for the *Deitel® Buzz Online* e-mail newsletter at

> http://www.deitel.com/newsletter/subscribe.html

and follow us on social media at

- Facebook—http://facebook.com/DeitelFan
- Twitter—http://twitter.com/deitel
- Google+—http://google.com/+DeitelFan

- YouTube—http://youtube.com/DeitelTV
- LinkedIn—http://bit.ly/DeitelLinkedIn

To learn more about Deitel & Associates' worldwide on-site programming training for your company or organization, visit

> http://www.deitel.com/training

or e-mail deitel@deitel.com. Good luck!

Self-Review Exercises

10.1 Fill in the blanks in each of the following statements:
- a) To sell your apps on Google Play, you'll need a(n) _____ merchant account.
- b) Before uploading your app to a device, to Google Play or to other app marketplaces, you must digitally sign the .apk file (Android app package file) using a(n) _____ that identifies you as the author of the app.
- c) The Google Play _____ allows you to manage your account and your apps, check users' star ratings for your apps (0 to 5 stars), track the overall number of installs of each app and the number of active installs (installs minus uninstalls).

10.2 State whether each of the following is *true* or *false*. If *false*, explain why.
- a) When an app works perfectly using the emulator on your computer, it will run on your Android device.
- b) You might use a licensing policy to limit how often the app checks in with the server, how many simultaneous device installs are allowed, and what happens when an unlicensed app is identified.
- c) The title of your app as it will appear in Google Play must be unique among all Android apps.
- d) Selling virtual goods can generate higher revenue per user than in-app advertising.
- e) If you choose to sell your apps through other app marketplaces, several third-party mobile payment providers can enable you to build in-app purchase into your apps using APIs from mobile payment providers.

Answers to Self-Review Exercises

10.1 a) Google Payments. b) digital certificate. c) Developer Console.

10.2 a) False. Although the app might work perfectly using the emulator on your computer, problems could arise when running it on a particular Android device. b) True. c) False. The title of your app as it will appear in Google Play does *not* need to be unique among all Android apps. d) True. e) True.

Exercises

10.3 Fill in the blanks in each of the following statements:
- a) _____ are displays of timely information on the user's **Home** screen, such as the current weather, stock prices and news.
- b) A(n) _____ is an agreement through which you license your software to the user. It typically stipulates terms of use, limitations on redistribution and reverse engineering, product liability, compliance with applicable laws and more.
- c) The _____ helps you debug your apps running on actual devices.

    d) The Google Play _____ allows you to limit how many simultaneous device installs are allowed.

    e) You can use the _____ to obtain a screen capture of your running app.

10.4   State whether each of the following is *true* or *false*. If *false*, explain why.

    a) You should "obfuscate" any apps you upload to Google Play to encourage reverse engineering of your code.

    b) There are more paid apps than free apps on Google Play, and they comprise the vast majority of downloads.

    c) Your app's version name is shown to the users, and the version code is an integer version number used internally by Google Play.

    d) Eclipse automatically digitally signs your app for publishing to Google Play.

    e) Google assigns a content rating to your app.

Introduction to Java Applications

Objectives

In this appendix you'll learn:

- To write simple Java applications.
- To use input and output statements.
- Java's primitive types.
- Basic memory concepts.
- To use arithmetic operators.
- The precedence of arithmetic operators.
- To write decision-making statements.
- To use relational and equality operators.

A.1 Introduction

This appendix introduces Java application programming. You'll use tools from the JDK to compile and run programs. At www.deitel.com/books/AndroidHTP3/, we've posted videos to help you get started with several popular integrated development environments (IDEs). The Android part of this book uses the Android Studio IDE, which is based on IntelliJ® IDEA.

A.2 Your First Program in Java: Printing a Line of Text

A Java **application** is a computer program that executes when you use the **java command** to launch the Java Virtual Machine (JVM). First we consider a simple application that displays a line of text. Figure A.1 shows the program followed by a box that displays its output.

```
1   // Fig. A.1: Welcome1.java
2   // Text-printing program.
3
4   public class Welcome1
5   {
6      // main method begins execution of Java application
7      public static void main( String[] args )
8      {
9         System.out.println( "Welcome to Java Programming!" );
10     } // end method main
11  } // end class Welcome1
```

```
Welcome to Java Programming!
```

Fig. A.1 | Text-printing program.

Commenting Your Programs

We insert **comments** to **document programs** and improve their readability. The Java compiler ignores comments, so they do *not* cause the computer to perform any action when the program is run.

The comment in line 1

```
// Fig. A.1: Welcome1.java
```

begins with **//**, indicating that it is an **end-of-line comment**—it terminates at the end of the line on which the **//** appears. Line 2 is a comment that describes the purpose of the program.

Java also has **traditional comments**, which can be spread over several lines as in

```
/* This is a traditional comment. It
   can be split over multiple lines */
```

These begin and end with delimiters, **/*** and ***/**. The compiler ignores all text between the delimiters.

Common Programming Error A.1

*A syntax error occurs when the compiler encounters code that violates Java's language rules (i.e., its syntax). Syntax errors are also called **compilation errors**, because the compiler detects them during the compilation phase. The compiler responds by issuing an error message and preventing your program from compiling.*

Using Blank Lines

Line 3 is a blank line. Blank lines, space characters and tabs make programs easier to read. Together, they're known as **white space** (or whitespace). The compiler ignores white space.

Declaring a Class

Line 4 begins a **class declaration** for class Welcome1. Every Java program consists of at least one class that you (the programmer) define. The **class keyword** introduces a class declaration and is immediately followed by the **class name** (Welcome1). **Keywords** are reserved for use by Java and are always spelled with all lowercase letters. The complete list of keywords can be viewed at:

    http://bit.ly/JavaKeywords

Class Names and Identifiers

By convention, class names begin with a capital letter and capitalize the first letter of each word they include (e.g., SampleClassName). A class name is an **identifier**—a series of characters consisting of letters, digits, underscores (_) and dollar signs ($) that does not begin with a digit and does not contain spaces. The name 7button is not a valid identifier because it begins with a digit, and the name input field is not a valid identifier because it contains a space. Java is **case sensitive**—uppercase and lowercase letters are distinct—so value and Value are different identifiers.

In Appendices A–E, every class we define begins with the keyword **public**. For our application, the file name is Welcome1.java.

Common Programming Error A.2

A public class must be placed in a file that has the same name as the class (in terms of both spelling and capitalization) plus the .java extension; otherwise, a compilation error occurs. For example, public class Welcome must be placed in a file named Welcome.java.

A **left brace** (as in line 5), **{**, begins the **body** of every class declaration. A corresponding **right brace**, **}**, must end each class declaration.

Good Programming Practice A.1

Indent the entire body of each class declaration one "level" between the left brace and the right brace that delimit the body of the class. We recommend using three spaces to form a level of indent. This format emphasizes the class declaration's structure and makes it easier to read.

Declaring a Method

Line 6 is an end-of-line comment indicating the purpose of lines 7–10 of the program. Line 7 is the starting point of every Java application. The **parentheses** after the identifier main indicate that it's a program building block called a **method**. For a Java application, one of the methods *must* be called main and must be defined as shown in line 7. Methods perform tasks and can return information when they complete their tasks. Keyword **void** indicates that this method will *not* return any information. In line 7, the String[] args in parentheses is a required part of the method main's declaration—we discuss this in Appendix E.

The left brace in line 8 begins the **body of the method declaration**. A corresponding right brace must end it (line 10).

Performing Output with System.out.println

Line 9 instructs the computer to perform an action—namely, to print the **string** of characters contained between the double quotation marks (but not the quotation marks themselves). A string is sometimes called a **character string** or a **string literal**. White-space characters in strings are *not* ignored by the compiler. Strings cannot span multiple lines of code.

The **System.out** object is known as the **standard output object**. It allows a Java applications to display information in the **command window** from which it executes. In recent versions of Microsoft Windows, the command window is the **Command Prompt**. In UNIX/Linux/Mac OS X, the command window is called a **terminal window** or a **shell**. Many programmers call it simply the **command line**.

Method **System.out.println** displays (or prints) a line of text in the command window. The string in the parentheses in line 9 is the **argument** to the method. When System.out.println completes its task, it positions the cursor (the location where the next character will be displayed) at the beginning of the next line in the command window.

The entire line 9, including System.out.println, the argument "Welcome to Java Programming!" in the parentheses and the **semicolon** (;), is called a **statement**. Most statements end with a semicolon. When the statement in line 9 executes, it displays Welcome to Java Programming! in the command window.

Using End-of-Line Comments on Right Braces for Readability

We include an end-of-line comment after a closing brace that ends a method declaration and after a closing brace that ends a class declaration. For example, line 10 indicates the closing brace of method main, and line 11 indicates the closing brace of class Welcome1.

Compiling and Executing Your First Java Application

We assume you're using the Java Development Kit's command-line tools, not an IDE. As we mentioned previously, we've posted videos at www.deitel.com/books/AndroidHTP3/ to help you get started with several popular IDEs.

To prepare to compile the program, open a command window and change to the directory where the program is stored. Many operating systems use the command cd to change directories. On Windows, for example,

```
cd c:\examples\appA\figA_01
```

changes to the figA_01 directory. On UNIX/Linux/Max OS X, the command

```
cd ~/examples/appA/figA_01
```

changes to the figA_01 directory.

To compile the program, type

```
javac Welcome1.java
```

If the program contains no syntax errors, this command creates a new file called Welcome1.class (known as the **class file** for Welcome1) containing the platform-independent Java bytecodes that represent our application. When we use the java command to execute the application on a given platform, the JVM will translate these bytecodes into instructions that are understood by the underlying operating system and hardware.

Error-Prevention Tip A.1

When attempting to compile a program, if you receive a message such as "bad command or filename," *"*javac: command not found*" or "'*javac' is not recognized as an internal or external command, operable program or batch file,*" then your Java software installation was not completed properly. If you're using the JDK, this indicates that the system's* PATH *environment variable was not set properly. Please carefully review the installation instructions in the Before You Begin section of this book. On some systems, after correcting the* PATH, *you may need to reboot your computer or open a new command window for these settings to take effect.*

Figure A.2 shows the program of Fig. A.1 executing in a Microsoft® Windows® 7 **Command Prompt** window. To execute the program, type java Welcome1. This command launches the JVM, which loads the .class file for class Welcome1. The command omits the .class file-name extension; otherwise, the JVM will not execute the program. The JVM calls method main. Next, the statement at line 9 of main displays "Welcome to Java Programming!"

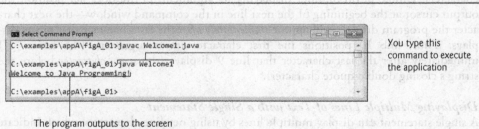

The program outputs to the screen
Welcome to Java Programming!

You type this command to execute the application

Fig. A.2 | Executing Welcome1 from the **Command Prompt**.

Error-Prevention Tip A.2

When attempting to run a Java program, if you receive a message such as "Exception in thread "main" java.lang.NoClassDefFoundError: Welcome1," your CLASSPATH environment variable has not been set properly. Please carefully review the installation instructions in the Before You Begin section of this book. On some systems, you may need to reboot your computer or open a new command window after configuring the CLASSPATH.

A.3 Modifying Your First Java Program

Welcome to Java Programming! can be displayed several ways. Class Welcome2, shown in Fig. A.3, uses two statements (lines 9–10) to produce the output shown in Fig. A.1.

```
1   // Fig. A.3: Welcome2.java
2   // Printing a line of text with multiple statements.
3
4   public class Welcome2
5   {
6      // main method begins execution of Java application
7      public static void main( String[] args )
8      {
9         System.out.print( "Welcome to " );
10        System.out.println( "Java Programming!" );
11     } // end method main
12  } // end class Welcome2
```

```
Welcome to Java Programming!
```

Fig. A.3 | Printing a line of text with multiple statements.

The program is similar to Fig. A.1, so we discuss only the changes here. Line 2 is a comment stating the purpose of the program. Line 4 begins the Welcome2 class declaration. Lines 9–10 of method main display one line of text. The first statement uses System.out's method print to display a string. Each print or println statement resumes displaying characters from where the last print or println statement stopped displaying characters. Unlike println, after displaying its argument, print does *not* position the output cursor at the beginning of the next line in the command window—the next character the program displays will appear *immediately after* the last character that print displays. Thus, line 10 positions the first character in its argument (the letter "J") immediately after the last character that line 9 displays (the *space character* before the string's closing double-quote character).

Displaying Multiple Lines of Text with a Single Statement

A single statement can display multiple lines by using **newline characters**, which indicate to System.out's print and println methods when to position the output cursor at the beginning of the next line in the command window. Like blank lines, space characters and tab characters, newline characters are white-space characters. The program in Fig. A.4 outputs four lines of text, using newline characters to determine when to begin each new line.

```
 1   // Fig. A.4: Welcome3.java
 2   // Printing multiple lines of text with a single statement.
 3
 4   public class Welcome3
 5   {
 6      // main method begins execution of Java application
 7      public static void main( String[] args )
 8      {
 9         System.out.println( "Welcome\nto\nJava\nProgramming!" );
10      } // end method main
11   } // end class Welcome3
```

```
Welcome
to
Java
Programming!
```

Fig. A.4 | Printing multiple lines of text with a single statement.

Line 2 is a comment stating the program's purpose. Line 4 begins the Welcome3 class declaration. Line 9 displays four separate lines of text in the command window. Normally, the characters in a string are displayed *exactly* as they appear in the double quotes. Note, however, that the paired characters \ and n (repeated three times in the statement) do not appear on the screen. The **backslash** (\) is an **escape character**. which has special meaning to System.out's print and println methods. When a backslash appears in a string, Java combines it with the next character to form an **escape sequence**. The escape sequence \n represents the newline character. When a newline character appears in a string being output with System.out, the newline character causes the screen's output cursor to move to the beginning of the next line in the command window.

Figure A.5 lists several common escape sequences and describes how they affect the display of characters in the command window.

Escape sequence	Description
\n	Newline. Position the screen cursor at the beginning of the next line.
\t	Horizontal tab. Move the screen cursor to the next tab stop.
\r	Carriage return. Position the screen cursor at the beginning of the current line—do *not* advance to the next line. Any characters output after the carriage return overwrite the characters previously output on that line.
\\	Backslash. Used to print a backslash character.
\"	Double quote. Used to print a double-quote character. For example, `System.out.println( "\"in quotes\"" );` displays "in quotes".

Fig. A.5 | Some common escape sequences.

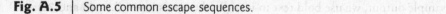

A.4 Displaying Text with `printf`

The **System.out.printf** method displays formatted data. Figure A.6 uses this method to output the strings "Welcome to" and "Java Programming!". Lines 9–10 call method Sys-tem.out.printf to display the program's output. The method call specifies three arguments—they're placed in a **comma-separated list**.

```
 1   // Fig. A.6: Welcome4.java
 2   // Displaying multiple lines with method System.out.printf.
 3
 4   public class Welcome4
 5   {
 6      // main method begins execution of Java application
 7      public static void main( String[] args )
 8      {
 9         System.out.printf( "%s\n%s\n",
10            "Welcome to", "Java Programming!" );
11      } // end method main
12   } // end class Welcome4
```

```
Welcome to
Java Programming!
```

Fig. A.6 | Displaying multiple lines with method `System.out.printf`.

Lines 9–10 represent only *one* statement. Java allows large statements to be split over many lines. We indent line 10 to indicate that it's a *continuation* of line 9.

Method printf's first argument is a **format string** that may consist of **fixed text** and **format specifiers**. Fixed text is output by printf just as it would be by print or println. Each format specifier is a placeholder for a value and specifies the type of data to output. Format specifiers also may include optional formatting information.

Format specifiers begin with a percent sign (%) followed by a character that represents the data type. For example, the format specifier **%s** is a placeholder for a string. The format string in line 9 specifies that printf should output two strings, each followed by a newline character. At the first format specifier's position, printf substitutes the value of the first argument after the format string. At each subsequent format specifier's position, printf substitutes the value of the next argument. So this example substitutes "Welcome to" for the first %s and "Java Programming!" for the second %s. The output shows that two lines of text are displayed.

A.5 Another Application: Adding Integers

Our next application reads (or inputs) two **integers** (whole numbers, such as –22, 7, 0 and 1024) typed by a user at the keyboard, computes their sum and displays it. Programs remember numbers and other data in the computer's memory and access that data through program elements called **variables**. The program of Fig. A.7 demonstrates these concepts. In the sample output, we use bold text to identify the user's input (i.e., **45** and **72**).

```
1    // Fig. A.7: Addition.java
2    // Addition program that displays the sum of two numbers.
3    import java.util.Scanner; // program uses class Scanner
4
5    public class Addition
6    {
7       // main method begins execution of Java application
8       public static void main( String[] args )
9       {
10          // create a Scanner to obtain input from the command window
11          Scanner input = new Scanner( System.in );
12
13          int number1; // first number to add
14          int number2; // second number to add
15          int sum; // sum of number1 and number2
16
17          System.out.print( "Enter first integer: " ); // prompt
18          number1 = input.nextInt(); // read first number from user
19
20          System.out.print( "Enter second integer: " ); // prompt
21          number2 = input.nextInt(); // read second number from user
22
23          sum = number1 + number2; // add numbers, then store total in sum
24
25          System.out.printf( "Sum is %d\n", sum ); // display sum
26       } // end method main
27    } // end class Addition
```

```
Enter first integer: 45
Enter second integer: 72
Sum is 117
```

Fig. A.7 | Addition program that displays the sum of two numbers.

Import Declarations

Lines 1–2 state the figure number, file name and purpose of the program. A great strength of Java is its rich set of predefined classes that you can *reuse* rather than "reinventing the wheel." These classes are grouped into **packages**—named groups of related classes—and are collectively referred to as the **Java class library**, or the **Java Application Programming Interface (Java API)**. Line 3 is an **import declaration** that helps the compiler locate a class that's used in this program. It indicates that this example uses Java's predefined Scanner class (discussed shortly) from package **java.util**.

Declaring Class Addition

Line 5 begins the declaration of class Addition. The file name for this public class must be Addition.java. Remember that the body of each class declaration starts with an opening left brace (line 6) and ends with a closing right brace (line 27).

The application begins execution with the main method (lines 8–26). The left brace (line 9) marks the beginning of method main's body, and the corresponding right brace (line 26) marks its end. Method main is indented one level in the body of class Addition, and the code in the body of main is indented another level for readability.

*Declaring and Creating a **Scanner** to Obtain User Input from the Keyboard*

A **variable** is a location in the computer's memory where a value can be stored for use later in a program. All Java variables *must* be declared with a **name** and a **type** *before* they can be used. A variable's name enables the program to access the value of the variable in memory. A variable's name can be any valid identifier. A variable's type specifies what kind of information is stored at that location in memory. Like other statements, declaration statements end with a semicolon (;).

Line 11 is a **variable declaration statement** that specifies the name (input) and type (Scanner) of a variable that's used in this program. A **Scanner** enables a program to read data (e.g., numbers and strings) for use in a program. The data can come from many sources, such as the user at the keyboard or a file on disk. Before using a Scanner, you must create it and specify the source of the data.

The = in line 11 indicates that Scanner variable input should be **initialized** (i.e., prepared for use in the program) in its declaration with the result of the expression to the right of the equals sign—new Scanner(System.in). This expression uses the **new** keyword to create a Scanner object that reads characters typed by the user at the keyboard. The **standard input object, System.in**, enables applications to read bytes of information typed by the user. The Scanner translates these bytes into types (like ints) that can be used in a program.

Declaring Variables to Store Integers

The variable declaration statements in lines 13–15 declare that variables number1, number2 and sum hold data of type **int**—that is, integer values (whole numbers such as 72, –1127 and 0). These variables are not yet initialized. The range of values for an int is –2,147,483,648 to +2,147,483,647. [*Note:* Actual int values may not contain commas.]

Other data types include **float** and **double**, for holding real numbers (such as 3.4, 0.0 and –11.19), and **char**, for holding character data. Variables of type char represent individual characters, such as an uppercase letter (e.g., A), a digit (e.g., 7), a special character (e.g., * or %) or an escape sequence (e.g., the newline character, \n). The types int, float, double and char are called **primitive types**. Primitive-type names are keywords and must appear in all lowercase letters. Appendix L summarizes the characteristics of the eight primitive types (boolean, byte, char, short, int, long, float and double).

Good Programming Practice A.2

By convention, variable-name identifiers begin with a lowercase letter, and every word in the name after the first word begins with a capital letter.

Prompting the User for Input

Line 17 uses System.out.print to display the message "Enter first integer: ". This message is called a **prompt** because it directs the user to take a specific action. We use method print here rather than println so that the user's input appears on the same line as the prompt. Recall from Section A.2 that identifiers starting with capital letters typically represent class names. So, System is a class. Class System is part of package **java.lang**. Class System is not imported with an import declaration at the beginning of the program.

Software Engineering Observation A.1

By default, package java.lang is imported in every Java program; thus, classes in java.lang are the only ones in the Java API that do not require an import declaration.

Obtaining an `int` as Input from the User

Line 18 uses Scanner object input's nextInt method to obtain an integer from the user at the keyboard. At this point the program waits for the user to type the number and press the *Enter* key to submit the number to the program.

Our program assumes that the user enters a valid integer value. If not, a runtime logic error will occur and the program will terminate. Appendix H discusses how to make your programs more robust by enabling them to handle such errors—this makes your program more *fault tolerant*.

In line 18, we place the result of the call to method nextInt (an int value) in variable number1 by using the **assignment operator**, =. The statement is read as "number1 gets the value of input.nextInt()." Operator = is called a **binary operator**, because it has two **operands**—number1 and the result of the method call input.nextInt(). This statement is called an assignment statement, because it assigns a value to a variable. Everything to the *right* of the assignment operator, =, is always evaluated *before* the assignment is performed.

Good Programming Practice A.3

Placing spaces on either side of a binary operator makes the program more readable.

Prompting for and Inputting a Second `int`

Line 20 prompts the user to input the second integer. Line 21 reads the second integer and assigns it to variable number2.

Using Variables in a Calculation

Line 23 is an assignment statement that calculates the sum of the variables number1 and number2 then assigns the result to variable sum by using the assignment operator, =. The statement is read as "sum *gets* the value of number1 + number2." In general, calculations are performed in assignment statements. When the program encounters the addition operation, it performs the calculation using the values stored in the variables number1 and number2. In the preceding statement, the addition operator is a *binary operator*—its *two* operands are the variables number1 and number2. Portions of statements that contain calculations are called **expressions**. In fact, an expression is any portion of a statement that has a *value* associated with it. For example, the value of the expression number1 + number2 is the *sum* of the numbers. Similarly, the value of the expression input.nextInt() is the integer typed by the user.

Displaying the Result of the Calculation

After the calculation has been performed, line 25 uses method System.out.printf to display the sum. The format specifier **%d** is a placeholder for an int value (in this case the value of sum)—the letter d stands for "decimal integer." The remaining characters in the format string are all fixed text. So, method printf displays "Sum is ", followed by the value of sum (in the position of the %d format specifier) and a newline.

Calculations can also be performed *inside* printf statements. We could have combined the statements at lines 23 and 25 into the statement

```
System.out.printf( "Sum is %d\n", ( number1 + number2 ) );
```

The parentheses around the expression number1 + number2 are not required—they're included to emphasize that the value of the *entire* expression is output in the position of the %d format specifier.

Java API Documentation

For each new Java API class we use, we indicate the package in which it's located. This information helps you locate descriptions of each package and class in the Java API documentation. A web-based version of this documentation can be found at

http://docs.oracle.com/javase/7/docs/api/

A.6 Memory Concepts

Variable names such as number1, number2 and sum actually correspond to locations in the computer's memory. Every variable has a **name**, a **type**, a **size** (in bytes) and a **value**.

In the addition program of Fig. A.7, when the following statement (line 18) executes:

number1 = input.nextInt(); // read first number from user

the number typed by the user is placed into a memory location corresponding to the name number1. Suppose that the user enters 45. The computer places that integer value into number1 (Fig. A.8), replacing the previous value (if any) in that location. The previous value is lost.

number1	45

Fig. A.8 | Memory location showing the name and value of variable number1.

When the statement (line 21)

number2 = input.nextInt(); // read second number from user

executes, suppose that the user enters 72. The computer places that integer value into location number2. The memory now appears as shown in Fig. A.9.

number1	45
number2	72

Fig. A.9 | Memory locations after storing values for number1 and number2.

After the program of Fig. A.7 obtains values for number1 and number2, it adds the values and places the total into variable sum. The statement (line 23)

sum = number1 + number2; // add numbers, then store total in sum

performs the addition, then replaces any previous value in sum. After sum has been calculated, memory appears as in Fig. A.10. number1 and number2 contain the values that were used in the calculation of sum. These values were used, but not destroyed, as the calculation was performed. When a value is read from a memory location, the process is nondestructive.

number1	45
number2	72
sum	117

Fig. A.10 | Memory locations after storing the sum of number1 and number2.

A.7 Arithmetic

Most programs perform arithmetic calculations. The **arithmetic operators** are summarized in Fig. A.11. Note the use of various special symbols not used in algebra. The **asterisk** (*) indicates multiplication, and the percent sign (%) is the **remainder operator**, which we'll discuss shortly. The arithmetic operators in Fig. A.11 are *binary* operators, because each operates on *two* operands. For example, the expression f + 7 contains the binary operator + and the two operands f and 7.

Java operation	Operator	Algebraic expression	Java expression
Addition	+	$f + 7$	f + 7
Subtraction	–	$p - c$	p - c
Multiplication	*	bm	b * m
Division	/	x/y or $\frac{x}{y}$ or $x \div y$	x / y
Remainder	%	$r \bmod s$	r % s

Fig. A.11 | Arithmetic operators.

Integer division yields an integer quotient. For example, the expression 7 / 4 evaluates to 1, and the expression 17 / 5 evaluates to 3. Any fractional part in integer division is simply *discarded* (i.e., *truncated*)—no rounding occurs. Java provides the remainder operator, %, which yields the remainder after division. The expression x % y yields the remainder after x is divided by y. Thus, 7 % 4 yields 3, and 17 % 5 yields 2. This operator is most commonly used with integer operands but can also be used with other arithmetic types.

Arithmetic Expressions in Straight-Line Form
Arithmetic expressions in Java must be written in **straight-line form** to facilitate entering programs into the computer. Thus, expressions such as "a divided by b" must be written as a / b, so that all constants, variables and operators appear in a straight line. The following algebraic notation is generally not acceptable to compilers:

$$\frac{a}{b}$$

Parentheses for Grouping Subexpressions

Parentheses are used to group terms in Java expressions in the same manner as in algebraic expressions. For example, to multiply a times the quantity b + c, we write

```
a * ( b + c )
```

If an expression contains **nested parentheses**, such as

```
( ( a + b ) * c )
```

the expression in the innermost set of parentheses (a + b in this case) is evaluated first.

Rules of Operator Precedence

Java applies the operators in arithmetic expressions in a precise sequence determined by the **rules of operator precedence**, which are generally the same as those followed in algebra:

1. Multiplication, division and remainder operations are applied first. If an expression contains several such operations, they're applied from left to right. Multiplication, division and remainder operators have the same level of precedence.

2. Addition and subtraction operations are applied next. If an expression contains several such operations, the operators are applied from left to right. Addition and subtraction operators have the same level of precedence.

These rules enable Java to apply operators in the correct order.[1] When we say that operators are applied from left to right, we're referring to their **associativity**. Some operators associate from right to left. Figure A.12 summarizes these rules of operator precedence. A complete precedence chart is included in Appendix K.

Operator(s)	Operation(s)	Order of evaluation (precedence)
* / %	Multiplication Division Remainder	Evaluated first. If there are several operators of this type, they're evaluated from left to right.
+ -	Addition Subtraction	Evaluated next. If there are several operators of this type, they're evaluated from left to right.
=	Assignment	Evaluated last.

Fig. A.12 | Precedence of arithmetic operators.

---

1. We use simple examples to explain the order of evaluation of expressions. Subtle issues occur in the more complex expressions you'll encounter. For more information on order of evaluation, see Chapter 15 of *The Java™ Language Specification* (https://docs.oracle.com/javase/specs/jls/se7/jls7.pdf).

Sample Algebraic and Java Expressions

Now let's consider several expressions in light of the rules of operator precedence. Each example lists an algebraic expression and its Java equivalent. The following is an example of an arithmetic mean (average) of five terms:

Algebra: $m = \dfrac{a + b + c + d + e}{5}$

Java: `m = ( a + b + c + d + e ) / 5;`

The parentheses are required because division has higher precedence than addition. The entire quantity (a + b + c + d + e) is to be divided by 5. If the parentheses are erroneously omitted, we obtain a + b + c + d + e / 5, which evaluates as

$$a + b + c + d + \frac{e}{5}$$

Here's an example of the equation of a straight line:

Algebra: $y = mx + b$

Java: `y = m * x + b;`

No parentheses are required. The multiplication operator is applied first because multiplication has a higher precedence than addition. The assignment occurs last because it has a lower precedence than multiplication or addition.

The following example contains remainder (%), multiplication, division, addition and subtraction operations:

Algebra: $z = pr \% q + w/x - y$

Java: `z = p * r % q + w / x - y;`

    ⑥ ① ② ④ ③ ⑤

The circled numbers under the statement indicate the order in which Java applies the operators. The *, % and / operations are evaluated first in left-to-right order (i.e., they associate from left to right), because they have higher precedence than + and -. The + and - operations are evaluated next. These operations are also applied from left to right. The assignment (=) operation is evaluated last.

Evaluation of a Second-Degree Polynomial

To develop a better understanding of the rules of operator precedence, consider the evaluation of an assignment expression that includes a second-degree polynomial $ax^2 + bx + c$:

`y = a * x * x + b * x + c;`

    ⑥ ① ② ④ ③ ⑤

The multiplication operations are evaluated first in left-to-right order (i.e., they associate from left to right), because they have higher precedence than addition. (Java has no arithmetic operator for exponentiation in Java, so x^2 is represented as x * x. Section C.16 shows an alternative for performing exponentiation.) The addition operations are evaluated next from left to right. Suppose that a, b, c and x are initialized (given values) as follows: a = 2, b = 3, c = 7 and x = 5. Figure A.13 illustrates the order in which the operators are applied.

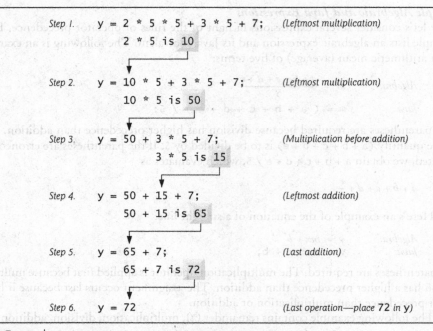

Step 1.   y = 2 * 5 * 5 + 3 * 5 + 7;   *(Leftmost multiplication)*
              2 * 5 is 10

Step 2.   y = 10 * 5 + 3 * 5 + 7;   *(Leftmost multiplication)*
              10 * 5 is 50

Step 3.   y = 50 + 3 * 5 + 7;   *(Multiplication before addition)*
              3 * 5 is 15

Step 4.   y = 50 + 15 + 7;   *(Leftmost addition)*
              50 + 15 is 65

Step 5.   y = 65 + 7;   *(Last addition)*
              65 + 7 is 72

Step 6.   y = 72   *(Last operation—place 72 in y)*

Fig. A.13 | Order in which a second-degree polynomial is evaluated.

A.8 Decision Making: Equality and Relational Operators

A **condition** is an expression that can be **true** or **false**. This section introduces Java's **if selection statement**, which allows a program to make a **decision** based on a condition's value. For example, the condition "grade is greater than or equal to 60" determines whether a student passed a test. If the condition in an if statement is true, the body of the if statement executes. If the condition is false, the body does not execute. We'll see an example shortly.

Conditions in if statements can be formed by using the **equality operators** (== and !=) and **relational operators** (>, <, >= and <=) summarized in Fig. A.14. Both equality operators have the same level of precedence, which is *lower* than that of the relational operators. The equality operators associate from left to right. The relational operators all have the same level of precedence and also associate from left to right.

Standard algebraic equality or relational operator	Java equality or relational operator	Sample Java condition	Meaning of Java condition
Equality operators			
=	==	x == y	x is equal to y
≠	!=	x != y	x is not equal to y

Fig. A.14 | Equality and relational operators. (Part 1 of 2.)

Standard algebraic equality or relational operator	Java equality or relational operator	Sample Java condition	Meaning of Java condition
Relational operators			
>	>	x > y	x is greater than y
<	<	x < y	x is less than y
≥	>=	x >= y	x is greater than or equal to y
≤	<=	x <= y	x is less than or equal to y

Fig. A.14 | Equality and relational operators. (Part 2 of 2.)

Figure A.15 uses six if statements to compare two integers input by the user. If the condition in any of these if statements is true, the statement associated with that if statement executes; otherwise, the statement is skipped. We use a Scanner to input the integers from the user and store them in variables number1 and number2. The program compares the numbers and displays the results of the comparisons that are true.

```java
1   // Fig. A.15: Comparison.java
2   // Compare integers using if statements, relational operators
3   // and equality operators.
4   import java.util.Scanner; // program uses class Scanner
5
6   public class Comparison
7   {
8      // main method begins execution of Java application
9      public static void main( String[] args )
10     {
11        // create Scanner to obtain input from command line
12        Scanner input = new Scanner( System.in );
13
14        int number1; // first number to compare
15        int number2; // second number to compare
16
17        System.out.print( "Enter first integer: " ); // prompt
18        number1 = input.nextInt(); // read first number from user
19
20        System.out.print( "Enter second integer: " ); // prompt
21        number2 = input.nextInt(); // read second number from user
22
23        if ( number1 == number2 )
24           System.out.printf( "%d == %d\n", number1, number2 );
25
26        if ( number1 != number2 )
27           System.out.printf( "%d != %d\n", number1, number2 );
28
```

Fig. A.15 | Compare integers using if statements, relational operators and equality operators. (Part 1 of 2.)

```
29          if ( number1 < number2 )
30              System.out.printf( "%d < %d\n", number1, number2 );
31
32          if ( number1 > number2 )
33              System.out.printf( "%d > %d\n", number1, number2 );
34
35          if ( number1 <= number2 )
36              System.out.printf( "%d <= %d\n", number1, number2 );
37
38          if ( number1 >= number2 )
39              System.out.printf( "%d >= %d\n", number1, number2 );
40      } // end method main
41  } // end class Comparison
```

```
Enter first integer: 777
Enter second integer: 777
777 == 777
777 <= 777
777 >= 777
```

```
Enter first integer: 1000
Enter second integer: 2000
1000 != 2000
1000 < 2000
1000 <= 2000
```

```
Enter first integer: 2000
Enter second integer: 1000
2000 != 1000
2000 > 1000
2000 >= 1000
```

Fig. A.15 | Compare integers using if statements, relational operators and equality operators. (Part 2 of 2.)

The declaration of class Comparison begins at line 6. The class's main method (lines 9–40) begins the execution of the program. Line 12 declares Scanner variable input and assigns it a Scanner that inputs data from the standard input (i.e., the keyboard).

Lines 14–15 declare the int variables used to store the values input from the user.

Lines 17–18 prompt the user to enter the first integer and input the value, respectively. The input value is stored in variable number1.

Lines 20–21 prompt the user to enter the second integer and input the value, respectively. The input value is stored in variable number2.

Lines 23–24 compare the values of number1 and number2 to determine whether they're equal. An if statement always begins with keyword if, followed by a condition in parentheses. An if statement expects one statement in its body, but may contain multiple statements if they're enclosed in a set of braces ({}). The indentation of the body statement shown here is not required, but it improves the program's readability by emphasizing that the statement in line 24 *is part of* the if statement that begins at line 23. Line 24 executes only if the numbers stored in variables number1 and number2 are equal (i.e., the condition is true). The if statements in lines 26–27, 29–30, 32–33, 35–36 and 38–39 compare number1 and number2 using the operators !=, <, >, <= and >=, respectively. If the condition in one or more of the if statements is true, the corresponding body statement executes.

> ### Common Programming Error A.3
>
> *Confusing the equality operator, ==, with the assignment operator, =, can cause a logic error or a syntax error. The equality operator should be read as "is equal to" and the assignment operator as "gets" or "gets the value of." To avoid confusion, some people read the equality operator as "double equals" or "equals equals."*

There's no semicolon (;) at the end of the first line of each if statement. Such a semicolon would result in a logic error at execution time. For example,

```
if ( number1 == number2 ); // logic error
    System.out.printf( "%d == %d\n", number1, number2 );
```

would actually be interpreted by Java as

```
if ( number1 == number2 )
    ; // empty statement
System.out.printf( "%d == %d\n", number1, number2 );
```

where the semicolon on the line by itself—called the **empty statement**—is the statement to execute if the condition in the if statement is true. When the empty statement executes, no task is performed. The program then continues with the output statement, which always executes, regardless of whether the condition is true or false, because the output statement is not part of the if statement.

Note the use of white space in Fig. A.15. Recall that the compiler normally ignores white space. So, statements may be split over several lines and may be spaced according to your preferences without affecting a program's meaning. It's incorrect to split identifiers and strings. Ideally, statements should be kept small, but this is not always possible.

Figure A.16 shows the operators discussed so far in decreasing order of precedence. All but the assignment operator, =, associate from left to right. The assignment operator, =, associates from right to left, so an expression like x = y = 0 is evaluated as if it had been written as x = (y = 0), which first assigns the value 0 to variable y, then assigns the result of that assignment, 0, to x.

Operators				Associativity	Type
*	/	%		left to right	multiplicative
+	-			left to right	additive
<	<=	>	>=	left to right	relational
==	!=			left to right	equality
=				right to left	assignment

Fig. A.16 | Precedence and associativity of operators discussed.

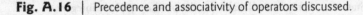

A.9 Wrap-Up

In this appendix, you learned many important features of Java, including displaying data on the screen in a **Command Prompt**, inputting data from the keyboard, performing calculations and making decisions. The applications presented here introduced you to basic programming concepts. As you'll see in Appendix B, Java applications typically contain just a few lines of code in method main—these statements normally create the objects that perform the work of the application. In Appendix B, you'll learn how to implement your own classes and use objects of those classes in applications.

Self-Review Exercises

A.1 Fill in the blanks in each of the following statements:

a) A(n) _____ begins the body of every method, and a(n) _____ ends the body of every method.

b) The _____ statement is used to make decisions.

c) _____ begins an end-of-line comment.

d) _____, _____ and _____ are called white space.

e) _____ are reserved for use by Java.

f) Java applications begin execution at method _____.

g) Methods _____, _____ and _____ display information in a command window.

A.2 State whether each of the following is *true* or *false*. If *false*, explain why.

a) Comments cause the computer to print the text after the // on the screen when the program executes.

b) All variables must be given a type when they're declared.

c) Java considers the variables number and NuMbEr to be identical.

d) The remainder operator (%) can be used only with integer operands.

e) The arithmetic operators *, /, %, + and - all have the same level of precedence.

A.3 Write statements to accomplish each of the following tasks:

a) Declare variables c, thisIsAVariable, q76354 and number to be of type int.

b) Prompt the user to enter an integer.

c) Input an integer and assign the result to int variable value. Assume Scanner variable input can be used to read a value from the keyboard.

d) Print "This is a Java program" on one line in the command window. Use method System.out.println.

e) Print "This is a Java program" on two lines in the command window. The first line should end with Java. Use method System.out.println.

f) Print "This is a Java program" on two lines in the command window. The first line should end with Java. Use method System.out.printf and two %s format specifiers.

g) If the variable number is not equal to 7, display "The variable number is not equal to 7".

A.4 Identify and correct the errors in each of the following statements:

a) if (c < 7);
    System.out.println("c is less than 7");

b) if (c => 7)
    System.out.println("c is equal to or greater than 7");

A.5 Write declarations, statements or comments that accomplish each of the following tasks:

a) State that a program will calculate the product of three integers.

b) Create a `Scanner` called `input` that reads values from the standard input.
c) Declare the variables x, y, z and `result` to be of type `int`.
d) Prompt the user to enter the first integer.
e) Read the first integer from the user and store it in the variable x.
f) Prompt the user to enter the second integer.
g) Read the second integer from the user and store it in the variable y.
h) Prompt the user to enter the third integer.
i) Read the third integer from the user and store it in the variable z.
j) Compute the product of the three integers contained in variables x, y and z, and assign the result to the variable `result`.
k) Display the message `"Product is"` followed by the value of the variable `result`.

A.6   Using the statements you wrote in Exercise A.5, write a complete program that calculates and prints the product of three integers.

Answers to Self-Review Exercises

A.1   a) left brace ({), right brace (}). b) `if`. c) `//`. d) Space characters, newlines and tabs. e) Keywords. f) `main`. g) `System.out.print`, `System.out.println` and `System.out.printf`.

A.2   a) False. Comments do not cause any action to be performed when the program executes. They're used to document programs and improve their readability. b) True. c) False. Java is case sensitive, so these variables are distinct. d) False. The remainder operator can also be used with non-integer operands in Java. e) False. The operators *, / and % are higher precedence than operators + and -.

A.3   a) `int c, thisIsAVariable, q76354, number;`
       or
       `int c;`
       `int thisIsAVariable;`
       `int q76354;`
       `int number;`
     b) `System.out.print( "Enter an integer: " );`
     c) `value = input.nextInt();`
     d) `System.out.println( "This is a Java program" );`
     e) `System.out.println( "This is a Java\nprogram" );`
     f) `System.out.printf( "%s\n%s\n", "This is a Java", "program" );`
     g) `if ( number != 7 )`
           `System.out.println( "The variable number is not equal to 7" );`

A.4   a) Error: Semicolon after the right parenthesis of the condition (c < 7) in the `if`.
       Correction: Remove the semicolon after the right parenthesis. [*Note:* As a result, the output statement will execute regardless of whether the condition in the `if` is true.]
     b) Error: The relational operator => is incorrect.
       Correction: Change => to >=.

A.5   a) `// Calculate the product of three integers`
     b) `Scanner input = new Scanner( System.in );`
     c) `int x, y, z, result;`
       or
       `int x;`
       `int y;`
       `int z;`
       `int result;`

d) `System.out.print( "Enter first integer: " );`
e) `x = input.nextInt();`
f) `System.out.print( "Enter second integer: " );`
g) `y = input.nextInt();`
h) `System.out.print( "Enter third integer: " );`
i) `z = input.nextInt();`
j) `result = x * y * z;`
k) `System.out.printf( "Product is %d\n", result );`

A.6   The solution to Self-Review Exercise A.6 is as follows:

```
1   // Exercise A.6: Product.java
2   // Calculate the product of three integers.
3   import java.util.Scanner; // program uses Scanner
4
5   public class Product
6   {
7      public static void main( String[] args )
8      {
9         // create Scanner to obtain input from command window
10        Scanner input = new Scanner( System.in );
11
12        int x; // first number input by user
13        int y; // second number input by user
14        int z; // third number input by user
15        int result; // product of numbers
16
17        System.out.print( "Enter first integer: " ); // prompt for input
18        x = input.nextInt(); // read first integer
19
20        System.out.print( "Enter second integer: " ); // prompt for input
21        y = input.nextInt(); // read second integer
22
23        System.out.print( "Enter third integer: " ); // prompt for input
24        z = input.nextInt(); // read third integer
25
26        result = x * y * z; // calculate product of numbers
27
28        System.out.printf( "Product is %d\n", result );
29     } // end method main
30  } // end class Product
```

```
Enter first integer: 10
Enter second integer: 20
Enter third integer: 30
Product is 6000
```

Exercises

A.7   Fill in the blanks in each of the following statements:

a) _____ are used to document a program and improve its readability.

b) A decision can be made in a Java program with a(n) _____.

c) Calculations are normally performed by _____ statements.

d) The arithmetic operators with the same precedence as multiplication are _____ and _____.

e) When parentheses in an arithmetic expression are nested, the _____ set of parentheses is evaluated first.

f) A location in the computer's memory that may contain different values at various times throughout the execution of a program is called a(n) _____.

A.8 Write Java statements that accomplish each of the following tasks:
a) Display the message "Enter an integer: ", leaving the cursor on the same line.
b) Assign the product of variables b and c to variable a.
c) Use a comment to state that a program performs a sample payroll calculation.

A.9 State whether each of the following is *true* or *false*. If *false*, explain why.
a) Java operators are evaluated from left to right.
b) The following are all valid variable names: _under_bar_, m928134, t5, j7, her_sales$, his_$account_total, a, b$, c, z and z2.
c) A valid Java arithmetic expression with no parentheses is evaluated from left to right.
d) The following are all invalid variable names: 3g, 87, 67h2, h22 and 2h.

A.10 Assuming that x = 2 and y = 3, what does each of the following statements display?
a) `System.out.printf( "x = %d\n", x );`
b) `System.out.printf( "Value of %d + %d is %d\n", x, x, ( x + x ) );`
c) `System.out.printf( "x =" );`
d) `System.out.printf( "%d = %d\n", ( x + y ), ( y + x ) );`

A.11 *(Arithmetic, Smallest and Largest)* Write an application that inputs three integers from the user and displays the sum, average, product, smallest and largest of the numbers. Use the techniques shown in Fig. A.15. [*Note:* The calculation of the average in this exercise should result in an integer representation of the average. So, if the sum of the values is 7, the average should be 2, not 2.3333....]

A.12 What does the following code print?

```
System.out.printf( "%s\n%s\n%s\n", "*", "***", "*****" );
```

A.13 *(Largest and Smallest Integers)* Write an application that reads five integers and determines and prints the largest and smallest integers in the group. Use only the programming techniques you learned in this appendix.

A.14 *(Odd or Even)* Write an application that reads an integer and determines and prints whether it's odd or even. [*Hint:* Use the remainder operator. An even number is a multiple of 2. Any multiple of 2 leaves a remainder of 0 when divided by 2.]

A.15 *(Multiples)* Write an application that reads two integers, determines whether the first is a multiple of the second and prints the result. [*Hint:* Use the remainder operator.]

A.16 *(Diameter, Circumference and Area of a Circle)* Here's a peek ahead. In this appendix, you learned about integers and the type int. Java can also represent floating-point numbers that contain decimal points, such as 3.14159. Write an application that inputs from the user the radius of a circle as an integer and prints the circle's diameter, circumference and area using the floating-point value 3.14159 for π. Use the techniques shown in Fig. A.7. [*Note:* You may also use the predefined constant Math.PI for the value of π. This constant is more precise than the value 3.14159. Class Math is defined in package java.lang. Classes in that package are imported automatically, so you do not need to import class Math to use it.] Use the following formulas (*r* is the radius):

$$diameter = 2r$$
$$circumference = 2\pi r$$
$$area = \pi r^2$$

Do not store the results of each calculation in a variable. Rather, specify each calculation as the value that will be output in a System.out.printf statement. The values produced by the circumference and area calculations are floating-point numbers. Such values can be output with the format specifier %f in a System.out.printf statement. You'll learn more about floating-point numbers in Appendix B.

A.17 *(Separating the Digits in an Integer)* Write an application that inputs one number consisting of five digits from the user, separates the number into its individual digits and prints the digits separated from one another by three spaces each. For example, if the user types in the number 42339, the program should print

```
4   2   3   3   9
```

Assume that the user enters the correct number of digits. What happens when you execute the program and type a number with more than five digits? What happens when you execute the program and type a number with fewer than five digits? [*Hint:* It's possible to do this exercise with the techniques you learned in this appendix. You'll need to use both division and remainder operations to "pick off" each digit.]

A.18 *(Table of Squares and Cubes)* Using only the programming techniques you learned in this appendix, write an application that calculates the squares and cubes of the numbers from 0 to 10 and prints the resulting values in table format, as shown below. [*Note:* This program does not require any input from the user.]

```
number   square   cube
0        0        0
1        1        1
2        4        8
3        9        27
4        16       64
5        25       125
6        36       216
7        49       343
8        64       512
9        81       729
10       100      1000
```

Introduction to Classes, Objects, Methods and Strings

Objectives

In this appendix you'll learn:

- How to declare a class and use it to create an object.
- How to implement a class's behaviors as methods.
- How to implement a class's attributes as instance variables and properties.
- How to call an object's methods to make them perform their tasks.
- What instance variables of a class and local variables of a method are.
- How to use a constructor to initialize an object's data.
- The differences between primitive and reference types.

B.1 Introduction

In this appendix, we introduce some key concepts of object-oriented programming in Java, including classes, objects, methods, instance variables and constructors. We explore the differences between primitive types and reference types, and we present a simple framework for organizing object-oriented applications.

B.2 Declaring a Class with a Method and Instantiating an Object of a Class

In this section, you'll create a *new* class, then use it to create an object. We begin by declaring classes GradeBook (Fig. B.1) and GradeBookTest (Fig. B.2). Class GradeBook (declared in the file GradeBook.java) will be used to display a message on the screen (Fig. B.2) welcoming the instructor to the grade book application. Class GradeBookTest (declared in the file GradeBookTest.java) is an application class in which the main method will create and use an object of class GradeBook. *Each class declaration that begins with keyword* public *must be stored in a file having the same name as the class and ending with the* .java *file-name extension.* Thus, classes GradeBook and GradeBookTest must be declared in *separate* files, because each class is declared public.

Class *GradeBook*

The GradeBook class declaration (Fig. B.1) contains a displayMessage method (lines 7–10) that displays a message on the screen. We'll need to make an object of this class and call its method to execute line 9 and display the message.

```java
1   // Fig. B.1: GradeBook.java
2   // Class declaration with one method.
3
4   public class GradeBook
5   {
6      // display a welcome message to the GradeBook user
7      public void displayMessage()
8      {
9         System.out.println( "Welcome to the Grade Book!" );
10     } // end method displayMessage
11  } // end class GradeBook
```

Fig. B.1 | Class declaration with one method.

The *class declaration* begins in line 4. The keyword public is an **access modifier**. For now, we'll simply declare every class public. Every class declaration contains keyword class followed immediately by the class's name. Every class's body is enclosed in a pair of left and right braces, as in lines 5 and 11 of class GradeBook.

In Appendix A, each class we declared had one method named main. Class GradeBook also has one method—displayMessage (lines 7–10). Recall that main is a special method that's *always* called automatically by the Java Virtual Machine (JVM) when you execute an application. Most methods do not get called automatically. As you'll soon see, you must call method displayMessage explicitly to tell it to perform its task.

The method declaration begins with keyword public to indicate that the method is "available to the public"—it can be called from methods of other classes. Next is the method's **return type**, which specifies the type of data the method returns to its caller after performing its task. The return type void indicates that this method will perform a task but will *not* return (i.e., give back) any information to its **calling method**. You've used methods that return information—for example, in Appendix A you used Scanner method nextInt to input an integer typed by the user at the keyboard. When nextInt reads a value from the user, it returns that value for use in the program.

The name of the method, displayMessage, follows the return type. By convention, method names begin with a lowercase first letter and subsequent words in the name begin with a capital letter. The *parentheses* after the method name indicate that this is a *method*. Empty parentheses, as in line 7, indicate that this method does not require additional information to perform its task. Line 7 is commonly referred to as the **method header**. Every method's body is delimited by left and right braces, as in lines 8 and 10.

The body of a method contains one or more statements that perform the method's task. In this case, the method contains one statement (line 9) that displays the message "Welcome to the Grade Book!" followed by a newline (because of println) in the command window. After this statement executes, the method has completed its task.

Class *GradeBookTest*

Next, we'll use class GradeBook in an application. As you learned in Appendix A, method main begins the execution of *every* application. A class that contains method main begins the execution of a Java application. Class GradeBook is *not* an application because it does *not* contain main. Therefore, if you try to execute GradeBook by typing java GradeBook in the command window, an error will occur. To fix this problem, we must either declare a separate class that contains a main method or place a main method in class GradeBook. To help you prepare for the larger programs you'll encounter later in this book and in industry, we use a separate class (GradeBookTest in this example) containing method main to test each new class we create. Some programmers refer to such a class as a *driver class*. The GradeBookTest class declaration (Fig. B.2) contains the main method that will control our application's execution.

Lines 7–14 declare method main. A key part of enabling the JVM to locate and call method main to begin the application's execution is the static keyword (line 7), which indicates that main is a static method. *A static method is special, because you can call it without first creating an object of the class in which the method is declared.* We discuss static methods in Appendix D.

```
1    // Fig. B.2: GradeBookTest.java
2    // Creating a GradeBook object and calling its displayMessage method.
3
4    public class GradeBookTest
5    {
6        // main method begins program execution
7        public static void main( String[] args )
8        {
9            // create a GradeBook object and assign it to myGradeBook
10           GradeBook myGradeBook = new GradeBook();
11
12           // call myGradeBook's displayMessage method
13           myGradeBook.displayMessage();
14       } // end main
15   } // end class GradeBookTest
```

```
Welcome to the Grade Book!
```

Fig. B.2 | Creating a GradeBook object and calling its displayMessage method.

In this application, we'd like to call class GradeBook's displayMessage method to display the welcome message in the command window. Typically, you cannot call a method that belongs to another class until you create an object of that class, as shown in line 10. We begin by declaring variable myGradeBook. The variable's type is GradeBook—the class we declared in Fig. B.1. Each new *class* you create becomes a new *type* that can be used to declare variables and create objects.

Variable myGradeBook is initialized (line 10) with the result of the **class instance creation expression** new GradeBook(). Keyword **new** creates a new object of the class specified to the right of the keyword (i.e., GradeBook). The parentheses to the right of GradeBook are required. As you'll learn in Section B.6, those parentheses in combination with a class name represent a call to a **constructor**, which is similar to a method but is used only at the time an object is *created* to *initialize* the object's data. You'll see that data can be placed in the parentheses to specify *initial values* for the object's data. For now, we simply leave the parentheses empty.

Just as we can use object System.out to call its methods print, printf and println, we can use object myGradeBook to call its method displayMessage. Line 13 calls the method displayMessage (lines 7–10 of Fig. B.1) using myGradeBook followed by a **dot separator** (.), the method name displayMessage and an empty set of parentheses. This call causes the displayMessage method to perform its task. This method call differs from those in Appendix A that displayed information in a command window—each of those method calls provided arguments that specified the data to display. At the beginning of line 13, "myGradeBook." indicates that main should use the myGradeBook object that was created in line 10. Line 7 of Fig. B.1 indicates that method displayMessage has an *empty parameter list*—that is, displayMessage does *not* require additional information to perform its task. For this reason, the method call (line 13 of Fig. B.2) specifies an empty set of parentheses after the method name to indicate that *no arguments* are being passed to method displayMessage. When method displayMessage completes its task, method main continues executing at line 14. This is the end of method main, so the program terminates.

Any class can contain a main method. The JVM invokes the main method *only* in the class used to execute the application. If an application has multiple classes that contain main, the one that's invoked is the one in the class named in the java command.

Compiling an Application with Multiple Classes

You must compile the classes in Fig. B.1 and Fig. B.2 before you can execute the application. First, change to the directory that contains the application's source-code files. Next, type the command

```
javac GradeBook.java GradeBookTest.java
```

to compile *both* classes at once. If the directory containing the application includes only this application's files, you can compile *all* the classes in the directory with the command

```
javac *.java
```

The asterisk (*) in *.java indicates that *all* files in the current directory that end with the file-name extension ".java" should be compiled.

B.3   Declaring a Method with a Parameter

In our car analogy from Section 1.8, we discussed the fact that pressing a car's gas pedal sends a *message* to the car to *perform a task*—to go faster. But *how fast* should the car accelerate? As you know, the farther down you press the pedal, the faster the car accelerates. So the message to the car actually includes the *task to perform* and *additional information* that helps the car perform the task. This additional information is known as a **parameter**—the value of the parameter helps the car determine how fast to accelerate. Similarly, a method can require one or more parameters that represent additional information it needs to perform its task. Parameters are defined in a comma-separated **parameter list**, which is located inside the parentheses that follow the method name. Each parameter must specify a *type* and a variable name. The parameter list may contain any number of parameters, including none at all. Empty parentheses following the method name (as in Fig. B.1, line 7) indicate that a method does *not* require any parameters.

Arguments to a Method

A method call supplies values—called *arguments*—for each of the method's parameters. For example, the method System.out.println requires an argument that specifies the data to output in a command window. Similarly, to make a deposit into a bank account, a deposit method specifies a parameter that represents the deposit amount. When the deposit method is called, an argument value representing the deposit amount is assigned to the method's parameter. The method then makes a deposit of that amount.

Class Declaration with a Method That Has One Parameter

We now declare class GradeBook (Fig. B.3) with a displayMessage method that displays the course name as part of the welcome message. (See the sample execution in Fig. B.4.) The new method requires a parameter that represents the course name to output.

Before discussing the new features of class GradeBook, let's see how the new class is used from the main method of class GradeBookTest (Fig. B.4). Line 12 creates a Scanner named input for reading the course name from the user. Line 15 creates the GradeBook object myGradeBook. Line 18 prompts the user to enter a course name. Line 19 reads the name from the user and assigns it to the nameOfCourse variable, using Scanner method **nextLine** to perform the input. The user types the course name and presses *Enter* to submit the course name to the program. Pressing *Enter* inserts a newline character at the end of the characters typed by the user. Method nextLine reads characters typed by the user until it encounters the newline character, then returns a String containing the characters up to, but *not* including, the newline. The newline character is *discarded*.

```
1   // Fig. B.3: GradeBook.java
2   // Class declaration with one method that has a parameter.
3
4   public class GradeBook
5   {
6      // display a welcome message to the GradeBook user
7      public void displayMessage( String courseName )
8      {
9         System.out.printf( "Welcome to the grade book for\n%s!\n",
10           courseName );
11     } // end method displayMessage
12  } // end class GradeBook
```

Fig. B.3 | Class declaration with one method that has a parameter.

```
1    // Fig. B.4: GradeBookTest.java
2    // Create a GradeBook object and pass a String to
3    // its displayMessage method.
4    import java.util.Scanner; // program uses Scanner
5
6    public class GradeBookTest
7    {
8       // main method begins program execution
9       public static void main( String[] args )
10      {
11         // create Scanner to obtain input from command window
12         Scanner input = new Scanner( System.in );
13
14         // create a GradeBook object and assign it to myGradeBook
15         GradeBook myGradeBook = new GradeBook();
16
17         // prompt for and input course name
18         System.out.println( "Please enter the course name:" );
19         String nameOfCourse = input.nextLine(); // read a line of text
20         System.out.println(); // outputs a blank line
21
22         // call myGradeBook's displayMessage method
23         // and pass nameOfCourse as an argument
24         myGradeBook.displayMessage( nameOfCourse );
25      } // end main
26   } // end class GradeBookTest
```

Fig. B.4 | Create a GradeBook object and pass a String to its displayMessage method. (Part 1 of 2.)

```
Please enter the course name:
CS101 Introduction to Java Programming

Welcome to the grade book for
CS101 Introduction to Java Programming!
```

Fig. B.4 | Create a GradeBook object and pass a String to its displayMessage method. (Part 2 of 2.)

Class Scanner also provides method **next** that reads individual words. When the user presses *Enter* after typing input, method next reads characters until it encounters a *white-space character* (such as a space, tab or newline), then returns a String containing the characters up to, but *not* including, the white-space character (which is discarded). All information after the first white-space character is not lost—it can be read by other statements that call the Scanner's methods later in the program. Line 20 outputs a blank line.

Line 24 calls myGradeBooks's displayMessage method. The variable nameOfCourse in parentheses is the *argument* that's passed to method displayMessage so that the method can perform its task. The value of variable nameOfCourse in main becomes the value of method displayMessage's *parameter* courseName in line 7 of Fig. B.3. When you execute this application, notice that method displayMessage outputs the name you type as part of the welcome message (Fig. B.4).

More on Arguments and Parameters

In Fig. B.3, displayMessage's parameter list (line 7) declares one parameter indicating that the method requires a String to perform its task. When the method is called, the argument value in the call is assigned to the corresponding parameter (courseName) in the method header. Then, the method body uses the value of the courseName parameter. Lines 9–10 of Fig. B.3 display parameter courseName's value, using the %s format specifier in printf's format string. The parameter variable's name (courseName in Fig. B.3, line 7) can be the *same or different* from the argument variable's name (nameOfCourse in Fig. B.4, line 24).

The number of arguments in a method call *must* match the number of parameters in the parameter list of the method's declaration. Also, the argument types in the method call must be "consistent with" the types of the corresponding parameters in the method's declaration. (As you'll learn in Appendix D, an argument's type and its corresponding parameter's type are not always required to be *identical*.) In our example, the method call passes one argument of type String (nameOfCourse is declared as a String in line 19 of Fig. B.4) and the method declaration specifies one parameter of type String (courseName is declared as a String in line 7 of Fig. B.3). So in this example the type of the argument in the method call exactly matches the type of the parameter in the method header.

Notes on **import** Declarations

Notice the import declaration in Fig. B.4 (line 4). This indicates to the compiler that the program uses class Scanner. Why do we need to import class Scanner, but not classes System, String or GradeBook? Classes System and String are in package java.lang, which is implicitly imported into *every* Java program, so all programs can use that package's classes *without* explicitly importing them. Most other classes you'll use in Java programs must be imported explicitly.

There's a special relationship between classes that are compiled in the same directory on disk, like classes `GradeBook` and `GradeBookTest`. By default, such classes are considered to be in the same package—known as the **default package**. Classes in the same package are *implicitly imported* into the source-code files of other classes in the same package. Thus, an import declaration is *not* required when one class in a package uses another in the same package—such as when class `GradeBookTest` uses class `GradeBook`.

The `import` declaration in line 4 is *not* required if we always refer to class `Scanner` as `java.util.Scanner`, which includes the *full package name and class name*. This is known as the class's **fully qualified class name**. For example, line 12 could be written as

```
java.util.Scanner input = new java.util.Scanner( System.in );
```

B.4 Instance Variables, *set* Methods and *get* Methods

In Appendix A, we declared all of an application's variables in the application's `main` method. Variables declared in the body of a particular method are known as **local variables** and can be used only in that method. When that method terminates, the values of its local variables are lost. Recall from Section 1.8 that an object has *attributes* that are carried with it as it's used in a program. Such attributes exist before a method is called on an object, while the method is executing and after the method completes execution.

A class normally consists of one or more methods that manipulate the attributes that belong to a particular object of the class. Attributes are represented as variables in a class declaration. Such variables are called **fields** and are declared *inside* a class declaration but *outside* the bodies of the class's method declarations. When each object of a class maintains its own copy of an attribute, the field that represents the attribute is also known as an **instance variable**—each object (instance) of the class has a separate instance of the variable in memory. The example in this section demonstrates a `GradeBook` class that contains a `courseName` instance variable to represent a particular `GradeBook` object's course name.

***GradeBook* Class with an Instance Variable, a *set* Method and a *get* Method**
In our next application (Figs. B.5–B.6), class `GradeBook` (Fig. B.5) maintains the course name as an instance variable so that it can be used or modified at any time during an application's execution. The class contains three methods—`setCourseName`, `getCourseName` and `displayMessage`. Method `setCourseName` stores a course name in a `GradeBook`. Method `getCourseName` obtains a `GradeBook`'s course name. Method `displayMessage`, which now specifies no parameters, still displays a welcome message that includes the course name; as you'll see, the method now obtains the course name by calling a method in the same class—`getCourseName`.

```
1  // Fig. B.5: GradeBook.java
2  // GradeBook class that contains a courseName instance variable
3  // and methods to set and get its value.
4
5  public class GradeBook
6  {
```

Fig. B.5 | GradeBook class that contains a `courseName` instance variable and methods to set and get its value. (Part 1 of 2.)

```
7       private String courseName; // course name for this GradeBook
8
9       // method to set the course name
10      public void setCourseName( String name )
11      {
12         courseName = name; // store the course name
13      } // end method setCourseName
14
15      // method to retrieve the course name
16      public String getCourseName()
17      {
18         return courseName;
19      } // end method getCourseName
20
21      // display a welcome message to the GradeBook user
22      public void displayMessage()
23      {
24         // calls getCourseName to get the name of
25         // the course this GradeBook represents
26         System.out.printf( "Welcome to the grade book for\n%s!\n",
27            getCourseName() );
28      } // end method displayMessage
29   } // end class GradeBook
```

Fig. B.5 | GradeBook class that contains a courseName instance variable and methods to set and get its value. (Part 2 of 2.)

A typical instructor teaches more than one course, each with its own course name. Line 7 declares courseName as a variable of type String. Because the variable is declared *in* the body of the class but *outside* the bodies of the class's methods (lines 10–13, 16–19 and 22–28), line 7 is a declaration for an *instance variable*. Every instance (i.e., object) of class GradeBook contains one copy of each instance variable. For example, if there are two GradeBook objects, each object has its own copy of courseName. A benefit of making courseName an instance variable is that all the methods of the class (in this case, Grade-Book) can manipulate any instance variables that appear in the class (in this case, course-Name).

Access Modifiers public and private

Most instance-variable declarations are preceded with the keyword private (as in line 7). Like public, keyword **private** is an *access modifier. Variables or methods declared with access modifier private are accessible only to methods of the class in which they're declared.* Thus, variable courseName can be used only in methods setCourseName, getCourseName and displayMessage of (every object of) class GradeBook.

Declaring instance variables with access modifier private is known as **data hiding** or information hiding. When a program creates (instantiates) an object of class GradeBook, variable courseName is *encapsulated* (hidden) in the object and can be accessed only by methods of the object's class. This prevents courseName from being modified accidentally by a class in another part of the program. In class GradeBook, methods setCourseName and getCourseName manipulate the instance variable courseName.

> **Software Engineering Observation B.1**
>
> *Precede each field and method declaration with an access modifier. Generally, instance variables should be declared* private *and methods* public. *(It's appropriate to declare certain methods* private, *if they'll be accessed only by other methods of the class.)*

Methods *setCourseName and getCourseName*

Method setCourseName (lines 10–13) does not return any data when it completes its task, so its return type is void. The method receives one parameter—name—which represents the course name that will be passed to the method as an argument. Line 12 assigns name to instance variable courseName.

Method getCourseName (lines 16–19) returns a particular GradeBook object's courseName. The method has an empty parameter list, so it does not require additional information to perform its task. The method specifies that it returns a String—this is the method's return type. When a method that specifies a return type other than void is called and completes its task, the method returns a *result* to its calling method. For example, when you go to an automated teller machine (ATM) and request your account balance, you expect the ATM to give you back a value that represents your balance. Similarly, when a statement calls method getCourseName on a GradeBook object, the statement expects to receive the GradeBook's course name (in this case, a String, as specified in the method declaration's return type).

The **return** statement in line 18 passes the value of instance variable courseName back to the statement that calls method getCourseName. Consider, method displayMessage's line 27, which calls method getCourseName. When the value is returned, the statement in lines 26–27 uses that value to output the course name. Similarly, if you have a method square that returns the square of its argument, you'd expect the statement

```
int result = square( 2 );
```

to return 4 from method square and assign 4 to the variable result. If you have a method maximum that returns the largest of three integer arguments, you'd expect the statement

```
int biggest = maximum( 27, 114, 51 );
```

to return 114 from method maximum and assign 114 to variable biggest.

The statements in lines 12 and 18 each use courseName *even though it was not declared in any of the methods*. We can use courseName in GradeBook's methods because course-Name is an instance variable of the class.

Method *displayMessage*

Method displayMessage (lines 22–28) does *not* return any data when it completes its task, so its return type is void. The method does *not* receive parameters, so the parameter list is empty. Lines 26–27 output a welcome message that includes the value of instance variable courseName, which is returned by the call to method getCourseName in line 27. Notice that one method of a class (displayMessage in this case) can call another method of the *same* class by using just the method name (getCourseName in this case).

GradeBookTest *Class That Demonstrates Class* GradeBook

Class GradeBookTest (Fig. B.6) creates one object of class GradeBook and demonstrates its methods. Line 14 creates a GradeBook object and assigns it to local variable myGradeBook of

```
 1    // Fig. B.6: GradeBookTest.java
 2    // Creating and manipulating a GradeBook object.
 3    import java.util.Scanner; // program uses Scanner
 4
 5    public class GradeBookTest
 6    {
 7       // main method begins program execution
 8       public static void main( String[] args )
 9       {
10          // create Scanner to obtain input from command window
11          Scanner input = new Scanner( System.in );
12
13          // create a GradeBook object and assign it to myGradeBook
14          GradeBook myGradeBook = new GradeBook();
15
16          // display initial value of courseName
17          System.out.printf( "Initial course name is: %s\n\n",
18             myGradeBook.getCourseName() );
19
20          // prompt for and read course name
21          System.out.println( "Please enter the course name:" );
22          String theName = input.nextLine(); // read a line of text
23          myGradeBook.setCourseName( theName ); // set the course name
24          System.out.println(); // outputs a blank line
25
26          // display welcome message after specifying course name
27          myGradeBook.displayMessage();
28       } // end main
29    } // end class GradeBookTest
```

```
Initial course name is: null

Please enter the course name:
CS101 Introduction to Java Programming

Welcome to the grade book for
CS101 Introduction to Java Programming!
```

Fig. B.6 | Creating and manipulating a GradeBook object.

type GradeBook. Lines 17–18 display the initial course name calling the object's getCourse-Name method. The first line of the output shows the name "null." *Unlike local variables, which are not automatically initialized, every field has a **default initial value**—a value provided by Java when you do not specify the field's initial value.* Thus, fields are *not* required to be explicitly initialized before they're used in a program—unless they must be initialized to values *other than* their default values. The default value for a field of type String (like courseName in this example) is null, which we say more about in Section B.5.

Line 21 prompts the user to enter a course name. Local String variable theName (declared in line 22) is initialized with the course name entered by the user, which is returned by the call to the nextLine method of the Scanner object input. Line 23 calls object myGradeBook's setCourseName method and supplies theName as the method's argument. When the method is called, the argument's value is assigned to parameter name (line

10, Fig. B.5) of method setCourseName (lines 10–13, Fig. B.5). Then the parameter's value is assigned to instance variable courseName (line 12, Fig. B.5). Line 24 (Fig. B.6) skips a line in the output, then line 27 calls object myGradeBook's displayMessage method to display the welcome message containing the course name.

set *and* get *Methods*

A class's private fields can be manipulated *only* by the class's methods. So a **client of an object**—that is, any class that calls the object's methods—calls the class's public methods to manipulate the private fields of an object of the class. This is why the statements in method main (Fig. B.6) call the setCourseName, getCourseName and displayMessage methods on a GradeBook object. Classes often provide public methods to allow clients to *set* (i.e., assign values to) or *get* (i.e., obtain the values of) private instance variables. The names of these methods need not begin with *set* or *get*, but this naming convention is recommended and is convention for special Java software components called JavaBeans, which can simplify programming in many Java integrated development environments (IDEs). The method that *sets* instance variable courseName in this example is called setCourseName, and the method that *gets* its value is called getCourseName.

B.5 Primitive Types vs. Reference Types

Java's types are divided into primitive types and **reference types**. The primitive types are boolean, byte, char, short, int, long, float and double. All nonprimitive types are reference types, so classes, which specify the types of objects, are reference types.

A primitive-type variable can store exactly one *value of its declared type* at a time. For example, an int variable can store one whole number (such as 7) at a time. When another value is assigned to that variable, its initial value is replaced. Primitive-type instance variables are *initialized by default*—variables of types byte, char, short, int, long, float and double are initialized to 0, and variables of type boolean are initialized to false. You can specify your own initial value for a primitive-type variable by assigning the variable a value in its declaration, as in

```
private int numberOfStudents = 10;
```

Recall that local variables are *not* initialized by default.

> **Error-Prevention Tip B.1**
>
> *An attempt to use an uninitialized local variable causes a compilation error.*

Programs use variables of reference types (normally called **references**) to store the *locations* of objects in the computer's memory. Such a variable is said to **refer to an object** in the program. Objects that are referenced may each contain many instance variables. Line 14 of Fig. B.6 creates an object of class GradeBook, and the variable myGradeBook contains a reference to that GradeBook object. *Reference-type instance variables are initialized by default to the value* null—a reserved word that represents a "reference to nothing." This is why the first call to getCourseName in line 18 of Fig. B.6 returned null—the value of courseName had not been set, so the default initial value null was returned.

When you use an object of another class, a reference to the object is required to **invoke** (i.e., call) its methods. In the application of Fig. B.6, the statements in method main use the variable myGradeBook to send messages to the GradeBook object. These messages are calls to methods (like setCourseName and getCourseName) that enable the program to interact with the GradeBook object. For example, the statement in line 23 uses myGrade-Book to send the setCourseName message to the GradeBook object. The message includes the argument that setCourseName requires to perform its task. The GradeBook object uses this information to set the courseName instance variable. Primitive-type variables do not refer to objects, so such variables cannot be used to invoke methods.

Software Engineering Observation B.2

A variable's declared type (e.g., int, double or GradeBook) indicates whether the variable is of a primitive or a reference type. If a variable is not of one of the eight primitive types, then it's of a reference type.

B.6 Initializing Objects with Constructors

As mentioned in Section B.4, when an object of class GradeBook (Fig. B.5) is created, its instance variable courseName is initialized to null by default. What if you want to provide a course name when you create a GradeBook object? Each class you declare can provide a special method called a constructor that can be used to initialize an object of a class when the object is created. In fact, Java *requires* a constructor call for *every* object that's created. Keyword new requests memory from the system to store an object, then calls the corresponding class's constructor to initialize the object. The call is indicated by the parentheses after the class name. A constructor *must* have the *same name* as the class. For example, line 14 of Fig. B.6 first uses new to create a GradeBook object. The empty parentheses after "new GradeBook" indicate a call to the class's constructor without arguments. By default, the compiler provides a **default constructor** with *no parameters* in any class that does *not* explicitly include a constructor. When a class has only the default constructor, its instance variables are initialized to their *default values*.

When you declare a class, you can provide your own constructor to specify custom initialization for objects of your class. For example, you might want to specify a course name for a GradeBook object when the object is created, as in

```
GradeBook myGradeBook =
    new GradeBook( "CS101 Introduction to Java Programming" );
```

In this case, the argument "CS101 Introduction to Java Programming" is passed to the GradeBook object's constructor and used to initialize the courseName. The preceding statement requires that the class provide a constructor with a String parameter. Figure B.7 contains a modified GradeBook class with such a constructor.

```
1   // Fig. B.7: GradeBook.java
2   // GradeBook class with a constructor to initialize the course name.
3
4   public class GradeBook
5   {
6       private String courseName; // course name for this GradeBook
7
```

Fig. B.7 | GradeBook class with a constructor to initialize the course name. (Part 1 of 2.)

```
 8      // constructor initializes courseName with String argument
 9      public GradeBook( String name ) // constructor name is class name
10      {
11         courseName = name; // initializes courseName
12      } // end constructor
13
14      // method to set the course name
15      public void setCourseName( String name )
16      {
17         courseName = name; // store the course name
18      } // end method setCourseName
19
20      // method to retrieve the course name
21      public String getCourseName()
22      {
23         return courseName;
24      } // end method getCourseName
25
26      // display a welcome message to the GradeBook user
27      public void displayMessage()
28      {
29         // this statement calls getCourseName to get the
30         // name of the course this GradeBook represents
31         System.out.printf( "Welcome to the grade book for\n%s!\n",
32            getCourseName() );
33      } // end method displayMessage
34   } // end class GradeBook
```

Fig. B.7 | GradeBook class with a constructor to initialize the course name. (Part 2 of 2.)

Lines 9–12 declare GradeBook's constructor. Like a method, a constructor's parameter list specifies the data it requires to perform its task. When you create a new object (as we'll do in Fig. B.8), this data is placed in the *parentheses that follow the class name*. Line 9 of Fig. B.7 indicates that the constructor has a String parameter called name. The name passed to the constructor is assigned to instance variable courseName in line 11.

Figure B.8 initializes GradeBook objects using the constructor. Lines 11–12 create and initialize the GradeBook object gradeBook1. The GradeBook constructor is called with the argument "CS101 Introduction to Java Programming" to initialize the course name. The class instance creation expression in lines 11–12 returns a reference to the new object, which is assigned to the variable gradeBook1. Lines 13–14 repeat this process, this time passing the argument "CS102 Data Structures in Java" to initialize the course name for gradeBook2. Lines 17–20 use each object's getCourseName method to obtain the course names and show that they were initialized when the objects were created. The output confirms that each GradeBook maintains its own copy of instance variable courseName.

An important difference between constructors and methods is that constructors cannot return values, so they cannot specify a return type (not even void). Normally, constructors are declared public. If a class does not include a constructor, the class's instance variables are initialized to their default values. *If you declare any constructors for a class, the Java compiler will not create a default constructor for that class.* Thus, we can no longer create a GradeBook object with new GradeBook() as we did in the earlier examples.

```
1   // Fig. B.8: GradeBookTest.java
2   // GradeBook constructor used to specify the course name at the
3   // time each GradeBook object is created.
4
5   public class GradeBookTest
6   {
7      // main method begins program execution
8      public static void main( String[] args )
9      {
10        // create GradeBook object
11        GradeBook gradeBook1 = new GradeBook(
12           "CS101 Introduction to Java Programming" );
13        GradeBook gradeBook2 = new GradeBook(
14           "CS102 Data Structures in Java" );
15
16        // display initial value of courseName for each GradeBook
17        System.out.printf( "gradeBook1 course name is: %s\n",
18           gradeBook1.getCourseName() );
19        System.out.printf( "gradeBook2 course name is: %s\n",
20           gradeBook2.getCourseName() );
21     } // end main
22  } // end class GradeBookTest
```

```
gradeBook1 course name is: CS101 Introduction to Java Programming
gradeBook2 course name is: CS102 Data Structures in Java
```

Fig. B.8 | GradeBook constructor used to specify the course name at the time each GradeBook object is created.

Constructors with Multiple Parameters

Sometimes you'll want to initialize objects with multiple data items. In Exercise B.11, we ask you to store the course name *and* the instructor's name in a GradeBook object. In this case, the GradeBook's constructor would be modified to receive two Strings, as in

```
public GradeBook( String courseName, String instructorName )
```

and you'd call the GradeBook constructor as follows:

```
GradeBook gradeBook = new GradeBook(
   "CS101 Introduction to Java Programming", "Sue Green" );
```

B.7 Floating-Point Numbers and Type double

We now depart temporarily from our GradeBook case study to declare an Account class that maintains the balance of a bank account. Most account balances are not whole numbers (such as 0, –22 and 1024). For this reason, class Account represents the account balance as a **floating-point number** (i.e., a number with a decimal point, such as 7.33, 0.0975 or 1000.12345). Java provides two primitive types for storing floating-point numbers in memory—float and double. They differ primarily in that double variables can store numbers with larger magnitude and finer detail (i.e., more digits to the right of the decimal point—also known as the number's **precision**) than float variables.

Floating-Point Number Precision and Memory Requirements

Variables of type **float** represent **single-precision floating-point numbers** and can represent up to *seven significant digits*. Variables of type **double** represent **double-precision floating-point numbers**. These require twice as much memory as float variables and provide *15 significant digits*—approximately double the precision of float variables. For the range of values required by most programs, variables of type float should suffice, but you can use double to "play it safe." In some applications, even double variables will be inadequate. Most programmers represent floating-point numbers with type double. In fact, Java treats all floating-point numbers you type in a program's source code (such as 7.33 and 0.0975) as double values by default. Such values in the source code are known as **floating-point literals**. See Appendix L for the ranges of values for floats and doubles.

Although floating-point numbers are not always 100% precise, they have numerous applications. For example, when we speak of a "normal" body temperature of 98.6, we do not need to be precise to a large number of digits. When we read the temperature on a thermometer as 98.6, it may actually be 98.5999473210643. Calling this number simply 98.6 is fine for most applications involving body temperatures. Owing to the imprecise nature of floating-point numbers, type double is preferred over type float, because double variables can represent floating-point numbers more accurately. For this reason, we primarily use type double throughout the book. For precise floating-point numbers, Java provides class BigDecimal (package java.math).

Floating-point numbers also arise as a result of division. In conventional arithmetic, when we divide 10 by 3, the result is 3.3333333..., with the sequence of 3s repeating infinitely. The computer allocates only a fixed amount of space to hold such a value, so clearly the stored floating-point value can be only an approximation.

Account Class with an Instance Variable of Type double

Our next application (Figs. B.9–B.10) contains a class named Account (Fig. B.9) that maintains the balance of a bank account. A typical bank services many accounts, each with its own balance, so line 7 declares an instance variable named balance of type double. It's an instance variable because it's declared in the body of the class but outside the class's method declarations (lines 10–16, 19–22 and 25–28). Every instance (i.e., object) of class Account contains its own copy of balance.

The class has a constructor and two methods. It's common for someone opening an account to deposit money immediately, so the constructor (lines 10–16) receives a parameter initialBalance of type double that represents the *starting balance*. Lines 14–15 ensure that initialBalance is greater than 0.0. If so, initialBalance's value is assigned to instance variable balance. Otherwise, balance remains at 0.0—its default initial value.

```
1   // Fig. B.9: Account.java
2   // Account class with a constructor to validate and
3   // initialize instance variable balance of type double.
4
5   public class Account
6   {
```

Fig. B.9 | Account class with a constructor to validate and initialize instance variable balance of type double. (Part 1 of 2.)

```
7     private double balance; // instance variable that stores the balance
8
9     // constructor
10    public Account( double initialBalance )
11    {
12        // validate that initialBalance is greater than 0.0;
13        // if it is not, balance is initialized to the default value 0.0
14        if ( initialBalance > 0.0 )
15            balance = initialBalance;
16    } // end Account constructor
17
18    // credit (add) an amount to the account
19    public void credit( double amount )
20    {
21        balance = balance + amount; // add amount to balance
22    } // end method credit
23
24    // return the account balance
25    public double getBalance()
26    {
27        return balance; // gives the value of balance to the calling method
28    } // end method getBalance
29 } // end class Account
```

Fig. B.9 | Account class with a constructor to validate and initialize instance variable balance of type double. (Part 2 of 2.)

Method credit (lines 19–22) does *not* return any data when it completes its task, so its return type is void. The method receives one parameter named amount—a double value that will be added to the balance. Line 21 adds amount to the current value of balance, then assigns the result to balance (thus replacing the prior balance amount).

Method getBalance (lines 25–28) allows clients of the class (i.e., other classes that use this class) to obtain the value of a particular Account object's balance. The method specifies return type double and an empty parameter list.

Once again, the statements in lines 15, 21 and 27 use instance variable balance even though it was *not* declared in any of the methods. We can use balance in these methods because it's an instance variable of the class.

AccountTest Class to Use Class Account

Class AccountTest (Fig. B.10) creates two Account objects (lines 10–11) and initializes them with 50.00 and -7.53, respectively. Lines 14–17 output the balance in each Account by calling the Account's getBalance method. When method getBalance is called for account1 from line 15, the value of account1's balance is returned from line 27 of Fig. B.9 and displayed by the System.out.printf statement (Fig. B.10, lines 14–15). Similarly, when method getBalance is called for account2 from line 17, the value of the account2's balance is returned from line 27 of Fig. B.9 and displayed by the System.out.printf statement (Fig. B.10, lines 16–17). The balance of account2 is 0.00, because the constructor ensured that the account could *not* begin with a negative balance. The value is output by printf with the format specifier %.2f. The format specifier %f is used to output values of type float or double. The .2 between % and f represents the number of decimal places (2) that should be output to the right of the decimal point in the floating-point number—also known as the number's **precision**. Any floating-point value output with %.2f will be rounded to the hundredths position—for example, 123.457 would be rounded to 123.46, 27.333 would be rounded to 27.33 and 123.455 would be rounded to 123.46.

```java
1   // Fig. B.10: AccountTest.java
2   // Inputting and outputting floating-point numbers with Account objects.
3   import java.util.Scanner;
4
5   public class AccountTest
6   {
7      // main method begins execution of Java application
8      public static void main( String[] args )
9      {
10        Account account1 = new Account( 50.00 ); // create Account object
11        Account account2 = new Account( -7.53 ); // create Account object
12
13        // display initial balance of each object
14        System.out.printf( "account1 balance: $%.2f\n",
15           account1.getBalance() );
16        System.out.printf( "account2 balance: $%.2f\n\n",
17           account2.getBalance() );
18
19        // create Scanner to obtain input from command window
20        Scanner input = new Scanner( System.in );
21        double depositAmount; // deposit amount read from user
22
23        System.out.print( "Enter deposit amount for account1: " ); // prompt
24        depositAmount = input.nextDouble(); // obtain user input
25        System.out.printf( "\nadding %.2f to account1 balance\n\n",
26           depositAmount );
27        account1.credit( depositAmount ); // add to account1 balance
28
29        // display balances
30        System.out.printf( "account1 balance: $%.2f\n",
31           account1.getBalance() );
32        System.out.printf( "account2 balance: $%.2f\n\n",
33           account2.getBalance() );
34
35        System.out.print( "Enter deposit amount for account2: " ); // prompt
36        depositAmount = input.nextDouble(); // obtain user input
37        System.out.printf( "\nadding %.2f to account2 balance\n\n",
38           depositAmount );
39        account2.credit( depositAmount ); // add to account2 balance
40
41        // display balances
42        System.out.printf( "account1 balance: $%.2f\n",
43           account1.getBalance() );
44        System.out.printf( "account2 balance: $%.2f\n",
45           account2.getBalance() );
46     } // end main
47  } // end class AccountTest
```

Fig. B.10 | Inputting and outputting floating-point numbers with Account objects. (Part 1 of 2.)

```
account1 balance: $50.00
account2 balance: $0.00

Enter deposit amount for account1: 25.53

adding 25.53 to account1 balance

account1 balance: $75.53
account2 balance: $0.00

Enter deposit amount for account2: 123.45

adding 123.45 to account2 balance

account1 balance: $75.53
account2 balance: $123.45
```

Fig. B.10 | Inputting and outputting floating-point numbers with Account objects. (Part 2 of 2.)

Line 21 declares local variable depositAmount to store each deposit amount entered by the user. Unlike the instance variable balance in class Account, local variable deposit-Amount in main is *not* initialized to 0.0 by default. However, this variable does not need to be initialized here, because its value will be determined by the user's input.

Line 23 prompts the user to enter a deposit amount for account1. Line 24 obtains the input from the user by calling Scanner object input's **nextDouble** method, which returns a double value entered by the user. Lines 25–26 display the deposit amount. Line 27 calls object account1's credit method and supplies depositAmount as the method's argument. When the method is called, the argument's value is assigned to parameter amount (line 19 of Fig. B.9) of method credit (lines 19–22 of Fig. B.9); then method credit adds that value to the balance (line 21 of Fig. B.9). Lines 30–33 (Fig. B.10) output the balances of both Accounts again to show that only account1's balance changed.

Line 35 prompts the user to enter a deposit amount for account2. Line 36 obtains the input from the user by calling Scanner object input's nextDouble method. Lines 37–38 display the deposit amount. Line 39 calls object account2's credit method and supplies depositAmount as the method's argument; then method credit adds that value to the balance. Finally, lines 42–45 output the balances of both Accounts again to show that only account2's balance changed.

B.8 Wrap-Up

In this appendix, you learned how to declare instance variables of a class to maintain data for each object of the class, and how to declare methods that operate on that data. You learned how to call a method to tell it to perform its task and how to pass information to methods as arguments. You learned the difference between a local variable of a method and an instance variable of a class and that only instance variables are initialized automatically. You also learned how to use a class's constructor to specify the initial values for an object's instance variables. Finally, you learned about floating-point numbers—how to store them with variables of primitive type double, how to input them with a Scanner object and how to format them with printf and format specifier %f for display purposes. In the next appendix we begin our introduction to control statements, which specify the order in which a program's actions are performed. You'll use these in your methods to specify how they should perform their tasks.

Self-Review Exercises

B.1   Fill in the blanks in each of the following:
   a) Each class declaration that begins with keyword _____ must be stored in a file that has exactly the same name as the class and ends with the .java file-name extension.
   b) Keyword _____ in a class declaration is followed immediately by the class's name.
   c) Keyword _____ requests memory from the system to store an object, then calls the corresponding class's constructor to initialize the object.
   d) Each parameter must specify both a(n) _____ and a(n) _____.
   e) By default, classes that are compiled in the same directory are considered to be in the same package, known as the _____.
   f) When each object of a class maintains its own copy of an attribute, the field that represents the attribute is also known as a(n) _____.
   g) Java provides two primitive types for storing floating-point numbers in memory: _____ and _____.
   h) Variables of type double represent _____ floating-point numbers.
   i) Scanner method _____ returns a double value.
   j) Keyword public is an access _____.
   k) Return type _____ indicates that a method will not return a value.
   l) Scanner method _____ reads characters until it encounters a newline character, then returns those characters as a String.
   m) Class String is in package _____.
   n) A(n) _____ is not required if you always refer to a class with its fully qualified class name.
   o) A(n) _____ is a number with a decimal point, such as 7.33, 0.0975 or 1000.12345.
   p) Variables of type float represent _____ floating-point numbers.
   q) The format specifier _____ is used to output values of type float or double.
   r) Types in Java are divided into two categories—_____ types and _____ types.

B.2   State whether each of the following is *true* or *false*. If *false*, explain why.
   a) By convention, method names begin with an uppercase first letter, and all subsequent words in the name begin with a capital first letter.
   b) An import declaration is not required when one class in a package uses another in the same package.
   c) Empty parentheses following a method name in a method declaration indicate that the method does not require any parameters to perform its task.
   d) Variables or methods declared with access modifier private are accessible only to methods of the class in which they're declared.
   e) A primitive-type variable can be used to invoke a method.
   f) Variables declared in the body of a particular method are known as instance variables and can be used in all methods of the class.
   g) Every method's body is delimited by left and right braces ({ and }).
   h) Primitive-type local variables are initialized by default.
   i) Reference-type instance variables are initialized by default to the value null.
   j) Any class that contains public static void main(String[] args) can be used to execute an application.
   k) The number of arguments in the method call must match the number of parameters in the method declaration's parameter list.
   l) Floating-point values that appear in source code are known as floating-point literals and are type float by default.

B.3   What is the difference between a local variable and a field?

B.4   Explain the purpose of a method parameter. What is the difference between a parameter and an argument?

Answers to Self-Review Exercises

B.1   a) public. b) class. c) new. d) type, name. e) default package. f) instance variable. g) float, double. h) double-precision. i) nextDouble. j) modifier. k) void. l) nextLine. m) java.lang. n) import declaration. o) floating-point number. p) single-precision. q) %f. r) primitive, reference.

B.2   a)   False. By convention, method names begin with a lowercase first letter and all subsequent words in the name begin with a capital first letter. b) True. c) True. d) True. e) False. A primitive-type variable cannot be used to invoke a method—a reference to an object is required to invoke the object's methods. f) False. Such variables are called local variables and can be used only in the method in which they're declared. g) True. h) False. Primitive-type instance variables are initialized by default. Each local variable must explicitly be assigned a value. i) True. j) True. k) True. l) False. Such literals are of type double by default.

B.3   A local variable is declared in the body of a method and can be used only from the point at which it's declared through the end of the method declaration. A field is declared in a class, but not in the body of any of the class's methods. Also, fields are accessible to all methods of the class. (We'll see an exception to this in Appendix F.)

B.4   A parameter represents additional information that a method requires to perform its task. Each parameter required by a method is specified in the method's declaration. An argument is the actual value for a method parameter. When a method is called, the argument values are passed to the corresponding parameters of the method so that it can perform its task.

Exercises

B.5   *(Keyword new)* What's the purpose of keyword new? Explain what happens when you use it.

B.6   *(Default Constructors)* What is a default constructor? How are an object's instance variables initialized if a class has only a default constructor?

B.7   *(Instance Variables)* Explain the purpose of an instance variable.

B.8   *(Using Classes Without Importing Them)* Most classes need to be imported before they can be used in an application. Why is every application allowed to use classes System and String without first importing them?

B.9   *(Using a Class Without Importing It)* Explain how a program could use class Scanner without importing it.

B.10   (set *and* get *Methods)* Explain why a class might provide a *set* method and a *get* method for an instance variable.

B.11   *(Modified GradeBook Class)* Modify class GradeBook (Fig. B.7) as follows:
   a)   Include a String instance variable that represents the name of the course's instructor.
   b)   Provide a *set* method to change the instructor's name and a *get* method to retrieve it.
   c)   Modify the constructor to specify two parameters—one for the course name and one for the instructor's name.
   d)   Modify method displayMessage to output the welcome message and course name, followed by "This course is presented by: " and the instructor's name.

Use your modified class in a test application that demonstrates the class's new capabilities.

B.12   *(Modified Account Class)* Modify class Account (Fig. B.9) to provide a method called debit that withdraws money from an Account. Ensure that the debit amount does not exceed the

Account's balance. If it does, the balance should be left unchanged and the method should print a message indicating "Debit amount exceeded account balance." Modify class AccountTest (Fig. B.10) to test method debit.

B.13 *(Invoice Class)* Create a class called Invoice that a hardware store might use to represent an invoice for an item sold at the store. An Invoice should include four pieces of information as instance variables—a part number (type String), a part description (type String), a quantity of the item being purchased (type int) and a price per item (double). Your class should have a constructor that initializes the four instance variables. Provide a *set* and a *get* method for each instance variable. In addition, provide a method named getInvoiceAmount that calculates the invoice amount (i.e., multiplies the quantity by the price per item), then returns the amount as a double value. If the quantity is not positive, it should be set to 0. If the price per item is not positive, it should be set to 0.0. Write a test application named InvoiceTest that demonstrates class Invoice's capabilities.

B.14 *(Employee Class)* Create a class called Employee that includes three instance variables—a first name (type String), a last name (type String) and a monthly salary (double). Provide a constructor that initializes the three instance variables. Provide a *set* and a *get* method for each instance variable. If the monthly salary is not positive, do not set its value. Write a test application named EmployeeTest that demonstrates class Employee's capabilities. Create two Employee objects and display each object's *yearly* salary. Then give each Employee a 10% raise and display each Employee's yearly salary again.

B.15 *(Date Class)* Create a class called Date that includes three instance variables—a month (type int), a day (type int) and a year (type int). Provide a constructor that initializes the three instance variables and assumes that the values provided are correct. Provide a *set* and a *get* method for each instance variable. Provide a method displayDate that displays the month, day and year separated by forward slashes (/). Write a test application named DateTest that demonstrates class Date's capabilities.

Control Statements

C

Objectives

In this appendix you'll:

- Learn basic problem-solving techniques.

- Develop algorithms through the process of top-down, stepwise refinement.

- Use the if and if...else selection statements to choose among alternative actions.

- Use the while repetition statement to execute statements in a program repeatedly.

- Use counter-controlled repetition and sentinel-controlled repetition.

- Use the compound assignment, increment and decrement operators.

- Learn the essentials of counter-controlled repetition.

- Use the for and do...while repetition statements to execute statements in a program repeatedly.

- Implement multiple selection using the switch statement.

- Use the break and continue statements .

- Use the logical operators in conditional expressions.

C.1 Introduction

In this appendix, we discuss the theory and principles of structured programming. The concepts presented here are crucial in building classes and manipulating objects. We introduce Java's compound assignment, increment and decrement operators, and we discuss the portability of Java's primitive types. We demonstrate Java's for, do...while and switch statements. Through a series of short examples using while and for, we explore the essentials of counter-controlled repetition. We create a version of class GradeBook that uses a switch statement to count the number of A, B, C, D and F grade equivalents in a set of numeric grades entered by the user. We introduce the break and continue program-control statements. We discuss Java's logical operators, which enable you to use more complex conditional expressions in control statements.

C.2 Algorithms

Any computing problem can be solved by executing a series of actions in a specific order. A procedure for solving a problem in terms of

1. the **actions** to execute and
2. the **order** in which these actions execute

is called an **algorithm**. Correctly specifying the order in which the actions execute is important.

Consider the "rise-and-shine algorithm" followed by one executive for getting out of bed and going to work: (1) Get out of bed; (2) take off pajamas; (3) take a shower; (4) get dressed; (5) eat breakfast; (6) carpool to work. This routine gets the executive to work well prepared to make critical decisions. Suppose that the same steps are performed in a slightly different order: (1) Get out of bed; (2) take off pajamas; (3) get dressed; (4) take a shower; (5) eat breakfast; (6) carpool to work. In this case, our executive shows up for work soaking wet. Specifying the order in which statements (actions) execute in a program is called **program control**. This appendix investigates program control using Java's **control statements**.

C.3 Pseudocode

Pseudocode is an informal language that helps you develop algorithms without having to worry about the strict details of Java language syntax. The pseudocode we present is particularly useful for developing algorithms that will be converted to structured portions of Java programs. Pseudocode is similar to everyday English—it's convenient and user friendly, but it's not an actual computer programming language.

Pseudocode does not execute on computers. Rather, it helps you "think out" a program before attempting to write it in a programming language, such as Java. Pseudocode normally describes only statements representing the actions that occur after you convert a program from pseudocode to Java and the program is run on a computer. Such actions might include input, output or calculations.

C.4 Control Structures

Normally, statements in a program are executed one after the other in the order in which they're written. This process is called **sequential execution**. Various Java statements, which we'll soon discuss, enable you to specify that the next statement to execute is *not* necessarily the *next* one in sequence. This is called **transfer of control**.

During the 1960s, it became clear that the indiscriminate use of transfers of control was the root of much difficulty experienced by software development groups. The blame was pointed at the **goto statement** (used in most programming languages of the time), which allows you to specify a transfer of control to one of a wide range of destinations in a program. The term **structured programming** became almost synonymous with "goto elimination." [*Note:* Java does *not* have a goto statement; however, the word goto is *reserved* by Java and should *not* be used as an identifier in programs.]

Research had demonstrated that programs could be written *without* any goto statements. The challenge of the era for programmers was to shift their styles to "goto-less programming." Not until the 1970s did most programmers start taking structured programming seriously. The results were impressive. The key to these successes was that structured programs were clearer, easier to debug and modify, and more likely to be bug free in the first place.

Researchers demonstrated that all programs could be written in terms of only three control structures—the **sequence structure**, the **selection structure** and the **repetition structure**. When we introduce Java's control structure implementations, we'll refer to them in the terminology of the *Java Language Specification* as "control statements."

Sequence Structure in Java

The sequence structure is built into Java. Unless directed otherwise, the computer executes Java statements one after the other in the order in which they're written—that is, in sequence. Java lets you have as many actions as you want in a sequence structure. As we'll soon see, anywhere a single action may be placed, we may place several actions in sequence.

Selection Statements in Java

Java has three types of **selection statements**. The if statement either performs (selects) an action, if a condition is true, or skips it, if the condition is false. The if...else statement performs an action if a condition is true and performs a different action if the condition is false. The switch statement performs one of many different actions, depending on the value of an expression.

The if statement is a **single-selection statement** because it selects or ignores a *single* action (or, as we'll soon see, a *single group of actions*). The if...else statement is called a **double-selection statement** because it selects between *two different actions* (or *groups of actions*). The switch statement is called a **multiple-selection statement** because it selects among *many different actions* (or *groups of actions*).

Repetition Statements in Java

Java provides three **repetition statements** (also called **looping statements**) that enable programs to perform statements repeatedly as long as a condition (called the **loop-continuation condition**) remains true. The repetition statements are the while, do...while and for statements. The while and for statements perform the action (or group of actions) in their bodies zero or more times—if the loop-continuation condition is initially false, the action (or group of actions) will not execute. The do...while statement performs the action (or group of actions) in its body *one or more* times. The words if, else, switch, while, do and for are Java keywords.

C.5 if Single-Selection Statement

Programs use selection statements to choose among alternative courses of action. For example, suppose that the passing grade on an exam is 60. The pseudocode statement

> *If student's grade is greater than or equal to 60*
> > *Print "Passed"*

determines whether the condition "student's grade is greater than or equal to 60" is true. If so, "Passed" is printed, and the next pseudocode statement in order is "performed." If the condition is false, the *Print* statement is ignored, and the next pseudocode statement in order is performed.

The preceding pseudocode *If* statement easily may be converted to the Java statement

```
if ( studentGrade >= 60 )
    System.out.println( "Passed" );
```

C.6 if...else Double-Selection Statement

The if single-selection statement performs an indicated action only when the condition is true; otherwise, the action is skipped. The **if...else double-selection statement** allows you to specify an action to perform when the condition is true and a different action when the condition is false. For example, the pseudocode statement

> *If student's grade is greater than or equal to 60*
> > *Print "Passed"*
> *Else*
> > *Print "Failed"*

prints "Passed" if the student's grade is greater than or equal to 60, but prints "Failed" if it's less than 60. In either case, after printing occurs, the next pseudocode statement in sequence is "performed."

The preceding *If...Else* pseudocode statement can be written in Java as

```
if ( grade >= 60 )
    System.out.println( "Passed" );
else
    System.out.println( "Failed" );
```

Conditional Operator (?:)

Java provides the **conditional operator** (**?:**) that can be used in place of an if...else statement. This is Java's only **ternary operator** (operator that takes three operands). Together, the operands and the ?: symbol form a **conditional expression.** The first operand (to the left of the ?) is a **boolean expression** (i.e., a condition that evaluates to a boolean value—**true** or **false**), the second operand (between the ? and :) is the value of the conditional expression if the boolean expression is true and the third operand (to the right of the :) is the value of the conditional expression if the boolean expression evaluates to false. For example, the statement

```
System.out.println( studentGrade >= 60 ? "Passed" : "Failed" );
```

prints the value of println's conditional-expression argument. The conditional expression in this statement evaluates to the string "Passed" if the boolean expression student-Grade >= 60 is true and to the string "Failed" if it's false. Thus, this statement with the conditional operator performs essentially the same function as the if...else statement shown earlier in this section. The precedence of the conditional operator is low, so the entire conditional expression is normally placed in parentheses.

Nested if...else Statements

A program can test multiple cases by placing if...else statements inside other if...else statements to create **nested if...else statements.** For example, the following pseudocode represents a nested if...else that prints A for exam grades greater than or equal to 90, B for grades 80 to 89, C for grades 70 to 79, D for grades 60 to 69 and F for all other grades:

If student's grade is greater than or equal to 90
    Print "A"
else
    If student's grade is greater than or equal to 80
        Print "B"
    else
        If student's grade is greater than or equal to 70
            Print "C"
        else
            If student's grade is greater than or equal to 60
                Print "D"
            else
                Print "F"

This pseudocode may be written in Java as

```
if ( studentGrade >= 90 )
    System.out.println( "A" );
else
    if ( studentGrade >= 80 )
        System.out.println( "B" );
    else
        if ( studentGrade >= 70 )
            System.out.println( "C" );
        else
            if ( studentGrade >= 60 )
                System.out.println( "D" );
            else
                System.out.println( "F" );
```

If variable studentGrade is greater than or equal to 90, the first four conditions in the nested if...else statement will be true, but only the statement in the if part of the first if...else statement will execute. After that statement executes, the else part of the "outermost" if...else statement is skipped. Many programmers prefer to write the preceding nested if...else statement as

```
if ( studentGrade >= 90 )
    System.out.println( "A" );
else if ( studentGrade >= 80 )
    System.out.println( "B" );
else if ( studentGrade >= 70 )
    System.out.println( "C" );
else if ( studentGrade >= 60 )
    System.out.println( "D" );
else
    System.out.println( "F" );
```

The two forms are identical except for the spacing and indentation, which the compiler ignores. The latter form avoids deep indentation of the code to the right.

Blocks

The if statement normally expects only one statement in its body. To include several statements in the body of an if (or the body of an else for an if...else statement), enclose the statements in braces. Statements contained in a pair of braces form a **block**. A block can be placed anywhere in a program that a single statement can be placed. The following example includes a block in the else part of an if...else statement:

```
if ( grade >= 60 )
    System.out.println( "Passed" );
else
{
    System.out.println( "Failed" );
    System.out.println( "You must take this course again." );
}
```

In this case, if grade is less than 60, the program executes *both* statements in the body of the else and prints

```
Failed
You must take this course again.
```

Note the braces surrounding the two statements in the else clause. These braces are important. Without the braces, the statement

```
System.out.println( "You must take this course again." );
```

would be outside the body of the else part of the if...else statement and would execute *regardless* of whether the grade was less than 60.

Syntax errors (e.g., when one brace in a block is left out of the program) are caught by the compiler. A **logic error** (e.g., when both braces in a block are left out of the program) has its effect at execution time. A **fatal logic error** causes a program to fail and terminate prematurely. A **nonfatal logic error** allows a program to continue executing but causes it to produce incorrect results.

C.7 while Repetition Statement

As an example of Java's **while repetition statement**, consider a program segment that finds the first power of 3 larger than 100. Suppose that the int variable product is initialized to 3. After the following while statement executes, product contains the result:

```
while ( product <= 100 )
    product = 3 * product;
```

When this while statement begins execution, the value of variable product is 3. Each iteration of the while statement multiplies product by 3, so product takes on the values 9, 27, 81 and 243 successively. When variable product becomes 243, the while-statement condition—product <= 100—becomes false. This terminates the repetition, so the final value of product is 243. At this point, program execution continues with the next statement after the while statement.

Common Programming Error C.1
*Not providing in the body of a while statement an action that eventually causes the condition in the while to become false normally results in a logic error called an **infinite loop** (the loop never terminates).*

C.8 Case Study: Counter-Controlled Repetition

To illustrate how algorithms are developed, we modify the GradeBook class of Appendix B to solve two variations of a problem that averages student grades. Consider the following problem statement:

> *A class of ten students took a quiz. The grades (integers in the range 0 to 100) for this quiz are available to you. Determine the class average on the quiz.*

The class average is equal to the sum of the grades divided by the number of students. The algorithm for solving this problem on a computer must input each grade, keep track of the total of all grades input, perform the averaging calculation and print the result.

Pseudocode Algorithm with Counter-Controlled Repetition

Let's use pseudocode to list the actions to execute and specify the order in which they should execute. We use **counter-controlled repetition** to input the grades one at a time. This technique uses a variable called a **counter** (or **control variable**) to control the number of times a set of statements will execute. In this example, repetition terminates when the counter exceeds 10. This section presents a fully developed pseudocode algorithm (Fig. C.1) and a version of class GradeBook (Fig. C.2) that implements the algorithm in a Java method. We then present an application (Fig. C.3) that demonstrates the algorithm in action.

Note the references in the algorithm of Fig. C.1 to a total and a counter. A **total** is a variable used to accumulate the sum of several values. A counter is a variable used to count—in this case, the grade counter indicates which of the 10 grades is about to be entered by the user. Variables used to store totals are normally initialized to zero before being used in a program.

```
 1    Set total to zero
 2    Set grade counter to one
 3
 4    While grade counter is less than or equal to ten
 5        Prompt the user to enter the next grade
 6        Input the next grade
 7        Add the grade into the total
 8        Add one to the grade counter
 9
10    Set the class average to the total divided by ten
11    Print the class average
```

Fig. C.1 | Pseudocode algorithm that uses counter-controlled repetition to solve the class-average problem.

Implementing Counter-Controlled Repetition in Class GradeBook

Class GradeBook (Fig. C.2) contains a constructor (lines 11–14) that assigns a value to the class's instance variable courseName (declared in line 8). Lines 17–20, 23–26 and 29–34 declare methods setCourseName, getCourseName and displayMessage, respectively. Lines 37–66 declare method determineClassAverage, which implements the class-averaging algorithm described by the pseudocode in Fig. C.1.

Line 40 declares and initializes Scanner variable input, which is used to read values entered by the user. Lines 42–45 declare local variables total, gradeCounter, grade and average to be of type int. Variable grade stores the user input.

```
1    // Fig. C.2: GradeBook.java
2    // GradeBook class that solves the class-average problem using
3    // counter-controlled repetition.
4    import java.util.Scanner; // program uses class Scanner
5
6    public class GradeBook
7    {
8        private String courseName; // name of course this GradeBook represents
```

Fig. C.2 | GradeBook class that solves the class-average problem using counter-controlled repetition. (Part 1 of 3.)

```
 9
10      // constructor initializes courseName
11      public GradeBook( String name )
12      {
13          courseName = name; // initializes courseName
14      } // end constructor
15
16      // method to set the course name
17      public void setCourseName( String name )
18      {
19          courseName = name; // store the course name
20      } // end method setCourseName
21
22      // method to retrieve the course name
23      public String getCourseName()
24      {
25          return courseName;
26      } // end method getCourseName
27
28      // display a welcome message to the GradeBook user
29      public void displayMessage()
30      {
31          // getCourseName gets the name of the course
32          System.out.printf( "Welcome to the grade book for\n%s!\n\n",
33              getCourseName() );
34      } // end method displayMessage
35
36      // determine class average based on 10 grades entered by user
37      public void determineClassAverage()
38      {
39          // create Scanner to obtain input from command window
40          Scanner input = new Scanner( System.in );
41
42          int total; // sum of grades entered by user
43          int gradeCounter; // number of the grade to be entered next
44          int grade; // grade value entered by user
45          int average; // average of grades
46
47          // initialization phase
48          total = 0; // initialize total
49          gradeCounter = 1; // initialize loop counter
50
51          // processing phase uses counter-controlled repetition
52          while ( gradeCounter <= 10 ) // loop 10 times
53          {
54              System.out.print( "Enter grade: " ); // prompt
55              grade = input.nextInt(); // input next grade
56              total = total + grade; // add grade to total
57              gradeCounter = gradeCounter + 1; // increment counter by 1
58          } // end while
59
```

Fig. C.2 | GradeBook class that solves the class-average problem using counter-controlled repetition. (Part 2 of 3.)

```
60          // termination phase
61          average = total / 10; // integer division yields integer result
62
63          // display total and average of grades
64          System.out.printf( "\nTotal of all 10 grades is %d\n", total );
65          System.out.printf( "Class average is %d\n", average );
66      } // end method determineClassAverage
67 } // end class GradeBook
```

Fig. C.2 | GradeBook class that solves the class-average problem using counter-controlled repetition. (Part 3 of 3.)

The declarations (in lines 42–45) appear in the body of method determineClassAverage. A local variable's declaration must appear *before* the variable is used in that method. A local variable cannot be accessed outside the method in which it's declared.

The assignments (in lines 48–49) initialize total to 0 and gradeCounter to 1. Line 52 indicates that the while statement should continue looping (also called **iterating**) as long as gradeCounter's value is less than or equal to 10. While this condition remains true, the while statement repeatedly executes the statements between the braces that delimit its body (lines 54–57).

Line 54 displays the prompt "Enter grade: ". Line 55 reads the grade entered by the user and assigns it to variable grade. Then line 56 adds the new grade entered by the user to the total and assigns the result to total, which replaces its previous value.

Line 57 adds 1 to gradeCounter to indicate that the program has processed a grade and is ready to input the next grade from the user. Incrementing gradeCounter eventually causes it to exceed 10. Then the loop terminates, because its condition (line 52) becomes false.

When the loop terminates, line 61 performs the averaging calculation and assigns its result to the variable average. Line 64 uses System.out's printf method to display the text "Total of all 10 grades is " followed by variable total's value. Line 65 then uses printf to display the text "Class average is " followed by variable average's value. After reaching line 66, method determineClassAverage returns control to the calling method (i.e., main in GradeBookTest of Fig. C.3).

Class *GradeBookTest*

Class GradeBookTest (Fig. C.3) creates an object of class GradeBook (Fig. C.2) and demonstrates its capabilities. Lines 10–11 of Fig. C.3 create a new GradeBook object and assign it to variable myGradeBook. The String in line 11 is passed to the GradeBook constructor (lines 11–14 of Fig. C.2). Line 13 calls myGradeBook's displayMessage method to display a welcome message to the user. Line 14 then calls myGradeBook's determineClassAverage method to allow the user to enter 10 grades, for which the method then calculates and prints the average—the method performs the algorithm shown in Fig. C.1.

```
1  // Fig. C.3: GradeBookTest.java
2  // Create GradeBook object and invoke its determineClassAverage method.
3
```

Fig. C.3 | GradeBookTest class creates an object of class GradeBook (Fig. C.2) and invokes its determineClassAverage method. (Part 1 of 2.)

```
4   public class GradeBookTest
5   {
6      public static void main( String[] args )
7      {
8         // create GradeBook object myGradeBook and
9         // pass course name to constructor
10        GradeBook myGradeBook = new GradeBook(
11           "CS101 Introduction to Java Programming" );
12
13        myGradeBook.displayMessage(); // display welcome message
14        myGradeBook.determineClassAverage(); // find average of 10 grades
15     } // end main
16  } // end class GradeBookTest
```

```
Welcome to the grade book for
CS101 Introduction to Java Programming!

Enter grade: 67
Enter grade: 78
Enter grade: 89
Enter grade: 67
Enter grade: 87
Enter grade: 98
Enter grade: 93
Enter grade: 85
Enter grade: 82
Enter grade: 100

Total of all 10 grades is 846
Class average is 84
```

Fig. C.3 | GradeBookTest class creates an object of class GradeBook (Fig. C.2) and invokes its determineClassAverage method. (Part 2 of 2.)

Notes on Integer Division and Truncation

The averaging calculation performed by method determineClassAverage in response to the method call at line 14 in Fig. C.3 produces an integer result. The program's output indicates that the sum of the grade values in the sample execution is 846, which, when divided by 10, should yield the floating-point number 84.6. However, the result of the calculation total / 10 (line 61 of Fig. C.2) is the integer 84, because total and 10 are both integers. Dividing two integers results in **integer division**—any fractional part of the calculation is lost (i.e., **truncated**).

C.9 Case Study: Sentinel-Controlled Repetition

Let's generalize Section C.8's class-average problem. Consider the following problem:

Develop a class-averaging program that processes grades for an arbitrary number of students each time it's run.

In the previous class-average example, the problem statement specified the number of students, so the number of grades (10) was known in advance. In this example, no indication is given of how many grades the user will enter during the program's execution. The program must process an arbitrary number of grades. How can it determine when to stop reading grades from the user? How will it know when to calculate and print the class average?

One way to solve this problem is to use a special value called a **sentinel value** (also called a **signal value**, a **dummy value** or a **flag value**) to indicate "end of data entry." The user enters grades until all legitimate grades have been entered. The user then types the sentinel value to indicate that no more grades will be entered. **Sentinel-controlled repetition** is often called **indefinite repetition** because the number of repetitions is *not* known before the loop begins executing.

Clearly, a sentinel value must be chosen that cannot be confused with an acceptable input value. Grades on a quiz are nonnegative integers, so –1 is an acceptable sentinel value for this problem. Thus, a run of the class-average program might process a stream of inputs such as 95, 96, 75, 74, 89 and –1. The program would then compute and print the class average for the grades 95, 96, 75, 74 and 89; since –1 is the sentinel value, it should *not* enter into the averaging calculation. The complete pseudocode for the class-average problem is shown in Fig. C.4.

1   *Initialize total to zero*
2   *Initialize counter to zero*
3
4   *Prompt the user to enter the first grade*
5   *Input the first grade (possibly the sentinel)*
6
7   *While the user has not yet entered the sentinel*
8   *Add this grade into the running total*
9   *Add one to the grade counter*
10   *Prompt the user to enter the next grade*
11   *Input the next grade (possibly the sentinel)*
12
13 *If the counter is not equal to zero*
14   *Set the average to the total divided by the counter*
15   *Print the average*
16 *else*
17   *Print "No grades were entered"*

Fig. C.4 | Class-average problem pseudocode algorithm with sentinel-controlled repetition.

Implementing Sentinel-Controlled Repetition in Class GradeBook

Figure C.5 shows the Java class GradeBook containing method determineClassAverage that implements the pseudocode algorithm of Fig. C.4. Although each grade is an integer, the averaging calculation is likely to produce a number with a decimal point—in other words, a real (i.e., floating-point) number. The type int cannot represent such a number, so this class uses type double to do so.

```java
1   // Fig. C.5: GradeBook.java
2   // GradeBook class that solves the class-average problem using
3   // sentinel-controlled repetition.
4   import java.util.Scanner; // program uses class Scanner
5
6   public class GradeBook
7   {
8      private String courseName; // name of course this GradeBook represents
9
10     // constructor initializes courseName
11     public GradeBook( String name )
12     {
13        courseName = name; // initializes courseName
14     } // end constructor
15
16     // method to set the course name
17     public void setCourseName( String name )
18     {
19        courseName = name; // store the course name
20     } // end method setCourseName
21
22     // method to retrieve the course name
23     public String getCourseName()
24     {
25        return courseName;
26     } // end method getCourseName
27
28     // display a welcome message to the GradeBook user
29     public void displayMessage()
30     {
31        // getCourseName gets the name of the course
32        System.out.printf( "Welcome to the grade book for\n%s!\n\n",
33           getCourseName() );
34     } // end method displayMessage
35
36     // determine the average of an arbitrary number of grades
37     public void determineClassAverage()
38     {
39        // create Scanner to obtain input from command window
40        Scanner input = new Scanner( System.in );
41
42        int total; // sum of grades
43        int gradeCounter; // number of grades entered
44        int grade; // grade value
45        double average; // number with decimal point for average
46
47        // initialization phase
48        total = 0; // initialize total
49        gradeCounter = 0; // initialize loop counter
50
```

Fig. C.5 | GradeBook class that solves the class-average problem using sentinel-controlled repetition. (Part 1 of 2.)

```
51          // processing phase
52          // prompt for input and read grade from user
53          System.out.print( "Enter grade or -1 to quit: " );
54          grade = input.nextInt();
55
56          // loop until sentinel value read from user
57          while ( grade != -1 )
58          {
59              total = total + grade; // add grade to total
60              gradeCounter = gradeCounter + 1; // increment counter
61
62              // prompt for input and read next grade from user
63              System.out.print( "Enter grade or -1 to quit: " );
64              grade = input.nextInt();
65          } // end while
66
67          // termination phase
68          // if user entered at least one grade...
69          if ( gradeCounter != 0 )
70          {
71              // calculate average of all grades entered
72              average = (double) total / gradeCounter;
73
74              // display total and average (with two digits of precision)
75              System.out.printf( "\nTotal of the %d grades entered is %d\n",
76                  gradeCounter, total );
77              System.out.printf( "Class average is %.2f\n", average );
78          } // end if
79          else // no grades were entered, so output appropriate message
80              System.out.println( "No grades were entered" );
81      } // end method determineClassAverage
82  } // end class GradeBook
```

Fig. C.5 | GradeBook class that solves the class-average problem using sentinel-controlled repetition. (Part 2 of 2.)

In this example, we see that control statements may be *stacked* on top of one another (in sequence). The while statement (lines 57–65) is followed in sequence by an if...else statement (lines 69–80). Much of the code in this program is identical to that in Fig. C.2, so we concentrate on the new concepts.

Line 45 declares double variable average, which allows us to store the class average as a floating-point number. Line 49 initializes gradeCounter to 0, because no grades have been entered yet. To keep an accurate record of the number of grades entered, the program increments gradeCounter only when the user enters a valid grade.

Program Logic for Sentinel-Controlled Repetition vs. Counter-Controlled Repetition
Compare the program logic for sentinel-controlled repetition in this application with that for counter-controlled repetition in Fig. C.2. In counter-controlled repetition, each iteration of the while statement (e.g., lines 52–58 of Fig. C.2) reads a value from the user, for the specified number of iterations. In sentinel-controlled repetition, the program reads the first value (lines 53–54 of Fig. C.5) before reaching the while. This value determines

whether the program's flow of control should enter the body of the `while`. If the condition of the `while` is false, the user entered the sentinel value, so the body of the `while` does not execute (i.e., no grades were entered). If, on the other hand, the condition is true, the body begins execution, and the loop adds the `grade` value to the `total` (line 59). Then lines 63–64 in the loop body input the next value from the user. Next, program control reaches the closing right brace of the loop body at line 65, so execution continues with the test of the `while`'s condition (line 57). The condition uses the most recent `grade` input by the user to determine whether the loop body should execute again. The value of variable `grade` is always input from the user immediately before the program tests the `while` condition. This allows the program to determine whether the value just input is the sentinel value *before* the program processes that value (i.e., adds it to the `total`). If the sentinel value is input, the loop terminates, and the program does not add –1 to the `total`.

After the loop terminates, the `if...else` statement at lines 69–80 executes. The condition at line 69 determines whether any grades were input. If none were input, the `else` part (lines 79–80) of the `if...else` statement executes and displays the message "No grades were entered" and the method returns control to the calling method.

Explicitly and Implicitly Converting Between Primitive Types

If at least one grade was entered, line 72 of Fig. C.5 calculates the average of the grades. Recall from Fig. C.2 that integer division yields an integer result. Even though variable average is declared as a `double` (line 45), the calculation

```
average = total / gradeCounter;
```

loses the fractional part of the quotient *before* the result of the division is assigned to average. This occurs because `total` and `gradeCounter` are *both* integers, and integer division yields an integer result. To perform a floating-point calculation with integer values, we must temporarily treat these values as floating-point numbers for use in the calculation. Java provides the **unary cast operator** to accomplish this task. Line 72 uses the **(double)** cast operator—a unary operator—to create a *temporary* floating-point copy of its operand `total` (which appears to the right of the operator). Using a cast operator in this manner is called **explicit conversion** or **type casting**. The value stored in `total` is still an integer.

The calculation now consists of a floating-point value (the temporary `double` version of `total`) divided by the integer `gradeCounter`. Java knows how to evaluate only arithmetic expressions in which the operands' types are *identical*. To ensure that the operands are of the same type, Java performs an operation called **promotion** (or **implicit conversion**) on selected operands. For example, in an expression containing values of the types `int` and `double`, the `int` values are promoted to `double` values for use in the expression. In this example, the value of `gradeCounter` is promoted to type `double`, then the floating-point division is performed and the result of the calculation is assigned to `average`. As long as the `(double)` cast operator is applied to *any* variable in the calculation, the calculation will yield a `double` result.

A cast operator is formed by placing parentheses around any type's name. The operator is a **unary operator** (i.e., an operator that takes only one operand). Java also supports unary versions of the plus (+) and minus (–) operators, so you can write expressions like –7 or +5. Cast operators associate from right to left and have the same precedence as other unary operators, such as unary + and unary -. (See the operator precedence chart in Appendix K.)

Line 77 displays the class average. In this example, we display the class average rounded to the nearest hundredth. The format specifier %.2f in printf's format control string indicates that variable average's value should be displayed with two digits of precision to the right of the decimal point—indicated by .2 in the format specifier. The three grades entered during the sample execution of class GradeBookTest (Fig. C.6) total 257, which yields the average 85.666666.... Method printf uses the precision in the format specifier to round the value to the specified number of digits. In this program, the average is rounded to the hundredths position and is displayed as 85.67.

```java
1   // Fig. C.6: GradeBookTest.java
2   // Create GradeBook object and invoke its determineClassAverage method.
3
4   public class GradeBookTest
5   {
6      public static void main( String[] args )
7      {
8         // create GradeBook object myGradeBook and
9         // pass course name to constructor
10        GradeBook myGradeBook = new GradeBook(
11           "CS101 Introduction to Java Programming" );
12
13        myGradeBook.displayMessage(); // display welcome message
14        myGradeBook.determineClassAverage(); // find average of grades
15     } // end main
16  } // end class GradeBookTest
```

```
Welcome to the grade book for
CS101 Introduction to Java Programming!

Enter grade or -1 to quit: 97
Enter grade or -1 to quit: 88
Enter grade or -1 to quit: 72
Enter grade or -1 to quit: -1

Total of the 3 grades entered is 257
Class average is 85.67
```

Fig. C.6 | GradeBookTest class creates an object of class GradeBook (Fig. C.5) and invokes its determineClassAverage method.

C.10 Case Study: Nested Control Statements

We've seen that control statements can be stacked on top of one another (in sequence). In this case study, we examine the only other structured way control statements can be connected— nesting one control statement within another.

Consider the following problem statement:

> *A college offers a course that prepares students for the state licensing exam for real estate brokers. Last year, ten of the students who completed this course took the exam.*

The college wants to know how well its students did on the exam. You've been asked to write a program to summarize the results. You've been given a list of these 10 students. Next to each name is written a 1 if the student passed the exam or a 2 if the student failed.

Your program should analyze the results of the exam as follows:

1. *Input each test result (i.e., a 1 or a 2). Display the message "Enter result" on the screen each time the program requests another test result.*

2. *Count the number of test results of each type.*

3. *Display a summary of the test results, indicating the number of students who passed and the number who failed.*

4. *If more than eight students passed the exam, print the message "Bonus to instructor!"*

The complete pseudocode appears in Fig. C.7. The Java class that implements the pseudocode algorithm and two sample executions are shown in Fig. C.8. Lines 13–16 of `main` declare the variables that method `processExamResults` of class `Analysis` uses to process the examination results. Several of these declarations use Java's ability to incorporate variable initialization into declarations (`passes` is assigned 0, `failures` 0 and `student-Counter` 1). Looping programs may require initialization at the beginning of each repetition—normally performed by assignment statements rather than in declarations. Java requires that local variables be initialized before their values are used in an expression.

1	*Initialize passes to zero*
2	*Initialize failures to zero*
3	*Initialize student counter to one*
4	
5	*While student counter is less than or equal to 10*
6	*Prompt the user to enter the next exam result*
7	*Input the next exam result*
8	
9	*If the student passed*
10	*Add one to passes*
11	*Else*
12	*Add one to failures*
13	
14	*Add one to student counter*
15	
16	*Print the number of passes*
17	*Print the number of failures*
18	
19	*If more than eight students passed*
20	*Print "Bonus to instructor!"*

Fig. C.7 | Pseudocode for examination-results problem.

The `while` statement (lines 19–33) loops 10 times. During each iteration, the loop inputs and processes one exam result. Notice that the `if...else` statement (lines 26–29) for processing each result is *nested* in the while statement. If the result is 1, the if...else statement increments passes; otherwise, it assumes the result is 2 and increments failures. Line 32 increments studentCounter before the loop condition is tested again at line 19. After 10 values have been input, the loop terminates and line 36 displays the number of passes and failures. The if statement at lines 39–40 determines whether more than eight students passed the exam and, if so, outputs the message "Bonus to instructor!".

```java
1   // Fig. C.8: Analysis.java
2   // Analysis of examination results using nested control statements.
3   import java.util.Scanner; // class uses class Scanner
4
5   public class Analysis
6   {
7      public static void main( String[] args )
8      {
9         // create Scanner to obtain input from command window
10        Scanner input = new Scanner( System.in );
11
12        // initializing variables in declarations
13        int passes = 0; // number of passes
14        int failures = 0; // number of failures
15        int studentCounter = 1; // student counter
16        int result; // one exam result (obtains value from user)
17
18        // process 10 students using counter-controlled loop
19        while ( studentCounter <= 10 )
20        {
21           // prompt user for input and obtain value from user
22           System.out.print( "Enter result (1 = pass, 2 = fail): " );
23           result = input.nextInt();
24
25           // if...else is nested in the while statement
26           if ( result == 1 )          // if result 1,
27              passes = passes + 1;     // increment passes;
28           else                        // else result is not 1, so
29              failures = failures + 1; // increment failures
30
31           // increment studentCounter so loop eventually terminates
32           studentCounter = studentCounter + 1;
33        } // end while
34
35        // termination phase; prepare and display results
36        System.out.printf( "Passed: %d\nFailed: %d\n", passes, failures );
37
38        // determine whether more than 8 students passed
39        if ( passes > 8 )
40           System.out.println( "Bonus to instructor!" );
41     } // end main
42  } // end class Analysis
```

Fig. C.8 | Analysis of examination results using nested control statements. (Part 1 of 2.)

```
Enter result (1 = pass, 2 = fail): 1
Enter result (1 = pass, 2 = fail): 2
Enter result (1 = pass, 2 = fail): 1
Enter result (1 = pass, 2 = fail): 1
Enter result (1 = pass, 2 = fail): 1
Enter result (1 = pass, 2 = fail): 1
Enter result (1 = pass, 2 = fail): 1
Enter result (1 = pass, 2 = fail): 1
Enter result (1 = pass, 2 = fail): 1
Enter result (1 = pass, 2 = fail): 1
Passed: 9
Failed: 1
Bonus to instructor!
```

Fig. C.8 | Analysis of examination results using nested control statements. (Part 2 of 2.)

During the sample execution, the condition at line 39 of method main is true—more than eight students passed the exam, so the program outputs a message to bonus the instructor.

This example contains only one class, with method main performing all the class's work. Occasionally, when it does not make sense to try to create a *reusable* class to demonstrate a concept, we'll place the program's statements entirely within the main method of a single class.

C.11 Compound Assignment Operators

The **compound assignment operators** abbreviate assignment expressions. Statements like

>   *variable* = *variable   operator   expression*;

where *operator* is one of the binary operators +, -, *, / or % (or others we discuss later in the text) can be written in the form

>   *variable   operator*= *expression*;

For example, you can abbreviate the statement

>   c = c + 3;

with the **addition compound assignment operator, +=**, as

>   c += 3;

The += operator adds the value of the expression on its right to the value of the variable on its left and stores the result in the variable on the left of the operator. Thus, the assignment expression c += 3 adds 3 to c. Figure C.9 shows the arithmetic compound assignment operators, sample expressions using the operators and explanations of what the operators do.

C.12 Increment and Decrement Operators

Java provides two unary operators (summarized in Fig. C.10) for adding 1 to or subtracting 1 from the value of a numeric variable. These are the unary **increment operator, ++**, and the unary **decrement operator, --**. A program can increment by 1 the value of a vari-

Assignment operator	Sample expression	Explanation	Assigns
Assume: `int c = 3, d = 5, e = 4, f = 6, g = 12;`			
+=	c += 7	c = c + 7	10 to c
-=	d -= 4	d = d - 4	1 to d
*=	e *= 5	e = e * 5	20 to e
/=	f /= 3	f = f / 3	2 to f
%=	g %= 9	g = g % 9	3 to g

Fig. C.9 | Arithmetic compound assignment operators.

Operator	Operator name	Sample expression	Explanation
++	prefix increment	++a	Increment a by 1, then use the new value of a in the expression in which a resides.
++	postfix increment	a++	Use the current value of a in the expression in which a resides, then increment a by 1.
--	prefix decrement	--b	Decrement b by 1, then use the new value of b in the expression in which b resides.
--	postfix decrement	b--	Use the current value of b in the expression in which b resides, then decrement b by 1.

Fig. C.10 | Increment and decrement operators.

able called c using the increment operator, ++, rather than the expression c = c + 1 or c += 1. An increment or decrement operator that's prefixed to (placed before) a variable is referred to as the **prefix increment** or **prefix decrement operator**, respectively. An increment or decrement operator that's postfixed to (placed after) a variable is referred to as the **postfix increment** or **postfix decrement operator**, respectively.

Using the prefix increment (or decrement) operator to add 1 to (or subtract 1 from) a variable is known as **preincrementing** (or **predecrementing**). This causes the variable to be incremented (decremented) by 1; then the new value of the variable is used in the expression in which it appears. Using the postfix increment (or decrement) operator to add 1 to (or subtract 1 from) a variable is known as **postincrementing** (or **postdecrementing**). This causes the current value of the variable to be used in the expression in which it appears; then the variable's value is incremented (decremented) by 1.

Figure C.11 demonstrates the difference between the prefix increment and postfix increment versions of the ++ increment operator. The decrement operator (--) works similarly. Line 11 initializes the variable c to 5, and line 12 outputs c's initial value. Line 13 outputs the value of the expression c++. This expression postincrements the variable c, so c's original value (5) is output, then c's value is incremented (to 6). Thus, line 13 outputs c's initial value (5) again. Line 14 outputs c's new value (6) to prove that the variable's value was indeed incremented in line 13.

```
1   // Fig. C.11: Increment.java
2   // Prefix increment and postfix increment operators.
3
4   public class Increment
5   {
6      public static void main( String[] args )
7      {
8         int c;
9
10        // demonstrate postfix increment operator
11        c = 5; // assign 5 to c
12        System.out.println( c );    // prints 5
13        System.out.println( c++ ); // prints 5 then postincrements
14        System.out.println( c );    // prints 6
15
16        System.out.println(); // skip a line
17
18        // demonstrate prefix increment operator
19        c = 5; // assign 5 to c
20        System.out.println( c );     // prints 5
21        System.out.println( ++c ); // preincrements then prints 6
22        System.out.println( c );     // prints 6
23     } // end main
24  } // end class Increment
```

```
5
5
6

5
6
6
```

Fig. C.11 | Preincrementing and postincrementing.

Line 19 resets c's value to 5, and line 20 outputs c's value. Line 21 outputs the value of the expression ++c. This expression preincrements c, so its value is incremented; then the new value (6) is output. Line 22 outputs c's value again to show that the value of c is still 6 after line 21 executes.

When incrementing or decrementing a variable in a statement by itself, the prefix increment and postfix increment forms have the same effect, and the prefix decrement and postfix decrement forms have the same effect. It's only when a variable appears in the context of a larger expression that preincrementing and postincrementing the variable have different effects (and similarly for predecrementing and postdecrementing).

C.13 Primitive Types

The table in Appendix L lists the eight primitive types in Java. Like its predecessor languages C and C++, Java requires all variables to have a type. For this reason, Java is referred to as a **strongly typed language**.

In C and C++, programmers frequently have to write separate versions of programs to support different computer platforms, because the primitive types are not guaranteed to be identical from computer to computer. For example, an int value on one machine might be represented by 16 bits (2 bytes) of memory, on a second machine by 32 bits (4 bytes) of memory, and on another machine by 64 bits (8 bytes) of memory. In Java, int values are always 32 bits (4 bytes).

Portability Tip C.1

The primitive types in Java are portable across all computer platforms that support Java.

Each type in Appendix L is listed with its size in bits (there are eight bits to a byte) and its range of values. Because the designers of Java want to ensure portability, they use internationally recognized standards for character formats (Unicode; for more information, visit www.unicode.org) and floating-point numbers (IEEE 754; for more information, visit grouper.ieee.org/groups/754/).

C.14 Essentials of Counter-Controlled Repetition

This section uses the while repetition statement introduced in Section C.7 to formalize the elements required to perform counter-controlled repetition, which requires

1. a **control variable** (or loop counter)

2. the **initial value** of the control variable

3. the **increment** (or **decrement**) by which the control variable is modified each time through the loop (also known as **each iteration of the loop**)

4. the **loop-continuation condition** that determines if looping should continue.

To see these elements of counter-controlled repetition, consider the application of Fig. C.12, which uses a loop to display the numbers from 1 through 10.

```java
1  // Fig. C.12: WhileCounter.java
2  // Counter-controlled repetition with the while repetition statement.
3
4  public class WhileCounter
5  {
6     public static void main( String[] args )
7     {
8        int counter = 1; // declare and initialize control variable
9
10       while ( counter <= 10 ) // loop-continuation condition
11       {
12          System.out.printf( "%d  ", counter );
13          ++counter; // increment control variable by 1
14       } // end while
15
16       System.out.println(); // output a newline
17    } // end main
18 } // end class WhileCounter
```

Fig. C.12 | Counter-controlled repetition with the while repetition statement. (Part 1 of 2.)

```
1  2  3  4  5  6  7  8  9  10
```

Fig. C.12 | Counter-controlled repetition with the while repetition statement. (Part 2 of 2.)

In Fig. C.12, the elements of counter-controlled repetition are defined in lines 8, 10 and 13. Line 8 declares the control variable (counter) as an int, reserves space for it in memory and sets its initial value to 1. Line 12 displays control variable counter's value during each iteration of the loop. Line 13 increments the control variable by 1 for each iteration of the loop. The loop-continuation condition in the while (line 10) tests whether the value of the control variable is less than or equal to 10 (the final value for which the condition is true). The program performs the body of this while even when the control variable is 10. The loop terminates when the control variable exceeds 10 (i.e., counter becomes 11).

C.15 for Repetition Statement

Java also provides the **for repetition statement**, which specifies the counter-controlled-repetition details in a single line of code. Figure C.13 reimplements the application of Fig. C.12 using for.

```java
1   // Fig. C.13: ForCounter.java
2   // Counter-controlled repetition with the for repetition statement.
3
4   public class ForCounter
5   {
6      public static void main( String[] args )
7      {
8         // for statement header includes initialization,
9         // loop-continuation condition and increment
10        for ( int counter = 1; counter <= 10; ++counter )
11           System.out.printf( "%d  ", counter );
12
13        System.out.println(); // output a newline
14     } // end main
15  } // end class ForCounter
```

```
1  2  3  4  5  6  7  8  9  10
s
```

Fig. C.13 | Counter-controlled repetition with the for repetition statement.

When the for statement (lines 10–11) begins executing, the control variable counter is declared and initialized to 1. Next, the program checks the loop-continuation condition, counter <= 10, which is between the two required semicolons. Because the initial value of counter is 1, the condition initially is true. Therefore, the body statement (line 11) displays control variable counter's value, namely 1. After executing the loop's body, the program increments counter in the expression ++counter, which appears to the right of the second semicolon. Then the loop-continuation test is performed again to determine whether the program should continue with the next iteration of the loop. At this point, the control variable's value is 2, so the condition is still true (the final value is not exceeded)—thus, the program performs the body statement again (i.e., the next iteration of the loop). This process continues until the numbers 1 through 10 have been displayed and the counter's value becomes 11, causing the loop-continuation test to fail and repetition to terminate (after 10 repetitions of the loop body). Then the program performs the first statement after the for—in this case, line 13.

Figure C.13 uses (in line 10) the loop-continuation condition counter <= 10. If you incorrectly specified counter < 10 as the condition, the loop would iterate only nine times. This is a common logic error called an **off-by-one error**.

A Closer Look at the for Statement's Header
Figure C.14 takes a closer look at the for statement in Fig. C.13. The for's first line (including the keyword for and everything in parentheses after for)—line 10 in Fig. C.13— is sometimes called the **for statement header**. The for header "does it all"—it specifies each item needed for counter-controlled repetition with a control variable. If there's more than one statement in the body of the for, braces are required to define the body of the loop. If the loop-continuation condition is initially false, the program does not execute the for statement's body—execution proceeds with the statement following the for.

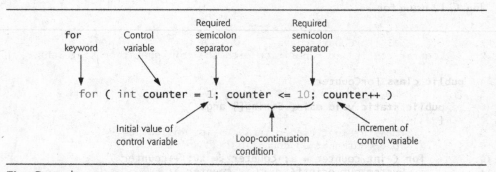

Fig. C.14 | for statement header components.

Scope of a for Statement's Control Variable
If the *initialization* expression in the for header declares the control variable (i.e., the control variable's type is specified before the variable name, as in Fig. C.13), the control variable can be used *only* in that for statement—it will not exist outside it. This restricted use is known as the variable's **scope**. The scope of a variable defines where it can be used in a program. For example, a local variable can be used *only* in the method that declares it and *only* from the point of declaration through the end of the method.

Expressions in a for Statement's Header Are Optional
All three expressions in a for header are optional. If the *loopContinuationCondition* is omitted, Java assumes that the loop-continuation condition is always *true*, thus creating an infinite loop. You might omit the *initialization* expression if the program initializes the control variable before the loop. You might omit the *increment* expression if the program calculates the increment with statements in the loop's body or if no increment is needed. The increment expression in a for acts as if it were a standalone statement at the end of the for's body.

C.16 Examples Using the for Statement

The following examples show techniques for varying the control variable in a for statement. In each case, we write the appropriate for header. Note the change in the relational operator for loops that *decrement* the control variable to count downward.

a) Vary the control variable from 1 to 100 in *increments* of 1.

```
for ( int i = 1; i <= 100; ++i )
```

b) Vary the control variable from 100 to 1 in *decrements* of 1.

```
for ( int i = 100; i >= 1; --i )
```

c) Vary the control variable from 7 to 77 in *increments* of 7.

```
for ( int i = 7; i <= 77; i += 7 )
```

d) Vary the control variable from 20 to 2 in *decrements* of 2.

```
for ( int i = 20; i >= 2; i -= 2 )
```

e) Vary the control variable over the values 2, 5, 8, 11, 14, 17, 20.

```
for ( int i = 2; i <= 20; i += 3 )
```

f) Vary the control variable over the values 99, 88, 77, 66, 55, 44, 33, 22, 11, 0.

```
for ( int i = 99; i >= 0; i -= 11 )
```

Application: Compound-Interest Calculations

Let's use the for statement to compute compound interest. Consider the following problem:

A person invests $1000 in a savings account yielding 5% interest. Assuming that all the interest is left on deposit, calculate and print the amount of money in the account at the end of each year for 10 years. Use the following formula to determine the amounts:

$$a = p (1 + r)^n$$

where

p is the original amount invested (i.e., the principal)
r is the annual interest rate (e.g., use 0.05 for 5%)
n is the number of years
a is the amount on deposit at the end of the nth year.

The solution to this problem (Fig. C.15) involves a loop that performs the indicated calculation for each of the 10 years the money remains on deposit. Lines 8–10 in method main declare double variables amount, principal and rate, and initialize principal to 1000.0 and rate to 0.05. Java treats floating-point constants like 1000.0 and 0.05 as type double. Similarly, Java treats whole-number constants like 7 and -22 as type int.

```
1   // Fig. C.15: Interest.java
2   // Compound-interest calculations with for.
3
```

Fig. C.15 | Compound-interest calculations with for. (Part 1 of 2.)

```
4    public class Interest
5    {
6       public static void main( String[] args )
7       {
8          double amount; // amount on deposit at end of each year
9          double principal = 1000.0; // initial amount before interest
10         double rate = 0.05; // interest rate
11
12         // display headers
13         System.out.printf( "%s%20s\n", "Year", "Amount on deposit" );
14
15         // calculate amount on deposit for each of ten years
16         for ( int year = 1; year <= 10; ++year )
17         {
18            // calculate new amount for specified year
19            amount = principal * Math.pow( 1.0 + rate, year );
20
21            // display the year and the amount
22            System.out.printf( "%4d%,20.2f\n", year, amount );
23         } // end for
24      } // end main
25   } // end class Interest
```

```
Year    Amount on deposit
   1            1,050.00
   2            1,102.50
   3            1,157.63
   4            1,215.51
   5            1,276.28
   6            1,340.10
   7            1,407.10
   8            1,477.46
   9            1,551.33
  10            1,628.89
```

Fig. C.15 | Compound-interest calculations with for. (Part 2 of 2.)

Formatting Strings with Field Widths and Justification

Line 13 outputs two column headers. The first column displays the year and the second the amount on deposit at the end of that year. We use the format specifier %20s to output the String "Amount on Deposit". The integer 20 between the % and the conversion character s indicates that the value should be displayed in a **field width** of 20—that is, printf displays the value with at least 20 character positions. If the value requires fewer than 20 character positions (17 in this example), the value is **right justified** in the field by default. If the year value to be output were more than four character positions wide, the field width would be extended to the right to accommodate the entire value—this would push the amount field to the right, upsetting the neat columns of our tabular output. To output values **left justified**, simply precede the field width with the **minus sign (–) formatting flag** (e.g., %-20s).

Performing the Interest Calculations

The for statement (lines 16–23) executes its body 10 times, varying control variable year from 1 to 10 in increments of 1. This loop terminates when year becomes 11. (Variable year represents *n* in the problem statement.)

Classes provide methods that perform common tasks on objects. In fact, most methods must be called on a specific object. For example, to output text in Fig. C.15, line 13 calls method printf on the System.out object. Many classes also provide methods that perform common tasks and do *not* require objects. These are called static methods. For example, Java does not include an exponentiation operator, so the designers of Java's Math class defined static method pow for raising a value to a power. You can call a static method by specifying the class name followed by a dot (.) and the method name, as in

ClassName.*methodName*(*arguments*)

In Appendix D, you'll learn how to implement static methods in your own classes.

We use static method **pow** of class **Math** to perform the compound-interest calculation in Fig. C.15. Math.pow(x, y) calculates the value of x raised to the yth power. The method receives two double arguments and returns a double value. Line 19 performs the calculation $a = p(1 + r)^n$, where a is amount, p is principal, r is rate and n is year. Class Math is defined in package java.lang, so you do *not* need to import class Math to use it.

Formatting Floating-Point Numbers

After each calculation, line 22 outputs the year and the amount on deposit at the end of that year. The year is output in a field width of four characters (as specified by %4d). The amount is output as a floating-point number with the format specifier %,20.2f. The **comma (,) formatting flag** indicates that the floating-point value should be output with a **grouping separator**. The actual separator used is specific to the user's locale (i.e., country). For example, in the United States, the number will be output using commas to separate every three digits and a decimal point to separate the fractional part of the number, as in 1,234.45. The number 20 in the format specification indicates that the value should be output right justified in a field width of 20 characters. The .2 specifies the formatted number's precision—in this case, the number is rounded to the nearest hundredth and output with two digits to the right of the decimal point.

C.17 do...while Repetition Statement

The **do...while repetition statement** is similar to the while statement. In the while, the program tests the loop-continuation condition at the beginning of the loop, before executing the loop's body; if the condition is false, the body *never* executes. The do...while statement tests the loop-continuation condition *after* executing the loop's body; therefore, *the body always executes at least once*. When a do...while statement terminates, execution continues with the next statement in sequence. Figure C.16 uses a do...while (lines 10–14) to output the numbers 1–10.

```
1   // Fig. C.16: DoWhileTest.java
2   // do...while repetition statement.
3
4   public class DoWhileTest
5   {
6      public static void main( String[] args )
7      {
```

Fig. C.16 | do...while repetition statement. (Part 1 of 2.)

```
8        int counter = 1; // initialize counter
9
10       do
11       {
12          System.out.printf( "%d  ", counter );
13          ++counter;
14       } while ( counter <= 10 ); // end do...while
15
16       System.out.println(); // outputs a newline
17    } // end main
18 } // end class DoWhileTest
```

```
1 2 3 4 5 6 7 8 9 10
```

Fig. C.16 | do...while repetition statement. (Part 2 of 2.)

Line 8 declares and initializes control variable counter. Upon entering the do...while statement, line 12 outputs counter's value and line 13 increments counter. Then the program evaluates the loop-continuation test at the *bottom* of the loop (line 14). If the condition is true, the loop continues from the first body statement (line 12). If the condition is false, the loop terminates and the program continues with the next statement after the loop.

C.18 switch Multiple-Selection Statement

Sections C.5–C.6 discussed the if single-selection and the if...else double-selection statements. The **switch multiple-selection statement** performs different actions based on the possible values of a **constant integral expression** of type byte, short, int or char.

GradeBook Class with switch Statement to Count A, B, C, D and F Grades
Figure C.17 enhances the GradeBook case study that we began presenting in Appendix B. The new version we now present not only calculates the average of a set of numeric grades entered by the user, but uses a switch statement to determine whether each grade is the equivalent of an A, B, C, D or F and to increment the appropriate grade counter. The class also displays a summary of the number of students who received each grade. Refer to Fig. C.18 for sample inputs and outputs of the GradeBookTest application that uses class GradeBook to process a set of grades.

```
1   // Fig. C.17: GradeBook.java
2   // GradeBook class uses the switch statement to count letter grades.
3   import java.util.Scanner; // program uses class Scanner
4
5   public class GradeBook
6   {
7      private String courseName; // name of course this GradeBook represents
8      // int instance variables are initialized to 0 by default
9      private int total; // sum of grades
10     private int gradeCounter; // number of grades entered
```

Fig. C.17 | GradeBook class uses the switch statement to count letter grades. (Part 1 of 4.)

```
11       private int aCount; // count of A grades
12       private int bCount; // count of B grades
13       private int cCount; // count of C grades
14       private int dCount; // count of D grades
15       private int fCount; // count of F grades
16
17       // constructor initializes courseName;
18       public GradeBook( String name )
19       {
20          courseName = name; // initializes courseName
21       } // end constructor
22
23       // method to set the course name
24       public void setCourseName( String name )
25       {
26          courseName = name; // store the course name
27       } // end method setCourseName
28
29       // method to retrieve the course name
30       public String getCourseName()
31       {
32          return courseName;
33       } // end method getCourseName
34
35       // display a welcome message to the GradeBook user
36       public void displayMessage()
37       {
38          // getCourseName gets the name of the course
39          System.out.printf( "Welcome to the grade book for\n%s!\n\n",
40             getCourseName() );
41       } // end method displayMessage
42
43       // input arbitrary number of grades from user
44       public void inputGrades()
45       {
46          Scanner input = new Scanner( System.in );
47
48          int grade; // grade entered by user
49
50          System.out.printf( "%s\n%s\n   %s\n   %s\n",
51             "Enter the integer grades in the range 0-100.",
52             "Type the end-of-file indicator to terminate input:",
53             "On UNIX/Linux/Mac OS X type <Ctrl> d then press Enter",
54             "On Windows type <Ctrl> z then press Enter" );
55
56          // loop until user enters the end-of-file indicator
57          while ( input.hasNext() )
58          {
59             grade = input.nextInt(); // read grade
60             total += grade; // add grade to total
61             ++gradeCounter; // increment number of grades
62
```

Fig. C.17 | GradeBook class uses the switch statement to count letter grades. (Part 2 of 4.)

```
63              // call method to increment appropriate counter
64              incrementLetterGradeCounter( grade );
65          } // end while
66      } // end method inputGrades
67
68      // add 1 to appropriate counter for specified grade
69      private void incrementLetterGradeCounter( int grade )
70      {
71          // determine which grade was entered
72          switch ( grade / 10 )
73          {
74              case 9:  // grade was between 90
75              case 10: // and 100, inclusive
76                  ++aCount; // increment aCount
77                  break; // necessary to exit switch
78
79              case 8: // grade was between 80 and 89
80                  ++bCount; // increment bCount
81                  break; // exit switch
82
83              case 7: // grade was between 70 and 79
84                  ++cCount; // increment cCount
85                  break; // exit switch
86
87              case 6: // grade was between 60 and 69
88                  ++dCount; // increment dCount
89                  break; // exit switch
90
91              default: // grade was less than 60
92                  ++fCount; // increment fCount
93                  break; // optional; will exit switch anyway
94          } // end switch
95      } // end method incrementLetterGradeCounter
96
97      // display a report based on the grades entered by the user
98      public void displayGradeReport()
99      {
100         System.out.println( "\nGrade Report:" );
101
102         // if user entered at least one grade...
103         if ( gradeCounter != 0 )
104         {
105             // calculate average of all grades entered
106             double average = (double) total / gradeCounter;
107
108             // output summary of results
109             System.out.printf( "Total of the %d grades entered is %d\n",
110                 gradeCounter, total );
111             System.out.printf( "Class average is %.2f\n", average );
112             System.out.printf( "%s\n%s%d\n%s%d\n%s%d\n%s%d\n%s%d\n",
113                 "Number of students who received each grade:",
114                 "A: ", aCount,   // display number of A grades
115                 "B: ", bCount,   // display number of B grades
```

Fig. C.17 | GradeBook class uses the switch statement to count letter grades. (Part 3 of 4.)

```
116                "C: ", cCount,   // display number of C grades
117                "D: ", dCount,   // display number of D grades
118                "F: ", fCount ); // display number of F grades
119            } // end if
120         else // no grades were entered, so output appropriate message
121            System.out.println( "No grades were entered" );
122      } // end method displayGradeReport
123 } // end class GradeBook
```

Fig. C.17 | GradeBook class uses the switch statement to count letter grades. (Part 4 of 4.)

Like earlier versions of the class, class GradeBook (Fig. C.17) declares instance variable courseName (line 7) and contains methods setCourseName (lines 24–27), getCourseName (lines 30–33) and displayMessage (lines 36–41), which set the course name, store the course name and display a welcome message to the user, respectively. The class also contains a constructor (lines 18–21) that initializes the course name.

Class GradeBook also declares instance variables total (line 9) and gradeCounter (line 10), which keep track of the sum of the grades entered by the user and the number of grades entered, respectively. Lines 11–15 declare counter variables for each grade category. Class GradeBook maintains total, gradeCounter and the five letter-grade counters as instance variables so that they can be used or modified in any of the class's methods. The class's constructor (lines 18–21) sets only the course name, because the remaining seven instance variables are ints and are initialized to 0 by default.

Class GradeBook contains three additional methods—inputGrades, incrementLetterGradeCounter and displayGradeReport. Method inputGrades (lines 44–66) reads an arbitrary number of integer grades from the user using sentinel-controlled repetition and updates instance variables total and gradeCounter. This method calls method incrementLetterGradeCounter (lines 69–95) to update the appropriate letter-grade counter for each grade entered. Method displayGradeReport (lines 98–122) outputs a report containing the total of all grades entered, the average of the grades and the number of students who received each letter grade. Let's examine these methods in more detail.

Method inputGrades

Line 48 in method inputGrades declares variable grade, which will store the user's input. Lines 50–54 prompt the user to enter integer grades and to type the end-of-file indicator to terminate the input. The **end-of-file indicator** is a system-dependent keystroke combination which the user enters to indicate that there's no more data to input.

On UNIX/Linux/Mac OS X systems, end-of-file is entered by typing the sequence

   <Ctrl> d

on a line by itself. This notation means to simultaneously press both the *Ctrl* key and the *d* key. On Windows systems, end-of-file can be entered by typing

   <Ctrl> z

[*Note:* On some systems, you must press *Enter* after typing the end-of-file key sequence. Also, Windows typically displays the characters ^Z on the screen when the end-of-file indicator is typed, as shown in the output of Fig. C.18.]

The `while` statement (lines 57–65) obtains the user input. The condition at line 57 calls `Scanner` method **hasNext** to determine whether there's more data to input. This method returns the `boolean` value `true` if there's more data; otherwise, it returns `false`. The returned value is then used as the value of the condition in the `while` statement. Method `hasNext` returns `false` once the user types the end-of-file indicator.

Line 59 inputs a grade value from the user. Line 60 adds `grade` to `total`. Line 61 increments `gradeCounter`. The class's `displayGradeReport` method uses these variables to compute the average of the grades. Line 64 calls the class's `incrementLetterGrade-Counter` method (declared in lines 69–95) to increment the appropriate letter-grade counter based on the numeric grade entered.

Method `incrementLetterGradeCounter`

Method `incrementLetterGradeCounter` contains a `switch` statement (lines 72–94) that determines which counter to increment. We assume that the user enters a valid grade in the range 0–100. A grade in the range 90–100 represents A, 80–89 represents B, 70–79 represents C, 60–69 represents D and 0–59 represents F. The `switch` statement consists of a block that contains a sequence of **case labels** and an optional **default case**. These are used in this example to determine which counter to increment based on the grade.

When the flow of control reaches the `switch`, the program evaluates the expression in the parentheses (`grade / 10`) following keyword `switch`. This is the `switch`'s **controlling expression**. The program compares this expression's value (which must evaluate to an integral value of type `byte`, `char`, `short` or `int`) with each `case` label. The controlling expression in line 72 performs integer division, which *truncates the fractional part* of the result. Thus, when we divide a value from 0 to 100 by 10, the result is always a value from 0 to 10. We use several of these values in our `case` labels. For example, if the user enters the integer 85, the controlling expression evaluates to 8. The `switch` compares 8 with each `case` label. If a match occurs (`case 8:` at line 79), the program executes that `case`'s statements. For the integer 8, line 80 increments `bCount`, because a grade in the 80s is a B. The **break statement** (line 81) causes program control to proceed with the first statement after the `switch`—in this program, we reach the end of method `incrementLetterGrade-Counter`'s body, so the method terminates and control returns to line 65 in method `inputGrades` (the first line after the call to `incrementLetterGradeCounter`). Line 65 is the end of a `while` loop's body, so control flows to the `while`'s condition (line 57) to determine whether the loop should continue executing.

The cases in our `switch` explicitly test for the values 10, 9, 8, 7 and 6. Note the cases at lines 74–75 that test for the values 9 and 10 (both of which represent the grade A). Listing cases consecutively in this manner with no statements between them enables the cases to perform the same set of statements—when the controlling expression evaluates to 9 or 10, the statements in lines 76–77 will execute. The `switch` statement does not provide a mechanism for testing ranges of values, so every value you need to test must be listed in a separate `case` label. Each `case` can have multiple statements. The `switch` statement differs from other control statements in that it does *not* require braces around multiple statements in a `case`.

Without `break` statements, each time a match occurs in the `switch`, the statements for that case and subsequent cases execute until a `break` statement or the end of the `switch` is encountered. (This feature is helpful for writing a concise program that displays the iterative song "The Twelve Days of Christmas").

If no match occurs between the controlling expression's value and a case label, the default case (lines 91–93) executes. We use the default case in this example to process all controlling-expression values that are less than 6—that is, all failing grades. If no match occurs and the switch does not contain a default case, program control simply continues with the first statement after the switch.

GradeBookTest Class That Demonstrates Class GradeBook

Class GradeBookTest (Fig. C.18) creates a GradeBook object (lines 10–11). Line 13 invokes the object's displayMessage method to output a welcome message to the user. Line 14 invokes the object's inputGrades method to read a set of grades from the user and keep track of the sum of all the grades entered and the number of grades. Recall that method inputGrades also calls method incrementLetterGradeCounter to keep track of the number of students who received each letter grade. Line 15 invokes method displayGradeReport of class GradeBook, which outputs a report based on the grades entered (as in the input/output window in Fig. C.18). Line 103 of class GradeBook (Fig. C.17) determines whether the user entered at least one grade—this helps us avoid dividing by zero. If so, line 106 calculates the average of the grades. Lines 109–118 then output the total of all the grades, the class average and the number of students who received each letter grade. If no grades were entered, line 121 outputs an appropriate message. The output in Fig. C.18 shows a sample grade report based on 10 grades.

```java
1   // Fig. C.18: GradeBookTest.java
2   // Create GradeBook object, input grades and display grade report.
3
4   public class GradeBookTest
5   {
6      public static void main( String[] args )
7      {
8         // create GradeBook object myGradeBook and
9         // pass course name to constructor
10        GradeBook myGradeBook = new GradeBook(
11           "CS101 Introduction to Java Programming" );
12
13        myGradeBook.displayMessage(); // display welcome message
14        myGradeBook.inputGrades(); // read grades from user
15        myGradeBook.displayGradeReport(); // display report based on grades
16     } // end main
17  } // end class GradeBookTest
```

```
Welcome to the grade book for
CS101 Introduction to Java Programming!

Enter the integer grades in the range 0-100.
Type the end-of-file indicator to terminate input:
   On UNIX/Linux/Mac OS X type <Ctrl> d then press Enter
   On Windows type <Ctrl> z then press Enter
99
92
```

Fig. C.18 | Create GradeBook object, input grades and display grade report. (Part 1 of 2.)

```
45
57
63
71
76
85
90
100
^Z

Grade Report:
Total of the 10 grades entered is 778
Class average is 77.80


Number of students who received each grade:
A: 4
B: 1
C: 2
D: 1
F: 2
```

Fig. C.18 | Create GradeBook object, input grades and display grade report. (Part 2 of 2.)

Class GradeBookTest (Fig. C.18) does not directly call GradeBook method incrementLetterGradeCounter (lines 69–95 of Fig. C.17). This method is used exclusively by method inputGrades of class GradeBook to update the appropriate letter-grade counter as each new grade is entered by the user. Method incrementLetterGradeCounter exists solely to support the operations of GradeBook's other methods, so it's declared private.

The break statement is not required for the switch's last case (or the optional default case, when it appears last), because execution continues with the next statement after the switch.

Notes on the Expression in Each **case** of a **switch**

When using the switch statement, remember that each case must contain a constant integral expression—that is, any combination of integer constants that evaluates to a constant integer value (e.g., –7, 0 or 221). An integer constant is simply an integer value. In addition, you can use **character constants**—specific characters in single quotes, such as 'A', '7' or '$'—which represent the integer values of characters and enum constants (introduced in Section D.10).

The expression in each case can also be a **constant variable**—a variable containing a value which does not change for the entire program. Such a variable is declared with keyword final (discussed in Appendix D). Java has a feature called *enumerations*, which we also present in Appendix D. Enumeration constants can also be used in case labels.

Using **Strings** in **switch** Statements (Java SE 7)

As of Java SE 7, you can use Strings in a switch statement's controlling expression and in case labels. For example, you might want to use a city's name to obtain the corresponding ZIP code. Assuming that city and zipCode are String variables, the following switch statement performs this task for three cities:

```
switch( city )
{
    case "Maynard":
        zipCode = "01754";
        break;
    case "Marlborough":
        zipCode = "01752";
        break;
    case "Framingham":
        zipCode = "01701";
        break;
} // end switch
```

C.19 break and continue Statements

In addition to selection and repetition statements, Java provides statements break and **continue** to alter the flow of control. The preceding section showed how break can be used to terminate a switch statement's execution. This section discusses how to use break in repetition statements.

break *Statement*

The break statement, when executed in a while, for, do...while or switch, causes immediate exit from that statement. Execution continues with the first statement after the control statement. Common uses of the break statement are to escape early from a loop or to skip the remainder of a switch.

continue *Statement*

The continue statement, when executed in a while, for or do...while, skips the remaining statements in the loop body and proceeds with the *next iteration* of the loop. In while and do...while statements, the program evaluates the loop-continuation test immediately after the continue statement executes. In a for statement, the increment expression executes, then the program evaluates the loop-continuation test.

C.20 Logical Operators

Java's **logical operators** enable you to form more complex conditions by *combining* simple conditions. The logical operators are && (conditional AND), || (conditional OR), & (boolean logical AND), | (boolean logical inclusive OR), ∧ (boolean logical exclusive OR) and ! (logical NOT). [*Note:* The &, | and ∧ operators are also bitwise operators when they're applied to integral operands.]

Conditional AND (&&) Operator

Suppose we wish to ensure at some point in a program that two conditions are *both* true before we choose a certain path of execution. In this case, we can use the && (**conditional AND**) operator, as follows:

```
if ( gender == FEMALE && age >= 65 )
    ++seniorFemales;
```

This if statement contains two simple conditions. The condition gender == FEMALE compares variable gender to the constant FEMALE to determine whether a person is female. The condition age >= 65 might be evaluated to determine whether a person is a senior citizen. The if statement considers the combined condition

```
gender == FEMALE && age >= 65
```

which is true if and only if *both* simple conditions are true. In this case, the if statement's body increments seniorFemales by 1. If either or both of the simple conditions are false, the program skips the increment. Some programmers find that the preceding combined condition is more readable when redundant parentheses are added, as in:

```
( gender == FEMALE ) && ( age >= 65 )
```

The table in Fig. C.19 summarizes the && operator. The table shows all four possible combinations of false and true values for *expression1* and *expression2*. Such tables are called **truth tables**. Java evaluates to false or true all expressions that include relational operators, equality operators or logical operators.

expression1	expression2	expression1 && expression2
false	false	false
false	true	false
true	false	false
true	true	true

Fig. C.19 | && (conditional AND) operator truth table.

Conditional OR (||) Operator

Now suppose we wish to ensure that *either or both* of two conditions are true before we choose a certain path of execution. In this case, we use the || (**conditional OR**) operator, as in the following program segment:

```
if ( ( semesterAverage >= 90 ) || ( finalExam >= 90 ) )
    System.out.println ( "Student grade is A" );
```

This statement also contains two simple conditions. The condition semesterAverage >= 90 evaluates to determine whether the student deserves an A in the course because of a solid performance throughout the semester. The condition finalExam >= 90 evaluates to determine whether the student deserves an A in the course because of an outstanding performance on the final exam. The if statement then considers the combined condition

```
( semesterAverage >= 90 ) || ( finalExam >= 90 )
```

and awards the student an A if *either or both* of the simple conditions are true. The only time the message "Student grade is A" is *not* printed is when *both* of the simple conditions are *false.* Figure C.20 is a truth table for operator conditional OR (||). Operator && has a higher precedence than operator ||. Both operators associate from left to right.

Short-Circuit Evaluation of Complex Conditions

The parts of an expression containing && or || operators are evaluated *only* until it's known whether the condition is true or false. Thus, evaluation of the expression

```
( gender == FEMALE ) && ( age >= 65 )
```

expression1	expression2	expression1 || expression2
false	false	false
false	true	true
true	false	true
true	true	true

Fig. C.20 | \|\| (conditional OR) operator truth table.

stops immediately if gender is not equal to FEMALE (i.e., the entire expression is false) and continues if gender *is* equal to FEMALE (i.e., the entire expression could still be true if the condition age >= 65 is true). This feature of conditional AND and conditional OR expressions is called **short-circuit evaluation**.

Boolean Logical AND (&) and Boolean Logical Inclusive OR (|) Operators

The **boolean logical AND (&)** and **boolean logical inclusive OR (|)** operators are identical to the && and || operators, except that the & and | operators *always* evaluate *both* of their operands (i.e., they do *not* perform short-circuit evaluation). So, the expression

```
( gender == 1 ) & ( age >= 65 )
```

evaluates age >= 65 *regardless* of whether gender is equal to 1. This is useful if the right operand of the boolean logical AND or boolean logical inclusive OR operator has a required **side effect**—a modification of a variable's value. For example, the expression

```
( birthday == true ) | ( ++age >= 65 )
```

guarantees that the condition ++age >= 65 will be evaluated. Thus, the variable age is incremented, regardless of whether the overall expression is true or false.

Error-Prevention Tip C.1

For clarity, avoid expressions with side effects in conditions. The side effects may seem clever, but they can make it harder to understand code and can lead to subtle logic errors.

Boolean Logical Exclusive OR (∧)

A simple condition containing the **boolean logical exclusive OR (∧)** operator is true *if and only if one of its operands is true and the other is false*. If both are true or both are false, the entire condition is false. Figure C.21 is a truth table for the boolean logical exclusive OR operator (∧). This operator is guaranteed to evaluate *both* of its operands.

expression1	expression2	expression1 ∧ expression2
false	false	false
false	true	true
true	false	true
true	true	false

Fig. C.21 | ∧ (boolean logical exclusive OR) operator truth table.

Logical Negation (!) Operator

The ! (**logical NOT**, also called **logical negation** or **logical complement**) operator "re-verses" the meaning of a condition. Unlike the logical operators &&, ||, &, | and ^, which are *binary* operators that combine two conditions, the logical negation operator is a *unary* operator that has only a single condition as an operand. The operator is placed *before* a condition to choose a path of execution if the original condition (without the logical negation operator) is false, as in the program segment

```
if ( ! ( grade == sentinelValue ) )
    System.out.printf( "The next grade is %d\n", grade );
```

which executes the printf call only if grade is *not* equal to sentinelValue. The parentheses around the condition grade == sentinelValue are needed because the logical negation operator has a higher precedence than the equality operator.

In most cases, you can avoid using logical negation by expressing the condition differently with an appropriate relational or equality operator. For example, the previous statement may also be written as follows:

```
if ( grade != sentinelValue )
    System.out.printf( "The next grade is %d\n", grade );
```

This flexibility can help you express a condition in a more convenient manner. Figure C.22 is a truth table for the logical negation operator.

expression	!expression
false	true
true	false

Fig. C.22 | ! (logical negation, or logical NOT) operator truth table.

C.21 Wrap-Up

This appendix presented basic problem solving for building classes and developing methods for these classes. We demonstrated how to construct an algorithm (i.e., an approach to solving a problem), then how to refine the algorithm through several phases of pseudocode development, resulting in Java code that can be executed as part of a method. The appendix showed how to use top-down, stepwise refinement to plan out the specific actions that a method must perform and the order in which the method must perform these actions.

Only three types of control structures—sequence, selection and repetition—are needed to develop any problem-solving algorithm. Specifically, this appendix demonstrated the if single-selection statement, the if...else double-selection statement and the while repetition statement. These are some of the building blocks used to construct solutions to many problems. We used control-statement stacking to total and compute the average of a set of student grades with counter- and sentinel-controlled repetition, and we used control-statement nesting to analyze and make decisions based on a set of exam results. We introduced Java's compound assignment operators and its increment and decrement operators. We discussed Java's primitive types.

We demonstrated the for, do...while and switch statements. We showed that any algorithm can be developed using combinations of the sequence structure (i.e., statements listed in the order in which they should execute), the three types of selection statements— if, if...else and switch—and the three types of repetition statements—while, do...while and for. We discussed how you can combine these building blocks to utilize proven program-construction and problem-solving techniques. We also introduced Java's logical operators, which enable you to use more complex conditional expressions in control statements. In Appendix D, we examine methods in greater depth.

Self-Review Exercises (Sections C.1–C.13)

C.1 Fill in the blanks in each of the following statements:
a) All programs can be written in terms of three types of control structures: _____, _____ and _____.
b) The _____ statement is used to execute one action when a condition is true and another when that condition is false.
c) When it's not known in advance how many times a set of statements will be repeated, a(n) _____ value can be used to terminate the repetition.
d) Java is a(n) _____ language; it requires all variables to have a type.
e) If the increment operator is _____ to a variable, first the variable is incremented by 1, then its new value is used in the expression.

C.2 State whether each of the following is *true* or *false*. If *false*, explain why.
a) A set of statements contained within a pair of parentheses is called a block.
b) A selection statement specifies that an action is to be repeated while some condition remains true.
c) A nested control statement appears in the body of another control statement.
d) Specifying the order in which statements execute in a program is called program control.
e) Instance variables of type boolean are given the value true by default.

C.3 Write Java statements to accomplish each of the following tasks:
a) Use one statement to assign the sum of x and y to z, then increment x by 1.
b) Test whether variable count is greater than 10. If it is, print "Count is greater than 10".
c) Use one statement to decrement the variable x by 1, then subtract it from variable total and store the result in variable total.
d) Calculate the remainder after q is divided by divisor, and assign the result to q. Write this statement in two different ways.

C.4 Write a Java statement to accomplish each of the following tasks:
a) Declare variables sum and x to be of type int.
b) Assign 1 to variable x.
c) Assign 0 to variable sum.
d) Add variable x to variable sum, and assign the result to sum.
e) Print "The sum is: ", followed by the value of variable sum.

C.5 Determine the value of the variables in the statement product *= x++; after the calculation is performed. Assume that all variables are type int and initially have the value 5.

C.6 Identify and correct the errors in each of the following sets of code:

a)
```
while ( c <= 5 )
{
    product *= c;
    ++c;
```

b)
```
if ( gender == 1 )
    System.out.println( "Woman" );
else;
    System.out.println( "Man" );
```

C.7 What is wrong with the following while statement?

```
while ( z >= 0 )
    sum += z;
```

Self-Review Exercises (Sections C.14–C.20)

C.8 Fill in the blanks in each of the following statements:

a) Typically, _____ statements are used for counter-controlled repetition and _____ statements for sentinel-controlled repetition.

b) The do...while statement tests the loop-continuation condition _____ executing the loop's body; therefore, the body always executes at least once.

c) The _____ statement selects among multiple actions based on the possible values of an integer variable or expression.

d) The _____ operator can be used to ensure that two conditions are *both* true before choosing a certain path of execution.

e) If the loop-continuation condition in a for header is initially _____, the program does not execute the for statement's body.

C.9 State whether each of the following is *true* or *false*. If *false*, explain why.

a) The default case is required in the switch selection statement.

b) The break statement is required in the last case of a switch selection statement.

c) The expression ((x > y) && (a < b)) is true if either x > y is true or a < b is true.

d) An expression containing the || operator is true if either or both of its operands are true.

e) Listing cases consecutively with no statements between them enables the cases to perform the same set of statements.

C.10 Write a Java statement or a set of Java statements to accomplish each of the following tasks:

a) Sum the odd integers between 1 and 99, using a for statement. Assume that the integer variables sum and count have been declared.

b) Calculate the value of 2.5 raised to the power of 3, using the pow method.

c) Print the integers from 1 to 20, using a while loop and the counter variable i. Assume that the variable i has been declared, but not initialized. Print only five integers per line. [*Hint:* Use the calculation i % 5. When the value of this expression is 0, print a newline character; otherwise, print a tab character. Assume that this code is an application. Use the System.out.println() method to output the newline character, and use the System.out.print('\t') method to output the tab character.]

d) Repeat part (c), using a for statement.

C.11 Find the error in each of the following code segments, and explain how to correct it:

a)
```
i = 1;

while ( i <= 10 );
    ++i;
}
```

b)
```
for ( k = 0.1; k != 1.0; k += 0.1 )
    System.out.println( k );
```
c)
```
switch ( n )
{
    case 1:
        System.out.println( "The number is 1" );
    case 2:
        System.out.println( "The number is 2" );
        break;
    default:
        System.out.println( "The number is not 1 or 2" );
        break;
}
```
d) The following code should print the values 1 to 10:
```
n = 1;
while ( n < 10 )
    System.out.println( n++ );
```

Answers to Self-Review Exercises (Sections C.1–C.13)

C.1 a) sequence, selection, repetition. b) if...else. c) sentinel, signal, flag or dummy. d) strongly typed. e) prefixed.

C.2 a) False. A set of statements contained within a pair of braces ({ and }) is called a block. b) False. A repetition statement specifies that an action is to be repeated while some condition remains true. c) True. d) True. e) False. Instance variables of type boolean are given the value false by default.

C.3 a) `z = x++ + y;`
b)
```
if ( count > 10 )
    System.out.println( "Count is greater than 10" );
```
c) `total -= --x;`
d)
```
q %= divisor;
q = q % divisor;
```

C.4 a)
```
int sum;
int x;
```
b) `x = 1;`
c) `sum = 0;`
d) `sum += x;` or `sum = sum + x;`
e) `System.out.printf( "The sum is: %d\n", sum );`

C.5 product = 25, x = 6

C.6 a) Error: The closing right brace of the while statement's body is missing.
Correction: Add a closing right brace after the statement ++c;.
b) Error: The semicolon after else results in a logic error. The second output statement will always be executed.
Correction: Remove the semicolon after else.

C.7 The value of the variable z is never changed in the while statement. Therefore, if the loop-continuation condition (z >= 0) is true, an infinite loop is created. To prevent an infinite loop from occurring, z must be decremented so that it eventually becomes less than 0.

Answers to Self-Review Exercises (Sections C.14–C.20)

C.8 a) for, while. b) after. c) switch. d) && (conditional AND). e) false.

C.9 a) False. The default case is optional. If no default action is needed, then there's no need for a default case. b) False. The break statement is used to exit the switch statement. The break statement is not required for the last case in a switch statement. c) False. Both of the relational expressions must be true for the entire expression to be true when using the && operator. d) True. e) True.

C.10 a)
```
sum = 0;
for ( count = 1; count <= 99; count += 2 )
   sum += count;
```
b)
```
double result = Math.pow( 2.5, 3 );
```
c)
```
i = 1;

while ( i <= 20 )
{
   System.out.print( i );

   if ( i % 5 == 0 )
      System.out.println();
   else
      System.out.print( '\t' );

   ++i;
}
```
d)
```
for ( i = 1; i <= 20; ++i )
{
   System.out.print( i );

   if ( i % 5 == 0 )
      System.out.println();
   else
      System.out.print( '\t' );
}
```

C.11 a) Error: The semicolon after the while header causes an infinite loop, and there's a missing left brace.
Correction: Replace the semicolon by a {, or remove both the ; and the }.
b) Error: Using a floating-point number to control a for statement may not work, because floating-point numbers are represented only approximately by most computers.
Correction: Use an integer, and perform the proper calculation in order to get the values you desire:
```
for ( k = 1; k != 10; ++k )
   System.out.println( (double) k / 10 );
```
c) Error: The missing code is the break statement in the statements for the first case.
Correction: Add a break statement at the end of the statements for the first case. This omission is not necessarily an error if you want the statement of case 2: to execute every time the case 1: statement executes.
d) Error: An improper relational operator is used in the while's continuation condition.
Correction: Use <= rather than <, or change 10 to 11.

Exercises (Sections C.1–C.13)

C.12 Explain what happens when a Java program attempts to divide one integer by another. What happens to the fractional part of the calculation? How can you avoid that outcome?

C.13 Describe the two ways in which control statements can be combined.

C.14 What type of repetition would be appropriate for calculating the sum of the first 100 positive integers? What type would be appropriate for calculating the sum of an arbitrary number of positive integers? Briefly describe how each of these tasks could be performed.

C.15 What is the difference between preincrementing and postincrementing a variable?

C.16 Identify and correct the errors in each of the following pieces of code. [*Note:* There may be more than one error in each piece of code.]

```
a) if ( age >= 65 );
      System.out.println( "Age is greater than or equal to 65" );
   else
      System.out.println( "Age is less than 65 )";
b) int x = 1, total;
   while ( x <= 10 )
   {
      total += x;
      ++x;
   }
c) while ( x <= 100 )
      total += x;
      ++x;
d) while ( y > 0 )
   {
      System.out.println( y );
      ++y;
```

For Exercise C.17 and Exercise C.18, perform each of the following steps:
   a) Read the problem statement.
   b) Write a Java program.
   c) Test, debug and execute the Java program.
   d) Process three complete sets of data.

C.17 *(Gas Mileage)* Drivers are concerned with the mileage their automobiles get. One driver has kept track of several trips by recording the miles driven and gallons used for each tankful. Develop a Java application that will input the miles driven and gallons used (both as integers) for each trip. The program should calculate and display the miles per gallon obtained for each trip and print the combined miles per gallon obtained for all trips up to this point. All averaging calculations should produce floating-point results. Use class Scanner and sentinel-controlled repetition to obtain the data from the user.

C.18 *(Credit Limit Calculator)* Develop a Java application that determines whether any of several department-store customers has exceeded the credit limit on a charge account. For each customer, the following facts are available:
   a) account number
   b) balance at the beginning of the month
   c) total of all items charged by the customer this month
   d) total of all credits applied to the customer's account this month
   e) allowed credit limit

The program should input all these facts as integers, calculate the new balance (= *beginning balance + charges − credits*), display the new balance and determine whether the new balance exceeds the customer's credit limit. For those customers whose credit limit is exceeded, the program should display the message "Credit limit exceeded".

C.19   *(Find the Largest Number)* The process of finding the largest value is used frequently in computer applications. For example, a program that determines the winner of a sales contest would input the number of units sold by each salesperson. The salesperson who sells the most units wins the contest. Write a pseudocode program, then a Java application that inputs a series of 10 integers and determines and prints the largest integer. Your program should use at least the following three variables:

   a) counter: A counter to count to 10 (i.e., to keep track of how many numbers have been input and to determine when all 10 numbers have been processed).
   b) number: The integer most recently input by the user.
   c) largest: The largest number found so far.

C.20   *(Tabular Output)* Write a Java application that uses looping to print the following table of values:

N	10*N	100*N	1000*N
1	10	100	1000
2	20	200	2000
3	30	300	3000
4	40	400	4000
5	50	500	5000

C.21   *(Multiples of 2 with an Infinite Loop)* Write an application that keeps displaying in the command window the multiples of the integer 2—namely, 2, 4, 8, 16, 32, 64, and so on. Your loop should not terminate (i.e., it should create an infinite loop). What happens when you run this program?

Exercises (Sections C.14–C.20)

C.22   Describe the four basic elements of counter-controlled repetition.

C.23   *(Find the Smallest Value)* Write an application that finds the smallest of several integers. Assume that the first value read specifies the number of values to input from the user.

C.24   Assume that $i = 1$, $j = 2$, $k = 3$ and $m = 2$. What does each of the following statements print?
   a) System.out.println(i == 1);
   b) System.out.println(j == 3);
   c) System.out.println((i >= 1) && (j < 4));
   d) System.out.println((m <= 99) & (k < m));
   e) System.out.println((j >= i) || (k == m));
   f) System.out.println((k + m < j) | (3 - j >= k));
   g) System.out.println(!(k > m));

C.25   *(Calculating the Value of π)* Calculate the value of π from the infinite series

$$\pi = 4 - \frac{4}{3} + \frac{4}{5} - \frac{4}{7} + \frac{4}{9} - \frac{4}{11} + \cdots$$

Print a table that shows the value of π approximated by computing the first 200,000 terms of this series. How many terms do you have to use before you first get a value that begins with 3.14159?

C.26   What does the following program segment do?

```
for ( i = 1; i <= 5; ++i )
{
   for ( j = 1; j <= 3; ++j )
   {
      for ( k = 1; k <= 4; ++k )
         System.out.print( '*' );

      System.out.println();
   } // end inner for

   System.out.println();
} // end outer for
```

C.27   (*"The Twelve Days of Christmas" Song*) Write (as concisely as possible) an application that uses repetition and one or more switch statements to print the song "The Twelve Days of Christmas."

D

Methods: A Deeper Look

Objectives

In this appendix you'll learn:

- How static methods and fields are associated with classes rather than objects.

- How the method call/return mechanism is supported by the method-call stack.

- How packages group related classes.

- To use random-number generation to implement game-playing applications.

- How the visibility of declarations is limited to specific regions of programs.

- What method overloading is and how to create overloaded methods.

D.1 Introduction

In this appendix, we study methods in more depth. You'll see that it's possible to call certain methods, called static methods, without the need for an object of the class to exist. You'll learn how to declare a method with more than one parameter. You'll also learn how Java keeps track of which method is currently executing, how local variables of methods are maintained in memory and how a method knows where to return after it completes execution.

We'll take a brief diversion into simulation techniques with random-number generation and develop a version of the casino dice game called craps that uses most of the programming techniques you've used to this point in the book. In addition, you'll learn how to declare values that cannot change (i.e., constants) in your programs.

Many of the classes you'll use or create while developing applications will have more than one method of the same name. This technique, called overloading, is used to implement methods that perform similar tasks for arguments of different types or for different numbers of arguments.

D.2 Program Modules in Java

You write Java programs by combining new methods and classes with predefined ones available in the **Java Application Programming Interface** (also referred to as the **Java API** or **Java class library**) and in various other class libraries. Related classes are typically grouped into *packages* so that they can be imported into programs and reused. You'll learn how to group your own classes into packages in Appendix F. The Java API provides a rich collection of predefined classes that contain methods for performing common mathematical calculations, string manipulations, character manipulations, input/output operations, database operations, networking operations, file processing, error checking and many other useful tasks.

Software Engineering Observation D.1

Familiarize yourself with the rich collection of classes and methods provided by the Java API (http://docs.oracle.com/javase/7/docs/api/) and reuse them when possible. This reduces program development time and avoids introducing programming errors.

Methods (called **functions** or **procedures** in some languages) help you modularize a program by separating its tasks into self-contained units. You've declared methods in every program you've written. The statements in the method bodies are written only once, are hidden from other methods and can be reused from several locations in a program.

One motivation for modularizing a program into methods is the divide-and-conquer approach, which makes program development more manageable by constructing programs from small, simple pieces. Another is **software reusability**—using existing methods as building blocks to create new programs. Often, you can create programs mostly from standardized methods rather than by building customized code. For example, in earlier programs, we did not define how to read data from the keyboard—Java provides these capabilities in the methods of class Scanner. A third motivation is to avoid repeating code. Dividing a program into meaningful methods makes the program easier to debug and maintain.

D.3 static Methods, static Fields and Class Math

Although most methods execute in response to method calls on *specific objects*, this is not always the case. Sometimes a method performs a task that does not depend on the contents of any object. Such a method applies to the class in which it's declared as a whole and is known as a static method or a **class method**. It's common for classes to contain convenient static methods to perform common tasks. For example, recall that we used static method pow of class Math to raise a value to a power in Fig. C.15. To declare a method as static, place the keyword static before the return type in the method's declaration. For any class imported into your program, you can call the class's static methods by specifying the name of the class in which the method is declared, followed by a dot (.) and the method name, as in

ClassName.methodName(arguments)

We use various Math class methods here to present the concept of static methods. Class Math provides a collection of methods that enable you to perform common mathematical calculations. For example, you can calculate the square root of 900.0 with the static method call

```
Math.sqrt( 900.0 )
```

The preceding expression evaluates to 30.0. Method sqrt takes an argument of type double and returns a result of type double. To output the value of the preceding method call in the command window, you might write the statement

```
System.out.println( Math.sqrt( 900.0 ) );
```

In this statement, the value that sqrt returns becomes the argument to method println. There was no need to create a Math object before calling method sqrt. Also *all* Math class methods are static—therefore, each is called by preceding its name with the class name Math and the dot (.) separator.

 Software Engineering Observation D.2

Class Math is part of the java.lang package, which is implicitly imported by the compiler, so it's not necessary to import class Math to use its methods.

Method arguments may be constants, variables or expressions. Figure D.1 summarizes several Math class methods. In the figure, *x* and *y* are of type double.

Method	Description	Example
abs(x)	absolute value of x	abs(23.7) is 23.7 abs(0.0) is 0.0 abs(-23.7) is 23.7
ceil(x)	rounds x to the smallest integer not less than x	ceil(9.2) is 10.0 ceil(-9.8) is -9.0
cos(x)	trigonometric cosine of x (x in radians)	cos(0.0) is 1.0
exp(x)	exponential method e^x	exp(1.0) is 2.71828 exp(2.0) is 7.38906
floor(x)	rounds x to the largest integer not greater than x	floor(9.2) is 9.0 floor(-9.8) is -10.0
log(x)	natural logarithm of x (base e)	log(Math.E) is 1.0 log(Math.E * Math.E) is 2.0
max(x, y)	larger value of x and y	max(2.3, 12.7) is 12.7 max(-2.3, -12.7) is -2.3
min(x, y)	smaller value of x and y	min(2.3, 12.7) is 2.3 min(-2.3, -12.7) is -12.7
pow(x, y)	x raised to the power y (i.e., x^y)	pow(2.0, 7.0) is 128.0 pow(9.0, 0.5) is 3.0
sin(x)	trigonometric sine of x (x in radians)	sin(0.0) is 0.0
sqrt(x)	square root of x	sqrt(900.0) is 30.0
tan(x)	trigonometric tangent of x (x in radians)	tan(0.0) is 0.0

Fig. D.1 | Math class methods.

Math Class Constants PI and E

Class Math declares two fields that represent commonly used mathematical constants—**Math.PI** and **Math.E**. Math.PI (3.141592653589793) is the ratio of a circle's circumference to its diameter. Math.E (2.718281828459045) is the base value for natural logarithms (calculated with static Math method log). These fields are declared in class Math with the modifiers public, final and static. Making them public allows you to use these fields in your own classes. Any field declared with keyword **final** is *constant*—its value cannot change after the field is initialized. PI and E are declared final because their values never change. Making these fields static allows them to be accessed via the class name Math and a dot (.) separator, just like class Math's methods. Recall from Section B.4 that when each object of a class maintains its own copy of an attribute, the field that represents the attribute is also known as an instance variable—each object (instance) of the class has a separate instance of the variable in memory. There are fields for which each object of a class does *not* have a separate instance of the field. That's the case with static fields, which are also known as **class variables.** When objects of a class containing static fields are created, all the objects of that class share one copy of the class's static fields. Together the class variables (i.e., static variables) and instance variables represent the fields of a class. You'll learn more about static fields in Section F.10.

Why Is Method main *Declared* static*?*

When you execute the Java Virtual Machine (JVM) with the java command, the JVM attempts to invoke the main method of the class you specify—when no objects of the class have been created. Declaring main as static allows the JVM to invoke main without creating an instance of the class. When you execute your application, you specify its class name as an argument to the command java, as in

java *ClassName argument1 argument2 ...*

The JVM loads the class specified by *ClassName* and uses that class name to invoke method main. In the preceding command, *ClassName* is a **command-line argument** to the JVM that tells it which class to execute. Following the *ClassName*, you can also specify a list of Strings (separated by spaces) as command-line arguments that the JVM will pass to your application. Such arguments might be used to specify options (e.g., a file name) to run the application. As you'll learn in Appendix E, your application can access those command-line arguments and use them to customize the application.

D.4 Declaring Methods with Multiple Parameters

We now consider how to write your own methods with *multiple* parameters. Figure D.2 uses a method called maximum to determine and return the largest of three double values. In main, lines 14–18 prompt the user to enter three double values, then read them from the user. Line 21 calls method maximum (declared in lines 28–41) to determine the largest of the three values it receives as arguments. When method maximum returns the result to line 21, the program assigns maximum's return value to local variable result. Then line 24 outputs the maximum value. At the end of this section, we'll discuss the use of operator + in line 24.

```java
1   // Fig. D.2: MaximumFinder.java
2   // Programmer-declared method maximum with three double parameters.
3   import java.util.Scanner;
4
5   public class MaximumFinder
6   {
7      // obtain three floating-point values and locate the maximum value
8      public static void main( String[] args )
9      {
10         // create Scanner for input from command window
11         Scanner input = new Scanner( System.in );
12
13         // prompt for and input three floating-point values
14         System.out.print(
15            "Enter three floating-point values separated by spaces: " );
16         double number1 = input.nextDouble(); // read first double
17         double number2 = input.nextDouble(); // read second double
18         double number3 = input.nextDouble(); // read third double
19
20         // determine the maximum value
21         double result = maximum( number1, number2, number3 );
22
```

Fig. D.2 | Programmer-declared method maximum with three double parameters. (Part 1 of 2.)

```
23          // display maximum value
24          System.out.println( "Maximum is: " + result );
25      } // end main
26
27      // returns the maximum of its three double parameters
28      public static double maximum( double x, double y, double z )
29      {
30          double maximumValue = x; // assume x is the largest to start
31
32          // determine whether y is greater than maximumValue
33          if ( y > maximumValue )
34              maximumValue = y;
35
36          // determine whether z is greater than maximumValue
37          if ( z > maximumValue )
38              maximumValue = z;
39
40          return maximumValue;
41      } // end method maximum
42  } // end class MaximumFinder
```

```
Enter three floating-point values separated by spaces: 9.35 2.74 5.1
Maximum is: 9.35
```

```
Enter three floating-point values separated by spaces: 5.8 12.45 8.32
Maximum is: 12.45
```

```
Enter three floating-point values separated by spaces: 6.46 4.12 10.54
Maximum is: 10.54
```

Fig. D.2 | Programmer-declared method maximum with three double parameters. (Part 2 of 2.)

The public and static Keywords

Method maximum's declaration begins with keyword public to indicate that the method is "available to the public"—it can be called from methods of other classes. The keyword static enables the main method (another static method) to call maximum as shown in line 21 without qualifying the method name with the class name MaximumFinder—static methods in the same class can call each other directly. Any other class that uses maximum must fully qualify the method name with the class name.

Method maximum

In maximum's declaration (lines 28–41), line 28 indicates that it returns a double value, that the its name is maximum and that it requires three double parameters (x, y and z) to accomplish its task. Multiple parameters are specified as a comma-separated list. When maximum is called (line 21), the parameters x, y and z are initialized with the values of arguments number1, number2 and number3, respectively. There must be one argument in the method call for each parameter in the method declaration. Also, each argument must be *consistent* with the type of the corresponding parameter. For example, a double parameter can receive values like 7.35, 22 or –0.03456, but not Strings like "hello" nor the boolean values true or false.

To determine the maximum value, we begin with the assumption that parameter x contains the largest value, so line 30 declares local variable maximumValue and initializes it with the value of parameter x. Of course, it's possible that parameter y or z contains the actual largest value, so we must compare each of these values with maximumValue. The if statement at lines 33–34 determines whether y is greater than maximumValue. If so, line 34 assigns y to maximumValue. The if statement at lines 37–38 determines whether z is greater than maximumValue. If so, line 38 assigns z to maximumValue. At this point the largest of the three values resides in maximumValue, so line 40 returns that value to line 21. When program control returns to the point in the program where maximum was called, maximum's parameters x, y and z no longer exist in memory.

Software Engineering Observation D.3

Variables should be declared as fields only if they're required for use in more than one method of the class or if the program should save their values between calls to the class's methods.

Implementing Method maximum by Reusing Method Math.max

The entire body of our maximum method could also be implemented with two calls to Math.max, as follows:

```
return Math.max( x, Math.max( y, z ) );
```

The first call to Math.max specifies arguments x and Math.max(y, z). *Before* any method can be called, its arguments must be evaluated to determine their values. If an argument is a method call, the method call must be performed to determine its return value. So, in the preceding statement, Math.max(y, z) is evaluated to determine the maximum of y and z. Then the result is passed as the second argument to the other call to Math.max, which returns the larger of its two arguments.

Assembling Strings with String Concatenation

Java allows you to assemble String objects into larger strings by using operators + or +=. This is known as **string concatenation**. When both operands of operator + are String objects, operator + creates a new String object in which the characters of the right operand are placed at the end of those in the left operand—e.g., the expression "hello " + "there" creates the String "hello there".

In line 24 of Fig. D.2, the expression "Maximum is: " + result uses operator + with operands of types String and double. *Every primitive value and object in Java has a String representation.* When one of the + operator's operands is a String, the other is converted to a String, then the two are *concatenated*. In line 24, the double value is converted to its String representation and placed at the end of the String "Maximum is: ". If there are any *trailing zeros* in a double value, these will be *discarded* when the number is converted to a String—for example 9.3500 would be represented as 9.35.

Primitive values used in String concatenation are converted to Strings. A boolean concatenated with a String is converted to the String "true" or "false". All objects have a toString method that returns a String representation of the object. When an object is concatenated with a String, the object's toString method is implicitly called to obtain the String representation of the object. ToString can be called explicitly.

Common Programming Error D.1
It's a syntax error to break a String literal across lines. If necessary, you can split a String into several smaller Strings and use concatenation to form the desired String.

Common Programming Error D.2
Confusing the + operator used for string concatenation with the + operator used for addition can lead to strange results. Java evaluates the operands of an operator from left to right. For example, if integer variable y has the value 5, the expression "y + 2 = " + y + 2 results in the string "y + 2 = 52", not "y + 2 = 7", because first the value of y (5) is concatenated to the string "y + 2 = ", then the value 2 is concatenated to the new larger string "y + 2 = 5". The expression "y + 2 = " + (y + 2) produces the desired result "y + 2 = 7".

D.5 Notes on Declaring and Using Methods

There are three ways to call a method:

1. Using a method name by itself to call another method of the *same* class—such as maximum(number1, number2, number3) in line 21 of Fig. D.2.

2. Using a variable that contains a reference to an object, followed by a dot (.) and the method name to call a non-static method of the referenced object—such as the method call in line 13 of Fig. C.3, myGradeBook.displayMessage(), which calls a method of class GradeBook from the main method of GradeBookTest.

3. Using the class name and a dot (.) to call a static method of a class—such as Math.sqrt(900.0) in Section D.3.

A static method can call *only* other static methods of the same class directly (i.e., using the method name by itself) and can manipulate *only* static variables in the same class directly. To access the class's non-static members, a static method must use a reference to an object of the class. Many objects of a class, each with its own copies of the instance variables, may exist at the same time. Suppose a static method were to invoke a non-static method directly. How would the method know which object's instance variables to manipulate? What would happen if no objects of the class existed at the time the non-static method was invoked? Thus, Java does not allow a static method to access non-static members of the same class directly.

There are three ways to return control to the statement that calls a method. If the method does not return a result, control returns when the program flow reaches the method-ending right brace or when the statement

```
return;
```

is executed. If the method returns a result, the statement

```
return expression;
```

evaluates the *expression*, then returns the result to the caller.

Common Programming Error D.3
Declaring a method outside the body of a class declaration or inside the body of another method is a syntax error.

Common Programming Error D.4

Redeclaring a parameter as a local variable in the method's body is a compilation error.

D.6 Method-Call Stack and Activation Records

To understand how Java performs method calls, we first need to consider a data structure (i.e., collection of related data items) known as a **stack**. You can think of a stack as analogous to a pile of dishes. When a dish is placed on the pile, it's normally placed at the top (referred to as **pushing** the dish onto the stack). Similarly, when a dish is removed from the pile, it's always removed from the top (referred to as **popping** the dish off the stack). Stacks are known as **last-in, first-out (LIFO) data structures**—the last item pushed (inserted) on the stack is the first item popped (removed) from the stack.

When a program calls a method, the called method must know how to return to its caller, so the return address of the calling method is pushed onto the **program-execution stack** (sometimes referred to as the **method-call stack**). If a series of method calls occurs, the successive return addresses are pushed onto the stack in last-in, first-out order so that each method can return to its caller.

The program-execution stack also contains the memory for the local variables used in each invocation of a method during a program's execution. This data, stored as a portion of the program-execution stack, is known as the **activation record** or **stack frame** of the method call. When a method call is made, the activation record for that method call is pushed onto the program-execution stack. When the method returns to its caller, the activation record for this method call is popped off the stack and those local variables are no longer known to the program. If a local variable holding a reference to an object is the only variable in the program with a reference to that object, then, when the activation record containing that local variable is popped off the stack, the object can no longer be accessed by the program and will eventually be deleted from memory by the JVM during "garbage collection." We discuss garbage collection in Section F.9.

Of course, a computer's memory is finite, so only a certain amount can be used to store activation records on the program-execution stack. If more method calls occur than can have their activation records stored, an error known as a **stack overflow** occurs.

D.7 Argument Promotion and Casting

Another important feature of method calls is **argument promotion**—converting an argument's value, if possible, to the type that the method expects to receive in its corresponding parameter. For example, a program can call Math method sqrt with an int argument even though a double argument is expected. The statement

```
System.out.println( Math.sqrt( 4 ) );
```

correctly evaluates Math.sqrt(4) and prints the value 2.0. The method declaration's parameter list causes Java to convert the int value 4 to the double value 4.0 before passing the value to method sqrt. Such conversions may lead to compilation errors if Java's **promotion rules** are not satisfied. These rules specify which conversions are allowed—that is, which ones can be performed without losing data. In the sqrt example above, an int is converted to a double without changing its value. However, converting a double to an int truncates the fractional part of the double value—thus, part of the value is lost. Converting large integer types to small integer types (e.g., long to int, or int to short) may also result in changed values.

The promotion rules apply to expressions containing values of two or more primitive types and to primitive-type values passed as arguments to methods. Each value is promoted to the "highest" type in the expression. Actually, the expression uses a temporary copy of each value—the types of the original values remain unchanged. Figure D.3 lists the primitive types and the types to which each can be promoted. The valid promotions for a given type are always to a type higher in the table. For example, an int can be promoted to the higher types long, float and double.

Type	Valid promotions
double	None
float	double
long	float or double
int	long, float or double
char	int, long, float or double
short	int, long, float or double (but not char)
byte	short, int, long, float or double (but not char)
boolean	None (boolean values are not considered to be numbers in Java)

Fig. D.3 | Promotions allowed for primitive types.

Converting values to types lower in the table of Fig. D.3 will result in different values if the lower type cannot represent the value of the higher type (e.g., the int value 2000000 cannot be represented as a short, and any floating-point number with digits after its decimal point cannot be represented in an integer type such as long, int or short). Therefore, in cases where information may be lost due to conversion, the Java compiler requires you to use a cast operator (introduced in Section C.9) to explicitly force the conversion to occur—otherwise a compilation error occurs. This enables you to "take control" from the compiler. You essentially say, "I know this conversion might cause loss of information, but for my purposes here, that's fine." Suppose method square calculates the square of an integer and thus requires an int argument. To call square with a double argument named doubleValue, we would be required to write the method call as

```
square( (int) doubleValue )
```

This method call explicitly casts (converts) a *copy* of variable doubleValue's value to an integer for use in method square. Thus, if doubleValue's value is 4.5, the method receives the value 4 and returns 16, not 20.25.

D.8 Java API Packages

As you've seen, Java contains many predefined classes that are grouped into categories of related classes called packages. Together, these are known as the Java Application Programming Interface (Java API), or the Java class library. A great strength of Java is the Java

API's thousands of classes. Some key Java API packages used in this book's appendices are described in Fig. D.4, which represents only a small portion of the reusable components in the Java API.

Package	Description
`java.awt.event`	The **Java Abstract Window Toolkit Event Package** contains classes and interfaces that enable event handling for GUI components in both the `java.awt` and `javax.swing` packages.
`java.io`	The **Java Input/Output Package** contains classes and interfaces that enable programs to input and output data.
`java.lang`	The **Java Language Package** contains classes and interfaces (discussed bookwide) that are required by many Java programs. This package is imported by the compiler into all programs.
`java.util`	The **Java Utilities Package** contains utility classes and interfaces that enable such actions as date and time manipulations, random-number processing (class `Random`) and the storing and processing of large amounts of data.
`java.util.` `concurrent`	The **Java Concurrency Package** contains utility classes and interfaces for implementing programs that can perform multiple tasks in parallel.
`javax.swing`	The **Java Swing GUI Components Package** contains classes and interfaces for Java's Swing GUI components that provide support for portable GUIs.

Fig. D.4 | Java API packages (a subset).

The set of packages available in Java is quite large. In addition to those summarized in Fig. D.4, Java includes packages for complex graphics, advanced graphical user interfaces, printing, advanced networking, security, database processing, multimedia, accessibility (for people with disabilities), concurrent programming, cryptography, XML processing and many other capabilities.

You can locate additional information about a predefined Java class's methods in the Java API documentation at `http://docs.oracle.com/javase/7/docs/api/`. When you visit this site, click the **Index** link to see an alphabetical listing of all the classes and methods in the Java API. Locate the class name and click its link to see the online description of the class. Click the **METHOD** link to see a table of the class's methods. Each `static` method will be listed with the word "`static`" preceding its return type.

D.9 Introduction to Random-Number Generation

We now take a brief diversion into a popular type of programming application—simulation and game playing. In this and the next section, we develop a nicely structured game-playing program with multiple methods. The program uses most of the control statements presented thus far in the appendices and introduces several new programming concepts.

Random numbers can be introduced in a program via an object of class **Random** (package java.util) or via the static method random of class Math. A Random object can produce random boolean, byte, float, double, int, long and Gaussian values, whereas Math method random can produce only double values in the range $0.0 \leq x < 1.0$, where x is the value returned by method random. In the next several examples, we use objects of class Random to produce random values. We discuss only random int values here. For more information on the Random class, see docs.oracle.com/javase/7/docs/api/java/util/Random.html.

A new random-number generator object can be created as follows:

```
Random randomNumbers = new Random();
```

Consider the following statement:

```
int randomValue = randomNumbers.nextInt();
```

Random method **nextInt** generates a random int value in the range −2,147,483,648 to +2,147,483,647, inclusive. If it truly produces values at random, then every value in the range should have an equal chance (or probability) of being chosen each time nextInt is called. The numbers are actually **pseudorandom numbers**—a sequence of values produced by a complex mathematical calculation. The calculation uses the current time of day (which, of course, changes constantly) to **seed** the random-number generator such that each execution of a program yields a different sequence of random values.

The range of values produced directly by method nextInt generally differs from the range of values required in a particular Java application. For example, a program that simulates coin tossing might require only 0 for "heads" and 1 for "tails." A program that simulates the rolling of a six-sided die might require random integers in the range 1–6. A program that randomly predicts the next type of spaceship (out of four possibilities) that will fly across the horizon in a video game might require random integers in the range 1–4. For cases like these, class Random provides another version of method nextInt that receives an int argument and returns a value from 0 up to, but not including, the argument's value. For example, for coin tossing, the following statement returns 0 or 1.

```
int randomValue = randomNumbers.nextInt( 2 );
```

D.9.1 Scaling and Shifting of Random Numbers

To demonstrate random numbers, let's show to simulate rolling a six-sided die. We begin by using nextInt to produce random values in the range 0–5, as follows:

```
face = randomNumbers.nextInt( 6 );
```

The argument 6—called the **scaling factor**—represents the number of unique values that nextInt should produce (in this case six—0, 1, 2, 3, 4 and 5). This manipulation is called **scaling** the range of values produced by Random method nextInt.

A six-sided die has the numbers 1–6 on its faces, not 0–5. So we **shift** the range of numbers produced by adding a **shifting value**—in this case 1—to our previous result, as in

```
face = 1 + randomNumbers.nextInt( 6 );
```

The shifting value (1) specifies the *first* value in the desired range of random integers. The preceding statement assigns face a random integer in the range 1–6. The numbers produced by nextInt occur with approximately equal likelihood.

Generalizing the Random Number Calculations

The preceding statement always assigns to variable face an integer in the range $1 \le$ face ≤ 6. The width of this range (i.e., the number of consecutive integers in the range) is 6, and the starting number in the range is 1. The width of the range is determined by the number 6 that's passed as an argument to Random method nextInt, and the starting number of the range is the number 1 that's added to the result of calling nextInt. We can generalize this result as

```
number = shiftingValue + randomNumbers.nextInt( scalingFactor );
```

where *shiftingValue* specifies the first number in the desired range of consecutive integers and *scalingFactor* specifies how many numbers are in the range.

It's also possible to choose integers at random from sets of values other than ranges of consecutive integers. For example, to obtain a random value from the sequence 2, 5, 8, 11 and 14, you could use the statement

```
number = 2 + 3 * randomNumbers.nextInt( 5 );
```

In this case, randomNumbers.nextInt(5) produces values in the range 0–4. Each value produced is multiplied by 3 to produce a number in the sequence 0, 3, 6, 9 and 12. We add 2 to that value to shift the range of values and obtain a value from the sequence 2, 5, 8, 11 and 14. We can generalize this result as

```
number = shiftingValue +
    differenceBetweenValues * randomNumbers.nextInt( scalingFactor );
```

where *shiftingValue* specifies the first number in the desired range of values, *difference-BetweenValues* represents the constant difference between consecutive numbers in the sequence and *scalingFactor* specifies how many numbers are in the range.

D.9.2 Random-Number Repeatability for Testing and Debugging

Class Random's methods actually generate pseudorandom numbers based on complex mathematical calculations—the sequence of numbers appears to be random. The calculation that produces the numbers uses the time of day as a **seed value** to change the sequence's starting point. Each new Random object seeds itself with a value based on the computer system's clock at the time the object is created, enabling each execution of a program to produce a different sequence of random numbers.

When debugging an application, it's often useful to repeat the exact same sequence of pseudorandom numbers during each execution of the program. This repeatability enables you to prove that your application is working for a specific sequence of random numbers before you test it with different sequences of random numbers. When repeatability is important, you can create a Random object as follows:

```
Random randomNumbers = new Random( seedValue );
```

The seedValue argument (of type long) seeds the random-number calculation. If the same seedValue is used every time, the Random object produces the same sequence of numbers. You can set a Random object's seed at any time during program execution by calling the object's set method, as in

```
randomNumbers.set( seedValue );
```

Error-Prevention Tip D.1

While developing a program, create the Random object with a specific seed value to produce a repeatable sequence of numbers each time the program executes. If a logic error occurs, fix the error and test the program again with the same seed value—this allows you to reconstruct the same sequence of numbers that caused the error. Once the logic errors have been removed, create the Random object without using a seed value, causing the Random object to generate a new sequence of random numbers each time the program executes.

D.10 Case Study: A Game of Chance; Introducing Enumerations

A popular game of chance is a dice game known as craps, which is played in casinos and back alleys throughout the world. The rules of the game are straightforward:

> *You roll two dice. Each die has six faces, which contain one, two, three, four, five and six spots, respectively. After the dice have come to rest, the sum of the spots on the two upward faces is calculated. If the sum is 7 or 11 on the first throw, you win. If the sum is 2, 3 or 12 on the first throw (called "craps"), you lose (i.e., the "house" wins). If the sum is 4, 5, 6, 8, 9 or 10 on the first throw, that sum becomes your "point." To win, you must continue rolling the dice until you "make your point" (i.e., roll that same point value). You lose by rolling a 7 before making your point.*

Figure D.5 simulates the game of craps, using methods to implement the game's logic. The main method (lines 21–65) calls the rollDice method (lines 68–81) as necessary to roll the dice and compute their sum. The sample outputs show winning and losing on the first roll, and winning and losing on a subsequent roll.

```java
 1  // Fig. D.5: Craps.java
 2  // Craps class simulates the dice game craps.
 3  import java.util.Random;
 4
 5  public class Craps
 6  {
 7     // create random number generator for use in method rollDice
 8     private static final Random randomNumbers = new Random();
 9
10     // enumeration with constants that represent the game status
11     private enum Status { CONTINUE, WON, LOST };
12
13     // constants that represent common rolls of the dice
14     private static final int SNAKE_EYES = 2;
15     private static final int TREY = 3;
16     private static final int SEVEN = 7;
17     private static final int YO_LEVEN = 11;
18     private static final int BOX_CARS = 12;
19
20     // plays one game of craps
21     public static void main( String[] args )
22     {
23        int myPoint = 0; // point if no win or loss on first roll
```

Fig. D.5 | Craps class simulates the dice game craps. (Part 1 of 3.)

```java
24          Status gameStatus; // can contain CONTINUE, WON or LOST
25
26          int sumOfDice = rollDice(); // first roll of the dice
27
28          // determine game status and point based on first roll
29          switch ( sumOfDice )
30          {
31             case SEVEN: // win with 7 on first roll
32             case YO_LEVEN: // win with 11 on first roll
33                gameStatus = Status.WON;
34                break;
35             case SNAKE_EYES: // lose with 2 on first roll
36             case TREY: // lose with 3 on first roll
37             case BOX_CARS: // lose with 12 on first roll
38                gameStatus = Status.LOST;
39                break;
40             default: // did not win or lose, so remember point
41                gameStatus = Status.CONTINUE; // game is not over
42                myPoint = sumOfDice; // remember the point
43                System.out.printf( "Point is %d\n", myPoint );
44                break; // optional at end of switch
45          } // end switch
46
47          // while game is not complete
48          while ( gameStatus == Status.CONTINUE ) // not WON or LOST
49          {
50             sumOfDice = rollDice(); // roll dice again
51
52             // determine game status
53             if ( sumOfDice == myPoint ) // win by making point
54                gameStatus = Status.WON;
55             else
56                if ( sumOfDice == SEVEN ) // lose by rolling 7 before point
57                   gameStatus = Status.LOST;
58          } // end while
59
60          // display won or lost message
61          if ( gameStatus == Status.WON )
62             System.out.println( "Player wins" );
63          else
64             System.out.println( "Player loses" );
65       } // end main
66
67       // roll dice, calculate sum and display results
68       public static int rollDice()
69       {
70          // pick random die values
71          int die1 = 1 + randomNumbers.nextInt( 6 ); // first die roll
72          int die2 = 1 + randomNumbers.nextInt( 6 ); // second die roll
73
74          int sum = die1 + die2; // sum of die values
75
```

Fig. D.5 | Craps class simulates the dice game craps. (Part 2 of 3.)

```
76          // display results of this roll
77          System.out.printf( "Player rolled %d + %d = %d\n",
78             die1, die2, sum );
79
80          return sum; // return sum of dice
81       } // end method rollDice
82   } // end class Craps
```

```
Player rolled 5 + 6 = 11
Player wins
```

```
Player rolled 5 + 4 = 9
Point is 9
Player rolled 4 + 2 = 6
Player rolled 3 + 6 = 9
Player wins
```

```
Player rolled 1 + 2 = 3
Player loses
```

```
Player rolled 2 + 6 = 8
Point is 8
Player rolled 5 + 1 = 6
Player rolled 2 + 1 = 3
Player rolled 1 + 6 = 7
Player loses
```

Fig. D.5 | Craps class simulates the dice game craps. (Part 3 of 3.)

Method `rollDice`

In the rules of the game, the player must roll two dice on the first roll and must do the same on all subsequent rolls. We declare method `rollDice` (Fig. D.5, lines 68–81) to roll the dice and compute and print their sum. Method `rollDice` is declared once, but it's called from two places (lines 26 and 50) in main, which contains the logic for one complete game of craps. Method `rollDice` takes no arguments, so it has an empty parameter list. Each time it's called, `rollDice` returns the sum of the dice, so the return type int is indicated in the method header (line 68). Although lines 71 and 72 look the same (except for the die names), they do not necessarily produce the same result. Each of these statements produces a random value in the range 1–6. Variable randomNumbers (used in lines 71–72) is *not* declared in the method. Instead it's declared as a private static final variable of the class and initialized in line 8. This enables us to create one Random object that's reused in each call to `rollDice`. If there were a program that contained multiple instances of class Craps, they'd all share this one Random object.

Method `main`'s Local Variables

The game is reasonably involved. The player may win or lose on the first roll, or may win or lose on any subsequent roll. Method main (lines 21–65) uses local variable myPoint (line 23) to store the "point" if the player does not win or lose on the first roll, local variable gameStatus (line 24) to keep track of the overall game status and local variable sumOfDice (line 26) to hold the sum of the dice for the most recent roll. Variable myPoint is initialized to 0 to ensure that the application will compile. If you do not initialize myPoint, the compiler issues an error, because myPoint is not assigned a value in *every* case of the switch statement, and thus the program could try to use myPoint before it's assigned a value. By contrast, gameStatus *is* assigned a value in *every* case of the switch statement—thus, it's guaranteed to be initialized before it's used and does not need to be initialized.

enum *Type* Status

Local variable gameStatus (line 24) is declared to be of a new type called Status (declared at line 11). Type Status is a private member of class Craps, because Status will be used only in that class. Status is a type called an **enumeration**, which, in its simplest form, declares a set of constants represented by identifiers. An enumeration is a special kind of class that's introduced by the keyword **enum** and a type name (in this case, Status). As with classes, braces delimit an enum declaration's body. Inside the braces is a comma-separated list of **enumeration constants**, each representing a unique value. The identifiers in an enum must be unique. You'll learn more about enumerations in Appendix E.

> ### Good Programming Practice D.1
>
> *It's a convention to use only uppercase letters in the names of enumeration constants. This makes them stand out and reminds you that they are not variables.*

Variables of type Status can be assigned only the three constants declared in the enumeration (line 11) or a compilation error will occur. When the game is won, the program sets local variable gameStatus to Status.WON (lines 33 and 54). When the game is lost, the program sets local variable gameStatus to Status.LOST (lines 38 and 57). Otherwise, the program sets local variable gameStatus to Status.CONTINUE (line 41) to indicate that the game is not over and the dice must be rolled again.

> ### Good Programming Practice D.2
>
> *Using enumeration constants (like Status.WON, Status.LOST and Status.CONTINUE) rather than literal values (such as 0, 1 and 2) makes programs easier to read and maintain.*

Logic of the main *Method*

Line 26 in main calls rollDice, which picks two random values from 1 to 6, displays the values of the first die, the second die and their sum, and returns the sum. Method main next enters the switch statement (lines 29–45), which uses the sumOfDice value from line 26 to determine whether the game has been won or lost, or should continue with another roll. The values that result in a win or loss on the first roll are declared as public static final int constants in lines 14–18. The identifier names use casino parlance for these sums. These constants, like enum constants, are declared by convention with all capital letters, to make them stand out in the program. Lines 31–34 determine whether the player won on the first roll with SEVEN (7) or YO_LEVEN (11). Lines 35–39 determine whether the player lost on the first roll with SNAKE_EYES (2), TREY (3), or BOX_CARS (12). After the first roll, if the game is not over, the default case (lines 40–44) sets gameStatus to Status.CONTINUE, saves sumOfDice in myPoint and displays the point.

If we're still trying to "make our point" (i.e., the game is continuing from a prior roll), lines 48–58 execute. Line 50 rolls the dice again. If sumOfDice matches myPoint (line 53), line 54 sets gameStatus to Status.WON, then the loop terminates because the game is complete. If sumOfDice is SEVEN (line 56), line 57 sets gameStatus to Status.LOST, and the loop terminates because the game is complete. When the game completes, lines 61–64 display a message indicating whether the player won or lost, and the program terminates.

The program uses the various program-control mechanisms we've discussed. The Craps class uses two methods—main and rollDice (called twice from main)—and the switch, while, if...else and nested if control statements. Note also the use of multiple case labels in the switch statement to execute the same statements for sums of SEVEN and YO_LEVEN (lines 31–32) and for sums of SNAKE_EYES, TREY and BOX_CARS (lines 35–37).

Why Some Constants Are Not Defined as **enum** *Constants*

You might be wondering why we declared the sums of the dice as public final static int constants rather than as enum constants. The reason is that the program must compare the int variable sumOfDice (line 26) to these constants to determine the outcome of each roll. Suppose we declared enum Sum containing constants (e.g., Sum.SNAKE_EYES) representing the five sums used in the game, then used these constants in the switch statement (lines 29–45). Doing so would prevent us from using sumOfDice as the switch statement's controlling expression, because Java does *not* allow an int to be compared to an enumeration constant. To achieve the same functionality as the current program, we would have to use a variable currentSum of type Sum as the switch's controlling expression. Unfortunately, Java does not provide an easy way to convert an int value to a particular enum constant. This could be done with a separate switch statement. Clearly this would be cumbersome and not improve the program's readability (thus defeating the purpose of using an enum).

D.11 Scope of Declarations

You've seen declarations of various Java entities, such as classes, methods, variables and parameters. Declarations introduce names that can be used to refer to such Java entities. The **scope** of a declaration is the portion of the program that can refer to the declared entity by its name. Such an entity is said to be "in scope" for that portion of the program. This section introduces several important scope issues.

The basic scope rules are as follows:

1. The scope of a parameter declaration is the body of the method in which the declaration appears.

2. The scope of a local-variable declaration is from the point at which the declaration appears to the end of that block.

3. The scope of a local-variable declaration that appears in the initialization section of a for statement's header is the body of the for statement and the other expressions in the header.

4. A method or field's scope is the entire body of the class. This enables non-static methods of a class to use the fields and other methods of the class.

Any block may contain variable declarations. If a local variable or parameter in a method has the same name as a field of the class, the field is "hidden" until the block terminates execution—this is called **shadowing**. In Appendix F, we discuss how to access shadowed fields.

Error-Prevention Tip D.2

Use different names for fields and local variables to help prevent subtle logic errors that occur when a method is called and a local variable of the method shadows a field in the class.

Figure D.6 demonstrates scoping issues with fields and local variables. Line 7 declares and initializes the field x to 1. This field is shadowed (hidden) in any block (or method) that declares a local variable named x. Method main (lines 11–23) declares a local variable x (line 13) and initializes it to 5. This local variable's value is output to show that the field x (whose value is 1) is shadowed in main. The program declares two other methods—use-LocalVariable (lines 26–35) and useField (lines 38–45)—that each take no arguments and return no results. Method main calls each method twice (lines 17–20). Method use-LocalVariable declares local variable x (line 28). When useLocalVariable is first called (line 17), it creates local variable x and initializes it to 25 (line 28), outputs the value of x (lines 30–31), increments x (line 32) and outputs the value of x again (lines 33–34). When useLocalVariable is called a second time (line 19), it recreates local variable x and re-initializes it to 25, so the output of each useLocalVariable call is identical.

```java
1   // Fig. D.6: Scope.java
2   // Scope class demonstrates field and local variable scopes.
3
4   public class Scope
5   {
6      // field that is accessible to all methods of this class
7      private static int x = 1;
8
9      // method main creates and initializes local variable x
10     // and calls methods useLocalVariable and useField
11     public static void main( String[] args )
12     {
13        int x = 5; // method's local variable x shadows field x
14
15        System.out.printf( "local x in main is %d\n", x );
16
17        useLocalVariable(); // useLocalVariable has local x
18        useField(); // useField uses class Scope's field x
19        useLocalVariable(); // useLocalVariable reinitializes local x
20        useField(); // class Scope's field x retains its value
21
22        System.out.printf( "\nlocal x in main is %d\n", x );
23     } // end main
24
25     // create and initialize local variable x during each call
26     public static void useLocalVariable()
27     {
28        int x = 25; // initialized each time useLocalVariable is called
29
30        System.out.printf(
31           "\nlocal x on entering method useLocalVariable is %d\n", x );
32        ++x; // modifies this method's local variable x
```

Fig. D.6 | Scope class demonstrates field and local variable scopes. (Part 1 of 2.)

```
33          System.out.printf(
34              "local x before exiting method useLocalVariable is %d\n", x );
35      } // end method useLocalVariable
36
37      // modify class Scope's field x during each call
38      public static void useField()
39      {
40          System.out.printf(
41              "\nfield x on entering method useField is %d\n", x );
42          x *= 10; // modifies class Scope's field x
43          System.out.printf(
44              "field x before exiting method useField is %d\n", x );
45      } // end method useField
46  } // end class Scope
```

```
local x in main is 5

local x on entering method useLocalVariable is 25
local x before exiting method useLocalVariable is 26

field x on entering method useField is 1
field x before exiting method useField is 10

local x on entering method useLocalVariable is 25
local x before exiting method useLocalVariable is 26

field x on entering method useField is 10
field x before exiting method useField is 100

local x in main is 5
```

Fig. D.6 | Scope class demonstrates field and local variable scopes. (Part 2 of 2.)

Method useField does not declare any local variables. Therefore, when it refers to x, field x (line 7) of the class is used. When method useField is first called (line 18), it outputs the value (1) of field x (lines 40–41), multiplies the field x by 10 (line 42) and outputs the value (10) of field x again (lines 43–44) before returning. The next time method use-Field is called (line 20), the field has its modified value (10), so the method outputs 10, then 100. Finally, in method main, the program outputs the value of local variable x again (line 22) to show that none of the method calls modified main's local variable x, because the methods all referred to variables named x in other scopes.

D.12 Method Overloading

Methods of the same name can be declared in the same class, as long as they have different sets of parameters (determined by the number, types and order of the parameters)—this is called **method overloading**. When an overloaded method is called, the compiler selects the appropriate method by examining the number, types and order of the arguments in the call. Method overloading is commonly used to create several methods with the *same* name that perform the *same* or *similar* tasks, but on different types or different numbers of arguments. For example, Math methods abs, min and max (summarized in Section D.3) are overloaded with four versions each:

1. One with two `double` parameters.
2. One with two `float` parameters.
3. One with two `int` parameters.
4. One with two `long` parameters.

Our next example demonstrates declaring and invoking overloaded methods. We demonstrate overloaded constructors in Appendix F.

Declaring Overloaded Methods

Class `MethodOverload` (Fig. D.7) includes two overloaded versions of method square—one that calculates the square of an `int` (and returns an `int`) and one that calculates the square of a `double` (and returns a `double`). Although these methods have the same name and similar parameter lists and bodies, think of them simply as *different* methods. It may help to think of the method names as "square of `int`" and "square of `double`," respectively.

```java
1   // Fig. D.7: MethodOverload.java
2   // Overloaded method declarations.
3
4   public class MethodOverload
5   {
6      // test overloaded square methods
7      public static void main( String[] args )
8      {
9         System.out.printf( "Square of integer 7 is %d\n", square( 7 ) );
10        System.out.printf( "Square of double 7.5 is %f\n", square( 7.5 ) );
11     } // end main
12
13     // square method with int argument
14     public static int square( int intValue )
15     {
16        System.out.printf( "\nCalled square with int argument: %d\n",
17           intValue );
18        return intValue * intValue;
19     } // end method square with int argument
20
21     // square method with double argument
22     public static double square( double doubleValue )
23     {
24        System.out.printf( "\nCalled square with double argument: %f\n",
25           doubleValue );
26        return doubleValue * doubleValue;
27     } // end method square with double argument
28  } // end class MethodOverload
```

```
Called square with int argument: 7
Square of integer 7 is 49

Called square with double argument: 7.500000
Square of double 7.5 is 56.250000
```

Fig. D.7 | Overloaded method declarations.

Line 9 invokes method square with the argument 7. Literal integer values are treated as type int, so the method call in line 9 invokes the version of square at lines 14–19 that specifies an int parameter. Similarly, line 10 invokes method square with the argument 7.5. Literal floating-point values are treated as type double, so the method call in line 10 invokes the version of square at lines 22–27 that specifies a double parameter. Each method first outputs a line of text to prove that the proper method was called in each case. The values in lines 10 and 24 are displayed with the format specifier %f. We did not specify a precision in either case. By default, floating-point values are displayed with six digits of precision if the precision is not specified in the format specifier.

Distinguishing Between Overloaded Methods

The compiler distinguishes overloaded methods by their **signature**—a combination of the method's name and the number, types and order of its parameters. If the compiler looked only at method names during compilation, the code in Fig. D.7 would be ambiguous— the compiler would not know how to distinguish between the two square methods (lines 14–19 and 22–27). Internally, the compiler uses longer method names that include the original method name, the types of each parameter and the exact order of the parameters to determine whether the methods in a class are unique in that class.

For example, in Fig. D.7, the compiler might use the logical name "square of int" for the square method that specifies an int parameter and "square of double" for the square method that specifies a double parameter (the actual names the compiler uses are messier). If method1's declaration begins as

```
void method1( int a, float b )
```

then the compiler might use the logical name "method1 of int and float." If the parameters are specified as

```
void method1( float a, int b )
```

then the compiler might use the logical name "method1 of float and int." The *order* of the parameter types is important—the compiler considers the preceding two method1 headers to be distinct.

Return Types of Overloaded Methods

In discussing the logical names of methods used by the compiler, we did not mention the return types of the methods. *Method calls cannot be distinguished by return type.* If you had overloaded methods that differed only by their return types and you called one of the methods in a standalone statement as in:

```
square( 2 );
```

the compiler would *not* be able to determine the version of the method to call, because the return value is ignored. When two methods have the same signature and different return types, the compiler issues an error message indicating that the method is already defined in the class. Overloaded methods *can* have different return types if the methods have different parameter lists. Also, overloaded methods need *not* have the same number of parameters.

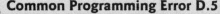

Common Programming Error D.5

Declaring overloaded methods with identical parameter lists is a compilation error regardless of whether the return types are different.

D.13 Wrap-Up

In this appendix, you learned more about method declarations. You also learned the difference between non-static and static methods and how to call static methods by preceding the method name with the name of the class in which it appears and the dot (.) separator. You learned how to use operators + and += to perform string concatenations. We discussed how the method-call stack and activation records keep track of the methods that have been called and where each method must return to when it completes its task. We also discussed Java's promotion rules for converting implicitly between primitive types and how to perform explicit conversions with cast operators. Next, you learned about some of the commonly used packages in the Java API.

You saw how to declare named constants using both enum types and public static final variables. You used class Random to generate random numbers for simulations. You also learned about the scope of fields and local variables in a class. Finally, you learned that multiple methods in one class can be overloaded by providing methods with the same name and different signatures. Such methods can be used to perform the same or similar tasks using different types or different numbers of parameters.

In Appendix E, you'll learn how to maintain lists and tables of data in arrays. You'll see a more elegant implementation of the application that rolls a die 6,000,000 times and two enhanced versions of our GradeBook case study that you studied in Appendices B–C. You'll also learn how to access an application's command-line arguments that are passed to method main when an application begins execution.

Self-Review Exercises

D.1 Fill in the blanks in each of the following statements:
   a) A method is invoked with a(n) _____.
   b) A variable known only within the method in which it's declared is called a(n) _____.
   c) The _____ statement in a called method can be used to pass the value of an expression back to the calling method.
   d) The keyword _____ indicates that a method does not return a value.
   e) Data can be added or removed only from the _____ of a stack.
   f) Stacks are known as _____ data structures; the last item pushed (inserted) on the stack is the first item popped (removed) from the stack.
   g) The three ways to return control from a called method to a caller are _____, _____ and _____.
   h) An object of class _____ produces random numbers.
   i) The program-execution stack contains the memory for local variables on each invocation of a method during a program's execution. This data, stored as a portion of the program-execution stack, is known as the _____ or _____ of the method call.
   j) If there are more method calls than can be stored on the program-execution stack, an error known as a(n) _____ occurs.
   k) The _____ of a declaration is the portion of a program that can refer to the entity in the declaration by name.
   l) It's possible to have several methods with the same name that each operate on different types or numbers of arguments. This feature is called method _____.
   m) The program-execution stack is also referred to as the _____ stack.

D.2   For the class `Craps` in Fig. D.5, state the scope of each of the following entities:

    a)   the variable `randomNumbers`.

    b)   the variable `die1`.

    c)   the method `rollDice`.

    d)   the method `main`.

    e)   the variable `sumOfDice`.

D.3   Write an application that tests whether the examples of the `Math` class method calls shown in Fig. D.1 actually produce the indicated results.

D.4   Give the method header for each of the following methods:

    a)   Method `hypotenuse`, which takes two double-precision, floating-point arguments `side1` and `side2` and returns a double-precision, floating-point result.

    b)   Method `smallest`, which takes three integers x, y and z and returns an integer.

    c)   Method `instructions`, which does not take any arguments and does not return a value. [*Note:* Such methods are commonly used to display instructions to a user.]

    d)   Method `intToFloat`, which takes integer argument `number` and returns a `float`.

D.5   Find the error in each of the following program segments. Explain how to correct the error.

    a)
```java
void g()
{
    System.out.println( "Inside method g" );

    void h()
    {
        System.out.println( "Inside method h" );
    }
}
```

    b)
```java
int sum( int x, int y )
{
    int result;
    result = x + y;
}
```

    c)
```java
void f( float a );
{
    float a;
    System.out.println( a );
}
```

D.6   Write a complete Java application to prompt the user for the `double` radius of a sphere, and call method `sphereVolume` to calculate and display the volume of the sphere. Use the following statement to calculate the volume:

```java
double volume = ( 4.0 / 3.0 ) * Math.PI * Math.pow( radius, 3 )
```

Answers to Self-Review Exercises

D.1   a) method call. b) local variable. c) return. d) void. e) top. f) last-in, first-out (LIFO). g) `return`; or `return` *expression*; or encountering the closing right brace of a method. h) `Random`. i) activation record, stack frame. j) stack overflow. k) scope. l) method overloading. m) method call.

D.2   a) class body. b) block that defines method `rollDice`'s body. c) class body. d) class body. e) block that defines method `main`'s body.

D.3   The following solution demonstrates the `Math` class methods in Fig. D.1:

```
1    // Exercise D.3: MathTest.java
2    // Testing the Math class methods.
3
4    public class MathTest
5    {
6       public static void main( String[] args )
7       {
8          System.out.printf( "Math.abs( 23.7 ) = %f\n", Math.abs( 23.7 ) );
9          System.out.printf( "Math.abs( 0.0 ) = %f\n", Math.abs( 0.0 ) );
10         System.out.printf( "Math.abs( -23.7 ) = %f\n", Math.abs( -23.7 ) );
11         System.out.printf( "Math.ceil( 9.2 ) = %f\n", Math.ceil( 9.2 ) );
12         System.out.printf( "Math.ceil( -9.8 ) = %f\n", Math.ceil( -9.8 ) );
13         System.out.printf( "Math.cos( 0.0 ) = %f\n", Math.cos( 0.0 ) );
14         System.out.printf( "Math.exp( 1.0 ) = %f\n", Math.exp( 1.0 ) );
15         System.out.printf( "Math.exp( 2.0 ) = %f\n", Math.exp( 2.0 ) );
16         System.out.printf( "Math.floor( 9.2 ) = %f\n", Math.floor( 9.2 ) );
17         System.out.printf( "Math.floor( -9.8 ) = %f\n",
18            Math.floor( -9.8 ) );
19         System.out.printf( "Math.log( Math.E ) = %f\n",
20            Math.log( Math.E ) );
21         System.out.printf( "Math.log( Math.E * Math.E ) = %f\n",
22            Math.log( Math.E * Math.E ) );
23         System.out.printf( "Math.max( 2.3, 12.7 ) = %f\n",
24            Math.max( 2.3, 12.7 ) );
25         System.out.printf( "Math.max( -2.3, -12.7 ) = %f\n",
26            Math.max( -2.3, -12.7 ) );
27         System.out.printf( "Math.min( 2.3, 12.7 ) = %f\n",
28            Math.min( 2.3, 12.7 ) );
29         System.out.printf( "Math.min( -2.3, -12.7 ) = %f\n",
30            Math.min( -2.3, -12.7 ) );
31         System.out.printf( "Math.pow( 2.0, 7.0 ) = %f\n",
32            Math.pow( 2.0, 7.0 ) );
33         System.out.printf( "Math.pow( 9.0, 0.5 ) = %f\n",
34            Math.pow( 9.0, 0.5 ) );
35         System.out.printf( "Math.sin( 0.0 ) = %f\n", Math.sin( 0.0 ) );
36         System.out.printf( "Math.sqrt( 900.0 ) = %f\n",
37            Math.sqrt( 900.0 ) );
38         System.out.printf( "Math.tan( 0.0 ) = %f\n", Math.tan( 0.0 ) );
39      } // end main
40   } // end class MathTest
```

```
Math.abs( 23.7 ) = 23.700000
Math.abs( 0.0 ) = 0.000000
Math.abs( -23.7 ) = 23.700000
Math.ceil( 9.2 ) = 10.000000
Math.ceil( -9.8 ) = -9.000000
Math.cos( 0.0 ) = 1.000000
Math.exp( 1.0 ) = 2.718282
Math.exp( 2.0 ) = 7.389056
Math.floor( 9.2 ) = 9.000000
Math.floor( -9.8 ) = -10.000000
Math.log( Math.E ) = 1.000000
Math.log( Math.E * Math.E ) = 2.000000
Math.max( 2.3, 12.7 ) = 12.700000
Math.max( -2.3, -12.7 ) = -2.300000
Math.min( 2.3, 12.7 ) = 2.300000
Math.min( -2.3, -12.7 ) = -12.700000
Math.pow( 2.0, 7.0 ) = 128.000000
Math.pow( 9.0, 0.5 ) = 3.000000
Math.sin( 0.0 ) = 0.000000
Math.sqrt( 900.0 ) = 30.000000
Math.tan( 0.0 ) = 0.000000
```

D.4 a) **double** hypotenuse(**double** side1, **double** side2)
      b) **int** smallest(**int** x, **int** y, **int** z)
      c) **void** instructions()
      d) **float** intToFloat(**int** number)

D.5 a) Error: Method h is declared within method g.
         Correction: Move the declaration of h outside the declaration of g.
      b) Error: The method is supposed to return an integer, but does not.
         Correction: Delete the variable result, and place the statement
            return x + y;
         to the method, or add the following statement at the end of the method body:
            return result;
      c) Error: The semicolon after the right parenthesis of the parameter list is incorrect, and
         the parameter a should not be redeclared in the method.
         Correction: Delete the semicolon after the right parenthesis of the parameter list, and
         delete the declaration float a;.

D.6 The following solution calculates the volume of a sphere, using the radius entered by the user:

```
1   // Exercise D.6: Sphere.java
2   // Calculate the volume of a sphere.
3   import java.util.Scanner;
4
5   public class Sphere
6   {
7      // obtain radius from user and display volume of sphere
8      public static void main( String[] args )
9      {
10         Scanner input = new Scanner( System.in );
11         System.out.print( "Enter radius of sphere: " );
12         double radius = input.nextDouble();
13         System.out.printf( "Volume is %f\n", sphereVolume( radius ) );
14      } // end method determineSphereVolume
15
16      // calculate and return sphere volume
17      public static double sphereVolume( double radius )
18      {
19         double volume = ( 4.0 / 3.0 ) * Math.PI * Math.pow( radius, 3 );
20         return volume;
21      } // end method sphereVolume
22   } // end class Sphere
```

```
Enter radius of sphere: 4
Volume is 268.082573
```

Exercises

D.7 What is the value of x after each of the following statements is executed?
      a) x = Math.abs(7.5);
      b) x = Math.floor(7.5);
      c) x = Math.abs(0.0);
      d) x = Math.ceil(0.0);
      e) x = Math.abs(-6.4);
      f) x = Math.ceil(-6.4);
      g) x = Math.ceil(-Math.abs(-8 + Math.floor(-5.5)));

D.8 *(Parking Charges)* A parking garage charges a $2.00 minimum fee to park for up to three hours. The garage charges an additional $0.50 per hour for each hour *or part thereof* in excess of three hours. The maximum charge for any given 24-hour period is $10.00. Assume that no car parks for longer than 24 hours at a time. Write an application that calculates and displays the parking charges for each customer who parked in the garage yesterday. You should enter the hours parked for each customer. The program should display the charge for the current customer and should calculate and display the running total of yesterday's receipts. It should use the method `calculateCharges` to determine the charge for each customer.

D.9 *(Rounding Numbers)* `Math.floor` can be used to round values to the nearest integer—e.g.,

```
y = Math.floor( x + 0.5 );
```

will round the number x to the nearest integer and assign the result to y. Write an application that reads `double` values and uses the preceding statement to round each of the numbers to the nearest integer. For each number processed, display both the original number and the rounded number.

D.10 *(Rounding Numbers)* To round numbers to specific decimal places, use a statement like

```
y = Math.floor( x * 10 + 0.5 ) / 10;
```

which rounds x to the tenths position (i.e., the first position to the right of the decimal point), or

```
y = Math.floor( x * 100 + 0.5 ) / 100;
```

which rounds x to the hundredths position (i.e., the second position to the right of the decimal point). Write an application that defines four methods for rounding a number x in various ways:

a) `roundToInteger( number )`
b) `roundToTenths( number )`
c) `roundToHundredths( number )`
d) `roundToThousandths( number )`

For each value read, your program should display the original value, the number rounded to the nearest integer, the number rounded to the nearest tenth, the number rounded to the nearest hundredth and the number rounded to the nearest thousandth.

D.11 Answer each of the following questions:

a) What does it mean to choose numbers "at random"?
b) Why is the `nextInt` method of class `Random` useful for simulating games of chance?
c) Why is it often necessary to scale or shift the values produced by a `Random` object?
d) Why is computerized simulation of real-world situations a useful technique?

D.12 Write statements that assign random integers to the variable n in the following ranges:

a) $1 \leq n \leq 2$.
b) $1 \leq n \leq 100$.
c) $0 \leq n \leq 9$.
d) $1000 \leq n \leq 1112$.
e) $-1 \leq n \leq 1$.
f) $-3 \leq n \leq 11$.

D.13 Write statements that will display a random number from each of the following sets:

a) 2, 4, 6, 8, 10.
b) 3, 5, 7, 9, 11.
c) 6, 10, 14, 18, 22.

D.14 *(Exponentiation)* Write a method `integerPower(base, exponent)` that returns the value of

$$base^{\,exponent}$$

For example, `integerPower(3, 4)` calculates 3^4 (or 3 * 3 * 3 * 3). Assume that `exponent` is a positive, nonzero integer and that `base` is an integer. Use a `for` or `while` statement to control the calculation. Do not use any Math class methods. Incorporate this method into an application that reads integer values for base and exponent and performs the calculation with the integerPower method.

D.15 *(Multiples)* Write a method isMultiple that determines, for a pair of integers, whether the second integer is a multiple of the first. The method should take two integer arguments and return true if the second is a multiple of the first and false otherwise. [*Hint:* Use the remainder operator.] Incorporate this method into an application that inputs a series of pairs of integers (one pair at a time) and determines whether the second value in each pair is a multiple of the first.

D.16 *(Even or Odd)* Write a method isEven that uses the remainder operator (%) to determine whether an integer is even. The method should take an integer argument and return true if the integer is even and false otherwise. Incorporate this method into an application that inputs a sequence of integers (one at a time) and determines whether each is even or odd.

D.17 *(Circle Area)* Write an application that prompts the user for the radius of a circle and uses a method called circleArea to calculate the area of the circle.

D.18 *(Temperature Conversions)* Implement the following integer methods:
a) Method celsius returns the Celsius equivalent of a Fahrenheit temperature, using the calculation

```
celsius = 5.0 / 9.0 * ( fahrenheit - 32 );
```

b) Method fahrenheit returns the Fahrenheit equivalent of a Celsius temperature, using the calculation

```
fahrenheit = 9.0 / 5.0 * celsius + 32;
```

c) Use the methods from parts (a) and (b) to write an application that enables the user either to enter a Fahrenheit temperature and display the Celsius equivalent or to enter a Celsius temperature and display the Fahrenheit equivalent.

D.19 *(Find the Minimum)* Write a method minimum3 that returns the smallest of three floating-point numbers. Use the Math.min method to implement minimum3. Incorporate the method into an application that reads three values from the user, determines the smallest value and displays the result.

D.20 *(Greatest Common Divisor)* The *greatest common divisor (GCD)* of two integers is the largest integer that evenly divides each of the two numbers. Write a method gcd that returns the greatest common divisor of two integers. [*Hint:* You might want to use Euclid's algorithm. You can find information about it at en.wikipedia.org/wiki/Euclidean_algorithm.] Incorporate the method into an application that reads two values from the user and displays the result.

D.21 *(Quality Points)* Write a method qualityPoints that inputs a student's average and returns 4 if it's 90–100, 3 if 80–89, 2 if 70–79, 1 if 60–69 and 0 if lower than 60. Incorporate the method into an application that reads a value from the user and displays the result.

D.22 *(Coin Tossing)* Write an application that simulates coin tossing. Let the program toss a coin each time the user chooses the "Toss Coin" menu option. Count the number of times each side of the coin appears. Display the results. The program should call a separate method flip that takes no arguments and returns a value from a Coin enum (HEADS and TAILS). [*Note:* If the program realistically simulates coin tossing, each side of the coin should appear approximately half the time.]

D.23 *(Guess the Number)* Write an application that plays "guess the number" as follows: Your program chooses the number to be guessed by selecting a random integer in the range 1 to 1000. The application displays the prompt Guess a number between 1 and 1000. The player inputs a first guess. If the player's guess is incorrect, your program should display "Too high. Try again." or "Too low. Try again." to help the player "zero in" on the correct answer. The program should prompt the user for the next guess. When the user enters the correct answer, display "Congratulations. You guessed the number!", and allow the user to choose whether to play again. The guessing technique employed in this problem is similar to a binary search.

D.24 *(Craps Game Modification)* Modify the craps program of Fig. D.5 to allow wagering. Initialize variable bankBalance to 1000 dollars. Prompt the player to enter a wager. Check that wager is less than or equal to bankBalance, and if it's not, have the user reenter wager until a valid wager is entered. Then, run one game of craps. If the player wins, increase bankBalance by wager and display the new bankBalance. If the player loses, decrease bankBalance by wager, display the new bankBalance, check whether bankBalance has become zero and, if so, display the message "Sorry. You busted!" As the game progresses, display various messages to create some "chatter," such as "Oh, you're going for broke, huh?" or "Aw c'mon, take a chance!" or "You're up big. Now's the time to cash in your chips!". Implement the "chatter" as a separate method that randomly chooses the string to display.

D.25 *(Computer-Assisted Instruction)* The use of computers in education is referred to as *computer-assisted instruction* (*CAI*). Write a program that will help an elementary school student learn multiplication. Use a Random object to produce two positive one-digit integers. The program should then prompt the user with a question, such as

How much is 6 times 7?

The student then inputs the answer. Next, the program checks the student's answer. If it's correct, display the message "Very good!" and ask another multiplication question. If the answer is wrong, display the message "No. Please try again." and let the student try the same question repeatedly until the student finally gets it right. A separate method should be used to generate each new question. This method should be called once when the application begins execution and each time the user answers the question correctly.

D.26 *(Computer-Assisted Instruction: Reducing Student Fatigue)* One problem in CAI environments is student fatigue. This can be reduced by varying the computer's responses to hold the student's attention. Modify the program of Exercise D.25 so that various comments are displayed for each answer as follows:

Possible responses to a correct answer:

Very good!
Excellent!
Nice work!
Keep up the good work!

Possible responses to an incorrect answer:

No. Please try again.
Wrong. Try once more.
Don't give up!
No. Keep trying.

Use random-number generation to choose a number from 1 to 4 that will be used to select one of the four appropriate responses to each correct or incorrect answer. Use a switch statement to issue the responses.

D.27 *(Computer-Assisted Instruction: Varying the Types of Problems)* Modify the previous program to allow the user to pick a type of arithmetic problem to study. An option of 1 means addition problems only, 2 means subtraction problems only, 3 means multiplication problems only, 4 means division problems only and 5 means a random mixture of all these types.

Arrays and ArrayLists

E

Objectives
In this appendix you'll learn:

- What arrays are.
- To use arrays to store data in and retrieve data from lists and tables of values.
- To declare arrays, initialize arrays and refer to individual elements of arrays.
- To iterate through arrays with the enhanced **for** statement.
- To pass arrays to methods.
- To declare and manipulate multidimensional arrays.
- To perform common array manipulations with the methods of class **Arrays**.
- To use class **ArrayList** to manipulate a dynamically resizable array-like data structure.

E.1 Introduction

This appendix introduces **data structures**—collections of related data items. **Arrays** are data structures consisting of related data items of the same type. Arrays make it convenient to process related groups of values. Arrays remain the same length once they're created, although an array variable may be reassigned such that it refers to a new array of a different length.

Although commonly used, arrays have limited capabilities. For instance, you must specify an array's size, and if at execution time you wish to modify it, you must do so manually by creating a new array. At the end of this appendix, we introduce one of Java's prebuilt data structures from the Java API's collection classes. These offer greater capabilities than traditional arrays. We focus on the **ArrayList** collection. **ArrayList**s are similar to arrays but provide additional functionality, such as **dynamic resizing**—they automatically increase their size at execution time to accommodate additional elements.

E.2 Arrays

An array is a group of variables (called **elements** or **components**) containing values that all have the same type. Arrays are *objects*, so they're considered reference types. As you'll soon see, what we typically think of as an array is actually a reference to an array object in memory. The *elements* of an array can be either primitive types or reference types (including arrays, as we'll see in Section E.9). To refer to a particular element in an array, we specify the name of the reference to the array and the *position number* of the element in the array. The position number of the element is called the element's **index** or **subscript**.

Figure E.1 shows a logical representation of an integer array called c. This array contains 12 elements. A program refers to any one of these elements with an **array-access expression** that includes the name of the array followed by the index of the particular element in **square brackets ([])**. The first element in every array has **index zero** and is sometimes called the **zeroth element**. Thus, the elements of array c are c[0], c[1], c[2] and so on. The highest index in array c is 11, which is 1 less than 12—the number of elements in the array. Array names follow the same conventions as other variable names.

Name of array (c) ⟶ c[0]	-45
c[1]	6
c[2]	0
c[3]	72
c[4]	1543
c[5]	-89
c[6]	0
c[7]	62
c[8]	-3
c[9]	1
Index (or subscript) of the c[10]	6453
element in array c c[11]	78

Fig. E.1 | A 12-element array.

An index must be a nonnegative integer. A program can use an expression as an index. For example, if we assume that variable a is 5 and variable b is 6, then the statement

```
c[ a + b ] += 2;
```

adds 2 to array element c[11]. An indexed array name is an array-access expression, which can be used on the left side of an assignment to place a new value into an array element.

Common Programming Error E.1

An index must be an int value or a value of a type that can be promoted to int—namely, byte, short or char, but not long; otherwise, a compilation error occurs.

Let's examine array c in Fig. E.1 more closely. The **name** of the array is c. Every array object knows its own length and stores it in a **length instance variable**. The expression c.length accesses array c's length field to determine the length of the array. Even though the length instance variable of an array is public, it cannot be changed because it's a final variable. This array's 12 elements are referred to as c[0], c[1], c[2], …, c[11]. The value of c[0] is -45, the value of c[1] is 6, the value of c[2] is 0, the value of c[7] is 62 and the value of c[11] is 78. To calculate the sum of the values contained in the first three elements of array c and store the result in variable sum, we would write

```
sum = c[ 0 ] + c[ 1 ] + c[ 2 ];
```

To divide the value of c[6] by 2 and assign the result to the variable x, we would write

```
x = c[ 6 ] / 2;
```

E.3 Declaring and Creating Arrays

Array objects occupy space in memory. Like other objects, arrays are created with keyword new. To create an array object, you specify the type of the array elements and the number of elements as part of an **array-creation expression** that uses keyword new. Such an expression returns a reference that can be stored in an array variable. The following declaration and array-creation expression create an array object containing 12 int elements and store the array's reference in array variable c:

```
int[] c = new int[ 12 ];
```

This expression can be used to create the array shown in Fig. E.1. When an array is created, each element of the array receives a default value—zero for the numeric primitive-type elements, false for boolean elements and null for references. As you'll soon see, you can provide nondefault initial element values when you create an array.

Creating the array in Fig. E.1 can also be performed in two steps as follows:

```
int[] c; // declare the array variable
c = new int[ 12 ]; // create the array; assign to array variable
```

In the declaration, the square brackets following the type indicate that c is a variable that will refer to an array (i.e., the variable will store an array reference). In the assignment statement, the array variable c receives the reference to a new array of 12 int elements.

A program can create several arrays in a single declaration. The following declaration reserves 100 elements for b and 27 elements for x:

```
String[] b = new String[ 100 ], x = new String[ 27 ];
```

When the type of the array and the square brackets are combined at the beginning of the declaration, all the identifiers in the declaration are array variables. In this case, variables b and x refer to String arrays. For readability, we prefer to declare only one variable per declaration. The preceding declaration is equivalent to:

```
String[] b = new String[ 100 ]; // create array b
String[] x = new String[ 27 ]; // create array x
```

When only one variable is declared in each declaration, the square brackets can be placed either after the type or after the array variable name, as in:

```
String b[] = new String[ 100 ]; // create array b
String x[] = new String[ 27 ]; // create array x
```

Common Programming Error E.2

Declaring multiple array variables in a single declaration can lead to subtle errors. Consider the declaration int[] a, b, c;. If a, b and c should be declared as array variables, then this declaration is correct—placing square brackets directly following the type indicates that all the identifiers in the declaration are array variables. However, if only a is intended to be an array variable, and b and c are intended to be individual int variables, then this declaration is incorrect—the declaration int a[], b, c; would achieve the desired result.

A program can declare arrays of any type. Every element of a primitive-type array contains a value of the array's declared element type. Similarly, in an array of a reference type, every element is a reference to an object of the array's declared element type. For example, every element of an int array is an int value, and every element of a String array is a reference to a String object.

E.4 Examples Using Arrays

This section presents several examples that demonstrate declaring arrays, creating arrays, initializing arrays and manipulating array elements.

Creating and Initializing an Array

The application of Fig. E.2 uses keyword new to create an array of 10 int elements, which are initially zero (the default for int variables). Line 8 declares array—a reference capable of referring to an array of int elements. Line 10 creates the array object and assigns its reference to variable array. Line 12 outputs the column headings. The first column contains the index (0–9) of each array element, and the second column contains the default value (0) of each array element.

```
1    // Fig. E.2: InitArray.java
2    // Initializing the elements of an array to default values of zero.
3
4    public class InitArray
5    {
6       public static void main( String[] args )
7       {
8          int[] array; // declare array named array
9
10         array = new int[ 10 ]; // create the array object
11
12         System.out.printf( "%s%8s\n", "Index", "Value" ); // column headings
13
14         // output each array element's value
15         for ( int counter = 0; counter < array.length; counter++ )
16            System.out.printf( "%5d%8d\n", counter, array[ counter ] );
17      } // end main
18   } // end class InitArray
```

```
Index   Value
    0       0
    1       0
    2       0
    3       0
    4       0
    5       0
    6       0
    7       0
    8       0
    9       0
```

Fig. E.2 | Initializing the elements of an array to default values of zero.

The for statement in lines 15–16 outputs the index number (represented by counter) and the value of each array element (represented by array[counter]). The loop-control variable counter is initially 0—index values start at 0, so using **zero-based counting** allows the loop to access every element of the array. The for's loop-continuation condition uses the expression array.length (line 15) to determine the length of the array. In this example, the length of the array is 10, so the loop continues executing as long as the value of control variable counter is less than 10. The highest index value of a 10-element array is 9, so using the less-than operator in the loop-continuation condition guarantees that the loop does not attempt to access an element *beyond* the end of the array (i.e., during the final iteration of the loop, counter is 9). We'll soon see what Java does when it encounters such an *out-of-range index* at execution time.

Using an Array Initializer

You can create an array and initialize its elements with an **array initializer**—a comma-separated list of expressions (called an **initializer list**) enclosed in braces. In this case, the array length is determined by the number of elements in the initializer list. For example,

```
int[] n = { 10, 20, 30, 40, 50 };
```

creates a five-element array with index values 0–4. Element n[0] is initialized to 10, n[1] is initialized to 20, and so on. When the compiler encounters an array declaration that includes an initializer list, it counts the number of initializers in the list to determine the size of the array, then sets up the appropriate new operation "behind the scenes."

The application in Fig. E.3 initializes an integer array with 10 values (line 9) and displays the array in tabular format. The code for displaying the array elements (lines 14–15) is identical to that in Fig. E.2 (lines 15–16).

```java
1   // Fig. E.3: InitArray.java
2   // Initializing the elements of an array with an array initializer.
3
4   public class InitArray
5   {
6      public static void main( String[] args )
7      {
8         // initializer list specifies the value for each element
9         int[] array = { 32, 27, 64, 18, 95, 14, 90, 70, 60, 37 };
10
11        System.out.printf( "%s%8s\n", "Index", "Value" ); // column headings
12
13        // output each array element's value
14        for ( int counter = 0; counter < array.length; counter++ )
15           System.out.printf( "%5d%8d\n", counter, array[ counter ] );
16     } // end main
17  } // end class InitArray
```

```
Index  Value
    0     32
    1     27
    2     64
    3     18
    4     95
    5     14
    6     90
    7     70
    8     60
    9     37
```

Fig. E.3 | Initializing the elements of an array with an array initializer.

Calculating the Values to Store in an Array

The application in Fig. E.4 creates a 10-element array and assigns to each element one of the even integers from 2 to 20 (2, 4, 6, …, 20). Then the application displays the array in tabular format. The for statement at lines 12–13 calculates an array element's value by multiplying the current value of the control variable counter by 2, then adding 2.

```
 1   // Fig. E.4: InitArray.java
 2   // Calculating the values to be placed into the elements of an array.
 3
 4   public class InitArray
 5   {
 6      public static void main( String[] args )
 7      {
 8         final int ARRAY_LENGTH = 10; // declare constant
 9         int[] array = new int[ ARRAY_LENGTH ]; // create array
10
11         // calculate value for each array element
12         for ( int counter = 0; counter < array.length; counter++ )
13            array[ counter ] = 2 + 2 * counter;
14
15         System.out.printf( "%s%8s\n", "Index", "Value" ); // column headings
16
17         // output each array element's value
18         for ( int counter = 0; counter < array.length; counter++ )
19            System.out.printf( "%5d%8d\n", counter, array[ counter ] );
20      } // end main
21   } // end class InitArray
```

```
Index   Value
    0       2
    1       4
    2       6
    3       8
    4      10
    5      12
    6      14
    7      16
    8      18
    9      20
```

Fig. E.4 | Calculating the values to be placed into the elements of an array.

Line 8 uses the modifier final to declare the constant variable ARRAY_LENGTH with the value 10. Constant variables must be initialized before they're used and cannot be modified thereafter. If you attempt to *modify* a final variable after it's initialized in its declaration, the compiler issues an error message like

> cannot assign a value to final variable *variableName*

If an attempt is made to access the value of a final variable before it's initialized, the compiler issues an error message like

> variable *variableName* might not have been initialized

Good Programming Practice E.1

*Constant variables also are called **named constants**. They often make programs more readable than programs that use literal values (e.g., 10)—a named constant such as ARRAY_LENGTH clearly indicates its purpose, whereas a literal value could have different meanings based on its context.*

Using Bar Charts to Display Array Data Graphically

Many programs present data to users in a graphical manner. For example, numeric values are often displayed as bars in a bar chart. In such a chart, longer bars represent proportionally larger numeric values. One simple way to display numeric data graphically is with a bar chart that shows each numeric value as a bar of asterisks (*).

Professors often like to examine the distribution of grades on an exam. A professor might graph the number of grades in each of several categories to visualize the grade distribution. Suppose the grades on an exam were 87, 68, 94, 100, 83, 78, 85, 91, 76 and 87. They include one grade of 100, two grades in the 90s, four grades in the 80s, two grades in the 70s, one grade in the 60s and no grades below 60. Our next application (Fig. E.5) stores this grade distribution data in an array of 11 elements, each corresponding to a category of grades. For example, `array[0]` indicates the number of grades in the range 0–9, `array[7]` the number of grades in the range 70–79 and `array[10]` the number of 100 grades.

```java
1   // Fig. E.5: BarChart.java
2   // Bar chart printing program.
3
4   public class BarChart
5   {
6      public static void main( String[] args )
7      {
8         int[] array = { 0, 0, 0, 0, 0, 0, 1, 2, 4, 2, 1 };
9
10        System.out.println( "Grade distribution:" );
11
12        // for each array element, output a bar of the chart
13        for ( int counter = 0; counter < array.length; counter++ )
14        {
15           // output bar label ( "00-09: ", ..., "90-99: ", "100: " )
16           if ( counter == 10 )
17              System.out.printf( "%5d: ", 100 );
18           else
19              System.out.printf( "%02d-%02d: ",
20                 counter * 10, counter * 10 + 9 );
21
22           // print bar of asterisks
23           for ( int stars = 0; stars < array[ counter ]; stars++ )
24              System.out.print( "*" );
25
26           System.out.println(); // start a new line of output
27        } // end outer for
28     } // end main
29  } // end class BarChart
```

```
Grade distribution:
00-09:
10-19:
20-29:
30-39:
40-49:
```

Fig. E.5 | Bar chart printing program. (Part 1 of 2.)

```
50-59:
60-69: *
70-79: **
80-89: ****
90-99: **
  100: *
```

Fig. E.5 | Bar chart printing program. (Part 2 of 2.)

The application reads the numbers from the array and graphs the information as a bar chart. It displays each grade range followed by a bar of asterisks indicating the number of grades in that range. To label each bar, lines 16–20 output a grade range (e.g., "70-79: ") based on the current value of counter. When counter is 10, line 17 outputs 100 with a field width of 5, followed by a colon and a space, to align the label "100: " with the other bar labels. The nested for statement (lines 23–24) outputs the bars. Note the loop-continuation condition at line 23 (stars < array[counter]). Each time the program reaches the inner for, the loop counts from 0 up to array[counter], thus using a value in array to determine the number of asterisks to display. In this example, no students received a grade below 60, so array[0]–array[5] contain zeroes, and no asterisks are displayed next to the first six grade ranges. In line 19, the format specifier %02d indicates that an int value should be formatted as a field of two digits. The **0 flag** in the format specifier displays a leading 0 for values with fewer digits than the field width (2).

Using the Elements of an Array as Counters

Sometimes, programs use counter variables to summarize data, such as the results of a survey. Figure E.6 uses the array frequency (line 10) to count the occurrences of each side of the die that's rolled 6,000,000 times. Line 14 uses the random value to determine which frequency element to increment during each iteration of the loop. The calculation in line 14 produces random numbers from 1 to 6, so the array frequency must be large enough to store six counters. However, we use a seven-element array in which we ignore frequency[0]—it's more logical to have the face value 1 increment frequency[1] than frequency[0]. Thus, each face value is used as an index for array frequency. In line 14, the calculation inside the square brackets evaluates first to determine which element of the array to increment, then the ++ operator adds one to that element. Lines 19–20 loop through array frequency to output the results.

```
 1   // Fig. E.6: RollDie.java
 2   // Die-rolling program using arrays instead of switch.
 3   import java.util.Random;
 4
 5   public class RollDie
 6   {
 7      public static void main( String[] args )
 8      {
 9         Random randomNumbers = new Random(); // random number generator
10         int[] frequency = new int[ 7 ]; // array of frequency counters
11
```

Fig. E.6 | Die-rolling program using arrays instead of switch. (Part 1 of 2.)

```
12        // roll die 6,000,000 times; use die value as frequency index
13        for ( int roll = 1; roll <= 6000000; roll++ )
14           ++frequency[ 1 + randomNumbers.nextInt( 6 ) ];
15
16        System.out.printf( "%s%10s\n", "Face", "Frequency" );
17
18        // output each array element's value
19        for ( int face = 1; face < frequency.length; face++ )
20           System.out.printf( "%4d%10d\n", face, frequency[ face ] );
21     } // end main
22  } // end class RollDie
```

```
Face Frequency
  1    999690
  2    999512
  3   1000575
  4    999815
  5    999781
  6   1000627
```

Fig. E.6 | Die-rolling program using arrays instead of `switch`. (Part 2 of 2.)

Using Arrays to Analyze Survey Results

Our next example uses arrays to summarize data collected in a survey. Consider the following problem statement:

> Twenty students were asked to rate on a scale of 1 to 5 the quality of the food in the student cafeteria, with 1 being "awful" and 5 being "excellent." Place the 20 responses in an integer array and determine the frequency of each rating.

This is a typical array-processing application (Fig. E.7). We wish to summarize the number of responses of each type (that is, 1–5). Array `responses` (lines 9–10) is a 20-element integer array containing the students' survey responses. The last value in the array is intentionally an incorrect response (14). When a Java program executes, array element indices are checked for validity—all indices must be greater than or equal to 0 and less than the length of the array. Any attempt to access an element outside that range of indices results in a runtime error that's known as an `ArrayIndexOutOfBoundsException`. At the end of this section, we'll discuss the invalid response value, demonstrate array **bounds checking** and introduce Java's exception-handling mechanism, which can be used to detect and handle an `ArrayIndexOutOfBoundsException`.

```
1   // Fig. E.7: StudentPoll.java
2   // Poll analysis program.
3
4   public class StudentPoll
5   {
6      public static void main( String[] args )
7      {
8         // student response array (more typically, input at runtime)
9         int[] responses = { 1, 2, 5, 4, 3, 5, 2, 1, 3, 3, 1, 4, 3, 3, 3,
10           2, 3, 3, 2, 14 };
```

Fig. E.7 | Poll analysis program. (Part 1 of 2.)

```
11      int[] frequency = new int[ 6 ]; // array of frequency counters
12
13      // for each answer, select responses element and use that value
14      // as frequency index to determine element to increment
15      for ( int answer = 0; answer < responses.length; answer++ )
16      {
17         try
18         {
19            ++frequency[ responses[ answer ] ];
20         } // end try
21         catch ( ArrayIndexOutOfBoundsException e )
22         {
23            System.out.println( e );
24            System.out.printf( "   responses[%d] = %d\n\n",
25               answer, responses[ answer ] );
26         } // end catch
27      } // end for
28
29      System.out.printf( "%s%10s\n", "Rating", "Frequency" );
30
31      // output each array element's value
32      for ( int rating = 1; rating < frequency.length; rating++ )
33         System.out.printf( "%6d%10d\n", rating, frequency[ rating ] );
34   } // end main
35 } // end class StudentPoll
```

```
java.lang.ArrayIndexOutOfBoundsException: 14
   responses[19] = 14

Rating Frequency
     1         3
     2         4
     3         8
     4         2
     5         2
```

Fig. E.7 | Poll analysis program. (Part 2 of 2.)

The frequency Array

We use the *six-element* array frequency (line 11) to count the number of occurrences of each response. Each element is used as a counter for one of the possible types of survey responses—frequency[1] counts the number of students who rated the food as 1, frequency[2] counts the number of students who rated the food as 2, and so on.

Summarizing the Results

The for statement (lines 15–27) reads the responses from the array responses one at a time and increments one of the counters frequency[1] to frequency[5]; we ignore frequency[0] because the survey responses are limited to the range 1–5. The key statement in the loop appears in line 19. This statement increments the appropriate frequency counter as determined by the value of responses[answer].

Let's step through the first few iterations of the for statement:

- When the counter answer is 0, responses[answer] is the value of responses[0] (that is, 1—see line 9). In this case, frequency[responses[answer]] is interpreted as `frequency[1]`, and the counter `frequency[1]` is incremented by one. To evaluate the expression, we begin with the value in the *innermost* set of brackets (answer, currently 0). The value of answer is plugged into the expression, and the next set of brackets (`responses[answer]`) is evaluated. That value is used as the index for the `frequency` array to determine which counter to increment (in this case, `frequency[1]`).

- The next time through the loop answer is 1, `responses[answer]` is the value of `responses[1]` (that is, 2—see line 9), so `frequency[responses[answer]]` is interpreted as `frequency[2]`, causing `frequency[2]` to be incremented.

- When answer is 2, `responses[answer]` is the value of `responses[2]` (that is, 5—see line 9), so `frequency[responses[answer]]` is interpreted as `frequency[5]`, causing `frequency[5]` to be incremented, and so on.

Regardless of the number of responses processed in the survey, only a six-element array (in which we ignore element zero) is required to summarize the results, because all the correct response values are between 1 and 5, and the index values for a six-element array are 0–5. In the program's output, the `Frequency` column summarizes only 19 of the 20 values in the `responses` array—the last element of the array `responses` contains an incorrect response that was not counted.

Exception Handling: Processing the Incorrect Response

An **exception** indicates a problem that occurs while a program executes. The name "exception" suggests that the problem occurs infrequently—if the "rule" is that a statement normally executes correctly, then the problem represents the "exception to the rule." **Exception handling** enables you to create **fault-tolerant programs** that can resolve (or handle) exceptions. In many cases, this allows a program to continue executing as if no problems were encountered. For example, the `StudentPoll` application still displays results (Fig. E.7), even though one of the responses was out of range. More severe problems might prevent a program from continuing normal execution, instead requiring the program to notify the user of the problem, then terminate. When the JVM or a method detects a problem, such as an invalid array index or an invalid method argument, it **throws** an exception—that is, an exception occurs.

The try Statement

To handle an exception, place any code that might throw an exception in a **try statement** (lines 17–26). The **try block** (lines 17–20) contains the code that might *throw* an exception, and the **catch block** (lines 21–26) contains the code that *handles* the exception if one occurs. You can have many `catch` blocks to handle different types of exceptions that might be thrown in the corresponding `try` block. When line 19 correctly increments an element of the `frequency` array, lines 21–26 are ignored. The braces that delimit the bodies of the `try` and `catch` blocks are required.

Executing the catch Block

When the program encounters the value 14 in the `responses` array, it attempts to add 1 to `frequency[14]`, which is *outside* the bounds of the array—the `frequency` array has only six elements. Because array bounds checking is performed at execution time, the JVM generates an exception—specifically line 19 throws an **ArrayIndexOutOfBoundsException** to notify the program of this problem. At this point the try block terminates and the catch block begins executing—if you declared any variables in the try block, they're now out of scope and are not accessible in the catch block.

The catch block declares a type (IndexOutOfRangeException) and an exception parameter (e). The catch block can handle exceptions of the specified type. Inside the catch block, you can use the parameter's identifier to interact with a caught exception object.

> **Error-Prevention Tip E.1**
> *When writing code to access an array element, ensure that the array index remains greater than or equal to 0 and less than the length of the array. This helps prevent ArrayIndex-OutOfBoundsException in your program.*

toString *Method of the Exception Parameter*

When lines 21–26 *catch* the exception, the program displays a message indicating the problem that occurred. Line 23 implicitly calls the exception object's toString method to get the error message that is stored in the exception object and display it. Once the message is displayed in this example, the exception is considered handled and the program continues with the next statement after the catch block's closing brace. In this example, the end of the for statement is reached (line 27), so the program continues with the increment of the control variable in line 15. We use exception handling again in Appendix F, and Appendix H presents a deeper look at exception handling.

E.5 Case Study: Card Shuffling and Dealing Simulation

The examples in the appendix thus far have used arrays containing elements of primitive types. Recall from Section E.2 that the elements of an array can be either primitive types or reference types. This section uses random-number generation and an array of reference-type elements, namely objects representing playing cards, to develop a class that simulates card shuffling and dealing. This class can then be used to implement applications that play specific card games.

We first develop class Card (Fig. E.8), which represents a playing card that has a face (e.g., "Ace", "Deuce", "Three", ..., "Jack", "Queen", "King") and a suit (e.g., "Hearts", "Diamonds", "Clubs", "Spades"). Next, we develop the DeckOfCards class (Fig. E.9), which creates a deck of 52 playing cards in which each element is a Card object. We then build a test application (Fig. E.10) that demonstrates class DeckOfCards's card-shuffling and dealing capabilities.

Class *Card*

Class Card (Fig. E.8) contains two String instance variables—face and suit—that are used to store references to the face name and suit name for a specific Card. The constructor for the class (lines 10–14) receives two Strings that it uses to initialize face and suit. Method toString (lines 17–20) creates a String consisting of the face of the card, the String " of " and the suit of the card. Card's toString method can be invoked explicitly to obtain a string representation of a Card object (e.g., "Ace of Spades"). The toString method of an object is called *implicitly* when the object is used where a String is expected (e.g., when printf outputs the object as a String using the %s format specifier or when the object is concatenated to a String using the + operator). For this behavior to occur, toString must be declared with the header shown in Fig. E.8.

```
 1    // Fig. E.8: Card.java
 2    // Card class represents a playing card.
 3
 4    public class Card
 5    {
 6       private String face; // face of card ("Ace", "Deuce", ...)
 7       private String suit; // suit of card ("Hearts", "Diamonds", ...)
 8
 9       // two-argument constructor initializes card's face and suit
10       public Card( String cardFace, String cardSuit )
11       {
12          face = cardFace; // initialize face of card
13          suit = cardSuit; // initialize suit of card
14       } // end two-argument Card constructor
15
16       // return String representation of Card
17       public String toString()
18       {
19          return face + " of " + suit;
20       } // end method toString
21    } // end class Card
```

Fig. E.8 | Card class represents a playing card.

Class DeckOfCards

Class DeckOfCards (Fig. E.9) declares as an instance variable a Card array named deck (line 7). An array of a reference type is declared like any other array. Class DeckOfCards also declares an integer instance variable currentCard (line 8) representing the next Card to be dealt from the deck array and a named constant NUMBER_OF_CARDS (line 9) indicating the number of Cards in the deck (52).

```
 1    // Fig. E.9: DeckOfCards.java
 2    // DeckOfCards class represents a deck of playing cards.
 3    import java.util.Random;
 4
 5    public class DeckOfCards
 6    {
 7       private Card[] deck; // array of Card objects
 8       private int currentCard; // index of next Card to be dealt (0-51)
 9       private static final int NUMBER_OF_CARDS = 52; // constant # of Cards
10       // random number generator
11       private static final Random randomNumbers = new Random();
12
13       // constructor fills deck of Cards
14       public DeckOfCards()
15       {
```

Fig. E.9 | DeckOfCards class represents a deck of playing cards. (Part 1 of 2.)

```
16          String[] faces = { "Ace", "Deuce", "Three", "Four", "Five", "Six",
17              "Seven", "Eight", "Nine", "Ten", "Jack", "Queen", "King" };
18          String[] suits = { "Hearts", "Diamonds", "Clubs", "Spades" };
19
20          deck = new Card[ NUMBER_OF_CARDS ]; // create array of Card objects
21          currentCard = 0; // set currentCard so first Card dealt is deck[ 0 ]
22
23          // populate deck with Card objects
24          for ( int count = 0; count < deck.length; count++ )
25              deck[ count ] =
26                  new Card( faces[ count % 13 ], suits[ count / 13 ] );
27      } // end DeckOfCards constructor
28
29      // shuffle deck of Cards with one-pass algorithm
30      public void shuffle()
31      {
32          // after shuffling, dealing should start at deck[ 0 ] again
33          currentCard = 0; // reinitialize currentCard
34
35          // for each Card, pick another random Card (0-51) and swap them
36          for ( int first = 0; first < deck.length; first++ )
37          {
38              // select a random number between 0 and 51
39              int second = randomNumbers.nextInt( NUMBER_OF_CARDS );
40
41              // swap current Card with randomly selected Card
42              Card temp = deck[ first ];
43              deck[ first ] = deck[ second ];
44              deck[ second ] = temp;
45          } // end for
46      } // end method shuffle
47
48      // deal one Card
49      public Card dealCard()
50      {
51          // determine whether Cards remain to be dealt
52          if ( currentCard < deck.length )
53              return deck[ currentCard++ ]; // return current Card in array
54          else
55              return null; // return null to indicate that all Cards were dealt
56      } // end method dealCard
57  } // end class DeckOfCards
```

Fig. E.9 | DeckOfCards class represents a deck of playing cards. (Part 2 of 2.)

DeckOfCards Constructor

The class's constructor instantiates array deck (line 20) with NUMBER_OF_CARDS (52) elements that are all null by default. Lines 24–26 fill the deck with Cards. The loop initializes control variable count to 0 and loops while count is less than deck.length, causing count to take on each integer value from 0 to 51 (the indices of array deck). Each Card is instantiated and initialized with a String from the faces array (which contains "Ace" through "King") and a String from the suits array (which contains "Hearts", "Diamonds", "Clubs" and "Spades"). The calculation count % 13 always results in a value from

0 to 12 (the 13 indices of the faces array in lines 16–17), and the calculation count / 13 always results in a value from 0 to 3 (the four indices of the suits array in line 18). When the deck array is initialized, it contains the Cards with faces "Ace" through "King" in order for each suit ("Hearts" then "Diamonds" then "Clubs" then "Spades").

DeckOfCards Method shuffle

Method shuffle (lines 30–46) shuffles the Cards in the deck. The method loops through all 52 Cards. For each Card, a number between 0 and 51 is picked randomly to select another Card, then the current Card and the randomly selected Card are swapped in the array. This exchange is performed by the assignments in lines 42–44. The extra variable temp temporarily stores one of the two Card objects being swapped. The swap cannot be performed with only the two statements

```
deck[ first ] = deck[ second ];
deck[ second ] = deck[ first ];
```

If deck[first] is the "Ace" of "Spades" and deck[second] is the "Queen" of "Hearts", after the first assignment, both array elements contain the "Queen" of "Hearts" and the "Ace" of "Spades" is lost—hence, the extra variable temp is needed. After the for loop terminates, the Card objects are randomly ordered. A total of only 52 swaps are made in a single pass of the entire array, and the array of Card objects is shuffled!

[*Note:* It's recommended that you use a so-called unbiased shuffling algorithm for real card games. Such an algorithm ensures that all possible shuffled card sequences are equally likely to occur. A popular unbiased shuffling algorithm is the Fisher-Yates algorithm.]

DeckOfCards Method dealCard

Method dealCard (lines 49–56) deals one Card in the array. Recall that currentCard indicates the index of the next Card to be dealt (i.e., the Card at the top of the deck). Thus, line 52 compares currentCard to the array's length. If the deck is not empty (i.e., currentCard is less than 52), line 53 returns the "top" Card and postincrements currentCard to prepare for the next call to dealCard—otherwise, null is returned.

Shuffling and Dealing Cards

Figure E.10 demonstrates class DeckOfCards (Fig. E.9). Line 9 creates a DeckOfCards object named myDeckOfCards. The DeckOfCards constructor creates the deck with the 52 Card objects in order by suit and face. Line 10 invokes myDeckOfCards's shuffle method to rearrange the Card objects. Lines 13–20 deal all 52 Cards and print them in four columns of 13 Cards each. Line 16 deals one Card object by invoking myDeckOfCards's dealCard method, then displays the Card left justified in a field of 19 characters. When a Card is output as a String, the Card's toString method (lines 17–20 of Fig. E.8) is implicitly invoked. Lines 18–19 (Fig. E.10) start a new line after every four Cards.

```
1   // Fig. E.10: DeckOfCardsTest.java
2   // Card shuffling and dealing.
3
4   public class DeckOfCardsTest
5   {
```

Fig. E.10 | Card shuffling and dealing. (Part 1 of 2.)

```
6     // execute application
7     public static void main( String[] args )
8     {
9        DeckOfCards myDeckOfCards = new DeckOfCards();
10       myDeckOfCards.shuffle(); // place Cards in random order
11
12       // print all 52 Cards in the order in which they are dealt
13       for ( int i = 1; i <= 52; i++ )
14       {
15          // deal and display a Card
16          System.out.printf( "%-19s", myDeckOfCards.dealCard() );
17
18          if ( i % 4 == 0 ) // output a newline after every fourth card
19             System.out.println();
20       } // end for
21    } // end main
22 } // end class DeckOfCardsTest
```

Six of Spades	Eight of Spades	Six of Clubs	Nine of Hearts
Queen of Hearts	Seven of Clubs	Nine of Spades	King of Hearts
Three of Diamonds	Deuce of Clubs	Ace of Hearts	Ten of Spades
Four of Spades	Ace of Clubs	Seven of Diamonds	Four of Hearts
Three of Clubs	Deuce of Hearts	Five of Spades	Jack of Diamonds
King of Clubs	Ten of Hearts	Three of Hearts	Six of Diamonds
Queen of Clubs	Eight of Diamonds	Deuce of Diamonds	Ten of Diamonds
Three of Spades	King of Diamonds	Nine of Clubs	Six of Hearts
Ace of Spades	Four of Diamonds	Seven of Hearts	Eight of Clubs
Deuce of Spades	Eight of Hearts	Five of Hearts	Queen of Spades
Jack of Hearts	Seven of Spades	Four of Clubs	Nine of Diamonds
Ace of Diamonds	Queen of Diamonds	Five of Clubs	King of Spades
Five of Diamonds	Ten of Clubs	Jack of Spades	Jack of Clubs

Fig. E.10 | Card shuffling and dealing. (Part 2 of 2.)

E.6 Enhanced for Statement

The **enhanced for statement** iterates through the elements of an array *without* using a counter, thus avoiding the possibility of "stepping outside" the array. We show how to use the enhanced for statement with the Java API's prebuilt data structures (called collections) in Section E.12. The syntax of an enhanced for statement is:

> for (*parameter* : *arrayName*)
>   *statement*

where *parameter* has a type and an identifier (e.g., int number), and *arrayName* is the array through which to iterate. The type of the parameter must be consistent with the type of the elements in the array. As the next example illustrates, the identifier represents successive element values in the array on successive iterations of the loop.

Figure E.11 uses the enhanced for statement (lines 12–13) to sum the integers in an array of student grades. The enhanced for's parameter is of type int, because array contains int values—the loop selects one int value from the array during each iteration. The enhanced for statement iterates through successive values in the array one by one. The statement's header can be read as "for each iteration, assign the next element of array to int variable number, then execute the following statement." Thus, for each iteration, identifier number represents an int value in array. Lines 12–13 are equivalent to the following counter-controlled repetition statement, except that counter cannot be accessed in the body of the enhanced for statement:

```
for ( int counter = 0; counter < array.length; counter++ )
    total += array[ counter ];
```

```
1   // Fig. E.11: EnhancedForTest.java
2   // Using the enhanced for statement to total integers in an array.
3
4   public class EnhancedForTest
5   {
6      public static void main( String[] args )
7      {
8         int[] array = { 87, 68, 94, 100, 83, 78, 85, 91, 76, 87 };
9         int total = 0;
10
11        // add each element's value to total
12        for ( int number : array )
13           total += number;
14
15        System.out.printf( "Total of array elements: %d\n", total );
16     } // end main
17  } // end class EnhancedForTest
```

```
Total of array elements: 849
```

Fig. E.11 | Using the enhanced for statement to total integers in an array.

The enhanced for statement simplifies the code for iterating through an array. Note, however, that *the enhanced for statement can be used only to obtain array elements—it cannot be used to modify elements*. If your program needs to modify elements, use the traditional counter-controlled for statement.

The enhanced for statement can be used in place of the counter-controlled for statement whenever code looping through an array does *not* require access to the counter indicating the index of the current array element. For example, totaling the integers in an array requires access only to the element values—the index of each element is irrelevant. However, if a program must use a counter for some reason other than simply to loop through an array (e.g., to print an index number next to each array element value, as in the examples earlier in this appendix), use the counter-controlled for statement.

E.7 Passing Arrays to Methods

This section demonstrates how to pass arrays and individual array elements as arguments to methods. To pass an array argument to a method, specify the name of the array without any brackets. For example, if array hourlyTemperatures is declared as

```
double[] hourlyTemperatures = new double[ 24 ];
```

then the method call

```
        modifyArray( hourlyTemperatures );
```

passes the reference of array hourlyTemperatures to method modifyArray. Every array object "knows" its own length (via its length field). Thus, when we pass an array object's reference into a method, we need not pass the array length as an additional argument.

For a method to receive an array reference through a method call, the method's parameter list must specify an array parameter. For example, the method header for method modifyArray might be written as

```
        void modifyArray( double[] b )
```

indicating that modifyArray receives the reference of a double array in parameter b. The method call passes array hourlyTemperature's reference, so when the called method uses the array variable b, it *refers to* the same array object as hourlyTemperatures in the caller.

When an argument to a method is an entire array or an individual array element of a reference type, the called method receives a *copy* of the reference. However, when an argument to a method is an individual array element of a primitive type, the called method receives a copy of the element's *value*. Such primitive values are called **scalars** or **scalar quantities**. To pass an individual array element to a method, use the indexed name of the array element as an argument in the method call.

Figure E.12 demonstrates the difference between passing an entire array and passing a primitive-type array element to a method. Notice that main invokes static methods modifyArray (line 19) and modifyElement (line 30) directly. Recall from Section D.4 that a static method of a class can invoke other static methods of the same class directly.

```
 1   // Fig. E.12: PassArray.java
 2   // Passing arrays and individual array elements to methods.
 3
 4   public class PassArray
 5   {
 6      // main creates array and calls modifyArray and modifyElement
 7      public static void main( String[] args )
 8      {
 9         int[] array = { 1, 2, 3, 4, 5 };
10
11         System.out.println(
12            "Effects of passing reference to entire array:\n" +
13            "The values of the original array are:" );
14
15         // output original array elements
16         for ( int value : array )
17            System.out.printf( "   %d", value );
18
19         modifyArray( array ); // pass array reference
20         System.out.println( "\n\nThe values of the modified array are:" );
21
22         // output modified array elements
23         for ( int value : array )
24            System.out.printf( "   %d", value );
25
```

Fig. E.12 | Passing arrays and individual array elements to methods. (Part 1 of 2.)

```
26        System.out.printf(
27            "\n\nEffects of passing array element value:\n" +
28            "array[3] before modifyElement: %d\n", array[ 3 ] );
29
30        modifyElement( array[ 3 ] ); // attempt to modify array[ 3 ]
31        System.out.printf(
32            "array[3] after modifyElement: %d\n", array[ 3 ] );
33    } // end main
34
35    // multiply each element of an array by 2
36    public static void modifyArray( int[] array2 )
37    {
38        for ( int counter = 0; counter < array2.length; counter++ )
39            array2[ counter ] *= 2;
40    } // end method modifyArray
41
42    // multiply argument by 2
43    public static void modifyElement( int element )
44    {
45        element *= 2;
46        System.out.printf(
47            "Value of element in modifyElement: %d\n", element );
48    } // end method modifyElement
49 } // end class PassArray
```

```
Effects of passing reference to entire array:
The values of the original array are:
   1   2   3   4   5

The values of the modified array are:
   2   4   6   8   10

Effects of passing array element value:
array[3] before modifyElement: 8
Value of element in modifyElement: 16
array[3] after modifyElement: 8
```

Fig. E.12 | Passing arrays and individual array elements to methods. (Part 2 of 2.)

The enhanced for statement at lines 16–17 outputs the five int elements of array. Line 19 invokes method modifyArray, passing array as an argument. Method modify-Array (lines 36–40) receives a copy of array's reference and uses the reference to multiply each of array's elements by 2. To prove that array's elements were modified, lines 23–24 output the five elements of array again. As the output shows, method modifyArray doubled the value of each element. We could not use the enhanced for statement in lines 38–39 because we're modifying the array's elements.

Figure E.12 next demonstrates that when a copy of an individual primitive-type array element is passed to a method, modifying the *copy* in the called method does *not* affect the original value of that element in the calling method's array. Lines 26–28 output the value of array[3] *before* invoking method modifyElement. Remember that the value of this element is now 8 after it was modified in the call to modifyArray. Line 30 calls method modifyElement and passes array[3] as an argument. Remember that array[3] is actually one int value (8) in array. Therefore, the program passes a copy of the value of array[3]. Method modifyElement (lines 43–48) multiplies the value received as an argument by 2, stores the result in its parameter element, then outputs the value of element (16). Since method parameters, like local variables, cease to exist when the method in which they're declared completes execution, the method parameter element is destroyed when method modifyElement terminates. When the program returns control to main, lines 31–32 output the *unmodified* value of array[3] (i.e., 8).

Notes on Passing Arguments to Methods

The preceding example demonstrated how arrays and primitive-type array elements are passed as arguments to methods. We now take a closer look at how arguments in general are passed to methods. Two ways to pass arguments in method calls in many programming languages are **pass-by-value** and **pass-by-reference** (also called **call-by-value** and **call-by-reference**). When an argument is passed by value, a copy of the argument's *value* is passed to the called method. The called method works exclusively with the copy. Changes to the called method's copy do *not* affect the original variable's value in the caller.

When an argument is passed by reference, the called method can access the argument's value in the caller directly and modify that data, if necessary. Pass-by-reference improves performance by eliminating the need to copy possibly large amounts of data.

Unlike some other languages, Java does *not* allow you to choose pass-by-value or pass-by-reference—*all arguments are passed by value*. A method call can pass two types of values to a method—copies of primitive values (e.g., values of type int and double) and copies of references to objects. Objects themselves cannot be passed to methods. When a method modifies a primitive-type parameter, changes to the parameter have no effect on the original argument value in the calling method. For example, when line 30 in main of Fig. E.12 passes array[3] to method modifyElement, the statement in line 45 that doubles the value of parameter element has *no* effect on the value of array[3] in main. This is also true for reference-type parameters. If you modify a reference-type parameter so that it refers to another object, only the parameter refers to the new object—the reference stored in the caller's variable still refers to the original object.

Although an object's reference is passed by value, a method can still interact with the referenced object by calling its public methods using the copy of the object's reference. Since the reference stored in the parameter is a copy of the reference that was passed as an argument, the parameter in the called method and the argument in the calling method refer to the same object in memory. For example, in Fig. E.12, both parameter array2 in method modifyArray and variable array in main refer to the *same* array object in memory. Any changes made using the parameter array2 are carried out on the object that array references in the calling method. In Fig. E.12, the changes made in modifyArray using array2 affect the contents of the array object referenced by array in main. Thus, with a reference to an object, the called method *can* manipulate the caller's object directly.

Performance Tip E.1

Passing arrays by reference makes sense for performance reasons. If arrays were passed by value, a copy of each element would be passed. For large, frequently passed arrays, this would waste time and consume considerable storage for the copies of the arrays.

E.8 Case Study: Class GradeBook Using an Array to Store Grades

Previous versions of class GradeBook process a set of grades entered by the user, but do not maintain the individual grade values in instance variables of the class. Thus, repeat calculations require the user to reenter the same grades. One way to solve this problem would be to store each grade entered in an individual instance of the class. For example, we could create instance variables grade1, grade2, ..., grade10 in class GradeBook to store 10 student grades. But this would make the code to total the grades and determine the class average cumbersome, and the class would not be able to process any more than 10 grades at a time. We solve this problem by storing grades in an array.

Storing Student Grades in an Array in Class GradeBook

Class GradeBook (Fig. E.13) uses an array of ints to store several students' grades on a single exam. This eliminates the need to repeatedly input the same set of grades. Array grades is declared as an instance variable (line 7), so each GradeBook object maintains its own set of grades. The constructor (lines 10–14) has two parameters—the name of the course and an array of grades. When an application (e.g., class GradeBookTest in Fig. E.14) creates a GradeBook object, the application passes an existing int array to the constructor, which assigns the array's reference to instance variable grades (line 13). The grades array's size is determined by the length of the array that's passed to the constructor. Thus, a GradeBook object can process a variable number of grades. The grade values in the passed array could have been input from a user or read from a file on disk. In our test application, we initialize an array with grade values (Fig. E.14, line 10). Once the grades are stored in instance variable grades of class GradeBook, all the class's methods can access the elements of grades *as often as needed* to perform various calculations.

Method processGrades (lines 37–51) contains a series of method calls that output a report summarizing the grades. Line 40 calls method outputGrades to print the contents of the array grades. Lines 134–136 in method outputGrades use a for statement to output the students' grades. A counter-controlled for *must* be used in this case, because lines 135–136 use counter variable student's value to output each grade next to a particular student number (see output in Fig. E.14). Although array indices start at 0, a professor would typically number students starting at 1. Thus, lines 135–136 output student + 1 as the student number to produce grade labels "Student 1: ", "Student 2: ", and so on.

```
1   // Fig. E.13: GradeBook.java
2   // GradeBook class using an array to store test grades.
3
4   public class GradeBook
5   {
6      private String courseName; // name of course this GradeBook represents
7      private int[] grades; // array of student grades
8
9      // two-argument constructor initializes courseName and grades array
10     public GradeBook( String name, int[] gradesArray )
11     {
```

Fig. E.13 | GradeBook class using an array to store test grades. (Part 1 of 4.)

```
12            courseName = name; // initialize courseName
13            grades = gradesArray; // store grades
14         } // end two-argument GradeBook constructor
15
16         // method to set the course name
17         public void setCourseName( String name )
18         {
19            courseName = name; // store the course name
20         } // end method setCourseName
21
22         // method to retrieve the course name
23         public String getCourseName()
24         {
25            return courseName;
26         } // end method getCourseName
27
28         // display a welcome message to the GradeBook user
29         public void displayMessage()
30         {
31            // getCourseName gets the name of the course
32            System.out.printf( "Welcome to the grade book for\n%s!\n\n",
33               getCourseName() );
34         } // end method displayMessage
35
36         // perform various operations on the data
37         public void processGrades()
38         {
39            // output grades array
40            outputGrades();
41
42            // call method getAverage to calculate the average grade
43            System.out.printf( "\nClass average is %.2f\n", getAverage() );
44
45            // call methods getMinimum and getMaximum
46            System.out.printf( "Lowest grade is %d\nHighest grade is %d\n\n",
47               getMinimum(), getMaximum() );
48
49            // call outputBarChart to print grade distribution chart
50            outputBarChart();
51         } // end method processGrades
52
53         // find minimum grade
54         public int getMinimum()
55         {
56            int lowGrade = grades[ 0 ]; // assume grades[ 0 ] is smallest
57
58            // loop through grades array
59            for ( int grade : grades )
60            {
61               // if grade lower than lowGrade, assign it to lowGrade
62               if ( grade < lowGrade )
63                  lowGrade = grade; // new lowest grade
64            } // end for
```

Fig. E.13 | GradeBook class using an array to store test grades. (Part 2 of 4.)

```
65
66          return lowGrade; // return lowest grade
67      } // end method getMinimum
68
69      // find maximum grade
70      public int getMaximum()
71      {
72          int highGrade = grades[ 0 ]; // assume grades[ 0 ] is largest
73
74          // loop through grades array
75          for ( int grade : grades )
76          {
77              // if grade greater than highGrade, assign it to highGrade
78              if ( grade > highGrade )
79                  highGrade = grade; // new highest grade
80          } // end for
81
82          return highGrade; // return highest grade
83      } // end method getMaximum
84
85      // determine average grade for test
86      public double getAverage()
87      {
88          int total = 0; // initialize total
89
90          // sum grades for one student
91          for ( int grade : grades )
92              total += grade;
93
94          // return average of grades
95          return (double) total / grades.length;
96      } // end method getAverage
97
98      // output bar chart displaying grade distribution
99      public void outputBarChart()
100     {
101         System.out.println( "Grade distribution:" );
102
103         // stores frequency of grades in each range of 10 grades
104         int[] frequency = new int[ 11 ];
105
106         // for each grade, increment the appropriate frequency
107         for ( int grade : grades )
108             ++frequency[ grade / 10 ];
109
110         // for each grade frequency, print bar in chart
111         for ( int count = 0; count < frequency.length; count++ )
112         {
113             // output bar label ( "00-09: ", ..., "90-99: ", "100: " )
114             if ( count == 10 )
115                 System.out.printf( "%5d: ", 100 );
```

Fig. E.13 | GradeBook class using an array to store test grades. (Part 3 of 4.)

```
116              else
117                 System.out.printf( "%02d-%02d: ",
118                    count * 10, count * 10 + 9  );
119
120              // print bar of asterisks
121              for ( int stars = 0; stars < frequency[ count ]; stars++ )
122                 System.out.print( "*" );
123
124              System.out.println(); // start a new line of output
125           } // end outer for
126        } // end method outputBarChart
127
128        // output the contents of the grades array
129        public void outputGrades()
130        {
131           System.out.println( "The grades are:\n" );
132
133           // output each student's grade
134           for ( int student = 0; student < grades.length; student++ )
135              System.out.printf( "Student %2d: %3d\n",
136                 student + 1, grades[ student ] );
137        } // end method outputGrades
138     } // end class GradeBook
```

Fig. E.13 | GradeBook class using an array to store test grades. (Part 4 of 4.)

Method processGrades next calls method getAverage (line 43) to obtain the average of the grades in the array. Method getAverage (lines 86–96) uses an enhanced for statement to total the values in array grades before calculating the average. The parameter in the enhanced for's header (e.g., int grade) indicates that for each iteration, the int variable grade takes on a value in the array grades. The averaging calculation in line 95 uses grades.length to determine the number of grades being averaged.

Lines 46–47 in method processGrades call methods getMinimum and getMaximum to determine the lowest and highest grades of any student on the exam, respectively. Each of these methods uses an enhanced for statement to loop through array grades. Lines 59–64 in method getMinimum loop through the array. Lines 62–63 compare each grade to lowGrade; if a grade is less than lowGrade, lowGrade is set to that grade. When line 66 executes, lowGrade contains the lowest grade in the array. Method getMaximum (lines 70–83) works similarly to method getMinimum.

Finally, line 50 in method processGrades calls method outputBarChart to print a distribution chart of the grade data using a technique similar to that in Fig. E.5. In that example, we manually calculated the number of grades in each category (i.e., 0–9, 10–19, ..., 90–99 and 100) by simply looking at a set of grades. In this example, lines 107–108 use a technique similar to that in Figs. E.6 and 7.8 to calculate the frequency of grades in each category. Line 104 declares and creates array frequency of 11 ints to store the frequency of grades in each grade category. For each grade in array grades, lines 107–108 increment the appropriate element of the frequency array. To determine which element to increment, line 108 divides the current grade by 10 using integer division. For example, if grade is 85, line 108 increments frequency[8] to update the count of grades in the range 80–89. Lines 111–125 next print the bar chart (see Fig. E.14) based on the values in array frequency. Like lines 23–24 of Fig. E.5, lines 121–122 of Fig. E.13 use a value in array frequency to determine the number of asterisks to display in each bar.

Class *GradeBookTest* That Demonstrates Class *GradeBook*

The application of Fig. E.14 creates an object of class GradeBook (Fig. E.13) using the int array gradesArray (declared and initialized in line 10 of Fig. E.14). Lines 12–13 pass a course name and gradesArray to the GradeBook constructor. Line 14 displays a welcome message, and line 15 invokes the GradeBook object's processGrades method. The output summarizes the 10 grades in myGradeBook.

Software Engineering Observation E.1

A test harness (or test application) is responsible for creating an object of the class being tested and providing it with data. This data could come from any of several sources. Test data can be placed directly into an array with an array initializer, it can come from the user at the keyboard, it can come from a file, or it can come from a network. After passing this data to the class's constructor to instantiate the object, the test harness should call upon the object to test its methods and manipulate its data. Gathering data in the test harness like this allows the class to manipulate data from several sources.

```java
1   // Fig. E.14: GradeBookTest.java
2   // GradeBookTest creates a GradeBook object using an array of grades,
3   // then invokes method processGrades to analyze them.
4   public class GradeBookTest
5   {
6      // main method begins program execution
7      public static void main( String[] args )
8      {
9         // array of student grades
10        int[] gradesArray = { 87, 68, 94, 100, 83, 78, 85, 91, 76, 87 };
11
12        GradeBook myGradeBook = new GradeBook(
13           "CS101 Introduction to Java Programming", gradesArray );
14        myGradeBook.displayMessage();
15        myGradeBook.processGrades();
16     } // end main
17  } // end class GradeBookTest
```

```
Welcome to the grade book for
CS101 Introduction to Java Programming!

The grades are:

Student   1:   87
Student   2:   68
Student   3:   94
Student   4:  100
Student   5:   83
Student   6:   78
```

Fig. E.14 | GradeBookTest creates a GradeBook object using an array of grades, then invokes method processGrades to analyze them. (Part 1 of 2.)

```
Student  7:   85
Student  8:   91
Student  9:   76
Student 10:   87

Class average is 84.90
Lowest grade is 68
Highest grade is 100

Grade distribution:
00-09:
10-19:
20-29:
30-39:
40-49:
50-59:
60-69: *
70-79: **
80-89: ****
90-99: **
  100: *
```

Fig. E.14 | GradeBookTest creates a GradeBook object using an array of grades, then invokes method processGrades to analyze them. (Part 2 of 2.)

E.9 Multidimensional Arrays

Multidimensional arrays with two dimensions are often used to represent *tables* of values consisting of information arranged in *rows* and *columns*. To identify a particular table element, we must specify two indices. *By convention*, the first identifies the element's row and the second its column. Arrays that require two indices to identify a particular element are called **two-dimensional arrays**. (Multidimensional arrays can have more than two dimensions.) Java does not support multidimensional arrays directly, but it does allow you to specify one-dimensional arrays whose elements are also one-dimensional arrays, thus achieving the same effect. Figure E.15 illustrates a two-dimensional array named a that contains three rows and four columns (i.e., a three-by-four array). In general, an array with *m* rows and *n* columns is called an **m-by-n array**.

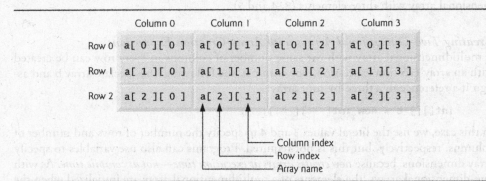

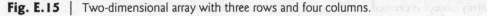

Fig. E.15 | Two-dimensional array with three rows and four columns.

Every element in array a is identified in Fig. E.15 by an *array-access expression* of the form a[*row*][*column*]; a is the name of the array, and *row* and *column* are the indices that uniquely identify each element in array a by row and column number. The names of the elements in *row* 0 all have a first index of 0, and the names of the elements in *column* 3 all have a second index of 3.

Arrays of One-Dimensional Arrays

Like one-dimensional arrays, multidimensional arrays can be initialized with array initializers in declarations. A two-dimensional array b with two rows and two columns could be declared and initialized with **nested array initializers** as follows:

```
int[][] b = { { 1, 2 }, { 3, 4 } };
```

The initial values are grouped by row in braces. So 1 and 2 initialize b[0][0] and b[0][1], respectively, and 3 and 4 initialize b[1][0] and b[1][1], respectively. The compiler counts the number of nested array initializers (represented by sets of braces within the outer braces) to determine the number of rows in array b. The compiler counts the initializer values in the nested array initializer for a row to determine the number of columns in that row. As we'll see momentarily, this means that *rows can have different lengths*.

Multidimensional arrays are maintained as arrays of one-dimensional arrays. Therefore array b in the preceding declaration is actually composed of two separate one-dimensional arrays—one containing the values in the first nested initializer list { 1, 2 } and one containing the values in the second nested initializer list { 3, 4 }. Thus, array b itself is an array of two elements, each a one-dimensional array of int values.

Two-Dimensional Arrays with Rows of Different Lengths

The manner in which multidimensional arrays are represented makes them quite flexible. In fact, the lengths of the rows in array b are *not* required to be the same. For example,

```
int[][] b = { { 1, 2 }, { 3, 4, 5 } };
```

creates integer array b with two elements (determined by the number of nested array initializers) that represent the rows of the two-dimensional array. Each element of b is a reference to a one-dimensional array of int variables. The int array for row 0 is a one-dimensional array with two elements (1 and 2), and the int array for row 1 is a one-dimensional array with three elements (3, 4 and 5).

Creating Two-Dimensional Arrays with Array-Creation Expressions

A multidimensional array with the same number of columns in every row can be created with an array-creation expression. For example, the following lines declare array b and assign it a reference to a three-by-four array:

```
int[][] b = new int[ 3 ][ 4 ];
```

In this case, we use the literal values 3 and 4 to specify the number of rows and number of columns, respectively, but this is not required. Programs can also use variables to specify array dimensions, because *new creates arrays at execution time—not at compile time*. As with one-dimensional arrays, the elements of a multidimensional array are initialized when the array object is created.

A multidimensional array in which each row has a different number of columns can be created as follows:

```
int[][] b = new int[ 2 ][ ];    // create 2 rows
b[ 0 ] = new int[ 5 ]; // create 5 columns for row 0
b[ 1 ] = new int[ 3 ]; // create 3 columns for row 1
```

The preceding statements create a two-dimensional array with two rows. Row 0 has five columns, and row 1 has three columns.

Two-Dimensional Array Example: Displaying Element Values

Figure E.16 demonstrates initializing two-dimensional arrays with array initializers and using nested for loops to **traverse** the arrays (i.e., manipulate every element of each array). Class InitArray's main declares two arrays. The declaration of array1 (line 9) uses nested array initializers of the *same* length to initialize the first row to the values 1, 2 and 3, and the second row to the values 4, 5 and 6. The declaration of array2 (line 10) uses nested initializers of *different* lengths. In this case, the first row is initialized to two elements with the values 1 and 2, respectively. The second row is initialized to one element with the value 3. The third row is initialized to three elements with the values 4, 5 and 6, respectively.

```java
1    // Fig. E.16: InitArray.java
2    // Initializing two-dimensional arrays.
3
4    public class InitArray
5    {
6       // create and output two-dimensional arrays
7       public static void main( String[] args )
8       {
9          int[][] array1 = { { 1, 2, 3 }, { 4, 5, 6 } };
10         int[][] array2 = { { 1, 2 }, { 3 }, { 4, 5, 6 } };
11
12         System.out.println( "Values in array1 by row are" );
13         outputArray( array1 ); // displays array1 by row
14
15         System.out.println( "\nValues in array2 by row are" );
16         outputArray( array2 ); // displays array2 by row
17      } // end main
18
19      // output rows and columns of a two-dimensional array
20      public static void outputArray( int[][] array )
21      {
22         // loop through array's rows
23         for ( int row = 0; row < array.length; row++ )
24         {
25            // loop through columns of current row
26            for ( int column = 0; column < array[ row ].length; column++ )
27               System.out.printf( "%d  ", array[ row ][ column ] );
28
29            System.out.println(); // start new line of output
30         } // end outer for
31      } // end method outputArray
32   } // end class InitArray
```

Fig. E.16 | Initializing two-dimensional arrays. (Part 1 of 2.)

```
Values in array1 by row are
1  2  3
4  5  6

Values in array2 by row are
1  2
3
4  5  6
```

Fig. E.16 | Initializing two-dimensional arrays. (Part 2 of 2.)

Lines 13 and 16 call method outputArray (lines 20–31) to output the elements of array1 and array2, respectively. Method outputArray's parameter—int[][] array—indicates that the method receives a two-dimensional array. The for statement (lines 23–30) outputs the rows of a two-dimensional array. In the loop-continuation condition of the outer for statement, the expression array.length determines the number of rows in the array. In the inner for statement, the expression array[row].length determines the number of columns in the current row of the array. The inner for statement's condition enables the loop to determine the exact number of columns in each row.

Common Multidimensional-Array Manipulations Performed with for Statements
Many common array manipulations use for statements. As an example, the following for statement sets all the elements in row 2 of array a in Fig. E.15 to zero:

```
for ( int column = 0; column < a[ 2 ].length; column++ )
    a[ 2 ][ column ] = 0;
```

We specified row 2; therefore, we know that the first index is always 2 (0 is the first row, and 1 is the second row). This for loop varies only the second index (i.e., the column index). If row 2 of array a contains four elements, then the preceding for statement is equivalent to the assignment statements

```
a[ 2 ][ 0 ] = 0;
a[ 2 ][ 1 ] = 0;
a[ 2 ][ 2 ] = 0;
a[ 2 ][ 3 ] = 0;
```

The following nested for statement totals the values of all the elements in array a:

```
int total = 0;
for ( int row = 0; row < a.length; row++ )
{
    for ( int column = 0; column < a[ row ].length; column++ )
        total += a[ row ][ column ];
} // end outer for
```

These nested for statements total the array elements one row at a time. The outer for statement begins by setting the row index to 0 so that the first row's elements can be totaled by the inner for statement. The outer for then increments row to 1 so that the second row can be totaled. Then, the outer for increments row to 2 so that the third row can be totaled. The variable total can be displayed when the outer for statement terminates. In the next example, we show how to process a two-dimensional array in a similar manner using nested enhanced for statements.

E.10 Case Study: Class GradeBook Using a Two-Dimensional Array

In Section E.8, we presented class GradeBook (Fig. E.13), which used a one-dimensional array to store student grades on a single exam. In most semesters, students take several exams. Professors are likely to want to analyze grades across the entire semester, both for a single student and for the class as a whole.

Storing Student Grades in a Two-Dimensional Array in Class GradeBook

Figure E.17 contains a GradeBook class that uses a two-dimensional array grades to store the grades of a number of students on multiple exams. Each row of the array represents a single student's grades for the entire course, and each column represents the grades of all the students who took a particular exam. Class GradeBookTest (Fig. E.18) passes the array as an argument to the GradeBook constructor. In this example, we use a ten-by-three array for ten students' grades on three exams. Five methods perform array manipulations to process the grades. Each method is similar to its counterpart in the earlier one-dimensional array version of GradeBook (Fig. E.13). Method getMinimum (lines 52–70) determines the lowest grade of any student for the semester. Method getMaximum (lines 73–91) determines the highest grade of any student for the semester. Method getAverage (lines 94–104) determines a particular student's semester average. Method outputBarChart (lines 107–137) outputs a grade bar chart for the entire semester's student grades. Method outputGrades (lines 140–164) outputs the array in a tabular format, along with each student's semester average.

```java
1   // Fig. E.17: GradeBook.java
2   // GradeBook class using a two-dimensional array to store grades.
3
4   public class GradeBook
5   {
6      private String courseName; // name of course this grade book represents
7      private int[][] grades; // two-dimensional array of student grades
8
9      // two-argument constructor initializes courseName and grades array
10     public GradeBook( String name, int[][] gradesArray )
11     {
12        courseName = name; // initialize courseName
13        grades = gradesArray; // store grades
14     } // end two-argument GradeBook constructor
15
16     // method to set the course name
17     public void setCourseName( String name )
18     {
19        courseName = name; // store the course name
20     } // end method setCourseName
21
22     // method to retrieve the course name
23     public String getCourseName()
24     {
25        return courseName;
26     } // end method getCourseName
```

Fig. E.17 | GradeBook class using a two-dimensional array to store grades. (Part 1 of 4.)

```
27
28      // display a welcome message to the GradeBook user
29      public void displayMessage()
30      {
31         // getCourseName gets the name of the course
32         System.out.printf( "Welcome to the grade book for\n%s!\n\n",
33            getCourseName() );
34      } // end method displayMessage
35
36      // perform various operations on the data
37      public void processGrades()
38      {
39         // output grades array
40         outputGrades();
41
42         // call methods getMinimum and getMaximum
43         System.out.printf( "\n%s %d\n%s %d\n\n",
44            "Lowest grade in the grade book is", getMinimum(),
45            "Highest grade in the grade book is", getMaximum() );
46
47         // output grade distribution chart of all grades on all tests
48         outputBarChart();
49      } // end method processGrades
50
51      // find minimum grade
52      public int getMinimum()
53      {
54         // assume first element of grades array is smallest
55         int lowGrade = grades[ 0 ][ 0 ];
56
57         // loop through rows of grades array
58         for ( int[] studentGrades : grades )
59         {
60            // loop through columns of current row
61            for ( int grade : studentGrades )
62            {
63               // if grade less than lowGrade, assign it to lowGrade
64               if ( grade < lowGrade )
65                  lowGrade = grade;
66            } // end inner for
67         } // end outer for
68
69         return lowGrade; // return lowest grade
70      } // end method getMinimum
71
72      // find maximum grade
73      public int getMaximum()
74      {
75         // assume first element of grades array is largest
76         int highGrade = grades[ 0 ][ 0 ];
77
```

Fig. E.17 | GradeBook class using a two-dimensional array to store grades. (Part 2 of 4.)

```
78         // loop through rows of grades array
79         for ( int[] studentGrades : grades )
80         {
81            // loop through columns of current row
82            for ( int grade : studentGrades )
83            {
84               // if grade greater than highGrade, assign it to highGrade
85               if ( grade > highGrade )
86                  highGrade = grade;
87            } // end inner for
88         } // end outer for
89
90         return highGrade; // return highest grade
91      } // end method getMaximum
92
93      // determine average grade for particular set of grades
94      public double getAverage( int[] setOfGrades )
95      {
96         int total = 0; // initialize total
97
98         // sum grades for one student
99         for ( int grade : setOfGrades )
100           total += grade;
101
102        // return average of grades
103        return (double) total / setOfGrades.length;
104     } // end method getAverage
105
106     // output bar chart displaying overall grade distribution
107     public void outputBarChart()
108     {
109        System.out.println( "Overall grade distribution:" );
110
111        // stores frequency of grades in each range of 10 grades
112        int[] frequency = new int[ 11 ];
113
114        // for each grade in GradeBook, increment the appropriate frequency
115        for ( int[] studentGrades : grades )
116        {
117           for ( int grade : studentGrades )
118              ++frequency[ grade / 10 ];
119        } // end outer for
120
121        // for each grade frequency, print bar in chart
122        for ( int count = 0; count < frequency.length; count++ )
123        {
124           // output bar label ( "00-09: ", ..., "90-99: ", "100: " )
125           if ( count == 10 )
126              System.out.printf( "%5d: ", 100 );
127           else
128              System.out.printf( "%02d-%02d: ",
129                 count * 10, count * 10 + 9 );
130
```

Fig. E.17 | GradeBook class using a two-dimensional array to store grades. (Part 3 of 4.)

```
131            // print bar of asterisks
132            for ( int stars = 0; stars < frequency[ count ]; stars++ )
133               System.out.print( "*" );
134
135            System.out.println(); // start a new line of output
136         } // end outer for
137      } // end method outputBarChart
138
139      // output the contents of the grades array
140      public void outputGrades()
141      {
142         System.out.println( "The grades are:\n" );
143         System.out.print( "            " ); // align column heads
144
145         // create a column heading for each of the tests
146         for ( int test = 0; test < grades[ 0 ].length; test++ )
147            System.out.printf( "Test %d ", test + 1 );
148
149         System.out.println( "Average" ); // student average column heading
150
151         // create rows/columns of text representing array grades
152         for ( int student = 0; student < grades.length; student++ )
153         {
154            System.out.printf( "Student %2d", student + 1 );
155
156            for ( int test : grades[ student ] ) // output student's grades
157               System.out.printf( "%8d", test );
158
159            // call method getAverage to calculate student's average grade;
160            // pass row of grades as the argument to getAverage
161            double average = getAverage( grades[ student ] );
162            System.out.printf( "%9.2f\n", average );
163         } // end outer for
164      } // end method outputGrades
165   } // end class GradeBook
```

Fig. E.17 | GradeBook class using a two-dimensional array to store grades. (Part 4 of 4.)

Methods getMinimum and getMaximum

Methods getMinimum, getMaximum, outputBarChart and outputGrades each loop through array grades by using nested for statements—for example, the nested enhanced for statement from the declaration of method getMinimum (lines 58–67). The outer enhanced for statement iterates through the two-dimensional array grades, assigning successive rows to parameter studentGrades on successive iterations. The square brackets following the parameter name indicate that studentGrades refers to a one-dimensional int array—namely, a row in array grades containing one student's grades. To find the lowest overall grade, the inner for statement compares the elements of the current one-dimensional array studentGrades to variable lowGrade. For example, on the first iteration of the outer for, row 0 of grades is assigned to parameter studentGrades. The inner enhanced for statement then loops through studentGrades and compares each grade value with lowGrade. If a grade is less than lowGrade, lowGrade is set to that grade. On the second iteration of the outer enhanced for statement, row 1 of grades is assigned to studentGrades, and the elements of this row are compared with variable lowGrade. This repeats until all rows of grades have been traversed. When execution of the nested statement is complete, lowGrade contains the lowest grade in the two-dimensional array. Method getMaximum works similarly to method getMinimum.

Method outputBarChart

Method outputBarChart (lines 107–137) is nearly identical to the one in Fig. E.13. However, to output the overall grade distribution for a whole semester, the method here uses nested enhanced for statements (lines 115–119) to create the one-dimensional array frequency based on all the grades in the two-dimensional array. The rest of the code in each of the two outputBarChart methods that displays the chart is identical.

Method outputGrades

Method outputGrades (lines 140–164) uses nested for statements to output values of the array grades and each student's semester average. The output (Fig. E.18) shows the result, which resembles the tabular format of a professor's physical grade book. Lines 146–147 print the column headings for each test. We use a counter-controlled for statement here so that we can identify each test with a number. Similarly, the for statement in lines 152–163 first outputs a row label using a counter variable to identify each student (line 154). Although array indices start at 0, lines 147 and 154 output test + 1 and student + 1, respectively, to produce test and student numbers starting at 1 (see Fig. E.18). The inner for statement (lines 156–157) uses the outer for statement's counter variable student to loop through a specific row of array grades and output each student's test grade. An enhanced for statement can be nested in a counter-controlled for statement, and vice versa. Finally, line 161 obtains each student's semester average by passing the current row of grades (i.e., grades[student]) to method getAverage.

Method getAverage

Method getAverage (lines 94–104) takes one argument—a one-dimensional array of test results for a particular student. When line 161 calls getAverage, the argument is grades[student], which specifies that a particular row of the two-dimensional array grades should be passed to getAverage. For example, based on the array created in Fig. E.18, the argument grades[1] represents the three values (a one-dimensional array of grades) stored in row 1 of the two-dimensional array grades. Recall that a two-dimensional array is one whose elements are one-dimensional arrays. Method getAverage calculates the sum of the array elements, divides the total by the number of test results and returns the floating-point result as a double value (line 103).

Class GradeBookTest That Demonstrates Class GradeBook

Figure E.18 creates an object of class GradeBook (Fig. E.17) using the two-dimensional array of ints named gradesArray (declared and initialized in lines 10–19). Lines 21–22 pass a course name and gradesArray to the GradeBook constructor. Lines 23–24 then invoke myGradeBook's displayMessage and processGrades methods to display a welcome message and obtain a report summarizing the students' grades for the semester, respectively.

```
 1    // Fig. E.18: GradeBookTest.java
 2    // GradeBookTest creates GradeBook object using a two-dimensional array
 3    // of grades, then invokes method processGrades to analyze them.
 4    public class GradeBookTest
 5    {
 6       // main method begins program execution
 7       public static void main( String[] args )
 8       {
 9          // two-dimensional array of student grades
10          int[][] gradesArray = { { 87, 96, 70 },
11                                  { 68, 87, 90 },
12                                  { 94, 100, 90 },
13                                  { 100, 81, 82 },
14                                  { 83, 65, 85 },
15                                  { 78, 87, 65 },
16                                  { 85, 75, 83 },
17                                  { 91, 94, 100 },
18                                  { 76, 72, 84 },
19                                  { 87, 93, 73 } };
20
21          GradeBook myGradeBook = new GradeBook(
22             "CS101 Introduction to Java Programming", gradesArray );
23          myGradeBook.displayMessage();
24          myGradeBook.processGrades();
25       } // end main
26    } // end class GradeBookTest
```

```
Welcome to the grade book for
CS101 Introduction to Java Programming!

The grades are:

              Test 1  Test 2  Test 3  Average
Student  1       87      96      70    84.33
Student  2       68      87      90    81.67
Student  3       94     100      90    94.67
Student  4      100      81      82    87.67
Student  5       83      65      85    77.67
Student  6       78      87      65    76.67
Student  7       85      75      83    81.00
Student  8       91      94     100    95.00
Student  9       76      72      84    77.33
Student 10       87      93      73    84.33

Lowest grade in the grade book is 65
Highest grade in the grade book is 100

Overall grade distribution:
00-09:
10-19:
20-29:
30-39:
```

Fig. E.18 | GradeBookTest creates GradeBook object using a two-dimensional array of grades, then invokes method processGrades to analyze them. (Part 1 of 2.)

```
40-49:
50-59:
60-69: ***
70-79: ******
80-89: ***********
90-99: *******
  100: ***
```

Fig. E.18 | GradeBookTest creates GradeBook object using a two-dimensional array of grades, then invokes method processGrades to analyze them. (Part 2 of 2.)

E.11 Class Arrays

Class **Arrays** helps you avoid reinventing the wheel by providing static methods for common array manipulations. These methods include **sort** for sorting an array (i.e., arranging elements into increasing order), **binarySearch** for searching an array (i.e., determining whether an array contains a specific value and, if so, where the value is located), **equals** for comparing arrays and **fill** for placing values into an array. These methods are overloaded for primitive-type arrays and for arrays of objects. Our focus in this section is on using the built-in capabilities provided by the Java API.

Figure E.19 uses Arrays methods sort, binarySearch, equals and fill, and shows how to copy arrays with class System's static **arraycopy method**. In main, line 11 sorts the elements of array doubleArray. The static method sort of class Arrays orders the array's elements in *ascending* order by default. Overloaded versions of sort allow you to sort a specific range of elements. Lines 12–15 output the sorted array.

```java
 1  // Fig. E.19: ArrayManipulations.java
 2  // Arrays class methods and System.arraycopy.
 3  import java.util.Arrays;
 4
 5  public class ArrayManipulations
 6  {
 7     public static void main( String[] args )
 8     {
 9        // sort doubleArray into ascending order
10        double[] doubleArray = { 8.4, 9.3, 0.2, 7.9, 3.4 };
11        Arrays.sort( doubleArray );
12        System.out.printf( "\ndoubleArray: " );
13
14        for ( double value : doubleArray )
15           System.out.printf( "%.1f ", value );
16
17        // fill 10-element array with 7s
18        int[] filledIntArray = new int[ 10 ];
19        Arrays.fill( filledIntArray, 7 );
20        displayArray( filledIntArray, "filledIntArray" );
21
```

Fig. E.19 | Arrays class methods and System.arraycopy. (Part 1 of 3.)

```
22          // copy array intArray into array intArrayCopy
23          int[] intArray = { 1, 2, 3, 4, 5, 6 };
24          int[] intArrayCopy = new int[ intArray.length ];
25          System.arraycopy( intArray, 0, intArrayCopy, 0, intArray.length );
26          displayArray( intArray, "intArray" );
27          displayArray( intArrayCopy, "intArrayCopy" );
28
29          // compare intArray and intArrayCopy for equality
30          boolean b = Arrays.equals( intArray, intArrayCopy );
31          System.out.printf( "\n\nintArray %s intArrayCopy\n",
32             ( b ? "==" : "!=" ) );
33
34          // compare intArray and filledIntArray for equality
35          b = Arrays.equals( intArray, filledIntArray );
36          System.out.printf( "intArray %s filledIntArray\n",
37             ( b ? "==" : "!=" ) );
38
39          // search intArray for the value 5
40          int location = Arrays.binarySearch( intArray, 5 );
41
42          if ( location >= 0 )
43             System.out.printf(
44                "Found 5 at element %d in intArray\n", location );
45          else
46             System.out.println( "5 not found in intArray" );
47
48          // search intArray for the value 8763
49          location = Arrays.binarySearch( intArray, 8763 );
50
51          if ( location >= 0 )
52             System.out.printf(
53                "Found 8763 at element %d in intArray\n", location );
54          else
55             System.out.println( "8763 not found in intArray" );
56       } // end main
57
58       // output values in each array
59       public static void displayArray( int[] array, String description )
60       {
61          System.out.printf( "\n%s: ", description );
62
63          for ( int value : array )
64             System.out.printf( "%d ", value );
65       } // end method displayArray
66    } // end class ArrayManipulations
```

```
doubleArray: 0.2 3.4 7.9 8.4 9.3
filledIntArray: 7 7 7 7 7 7 7 7 7 7
intArray: 1 2 3 4 5 6
intArrayCopy: 1 2 3 4 5 6
```

Fig. E.19 | Arrays class methods and System.arraycopy. (Part 2 of 3.)

```
intArray == intArrayCopy
intArray != filledIntArray
Found 5 at element 4 in intArray
8763 not found in intArray
```

Fig. E.19 | Arrays class methods and System.arraycopy. (Part 3 of 3.)

Line 19 calls static method fill of class Arrays to populate all 10 elements of filledIntArray with 7s. Overloaded versions of fill allow you to populate a specific range of elements with the same value. Line 20 calls our class's displayArray method (declared at lines 59–65) to output the contents of filledIntArray.

Line 25 copies the elements of intArray into intArrayCopy. The first argument (intArray) passed to System method arraycopy is the array from which elements are to be copied. The second argument (0) is the index that specifies the starting point in the range of elements to copy from the array. This value can be any valid array index. The third argument (intArrayCopy) specifies the destination array that will store the copy. The fourth argument (0) specifies the index in the destination array where the first copied element should be stored. The last argument specifies the number of elements to copy from the array in the first argument. In this case, we copy all the elements in the array.

Lines 30 and 35 call static method equals of class Arrays to determine whether all the elements of two arrays are equivalent. If the arrays contain the same elements in the same order, the method returns true; otherwise, it returns false.

Lines 40 and 49 call static method binarySearch of class Arrays to perform a binary search on intArray, using the second argument (5 and 8763, respectively) as the key. If value is found, binarySearch returns the index of the element; otherwise, binarySearch returns a negative value. The negative value returned is based on the search key's insertion point—the index where the key would be inserted in the array if we were performing an insert operation. After binarySearch determines the insertion point, it changes its sign to negative and subtracts 1 to obtain the return value. For example, in Fig. E.19, the insertion point for the value 8763 is the element with index 6 in the array. Method binarySearch changes the insertion point to –6, subtracts 1 from it and returns the value –7. Subtracting 1 from the insertion point guarantees that method binarySearch returns positive values (>= 0) if and only if the key is found. This return value is useful for inserting elements in a sorted array.

Common Programming Error E.3

Passing an unsorted array to binarySearch is a logic error—the value returned is undefined.

E.12 Introduction to Collections and Class ArrayList

The Java API provides several predefined data structures, called **collections**, used to store groups of related objects. These classes provide efficient methods that organize, store and retrieve your data without requiring knowledge of how the data is being stored. This reduces application-development time.

You've used arrays to store sequences of objects. Arrays do not automatically change their size at execution time to accommodate additional elements. The collection class

`ArrayList<T>` (from package `java.util`) provides a convenient solution to this problem—it can *dynamically* change its size to accommodate more elements. The `T` (by convention) is a *placeholder*—when declaring a new `ArrayList`, replace it with the type of elements that you want the `ArrayList` to hold. This is similar to specifying the type when declaring an array, except that *only nonprimitive types can be used with these collection classes*. For example,

```
ArrayList< String > list;
```

declares `list` as an `ArrayList` collection that can store only `Strings`. Classes with this kind of placeholder that can be used with any type are called **generic classes**. Additional generic collection classes and generics are discussed in Appendix J. Figure E.20 shows some common methods of class `ArrayList<T>`.

Method	Description
add	Adds an element to the end of the `ArrayList`.
clear	Removes all the elements from the `ArrayList`.
contains	Returns `true` if the `ArrayList` contains the specified element; otherwise, returns `false`.
get	Returns the element at the specified index.
indexOf	Returns the index of the first occurrence of the specified element in the `ArrayList`.
remove	Overloaded. Removes the first occurrence of the specified value or the element at the specified index.
size	Returns the number of elements stored in the `ArrayList`.
trimToSize	Trims the capacity of the `ArrayList` to current number of elements.

Fig. E.20 | Some methods and properties of class `ArrayList<T>`.

Figure E.21 demonstrates some common `ArrayList` capabilities. Line 10 creates a new empty `ArrayList` of `Strings` with a default initial capacity of 10 elements. The capacity indicates how many items the `ArrayList` can hold without growing. `ArrayList` is implemented using an array behind the scenes. When the `ArrayList` grows, it must create a larger internal array and copy each element to the new array. This is a time-consuming operation. It would be inefficient for the `ArrayList` to grow each time an element is added. Instead, it grows only when an element is added *and* the number of elements is equal to the capacity—i.e., there's no space for the new element.

```java
1    // Fig. E.21: ArrayListCollection.java
2    // Generic ArrayList<T> collection demonstration.
3    import java.util.ArrayList;
4
5    public class ArrayListCollection
6    {
```

Fig. E.21 | Generic `ArrayList<T>` collection demonstration. (Part 1 of 3.)

```
7      public static void main( String[] args )
8      {
9         // create a new ArrayList of Strings with an initial capacity of 10
10        ArrayList< String > items = new ArrayList< String >();
11
12        items.add( "red" ); // append an item to the list
13        items.add( 0, "yellow" ); // insert the value at index 0
14
15        // header
16        System.out.print(
17           "Display list contents with counter-controlled loop:" );
18
19        // display the colors in the list
20        for ( int i = 0; i < items.size(); i++ )
21           System.out.printf( " %s", items.get( i ) );
22
23        // display colors using foreach in the display method
24        display( items,
25           "\nDisplay list contents with enhanced for statement:" );
26
27        items.add( "green" ); // add "green" to the end of the list
28        items.add( "yellow" ); // add "yellow" to the end of the list
29        display( items, "List with two new elements:" );
30
31        items.remove( "yellow" ); // remove the first "yellow"
32        display( items, "Remove first instance of yellow:" );
33
34        items.remove( 1 ); // remove item at index 1
35        display( items, "Remove second list element (green):" );
36
37        // check if a value is in the List
38        System.out.printf( "\"red\" is %sin the list\n",
39           items.contains( "red" ) ? "": "not " );
40
41        // display number of elements in the List
42        System.out.printf( "Size: %s\n", items.size() );
43     } // end main
44
45     // display the ArrayList's elements on the console
46     public static void display( ArrayList< String > items, String header )
47     {
48        System.out.print( header ); // display header
49
50        // display each element in items
51        for ( String item : items )
52           System.out.printf( " %s", item );
53
54        System.out.println(); // display end of line
55     } // end method display
56  } // end class ArrayListCollection
```

Fig. E.21 | Generic `ArrayList<T>` collection demonstration. (Part 2 of 3.)

```
Display list contents with counter-controlled loop: yellow red
Display list contents with enhanced for statement: yellow red
List with two new elements: yellow red green yellow
Remove first instance of yellow: red green yellow
Remove second list element (green): red yellow
"red" is in the list
Size: 2
```

Fig. E.21 | Generic `ArrayList<T>` collection demonstration. (Part 3 of 3.)

The **add** method adds elements to the `ArrayList` (lines 12–13). The add method with *one* argument appends its argument to the end of the `ArrayList`. The add method with *two* arguments inserts a new element at the specified position. The first argument is an index. As with arrays, collection indices start at zero. The second argument is the value to insert at that index. The indices of all subsequent elements are incremented by one. Inserting an element is usually slower than adding an element to the end of the `ArrayList`.

Lines 20–21 display the items in the `ArrayList`. The **size** method returns the number of elements currently in the `ArrayList`. `ArrayLists` method **get** (line 21) obtains the element at a specified index. Lines 24–25 display the elements again by invoking method display (defined at lines 46–55). Lines 27–28 add two more elements to the `ArrayList`, then line 29 displays the elements again to confirm that the two elements were added to the end of the collection.

The **remove** method is used to remove an element with a specific value (line 31). It removes only the first such element. If no such element is in the `ArrayList`, remove does nothing. An overloaded version of the method removes the element at the specified index (line 34). When an element is removed, the indices of all elements after the removed element decrease by one.

Line 39 uses the **contains** method to check if an item is in the `ArrayList`. The contains method returns true if the element is found in the `ArrayList`, and false otherwise. The method compares its argument to each element of the `ArrayList` in order, so using contains on a large `ArrayList` can be inefficient. Line 42 displays the `ArrayList`'s size.

E.13 Wrap-Up

This appendix began our introduction to data structures, exploring the use of arrays to store data in and retrieve data from lists and tables of values. The appendix examples demonstrated how to declare an array, initialize an array and refer to individual elements of an array. The appendix introduced the enhanced for statement to iterate through arrays. We used exception handling to test for `ArrayIndexOutOfBoundsExceptions` that occur when a program attempts to access an array element outside the bounds of an array. We also illustrated how to pass arrays to methods and how to declare and manipulate multidimensional arrays.

We introduced the `ArrayList<T>` generic collection, which provides all the functionality and performance of arrays, along with other useful capabilities such as dynamic resizing. We used the add methods to add new items to the end of an `ArrayList` and to insert items in an `ArrayList`. The remove method was used to remove the first occurrence of a specified item, and an overloaded version of remove was used to remove an item at a specified index. We used the size method to obtain number of items in the ArrayList.

We continue our coverage of data structures in Appendix J. Appendix J introduces the Java Collections Framework, which uses generics to allow you to specify the exact types of objects that a particular data structure will store. Appendix J also introduces Java's other predefined data structures. The Collections API provides class Arrays, which contains utility methods for array manipulation. Appendix J uses several static methods of class Arrays to perform such manipulations as sorting and searching the data in an array.

We've now introduced the basic concepts of classes, objects, control statements, methods, arrays and collections. In Appendix F, we take a deeper look at classes and objects.

Self-Review Exercises

E.1   Fill in the blank(s) in each of the following statements:
  a) Lists and tables of values can be stored in _____.
  b) An array is a group of _____ (called elements or components) containing values that all have the same _____.
  c) The _____ allows you to iterate through the elements in an array without using a counter.
  d) The number used to refer to a particular array element is called the element's _____.
  e) An array that uses two indices is referred to as a(n) _____ array.
  f) Use the enhanced for statement _____ to walk through double array numbers.
  g) Command-line arguments are stored in _____.

E.2   Determine whether each of the following is *true* or *false*. If *false*, explain why.
  a) An array can store many different types of values.
  b) An array index should normally be of type float.
  c) An individual array element that's passed to a method and modified in that method will contain the modified value when the called method completes execution.

E.3   Perform the following tasks for an array called fractions:
  a) Declare a constant ARRAY_SIZE that's initialized to 10.
  b) Declare an array with ARRAY_SIZE elements of type double, and initialize the elements to 0.
  c) Refer to array element 4.
  d) Assign the value 1.667 to array element 9.
  e) Assign the value 3.333 to array element 6.
  f) Sum all the elements of the array, using a for statement. Declare the integer variable x as a control variable for the loop.

E.4   Perform the following tasks for an array called table:
  a) Declare and create the array as an integer array that has three rows and three columns. Assume that the constant ARRAY_SIZE has been declared to be 3.
  b) How many elements does the array contain?
  c) Use a for statement to initialize each element of the array to the sum of its indices. Assume that the integer variables x and y are declared as control variables.

E.5 Find and correct the error in each of the following program segments:

a) ```
final int ARRAY_SIZE = 5;
ARRAY_SIZE = 10;
```

b) Assume ```int[] b = new int[ 10 ];```
```
for (int i = 0; i <= b.length; i++)
   b[i] = 1;
```

c) Assume ```int[][] a = { { 1, 2 }, { 3, 4 } };```
```
a[1, 1] = 5;
```

## Answers to Self-Review Exercises

**E.1**   a)   arrays. b) variables, type. c) enhanced for statement. d) index (or subscript or position number). e) two-dimensional. f) for ( double d : numbers ). g) an array of Strings, called args by convention.

**E.2**   a)   False. An array can store only values of the same type. b) False. An array index must be an integer or an integer expression. c) For individual primitive-type elements of an array: False. A called method receives and manipulates a copy of the value of such an element, so modifications do not affect the original value. If the reference of an array is passed to a method, however, modifications to the array elements made in the called method are indeed reflected in the original. For individual elements of a reference type: True. A called method receives a copy of the reference of such an element, and changes to the referenced object will be reflected in the original array element.

**E.3**   a)   ```final int ARRAY_SIZE = 10;```

b) ```double[] fractions = new double[ ARRAY_SIZE ];```

c) ```fractions[ 4 ]```

d) ```fractions[ 9 ] = 1.667;```

e) ```fractions[ 6 ] = 3.333;```

f) ```double total = 0.0;```
```
for (int x = 0; x < fractions.length; x++)
   total += fractions[x];
```

**E.4**   a)   ```int[][] table = new int[ ARRAY_SIZE ][ ARRAY_SIZE ];```

b) Nine.

c) ```for ( int x = 0; x < table.length; x++ )```
```
   for (int y = 0; y < table[x].length; y++)
      table[x][y] = x + y;
```

**E.5**   a)   Error: Assigning a value to a constant after it has been initialized.
Correction: Assign the correct value to the constant in a final int ARRAY_SIZE declaration or declare another variable.

b) Error: Referencing an array element outside the bounds of the array (b[10]).
Correction: Change the <= operator to <.

c) Error: Array indexing is performed incorrectly.
Correction: Change the statement to a[ 1 ][ 1 ] = 5;.

## Exercises

**E.6** Fill in the blanks in each of the following statements:

a) One-dimensional array p contains four elements. The names of those elements are _____, _____, _____ and _____.

b) Naming an array, stating its type and specifying the number of dimensions in the array is called _____ the array.
```

c) In a two-dimensional array, the first index identifies the _____ of an element and the second index identifies the _____ of an element.

d) An *m*-by-*n* array contains _____ rows, _____ columns and _____ elements.

e) The name of the element in row 3 and column 5 of array d is _____.

E.7 Determine whether each of the following is *true* or *false*. If *false*, explain why.

a) To refer to a particular location or element within an array, we specify the name of the array and the value of the particular element.

b) An array declaration reserves space for the array.

c) To indicate that 100 locations should be reserved for integer array p, you write the declaration

```
p[ 100 ];
```

d) An application that initializes the elements of a 15-element array to zero must contain at least one for statement.

e) An application that totals the elements of a two-dimensional array must contain nested for statements.

E.8 Consider a two-by-three integer array t.

a) Write a statement that declares and creates t.

b) How many rows does t have?

c) How many columns does t have?

d) How many elements does t have?

e) Write access expressions for all the elements in row 1 of t.

f) Write access expressions for all the elements in column 2 of t.

g) Write a single statement that sets the element of t in row 0 and column 1 to zero.

h) Write individual statements to initialize each element of t to zero.

i) Write a nested for statement that initializes each element of t to zero.

j) Write a nested for statement that inputs the values for the elements of t from the user.

k) Write a series of statements that determines and displays the smallest value in t.

l) Write a single printf statement that displays the elements of the first row of t.

m) Write a statement that totals the elements of the third column of t. Do not use repetition.

n) Write a series of statements that displays the contents of t in tabular format. List the column indices as headings across the top, and list the row indices at the left of each row.

E.9 *(Duplicate Elimination)* Use a one-dimensional array to solve the following problem: Write an application that inputs five numbers, each between 10 and 100, inclusive. As each number is read, display it only if it's not a duplicate of a number already read. Provide for the "worst case," in which all five numbers are different. Use the smallest possible array to solve this problem. Display the complete set of unique values input after the user enters each new value.

E.10 Label the elements of three-by-five two-dimensional array sales to indicate the order in which they're set to zero by the following program segment:

```
for ( int row = 0; row < sales.length; row++ )
{
    for ( int col = 0; col < sales[ row ].length; col++ )
    {
        sales[ row ][ col ] = 0;
    }
}
```

E.11 *(Sieve of Eratosthenes)* A prime number is any integer greater than 1 that's evenly divisible only by itself and 1. The Sieve of Eratosthenes is a method of finding prime numbers. It operates as follows:

a) Create a primitive-type `boolean` array with all elements initialized to `true`. Array elements with prime indices will remain `true`. All other array elements will eventually be set to `false`.

b) Starting with array index 2, determine whether a given element is `true`. If so, loop through the remainder of the array and set to `false` every element whose index is a multiple of the index for the element with value `true`. Then continue the process with the next element with value `true`. For array index 2, all elements beyond element 2 in the array that have indices which are multiples of 2 (indices 4, 6, 8, 10, etc.) will be set to `false`; for array index 3, all elements beyond element 3 in the array that have indices which are multiples of 3 (indices 6, 9, 12, 15, etc.) will be set to `false`; and so on.

When this process completes, the array elements that are still `true` indicate that the index is a prime number. These indices can be displayed. Write an application that uses an array of 1000 elements to determine and display the prime numbers between 2 and 999. Ignore array elements 0 and 1.

E.12 *(Fibonacci Series)* The Fibonacci series

$$0, 1, 1, 2, 3, 5, 8, 13, 21, \ldots$$

begins with the terms 0 and 1 and has the property that each succeeding term is the sum of the two preceding terms.

a) Write a method `fibonacci( n )` that calculates the *n*th Fibonacci number. Incorporate this method into an application that enables the user to enter the value of n.

b) Determine the largest Fibonacci number that can be displayed on your system.

c) Modify the application you wrote in part (a) to use `double` instead of `int` to calculate and return Fibonacci numbers, and use this modified application to repeat part (b).

Classes and Objects:
A Deeper Look

F

Objectives

In this appendix you'll learn:

- Encapsulation and data hiding.
- To use keyword **this**.
- To use **static** variables and methods.
- To import **static** members of a class.
- To use the **enum** type to create sets of constants with unique identifiers.
- To declare **enum** constants with parameters.
- To organize classes in packages to promote reuse.

F.1 Introduction

We now take a deeper look at building classes, controlling access to members of a class and creating constructors. We discuss composition—a capability that allows a class to have references to objects of other classes as members. Recall that Section D.10 introduced the basic enum type to declare a set of constants. In this appendix, we discuss the relationship between enum types and classes, demonstrating that an enum, like a class, can be declared in its own file with constructors, methods and fields. The appendix also discusses static class members and final instance variables in detail. Finally, we explain how to organize classes in packages to help manage large applications and promote reuse, then show a special relationship between classes in the same package.

F.2 Time Class Case Study

Our first example consists of two classes—Time1 (Fig. F.1) and Time1Test (Fig. F.2). Class Time1 represents the time of day. Class Time1Test is an application class in which the main method creates one object of class Time1 and invokes its methods. These classes must be declared in *separate* files because they're both public classes. The output of this program appears in Fig. F.2.

Time1 Class Declaration

Class Time1's private int instance variables hour, minute and second (Fig. F.1, lines 6–8) represent the time in universal-time format (24-hour clock format in which hours are in the range 0–23). Class Time1 contains public methods setTime (lines 12–25), toUniversalString (lines 28–31) and toString (lines 34–39). These methods are also called the **public services** or the **public interface** that the class provides to its clients.

Default Constructor

In this example, class Time1 does not declare a constructor, so the class has a default constructor that's supplied by the compiler. Each instance variable implicitly receives the default value 0 for an int. Instance variables also can be initialized when they're declared in the class body, using the same initialization syntax as with a local variable.

```
1    // Fig. F.1: Time1.java
2    // Time1 class declaration maintains the time in 24-hour format.
3
4    public class Time1
5    {
6       private int hour;   // 0 - 23
7       private int minute; // 0 - 59
8       private int second; // 0 - 59
9
10      // set a new time value using universal time; throw an
11      // exception if the hour, minute or second is invalid
12      public void setTime( int h, int m, int s )
13      {
14         // validate hour, minute and second
15         if ( ( h >= 0 && h < 24 ) && ( m >= 0 && m < 60 ) &&
16            ( s >= 0 && s < 60 ) )
17         {
18            hour = h;
19            minute = m;
20            second = s;
21         } // end if
22         else
23            throw new IllegalArgumentException(
24               "hour, minute and/or second was out of range" );
25      } // end method setTime
26
27      // convert to String in universal-time format (HH:MM:SS)
28      public String toUniversalString()
29      {
30         return String.format( "%02d:%02d:%02d", hour, minute, second );
31      } // end method toUniversalString
32
33      // convert to String in standard-time format (H:MM:SS AM or PM)
34      public String toString()
35      {
36         return String.format( "%d:%02d:%02d %s",
37            ( ( hour == 0 || hour == 12 ) ? 12 : hour % 12 ),
38            minute, second, ( hour < 12 ? "AM" : "PM" ) );
39      } // end method toString
40   } // end class Time1
```

Fig. F.I | Time1 class declaration maintains the time in 24-hour format.

Method setTime and Throwing Exceptions

Method setTime (lines 12–25) is a public method that declares three int parameters and uses them to set the time. Lines 15–16 test each argument to determine whether the value is in the proper range, and, if so, lines 18–20 assign the values to the hour, minute and second instance variables. The hour value must be greater than or equal to 0 and less than 24, because universal-time format represents hours as integers from 0 to 23 (e.g., 1 PM is hour 13 and 11 PM is hour 23; midnight is hour 0 and noon is hour 12). Similarly, both minute and second values must be greater than or equal to 0 and less than 60. For values outside these ranges, SetTime **throws an exception** of type **IllegalArgumentException** (lines 23–24), which notifies the client code that an invalid argument was passed to the method. As you learned in Appendix E, you can use try...catch to catch exceptions and attempt to recover from them, which we'll do in Fig. F.2. The **throw statement** (line 23) creates a new object of type IllegalArgumentException. The parentheses following the class name indicate a call to the IllegalArgumentException constructor. In this case, we call the constructor that allows us to specify a custom error message. After the exception object is created, the throw statement immediately terminates method setTime and the exception is returned to the code that attempted to set the time.

Method toUniversalString

Method toUniversalString (lines 28–31) takes no arguments and returns a String in universal-time format, consisting of two digits each for the hour, minute and second. For example, if the time were 1:30:07 PM, the method would return 13:30:07. Line 30 uses static method **format** of class String to return a String containing the formatted hour, minute and second values, each with two digits and possibly a leading 0 (specified with the 0 flag). Method format is similar to method System.out.printf except that format *returns* a formatted String rather than displaying it in a command window. The formatted String is returned by method toUniversalString.

Method toString

Method toString (lines 34–39) takes no arguments and returns a String in standard-time format, consisting of the hour, minute and second values separated by colons and followed by AM or PM (e.g., 1:27:06 PM). Like method toUniversalString, method toString uses static String method format to format the minute and second as two-digit values, with leading zeros if necessary. Line 37 uses a conditional operator (?:) to determine the value for hour in the String—if the hour is 0 or 12 (AM or PM), it appears as 12; otherwise, it appears as a value from 1 to 11. The conditional operator in line 38 determines whether AM or PM will be returned as part of the String.

Recall from Section D.4 that all objects in Java have a toString method that returns a String representation of the object. We chose to return a String containing the time in standard-time format. Method toString is called implicitly whenever a Time1 object appears in the code where a String is needed, such as the value to output with a %s format specifier in a call to System.out.printf.

Using Class Time1

As you learned in Appendix B, each class you declare represents a new *type* in Java. Therefore, after declaring class Time1, we can use it as a type in declarations such as

```
Time1 sunset; // sunset can hold a reference to a Time1 object
```

The Time1Test application class (Fig. F.2) uses class Time1. Line 9 declares and creates a Time1 object and assigns it to local variable time. Operator new implicitly invokes class Time1's default constructor, since Time1 does not declare any constructors. Lines 12–16 output the time first in universal-time format (by invoking time's toUniversalString method in line 13), then in standard-time format (by explicitly invoking time's toString method in line 15) to confirm that the Time1 object was initialized properly. Next, line 19 invokes method setTime of the time object to change the time. Then lines 20–24 output the time again in both formats to confirm that it was set correctly.

```
 1   // Fig. F.2: Time1Test.java
 2   // Time1 object used in an application.
 3
 4   public class Time1Test
 5   {
 6      public static void main( String[] args )
 7      {
 8         // create and initialize a Time1 object
 9         Time1 time = new Time1(); // invokes Time1 constructor
10
11         // output string representations of the time
12         System.out.print( "The initial universal time is: " );
13         System.out.println( time.toUniversalString() );
14         System.out.print( "The initial standard time is: " );
15         System.out.println( time.toString() );
16         System.out.println(); // output a blank line
17
18         // change time and output updated time
19         time.setTime( 13, 27, 6 );
20         System.out.print( "Universal time after setTime is: " );
21         System.out.println( time.toUniversalString() );
22         System.out.print( "Standard time after setTime is: " );
23         System.out.println( time.toString() );
24         System.out.println(); // output a blank line
25
26         // attempt to set time with invalid values
27         try
28         {
29            time.setTime( 99, 99, 99 ); // all values out of range
30         } // end try
31         catch ( IllegalArgumentException e )
32         {
33            System.out.printf( "Exception: %s\n\n", e.getMessage() );
34         } // end catch
35
36         // display time after attempt to set invalid values
37         System.out.println( "After attempting invalid settings:" );
38         System.out.print( "Universal time: " );
39         System.out.println( time.toUniversalString() );
40         System.out.print( "Standard time: " );
41         System.out.println( time.toString() );
42      } // end main
43   } // end class Time1Test
```

```
The initial universal time is: 00:00:00
The initial standard time is: 12:00:00 AM

Universal time after setTime is: 13:27:06
Standard time after setTime is: 1:27:06 PM

Exception: hour, minute and/or second was out of range

After attempting invalid settings:
Universal time: 13:27:06
Standard time: 1:27:06 PM
```

Fig. F.2 | Time1 object used in an application.

*Calling **Time1** Method **setTime** with Invalid Values*

To illustrate that method setTime validates its arguments, line 29 calls method setTime with invalid arguments of 99 for the hour, minute and second. This statement is placed in a try block (lines 27–30) in case setTime throws an IllegalArgumentException, which it will do since the arguments are all invalid. When this occurs, the exception is caught at lines 31–34, and line 33 displays the exception's error message by calling its getMessage method. Lines 37–41 output the time again in both formats to confirm that setTime did not change the time when invalid arguments were supplied.

*Notes on the **Time1** Class Declaration*

Consider several issues of class design with respect to class Time1. The instance variables hour, minute and second are each declared private. The actual data representation used within the class is of no concern to the class's clients. For example, it would be perfectly reasonable for Time1 to represent the time internally as the number of seconds since midnight or the number of minutes and seconds since midnight. Clients could use the same public methods and get the same results without being aware of this.

F.3 Controlling Access to Members

The access modifiers public and private control access to a class's variables and methods. In Appendix G, we'll introduce the access modifier protected. As you know, the primary purpose of public methods is to present to the class's clients a view of the services the class provides (the class's public interface). Clients need not be concerned with how the class accomplishes its tasks. For this reason, the class's private variables and private methods (i.e., its implementation details) are *not* accessible to its clients.

Figure F.3 demonstrates that private class members are not accessible outside the class. Lines 9–11 attempt to access directly the private instance variables hour, minute and second of the Time1 object time. When this program is compiled, the compiler generates error messages that these private members are not accessible. This program assumes that the Time1 class from Fig. F.1 is used.

```
1   // Fig. F.3: MemberAccessTest.java
2   // Private members of class Time1 are not accessible.
3   public class MemberAccessTest
4   {
5      public static void main( String[] args )
6      {
7         Time1 time = new Time1(); // create and initialize Time1 object
8
9         time.hour = 7; // error: hour has private access in Time1
10        time.minute = 15; // error: minute has private access in Time1
11        time.second = 30; // error: second has private access in Time1
12     } // end main
13  } // end class MemberAccessTest
```

Fig. F.3 | Private members of class Time1 are not accessible. (Part I of 2.)

```
MemberAccessTest.java:9: hour has private access in Time1
      time.hour = 7; // error: hour has private access in Time1
           ^
MemberAccessTest.java:10: minute has private access in Time1
      time.minute = 15; // error: minute has private access in Time1
           ^
MemberAccessTest.java:11: second has private access in Time1
      time.second = 30; // error: second has private access in Time1
           ^
3 errors
```

Fig. F.3 | Private members of class Time1 are not accessible. (Part 2 of 2.)

F.4 Referring to the Current Object's Members with the this Reference

Every object can access a reference to itself with keyword **this** (sometimes called the **this reference**). When a non-static method is called for a particular object, the method's body implicitly uses keyword this to refer to the object's instance variables and other methods. This enables the class's code to know which object should be manipulated. As you'll see in Fig. F.4, you can also use keyword this explicitly in a non-static method's body. Section F.5 shows another interesting use of keyword this. Section F.10 explains why keyword this cannot be used in a static method.

We now demonstrate implicit and explicit use of the this reference (Fig. F.4). This example is the first in which we declare *two* classes in one file—class ThisTest is declared in lines 4–11, and class SimpleTime in lines 14–47. We do this to demonstrate that when you compile a .java file containing more than one class, the compiler produces a separate class file with the .class extension for every compiled class. In this case, two separate files are produced—SimpleTime.class and ThisTest.class. When one source-code (.java) file contains multiple class declarations, the compiler places both class files for those classes in the same directory. Note also in Fig. F.4 that only class ThisTest is declared public. A source-code file can contain only one public class—otherwise, a compilation error occurs. Non-public classes can be used only by other classes in the same package. So, in this example, class SimpleTime can be used only by class ThisTest.

```
 1   // Fig. F.4: ThisTest.java
 2   // this used implicitly and explicitly to refer to members of an object.
 3
 4   public class ThisTest
 5   {
 6      public static void main( String[] args )
 7      {
 8         SimpleTime time = new SimpleTime( 15, 30, 19 );
 9         System.out.println( time.buildString() );
10      } // end main
11   } // end class ThisTest
12
```

Fig. F.4 | this used implicitly and explicitly to refer to members of an object. (Part 1 of 2.)

```
13    // class SimpleTime demonstrates the "this" reference
14    class SimpleTime
15    {
16        private int hour;   // 0-23
17        private int minute; // 0-59
18        private int second; // 0-59
19
20        // if the constructor uses parameter names identical to
21        // instance variable names the "this" reference is
22        // required to distinguish between the names
23        public SimpleTime( int hour, int minute, int second )
24        {
25            this.hour = hour;     // set "this" object's hour
26            this.minute = minute; // set "this" object's minute
27            this.second = second; // set "this" object's second
28        } // end SimpleTime constructor
29
30        // use explicit and implicit "this" to call toUniversalString
31        public String buildString()
32        {
33            return String.format( "%24s: %s\n%24s: %s",
34                "this.toUniversalString()", this.toUniversalString(),
35                "toUniversalString()", toUniversalString() );
36        } // end method buildString
37
38        // convert to String in universal-time format (HH:MM:SS)
39        public String toUniversalString()
40        {
41            // "this" is not required here to access instance variables,
42            // because method does not have local variables with same
43            // names as instance variables
44            return String.format( "%02d:%02d:%02d",
45                this.hour, this.minute, this.second );
46        } // end method toUniversalString
47    } // end class SimpleTime
```

```
this.toUniversalString(): 15:30:19
    toUniversalString(): 15:30:19
```

Fig. F.4 | this used implicitly and explicitly to refer to members of an object. (Part 2 of 2.)

Class SimpleTime (lines 14–47) declares three private instance variables—hour, minute and second (lines 16–18). The constructor (lines 23–28) receives three int arguments to initialize a SimpleTime object. We used parameter names for the constructor (line 23) that are identical to the class's instance-variable names (lines 16–18). We don't recommend this practice, but we did it here to shadow (hide) the corresponding instance variables so that we could illustrate a case in which *explicit* use of the this reference is required. If a method contains a local variable with the *same* name as a field, that method will refer to the local variable rather than the field. In this case, the local variable shadows the field in the method's scope. However, the method can use the this reference to refer to the shadowed field explicitly, as shown on the left sides of the assignments in lines 25–27 for SimpleTime's shadowed instance variables.

Method buildString (lines 31–36) returns a String created by a statement that uses the this reference explicitly and implicitly. Line 34 uses it explicitly to call method toUniversalString. Line 35 uses it implicitly to call the same method. Both lines perform the same task. You typically will not use this explicitly to reference other methods within the current object. Also, line 45 in method toUniversalString explicitly uses the this reference to access each instance variable. This is *not* necessary here, because the method does *not* have any local variables that shadow the instance variables of the class.

Common Programming Error F.1
It's often a logic error when a method contains a parameter or local variable that has the same name as a field of the class. In this case, use reference this if you wish to access the field of the class—otherwise, the method parameter or local variable will be referenced.

Error-Prevention Tip F.1
Avoid method-parameter names or local-variable names that conflict with field names. This helps prevent subtle, hard-to-locate bugs.

Performance Tip F.1
Java conserves storage by maintaining only one copy of each method per class—this method is invoked by every object of the class. Each object, on the other hand, has its own copy of the class's instance variables (i.e., non-static fields). Each method of the class implicitly uses this to determine the specific object of the class to manipulate.

Application class ThisTest (lines 4–11) demonstrates class SimpleTime. Line 8 creates an instance of class SimpleTime and invokes its constructor. Line 9 invokes the object's buildString method, then displays the results.

F.5 Time Class Case Study: Overloaded Constructors

As you know, you can declare your own constructor to specify how objects of a class should be initialized. Next, we demonstrate a class with several **overloaded constructors** that enable objects of that class to be initialized in different ways. To overload constructors, simply provide multiple constructor declarations with different signatures.

Class *Time2 with Overloaded Constructors*
The default constructor for class Time1 (Fig. F.1) initialized hour, minute and second to their default 0 values (which is midnight in universal time). The default constructor does not enable the class's clients to initialize the time with specific nonzero values. Class Time2 (Fig. F.5) contains five overloaded constructors that provide convenient ways to initialize objects of the new class Time2. Each constructor initializes the object to begin in a consistent state. In this program, four of the constructors invoke a fifth, which in turn calls method setTime to ensure that the value supplied for hour is in the range 0 to 23, and the values for minute and second are each in the range 0 to 59. The compiler invokes the appropriate constructor by matching the number, types and order of the types of the arguments specified in the constructor call with the number, types and order of the types of the parameters specified in each constructor declaration. Class Time2 also provides *set* and *get* methods for each instance variable.

```
1    // Fig. F.5: Time2.java
2    // Time2 class with overloaded constructors.
3
4    public class Time2
5    {
6       private int hour;   // 0 - 23
7       private int minute; // 0 - 59
8       private int second; // 0 - 59
9
10      // Time2 no-argument constructor:
11      // initializes each instance variable to zero
12      public Time2()
13      {
14         this( 0, 0, 0 ); // invoke Time2 constructor with three arguments
15      } // end Time2 no-argument constructor
16
17      // Time2 constructor: hour supplied, minute and second defaulted to 0
18      public Time2( int h )
19      {
20         this( h, 0, 0 ); // invoke Time2 constructor with three arguments
21      } // end Time2 one-argument constructor
22
23      // Time2 constructor: hour and minute supplied, second defaulted to 0
24      public Time2( int h, int m )
25      {
26         this( h, m, 0 ); // invoke Time2 constructor with three arguments
27      } // end Time2 two-argument constructor
28
29      // Time2 constructor: hour, minute and second supplied
30      public Time2( int h, int m, int s )
31      {
32         setTime( h, m, s ); // invoke setTime to validate time
33      } // end Time2 three-argument constructor
34
35      // Time2 constructor: another Time2 object supplied
36      public Time2( Time2 time )
37      {
38         // invoke Time2 three-argument constructor
39         this( time.getHour(), time.getMinute(), time.getSecond() );
40      } // end Time2 constructor with a Time2 object argument
41
42      // Set Methods
43      // set a new time value using universal time;
44      // validate the data
45      public void setTime( int h, int m, int s )
46      {
47         setHour( h );   // set the hour
48         setMinute( m ); // set the minute
49         setSecond( s ); // set the second
50      } // end method setTime
51
```

Fig. F.5 | Time2 class with overloaded constructors. (Part 1 of 3.)

```
52      // validate and set hour
53      public void setHour( int h )
54      {
55          if ( h >= 0 && h < 24 )
56              hour = h;
57          else
58              throw new IllegalArgumentException( "hour must be 0-23" );
59      } // end method setHour
60
61      // validate and set minute
62      public void setMinute( int m )
63      {
64          if ( m >= 0 && m < 60 )
65              minute = m;
66          else
67              throw new IllegalArgumentException( "minute must be 0-59" );
68      } // end method setMinute
69
70      // validate and set second
71      public void setSecond( int s )
72      {
73          if ( s >= 0 && s < 60 )
74              second = ( ( s >= 0 && s < 60 ) ? s : 0 );
75          else
76              throw new IllegalArgumentException( "second must be 0-59" );
77      } // end method setSecond
78
79      // Get Methods
80      // get hour value
81      public int getHour()
82      {
83          return hour;
84      } // end method getHour
85
86      // get minute value
87      public int getMinute()
88      {
89          return minute;
90      } // end method getMinute
91
92      // get second value
93      public int getSecond()
94      {
95          return second;
96      } // end method getSecond
97
98      // convert to String in universal-time format (HH:MM:SS)
99      public String toUniversalString()
100     {
101         return String.format(
102             "%02d:%02d:%02d", getHour(), getMinute(), getSecond() );
103     } // end method toUniversalString
104
```

Fig. F.5 | Time2 class with overloaded constructors. (Part 2 of 3.)

```
105      // convert to String in standard-time format (H:MM:SS AM or PM)
106      public String toString()
107      {
108         return String.format( "%d:%02d:%02d %s",
109            ( (getHour() == 0 || getHour() == 12) ? 12 : getHour() % 12 ),
110            getMinute(), getSecond(), ( getHour() < 12 ? "AM" : "PM" ) );
111      } // end method toString
112   } // end class Time2
```

Fig. F.5 | `Time2` class with overloaded constructors. (Part 3 of 3.)

Class Time2's Constructors

Lines 12–15 declare a so-called **no-argument constructor** that's invoked without arguments. Once you declare any constructors in a class, the compiler will *not* provide a default constructor. This no-argument constructor ensures that class `Time2`'s clients can create `Time2` objects with default values. Such a constructor simply initializes the object as specified in the constructor's body. In the body, we introduce a use of the `this` reference that's allowed only as the *first* statement in a constructor's body. Line 14 uses `this` in method-call syntax to invoke the `Time2` constructor that takes three parameters (lines 30–33) with values of 0 for the `hour`, `minute` and `second`. Using the `this` reference as shown here is a popular way to reuse initialization code provided by another of the class's constructors rather than defining similar code in the no-argument constructor's body. We use this syntax in four of the five `Time2` constructors to make the class easier to maintain and modify. If we need to change how objects of class `Time2` are initialized, only the constructor that the class's other constructors call will need to be modified. In fact, even that constructor might not need modification in this example. That constructor simply calls the `setTime` method to perform the actual initialization, so it's possible that the changes the class might require would be localized to the *set* methods.

Common Programming Error F.2

It's a compilation error when `this` *is used in a constructor's body to call another constructor of the same class if that call is not the* first *statement in the constructor. It's also a compilation error when a method attempts to invoke a constructor directly via* `this`.

Common Programming Error F.3

A constructor can call methods of the class. Be aware that the instance variables might not yet be initialized, because the constructor is in the process of initializing the object. Using instance variables before they've been initialized properly is a logic error.

Lines 18–21 declare a `Time2` constructor with a single `int` parameter representing the hour, which is passed with 0 for the `minute` and `second` to the constructor at lines 30–33. Lines 24–27 declare a `Time2` constructor that receives two `int` parameters representing the hour and `minute`, which are passed with 0 for the `second` to the constructor at lines 30–33. Like the no-argument constructor, each of these constructors invokes the constructor at lines 30–33 to minimize code duplication. Lines 30–33 declare the `Time2` constructor that receives three `int` parameters representing the hour, `minute` and `second`. This constructor calls `setTime` to initialize the instance variables.

Lines 36–40 declare a Time2 constructor that receives a reference to another Time2 object. In this case, the values from the Time2 argument are passed to the three-argument constructor at lines 30–33 to initialize the hour, minute and second. Line 39 could have directly accessed the hour, minute and second values of the constructor's argument time with the expressions time.hour, time.minute and time.second—even though hour, minute and second are declared as private variables of class Time2. This is due to a special relationship between objects of the same class. We'll see in a moment why it's preferable to use the *get* methods.

Software Engineering Observation F.1

When one object of a class has a reference to another object of the same class, the first object can access all *the second object's data and methods (including those that are private).*

Class Time2's setTime Method

Method setTime (lines 45–50) invokes the setHour (lines 53–59), setMinute (lines 62–68) and setSecond (lines 71–77) methods, which ensure that the value supplied for hour is in the range 0 to 23 and the values for minute and second are each in the range 0 to 59. If a value is out of range, each of these methods throws an IllegalArgumentException (lines 58, 67 and 76) indicating which value was out of range.

Notes Regarding Class Time2's set and get Methods and Constructors

Time2's *set* and *get* methods are called throughout the class. In particular, method setTime calls methods setHour, setMinute and setSecond in lines 47–49, and methods toUniversalString and toString call methods getHour, getMinute and getSecond in line 102 and lines 109–110, respectively. In each case, these methods could have accessed the class's private data directly without calling the *set* and *get* methods. However, consider changing the representation of the time from three int values (requiring 12 bytes of memory) to a single int value representing the total number of seconds that have elapsed since midnight (requiring only 4 bytes of memory). If we made such a change, only the bodies of the methods that access the private data directly would need to change—in particular, the individual *set* and *get* methods for the hour, minute and second. There would be no need to modify the bodies of methods setTime, toUniversalString or toString because they do not access the data directly. Designing the class in this manner reduces the likelihood of programming errors when altering the class's implementation.

Similarly, each Time2 constructor could include a copy of the appropriate statements from methods setHour, setMinute and setSecond. Doing so may be slightly more efficient, because the extra calls to the constructor and setTime are eliminated. However, *duplicating* statements in multiple methods or constructors makes changing the class's internal data representation more difficult. Having the Time2 constructors call the constructor with three arguments (or even call setTime directly) requires that any changes to the implementation of setTime be made only once. Also, the compiler can optimize programs by removing calls to simple methods and replacing them with the expanded code of their declarations—a technique known as **inlining the code**, which improves program performance.

Software Engineering Observation F.2

When implementing a method of a class, use the class's set and get methods to access the class's private data. This simplifies code maintenance and reduces the likelihood of errors.

Using Class Time2's Overloaded Constructors

Class Time2Test (Fig. F.6) invokes the overloaded Time2 constructors (lines 8–12 and 40). Line 8 invokes the no-argument constructor (Fig. F.5, lines 12–15). Lines 9–13 of the program demonstrate passing arguments to the other Time2 constructors. Line 9 invokes the single-argument constructor that receives an int at lines 18–21 of Fig. F.5. Line 10 invokes the two-argument constructor at lines 24–27 of Fig. F.5. Line 11 invokes the three-argument constructor at lines 30–33 of Fig. F.5. Line 12 invokes the single-argument constructor that takes a Time2 at lines 36–40 of Fig. F.5. Next, the application displays the String representations of each Time2 object to confirm that it was initialized properly. Line 40 attempts to intialize t6 by creating a new Time2 object and passing three invalid values to the constructor. When the constructor attempts to use the invalid hour value to initialize the object's hour, an IllegalArgumentException occurs. We catch this exception at line 42 and display its error message, which results in the last line of the output.

```
1   // Fig. F.6: Time2Test.java
2   // Overloaded constructors used to initialize Time2 objects.
3
4   public class Time2Test
5   {
6      public static void main( String[] args )
7      {
8         Time2 t1 = new Time2(); // 00:00:00
9         Time2 t2 = new Time2( 2 ); // 02:00:00
10        Time2 t3 = new Time2( 21, 34 ); // 21:34:00
11        Time2 t4 = new Time2( 12, 25, 42 ); // 12:25:42
12        Time2 t5 = new Time2( t4 ); // 12:25:42
13
14        System.out.println( "Constructed with:" );
15        System.out.println( "t1: all arguments defaulted" );
16        System.out.printf( "   %s\n", t1.toUniversalString() );
17        System.out.printf( "   %s\n", t1.toString() );
18
19        System.out.println(
20           "t2: hour specified; minute and second defaulted" );
21        System.out.printf( "   %s\n", t2.toUniversalString() );
22        System.out.printf( "   %s\n", t2.toString() );
23
24        System.out.println(
25           "t3: hour and minute specified; second defaulted" );
26        System.out.printf( "   %s\n", t3.toUniversalString() );
27        System.out.printf( "   %s\n", t3.toString() );
28
29        System.out.println( "t4: hour, minute and second specified" );
30        System.out.printf( "   %s\n", t4.toUniversalString() );
31        System.out.printf( "   %s\n", t4.toString() );
32
33        System.out.println( "t5: Time2 object t4 specified" );
34        System.out.printf( "   %s\n", t5.toUniversalString() );
35        System.out.printf( "   %s\n", t5.toString() );
36
```

Fig. F.6 | Overloaded constructors used to initialize Time2 objects. (Part I of 2.)

```
37          // attempt to initialize t6 with invalid values
38          try
39          {
40              Time2 t6 = new Time2( 27, 74, 99 ); // invalid values
41          } // end try
42          catch ( IllegalArgumentException e )
43          {
44              System.out.printf( "\nException while initializing t6: %s\n",
45                  e.getMessage() );
46          } // end catch
47      } // end main
48  } // end class Time2Test
```

```
Constructed with:
t1: all arguments defaulted
    00:00:00
    12:00:00 AM
t2: hour specified; minute and second defaulted
    02:00:00
    2:00:00 AM
t3: hour and minute specified; second defaulted
    21:34:00
    9:34:00 PM
t4: hour, minute and second specified
    12:25:42
    12:25:42 PM
t5: Time2 object t4 specified
    12:25:42
    12:25:42 PM

Exception while initializing t6: hour must be 0-23
```

Fig. F.6 | Overloaded constructors used to initialize Time2 objects. (Part 2 of 2.)

F.6 Default and No-Argument Constructors

Every class must have at least one constructor. If you do not provide any in a class's declaration, the compiler creates a default constructor that takes no arguments when it's invoked. The default constructor initializes the instance variables to the initial values specified in their declarations or to their default values (zero for primitive numeric types, false for boolean values and null for references). In Section G.4.1, you'll learn that the default constructor performs another task also.

If your class declares constructors, the compiler will *not* create a default constructor. In this case, you must declare a no-argument constructor if default initialization is required. Like a default constructor, a no-argument constructor is invoked with empty parentheses. The Time2 no-argument constructor (lines 12–15 of Fig. F.5) explicitly initializes a Time2 object by passing to the three-argument constructor 0 for each parameter. Since 0 is the default value for int instance variables, the no-argument constructor in this example could actually be declared with an empty body. In this case, each instance variable would receive its default value when the no-argument constructor was called. If we omit the no-argument constructor, clients of this class would not be able to create a Time2 object with the expression new Time2().

F.7 Composition

A class can have references to objects of other classes as members. This is called **composition** and is sometimes referred to as a *has-a* relationship. For example, an AlarmClock object needs to know the current time *and* the time when it's supposed to sound its alarm, so it's reasonable to include *two* references to Time objects in an AlarmClock object.

Class Date

This composition example contains classes Date (Fig. F.7), Employee (Fig. F.8) and EmployeeTest (Fig. F.9). Class Date (Fig. F.7) declares instance variables month, day and year (lines 6–8) to represent a date. The constructor receives three int parameters. Line 17 invokes utility method checkMonth (lines 26–32) to validate the month—if the value is out of range the method throws an exception. Line 15 assumes that the value for year is correct and doesn't validate it. Line 19 invokes utility method checkDay (lines 35–48) to validate the day based on the current month and year. Line 38 determines whether the day is correct based on the number of days in the particular month. If the day is not correct, lines 42–43 determine whether the month is February, the day is 29 and the year is a leap year. If the day is still invalid, the method throws an exception. Lines 21–22 in the constructor output the this reference as a String. Since this is a reference to the current Date object, the object's toString method (lines 51–54) is called *implicitly* to obtain the object's String representation.

```
1    // Fig. F.7: Date.java
2    // Date class declaration.
3
4    public class Date
5    {
6       private int month; // 1-12
7       private int day; // 1-31 based on month
8       private int year; // any year
9
10      private static final int[] daysPerMonth = // days in each month
11         { 0, 31, 28, 31, 30, 31, 30, 31, 31, 30, 31, 30, 31 };
12
13      // constructor: call checkMonth to confirm proper value for month;
14      // call checkDay to confirm proper value for day
15      public Date( int theMonth, int theDay, int theYear )
16      {
17         month = checkMonth( theMonth ); // validate month
18         year = theYear; // could validate year
19         day = checkDay( theDay ); // validate day
20
21         System.out.printf(
22            "Date object constructor for date %s\n", this );
23      } // end Date constructor
24
25      // utility method to confirm proper month value
26      private int checkMonth( int testMonth )
27      {
28         if ( testMonth > 0 && testMonth <= 12 ) // validate month
29            return testMonth;
```

Fig. F.7 | Date class declaration. (Part 1 of 2.)

```
30          else // month is invalid
31              throw new IllegalArgumentException( "month must be 1-12" );
32       } // end method checkMonth
33
34       // utility method to confirm proper day value based on month and year
35       private int checkDay( int testDay )
36       {
37          // check if day in range for month
38          if ( testDay > 0 && testDay <= daysPerMonth[ month ] )
39              return testDay;
40
41          // check for leap year
42          if ( month == 2 && testDay == 29 && ( year % 400 == 0 ||
43              ( year % 4 == 0 && year % 100 != 0 ) ) )
44              return testDay;
45
46          throw new IllegalArgumentException(
47              "day out-of-range for the specified month and year" );
48       } // end method checkDay
49
50       // return a String of the form month/day/year
51       public String toString()
52       {
53          return String.format( "%d/%d/%d", month, day, year );
54       } // end method toString
55    } // end class Date
```

Fig. F.7 | Date class declaration. (Part 2 of 2.)

Class Employee

Class Employee (Fig. F.8) has instance variables firstName, lastName, birthDate and hireDate. Members firstName and lastName (lines 6–7) are references to String objects. Members birthDate and hireDate (lines 8–9) are references to Date objects. This demonstrates that a class can have as instance variables references to objects of other classes. The Employee constructor (lines 12–19) takes four parameters—first, last, dateOfBirth and dateOfHire. The objects referenced by the parameters are assigned to the Employee object's instance variables. When class Employee's toString method is called, it returns a String containing the employee's name and the String representations of the two Date objects. Each of these Strings is obtained with an *implicit* call to the Date class's toString method.

```
1   // Fig. F.8: Employee.java
2   // Employee class with references to other objects.
3
4   public class Employee
5   {
6       private String firstName;
7       private String lastName;
8       private Date birthDate;
9       private Date hireDate;
```

Fig. F.8 | Employee class with references to other objects. (Part 1 of 2.)

```
10
11      // constructor to initialize name, birth date and hire date
12      public Employee( String first, String last, Date dateOfBirth,
13         Date dateOfHire )
14      {
15         firstName = first;
16         lastName = last;
17         birthDate = dateOfBirth;
18         hireDate = dateOfHire;
19      } // end Employee constructor
20
21      // convert Employee to String format
22      public String toString()
23      {
24         return String.format( "%s, %s  Hired: %s  Birthday: %s",
25            lastName, firstName, hireDate, birthDate );
26      } // end method toString
27   } // end class Employee
```

Fig. F.8 | Employee class with references to other objects. (Part 2 of 2.)

Class EmployeeTest

Class EmployeeTest (Fig. F.9) creates two Date objects (lines 8–9) to represent an Employee's birthday and hire date, respectively. Line 10 creates an Employee and initializes its instance variables by passing to the constructor two Strings (representing the Employee's first and last names) and two Date objects (representing the birthday and hire date). Line 12 implicitly invokes the Employee's toString method to display the values of its instance variables and demonstrate that the object was initialized properly.

```
1    // Fig. F.9: EmployeeTest.java
2    // Composition demonstration.
3
4    public class EmployeeTest
5    {
6       public static void main( String[] args )
7       {
8          Date birth = new Date( 7, 24, 1949 );
9          Date hire = new Date( 3, 12, 1988 );
10         Employee employee = new Employee( "Bob", "Blue", birth, hire );
11
12         System.out.println( employee );
13      } // end main
14   } // end class EmployeeTest
```

```
Date object constructor for date 7/24/1949
Date object constructor for date 3/12/1988
Blue, Bob  Hired: 3/12/1988  Birthday: 7/24/1949
```

Fig. F.9 | Composition demonstration.

F.8 Enumerations

In Fig. D.5, we introduced the basic enum type, which defines a set of constants represented as unique identifiers. In that program the enum constants represented the game's status. In this section we discuss the relationship between enum types and classes. Like classes, all enum types are reference types. An enum type is declared with an **enum declaration**, which is a comma-separated list of enum constants—the declaration may optionally include other components of traditional classes, such as constructors, fields and methods. Each enum declaration declares an enum class with the following restrictions:

1. enum constants are implicitly final, because they declare constants that shouldn't be modified.

2. enum constants are implicitly static.

3. Any attempt to create an object of an enum type with operator new results in a compilation error.

The enum constants can be used anywhere constants can be used, such as in the case labels of switch statements and to control enhanced for statements.

Figure F.10 illustrates how to declare instance variables, a constructor and methods in an enum type. The enum declaration (lines 5–37) contains two parts—the enum constants and the other members of the enum type. The first part (lines 8–13) declares six enum constants. Each is optionally followed by arguments which are passed to the **enum constructor** (lines 20–24). Like the constructors you've seen in classes, an enum constructor can specify any number of parameters and can be overloaded. In this example, the enum constructor requires two String parameters. To properly initialize each enum constant, we follow it with parentheses containing two String arguments, which are passed to the enum's constructor. The second part (lines 16–36) declares the other members of the enum type—two instance variables (lines 16–17), a constructor (lines 20–24) and two methods (lines 27–30 and 33–36).

```
 1   // Fig. F.10: Book.java
 2   // Declaring an enum type with constructor and explicit instance fields
 3   // and accessors for these fields
 4
 5   public enum Book
 6   {
 7      // declare constants of enum type
 8      JHTP( "Java How to Program", "2012" ),
 9      CHTP( "C How to Program", "2007" ),
10      IW3HTP( "Internet & World Wide Web How to Program", "2008" ),
11      CPPHTP( "C++ How to Program", "2012" ),
12      VBHTP( "Visual Basic 2010 How to Program", "2011" ),
13      CSHARPHTP( "Visual C# 2010 How to Program", "2011" );
14
15      // instance fields
16      private final String title; // book title
17      private final String copyrightYear; // copyright year
```

Fig. F.10 | Declaring an enum type with constructor and explicit instance fields and accessors for these fields. (Part 1 of 2.)

```
18
19      // enum constructor
20      Book( String bookTitle, String year )
21      {
22         title = bookTitle;
23         copyrightYear = year;
24      } // end enum Book constructor
25
26      // accessor for field title
27      public String getTitle()
28      {
29         return title;
30      } // end method getTitle
31
32      // accessor for field copyrightYear
33      public String getCopyrightYear()
34      {
35         return copyrightYear;
36      } // end method getCopyrightYear
37   } // end enum Book
```

Fig. F.10 | Declaring an enum type with constructor and explicit instance fields and accessors for these fields. (Part 2 of 2.)

Lines 16–17 declare the instance variables title and copyrightYear. Each enum constant in Book is actually an object of type Book that has its own copy of instance variables title and copyrightYear. The constructor (lines 20–24) takes two String parameters, one that specifies the book's title and one that specifies its copyright year. Lines 22–23 assign these parameters to the instance variables. Lines 27–36 declare two methods, which return the book title and copyright year, respectively.

Figure F.11 tests the enum type Book and illustrates how to iterate through a range of enum constants. For every enum, the compiler generates the static method **values** (called in line 12) that returns an array of the enum's constants in the order they were declared. Lines 12–14 use the enhanced for statement to display all the constants declared in the enum Book. Line 14 invokes the enum Book's getTitle and getCopyrightYear methods to get the title and copyright year associated with the constant. When an enum constant is converted to a String (e.g., book in line 13), the constant's identifier is used as the String representation (e.g., JHTP for the first enum constant).

```
1    // Fig. F.11: EnumTest.java
2    // Testing enum type Book.
3    import java.util.EnumSet;
4
5    public class EnumTest
6    {
7       public static void main( String[] args )
8       {
9          System.out.println( "All books:\n" );
```

Fig. F.11 | Testing enum type Book. (Part 1 of 2.)

```
10
11          // print all books in enum Book
12          for ( Book book : Book.values() )
13             System.out.printf( "%-10s%-45s%s\n", book,
14                book.getTitle(), book.getCopyrightYear() );
15
16          System.out.println( "\nDisplay a range of enum constants:\n" );
17
18          // print first four books
19          for ( Book book : EnumSet.range( Book.JHTP, Book.CPPHTP ) )
20             System.out.printf( "%-10s%-45s%s\n", book,
21                book.getTitle(), book.getCopyrightYear() );
22       } // end main
23    } // end class EnumTest
```

```
All books:

JHTP       Java How to Program                            2012
CHTP       C How to Program                               2007
IW3HTP     Internet & World Wide Web How to Program       2008
CPPHTP     C++ How to Program                             2012
VBHTP      Visual Basic 2010 How to Program               2011
CSHARPHTP  Visual C# 2010 How to Program                  2011

Display a range of enum constants:

JHTP       Java How to Program                            2012
CHTP       C How to Program                               2007
IW3HTP     Internet & World Wide Web How to Program       2008
CPPHTP     C++ How to Program                             2012
```

Fig. F.11 | Testing enum type Book. (Part 2 of 2.)

Lines 19–21 use the static method **range** of class **EnumSet** (declared in package
java.util) to display a range of the enum Book's constants. Method range takes two
parameters—the first and the last enum constants in the range—and returns an EnumSet
that contains all the constants between these two constants, inclusive. For example, the
expression EnumSet.range(Book.JHTP, Book.CPPHTP) returns an EnumSet containing
Book.JHTP, Book.CHTP, Book.IW3HTP and Book.CPPHTP. The enhanced for statement can
be used with an EnumSet just as it can with an array, so lines 12–14 use it to display the
title and copyright year of every book in the EnumSet. Class EnumSet provides several other
static methods for creating sets of enum constants from the same enum type.

Common Programming Error F.4

In an enum *declaration, it's a syntax error to declare* enum *constants after the* enum *type's
constructors, fields and methods.*

F.9 Garbage Collection

Every object uses system resources, such as memory. We need a disciplined way to give
resources back to the system when they're no longer needed; otherwise, "resource leaks"
might occur that would prevent them from being reused by your program or possibly by
other programs. The JVM performs automatic **garbage collection** to reclaim the memory

occupied by objects that are no longer used. When there are no more references to an object, the object is eligible to be collected. This typically occurs when the JVM executes its **garbage collector**. So, memory leaks that are common in other languages like C and C++ (because memory is not automatically reclaimed in those languages) are less likely in Java, but some can still happen in subtle ways. Other types of resource leaks can occur. For example, an application may open a file on disk to modify its contents. If it does not close the file, the application must terminate before any other application can use it.

Software Engineering Observation F.3

A class that uses system resources, such as files on disk, should provide a method that programmers can call to release resources when they're no longer needed in a program. Many Java API classes provide close or dispose methods for this purpose. For example, class Scanner has a close method.

F.10 static Class Members

Every object has its own copy of all the instance variables of the class. In certain cases, only one copy of a particular variable should be *shared* by all objects of a class. A **static field**—called a **class variable**—is used in such cases. A static variable represents **classwide information**—all objects of the class share the *same* piece of data. The declaration of a static variable begins with the keyword static.

Let's motivate static data with an example. Suppose that we have a video game with Martians and other space creatures. Each Martian tends to be brave and willing to attack other space creatures when the Martian is aware that at least four other Martians are present. If fewer than five Martians are present, each of them becomes cowardly. Thus, each Martian needs to know the martianCount. We could endow class Martian with martianCount as an instance variable. If we do this, then every Martian will have *a separate copy* of the instance variable, and every time we create a new Martian, we'll have to update the instance variable martianCount in every Martian object. This wastes space with the redundant copies, wastes time in updating the separate copies and is error prone. Instead, we declare martianCount to be static, making martianCount classwide data. Every Martian can see the martianCount as if it were an instance variable of class Martian, but only one copy of the static martianCount is maintained. This saves space. We save time by having the Martian constructor increment the static martianCount—there's only one copy, so we do not have to increment separate copies for each Martian object.

Software Engineering Observation F.4

Use a static variable when all objects of a class must use the same copy of the variable.

Static variables have class scope. We can access a class's public static members through a reference to any object of the class, or by qualifying the member name with the class name and a dot (.), as in Math.random(). A class's private static class members can be accessed by client code only through methods of the class. Actually, *static class members exist even when no objects of the class exist*—they're available as soon as the class is loaded into memory at execution time. To access a public static member when no objects of the class exist (and even when they do), prefix the class name and a dot (.) to the static member, as in Math.PI. To access a private static member when no objects of the class exist, provide a public static method and call it by qualifying its name with the class name and a dot.

Software Engineering Observation F.5

Static class variables and methods exist, and can be used, even if no objects of that class have been instantiated.

A static method cannot access non-static class members, because a static method can be called even when no objects of the class have been instantiated. For the same reason, the this reference cannot be used in a static method. The this reference must refer to a specific object of the class, and when a static method is called, there might not be any objects of its class in memory.

Common Programming Error F.5

A compilation error occurs if a static method calls an instance (non-static) method in the same class by using only the method name. Similarly, a compilation error occurs if a static method attempts to access an instance variable in the same class by using only the variable name.

Common Programming Error F.6

Referring to this in a static method is a compilation error.

Tracking the Number of Employee Objects That Have Been Created

Our next program declares two classes—Employee (Fig. F.12) and EmployeeTest (Fig. F.13). Class Employee declares private static variable count (Fig. F.12, line 9) and public static method getCount (lines 36–39). The static variable count is initialized to zero in line 9. If a static variable is not initialized, the compiler assigns it a default value—in this case 0, the default value for type int. Variable count maintains a count of the number of objects of class Employee that have been created so far.

```
1  // Fig. F.12: Employee.java
2  // Static variable used to maintain a count of the number of
3  // Employee objects in memory.
4
5  public class Employee
6  {
7     private String firstName;
8     private String lastName;
9     private static int count = 0; // number of Employees created
10
11    // initialize Employee, add 1 to static count and
12    // output String indicating that constructor was called
13    public Employee( String first, String last )
14    {
```

Fig. F.12 | static variable used to maintain a count of the number of Employee objects in memory. (Part 1 of 2.)

```
15          firstName = first;
16          lastName = last;
17
18          ++count;  // increment static count of employees
19          System.out.printf( "Employee constructor: %s %s; count = %d\n",
20              firstName, lastName, count );
21       } // end Employee constructor
22
23       // get first name
24       public String getFirstName()
25       {
26          return firstName;
27       } // end method getFirstName
28
29       // get last name
30       public String getLastName()
31       {
32          return lastName;
33       } // end method getLastName
34
35       // static method to get static count value
36       public static int getCount()
37       {
38          return count;
39       } // end method getCount
40    } // end class Employee
```

Fig. F.12 | `static` variable used to maintain a count of the number of `Employee` objects in memory. (Part 2 of 2.)

When `Employee` objects exist, variable `count` can be used in any method of an `Employee` object—this example increments `count` in the constructor (line 18). The `public static` method `getCount` (lines 36–39) returns the number of `Employee` objects that have been created so far. When no objects of class `Employee` exist, client code can access variable `count` by calling method `getCount` via the class name, as in `Employee.getCount()`. When objects exist, method `getCount` can also be called via any reference to an `Employee` object.

Good Programming Practice F.1
Invoke every static *method by using the class name and a dot (.) to emphasize that the method being called is a* static *method.*

`EmployeeTest` method main (Fig. F.13) instantiates two `Employee` objects (lines 13–14). When each `Employee` object's constructor is invoked, lines 15–16 of Fig. F.12 assign the `Employee`'s first name and last name to instance variables `firstName` and `lastName`. These two statements do *not* make copies of the original `String` arguments. Actually, `String` objects in Java are **immutable**—they cannot be modified after they're created. Therefore, it's safe to have many references to one `String` object. This is not normally the case for objects of most other classes in Java. If `String` objects are immutable, you might wonder why we're able to use operators + and += to concatenate `String` objects. String-concatenation operations actually result in a *new* `Strings` object containing the concatenated values. The original `String` objects are not modified.

When main has finished using the two Employee objects, the references e1 and e2 are set to null at lines 31–32 (Fig. F.13). At this point, references e1 and e2 no longer refer to the objects that were instantiated in lines 13–14. The objects become "eligible for garbage collection" because there are no more references to them in the program.

```java
1   // Fig. F.13: EmployeeTest.java
2   // static member demonstration.
3
4   public class EmployeeTest
5   {
6      public static void main( String[] args )
7      {
8         // show that count is 0 before creating Employees
9         System.out.printf( "Employees before instantiation: %d\n",
10           Employee.getCount() );
11
12        // create two Employees; count should be 2
13        Employee e1 = new Employee( "Susan", "Baker" );
14        Employee e2 = new Employee( "Bob", "Blue" );
15
16        // show that count is 2 after creating two Employees
17        System.out.println( "\nEmployees after instantiation: " );
18        System.out.printf( "via e1.getCount(): %d\n", e1.getCount() );
19        System.out.printf( "via e2.getCount(): %d\n", e2.getCount() );
20        System.out.printf( "via Employee.getCount(): %d\n",
21           Employee.getCount() );
22
23        // get names of Employees
24        System.out.printf( "\nEmployee 1: %s %s\nEmployee 2: %s %s\n",
25           e1.getFirstName(), e1.getLastName(),
26           e2.getFirstName(), e2.getLastName() );
27
28        // in this example, there is only one reference to each Employee,
29        // so the following two statements indicate that these objects
30        // are eligible for garbage collection
31        e1 = null;
32        e2 = null;
33     } // end main
34  } // end class EmployeeTest
```

```
Employees before instantiation: 0
Employee constructor: Susan Baker; count = 1
Employee constructor: Bob Blue; count = 2

Employees after instantiation:
via e1.getCount(): 2
via e2.getCount(): 2
via Employee.getCount(): 2

Employee 1: Susan Baker
Employee 2: Bob Blue
```

Fig. F.13 | static member demonstration.

Eventually, the garbage collector might reclaim the memory for these objects (or the operating system will reclaim the memory when the program terminates). The JVM does not guarantee when, or even whether, the garbage collector will execute. When it does, it's possible that no objects or only a subset of the eligible objects will be collected.

F.11 final Instance Variables

The **principle of least privilege** is fundamental to good software engineering. In the context of an application, it states that code should be granted only the amount of privilege and access that it needs to accomplish its designated task, but no more. This makes your programs more robust by preventing code from accidentally (or maliciously) modifying variable values and calling methods that should not be accessible.

Let's see how this principle applies to instance variables. Some of them need to be modifiable and some do not. You can use the keyword final to specify that a variable is not modifiable (i.e., it's a constant) and that any attempt to modify it is an error. For example,

```
private final int INCREMENT;
```

declares a final (constant) instance variable INCREMENT of type int. Such variables can be initialized when they're declared. If they are not, they *must* be initialized in every constructor of the class. Initializing constants in constructors enables each object of the class to have a different value for the constant. If a final variable is not initialized in its declaration or in every constructor, a compilation error occurs.

Software Engineering Observation F.6

Declaring an instance variable as final helps enforce the principle of least privilege. If an instance variable should not be modified, declare it to be final to prevent modification.

Common Programming Error F.7

Attempting to modify a final instance variable after it's initialized is a compilation error.

Error-Prevention Tip F.2

Attempts to modify a final instance variable are caught at compilation time rather than causing execution-time errors. It's always preferable to get bugs out at compilation time, if possible, rather than allow them to slip through to execution time (where experience has found that repair is often many times more expensive).

Software Engineering Observation F.7

A final field should also be declared static if it's initialized in its declaration to a value that's the same for all objects of the class. After this initialization, its value can never change. Therefore, we don't need a separate copy of the field for every object of the class. Making the field static enables all objects of the class to share the final field.

F.12 Packages

We've seen in almost every example in the text that classes from preexisting libraries, such as the Java API, can be imported into a Java program. Each class in the Java API belongs to a package that contains a group of related classes. These packages are defined once, but can be imported into many programs. As applications become more complex, packages help you manage the complexity of application components. Packages also facilitate software reuse by enabling programs to *import* classes from other packages (as we've done in most examples), rather than *copying* the classes into each program that uses them. Another benefit of packages is that they provide a convention for unique class names, which helps prevent class-name conflicts.

F.13 Package Access

If no access modifier (public, protected or private) is specified for a method or variable when it's declared in a class, the method or variable has **package access**. In a program that consists of one class declaration, this has no specific effect. However, if a program uses multiple classes from the same package (i.e., a group of related classes), these classes can access each other's package-access members directly through references to objects of the appropriate classes, or in the case of static members through the class name. Package access is rarely used.

F.14 Wrap-Up

In this appendix, we presented additional class concepts. The Time class case study presented a complete class declaration consisting of private data, overloaded public constructors for initialization flexibility, *set* and *get* methods for manipulating the class's data, and methods that returned String representations of a Time object in two different formats. You also learned that every class can declare a toString method that returns a String representation of an object of the class and that method toString can be called implicitly whenever an object of a class appears in the code where a String is expected.

You learned that the this reference is used implicitly in a class's non-static methods to access the class's instance variables and other non-static methods. You also saw explicit uses of the this reference to access the class's members (including shadowed fields) and how to use keyword this in a constructor to call another constructor of the class.

We discussed the differences between default constructors provided by the compiler and no-argument constructors provided by the programmer. You learned that a class can have references to objects of other classes as members—a concept known as composition. You saw the enum class type and learned how it can be used to create a set of constants for use in a program. You learned about Java's garbage-collection capability and how it (unpredictably) reclaims the memory of objects that are no longer used. We explained the motivation for static fields in a class and demonstrated how to declare and use static fields and methods in your own classes. You also learned how to declare and initialize final variables.

You learned that fields declared without an access modifier are given package access by default and that classes in the same package can access the package-access members of other classes in the package.

In the next appendix, you'll learn about two important aspects of object-oriented programming in Java—inheritance and polymorphism. You'll see that all classes in Java are related directly or indirectly to the class called Object. You'll also begin to understand how the relationships between classes enable you to build more powerful applications.

Self-Review Exercise

F.1 Fill in the blanks in each of the following statements:

a) The `public` methods of a class are also known as the class's _____ or _____.

b) `String` class `static` method _____ is similar to method `System.out.printf`, but returns a formatted `String` rather than displaying a `String` in a command window.

c) If a method contains a local variable with the same name as one of its class's fields, the local variable _____ the field in that method's scope.

d) Keyword _____ specifies that a variable is not modifiable.

e) The _____ states that code should be granted only the amount of privilege and access that it needs to accomplish its designated task.

f) If a class declares constructors, the compiler will not create a(n) _____.

g) An object's _____ method is called implicitly when an object appears in code where a `String` is needed.

h) For every enum, the compiler generates a `static` method called _____ that returns an array of the enum's constants in the order in which they were declared.

i) Composition is sometimes referred to as a(n) _____ relationship.

j) A(n) _____ declaration contains a comma-separated list of constants.

k) A(n) _____ variable represents classwide information that's shared by all the objects of the class.

Answers to Self-Review Exercise

F.1 a) public services, public interface. b) `format`. c) shadows. d) `final`. e) principle of least privilege. f) default constructor. g) `toString`. h) `values`. i) *has-a*. j) enum. k) `static`.

Exercises

F.2 *(Rectangle Class)* Create a class `Rectangle` with attributes `length` and `width`, each of which defaults to 1. Provide methods that calculate the rectangle's perimeter and area. Provide *set* and *get* methods for both `length` and `width`. The *set* methods should verify that `length` and `width` are each floating-point numbers larger than 0.0 and less than 20.0. Write a program to test class `Rectangle`.

F.3 *(Savings Account Class)* Create class `SavingsAccount`. Use a `static` variable `annualInterestRate` to store the annual interest rate for all account holders. Each object of the class should contain a `private` instance variable `savingsBalance` indicating the amount the saver currently has on deposit. Provide method `calculateMonthlyInterest` to calculate the monthly interest by multiplying the `savingsBalance` by `annualInterestRate` divided by 12—this interest should be added to `savingsBalance`. Provide a `static` method `modifyInterestRate` that sets the `annualInterestRate` to a new value. Write a program to test class `SavingsAccount`. Instantiate two `savingsAccount` objects, `saver1` and `saver2`, with balances of $2000.00 and $3000.00, respectively. Set `annualInterestRate` to 4%, then calculate the monthly interest for each of 12 months and print the new balances for both savers. Next, set the `annualInterestRate` to 5%, calculate the next month's interest and print the new balances for both savers.

F.4 *(Enhancing Class Time2)* Modify class `Time2` of Fig. F.5 to include a `tick` method that increments the time stored in a `Time2` object by one second. Provide method `incrementMinute` to increment the minute by one and method `incrementHour` to increment the hour by one. Write a program that tests the `tick` method, the `incrementMinute` method and the `incrementHour` method to ensure that they work correctly. Be sure to test the following cases:

a) incrementing into the next minute,

b) incrementing into the next hour and

c) incrementing into the next day (i.e., 11:59:59 PM to 12:00:00 AM).

F.5   Write an enum type TrafficLight, whose constants (RED, GREEN, YELLOW) take one parameter—the duration of the light. Write a program to test the TrafficLight enum so that it displays the enum constants and their durations.

F.6   *(Date Class)* Create class Date with the following capabilities:

a) Output the date in multiple formats, such as

```
MM/DD/YYYY
June 14, 1992
DDD YYYY
```

b) Use overloaded constructors to create Date objects initialized with dates of the formats in part (a). In the first case the constructor should receive three integer values. In the second case it should receive a String and two integer values. In the third case it should receive two integer values, the first of which represents the day number in the year. [*Hint:* To convert the String representation of the month to a numeric value, compare Strings using the equals method. For example, if s1 and s2 are Strings, the method call s1.equals(s2) returns true if the Strings are identical and otherwise returns false.]

F.7   *(Huge Integer Class)* Create a class HugeInteger which uses a 40-element array of digits to store integers as large as 40 digits each. Provide methods parse, toString, add and subtract. Method parse should receive a String, extract each digit using method charAt and place the integer equivalent of each digit into the integer array. For comparing HugeInteger objects, provide the following methods: isEqualTo, isNotEqualTo, isGreaterThan, isLessThan, isGreaterThanOrEqualTo and isLessThanOrEqualTo. Each of these so-called *predicate methods* (that is, methods that test a condition and return true or false) returns true if the relationship holds between the two HugeInteger objects and returns false if the relationship does not hold. Provide a predicate method isZero. If you feel ambitious, also provide methods multiply, divide and remainder. [*Note:* Primitive boolean values can be output as the word "true" or the word "false" with format specifier %b.]

F.8   *(Tic-Tac-Toe)* Create a class TicTacToe that will enable you to write a program to play Tic-Tac-Toe. The class contains a private 3-by-3 two-dimensional array. Use an enumeration to represent the value in each cell of the array. The enumeration's constants should be named X, O and EMPTY (for a position that does not contain an X or an O). The constructor should initialize the board elements to EMPTY. Allow two human players. Wherever the first player moves, place an X in the specified square, and place an O wherever the second player moves. Each move must be to an empty square. After each move, determine whether the game has been won and whether it's a draw. If you feel ambitious, modify your program so that the computer makes the moves for one of the players. Also, allow the player to specify whether he or she wants to go first or second. If you feel exceptionally ambitious, develop a program that will play three-dimensional Tic-Tac-Toe on a 4-by-4-by-4 board [*Note:* This is an extremely challenging project!].

G

Object-Oriented Programming: Inheritance and Polymorphism

Objectives

In this appendix you'll:

- Learn how inheritance promotes software resuse.

- Understand the relationships between superclasses and subclasses.

- Use keyword **extends** to effect inheritance.

- Use **protected** to give subclass methods access to superclass members.

- Reference superclass members with **super**.

- Learn the methods of class **Object**.

- Learn the concept of polymorphism.

- Use overridden methods to effect polymorphism.

- Distinguish between abstract and concrete classes.

- Declare abstract methods to create abstract classes.

- Learn how polymorphism makes systems extensible and maintainable.

- Determine an object's type at execution time.

- Declare and implement interfaces.

G.I   Introduction to Inheritance

The first part of this appendix continues our discussion of object-oriented programming (OOP) by introducing one of its primary capabilities—**inheritance**, which is a form of software reuse in which a new class is created by absorbing an existing class's members and embellishing them with new or modified capabilities. With inheritance, you can save time during program development by basing new classes on existing proven and debugged high-quality software. The existing class is called the **superclass**, and the new class is the **subclass.** Each subclass can become a superclass for future subclasses.

A subclass can add its own fields and methods. Therefore, a subclass is *more specific* than its superclass and represents a more specialized group of objects. The subclass exhibits the behaviors of its superclass and can modify those behaviors so that they operate appropriately for the subclass. This is why inheritance is sometimes referred to as **specialization**.

The **direct superclass** is the superclass from which the subclass explicitly inherits. An **indirect superclass** is any class above the direct superclass in the **class hierarchy**, which defines the inheritance relationships between classes. In Java, the class hierarchy begins with class `Object` (in package `java.lang`), which *every* class in Java directly or indirectly **extends** (or "inherits from"). Section G.5 lists the methods of class `Object` that are inherited by all other Java classes.

We distinguish between the *is-a* **relationship** and the *has-a* **relationship.** *Is-a* represents inheritance. In an *is-a* relationship, *an object of a subclass can also be treated as an object of its superclass*—e.g., a car *is a* vehicle. By contrast, *has-a* represents composition (see Appendix F). In a *has-a* relationship, *an object contains as members references to other objects*—e.g., a car *has a* steering wheel (and a car object has a reference to a steering-wheel object).

Later in the appendix, we discuss the concept of polymorphism, which simplifies programming with objects from the same class hierarchy. You'll see that polymorphism also makes it possible to extend systems to add new capabilities. Finally, we discuss interfaces, which are useful for assigning common functionality to possibly *unrelated* classes. This allows objects of unrelated classes to be processed polymorphically—objects of classes that implement the same interface can respond to all of the interface method calls in their own customized way.

G.2 Superclasses and Subclasses

Often, an object of one class *is an* object of another class as well. Figure G.1 lists several examples of superclasses and subclasses—superclasses tend to be "more general" and subclasses "more specific." For example, a CarLoan *is a* Loan as are HomeImprovementLoans and MortgageLoans. Thus, in Java, class CarLoan can be said to inherit from class Loan. In this context, class Loan is a superclass and class CarLoan is a subclass. A CarLoan *is a* specific type of Loan, but it's incorrect to claim that every Loan *is a* CarLoan—the Loan could be any type of loan.

Superclass	Subclasses
Student	GraduateStudent, UndergraduateStudent
Shape	Circle, Triangle, Rectangle, Sphere, Cube
Loan	CarLoan, HomeImprovementLoan, MortgageLoan
Employee	Faculty, Staff
BankAccount	CheckingAccount, SavingsAccount

Fig. G.1 | Inheritance examples.

Because every subclass object *is an* object of its superclass, and one superclass can have many subclasses, the set of objects represented by a superclass is often larger than the set of objects represented by any of its subclasses. For example, the superclass Vehicle represents all vehicles, including cars, trucks, boats, bicycles and so on. By contrast, subclass Car represents a smaller, more specific subset of vehicles.

University Community Member Hierarchy
Inheritance relationships form treelike hierarchical structures. A superclass exists in a hierarchical relationship with its subclasses. Let's develop a sample class hierarchy (Fig. G.2), also called an **inheritance hierarchy**. A university community has thousands of members, including employees, students and alumni. Employees are either faculty or staff members.

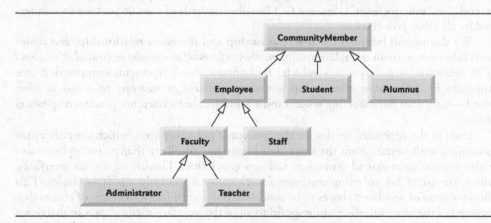

Fig. G.2 | Inheritance hierarchy for university CommunityMembers.

Faculty members are either administrators (e.g., deans and department chairpersons) or teachers. The hierarchy could contain many other classes. For example, students can be graduate or undergraduate students. Undergraduate students can be freshmen, sophomores, juniors or seniors.

Each arrow in the hierarchy represents an *is-a* relationship. As we follow the arrows upward in this class hierarchy, we can state, for instance, that "an Employee *is a* CommunityMember" and "a Teacher *is a* Faculty member." CommunityMember is the direct superclass of Employee, Student and Alumnus and is an indirect superclass of all the other classes in the diagram. Starting from the bottom, you can follow the arrows and apply the *is-a* relationship up to the topmost superclass. For example, an Administrator *is a* Faculty member, *is an* Employee, *is a* CommunityMember and, of course, *is an* Object.

Shape Hierarchy

Now consider the Shape inheritance hierarchy in Fig. G.3. This hierarchy begins with superclass Shape, which is extended by subclasses TwoDimensionalShape and ThreeDimensionalShape—Shapes are either TwoDimensionalShapes or ThreeDimensionalShapes. The third level of this hierarchy contains specific types of TwoDimensionalShapes and ThreeDimensionalShapes. As in Fig. G.2, we can follow the arrows from the bottom of the diagram to the topmost superclass in this class hierarchy to identify several *is-a* relationships. For instance, a Triangle *is a* TwoDimensionalShape and *is a* Shape, while a Sphere *is a* ThreeDimensionalShape and *is a* Shape. This hierarchy could contain many other classes. For example, ellipses and trapezoids are TwoDimensionalShapes.

It's possible to treat superclass objects and subclass objects similarly—their commonalities are expressed in the superclass's members. Objects of all classes that extend a common superclass can be treated as objects of that superclass—such objects have an *is-a* relationship with the superclass. Later in this appendix, we consider many examples that take advantage of the *is-a* relationship.

A subclass can customize methods that it inherits from its superclass. To do this, the subclass **overrides** (redefines) the superclass method with an appropriate implementation, as we'll see often in this appendix's code examples.

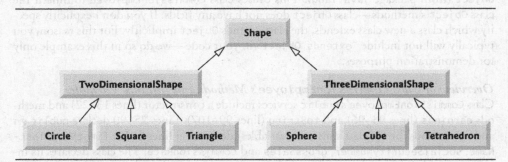

Fig. G.3 | Inheritance hierarchy for Shapes.

G.3 **protected** Members

In this section, we introduce access modifier **protected**. Using protected access offers an intermediate level of access between public and private. A superclass's protected members can be accessed by the class, by members of its subclasses and by members of other classes in the same package—protected members also have package access.

All public and protected superclass members retain their original access modifier when they become members of the subclass—public members of the superclass become public members of the subclass, and protected members of the superclass become protected members of the subclass. A superclass's private members are *not* accessible outside the class itself. Rather, they're *hidden* in its subclasses and can be accessed only through the public or protected methods inherited from the superclass.

Subclass methods can refer to public and protected members inherited from the superclass simply by using the member names. When a subclass method overrides an inherited superclass method, the *superclass* method can be accessed from the *subclass* by preceding the superclass method name with keyword **super** and a dot (.) separator. We discuss accessing overridden members of the superclass in Section G.4.

G.4 Relationship between Superclasses and Subclasses

We now use an inheritance hierarchy containing types of employees in a company's payroll application to discuss the relationship between a superclass and its subclass. In this company, commission employees (who will be represented as objects of a superclass) are paid a percentage of their sales, while base-salaried commission employees (who will be represented as objects of a subclass) receive a base salary *plus* a percentage of their sales.

We create an example that sets the CommissionEmployee instance variables to private to enforce good software engineering. Then we show how the BasePlusCommissionEmployee subclass can use CommissionEmployee's public methods to manipulate (in a controlled manner) the private instance variables inherited from CommissionEmployee.

G.4.1 Creating and Using a CommissionEmployee Class

We begin by declaring class CommissionEmployee (Fig. G.4). Line 4 begins the class declaration and indicates that class CommissionEmployee **extends** (i.e., inherits from) class **Object** (from package java.lang). This causes class CommissionEmployee to inherit the class Object's methods—class Object does not have any fields. If you don't explicitly specify which class a new class extends, the class extends Object implicitly. For this reason, you typically will not include "extends Object" in your code—we do so in this example only for demonstration purposes.

*Overview of Class **CommissionEmployee**'s Methods and Instance Variables*
Class CommissionEmployee's public services include a constructor (lines 13–22) and methods earnings (lines 93–96) and toString (lines 99–107). Lines 25–90 declare public *get* and *set* methods for the class's instance variables (declared in lines 6–10) firstName, lastName, socialSecurityNumber, grossSales and commissionRate. The class declares its instance variables as private, so objects of other classes cannot directly access these variables. Declaring instance variables as private and providing *get* and *set* methods to manipulate and validate them helps enforce good software engineering. Methods setGrossSales and setCommissionRate, for example, validate their arguments before assigning the values to instance variables grossSales and commissionRate, respectively. In a real-world, business-critical application, we'd also perform validation in the class's other *set* methods.

```java
1   // Fig. G.4: CommissionEmployee.java
2   // CommissionEmployee class represents an employee paid a
3   // percentage of gross sales.
4   public class CommissionEmployee extends Object
5   {
6      private String firstName;
7      private String lastName;
8      private String socialSecurityNumber;
9      private double grossSales; // gross weekly sales
10     private double commissionRate; // commission percentage
11
12     // five-argument constructor
13     public CommissionEmployee( String first, String last, String ssn,
14        double sales, double rate )
15     {
16        // implicit call to Object constructor occurs here
17        firstName = first;
18        lastName = last;
19        socialSecurityNumber = ssn;
20        setGrossSales( sales ); // validate and store gross sales
21        setCommissionRate( rate ); // validate and store commission rate
22     } // end five-argument CommissionEmployee constructor
23
24     // set first name
25     public void setFirstName( String first )
26     {
27        firstName = first; // should validate
28     } // end method setFirstName
29
30     // return first name
31     public String getFirstName()
32     {
33        return firstName;
34     } // end method getFirstName
35
36     // set last name
37     public void setLastName( String last )
38     {
39        lastName = last; // should validate
40     } // end method setLastName
41
42     // return last name
43     public String getLastName()
44     {
45        return lastName;
46     } // end method getLastName
47
48     // set social security number
49     public void setSocialSecurityNumber( String ssn )
50     {
51        socialSecurityNumber = ssn; // should validate
52     } // end method setSocialSecurityNumber
```

Fig. G.4 | CommissionEmployee class represents an employee paid a percentage of gross sales. (Part 1 of 3.)

```
53
54    // return social security number
55    public String getSocialSecurityNumber()
56    {
57       return socialSecurityNumber;
58    } // end method getSocialSecurityNumber
59
60    // set gross sales amount
61    public void setGrossSales( double sales )
62    {
63       if ( sales >= 0.0 )
64          grossSales = sales;
65       else
66          throw new IllegalArgumentException(
67             "Gross sales must be >= 0.0" );
68    } // end method setGrossSales
69
70    // return gross sales amount
71    public double getGrossSales()
72    {
73       return grossSales;
74    } // end method getGrossSales
75
76    // set commission rate
77    public void setCommissionRate( double rate )
78    {
79       if ( rate > 0.0 && rate < 1.0 )
80          commissionRate = rate;
81       else
82          throw new IllegalArgumentException(
83             "Commission rate must be > 0.0 and < 1.0" );
84    } // end method setCommissionRate
85
86    // return commission rate
87    public double getCommissionRate()
88    {
89       return commissionRate;
90    } // end method getCommissionRate
91
92    // calculate earnings
93    public double earnings()
94    {
95       return commissionRate * grossSales;
96    } // end method earnings
97
98    // return String representation of CommissionEmployee object
99    @Override // indicates that this method overrides a superclass method
100   public String toString()
101   {
102      return String.format( "%s: %s %s\n%s: %s\n%s: %.2f\n%s: %.2f",
103         "commission employee", firstName, lastName,
104         "social security number", socialSecurityNumber,
```

Fig. G.4 | CommissionEmployee class represents an employee paid a percentage of gross sales. (Part 2 of 3.)

```
105              "gross sales", grossSales,
106              "commission rate", commissionRate );
107    } // end method toString
108 } // end class CommissionEmployee
```

Fig. G.4 | CommissionEmployee class represents an employee paid a percentage of gross sales. (Part 3 of 3.)

Class CommissionEmployee's Constructor

Constructors are *not* inherited, so class CommissionEmployee does not inherit class Object's constructor. However, a superclass's constructors are still available to subclasses. In fact, *the first task of any subclass constructor is to call its direct superclass's constructor*, either explicitly or implicitly (if no constructor call is specified), to ensure that the instance variables inherited from the superclass are initialized properly. In this example, class CommissionEmployee's constructor calls class Object's constructor implicitly. The syntax for calling a superclass constructor explicitly is discussed in Section G.4.3. If the code does not include an explicit call to the superclass constructor, Java *implicitly* calls the superclass's default or no-argument constructor. The comment in line 16 of Fig. G.4 indicates where the implicit call to the superclass Object's default constructor is made (you do not write the code for this call). Object's default (empty) constructor does nothing. Even if a class does not have constructors, the default constructor that the compiler implicitly declares for the class will call the superclass's default or no-argument constructor.

After the implicit call to Object's constructor, lines 17–21 of CommissionEmployee's constructor assign values to the class's instance variables. We do not validate the values of arguments first, last and ssn before assigning them to the corresponding instance variables. We could validate the first and last names—perhaps to ensure that they're of a reasonable length. Similarly, a social security number could be validated using regular expressions to ensure that it contains nine digits, with or without dashes (e.g., 123-45-6789 or 123456789).

Class CommissionEmployee's earnings Method

Method earnings (lines 93–96) calculates a CommissionEmployee's earnings. Line 95 multiplies the commissionRate by the grossSales and returns the result.

Class CommissionEmployee's toString Method and the @Override Annotation

Method toString (lines 99–107) is special—it's one of the methods that *every* class inherits directly or indirectly from class Object (summarized in Section G.5). Method toString returns a String representing an object. It's called implicitly whenever an object must be converted to a String representation, such as when an object is output by printf or output by String method format via the %s format specifier. Class Object's toString method returns a String that includes the name of the object's class. It's primarily a placeholder that can be overridden by a subclass to specify an appropriate String representation of the data in a subclass object. Method toString of class CommissionEmployee overrides (redefines) class Object's toString method. When invoked, CommissionEmployee's toString method uses String method format to return a String containing information about the CommissionEmployee. To override a superclass method, a subclass must declare a method with the same signature (method name, number of parameters, parameter types and order of parameter types) as the superclass method—Object's toString method takes no parameters, so CommissionEmployee declares toString with no parameters.

Line 99 uses the **@Override annotation** to indicate that method toString should override a superclass method. Annotations have several purposes. For example, when you attempt to override a superclass method, common errors include naming the subclass method incorrectly, or using the wrong number or types of parameters in the parameter list. Each of these problems creates an *unintentional overload* of the superclass method. If you then attempt to call the method on a subclass object, the superclass's version is invoked and the subclass version is ignored—potentially leading to subtle logic errors. When the compiler encounters a method declared with @Override, it compares the method's signature with the superclass's method signatures. If there isn't an exact match, the compiler issues an error message, such as "method does not override or implement a method from a supertype." This indicates that you've accidentally overloaded a superclass method. You can then fix your method's signature so that it matches one in the superclass.

In web applications and web services, annotations can also add complex support code to your classes to simplify the development process and can be used by servers to configure certain aspects of web applications.

> ### Common Programming Error G.1
> *It's a syntax error to override a method with a more restricted access modifier—a* public *method of the superclass cannot become a* protected *or* private *method in the subclass; a* protected *method of the superclass cannot become a* private *method in the subclass. Doing so would break the* is-a *relationship in which it's required that all subclass objects be able to respond to method calls that are made to* public *methods declared in the superclass. If a* public *method, for example, could be overridden as a* protected *or* private *method, the subclass objects would not be able to respond to the same method calls as superclass objects. Once a method is declared* public *in a superclass, the method remains* public *for all that class's direct and indirect subclasses.*

Class CommissionEmployeeTest
Figure G.5 tests class CommissionEmployee. Lines 9–10 instantiate a CommissionEmployee object and invoke CommissionEmployee's constructor (lines 13–22 of Fig. G.4) to initialize it with "Sue" as the first name, "Jones" as the last name, "222-22-2222" as the social security number, 10000 as the gross sales amount and .06 as the commission rate. Lines 15–24 use CommissionEmployee's *get* methods to retrieve the object's instance-variable values for output. Lines 26–27 invoke the object's methods setGrossSales and setCommissionRate to change the values of instance variables grossSales and commissionRate. Lines 29–30 output the String representation of the updated CommissionEmployee. When an object is output using the %s format specifier, the object's toString method is invoked implicitly to obtain the object's String representation. [*Note:* Early in this appendix, we do not use the earnings methods of our classes—they're used extensively in the polymorphism part of the appendix.]

```
1   // Fig. G.5: CommissionEmployeeTest.java
2   // CommissionEmployee class test program.
3
```

Fig. G.5 | CommissionEmployee class test program. (Part 1 of 2.)

```
 4   public class CommissionEmployeeTest
 5   {
 6      public static void main( String[] args )
 7      {
 8         // instantiate CommissionEmployee object
 9         CommissionEmployee employee = new CommissionEmployee(
10            "Sue", "Jones", "222-22-2222", 10000, .06 );
11
12         // get commission employee data
13         System.out.println(
14            "Employee information obtained by get methods: \n" );
15         System.out.printf( "%s %s\n", "First name is",
16            employee.getFirstName() );
17         System.out.printf( "%s %s\n", "Last name is",
18            employee.getLastName() );
19         System.out.printf( "%s %s\n", "Social security number is",
20            employee.getSocialSecurityNumber() );
21         System.out.printf( "%s %.2f\n", "Gross sales is",
22            employee.getGrossSales() );
23         System.out.printf( "%s %.2f\n", "Commission rate is",
24            employee.getCommissionRate() );
25
26         employee.setGrossSales( 500 ); // set gross sales
27         employee.setCommissionRate( .1 ); // set commission rate
28
29         System.out.printf( "\n%s:\n\n%s\n",
30            "Updated employee information obtained by toString", employee );
31      } // end main
32   } // end class CommissionEmployeeTest
```

```
Employee information obtained by get methods:

First name is Sue
Last name is Jones
Social security number is 222-22-2222
Gross sales is 10000.00
Commission rate is 0.06

Updated employee information obtained by toString:

commission employee: Sue Jones
social security number: 222-22-2222
gross sales: 500.00
commission rate: 0.10
```

Fig. G.5 | CommissionEmployee class test program. (Part 2 of 2.)

G.4.2 Creating and Using a BasePlusCommissionEmployee Class

We now discuss the second part of our introduction to inheritance by declaring and testing (a completely new and independent) class BasePlusCommissionEmployee (Fig. G.6), which contains a first name, last name, social security number, gross sales amount, commission rate *and* base salary. Class BasePlusCommissionEmployee's public services include a BasePlusCommissionEmployee constructor (lines 15–25) and methods earnings (lines 112–115) and toString (lines 118–127). Lines 28–109 declare public *get* and *set* methods for the class's private instance variables (declared in lines 7–12) firstName, lastName, socialSecurityNumber, grossSales, commissionRate *and* baseSalary. These variables and methods encapsulate all the necessary features of a base-salaried commission employee. Note the *similarity* between this class and class CommissionEmployee (Fig. G.4)—in this example, we'll not yet exploit that similarity.

```java
1   // Fig. G.6: BasePlusCommissionEmployee.java
2   // BasePlusCommissionEmployee class represents an employee who receives
3   // a base salary in addition to a commission.
4
5   public class BasePlusCommissionEmployee
6   {
7      private String firstName;
8      private String lastName;
9      private String socialSecurityNumber;
10     private double grossSales; // gross weekly sales
11     private double commissionRate; // commission percentage
12     private double baseSalary; // base salary per week
13
14     // six-argument constructor
15     public BasePlusCommissionEmployee( String first, String last,
16        String ssn, double sales, double rate, double salary )
17     {
18        // implicit call to Object constructor occurs here
19        firstName = first;
20        lastName = last;
21        socialSecurityNumber = ssn;
22        setGrossSales( sales ); // validate and store gross sales
23        setCommissionRate( rate ); // validate and store commission rate
24        setBaseSalary( salary ); // validate and store base salary
25     } // end six-argument BasePlusCommissionEmployee constructor
26
27     // set first name
28     public void setFirstName( String first )
29     {
30        firstName = first; // should validate
31     } // end method setFirstName
32
33     // return first name
34     public String getFirstName()
35     {
36        return firstName;
37     } // end method getFirstName
38
39     // set last name
40     public void setLastName( String last )
41     {
42        lastName = last; // should validate
43     } // end method setLastName
```

Fig. G.6 | BasePlusCommissionEmployee class represents an employee who receives a base salary in addition to a commission. (Part 1 of 3.)

```
44
45       // return last name
46       public String getLastName()
47       {
48          return lastName;
49       } // end method getLastName
50
51       // set social security number
52       public void setSocialSecurityNumber( String ssn )
53       {
54          socialSecurityNumber = ssn; // should validate
55       } // end method setSocialSecurityNumber
56
57       // return social security number
58       public String getSocialSecurityNumber()
59       {
60          return socialSecurityNumber;
61       } // end method getSocialSecurityNumber
62
63       // set gross sales amount
64       public void setGrossSales( double sales )
65       {
66          if ( sales >= 0.0 )
67             grossSales = sales;
68          else
69             throw new IllegalArgumentException(
70                "Gross sales must be >= 0.0" );
71       } // end method setGrossSales
72
73       // return gross sales amount
74       public double getGrossSales()
75       {
76          return grossSales;
77       } // end method getGrossSales
78
79       // set commission rate
80       public void setCommissionRate( double rate )
81       {
82          if ( rate > 0.0 && rate < 1.0 )
83             commissionRate = rate;
84          else
85             throw new IllegalArgumentException(
86                "Commission rate must be > 0.0 and < 1.0" );
87       } // end method setCommissionRate
88
89       // return commission rate
90       public double getCommissionRate()
91       {
92          return commissionRate;
93       } // end method getCommissionRate
```

Fig. G.6 | BasePlusCommissionEmployee class represents an employee who receives a base salary in addition to a commission. (Part 2 of 3.)

```
 94
 95      // set base salary
 96      public void setBaseSalary( double salary )
 97      {
 98         if ( salary >= 0.0 )
 99            baseSalary = salary;
100         else
101            throw new IllegalArgumentException(
102               "Base salary must be >= 0.0" );
103      } // end method setBaseSalary
104
105      // return base salary
106      public double getBaseSalary()
107      {
108         return baseSalary;
109      } // end method getBaseSalary
110
111      // calculate earnings
112      public double earnings()
113      {
114         return baseSalary + ( commissionRate * grossSales );
115      } // end method earnings
116
117      // return String representation of BasePlusCommissionEmployee
118      @Override // indicates that this method overrides a superclass method
119      public String toString()
120      {
121         return String.format(
122            "%s: %s %s\n%s: %s\n%s: %.2f\n%s: %.2f\n%s: %.2f",
123            "base-salaried commission employee", firstName, lastName,
124            "social security number", socialSecurityNumber,
125            "gross sales", grossSales, "commission rate", commissionRate,
126            "base salary", baseSalary );
127      } // end method toString
128   } // end class BasePlusCommissionEmployee
```

Fig. G.6 | BasePlusCommissionEmployee class represents an employee who receives a base salary in addition to a commission. (Part 3 of 3.)

Class BasePlusCommissionEmployee does not specify "extends Object" in line 5, so the class implicitly extends Object. Also, like class CommissionEmployee's constructor (lines 13–22 of Fig. G.4), class BasePlusCommissionEmployee's constructor invokes class Object's default constructor implicitly, as noted in the comment in line 18.

Class BasePlusCommissionEmployee's earnings method (lines 112–115) returns the result of adding the BasePlusCommissionEmployee's base salary to the product of the commission rate and the employee's gross sales.

Class BasePlusCommissionEmployee overrides Object method toString to return a String containing the BasePlusCommissionEmployee's information. Once again, we use format specifier %.2f to format the gross sales, commission rate and base salary with two digits of precision to the right of the decimal point (line 122).

Testing Class BasePlusCommissionEmployee
Figure G.7 tests class BasePlusCommissionEmployee. Lines 9–11 create a BasePlusCommissionEmployee object and pass "Bob", "Lewis", "333-33-3333", 5000, .04 and 300 to the constructor as the first name, last name, social security number, gross sales, commission rate and base salary, respectively. Lines 16–27 use BasePlusCommissionEmployee's *get* methods to retrieve the values of the object's instance variables for output. Line 29 invokes the object's setBaseSalary method to change the base salary. Method setBaseSalary (Fig. G.6, lines 96–103) ensures that instance variable baseSalary is not assigned a negative value. Lines 31–33 of Fig. G.7 invoke method toString explicitly to get the object's String representation.

Notes on Class BasePlusCommissionEmployee
Much of class BasePlusCommissionEmployee's code (Fig. G.6) is similar, or identical, to that of class CommissionEmployee (Fig. G.4). For example, private instance variables

```
1   // Fig. G.7: BasePlusCommissionEmployeeTest.java
2   // BasePlusCommissionEmployee test program.
3
4   public class BasePlusCommissionEmployeeTest
5   {
6      public static void main( String[] args )
7      {
8         // instantiate BasePlusCommissionEmployee object
9         BasePlusCommissionEmployee employee =
10           new BasePlusCommissionEmployee(
11           "Bob", "Lewis", "333-33-3333", 5000, .04, 300 );
12
13        // get base-salaried commission employee data
14        System.out.println(
15           "Employee information obtained by get methods: \n" );
16        System.out.printf( "%s %s\n", "First name is",
17           employee.getFirstName() );
18        System.out.printf( "%s %s\n", "Last name is",
19           employee.getLastName() );
20        System.out.printf( "%s %s\n", "Social security number is",
21           employee.getSocialSecurityNumber() );
22        System.out.printf( "%s %.2f\n", "Gross sales is",
23           employee.getGrossSales() );
24        System.out.printf( "%s %.2f\n", "Commission rate is",
25           employee.getCommissionRate() );
26        System.out.printf( "%s %.2f\n", "Base salary is",
27           employee.getBaseSalary() );
28
29        employee.setBaseSalary( 1000 ); // set base salary
30
31        System.out.printf( "\n%s:\n\n%s\n",
32           "Updated employee information obtained by toString",
33           employee.toString() );
34     } // end main
35  } // end class BasePlusCommissionEmployeeTest
```

Fig. G.7 | BasePlusCommissionEmployee test program. (Part 1 of 2.)

```
Employee information obtained by get methods:

First name is Bob
Last name is Lewis
Social security number is 333-33-3333
Gross sales is 5000.00
Commission rate is 0.04
Base salary is 300.00

Updated employee information obtained by toString:

base-salaried commission employee: Bob Lewis
social security number: 333-33-3333
gross sales: 5000.00
commission rate: 0.04
base salary: 1000.00
```

Fig. G.7 | BasePlusCommissionEmployee test program. (Part 2 of 2.)

firstName and lastName and methods setFirstName, getFirstName, setLastName and getLastName are identical to those of class CommissionEmployee. The classes also both contain private instance variables socialSecurityNumber, commissionRate and grossSales, and corresponding *get* and *set* methods. In addition, the BasePlusCommissionEmployee constructor is almost identical to that of class CommissionEmployee, except that BasePlusCommissionEmployee's constructor also sets the baseSalary. The other additions to class BasePlusCommissionEmployee are private instance variable baseSalary and methods setBaseSalary and getBaseSalary. Class BasePlusCommissionEmployee's toString method is nearly identical to that of class CommissionEmployee except that it also outputs instance variable baseSalary with two digits of precision to the right of the decimal point.

We literally *copied* code from class CommissionEmployee and *pasted* it into class BasePlusCommissionEmployee, then modified class BasePlusCommissionEmployee to include a base salary and methods that manipulate the base salary. This *"copy-and-paste" approach* is often error prone and time consuming. Worse yet, it spreads copies of the same code throughout a system, creating a code-maintenance nightmare. Is there a way to "absorb" the instance variables and methods of one class in a way that makes them part of other classes *without duplicating code*? Next we answer this question, using a more elegant approach to building classes that emphasizes the benefits of inheritance.

> **Software Engineering Observation G.1**
>
> *With inheritance, the* common *instance variables and methods of all the classes in the hierarchy are declared in a superclass. When changes are made for these common features in the superclass—subclasses then inherit the changes. Without inheritance, changes would need to be made to* all *the source-code files that contain a* copy *of the code in question.*

G.4.3 Creating a CommissionEmployee–BasePlusCommissionEmployee Inheritance Hierarchy

Now we redeclare class BasePlusCommissionEmployee (Fig. G.8) to *extend* class CommissionEmployee (Fig. G.4). A BasePlusCommissionEmployee object *is a* CommissionEmployee, because inheritance passes on class CommissionEmployee's capabilities. Class BasePlus-CommissionEmployee also has instance variable baseSalary (Fig. G.8, line 6).

Keyword extends (line 4) indicates inheritance. BasePlusCommissionEmployee *inherits* CommissionEmployee's instance variables and methods, but only the superclass's public and protected members are directly accessible in the subclass. The CommissionEmployee constructor is *not* inherited. So, the public BasePlusCommissionEmployee services include its constructor (lines 9–16), public methods inherited from CommissionEmployee, and methods setBaseSalary (lines 19–26), getBaseSalary (lines 29–32), earnings (lines 35–40) and toString (lines 43–53). Methods earnings and toString *override* the corresponding methods in class CommissionEmployee because their superclass versions do not properly calculate a BasePlusCommissionEmployee's earnings or return an appropriate String representation.

```java
1   // Fig. G.8: BasePlusCommissionEmployee.java
2   // private superclass members cannot be accessed in a subclass.
3
4   public class BasePlusCommissionEmployee extends CommissionEmployee
5   {
6      private double baseSalary; // base salary per week
7
8      // six-argument constructor
9      public BasePlusCommissionEmployee( String first, String last,
10        String ssn, double sales, double rate, double salary )
11     {
12        // explicit call to superclass CommissionEmployee constructor
13        super( first, last, ssn, sales, rate );
14
15        setBaseSalary( salary ); // validate and store base salary
16     } // end six-argument BasePlusCommissionEmployee constructor
17
18     // set base salary
19     public void setBaseSalary( double salary )
20     {
21        if ( salary >= 0.0 )
22           baseSalary = salary;
23        else
24           throw new IllegalArgumentException(
25              "Base salary must be >= 0.0" );
26     } // end method setBaseSalary
27
28     // return base salary
29     public double getBaseSalary()
30     {
31        return baseSalary;
32     } // end method getBaseSalary
33
34     // calculate earnings
35     @Override // indicates that this method overrides a superclass method
36     public double earnings()
37     {
38        // not allowed: commissionRate and grossSales private in superclass
39        return baseSalary + ( commissionRate * grossSales );
40     } // end method earnings
```

Fig. G.8 | private superclass members cannot be accessed in a subclass. (Part 1 of 2.)

```
41
42      // return String representation of BasePlusCommissionEmployee
43      @Override // indicates that this method overrides a superclass method
44      public String toString()
45      {
46          // not allowed: attempts to access private superclass members
47          return String.format(
48              "%s: %s %s\n%s: %s\n%s: %.2f\n%s: %.2f\n%s: %.2f",
49              "base-salaried commission employee", firstName, lastName,
50              "social security number", socialSecurityNumber,
51              "gross sales", grossSales, "commission rate", commissionRate,
52              "base salary", baseSalary );
53      } // end method toString
54  } // end class BasePlusCommissionEmployee
```

```
BasePlusCommissionEmployee.java:39: commissionRate has private access in
CommissionEmployee
      return baseSalary + ( commissionRate * grossSales );
                            ^
BasePlusCommissionEmployee.java:39: grossSales has private access in
CommissionEmployee
      return baseSalary + ( commissionRate * grossSales );
                                             ^
BasePlusCommissionEmployee.java:49: firstName has private access in
CommissionEmployee
          "base-salaried commission employee", firstName, lastName,
                                                ^
BasePlusCommissionEmployee.java:49: lastName has private access in
CommissionEmployee
          "base-salaried commission employee", firstName, lastName,
                                                           ^
BasePlusCommissionEmployee.java:50: socialSecurityNumber has private access
in CommissionEmployee
          "social security number", socialSecurityNumber,
                                    ^
BasePlusCommissionEmployee.java:51: grossSales has private access in
CommissionEmployee
          "gross sales", grossSales, "commission rate", commissionRate,
                         ^
BasePlusCommissionEmployee.java:51: commissionRate has private access in
CommissionEmployee
          "gross sales", grossSales, "commission rate", commissionRate,
                                                        ^
7 errors
```

Fig. G.8 | private superclass members cannot be accessed in a subclass. (Part 2 of 2.)

A Subclass's Constructor Must Call Its Superclass's Constructor

Each subclass constructor must implicitly or explicitly call its superclass constructor to initialize the instance variables inherited from the superclass. Line 13 in BasePlusCommissionEmployee's six-argument constructor (lines 9–16) explicitly calls class CommissionEmployee's five-argument constructor (declared at lines 13–22 of Fig. G.4) to initialize the superclass portion of a BasePlusCommissionEmployee object (i.e., variables firstName, lastName, socialSecurityNumber, grossSales and commissionRate). We do this by using the **superclass constructor call syntax**—keyword super, followed by a set of parentheses containing the superclass constructor arguments. The arguments first, last, ssn, sales and rate are used to initialize superclass members firstName, lastName, socialSecurityNumber, grossSales and commissionRate, respectively. If BasePlusCommissionEmployee's constructor did not invoke the superclass's constructor explicitly, Java would attempt to invoke the superclass's no-argument or default constructor. Class CommissionEmployee does not have such a constructor, so the compiler would issue an error. The explicit superclass constructor call in line 13 of Fig. G.8 must be the *first* statement in the subclass constructor's body. When a superclass contains a no-argument constructor, you can use super() to call that constructor explicitly, but this is rarely done.

BasePlusCommissionEmployee Method Earnings
The compiler generates errors for line 39 because superclass CommissionEmployee's instance variables commissionRate and grossSales are private—subclass BasePlusCommissionEmployee's methods are not allowed to access superclass CommissionEmployee's private instance variables. We highlighted the erroneous code. The compiler issues additional errors at lines 49–51 of BasePlusCommissionEmployee's toString method for the same reason. The errors in BasePlusCommissionEmployee could have been prevented by using the *get* methods inherited from class CommissionEmployee. For example, line 39 could have used getCommissionRate and getGrossSales to access CommissionEmployee's private instance variables commissionRate and grossSales, respectively. Lines 49–51 also could have used appropriate *get* methods to retrieve the values of the superclass's instance variables.

G.4.4 CommissionEmployee–BasePlusCommissionEmployee Inheritance Hierarchy Using protected Instance Variables
To enable class BasePlusCommissionEmployee to directly access superclass instance variables firstName, lastName, socialSecurityNumber, grossSales and commissionRate, we can declare those members as protected in the superclass. As we discussed in Section G.3, a superclass's protected members are accessible by all subclasses of that superclass. In the new CommissionEmployee class, we modified only lines 6–10 of Fig. G.4 to declare the instance variables with the protected access modifier as follows:

```
protected String firstName;
protected String lastName;
protected String socialSecurityNumber;
protected double grossSales; // gross weekly sales
protected double commissionRate; // commission percentage
```

The rest of the class declaration (which is not shown here) is identical to that of Fig. G.4.

We could have declared CommissionEmployee's instance variables public to enable subclass BasePlusCommissionEmployee to access them. However, declaring public instance variables is poor software engineering because it allows unrestricted access to the these variables, greatly increasing the chance of errors. With protected instance variables, the subclass gets access to the instance variables, but classes that are not subclasses and classes that are not in the same package cannot access these variables directly—recall that protected class members are also visible to other classes in the same package.

Class *BasePlusCommissionEmployee*

Class BasePlusCommissionEmployee (Fig. G.9) extends the new version of class CommissionEmployee with protected instance variables. BasePlusCommissionEmployee objects inherit CommissionEmployee's protected instance variables firstName, lastName, socialSecurityNumber, grossSales and commissionRate—all these variables are now protected members of BasePlusCommissionEmployee. As a result, the compiler does not generate errors when compiling line 37 of method earnings and lines 46–48 of method toString. If another class extends this version of class BasePlusCommissionEmployee, the new subclass also can access the protected members.

```
1   // Fig. G.9: BasePlusCommissionEmployee.java
2   // BasePlusCommissionEmployee inherits protected instance
3   // variables from CommissionEmployee.
4
5   public class BasePlusCommissionEmployee extends CommissionEmployee
6   {
7      private double baseSalary; // base salary per week
8
9      // six-argument constructor
10     public BasePlusCommissionEmployee( String first, String last,
11        String ssn, double sales, double rate, double salary )
12     {
13        super( first, last, ssn, sales, rate );
14        setBaseSalary( salary ); // validate and store base salary
15     } // end six-argument BasePlusCommissionEmployee constructor
16
17     // set base salary
18     public void setBaseSalary( double salary )
19     {
20        if ( salary >= 0.0 )
21           baseSalary = salary;
22        else
23           throw new IllegalArgumentException(
24              "Base salary must be >= 0.0" );
25     } // end method setBaseSalary
26
27     // return base salary
28     public double getBaseSalary()
29     {
30        return baseSalary;
31     } // end method getBaseSalary
32
33     // calculate earnings
34     @Override // indicates that this method overrides a superclass method
35     public double earnings()
36     {
37        return baseSalary + ( commissionRate * grossSales );
38     } // end method earnings
39
```

Fig. G.9 | BasePlusCommissionEmployee inherits protected instance variables from CommissionEmployee. (Part 1 of 2.)

```
40       // return String representation of BasePlusCommissionEmployee
41       @Override // indicates that this method overrides a superclass method
42       public String toString()
43       {
44          return String.format(
45             "%s: %s %s\n%s: %s\n%s: %.2f\n%s: %.2f\n%s: %.2f",
46             "base-salaried commission employee", firstName, lastName,
47             "social security number", socialSecurityNumber,
48             "gross sales", grossSales, "commission rate", commissionRate,
49             "base salary", baseSalary );
50       } // end method toString
51    } // end class BasePlusCommissionEmployee
```

Fig. G.9 | BasePlusCommissionEmployee inherits protected instance variables from CommissionEmployee. (Part 2 of 2.)

When you create a BasePlusCommissionEmployee object, it contains all instance variables declared in the class hierarchy to that point—i.e., those from classes Object, CommissionEmployee and BasePlusCommissionEmployee. Class BasePlusCommissionEmployee does not inherit class CommissionEmployee's constructor. However, class BasePlusCommissionEmployee's six-argument constructor (lines 10–15) calls class CommissionEmployee's five-argument constructor *explicitly* to initialize the instance variables that BasePlusCommissionEmployee inherited from class CommissionEmployee. Similarly, class CommissionEmployee's constructor *implicitly* calls class Object's constructor. BasePlusCommissionEmployee's constructor must do this *explicitly* because CommissionEmployee does *not* provide a no-argument constructor that could be invoked implicitly.

Testing Class *BasePlusCommissionEmployee*
The BasePlusCommissionEmployeeTest class for this example is identical to that of Fig. G.7 and produces the same output, so we do not show it here. Although the version of class BasePlusCommissionEmployee in Fig. G.6 does not use inheritance and the version in Fig. G.9 does, *both classes provide the same functionality*. The source code in Fig. G.9 (51 lines) is considerably shorter than that in Fig. G.6 (128 lines), because most of BasePlusCommissionEmployee's functionality is now inherited from CommissionEmployee—there's now only one copy of the CommissionEmployee functionality. This makes the code easier to maintain, modify and debug, because the code related to a commission employee exists only in class CommissionEmployee.

Notes on Using *protected* Instance Variables
In this example, we declared superclass instance variables as protected so that subclasses could access them. Inheriting protected instance variables slightly increases performance, because we can directly access the variables in the subclass without incurring the overhead of a *set* or *get* method call. In most cases, however, it's better to use private instance variables to encourage proper software engineering, and leave code optimization issues to the compiler. Your code will be easier to maintain, modify and debug.

Using protected instance variables creates several potential problems. First, the subclass object can set an inherited variable's value directly without using a *set* method. Therefore, a subclass object can assign an invalid value to the variable, possibly leaving the object in an inconsistent state. For example, if we were to declare CommissionEmployee's instance variable grossSales as protected, a subclass object (e.g., BasePlusCommissionEmployee) could then assign a negative value to grossSales. Another problem with using protected instance variables is that subclass methods are more likely to be written so that they depend on the superclass's data implementation. In practice, subclasses should depend only on the superclass services (i.e., non-private methods) and not on the superclass data implementation. With protected instance variables in the superclass, we may need to modify all the subclasses of the superclass if the superclass implementation changes. For example, if for some reason we were to change the names of instance variables firstName and lastName to first and last, then we would have to do so for all occurrences in which a subclass directly references superclass instance variables firstName and lastName. In such a case, the software is said to be **fragile** or **brittle**, because a small change in the superclass can "break" subclass implementation. You should be able to change the superclass implementation while still providing the same services to the subclasses. Of course, if the superclass services change, we must reimplement our subclasses. A third problem is that a class's protected members are visible to all classes in the same package as the class containing the protected members—this is not always desirable.

Software Engineering Observation G.2

Use the protected access modifier when a superclass should provide a method only to its subclasses and other classes in the same package, but not to other clients.

Software Engineering Observation G.3

Declaring superclass instance variables private (as opposed to protected) enables the superclass implementation of these instance variables to change without affecting subclass implementations.

Error-Prevention Tip G.1

When possible, do not include protected instance variables in a superclass. Instead, include non-private methods that access private instance variables. This will help ensure that objects of the class maintain consistent states.

G.4.5 CommissionEmployee–BasePlusCommissionEmployee Inheritance Hierarchy Using private Instance Variables

Let's reexamine our hierarchy once more, this time using good software engineering practices. Class CommissionEmployee (Fig. G.10) declares instance variables firstName, lastName, socialSecurityNumber, grossSales and commissionRate as *private* (lines 6–10) and provides public methods setFirstName, getFirstName, setLastName, getLastName, setSocialSecurityNumber, getSocialSecurityNumber, setGrossSales, getGrossSales, setCommissionRate, getCommissionRate, earnings and toString for manipulating these values. Methods earnings (lines 93–96) and toString (lines 99–107) use the class's *get* methods to obtain the values of its instance variables. If we decide to change the instance-variable names, the earnings and toString declarations will not require modification—only the bodies of the *get* and *set* methods that directly manipulate the instance variables will need to change. These changes occur solely within the superclass—no changes to the subclass are needed. *Localizing the effects of changes* like this is a good software engineering practice.

```java
1   // Fig. G.10: CommissionEmployee.java
2   // CommissionEmployee class uses methods to manipulate its
3   // private instance variables.
4   public class CommissionEmployee
5   {
6      private String firstName;
7      private String lastName;
8      private String socialSecurityNumber;
9      private double grossSales; // gross weekly sales
10     private double commissionRate; // commission percentage
11
12     // five-argument constructor
13     public CommissionEmployee( String first, String last, String ssn,
14        double sales, double rate )
15     {
16        // implicit call to Object constructor occurs here
17        firstName = first;
18        lastName = last;
19        socialSecurityNumber = ssn;
20        setGrossSales( sales ); // validate and store gross sales
21        setCommissionRate( rate ); // validate and store commission rate
22     } // end five-argument CommissionEmployee constructor
23
24     // set first name
25     public void setFirstName( String first )
26     {
27        firstName = first; // should validate
28     } // end method setFirstName
29
30     // return first name
31     public String getFirstName()
32     {
33        return firstName;
34     } // end method getFirstName
35
36     // set last name
37     public void setLastName( String last )
38     {
39        la5stName = last; // should validate
40     } // end method setLastName
41
42     // return last name
43     public String getLastName()
44     {
45        return lastName;
46     } // end method getLastName
47
48     // set social security number
49     public void setSocialSecurityNumber( String ssn )
50     {
51        socialSecurityNumber = ssn; // should validate
52     } // end method setSocialSecurityNumber
```

Fig. G.10 | CommissionEmployee class uses methods to manipulate its private instance variables. (Part 1 of 3.)

```
53
54      // return social security number
55      public String getSocialSecurityNumber()
56      {
57         return socialSecurityNumber;
58      } // end method getSocialSecurityNumber
59
60      // set gross sales amount
61      public void setGrossSales( double sales )
62      {
63         if ( sales >= 0.0 )
64            grossSales = sales;
65         else
66            throw new IllegalArgumentException(
67               "Gross sales must be >= 0.0" );
68      } // end method setGrossSales
69
70      // return gross sales amount
71      public double getGrossSales()
72      {
73         return grossSales;
74      } // end method getGrossSales
75
76      // set commission rate
77      public void setCommissionRate( double rate )
78      {
79         if ( rate > 0.0 && rate < 1.0 )
80            commissionRate = rate;
81         else
82            throw new IllegalArgumentException(
83               "Commission rate must be > 0.0 and < 1.0" );
84      } // end method setCommissionRate
85
86      // return commission rate
87      public double getCommissionRate()
88      {
89         return commissionRate;
90      } // end method getCommissionRate
91
92      // calculate earnings
93      public double earnings()
94      {
95         return getCommissionRate() * getGrossSales();
96      } // end method earnings
97
98      // return String representation of CommissionEmployee object
99      @Override // indicates that this method overrides a superclass method
100     public String toString()
101     {
102        return String.format( "%s: %s %s\n%s: %s\n%s: %.2f\n%s: %.2f",
103           "commission employee", getFirstName(), getLastName(),
104           "social security number", getSocialSecurityNumber(),
```

Fig. G.10 | CommissionEmployee class uses methods to manipulate its private instance variables. (Part 2 of 3.)

```
105            "gross sales", getGrossSales(),
106            "commission rate", getCommissionRate() );
107    } // end method toString
108 } // end class CommissionEmployee
```

Fig. G.10 | CommissionEmployee class uses methods to manipulate its private instance variables. (Part 3 of 3.)

Subclass BasePlusCommissionEmployee (Fig. G.11) inherits CommissionEmployee's non-private methods and can access the private superclass members via those methods. Class BasePlusCommissionEmployee has several changes that distinguish it from Fig. G.9. Methods earnings (lines 35–39) and toString (lines 42–47) each invoke method get-BaseSalary to obtain the base salary value, rather than accessing baseSalary directly. If we decide to rename instance variable baseSalary, only the bodies of method setBase-Salary and getBaseSalary will need to change.

```
1  // Fig. G.11: BasePlusCommissionEmployee.java
2  // BasePlusCommissionEmployee class inherits from CommissionEmployee
3  // and accesses the superclass's private data via inherited
4  // public methods.
5
6  public class BasePlusCommissionEmployee extends CommissionEmployee
7  {
8     private double baseSalary; // base salary per week
9
10    // six-argument constructor
11    public BasePlusCommissionEmployee( String first, String last,
12       String ssn, double sales, double rate, double salary )
13    {
14       super( first, last, ssn, sales, rate );
15       setBaseSalary( salary ); // validate and store base salary
16    } // end six-argument BasePlusCommissionEmployee constructor
17
18    // set base salary
19    public void setBaseSalary( double salary )
20    {
21       if ( salary >= 0.0 )
22          baseSalary = salary;
23       else
24          throw new IllegalArgumentException(
25             "Base salary must be >= 0.0" );
26    } // end method setBaseSalary
27
28    // return base salary
29    public double getBaseSalary()
30    {
31       return baseSalary;
32    } // end method getBaseSalary
33
```

Fig. G.11 | BasePlusCommissionEmployee class inherits from CommissionEmployee and accesses the superclass's private data via inherited public methods. (Part 1 of 2.)

```
34     // calculate earnings
35     @Override // indicates that this method overrides a superclass method
36     public double earnings()
37     {
38        return getBaseSalary() + super.earnings();
39     } // end method earnings
40
41     // return String representation of BasePlusCommissionEmployee
42     @Override // indicates that this method overrides a superclass method
43     public String toString()
44     {
45        return String.format( "%s %s\n%s: %.2f", "base-salaried",
46           super.toString(), "base salary", getBaseSalary() );
47     } // end method toString
48  } // end class BasePlusCommissionEmployee
```

Fig. G.11 | BasePlusCommissionEmployee class inherits from CommissionEmployee and accesses the superclass's private data via inherited public methods. (Part 2 of 2.)

Class *BasePlusCommissionEmployee's earnings Method*

Method earnings (lines 35–39) overrides class CommissionEmployee's earnings method (Fig. G.10, lines 93–96) to calculate a base-salaried commission employee's earnings. The new version obtains the portion of the earnings based on commission alone by calling CommissionEmployee's earnings method with super.earnings() (line 38), then adds the base salary to this value to calculate the total earnings. Note the syntax used to invoke an overridden superclass method from a subclass—place the keyword super and a dot (.) separator before the superclass method name. This method invocation is a good software engineering practice—if a method performs all or some of the actions needed by another method, call that method rather than duplicate its code. By having BasePlusCommission-Employee's earnings method invoke CommissionEmployee's earnings method to calculate part of a BasePlusCommissionEmployee object's earnings, we *avoid duplicating the code* and *reduce code-maintenance problems*. If we did not use "super." then BasePlusCommissionEmployee's earnings method would *call itself* rather than the superclass version. This would result in a phenomenon called *infinite recursion*, which would eventually cause the method-call stack to overflow—a fatal runtime error.

Class *BasePlusCommissionEmployee's toString Method*

Similarly, BasePlusCommissionEmployee's toString method (Fig. G.11, lines 42–47) overrides class CommissionEmployee's toString method (Fig. G.10, lines 99–107) to return a String representation that's appropriate for a base-salaried commission employee. The new version creates part of a BasePlusCommissionEmployee object's String representation (i.e., the String "commission employee" and the values of class CommissionEmployee's private instance variables) by calling CommissionEmployee's toString method with the expression super.toString() (Fig. G.11, line 46). BasePlusCommissionEmployee's toString method then outputs the remainder of a BasePlusCommissionEmployee object's String representation (i.e., the value of class BasePlusCommissionEmployee's base salary).

Common Programming Error G.2

When a superclass method is overridden in a subclass, the subclass version often calls the superclass version to do a portion of the work. Failure to prefix the superclass method name with the keyword super and a dot (.) separator when calling the superclass's method causes the subclass method to call itself, potentially creating an error called infinite recursion. Recursion, used correctly, is a powerful capability.

Testing Class BasePlusCommissionEmployee

Class BasePlusCommissionEmployeeTest performs the same manipulations on a Base-PlusCommissionEmployee object as in Fig. G.7 and produces the same output, so we do not show it here. Although each BasePlusCommissionEmployee class you've seen behaves identically, the version in Fig. G.11 is the best engineered. By using inheritance and by calling methods that hide the data and ensure consistency, we've efficiently and effectively constructed a well-engineered class.

G.5 Class Object

As we discussed earlier in this appendix, all classes in Java inherit directly or indirectly from the Object class (package java.lang), so its 11 methods (some are overloaded) are inherited by all other classes. Figure G.12 summarizes Object's methods. We discuss several Object methods throughout this book (as indicated in Fig. G.12).

Method	Description
clone	This protected method, which takes no arguments and returns an Object reference, makes a copy of the object on which it's called. The default implementation performs a so-called **shallow copy**—instance-variable values in one object are copied into another object of the same type. For reference types, only the references are copied. A typical overridden clone method's implementation would perform a **deep copy** that creates a new object for each reference-type instance variable. Implementing clone correctly is difficult. For this reason, its use is discouraged. Many industry experts suggest that object serialization should be used instead. We introduce object serialization in Appendix J.
equals	This method compares two objects for equality and returns true if they're equal and false otherwise. The method takes any Object as an argument. When objects of a particular class must be compared for equality, the class should override method equals to compare the *contents* of the two objects. The default equals implementation uses operator == to determine whether two references *refer to the same object* in memory.
finalize	This protected method (introduced in Section F.9) is called by the garbage collector to perform termination housekeeping on an object just before the garbage collector reclaims the object's memory. Recall that it's unclear whether, or when, method finalize will be called. For this reason, most programmers should avoid method finalize.

Fig. G.12 | Object methods. (Part 1 of 2.)

Method	Description
getClass	Every object in Java knows its own type at execution time. Method get-Class returns an object of class Class (package java.lang) that contains information about the object's type, such as its class name (returned by Class method getName).
hashCode	Hashcodes are int values that are useful for high-speed storage and retrieval of information stored in a data structure that's known as a hashtable (discussed in Section J.9). This method is also called as part of class Object's default toString method implementation.
wait, notify, notifyAll	Methods notify, notifyAll and the three overloaded versions of wait are related to multithreading, which is discussed in Appendix J.
toString	This method (introduced in Section G.4.1) returns a String representation of an object. The default implementation of this method returns the package name and class name of the object's class followed by a hexadecimal representation of the value returned by the object's hashCode method.

Fig. G.12 | Object methods. (Part 2 of 2.)

Recall from Appendix E that arrays are objects. As a result, like all other objects, arrays inherit the members of class Object. Every array has an overridden clone method that copies the array. However, if the array stores references to objects, the objects are not copied—a *shallow copy is* performed.

G.6 Introduction to Polymorphism

We continue our study of object-oriented programming by explaining and demonstrating **polymorphism** with inheritance hierarchies. Polymorphism enables you to "program in the general" rather than "program in the specific." In particular, polymorphism enables you to write programs that process objects that share the same superclass (either directly or indirectly) as if they're all objects of the superclass; this can simplify programming.

Consider the following example of polymorphism. Suppose we create a program that simulates the movement of several types of animals for a biological study. Classes Fish, Frog and Bird represent the types of animals under investigation. Imagine that each class extends superclass Animal, which contains a method move and maintains an animal's current location as *x-y* coordinates. Each subclass implements method move. Our program maintains an Animal array containing references to objects of the various Animal subclasses. To simulate the animals' movements, the program sends each object the *same* message once per second—namely, move. Each specific type of Animal responds to a move message in its own way—a Fish might swim three feet, a Frog might jump five feet and a Bird might fly ten feet. Each object knows how to modify its *x-y* coordinates appropriately for its *specific* type of movement. Relying on each object to know how to "do the right thing" (i.e., do what is appropriate for that type of object) in response to the same method call is the key concept of polymorphism. The same message (in this case, move) sent to a variety of objects has "many forms" of results—hence the term polymorphism.

Programming in the Specific

Occasionally, when performing polymorphic processing, we need to program "in the specific." We'll demonstrate that a program can determine the type of an object at *execution time* and act on that object accordingly.

Interfaces

The appendix continues with an introduction to Java interfaces. An interface describes a set of methods that can be called on an object, but does *not* provide concrete implementations for all the methods. You can declare classes that **implement** (i.e., provide concrete implementations for the methods of) one or more interfaces. Each interface method must be declared in all the classes that explicitly implement the interface. Once a class implements an interface, all objects of that class have an *is-a* relationship with the interface type, and all objects of the class are guaranteed to provide the functionality described by the interface. This is true of all subclasses of that class as well.

Interfaces are particularly useful for assigning common functionality to possibly *unrelated* classes. This allows objects of unrelated classes to be processed polymorphically—objects of classes that implement the same interface can respond to all of the interface method calls. To demonstrate creating and using interfaces, we modify our payroll application to create a general accounts payable application that can calculate payments due for company employees and invoice amounts to be billed for purchased goods. As you'll see, interfaces enable polymorphic capabilities similar to those possible with inheritance.

G.7 Polymorphism: An Example

Space Objects in a Video Game

Suppose we design a video game that manipulates objects of classes Martian, Venusian, Plutonian, SpaceShip and LaserBeam. Imagine that each class inherits from the superclass SpaceObject, which contains method draw. Each subclass implements this method. A screen manager maintains a collection (e.g., a SpaceObject array) of references to objects of the various classes. To refresh the screen, the screen manager periodically sends each object the same message—namely, draw. However, each object responds its own way, based on its class. For example, a Martian object might draw itself in red with green eyes and the appropriate number of antennae. A SpaceShip object might draw itself as a bright silver flying saucer. A LaserBeam object might draw itself as a bright red beam across the screen. Again, the *same* message (in this case, draw) sent to a variety of objects has "many forms" of results.

A screen manager might use polymorphism to facilitate adding new classes to a system with minimal modifications to the system's code. Suppose that we want to add Mercurian objects to our video game. To do so, we'd build a class Mercurian that extends SpaceObject and provides its own draw method implementation. When Mercurian objects appear in the SpaceObject collection, the screen manager code *invokes method draw, exactly as it does for every other object in the collection, regardless of its type.* So the new Mercurian objects simply "plug right in" without any modification of the screen manager code by the programmer. Thus, without modifying the system (other than to build new classes and modify the code that creates new objects), you can use polymorphism to conveniently include additional types that were not envisioned when the system was created.

Software Engineering Observation G.4

Polymorphism enables you to deal in generalities and let the execution-time environment handle the specifics. You can command objects to behave in manners appropriate to those objects, without knowing their types (as long as the objects belong to the same inheritance hierarchy).

Software Engineering Observation G.5

Polymorphism promotes extensibility: Software that invokes polymorphic behavior is independent of the object types to which messages are sent. New object types that can respond to existing method calls can be incorporated into a system without modifying the base system. Only client code that instantiates new objects must be modified to accommodate new types.

G.8 Demonstrating Polymorphic Behavior

Section G.4 created a class hierarchy, in which class BasePlusCommissionEmployee inherited from CommissionEmployee. The examples in that section manipulated CommissionEmployee and BasePlusCommissionEmployee objects by using references to them to invoke their methods—we aimed superclass variables at superclass objects and subclass variables at subclass objects. These assignments are natural and straightforward—superclass variables are *intended* to refer to superclass objects, and subclass variables are *intended* to refer to subclass objects. However, as you'll soon see, other assignments are possible.

In the next example, we aim a *superclass* reference at *a subclass* object. We then show how invoking a method on a subclass object via a superclass reference invokes the *subclass* functionality—the type of the *referenced object*, not the type of the *variable*, determines which method is called. This example demonstrates that *an object of a subclass can be treated as an object of its superclass,* enabling various interesting manipulations. A program can create an array of superclass variables that refer to objects of many subclass types. This is allowed because each subclass object *is an* object of its superclass. For instance, we can assign the reference of a BasePlusCommissionEmployee object to a superclass CommissionEmployee variable, because a BasePlusCommissionEmployee *is a* CommissionEmployee—we can treat a BasePlusCommissionEmployee as a CommissionEmployee.

As you'll learn later in this appendix, you *cannot treat a superclass object as a subclass object,* because a superclass object is *not* an object of any of its subclasses. For example, we cannot assign the reference of a CommissionEmployee object to a subclass BasePlusCommissionEmployee variable, because a CommissionEmployee is *not* a BasePlusCommissionEmployee—a CommissionEmployee does *not* have a baseSalary instance variable and does *not* have methods setBaseSalary and getBaseSalary. The *is-a* relationship applies only *up the hierarchy* from a subclass to its direct and *indirect* superclasses, and *not* vice versa (i.e., *not down the hierarchy* from a superclass to its subclasses).

The Java compiler *does* allow the assignment of a superclass reference to a subclass variable if we explicitly *cast* the superclass reference to the subclass type—a technique we discuss in Section G.10. Why would we ever want to perform such an assignment? A superclass reference can be used to invoke only the methods declared in the superclass—attempting to invoke subclass-only methods through a superclass reference results in compilation errors. If a program needs to perform a subclass-specific operation on a subclass object referenced by a superclass variable, the program must first cast the superclass reference to a subclass reference through a technique known as **downcasting**. This enables the program to invoke subclass methods that are *not* in the superclass. We show a downcasting example in Section G.10.

The example in Fig. G.13 demonstrates three ways to use superclass and subclass variables to store references to superclass and subclass objects. The first two are straightforward—as in Section G.4, we assign a superclass reference to a superclass variable, and a subclass reference to a subclass variable. Then we demonstrate the relationship between subclasses and superclasses (i.e., the *is-a* relationship) by assigning a subclass reference to a superclass variable. This program uses classes CommissionEmployee and BasePlusCommissionEmployee from Fig. G.10 and Fig. G.11, respectively.

```java
 1  // Fig. G.13: PolymorphismTest.java
 2  // Assigning superclass and subclass references to superclass and
 3  // subclass variables.
 4
 5  public class PolymorphismTest
 6  {
 7     public static void main( String[] args )
 8     {
 9        // assign superclass reference to superclass variable
10        CommissionEmployee commissionEmployee = new CommissionEmployee(
11           "Sue", "Jones", "222-22-2222", 10000, .06 );
12
13        // assign subclass reference to subclass variable
14        BasePlusCommissionEmployee basePlusCommissionEmployee =
15           new BasePlusCommissionEmployee(
16           "Bob", "Lewis", "333-33-3333", 5000, .04, 300 );
17
18        // invoke toString on superclass object using superclass variable
19        System.out.printf( "%s %s:\n\n%s\n\n",
20           "Call CommissionEmployee's toString with superclass reference ",
21           "to superclass object", commissionEmployee.toString() );
22
23        // invoke toString on subclass object using subclass variable
24        System.out.printf( "%s %s:\n\n%s\n\n",
25           "Call BasePlusCommissionEmployee's toString with subclass",
26           "reference to subclass object",
27           basePlusCommissionEmployee.toString() );
28
29        // invoke toString on subclass object using superclass variable
30        CommissionEmployee commissionEmployee2 =
31           basePlusCommissionEmployee;
32        System.out.printf( "%s %s:\n\n%s\n",
33           "Call BasePlusCommissionEmployee's toString with superclass",
34           "reference to subclass object", commissionEmployee2.toString() );
35     } // end main
36  } // end class PolymorphismTest
```

Fig. G.13 | Assigning superclass and subclass references to superclass and subclass variables. (Part 1 of 2.)

```
Call CommissionEmployee's toString with superclass reference to superclass
object:

commission employee: Sue Jones
social security number: 222-22-2222
gross sales: 10000.00
commission rate: 0.06

Call BasePlusCommissionEmployee's toString with subclass reference to
subclass object:

base-salaried commission employee: Bob Lewis
social security number: 333-33-3333
gross sales: 5000.00
commission rate: 0.04
base salary: 300.00

Call BasePlusCommissionEmployee's toString with superclass reference to
subclass object:

base-salaried commission employee: Bob Lewis
social security number: 333-33-3333
gross sales: 5000.00
commission rate: 0.04
base salary: 300.00
```

Fig. G.13 | Assigning superclass and subclass references to superclass and subclass variables. (Part 2 of 2.)

In Fig. G.13, lines 10–11 create a CommissionEmployee object and assign its reference to a CommissionEmployee variable. Lines 14–16 create a BasePlusCommissionEmployee object and assign its reference to a BasePlusCommissionEmployee variable. These assignments are natural—for example, a CommissionEmployee variable's primary purpose is to hold a reference to a CommissionEmployee object. Lines 19–21 use commissionEmployee to invoke toString explicitly. Because commissionEmployee refers to a CommissionEmployee object, superclass CommissionEmployee's version of toString is called. Similarly, lines 24–27 use basePlusCommissionEmployee to invoke toString explicitly on the BasePlusCommissionEmployee object. This invokes subclass BasePlusCommissionEmployee's version of toString.

Lines 30–31 then assign the reference of subclass object basePlusCommissionEmployee to a superclass CommissionEmployee variable, which lines 32–34 use to invoke method toString. *When a superclass variable contains a reference to a subclass object, and that reference is used to call a method, the subclass version of the method is called.* Hence, commissionEmployee2.toString() in line 34 actually calls class BasePlusCommissionEmployee's toString method. The Java compiler allows this "crossover" because an object of a subclass *is an* object of its superclass (but not vice versa). When the compiler encounters a method call made through a variable, the compiler determines if the method can be called by checking the variable's class type. If that class contains the proper method declaration (or inherits one), the call is compiled. At execution time, the type of the object to which the variable refers determines the actual method to use. This process, called *dynamic binding*, is discussed in detail in Section G.10.

G.9 Abstract Classes and Methods

When we think of a class, we assume that programs will create objects of that type. Sometimes it's useful to declare classes—called **abstract classes**—for which you *never* intend to create objects. Because they're used only as superclasses in inheritance hierarchies, we refer to them as **abstract superclasses**. These classes cannot be used to instantiate objects, because, as we'll soon see, abstract classes are *incomplete*. Subclasses must declare the "missing pieces" to become "concrete" classes, from which you *can* instantiate objects. Otherwise, these subclasses, too, will be abstract. We demonstrate abstract classes in Section G.10.

Purpose of Abstract Classes

An abstract class's purpose is to provide an appropriate superclass from which other classes can inherit and thus share a common design. In the Shape hierarchy of Fig. G.3, for example, subclasses inherit the notion of what it means to be a Shape—perhaps common attributes such as location, color and borderThickness, and behaviors such as draw, move, resize and changeColor. Classes that can be used to instantiate objects are called **concrete classes**. Such classes provide implementations of *every* method they declare (some of the implementations can be inherited). For example, we could derive concrete classes Circle, Square and Triangle from abstract superclass TwoDimensionalShape. Similarly, we could derive concrete classes Sphere, Cube and Tetrahedron from abstract superclass ThreeDimensionalShape. Abstract superclasses are *too general* to create real objects—they specify only what is *common* among subclasses. We need to be more *specific* before we can create objects. For example, if you send the draw message to abstract class TwoDimensionalShape, the class knows that two-dimensional shapes should be *drawable*, but it does not know what *specific* shape to draw, so it cannot implement a real draw method. Concrete classes provide the *specifics* that make it reasonable to instantiate objects.

Not all hierarchies contain abstract classes. However, you'll often write client code that uses only abstract superclass types to reduce the client code's dependencies on a range of subclass types. For example, you can write a method with a parameter of an abstract superclass type. When called, such a method can receive an object of *any* concrete class that directly or indirectly extends the superclass specified as the parameter's type.

Abstract classes sometimes constitute several levels of a hierarchy. For example, the Shape hierarchy of Fig. G.3 begins with abstract class Shape. On the next level of the hierarchy are *abstract* classes TwoDimensionalShape and ThreeDimensionalShape. The next level of the hierarchy declares *concrete* classes for TwoDimensionalShapes (Circle, Square and Triangle) and for ThreeDimensionalShapes (Sphere, Cube and Tetrahedron).

Declaring an Abstract Class and Abstract Methods

You make a class abstract by declaring it with keyword **abstract**. An abstract class normally contains one or more **abstract methods**. An abstract method is one with keyword abstract in its declaration, as in

```
public abstract void draw(); // abstract method
```

Abstract methods do *not* provide implementations. A class that contains *any* abstract methods must be explicitly declared abstract even if that class contains some concrete (nonabstract) methods. Each concrete subclass of an abstract superclass also must provide concrete implementations of each of the superclass's abstract methods. Constructors and static methods cannot be declared abstract. Constructors are not inherited, so an abstract constructor could never be implemented. Though non-private static methods *are* inherited, they *cannot* be overridden. Since abstract methods are meant to be overridden so that they can process objects based on their types, it would not make sense to declare a static method as abstract.

> ### Software Engineering Observation G.6
>
> *An abstract class declares common attributes and behaviors (both abstract and concrete) of the various classes in a class hierarchy. An abstract class typically contains one or more abstract methods that subclasses must override if they are to be concrete. The instance variables and concrete methods of an abstract class are subject to the normal rules of inheritance.*

Using Abstract Classes to Declare Variables

Although we cannot instantiate objects of abstract superclasses, you'll soon see that we *can* use abstract superclasses to declare variables that can hold references to objects of any concrete class derived from those abstract superclasses. Programs typically use such variables to manipulate subclass objects polymorphically. You also can use abstract superclass names to invoke static methods declared in those abstract superclasses.

Consider another application of polymorphism. A drawing program needs to display many shapes, including types of new shapes that you'll add to the system after writing the drawing program. The drawing program might need to display shapes, such as Circles, Triangles, Rectangles or others, that derive from abstract class Shape. The drawing program uses Shape variables to manage the objects that are displayed. To draw any object in this inheritance hierarchy, the drawing program uses a superclass Shape variable containing a reference to the subclass object to invoke the object's draw method. This method is declared abstract in superclass Shape, so each concrete subclass *must* implement method draw in a manner *specific* to that shape—each object in the Shape inheritance hierarchy *knows how to draw itself*. The drawing program does not have to worry about the type of each object or whether the program has ever encountered objects of that type.

G.10 Case Study: Payroll System Using Polymorphism

This section reexamines the CommissionEmployee-BasePlusCommissionEmployee hierarchy that we explored throughout Section G.4. Now we use an abstract method and polymorphism to perform payroll calculations based on an enhanced employee inheritance hierarchy that meets the following requirements:

> *A company pays its employees on a weekly basis. The employees are of four types: Salaried employees are paid a fixed weekly salary regardless of the number of hours worked, hourly employees are paid by the hour and receive overtime pay (i.e., 1.5 times their hourly salary rate) for all hours worked in excess of 40 hours, commission employees are paid a percentage of their sales and base-salaried commission employees receive a base salary plus a percentage of their sales. For the current pay period, the company has decided to reward salaried-commission employees by adding 10% to their base salaries. The company wants to write an application that performs its payroll calculations polymorphically.*

We use abstract class Employee to represent the general concept of an employee. The classes that extend Employee are SalariedEmployee, CommissionEmployee and Hourly-

Employee. Class `BasePlusCommissionEmployee`—which extends `CommissionEmployee`—represents the last employee type. The UML class diagram in Fig. G.14 shows the inheritance hierarchy for our polymorphic employee-payroll application. Abstract class name `Employee` is italicized—a convention of the UML.

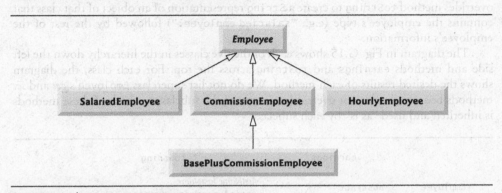

Fig. G.14 | `Employee` hierarchy UML class diagram.

Abstract superclass `Employee` declares the "interface" to the hierarchy—that is, the set of methods that a program can invoke on all `Employee` objects. We use the term "interface" here in a general sense to refer to the various ways programs can communicate with objects of any `Employee` subclass. Be careful not to confuse the general notion of an "interface" with the formal notion of a Java interface, the subject of Section G.12. Each employee, regardless of the way his or her earnings are calculated, has a first name, a last name and a social security number, so `private` instance variables `firstName`, `lastName` and `socialSecurityNumber` appear in abstract superclass `Employee`.

The following sections implement the `Employee` class hierarchy of Fig. G.14. The first section implements abstract superclass `Employee`. The next four sections each implement one of the concrete classes. The last section implements a test program that builds objects of all these classes and processes those objects polymorphically.

G.10.1 Abstract Superclass Employee

Class `Employee` (Fig. G.16) provides methods `earnings` and `toString`, in addition to the *get* and *set* methods that manipulate `Employee`'s instance variables. An `earnings` method certainly applies generically to all employees. But each earnings calculation depends on the employee's class. So we declare `earnings` as abstract in superclass `Employee` because a default implementation does not make sense for that method—there isn't enough information to determine what amount `earnings` should return. Each subclass overrides `earnings` with an appropriate implementation. To calculate an employee's earnings, the program assigns to a superclass `Employee` variable a reference to the employee's object, then invokes the `earnings` method on that variable. We maintain an array of `Employee` variables, each holding a reference to an `Employee` object. (Of course, there cannot be `Employee` objects, because `Employee` is an abstract class. Because of inheritance, however, all objects of all subclasses of `Employee` may nevertheless be thought of as `Employee` objects.) The program will iterate through the array and call method `earnings` for each `Employee` object. Java processes these method calls polymorphically. Declaring `earnings` as an abstract method in Employee enables the calls to earnings through Employee variables to compile and forces every direct concrete subclass of Employee to override earnings.

Method toString in class Employee returns a String containing the first name, last name and social security number of the employee. As we'll see, each subclass of Employee overrides method toString to create a String representation of an object of that class that contains the employee's type (e.g., "salaried employee:") followed by the rest of the employee's information.

The diagram in Fig. G.15 shows each of the five classes in the hierarchy down the left side and methods earnings and toString across the top. For each class, the diagram shows the desired results of each method. We do not list superclass Employee's *get* and *set* methods because they're not overridden in any of the subclasses—each of these methods is inherited and used "as is" by each subclass.

	earnings	toString
Employee	abstract	*firstName lastName* social security number: *SSN*
Salaried- Employee	weeklySalary	salaried employee: *firstName lastName* social security number: *SSN* weekly salary: *weeklySalary*

Hourly-
Employee
	if (hours <= 40)
	  wage * hours
	else if (hours > 40)
	{
	  40 * wage +
	  (hours - 40) *
	  wage * 1.5
	}
		hourly employee: *firstName lastName*
		social security number: *SSN*
		hourly wage: *wage*; hours worked: *hours*

Commission- Employee	commissionRate * grossSales	commission employee: *firstName lastName* social security number: *SSN* gross sales: *grossSales*; commission rate: *commissionRate*
BasePlus- Commission- Employee	(commissionRate * grossSales) + baseSalary	base salaried commission employee: *firstName lastName* social security number: *SSN* gross sales: *grossSales*; commission rate: *commissionRate*; base salary: *baseSalary*

Fig. G.15 | Polymorphic interface for the Employee hierarchy classes.

Let's consider class Employee's declaration (Fig. G.16). The class includes a constructor that takes the first name, last name and social security number as arguments (lines 11–16); *get* methods that return the first name, last name and social security number (lines 25–28, 37–40 and 49–52, respectively); *set* methods that set the first name, last name and social security number (lines 19–22, 31–34 and 43–46, respectively); method toString (lines 55–60), which returns the String representation of an Employee; and abstract method earnings (line 63), which will be implemented by each of the concrete subclasses. The Employee constructor does not validate its parameters in this example; normally, such validation should be provided.

```java
1   // Fig. G.16: Employee.java
2   // Employee abstract superclass.
3
4   public abstract class Employee
5   {
6       private String firstName;
7       private String lastName;
8       private String socialSecurityNumber;
9
10      // three-argument constructor
11      public Employee( String first, String last, String ssn )
12      {
13          firstName = first;
14          lastName = last;
15          socialSecurityNumber = ssn;s
16      } // end three-argument Employee constructor
17
18      // set first name
19      public void setFirstName( String first )
20      {
21          firstName = first; // should validate
22      } // end method setFirstName
23
24      // return first name
25      public String getFirstName()
26      {
27          return firstName;
28      } // end method getFirstName
29
30      // set last name
31      public void setLastName( String last )
32      {
33          lastName = last; // should validate
34      } // end method setLastName
35
36      // return last name
37      public String getLastName()
38      {
39          return lastName;
40      } // end method getLastName
41
42      // set social security number
43      public void setSocialSecurityNumber( String ssn )
44      {
45          socialSecurityNumber = ssn; // should validate
46      } // end method setSocialSecurityNumber
47
```

Fig. G.16 | Employee abstract superclass. (Part 1 of 2.)

```
48      // return social security number
49      public String getSocialSecurityNumber()
50      {
51          return socialSecurityNumber;
52      } // end method getSocialSecurityNumber
53
54      // return String representation of Employee object
55      @Override
56      public String toString()
57      {
58          return String.format( "%s %s\nsocial security number: %s",
59              getFirstName(), getLastName(), getSocialSecurityNumber() );
60      } // end method toString
61
62      // abstract method overridden by concrete subclasses
63      public abstract double earnings(); // no implementation here
64  } // end abstract class Employee
```

Fig. G.16 | Employee abstract superclass. (Part 2 of 2.)

Why did we decide to declare earnings as an abstract method? It simply does not make sense to provide an implementation of this method in class Employee. We cannot calculate the earnings for a *general* Employee—we first must know the *specific* type of Employee to determine the appropriate earnings calculation. By declaring this method abstract, we indicate that each concrete subclass *must* provide an appropriate earnings implementation and that a program will be able to use superclass Employee variables to invoke method earnings polymorphically for any type of Employee.

G.10.2 Concrete Subclass SalariedEmployee

Class SalariedEmployee (Fig. G.17) extends class Employee (line 4) and overrides abstract method earnings (lines 33–37), which makes SalariedEmployee a concrete class. The class includes a constructor (lines 9–14) that takes a first name, a last name, a social security number and a weekly salary as arguments; a *set* method to assign a new nonnegative value to instance variable weeklySalary (lines 17–24); a *get* method to return weeklySalary's value (lines 27–30); a method earnings (lines 33–37) to calculate a SalariedEmployee's earnings; and a method toString (lines 40–45), which returns a String including the employee's type, namely, "salaried employee: " followed by employee-specific information produced by superclass Employee's toString method and Salaried-Employee's getWeeklySalary method. Class SalariedEmployee's constructor passes the first name, last name and social security number to the Employee constructor (line 12) to initialize the private instance variables not inherited from the superclass. Method earnings overrides Employee's abstract method earnings to provide a concrete implementation that returns the SalariedEmployee's weekly salary. If we do not implement earnings, class SalariedEmployee must be declared abstract—otherwise, class SalariedEmployee will not compile. Of course, we want SalariedEmployee to be a concrete class in this example.

Method toString (lines 40–45) overrides Employee method toString. If class SalariedEmployee did not override toString, SalariedEmployee would have inherited the Employee version of toString. In that case, SalariedEmployee's toString method would

```
1   // Fig. G.17: SalariedEmployee.java
2   // SalariedEmployee concrete class extends abstract class Employee.
3
4   public class SalariedEmployee extends Employee
5   {
6       private double weeklySalary;
7
8       // four-argument constructor
9       public SalariedEmployee( String first, String last, String ssn,
10          double salary )
11      {
12          super( first, last, ssn ); // pass to Employee constructor
13          setWeeklySalary( salary ); // validate and store salary
14      } // end four-argument SalariedEmployee constructor
15
16      // set salary
17      public void setWeeklySalary( double salary )
18      {
19          if ( salary >= 0.0 )
20              baseSalary = salary;
21          else
22              throw new IllegalArgumentException(
23                  "Weekly salary must be >= 0.0" );
24      } // end method setWeeklySalary
25
26      // return salary
27      public double getWeeklySalary()
28      {
29          return weeklySalary;
30      } // end method getWeeklySalary
31
32      // calculate earnings; override abstract method earnings in Employee
33      @Override
34      public double earnings()
35      {
36          return getWeeklySalary();
37      } // end method earnings
38
39      // return String representation of SalariedEmployee object
40      @Override
41      public String toString()
42      {
43          return String.format( "salaried employee: %s\n%s: $%,.2f",
44              super.toString(), "weekly salary", getWeeklySalary() );
45      } // end method toString
46  } // end class SalariedEmployee
```

Fig. G.17 | SalariedEmployee concrete class extends abstract class Employee.

simply return the employee's full name and social security number, which does not adequately represent a SalariedEmployee. To produce a complete String representation of a SalariedEmployee, the subclass's toString method returns "salaried employee: " followed by the superclass Employee-specific information (i.e., first name, last name and social security number) obtained by invoking the superclass's toString method (line

44)—this is a nice example of code reuse. The String representation of a SalariedEmployee also contains the employee's weekly salary obtained by invoking the class's getWeeklySalary method.

G.10.3 Concrete Subclass HourlyEmployee

Class HourlyEmployee (Fig. G.18) also extends Employee (line 4). The class includes a constructor (lines 10–16) that takes as arguments a first name, a last name, a social security number, an hourly wage and the number of hours worked. Lines 19–26 and 35–42 declare *set* methods that assign new values to instance variables wage and hours, respectively. Method setWage (lines 19–26) ensures that wage is nonnegative, and method setHours (lines 35–42) ensures that hours is between 0 and 168 (the total number of hours in a week) inclusive. Class HourlyEmployee also includes *get* methods (lines 29–32 and 45–48) to return the values of wage and hours, respectively; a method earnings (lines 51–58) to calculate an HourlyEmployee's earnings; and a method toString (lines 61–67), which returns a String containing the employee's type ("hourly employee: ") and the employee-specific information. The HourlyEmployee constructor, like the SalariedEmployee constructor, passes the first name, last name and social security number to the superclass Employee constructor (line 13) to initialize the private instance variables. In addition, method toString calls superclass method toString (line 65) to obtain the Employee-specific information (i.e., first name, last name and social security number)—this is another nice example of code reuse.

```java
 1   // Fig. G.18: HourlyEmployee.java
 2   // HourlyEmployee class extends Employee.
 3
 4   public class HourlyEmployee extends Employee
 5   {
 6      private double wage; // wage per hour
 7      private double hours; // hours worked for week
 8
 9      // five-argument constructor
10      public HourlyEmployee( String first, String last, String ssn,
11         double hourlyWage, double hoursWorked )
12      {
13         super( first, last, ssn );
14         setWage( hourlyWage ); // validate hourly wage
15         setHours( hoursWorked ); // validate hours worked
16      } // end five-argument HourlyEmployee constructor
17
18      // set wage
19      public void setWage( double hourlyWage )
20      {
21         if ( hourlyWage >= 0.0 )
22            wage = hourlyWage;
23         else
24            throw new IllegalArgumentException(
25               "Hourly wage must be >= 0.0" );
26      } // end method setWage
```

Fig. G.18 | HourlyEmployee class extends Employee. (Part 1 of 2.)

```
27
28         // return wage
29         public double getWage()
30         {
31            return wage;
32         } // end method getWage
33
34         // set hours worked
35         public void setHours( double hoursWorked )
36         {
37            if ( ( hoursWorked >= 0.0 ) && ( hoursWorked <= 168.0 ) )
38               hours = hoursWorked;
39            else
40               throw new IllegalArgumentException(
41                  "Hours worked must be >= 0.0 and <= 168.0" );
42         } // end method setHours
43
44         // return hours worked
45         public double getHours()
46         {
47            return hours;
48         } // end method getHours
49
50         // calculate earnings; override abstract method earnings in Employee
51         @Override
52         public double earnings()
53         {
54            if ( getHours() <= 40 ) // no overtime
55               return getWage() * getHours();
56            else
57               return 40 * getWage() + ( getHours() - 40 ) * getWage() * 1.5;
58         } // end method earnings
59
60         // return String representation of HourlyEmployee object
61         @Override
62         public String toString()
63         {
64            return String.format( "hourly employee: %s\n%s: $%,.2f; %s: %,.2f",
65               super.toString(), "hourly wage", getWage(),
66               "hours worked", getHours() );
67         } // end method toString
68      } // end class HourlyEmployee
```

Fig. G.18 | HourlyEmployee class extends Employee. (Part 2 of 2.)

G.10.4 Concrete Subclass CommissionEmployee

Class CommissionEmployee (Fig. G.19) extends class Employee (line 4). The class includes a constructor (lines 10–16) that takes a first name, a last name, a social security number, a sales amount and a commission rate; *set* methods (lines 19–26 and 35–42) to assign new values to instance variables commissionRate and grossSales, respectively; *get* methods (lines 29–32 and 45–48) that retrieve the values of these instance variables; method earnings (lines 51–55) to calculate a CommissionEmployee's earnings; and method toString (lines 58–65), which returns the employee's type, namely, "commission employee: " and employee-specific information. The constructor also passes the first name, last name and social security number to Employee's constructor (line 13) to initialize Employee's private instance variables. Method toString calls superclass method toString (line 62) to obtain the Employee-specific information (i.e., first name, last name and social security number).

```java
1   // Fig. G.19: CommissionEmployee.java
2   // CommissionEmployee class extends Employee.
3
4   public class CommissionEmployee extends Employee
5   {
6      private double grossSales; // gross weekly sales
7      private double commissionRate; // commission percentage
8
9      // five-argument constructor
10     public CommissionEmployee( String first, String last, String ssn,
11        double sales, double rate )
12     {
13        super( first, last, ssn );
14        setGrossSales( sales );
15        setCommissionRate( rate );
16     } // end five-argument CommissionEmployee constructor
17
18     // set commission rate
19     public void setCommissionRate( double rate )
20     {
21        if ( rate > 0.0 && rate < 1.0 )
22           commissionRate = rate;
23        else
24           throw new IllegalArgumentException(
25              "Commission rate must be > 0.0 and < 1.0" );
26     } // end method setCommissionRate
27
28     // return commission rate
29     public double getCommissionRate()
30     {
31        return commissionRate;
32     } // end method getCommissionRate
33
34     // set gross sales amount
35     public void setGrossSales( double sales )
36     {
37        if ( sales >= 0.0 )
38           grossSales = sales;
39        else
40           throw new IllegalArgumentException(
41              "Gross sales must be >= 0.0" );
42     } // end method setGrossSales
43
44     // return gross sales amount
45     public double getGrossSales()
46     {
```

Fig. G.19 | CommissionEmployee class extends Employee. (Part I of 2.)

```
47        return grossSales;
48     } // end method getGrossSales
49
50     // calculate earnings; override abstract method earnings in Employee
51     @Override
52     public double earnings()
53     {
54        return getCommissionRate() * getGrossSales();
55     } // end method earnings
56
57     // return String representation of CommissionEmployee object
58     @Override
59     public String toString()
60     {
61        return String.format( "%s: %s\n%s: $%,.2f; %s: %.2f",
62           "commission employee", super.toString(),
63           "gross sales", getGrossSales(),
64           "commission rate", getCommissionRate() );
65     } // end method toString
66  } // end class CommissionEmployee
```

Fig. G.19 | CommissionEmployee class extends Employee. (Part 2 of 2.)

G.10.5 Indirect Concrete Subclass BasePlusCommissionEmployee

Class BasePlusCommissionEmployee (Fig. G.20) extends class CommissionEmployee (line 4) and therefore is an *indirect* subclass of class Employee. Class BasePlusCommission-Employee has a constructor (lines 9–14) that takes as arguments a first name, a last name, a social security number, a sales amount, a commission rate and a base salary. It then passes all of these except the base salary to the CommissionEmployee constructor (line 12) to initialize the inherited members. BasePlusCommissionEmployee also contains a *set* method (lines 17–24) to assign a new value to instance variable baseSalary and a *get* method (lines 27–30) to return baseSalary's value. Method earnings (lines 33–37) calculates a Base-PlusCommissionEmployee's earnings. Line 36 in method earnings calls superclass CommissionEmployee's earnings method to calculate the commission-based portion of the employee's earnings—this is another nice example of code reuse. BasePlusCommis-sionEmployee's toString method (lines 40–46) creates a String representation of a BasePlusCommissionEmployee that contains "base-salaried", followed by the String

```
1   // Fig. G.20: BasePlusCommissionEmployee.java
2   // BasePlusCommissionEmployee class extends CommissionEmployee.
3
4   public class BasePlusCommissionEmployee extends CommissionEmployee
5   {
6      private double baseSalary; // base salary per week
7
8      // six-argument constructor
9      public BasePlusCommissionEmployee( String first, String last,
10        String ssn, double sales, double rate, double salary )
11     {
```

Fig. G.20 | BasePlusCommissionEmployee class extends CommissionEmployee. (Part 1 of 2.)

```
12          super( first, last, ssn, sales, rate );
13          setBaseSalary( salary ); // validate and store base salary
14      } // end six-argument BasePlusCommissionEmployee constructor
15
16      // set base salary
17      public void setBaseSalary( double salary )
18      {
19          if ( salary >= 0.0 )
20              baseSalary = salary;
21          else
22              throw new IllegalArgumentException(
23                  "Base salary must be >= 0.0" );
24      } // end method setBaseSalary
25
26      // return base salary
27      public double getBaseSalary()
28      {
29          return baseSalary;
30      } // end method getBaseSalary
31
32      // calculate earnings; override method earnings in CommissionEmployee
33      @Override
34      public double earnings()
35      {
36          return getBaseSalary() + super.earnings();
37      } // end method earnings
38
39      // return String representation of BasePlusCommissionEmployee object
40      @Override
41      public String toString()
42      {
43          return String.format( "%s %s; %s: $%,.2f",
44              "base-salaried", super.toString(),
45              "base salary", getBaseSalary() );
46      } // end method toString
47  } // end class BasePlusCommissionEmployee
```

Fig. G.20 | BasePlusCommissionEmployee class extends CommissionEmployee. (Part 2 of 2.)

obtained by invoking superclass CommissionEmployee's toString method (another example of code reuse), then the base salary. The result is a String beginning with "base-salaried commission employee" followed by the rest of the BasePlusCommissionEmployee's information. Recall that CommissionEmployee's toString obtains the employee's first name, last name and social security number by invoking the toString method of its superclass (i.e., Employee)—yet another example of code reuse. BasePlusCommissionEmployee's toString initiates a chain of method calls that span all three levels of the Employee hierarchy.

G.10.6 Polymorphic Processing, Operator instanceof and Downcasting

To test our Employee hierarchy, the application in Fig. G.21 creates an object of each of the four concrete classes SalariedEmployee, HourlyEmployee, CommissionEmployee and BasePlusCommissionEmployee. The program manipulates these objects nonpolymorphically, via variables of each object's own type, then polymorphically, using an array of Employee variables. While processing the objects polymorphically, the program increases the base salary of each BasePlusCommissionEmployee by 10%—this requires *determining the object's type at execution time*. Finally, the program polymorphically determines and outputs the type of each object in the Employee array. Lines 9–18 create objects of each of the four concrete Employee subclasses. Lines 22–30 output the String representation and earnings of each of these objects *nonpolymorphically*. Each object's toString method is called *implicitly* by printf when the object is output as a String with the %s format specifier.

```java
1   // Fig. G.21: PayrollSystemTest.java
2   // Employee hierarchy test program.
3
4   public class PayrollSystemTest
5   {
6      public static void main( String[] args )
7      {
8         // create subclass objects
9         SalariedEmployee salariedEmployee =
10           new SalariedEmployee( "John", "Smith", "111-11-1111", 800.00 );
11        HourlyEmployee hourlyEmployee =
12           new HourlyEmployee( "Karen", "Price", "222-22-2222", 16.75, 40 );
13        CommissionEmployee commissionEmployee =
14           new CommissionEmployee(
15           "Sue", "Jones", "333-33-3333", 10000, .06 );
16        BasePlusCommissionEmployee basePlusCommissionEmployee =
17           new BasePlusCommissionEmployee(
18           "Bob", "Lewis", "444-44-4444", 5000, .04, 300 );
19
20        System.out.println( "Employees processed individually:\n" );
21
22        System.out.printf( "%s\n%s: $%,.2f\n\n",
23           salariedEmployee, "earned", salariedEmployee.earnings() );
24        System.out.printf( "%s\n%s: $%,.2f\n\n",
25           hourlyEmployee, "earned", hourlyEmployee.earnings() );
26        System.out.printf( "%s\n%s: $%,.2f\n\n",
27           commissionEmployee, "earned", commissionEmployee.earnings() );
28        System.out.printf( "%s\n%s: $%,.2f\n\n",
29           basePlusCommissionEmployee,
30           "earned", basePlusCommissionEmployee.earnings() );
31
32        // create four-element Employee array
33        Employee[] employees = new Employee[ 4 ];
34
35        // initialize array with Employees
36        employees[ 0 ] = salariedEmployee;
37        employees[ 1 ] = hourlyEmployee;
38        employees[ 2 ] = commissionEmployee;
39        employees[ 3 ] = basePlusCommissionEmployee;
40
41        System.out.println( "Employees processed polymorphically:\n" );
42
```

Fig. G.21 | Employee hierarchy test program. (Part 1 of 3.)

```
43          // generically process each element in array employees
44          for ( Employee currentEmployee : employees )
45          {
46              System.out.println( currentEmployee ); // invokes toString
47
48              // determine whether element is a BasePlusCommissionEmployee
49              if ( currentEmployee instanceof BasePlusCommissionEmployee )
50              {
51                  // downcast Employee reference to
52                  // BasePlusCommissionEmployee reference
53                  BasePlusCommissionEmployee employee =
54                      ( BasePlusCommissionEmployee ) currentEmployee;
55
56                  employee.setBaseSalary( 1.10 * employee.getBaseSalary() );
57
58                  System.out.printf(
59                      "new base salary with 10%% increase is: $%,.2f\n",
60                      employee.getBaseSalary() );
61              } // end if
62
63              System.out.printf(
64                  "earned $%,.2f\n\n", currentEmployee.earnings() );
65          } // end for
66
67          // get type name of each object in employees array
68          for ( int j = 0; j < employees.length; j++ )
69              System.out.printf( "Employee %d is a %s\n", j,
70                  employees[ j ].getClass().getName() );
71      } // end main
72  } // end class PayrollSystemTest
```

```
Employees processed individually:

salaried employee: John Smith
social security number: 111-11-1111
weekly salary: $800.00
earned: $800.00

hourly employee: Karen Price
social security number: 222-22-2222
hourly wage: $16.75; hours worked: 40.00
earned: $670.00

commission employee: Sue Jones
social security number: 333-33-3333
gross sales: $10,000.00; commission rate: 0.06
earned: $600.00

base-salaried commission employee: Bob Lewis
social security number: 444-44-4444
gross sales: $5,000.00; commission rate: 0.04; base salary: $300.00
earned: $500.00
```

Fig. G.21 | Employee hierarchy test program. (Part 2 of 3.)

```
Employees processed polymorphically:

salaried employee: John Smith
social security number: 111-11-1111
weekly salary: $800.00
earned $800.00

hourly employee: Karen Price
social security number: 222-22-2222
hourly wage: $16.75; hours worked: 40.00
earned $670.00

commission employee: Sue Jones
social security number: 333-33-3333
gross sales: $10,000.00; commission rate: 0.06
earned $600.00

base-salaried commission employee: Bob Lewis
social security number: 444-44-4444
gross sales: $5,000.00; commission rate: 0.04; base salary: $300.00
new base salary with 10% increase is: $330.00
earned $530.00

Employee 0 is a SalariedEmployee
Employee 1 is a HourlyEmployee
Employee 2 is a CommissionEmployee
Employee 3 is a BasePlusCommissionEmployee
```

Fig. G.21 | Employee hierarchy test program. (Part 3 of 3.)

Creating the Array of Employees

Line 33 declares employees and assigns it an array of four Employee variables. Line 36 assigns the reference to a SalariedEmployee object to employees[0]. Line 37 assigns the reference to an HourlyEmployee object to employees[1]. Line 38 assigns the reference to a CommissionEmployee object to employees[2]. Line 39 assigns the reference to a BasePlusCommissionEmployee object to employee[3]. These assignments are allowed, because a SalariedEmployee *is an* Employee, an HourlyEmployee *is an* Employee, a CommissionEmployee *is an* Employee and a BasePlusCommissionEmployee *is an* Employee. Therefore, we can assign the references of SalariedEmployee, HourlyEmployee, CommissionEmployee and BasePlusCommissionEmployee objects to superclass Employee variables, *even though Employee is an abstract class.*

Polymorphically Processing Employees

Lines 44–65 iterate through array employees and invoke methods toString and earnings with Employee variable currentEmployee, which is assigned the reference to a different Employee in the array on each iteration. The output illustrates that the appropriate methods for each class are indeed invoked. All calls to method toString and earnings are resolved at execution time, based on the type of the object to which currentEmployee refers. This process is known as **dynamic binding** or **late binding**. For example, line 46 *implicitly* invokes method toString of the object to which currentEmployee refers. As a result of dynamic binding, Java decides which class's toString method to call *at execution time rather than at compile time.* Only the methods of class Employee can be called via an

Employee variable (and Employee, of course, includes the methods of class Object). A superclass reference can be used to invoke only methods of the superclass—the subclass method implementations are invoked polymorphically.

Performing Type-Specific Operations on BasePlusCommissionEmployees

We perform special processing on BasePlusCommissionEmployee objects—as we encounter these objects at execution time, we increase their base salary by 10%. When processing objects polymorphically, we typically do not need to worry about the "specifics," but to adjust the base salary, we *do* have to determine the specific type of Employee object at execution time. Line 49 uses the **instanceof** operator to determine whether a particular Employee object's type is BasePlusCommissionEmployee. The condition in line 49 is true if the object referenced by currentEmployee *is a* BasePlusCommissionEmployee. This would also be true for any object of a BasePlusCommissionEmployee subclass because of the *is-a* relationship a subclass has with its superclass. Lines 53–54 downcast currentEmployee from type Employee to type BasePlusCommissionEmployee—this cast is allowed only if the object has an *is-a* relationship with BasePlusCommissionEmployee. The condition at line 49 ensures that this is the case. This cast is required if we're to invoke subclass BasePlusCommissionEmployee methods getBaseSalary and setBaseSalary on the current Employee object—as you'll see momentarily, *attempting to invoke a subclass-only method directly on a superclass reference is a compilation error.*

Common Programming Error G.3

Assigning a superclass variable to a subclass variable (without an explicit cast) is a compilation error.

Software Engineering Observation G.7

If a subclass object's reference has been assigned to a variable of one of its direct or indirect superclasses at execution time, it's acceptable to downcast the reference stored in that superclass variable back to a subclass-type reference. Before performing such a cast, use the instanceof *operator to ensure that the object is indeed an object of an appropriate subclass.*

Common Programming Error G.4

When downcasting a reference, a ClassCastException *occurs if the referenced object at execution time does not have an* is-a *relationship with the type specified in the cast operator.*

If the instanceof expression in line 49 is true, lines 53–60 perform the special processing required for the BasePlusCommissionEmployee object. Using BasePlusCommissionEmployee variable employee, line 56 invokes subclass-only methods getBaseSalary and setBaseSalary to retrieve and update the employee's base salary with the 10% raise.

Calling earnings Polymorphically

Lines 63–64 invoke method earnings on currentEmployee, which polymorphically calls the appropriate subclass object's earnings method. Obtaining the earnings of the SalariedEmployee, HourlyEmployee and CommissionEmployee polymorphically in lines 63–64 produces the same results as obtaining these employees' earnings individually in lines 22–27. The earnings amount obtained for the BasePlusCommissionEmployee in lines 63–64 is higher than that obtained in lines 28–30, due to the 10% increase in its base salary.

Using Reflection to Get Each Employee's Class Name

Lines 68–70 display each employee's type as a String, using basic features of Java's so-called reflection capabilities. Every object knows its own class and can access this information through the **getClass** method, which all classes inherit from class Object. Method getClass returns an object of type **Class** (from package java.lang), which contains information about the object's type, including its class name. Line 70 invokes getClass on the current object to get its runtime class. The result of the getClass call is used to invoke **getName** to get the object's class name.

Avoiding Compilation Errors with Downcasting

In the previous example, we avoided several compilation errors by downcasting an Employee variable to a BasePlusCommissionEmployee variable in lines 53–54. If you remove the cast operator (BasePlusCommissionEmployee) from line 54 and attempt to assign Employee variable currentEmployee directly to BasePlusCommissionEmployee variable employee, you'll receive an "incompatible types" compilation error. This error indicates that the attempt to assign the reference of superclass object currentEmployee to subclass variable employee is not allowed. The compiler prevents this assignment because a CommissionEmployee is not a BasePlusCommissionEmployee—*the is-a relationship applies only between the subclass and its superclasses, not vice versa.*

Similarly, if lines 56 and 60 used superclass variable currentEmployee to invoke subclass-only methods getBaseSalary and setBaseSalary, we'd receive "cannot find symbol" compilation errors at these lines. Attempting to invoke subclass-only methods via a superclass variable is not allowed—even though lines 56 and 60 execute only if instanceof in line 49 returns true to indicate that currentEmployee holds a reference to a BasePlusCommissionEmployee object. Using a superclass Employee variable, we can invoke only methods found in class Employee—earnings, toString and Employee's *get* and *set* methods.

Software Engineering Observation G.8

Although the actual method that's called depends on the runtime type of the object to which a variable refers, a variable can be used to invoke only those methods that are members of that variable's type, which the compiler verifies.

G.10.7 Summary of the Allowed Assignments Between Superclass and Subclass Variables

Now that you've seen a complete application that processes diverse subclass objects polymorphically, we summarize what you can and cannot do with superclass and subclass objects and variables. Although a subclass object also *is a* superclass object, the two objects are nevertheless different. As discussed previously, subclass objects can be treated as objects of their superclass. But because the subclass can have additional subclass-only members, assigning a superclass reference to a subclass variable is not allowed without an explicit cast—such an assignment would leave the subclass members undefined for the superclass object.

We've discussed four ways to assign superclass and subclass references to variables of superclass and subclass types:

1. Assigning a superclass reference to a superclass variable is straightforward.

2. Assigning a subclass reference to a subclass variable is straightforward.

3. Assigning a subclass reference to a superclass variable is safe, because the subclass object *is an* object of its superclass. However, the superclass variable can be used to refer *only* to superclass members. If this code refers to subclass-only members through the superclass variable, the compiler reports errors.

4. Attempting to assign a superclass reference to a subclass variable is a compilation error. To avoid this error, the superclass reference must be cast to a subclass type explicitly. At *execution time*, if the object to which the reference refers is *not* a subclass object, an exception will occur. (For more on exception handling, see Appendix H.) You should use the instanceof operator to ensure that such a cast is performed only if the object is a subclass object.

G.11 final Methods and Classes

We saw in Sections D.3 and D.10 that variables can be declared final to indicate that they cannot be modified after they're initialized—such variables represent constant values. It's also possible to declare methods, method parameters and classes with the final modifier.

Final Methods Cannot Be Overridden

A **final method** in a superclass *cannot* be overridden in a subclass—this guarantees that the final method implementation will be used by all direct and indirect subclasses in the hierarchy. Methods that are declared private are implicitly final, because it's not possible to override them in a subclass. Methods that are declared static are also implicitly final. A final method's declaration can never change, so all subclasses use the same method implementation, and calls to final methods are resolved at compile time—this is known as **static binding**.

Final Classes Cannot Be Superclasses

A **final class** that's declared final cannot be a superclass (i.e., a class cannot extend a final class). All methods in a final class are implicitly final. Class String is an example of a final class. If you were allowed to create a subclass of String, objects of that subclass could be used wherever Strings are expected. Since class String cannot be extended, programs that use Strings can rely on the functionality of String objects as specified in the Java API. Making the class final also prevents programmers from creating subclasses that might bypass security restrictions. For more insights on the use of keyword final, visit

    docs.oracle.com/javase/tutorial/java/IandI/final.html

and

    www.ibm.com/developerworks/java/library/j-jtp1029.html

Common Programming Error G.5

Attempting to declare a subclass of a final class is a compilation error.

Software Engineering Observation G.9

In the Java API, the vast majority of classes are not declared final. This enables inheritance and polymorphism. However, in some cases, it's important to declare classes final—typically for security reasons.

G.12 Case Study: Creating and Using Interfaces

Our next example (Figs. G.23–G.27) reexamines the payroll system of Section G.10. Suppose that the company involved wishes to perform several accounting operations in a single accounts payable application—in addition to calculating the earnings that must be paid to each employee, the company must also calculate the payment due on each of several invoices (i.e., bills for goods purchased). Though applied to unrelated things (i.e., employees and invoices), both operations have to do with obtaining some kind of payment amount. For an employee, the payment refers to the employee's earnings. For an invoice, the payment refers to the total cost of the goods listed on the invoice. Can we calculate such *different* things as the payments due for employees and invoices in *a single* application polymorphically? Does Java offer a capability requiring that *unrelated* classes implement a set of *common* methods (e.g., a method that calculates a payment amount)? Java **interfaces** offer exactly this capability.

Standardizing Interactions

Interfaces define and standardize the ways in which things such as people and systems can interact with one another. For example, the controls on a radio serve as an interface between radio users and a radio's internal components. The controls allow users to perform only a limited set of operations (e.g., change the station, adjust the volume, choose between AM and FM), and different radios may implement the controls in different ways (e.g., using push buttons, dials, voice commands). The interface specifies *what* operations a radio must permit users to perform but does not specify *how* the operations are performed.

Software Objects Communicate Via Interfaces

Software objects also communicate via interfaces. A Java interface describes a set of methods that can be called on an object to tell it, for example, to perform some task or return some piece of information. The next example introduces an interface named `Payable` to describe the functionality of any object that must be capable of being paid and thus must offer a method to determine the proper payment amount due. An **interface declaration** begins with the keyword **interface** and contains only constants and abstract methods. Unlike classes, all interface members must be `public`, and *interfaces may not specify any implementation details*, such as concrete method declarations and instance variables. All methods declared in an interface are implicitly `public abstract` methods, and all fields are implicitly `public`, `static` and `final`. [*Note:* As of Java SE 5, it became a better programming practice to declare sets of constants as enumerations with keyword enum. See Section D.10 for an introduction to enum and Section F.8 for additional enum details.]

Good Programming Practice G.1

According to Chapter 9 of the Java Language Specification, *it's proper style to declare an interface's methods without keywords* public *and* abstract, *because they're redundant in interface method declarations. Similarly, constants should be declared without keywords* public, static *and* final, *because they, too, are redundant.*

Using an Interface

To use an interface, a concrete class must specify that it **implements** the interface and must declare each method in the interface with the signature specified in the interface declaration. To specify that a class implements an interface add the `implements` keyword and the name of the interface to the end of your class declaration's first line. A class that does not implement *all* the methods of the interface is an *abstract* class and must be declared abstract. Implementing an interface is like signing a *contract* with the compiler that states, "I will declare all the methods specified by the interface or I will declare my class abstract."

Common Programming Error G.6

Failing to implement any method of an interface in a concrete class that implements the interface results in a compilation error indicating that the class must be declared abstract.

Relating Disparate Types

An interface is often used when disparate (i.e., unrelated) classes need to share common methods and constants. This allows objects of unrelated classes to be processed polymorphically—objects of classes that implement the same interface can respond to the same method calls. You can create an interface that describes the desired functionality, then implement this interface in any classes that require that functionality. For example, in the accounts payable application developed in this section, we implement interface Payable in any class that must be able to calculate a payment amount (e.g., Employee, Invoice).

Interfaces vs. Abstract Classes

An interface is often used in place of an abstract class when there's no default implementation to inherit—that is, no fields and no default method implementations. Like public abstract classes, interfaces are typically public types. Like a public class, a public interface must be declared in a file with the same name as the interface and the .java file-name extension.

Tagging Interfaces

We'll see in Appendix J, the notion of "tagging interfaces"—empty interfaces that have *no* methods or constant values. They're used to add *is-a* relationships to classes. For example, in Appendix J we'll discuss a mechanism called object serialization, which can convert objects to byte representations and can convert those byte representations back to objects. To enable this mechanism to work with your objects, you simply have to mark them as Serializable by adding implements Serializable to the end of your class declaration's first line. Then, all the objects of your class have the *is-a* relationship with Serializable.

G.12.1 Developing a Payable Hierarchy

To build an application that can determine payments for employees and invoices alike, we first create interface Payable, which contains method getPaymentAmount that returns a double amount that must be paid for an object of any class that implements the interface. Method getPaymentAmount is a general-purpose version of method earnings of the Employee hierarchy—method earnings calculates a payment amount specifically for an Employee, while getPaymentAmount can be applied to a broad range of unrelated objects. After declaring interface Payable, we introduce class Invoice, which implements interface Payable. We then modify class Employee such that it also implements interface Payable. Finally, we update Employee subclass SalariedEmployee to "fit" into the Payable hierarchy by renaming SalariedEmployee method earnings as getPaymentAmount.

Good Programming Practice G.2

When declaring a method in an interface, choose a method name that describes the method's purpose in a general manner, because the method may be implemented by many unrelated classes.

Classes `Invoice` and `Employee` both represent things for which the company must be able to calculate a payment amount. Both classes implement the `Payable` interface, so a program can invoke method `getPaymentAmount` on `Invoice` objects and `Employee` objects alike. As we'll soon see, this enables the polymorphic processing of `Invoices` and `Employees` required for the company's accounts payable application.

The UML class diagram in Fig. G.22 shows the hierarchy used in our accounts payable application. The hierarchy begins with interface `Payable`. The UML distinguishes an interface from other classes by placing the word "interface" in guillemets (« and ») above the interface name. The UML expresses the relationship between a class and an interface through a relationship known as **realization**. A class is said to "realize," or implement, the methods of an interface. A class diagram models a realization as a dashed arrow with a hollow arrowhead pointing from the implementing class to the interface. The diagram in Fig. G.22 indicates that classes `Invoice` and `Employee` each realize (i.e., implement) interface `Payable`. As in the class diagram of Fig. G.14, class `Employee` appears in italics, indicating that it's an abstract class. Concrete class `SalariedEmployee` extends `Employee` and *inherits its superclass's realization relationship* with interface `Payable`.

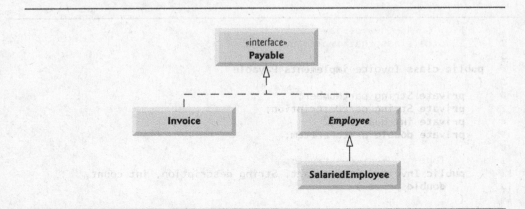

Fig. G.22 | `Payable` interface hierarchy UML class diagram.

G.12.2 Interface `Payable`

The declaration of interface `Payable` begins in Fig. G.23 at line 4. Interface `Payable` contains public abstract method `getPaymentAmount` (line 6). The method is not explicitly declared `public` or `abstract`. Interface methods are always `public` and `abstract`, so they do not need to be declared as such. Interface `Payable` has only one method—interfaces can have any number of methods. In addition, method `getPaymentAmount` has no parameters, but interface methods *can* have parameters. Interfaces may also contain fields that are implicitly `final` and `static`.

```
1   // Fig. G.23: Payable.java
2   // Payable interface declaration.
3
4   public interface Payable
5   {
6      double getPaymentAmount(); // calculate payment; no implementation
7   } // end interface Payable
```

Fig. G.23 | Payable interface declaration.

G.12.3 Class Invoice

We now create class Invoice (Fig. G.24) to represent a simple invoice that contains billing information for only one kind of part. The class declares private instance variables part-Number, partDescription, quantity and pricePerItem (in lines 6–9) that indicate the part number, a description of the part, the quantity of the part ordered and the price per item. Class Invoice also contains a constructor (lines 12–19), *get* and *set* methods (lines 22–74) that manipulate the class's instance variables and a toString method (lines 77–83) that returns a String representation of an Invoice object. Methods setQuantity (lines 46–52) and setPricePerItem (lines 61–68) ensure that quantity and pricePer-Item obtain only nonnegative values.

```
1    // Fig. G.24: Invoice.java
2    // Invoice class that implements Payable.
3
4    public class Invoice implements Payable
5    {
6       private String partNumber;
7       private String partDescription;
8       private int quantity;2
9       private double pricePerItem;
10
11      // four-argument constructor
12      public Invoice( String part, String description, int count,
13         double price )
14      {
15         partNumber = part;
16         partDescription = description;
17         setQuantity( count ); // validate and store quantity
18         setPricePerItem( price ); // validate and store price per item
19      } // end four-argument Invoice constructor
20
21      // set part number
22      public void setPartNumber( String part )
23      {
24         partNumber = part; // should validate
25      } // end method setPartNumber
26
```

Fig. G.24 | Invoice class that implements Payable. (Part 1 of 3.)

```
27       // get part number
28       public String getPartNumber()
29       {
30           return partNumber;
31       } // end method getPartNumber
32
33       // set description
34       public void setPartDescription( String description )
35       {
36           partDescription = description; // should validate
37       } // end method setPartDescription
38
39       // get description
40       public String getPartDescription()
41       {
42           return partDescription;
43       } // end method getPartDescription
44
45       // set quantity
46       public void setQuantity( int count )
47       {
48           if ( count >= 0 )
49               quantity = count;
50           else
51               throw new IllegalArgumentException( "Quantity must be >= 0" );
52       } // end method setQuantity
53
54       // get quantity
55       public int getQuantity()
56       {
57           return quantity;
58       } // end method getQuantity
59
60       // set price per item
61       public void setPricePerItem( double price )
62       {
63           if ( price >= 0.0 )
64               pricePerItem = price;
65           else
66               throw new IllegalArgumentException(
67                   "Price per item must be >= 0" );
68       } // end method setPricePerItem
69
70       // get price per item
71       public double getPricePerItem()
72       {
73           return pricePerItem;
74       } // end method getPricePerItem
75
76       // return String representation of Invoice object
77       @Override
78       public String toString()
79       {
```

Fig. G.24 | Invoice class that implements Payable. (Part 2 of 3.)

```
80            return String.format( "%s: \n%s: %s (%s) \n%s: %d \n%s: $%,.2f",
81               "invoice", "part number", getPartNumber(), getPartDescription(),
82               "quantity", getQuantity(), "price per item", getPricePerItem() );
83         } // end method toString
84
85         // method required to carry out contract with interface Payable
86         @Override
87         public double getPaymentAmount()
88         {
89            return getQuantity() * getPricePerItem(); // calculate total cost
90         } // end method getPaymentAmount
91   } // end class Invoice
```

Fig. G.24 | `Invoice` class that implements `Payable`. (Part 3 of 3.)

Line 4 indicates that class `Invoice` implements interface `Payable`. Like all classes, class `Invoice` also implicitly extends `Object`. Java does not allow subclasses to inherit from more than one superclass, but it allows a class to inherit from one superclass and implement as many interfaces as it needs. To implement more than one interface, use a comma-separated list of interface names after keyword `implements` in the class declaration, as in:

> `public class` *ClassName* `extends` *SuperclassName* `implements` *FirstInterface*,
> *SecondInterface*, ...

Software Engineering Observation G.10

All objects of a class that implement multiple interfaces have the is-a *relationship with each implemented interface type.*

Class `Invoice` implements the one method in interface `Payable`—method `getPaymentAmount` is declared in lines 86–90. The method calculates the total payment required to pay the invoice. The method multiplies the values of `quantity` and `pricePerItem` (obtained through the appropriate *get* methods) and returns the result (line 89). This method satisfies the implementation requirement for this method in interface `Payable`—we've fulfilled the interface contract with the compiler.

G.12.4 Modifying Class `Employee` to Implement Interface `Payable`

We now modify class `Employee` such that it implements interface `Payable`. Figure G.25 contains the modified class, which is identical to that of Fig. G.16 with two exceptions. First, line 4 of Fig. G.25 indicates that class `Employee` now `implements` interface `Payable`. So we must rename `earnings` to `getPaymentAmount` throughout the `Employee` hierarchy. As with method `earnings` in the version of class `Employee` in Fig. G.16, however, it does not make sense to implement method `getPaymentAmount` in class `Employee` because we cannot calculate the earnings payment owed to a general `Employee`—we must first know the specific type of `Employee`. In Fig. G.16, we declared method `earnings` as `abstract` for this reason, so class `Employee` had to be declared `abstract`. This forced each `Employee` concrete subclass to override `earnings` with an implementation.

In Fig. G.25, we handle this situation differently. Recall that when a class implements an interface, it makes a *contract* with the compiler stating either that the class will implement *each* of the methods in the interface or that the class will be declared `abstract`. If

```java
1    // Fig. G.25: Employee.java
2    // Employee abstract superclass that implements Payable.
3
4    public abstract class Employee implements Payable
5    {
6       private String firstName;
7       private String lastName;
8       private String socialSecurityNumber;
9
10      // three-argument constructor
11      public Employee( String first, String last, String ssn )
12      {
13         firstName = first;
14         lastName = last;
15         socialSecurityNumber = ssn;
16      } // end three-argument Employee constructor
17
18      // set first name
19      public void setFirstName( String first )
20      {
21         firstName = first; // should validate
22      } // end method setFirstName
23
24      // return first name
25      public String getFirstName()
26      {
27         return firstName;
28      } // end method getFirstName
29
30      // set last name
31      public void setLastName( String last )
32      {
33         lastName = last; // should validate
34      } // end method setLastName
35
36      // return last name
37      public String getLastName()
38      {
39         return lastName;
40      } // end method getLastName
41
42      // set social security number
43      public void setSocialSecurityNumber( String ssn )
44      {
45         socialSecurityNumber = ssn; // should validate
46      } // end method setSocialSecurityNumber
47
48      // return social security number
49      public String getSocialSecurityNumber()
50      {
51         return socialSecurityNumber;
52      } // end method getSocialSecurityNumber
53
```

Fig. G.25 | Employee abstract superclass that implements Payable. (Part 1 of 2.)

```
54        // return String representation of Employee object
55        @Override
56        public String toString()
57        {
58           return String.format( "%s %s\nsocial security number: %s",
59              getFirstName(), getLastName(), getSocialSecurityNumber() );
60        } // end method toString
61
62        // Note: We do not implement Payable method getPaymentAmount here so
63        // this class must be declared abstract to avoid a compilation error.
64  } // end abstract class Employee
```

Fig. G.25 | Employee abstract superclass that implements Payable. (Part 2 of 2.)

the latter option is chosen, we do not need to declare the interface methods as abstract in the abstract class—they're already implicitly declared as such in the interface. Any concrete subclass of the abstract class must implement the interface methods to fulfill the superclass's contract with the compiler. If the subclass does not do so, it too must be declared abstract. As indicated by the comments in lines 62–63, class Employee of Fig. G.25 does *not* implement method getPaymentAmount, so the class is declared abstract. Each direct Employee subclass *inherits the superclass's contract* to implement method getPaymentAmount and thus must implement this method to become a concrete class for which objects can be instantiated. A class that extends one of Employee's concrete subclasses will inherit an implementation of getPaymentAmount and thus will also be a concrete class.

G.12.5 Modifying Class SalariedEmployee for Use in the Payable Hierarchy

Figure G.26 contains a modified SalariedEmployee class that extends Employee and fulfills superclass Employee's contract to implement Payable method getPaymentAmount. This version of SalariedEmployee is identical to that of Fig. G.17, but it replaces method earnings with method getPaymentAmount (lines 34–38). Recall that the Payable version of the method has a more *general* name to be applicable to possibly *disparate* classes. The remaining Employee subclasses (e.g., HourlyEmployee, CommissionEmployee and BasePlusCommissionEmployee) also must be modified to contain method getPaymentAmount in place of earnings to reflect the fact that Employee now implements Payable. We leave these modifications as an exercise (Exercise G.16) and use only SalariedEmployee in our test program here. Exercise G.17 asks you to implement interface Payable in the entire Employee class hierarchy of Figs. G.16–G.21 without modifying the Employee subclasses.

When a class implements an interface, the same *is-a* relationship provided by inheritance applies. Class Employee implements Payable, so we can say that an Employee *is a* Payable. In fact, objects of any classes that extend Employee are also Payable objects. SalariedEmployee objects, for instance, are Payable objects. Objects of any subclasses of the class that implements the interface can also be thought of as objects of the interface type. Thus, just as we can assign the reference of a SalariedEmployee object to a superclass Employee variable, we can assign the reference of a SalariedEmployee object to an interface Payable variable. Invoice implements Payable, so an Invoice object also *is a* Payable object, and we can assign the reference of an Invoice object to a Payable variable.

Software Engineering Observation G.11

When a method parameter is declared with a superclass or interface type, the method processes the object received as an argument polymorphically.

Software Engineering Observation G.12

Using a superclass reference, we can polymorphically invoke any method declared in the superclass and its superclasses (e.g., class Object). Using an interface reference, we can polymorphically invoke any method declared in the interface, its superinterfaces (one interface can extend another) and in class Object—a variable of an interface type must refer to an object to call methods, and all objects have the methods of class Object.

```java
1   // Fig. G.26: SalariedEmployee.java
2   // SalariedEmployee class extends Employee, which implements Payable.
3
4   public class SalariedEmployee extends Employee
5   {
6      private double weeklySalary;
7
8      // four-argument constructor
9      public SalariedEmployee( String first, String last, String ssn,
10        double salary )
11     {
12        super( first, last, ssn ); // pass to Employee constructor
13        setWeeklySalary( salary ); // validate and store salary
14     } // end four-argument SalariedEmployee constructor
15
16     // set salary
17     public void setWeeklySalary( double salary )
18     {
19        if ( salary >= 0.0 )
20           baseSalary = salary;
21        else
22           throw new IllegalArgumentException(
23              "Weekly salary must be >= 0.0" );
24     } // end method setWeeklySalary
25
26     // return salary
27     public double getWeeklySalary()
28     {
29        return weeklySalary;
30     } // end method getWeeklySalary
31
32     // calculate earnings; implement interface Payable method that was
33     // abstract in superclass Employee
34     @Override
35     public double getPaymentAmount()
36     {
37        return getWeeklySalary();
38     } // end method getPaymentAmount
```

Fig. G.26 | SalariedEmployee class that implements interface Payable method getPaymentAmount. (Part 1 of 2.)

```
39
40     // return String representation of SalariedEmployee object
41     @Override
42     public String toString()
43     {
44        return String.format( "salaried employee: %s\n%s: $%,.2f",
45           super.toString(), "weekly salary", getWeeklySalary() );
46     } // end method toString
47  } // end class SalariedEmployee
```

Fig. G.26 | SalariedEmployee class that implements interface Payable method getPaymentAmount. (Part 2 of 2.)

G.12.6 Using Interface Payable to Process Invoices and Employees Polymorphically

PayableInterfaceTest (Fig. G.27) illustrates that interface Payable can be used to process a set of Invoices and Employees polymorphically in a single application. Line 9 declares payableObjects and assigns it an array of four Payable variables. Lines 12–13 assign the references of Invoice objects to the first two elements of payableObjects. Lines 14–17 then assign the references of SalariedEmployee objects to the remaining two elements of payableObjects. These assignments are allowed because an Invoice *is a* Payable, a SalariedEmployee *is an* Employee and an Employee *is a* Payable. Lines 23–29 use the enhanced for statement to polymorphically process each Payable object in payableObjects, printing the object as a String, along with the payment amount due. Line 27 invokes method toString via a Payable interface reference, even though toString is not declared in interface Payable—*all references (including those of interface types) refer to objects that extend Object and therefore have a toString method.* (Method toString also can be invoked *implicitly* here.) Line 28 invokes Payable method getPaymentAmount to obtain the payment amount for each object in payableObjects, regardless of the actual type of the object. The output reveals that the method calls in lines 27–28 invoke the appropriate class's implementation of methods toString and getPaymentAmount. For instance, when currentPayable refers to an Invoice during the first iteration of the for loop, class Invoice's toString and getPaymentAmount execute.

```
1   // Fig. G.27: PayableInterfaceTest.java
2   // Tests interface Payable.
3
4   public class PayableInterfaceTest
5   {
6      public static void main( String[] args )
7      {
8         // create four-element Payable array
9         Payable[] payableObjects = new Payable[ 4 ];
10
11        // populate array with objects that implement Payable
12        payableObjects[ 0 ] = new Invoice( "01234", "seat", 2, 375.00 );
```

Fig. G.27 | Payable interface test program processing Invoices and Employees polymorphically. (Part 1 of 2.)

```
13          payableObjects[ 1 ] = new Invoice( "56789", "tire", 4, 79.95 );
14          payableObjects[ 2 ] =
15             new SalariedEmployee( "John", "Smith", "111-11-1111", 800.00 );
16          payableObjects[ 3 ] =
17             new SalariedEmployee( "Lisa", "Barnes", "888-88-8888", 1200.00 );
18
19          System.out.println(
20             "Invoices and Employees processed polymorphically:\n" );
21
22          // generically process each element in array payableObjects
23          for ( Payable currentPayable : payableObjects )
24          {
25             // output currentPayable and its appropriate payment amount
26             System.out.printf( "%s \n%s: $%,.2f\n\n",
27                currentPayable.toString(),
28                "payment due", currentPayable.getPaymentAmount() );
29          } // end for
30       } // end main
31    } // end class PayableInterfaceTest
```

```
Invoices and Employees processed polymorphically:

invoice:
part number: 01234 (seat)
quantity: 2
price per item: $375.00
payment due: $750.00

invoice:
part number: 56789 (tire)
quantity: 4
price per item: $79.95
payment due: $319.80

salaried employee: John Smith
social security number: 111-11-1111
weekly salary: $800.00
payment due: $800.00

salaried employee: Lisa Barnes
social security number: 888-88-8888
weekly salary: $1,200.00
payment due: $1,200.00
```

Fig. G.27 | Payable interface test program processing Invoices and Employees polymorphically. (Part 2 of 2.)

G.13 Common Interfaces of the Java API

In this section, we overview several common interfaces found in the Java API. The power and flexibility of interfaces is used frequently throughout the Java API. These interfaces are implemented and used in the same manner as the interfaces you create (e.g., interface Payable in Section G.12.2). The Java API's interfaces enable you to use your own classes within the frameworks provided by Java, such as comparing objects of your own types and creating tasks that can execute concurrently with other tasks in the same program. Figure G.28 overviews a few commonly used interfaces of the Java API.

Interface	Description
Comparable	Java contains several comparison operators (e.g., <, <=, >, >=, ==, !=) that allow you to compare primitive values. However, these operators *cannot* be used to compare objects. Interface Comparable is used to allow objects of a class that implements the interface to be compared to one another. Interface Comparable is commonly used for ordering objects in a collection such as an array.
Serializable	An interface used to identify classes whose objects can be written to (i.e., serialized) or read from (i.e., deserialized) some type of storage (e.g., file on disk, database field) or transmitted across a network.
Runnable	Implemented by any class for which objects of that class should be able to execute in parallel using a technique called multithreading (discussed in Appendix J). The interface contains one method, run, which describes the behavior of an object when executed.
GUI event-listener interfaces	You work with graphical user interfaces (GUIs) every day. In your web browser, you might type the address of a website to visit, or you might click a button to return to a previous site. The browser responds to your interaction and performs the desired task. Your interaction is known as an event, and the code that the browser uses to respond to an event is known as an event handler.
SwingConstants	Contains a set of constants used in GUI programming to position GUI elements on the screen.

Fig. G.28 | Common interfaces of the Java API.

G.14 Wrap-Up

We introduced inheritance—the ability to create classes by absorbing an existing class's members and embellishing them with new capabilities. You learned the notions of super-classes and subclasses and used keyword extends to create a subclass that inherits members from a superclass. We showed how to use the @Override annotation to prevent unintended overloading by indicating that a method overrides a superclass method. We introduced the access modifier protected; subclass methods can directly access protected superclass members. You learned how to use super to access overridden superclass members. You also saw how constructors are used in inheritance hierarchies. Next, you learned about the methods of class Object, the direct or indirect superclass of all Java classes.

We discussed polymorphism—the ability to process objects that share the same super-class in a class hierarchy as if they're all objects of the superclass. We considered how poly-morphism makes systems extensible and maintainable, then demonstrated how to use overridden methods to effect polymorphic behavior. We introduced abstract classes, which allow you to provide an appropriate superclass from which other classes can inherit. You learned that an abstract class can declare abstract methods that each subclass must implement to become a concrete class and that a program can use variables of an abstract class to invoke the subclasses' implementations of abstract methods polymorphically. You also learned how to determine an object's type at execution time. We discussed the concepts of final methods and classes. Finally, we discussed declaring and implementing an interface as another way to achieve polymorphic behavior.

You should now be familiar with classes, objects, encapsulation, inheritance, polymorphism and interfaces—the most essential aspects of object-oriented programming.

Next, you'll learn about exceptions, useful for handling errors during a program's execution. Exception handling helps you build more robust programs.

Self-Review Exercises (Sections G.1–G.5)

G.1 Fill in the blanks in each of the following statements:
- a) _____ is a form of software reusability in which new classes acquire the members of existing classes and embellish those classes with new capabilities.
- b) A superclass's _____ members can be accessed in the superclass declaration *and in* subclass declarations.
- c) In a(n) _____ relationship, an object of a subclass can also be treated as an object of its superclass.
- d) In a(n) _____ relationship, a class object has references to objects of other classes as members.
- e) In single inheritance, a class exists in a(n) _____ relationship with its subclasses.
- f) A superclass's _____ members are accessible anywhere that the program has a reference to an object of that superclass or to an object of one of its subclasses.
- g) When an object of a subclass is instantiated, a superclass _____ is called implicitly or explicitly.
- h) Subclass constructors can call superclass constructors via the _____ keyword.

G.2 State whether each of the following is *true* or *false*. If a statement is *false*, explain why.
- a) Superclass constructors are not inherited by subclasses.
- b) A *has-a* relationship is implemented via inheritance.
- c) A Car class has an *is-a* relationship with the SteeringWheel and Brakes classes.
- d) When a subclass redefines a superclass method by using the same signature, the subclass is said to overload that superclass method.

Self-Review Exercises (Sections G.6–G.13)

G.3 Fill in the blanks in each of the following statements:
- a) If a class contains at least one abstract method, it's a(n) _____ class.
- b) Classes from which objects can be instantiated are called _____ classes.
- c) _____ involves using a superclass variable to invoke methods on superclass and subclass objects, enabling you to "program in the general."
- d) Methods that are not interface methods and that do not provide implementations must be declared using keyword _____.
- e) Casting a reference stored in a superclass variable to a subclass type is called _____.

G.4 State whether each of the statements that follows is *true* or *false*. If *false*, explain why.
- a) All methods in an abstract class must be declared as abstract methods.
- b) Invoking a subclass-only method through a subclass variable is not allowed.
- c) If a superclass declares an abstract method, a subclass must implement that method.

d) An object of a class that implements an interface may be thought of as an object of that interface type.

Answers to Self-Review Exercises (Sections G.1–G.5)

G.1 a) Inheritance. b) public and protected. c) *is-a* or inheritance. d) *has-a* or composition. e) hierarchical. f) public. g) constructor. h) super.

G.2 a) True. b) False. A *has-a* relationship is implemented via composition. An *is-a* relationship is implemented via inheritance. c) False. This is an example of a *has-a* relationship. Class Car has an *is-a* relationship with class Vehicle. d) False. This is known as overriding, not overloading—an overloaded method has the same name, but a different signature.

Answers to Self-Review Exercises (Sections G.6–G.13)

G.3 a) abstract. b) concrete. c) Polymorphism. d) abstract. e) downcasting.

G.4 a) False. An abstract class can include methods with implementations and abstract methods. b) False. Trying to invoke a subclass-only method with a superclass variable is not allowed. c) False. Only a concrete subclass must implement the method. d) True.

Exercises (Sections G.1–G.5)

G.5 Discuss the ways in which inheritance promotes software reuse, saves time during program development and helps prevent errors.

G.6 Draw an inheritance hierarchy for students at a university similar to the hierarchy shown in Fig. G.2. Use Student as the superclass of the hierarchy, then extend Student with classes UndergraduateStudent and GraduateStudent. Continue to extend the hierarchy as deep (i.e., as many levels) as possible. For example, Freshman, Sophomore, Junior and Senior might extend UndergraduateStudent, and DoctoralStudent and MastersStudent might be subclasses of GraduateStudent. After drawing the hierarchy, discuss the relationships that exist between the classes. [*Note:* You do not need to write any code for this exercise.]

G.7 Some programmers prefer not to use protected access, because they believe it breaks the encapsulation of the superclass. Discuss the relative merits of using protected access vs. using private access in superclasses.

G.8 Write an inheritance hierarchy for classes Quadrilateral, Trapezoid, Parallelogram, Rectangle and Square. Use Quadrilateral as the superclass of the hierarchy. Create and use a Point class to represent the points in each shape. Make the hierarchy as deep (i.e., as many levels) as possible. Specify the instance variables and methods for each class. The private instance variables of Quadrilateral should be the *x-y* coordinate pairs for the four endpoints of the Quadrilateral. Write a program that instantiates objects of your classes and outputs each object's area (except Quadrilateral).

Exercises (Sections G.6–G.13)

G.9 How does polymorphism enable you to program "in the general" rather than "in the specific"? Discuss the key advantages of programming "in the general."

G.10 What are abstract methods? Describe the circumstances in which an abstract method would be appropriate.

G.11 How does polymorphism promote extensibility?

G.12 Discuss four ways in which you can assign superclass and subclass references to variables of superclass and subclass types.

G.13 Compare and contrast abstract classes and interfaces. Why would you use an abstract class? Why would you use an interface?

G.14 *(Payroll System Modification)* Modify the payroll system of Figs. G.16–G.21 to include `private` instance variable `birthDate` in class `Employee`. Use class `Date` of Fig. F.7 to represent an employee's birthday. Add *get* methods to class `Date`. Assume that payroll is processed once per month. Create an array of `Employee` variables to store references to the various employee objects. In a loop, calculate the payroll for each `Employee` (polymorphically), and add a $100.00 bonus to the person's payroll amount if the current month is the one in which the `Employee`'s birthday occurs.

G.15 *(Payroll System Modification)* Modify the payroll system of Figs. G.16–G.21 to include an additional `Employee` subclass `PieceWorker` that represents an employee whose pay is based on the number of pieces of merchandise produced. Class `PieceWorker` should contain `private` instance variables `wage` (to store the employee's wage per piece) and `pieces` (to store the number of pieces produced). Provide a concrete implementation of method `earnings` in class `PieceWorker` that calculates the employee's earnings by multiplying the number of pieces produced by the wage per piece. Create an array of `Employee` variables to store references to objects of each concrete class in the new `Employee` hierarchy. For each `Employee`, display its `String` representation and earnings.

G.16 *(Accounts Payable System Modification)* In this exercise, we modify the accounts payable application of Figs. G.23–G.27 to include the complete functionality of the payroll application of Figs. G.16–G.21. The application should still process two `Invoice` objects, but now should process one object of each of the four `Employee` subclasses. If the object currently being processed is a `BasePlusCommissionEmployee`, the application should increase the `BasePlusCommissionEmployee`'s base salary by 10%. Finally, the application should output the payment amount for each object. Complete the following steps to create the new application:

  a) Modify classes `HourlyEmployee` (Fig. G.18) and `CommissionEmployee` (Fig. G.19) to place them in the `Payable` hierarchy as subclasses of the version of `Employee` (Fig. G.25) that implements `Payable`. [*Hint:* Change the name of method `earnings` to `getPaymentAmount` in each subclass so that the class satisfies its inherited contract with interface `Payable`.]

  b) Modify class `BasePlusCommissionEmployee` (Fig. G.20) such that it extends the version of class `CommissionEmployee` created in part (a).

  c) Modify `PayableInterfaceTest` (Fig. G.27) to polymorphically process two `Invoices`, one `SalariedEmployee`, one `HourlyEmployee`, one `CommissionEmployee` and one `BasePlusCommissionEmployee`. First output a `String` representation of each `Payable` object. Next, if an object is a `BasePlusCommissionEmployee`, increase its base salary by 10%. Finally, output the payment amount for each `Payable` object.

G.17 *(Accounts Payable System Modification)* It's possible to include the functionality of the payroll application (Figs. G.16–G.21) in the accounts payable application without modifying `Employee` subclasses `SalariedEmployee`, `HourlyEmployee`, `CommissionEmployee` or `BasePlusCommissionEmplyee`. To do so, you can modify class `Employee` (Fig. G.16) to implement interface `Payable` and declare method `getPaymentAmount` to invoke method `earnings`. Method `getPaymentAmount` would then be inherited by the subclasses in the `Employee` hierarchy. When `getPaymentAmount` is called for a particular subclass object, it polymorphically invokes the appropriate `earnings` method for that subclass. Reimplement Exercise G.16 using the original `Employee` hierarchy from the payroll application of Figs. G.16–G.21. Modify class `Employee` as described in this exercise, and *do not* modify any of class `Employee`'s subclasses.

H

Exception Handling: A Deeper Look

Objectives

In this appendix you'll:

- Learn what exceptions are and how they're handled.
- Understand when to use exception handling.
- Use `try` blocks to delimit code in which exceptions might occur.
- `throw` exceptions to indicate a problem.
- Use `catch` blocks to specify exception handlers.
- Use the `finally` block to release resources.
- Become familiar with the exception class hierarchy.

H.1 Introduction

An exception is an indication of a problem that occurs during a program's execution. Exception handling enables you to create applications that can resolve (or handle) exceptions. In many cases, handling an exception allows a program to continue executing as if no problem had been encountered. The features presented in this appendix help you write robust programs that can deal with problems and continue executing or terminate gracefully.

H.2 Example: Divide by Zero without Exception Handling

First we demonstrate what happens when errors arise in an application that does not use exception handling. Figure H.1 prompts the user for two integers and passes them to method quotient, which calculates the integer quotient and returns an int result. In this example, you'll see that exceptions are **thrown** (i.e., the exception occurs) when a method detects a problem and is unable to handle it.

```java
1   // Fig. H.1: DivideByZeroNoExceptionHandling.java
2   // Integer division without exception handling.
3   import java.util.Scanner;
4
5   public class DivideByZeroNoExceptionHandling
6   {
7      // demonstrates throwing an exception when a divide-by-zero occurs
8      public static int quotient( int numerator, int denominator )
9      {
10         return numerator / denominator; // possible division by zero
11      } // end method quotient
12
13      public static void main( String[] args )
14      {
15         Scanner scanner = new Scanner( System.in ); // scanner for input
16
17         System.out.print( "Please enter an integer numerator: " );
18         int numerator = scanner.nextInt();
19         System.out.print( "Please enter an integer denominator: " );
20         int denominator = scanner.nextInt();
21
```

Fig. H.1 | Integer division without exception handling. (Part 1 of 2.)

```
22            int result = quotient( numerator, denominator );
23            System.out.printf(
24               "\nResult: %d / %d = %d\n", numerator, denominator, result );
25        } // end main
26    } // end class DivideByZeroNoExceptionHandling
```

```
Please enter an integer numerator: 100
Please enter an integer denominator: 7

Result: 100 / 7 = 14
```

```
Please enter an integer numerator: 100
Please enter an integer denominator: 0
Exception in thread "main" java.lang.ArithmeticException: / by zero
        at DivideByZeroNoExceptionHandling.quotient(
           DivideByZeroNoExceptionHandling.java:10)
        at DivideByZeroNoExceptionHandling.main(
           DivideByZeroNoExceptionHandling.java:22)
```

```
Please enter an integer numerator: 100
Please enter an integer denominator: hello
Exception in thread "main" java.util.InputMismatchException
        at java.util.Scanner.throwFor(Unknown Source)
        at java.util.Scanner.next(Unknown Source)
        at java.util.Scanner.nextInt(Unknown Source)
        at java.util.Scanner.nextInt(Unknown Source)
        at DivideByZeroNoExceptionHandling.main(
           DivideByZeroNoExceptionHandling.java:20)
```

Fig. H.1 | Integer division without exception handling. (Part 2 of 2.)

The first sample execution in Fig. H.1 shows a successful division. In the second execution, the user enters the value 0 as the denominator. Several lines of information are displayed in response to this invalid input. This information is known as a **stack trace**, which includes the name of the exception (java.lang.ArithmeticException) in a descriptive message that indicates the problem that occurred and the method-call stack (i.e., the call chain) at the time it occurred. The stack trace includes the path of execution that led to the exception method by method. This helps you debug the program. The first line specifies that an ArithmeticException has occurred. The text after the name of the exception ("/ by zero") indicates that this exception occurred as a result of an attempt to divide by zero. Java does not allow division by zero in integer arithmetic. When this occurs, Java throws an **ArithmeticException**. ArithmeticExceptions can arise from a number of different problems in arithmetic, so the extra data ("/ by zero") provides more specific information. Java *does* allow division by zero with floating-point values. Such a calculation results in the value positive or negative infinity, which is represented in Java as a floating-point value (but displays as the string Infinity or -Infinity). If 0.0 is divided by 0.0, the result is NaN (not a number), which is also represented in Java as a floating-point value (but displays as NaN).

Starting from the last line of the stack trace, we see that the exception was detected in line 22 of method main. Each line of the stack trace contains the class name and method (DivideByZeroNoExceptionHandling.main) followed by the file name and line number (DivideByZeroNoExceptionHandling.java:22). Moving up the stack trace, we see that the exception occurs in line 10, in method quotient. The top row of the call chain indicates the **throw point**—the initial point at which the exception occurs. The throw point of this exception is in line 10 of method quotient.

In the third execution, the user enters the string "hello" as the denominator. Notice again that a stack trace is displayed. This informs us that an InputMismatchException has occurred (package java.util). Our prior examples that read numeric values from the user assumed that the user would input a proper integer value. However, users sometimes make mistakes and input noninteger values. An **InputMismatchException** occurs when Scanner method nextInt receives a string that does not represent a valid integer. Starting from the end of the stack trace, we see that the exception was detected in line 20 of method main. Moving up the stack trace, we see that the exception occurred in method nextInt. Notice that in place of the file name and line number, we're provided with the text Unknown Source. This means that the so-called debugging symbols that provide the filename and line number information for that method's class were not available to the JVM—this is typically the case for the classes of the Java API. Many IDEs have access to the Java API source code and will display file names and line numbers in stack traces.

In the sample executions of Fig. H.1 when exceptions occur and stack traces are displayed, the program also exits. This does not always occur in Java—sometimes a program may continue even though an exception has occurred and a stack trace has been printed. In such cases, the application may produce unexpected results. For example, a graphical user interface (GUI) application will often continue executing. The next section demonstrates how to handle these exceptions.

In Fig. H.1 both types of exceptions were detected in method main. In the next example, we'll see how to handle these exceptions to enable the program to run to normal completion.

H.3 Example: Handling ArithmeticExceptions and InputMismatchExceptions

The application in Fig. H.2, which is based on Fig. H.1, uses exception handling to process any ArithmeticExceptions and InputMismatchExceptions that arise. The application still prompts the user for two integers and passes them to method quotient, which calculates the quotient and returns an int result. This version of the application uses exception handling so that if the user makes a mistake, the program catches and handles (i.e., deals with) the exception—in this case, allowing the user to enter the input again.

```
1   // Fig. H.2: DivideByZeroWithExceptionHandling.java
2   // Handling ArithmeticExceptions and InputMismatchExceptions.
3   import java.util.InputMismatchException;
4   import java.util.Scanner;
```

Fig. H.2 | Handling ArithmeticExceptions and InputMismatchExceptions. (Part 1 of 3.)

```java
5
6    public class DivideByZeroWithExceptionHandling
7    {
8       // demonstrates throwing an exception when a divide-by-zero occurs
9       public static int quotient( int numerator, int denominator )
10         throws ArithmeticException
11      {
12         return numerator / denominator; // possible division by zero
13      } // end method quotient
14
15      public static void main( String[] args )
16      {
17         Scanner scanner = new Scanner( System.in ); // scanner for input
18         boolean continueLoop = true; // determines if more input is needed
19
20         do
21         {
22            try // read two numbers and calculate quotient
23            {
24               System.out.print( "Please enter an integer numerator: " );
25               int numerator = scanner.nextInt();
26               System.out.print( "Please enter an integer denominator: " );
27               int denominator = scanner.nextInt();
28
29               int result = quotient( numerator, denominator );
30               System.out.printf( "\nResult: %d / %d = %d\n", numerator,
31                  denominator, result );
32               continueLoop = false; // input successful; end looping
33            } // end try
34            catch ( InputMismatchException inputMismatchException )
35            {
36               System.err.printf( "\nException: %s\n",
37                  inputMismatchException );
38               scanner.nextLine(); // discard input so user can try again
39               System.out.println(
40                  "You must enter integers. Please try again.\n" );
41            } // end catch
42            catch ( ArithmeticException arithmeticException )
43            {
44               System.err.printf( "\nException: %s\n", arithmeticException );
45               System.out.println(
46                  "Zero is an invalid denominator. Please try again.\n" );
47            } // end catch
48         } while ( continueLoop ); // end do...while
49      } // end main
50   } // end class DivideByZeroWithExceptionHandling
```

```
Please enter an integer numerator: 100
Please enter an integer denominator: 7

Result: 100 / 7 = 14
```

Fig. H.2 | Handling ArithmeticExceptions and InputMismatchExceptions. (Part 2 of 3.)

```
Please enter an integer numerator: 100
Please enter an integer denominator: 0

Exception: java.lang.ArithmeticException: / by zero
Zero is an invalid denominator. Please try again.

Please enter an integer numerator: 100
Please enter an integer denominator: 7

Result: 100 / 7 = 14
```

```
Please enter an integer numerator: 100
Please enter an integer denominator: hello

Exception: java.util.InputMismatchException
You must enter integers. Please try again.

Please enter an integer numerator: 100
Please enter an integer denominator: 7

Result: 100 / 7 = 14
```

Fig. H.2 | Handling ArithmeticExceptions and InputMismatchExceptions. (Part 3 of 3.)

The first sample execution in Fig. H.2 is a successful one that does not encounter any problems. In the second execution the user enters a zero denominator, and an ArithmeticException exception occurs. In the third execution the user enters the string "hello" as the denominator, and an InputMismatchException occurs. For each exception, the user is informed of the mistake and asked to try again, then is prompted for two new integers. In each sample execution, the program runs successfully to completion.

Class InputMismatchException is imported in line 3. Class ArithmeticException does not need to be imported because it's in package java.lang. Line 18 creates the boolean variable continueLoop, which is true if the user has not yet entered valid input. Lines 20–48 repeatedly ask users for input until a valid input is received.

Enclosing Code in a try Block

Lines 22–33 contain a **try block**, which encloses the code that might throw an exception and the code that should not execute if an exception occurs (i.e., if an exception occurs, the remaining code in the try block will be skipped). A try block consists of the keyword try followed by a block of code enclosed in curly braces. [*Note:* The term "try block" sometimes refers only to the block of code that follows the try keyword (not including the try keyword itself). For simplicity, we use the term "try block" to refer to the block of code that follows the try keyword, as well as the try keyword.] The statements that read the integers from the keyboard (lines 25 and 27) each use method nextInt to read an int value. Method nextInt throws an InputMismatchException if the value read in is not an integer.

The division that can cause an ArithmeticException is not performed in the try block. Rather, the call to method quotient (line 29) invokes the code that attempts the division (line 12); the JVM throws an ArithmeticException object when the denominator is zero.

Software Engineering Observation H.1

Exceptions may surface through explicitly mentioned code in a try block, through calls to other methods, through deeply nested method calls initiated by code in a try block or from the Java Virtual Machine as it executes Java bytecodes.

Catching Exceptions

The try block in this example is followed by two catch blocks—one that handles an InputMismatchException (lines 34–41) and one that handles an ArithmeticException (lines 42–47). A **catch block** (also called a **catch clause** or **exception handler**) catches (i.e., receives) and handles an exception. A catch block begins with the keyword catch and is followed by a parameter in parentheses (called the exception parameter, discussed shortly) and a block of code enclosed in curly braces. [*Note:* The term "catch clause" is sometimes used to refer to the keyword catch followed by a block of code, whereas the term "catch block" refers to only the block of code following the catch keyword, but not including it. For simplicity, we use the term "catch block" to refer to the block of code following the catch keyword, as well as the keyword itself.]

At least one catch block or a **finally block** (discussed in Section H.6) must immediately follow the try block. Each catch block specifies in parentheses an **exception parameter** that identifies the exception type the handler can process. When an exception occurs in a try block, the catch block that executes is the *first* one whose type matches the type of the exception that occurred (i.e., the type in the catch block matches the thrown exception type exactly or is a superclass of it). The exception parameter's name enables the catch block to interact with a caught exception object—e.g., to implicitly invoke the caught exception's toString method (as in lines 37 and 44), which displays basic information about the exception. Notice that we use the **System.err (standard error stream) object** to output error messages. By default, System.err's print methods, like those of System.out, display data to the command prompt.

Line 38 of the first catch block calls Scanner method nextLine. Because an InputMismatchException occurred, the call to method nextInt never successfully read in the user's data—so we read that input with a call to method nextLine. We do not do anything with the input at this point, because we know that it's invalid. Each catch block displays an error message and asks the user to try again. After either catch block terminates, the user is prompted for input. We'll soon take a deeper look at how this flow of control works in exception handling.

Common Programming Error H.1

It's a syntax error to place code between a try block and its corresponding catch blocks.

Common Programming Error H.2

Each catch block can have only a single parameter—specifying a comma-separated list of exception parameters is a syntax error.

An **uncaught exception** is one for which there are no matching catch blocks. You saw uncaught exceptions in the second and third outputs of Fig. H.1. Recall that when exceptions occurred in that example, the application terminated early (after displaying the exception's stack trace). This does not always occur as a result of uncaught exceptions. Java uses a "multithreaded" model of program execution—each **thread** is a parallel activity. One program can have many threads. If a program has only one thread, an uncaught exception will cause the program to terminate. If a program has multiple threads, an uncaught exception will terminate *only* the thread where the exception occurred. In such programs, however, certain threads may rely on others, and if one thread terminates due to an uncaught exception, there may be adverse effects to the rest of the program. Appendix J discusses these issues.

Termination Model of Exception Handling

If an exception occurs in a try block (such as an InputMismatchException being thrown as a result of the code at line 25 of Fig. H.2), the try block terminates immediately and program control transfers to the *first* of the following catch blocks in which the exception parameter's type matches the thrown exception's type. In Fig. H.2, the first catch block catches InputMismatchExceptions (which occur if invalid input is entered) and the second catch block catches ArithmeticExceptions (which occur if an attempt is made to divide by zero). After the exception is handled, program control does *not* return to the throw point, because the try block has *expired* (and its local variables have been lost). Rather, control resumes after the last catch block. This is known as the **termination model of exception handling**. Some languages use the **resumption model of exception handling**, in which, after an exception is handled, control resumes just after the throw point.

Notice that we name our exception parameters (inputMismatchException and arithmeticException) based on their type. Java programmers often simply use the letter e as the name of their exception parameters.

After executing a catch block, this program's flow of control proceeds to the first statement after the last catch block (line 48 in this case). The condition in the do...while statement is true (variable continueLoop contains its initial value of true), so control returns to the beginning of the loop and the user is once again prompted for input. This control statement will loop until valid input is entered. At that point, program control reaches line 32, which assigns false to variable continueLoop. The try block then terminates. If no exceptions are thrown in the try block, the catch blocks are skipped and control continues with the first statement after the catch blocks (we'll learn about another possibility when we discuss the finally block in Section H.6). Now the condition for the do...while loop is false, and method main ends.

The try block and its corresponding catch and/or finally blocks form a **try statement**. Do not confuse the terms "try block" and "try statement"—the latter includes the try block as well as the following catch blocks and/or finally block.

As with any other block of code, when a try block terminates, local variables declared in the block go out of scope and are no longer accessible; thus, the local variables of a try block are not accessible in the corresponding catch blocks. When a catch block terminates, local variables declared within the catch block (including the exception parameter of that catch block) also go out of scope and are destroyed. Any remaining catch blocks in the try statement are ignored, and execution resumes at the first line of code after the try...catch sequence—this will be a finally block, if one is present.

*Using the **throws** Clause*

Now let's examine method quotient (Fig. H.2, lines 9–13). The portion of the method declaration located at line 10 is known as a **throws clause**. It specifies the exceptions the method throws. This clause appears *after* the method's parameter list and *before* the method's body. It contains a comma-separated list of the exceptions that the method will throw if various problems occur. Such exceptions may be thrown by statements in the method's body or by methods called from the body. A method can throw exceptions of the classes listed in its throws clause or of their subclasses. We've added the throws clause to this application to indicate to the rest of the program that this method may throw an ArithmeticException. Clients of method quotient are thus informed that the method may throw an ArithmeticException. You'll learn more about the throws clause in Section H.5.

When line 12 executes, if the denominator is zero, the JVM throws an ArithmeticException object. This object will be caught by the catch block at lines 42–47, which displays basic information about the exception by implicitly invoking the exception's toString method, then asks the user to try again.

If the denominator is not zero, method quotient performs the division and returns the result to the point of invocation of method quotient in the try block (line 29). Lines 30–31 display the result of the calculation and line 32 sets continueLoop to false. In this case, the try block completes successfully, so the program skips the catch blocks and fails the condition at line 48, and method main completes execution normally.

When quotient throws an ArithmeticException, quotient terminates and does not return a value, and quotient's local variables go out of scope (and are destroyed). If quotient contained local variables that were references to objects and there were no other references to those objects, the objects would be marked for garbage collection. Also, when an exception occurs, the try block from which quotient was called terminates before lines 30–32 can execute. Here, too, if local variables were created in the try block prior to the exception's being thrown, these variables would go out of scope.

If an InputMismatchException is generated by lines 25 or 27, the try block terminates and execution continues with the catch block at lines 34–41. In this case, method quotient is not called. Then method main continues after the last catch block (line 48).

H.4 When to Use Exception Handling

Exception handling is designed to process **synchronous errors**, which occur when a statement executes. Common examples we'll see throughout the book are out-of-range array indices, arithmetic overflow (i.e., a value outside the representable range of values), division by zero, invalid method parameters, thread interruption (as we'll see in Appendix J) and unsuccessful memory allocation (due to lack of memory). Exception handling is not designed to process problems associated with **asynchronous events** (e.g., disk I/O completions, network message arrivals, mouse clicks and keystrokes), which occur in parallel with, and independent of, the program's flow of control.

H.5 Java Exception Hierarchy

All Java exception classes inherit directly or indirectly from class **Exception**, forming an inheritance hierarchy. You can extend this hierarchy with your own exception classes. Class **Throwable** (a subclass of Object) is the superclass of class Exception. Only Throwable objects can be used with the exception-handling mechanism. Class Throwable has two subclasses: Exception and Error. Class Exception and its subclasses—for instance, RuntimeException (package java.lang) and IOException (package java.io)—represent exceptional situations that can occur in a Java program and that can be caught by the application. Class **Error** and its subclasses represent abnormal situations that happen in the JVM. Most *Errors happen infrequently and should not be caught by applications—it's usually not possible for applications to recover from Errors.*

Checked vs. Unchecked Exceptions

Java distinguishes between **checked exceptions** and **unchecked exceptions**. This distinction is important, because the Java compiler enforces a **catch-or-declare requirement** for checked exceptions. An exception's type determines whether it's checked or unchecked. All exception types that are direct or indirect subclasses of class **RuntimeException** (package java.lang) are unchecked exceptions. These are typically caused by defects in your program's code. Examples of unchecked exceptions include ArrayIndexOutOfBoundsExceptions (discussed in Appendix E) and ArithmeticExceptions. All classes that inherit from class Exception but not class RuntimeException are considered to be checked exceptions. Such exceptions are typically caused by conditions that are not under the control of the program—for example, in file processing, the program can't open a file because the file does not exist. Classes that inherit from class Error are considered to be unchecked.

The compiler *checks* each method call and method declaration to determine whether the method throws checked exceptions. If so, the compiler verifies that the checked exception is caught or is declared in a throws clause. We show how to catch and declare checked exceptions in the next several examples. Recall from Section H.3 that the throws clause specifies the exceptions a method throws. Such exceptions are not caught in the method's body. To satisfy the *catch* part of the catch-or-declare requirement, the code that generates the exception must be wrapped in a try block and must provide a catch handler for the checked-exception type (or one of its superclass types). To satisfy the *declare* part of the catch-or-declare requirement, the method containing the code that generates the exception must provide a throws clause containing the checked-exception type after its parameter list and before its method body. If the catch-or-declare requirement is not satisfied, the compiler will issue an error message indicating that the exception must be caught or declared. This forces you to think about the problems that may occur when a method that throws checked exceptions is called.

Software Engineering Observation H.2
You must deal with checked exceptions. This results in more robust code than would be created if you were able to simply ignore the exceptions.

Common Programming Error H.3
A compilation error occurs if a method explicitly attempts to throw a checked exception (or calls another method that throws a checked exception) and that exception is not listed in that method's throws clause.

Common Programming Error H.4
If a subclass method overrides a superclass method, it's an error for the subclass method to list more exceptions in its throws clause than the overridden superclass method does. However, a subclass's throws clause can contain a subset of a superclass's throws list.

Software Engineering Observation H.3

If your method calls other methods that throw checked exceptions, those exceptions must be caught or declared in your method. If an exception can be handled meaningfully in a method, the method should catch the exception rather than declare it.

Unlike checked exceptions, the Java compiler does *not* check the code to determine whether an unchecked exception is caught or declared. Unchecked exceptions typically can be prevented by proper coding. For example, the unchecked ArithmeticException thrown by method quotient (lines 9–13) in Fig. H.2 can be avoided if the method ensures that the denominator is not zero *before* attempting to perform the division. Unchecked exceptions are not required to be listed in a method's throws clause—even if they are, it's not required that such exceptions be caught by an application.

Software Engineering Observation H.4

Although the compiler does not enforce the catch-or-declare requirement for unchecked exceptions, provide appropriate exception-handling code when it's known that such exceptions might occur. For example, a program should process the NumberFormatException from Integer method parseInt, even though NumberFormatException (an indirect subclass of RuntimeException) is an unchecked exception type. This makes your programs more robust.

Catching Subclass Exceptions

If a catch handler is written to catch superclass-type exception objects, it can also catch all objects of that class's subclasses. This enables catch to handle related errors with a concise notation and allows for polymorphic processing of related exceptions. You can certainly catch each subclass type individually if those exceptions require different processing.

Only the First Matching catch Executes

If there are *multiple* catch blocks that match a particular exception type, only the *first* matching catch block executes when an exception of that type occurs. It's a compilation error to catch the *exact same type* in two different catch blocks associated with a particular try block. However, there may be several catch blocks that match an exception—i.e., several catch blocks whose types are the same as the exception type or a superclass of that type. For instance, we could follow a catch block for type ArithmeticException with a catch block for type Exception—both would match ArithmeticExceptions, but only the first matching catch block would execute.

Error-Prevention Tip H.1

Catching subclass types individually is subject to error if you forget to test for one or more of the subclass types explicitly; catching the superclass guarantees that objects of all subclasses will be caught. Positioning a catch block for the superclass type after all other subclass catch blocks ensures that all subclass exceptions are eventually caught.

Common Programming Error H.5

Placing a catch block for a superclass exception type before other catch blocks that catch subclass exception types would prevent those catch blocks from executing, so a compilation error occurs.

H.6 finally Block

Programs that obtain certain types of resources must return them to the system explicitly to avoid so-called **resource leaks.** In programming languages such as C and C++, the most common kind of resource leak is a memory leak. Java performs automatic garbage collection of memory no longer used by programs, thus avoiding most memory leaks. However, other types of resource leaks can occur. For example, files, database connections and network connections that are not closed properly after they're no longer needed might not be available for use in other programs.

Error-Prevention Tip H.2

A subtle issue is that Java does not entirely eliminate memory leaks. Java will not garbage-collect an object until there are no remaining references to it. Thus, if you erroneously keep references to unwanted objects, memory leaks can occur. To help avoid this problem, set reference-type variables to null when they're no longer needed.

The finally block (which consists of the finally keyword, followed by code enclosed in curly braces), sometimes referred to as the **finally clause,** is optional. If it's present, it's placed after the last catch block. If there are no catch blocks, the finally block immediately follows the try block.

The finally block will execute whether or not an exception is thrown in the corresponding try block. The finally block also will execute if a try block exits by using a return, break or continue statement or simply by reaching its closing right brace. The finally block will *not* execute if the application exits early from a try block by calling method **System.exit.** This method immediately terminates an application.

Because a finally block almost always executes, it typically contains resource-release code. Suppose a resource is allocated in a try block. If no exception occurs, the catch blocks are skipped and control proceeds to the finally block, which frees the resource. Control then proceeds to the first statement after the finally block. If an exception occurs in the try block, the try block terminates. If the program catches the exception in one of the corresponding catch blocks, it processes the exception, then the finally block releases the resource and control proceeds to the first statement after the finally block. If the program doesn't catch the exception, the finally block *still* releases the resource and an attempt is made to catch the exception in a calling method.

Error-Prevention Tip H.3

The finally block is an ideal place to release resources acquired in a try block (such as opened files), which helps eliminate resource leaks.

Performance Tip H.1

Always release a resource explicitly and at the earliest possible moment at which it's no longer needed. This makes resources available for reuse as early as possible, thus improving resource utilization.

If an exception that occurs in a try block cannot be caught by one of that try block's catch handlers, the program skips the rest of the try block and control proceeds to the finally block. Then the program passes the exception to the next outer try block—normally in the calling method—where an associated catch block might catch it. This process can occur through many levels of try blocks. Also, the exception could go uncaught.

If a catch block throws an exception, the finally block still executes. Then the exception is passed to the next outer try block—again, normally in the calling method.

Figure H.3 demonstrates that the finally block executes even if an exception is not thrown in the corresponding try block. The program contains static methods main (lines 6–18), throwException (lines 21–44) and doesNotThrowException (lines 47–64). Methods throwException and doesNotThrowException are declared static, so main can call them directly without instantiating a UsingExceptions object.

```
1   // Fig. H.3: UsingExceptions.java
2   // try...catch...finally exception handling mechanism.
3
4   public class UsingExceptions
5   {
6      public static void main( String[] args )
7      {
8         try
9         {
10           throwException(); // call method throwException
11        } // end try
12        catch ( Exception exception ) // exception thrown by throwException
13        {
14           System.err.println( "Exception handled in main" );
15        } // end catch
16
17        doesNotThrowException();
18     } // end main
19
20     // demonstrate try...catch...finally
21     public static void throwException() throws Exception
22     {
23        try // throw an exception and immediately catch it
24        {
25           System.out.println( "Method throwException" );
26           throw new Exception(); // generate exception
27        } // end try
28        catch ( Exception exception ) // catch exception thrown in try
29        {
30           System.err.println(
31              "Exception handled in method throwException" );
32           throw exception; // rethrow for further processing
33
34           // code here would not be reached; would cause compilation errors
35
36        } // end catch
37        finally // executes regardless of what occurs in try...catch
38        {
39           System.err.println( "Finally executed in throwException" );
40        } // end finally
41
```

Fig. H.3 | try...catch...finally exception-handling mechanism. (Part 1 of 2.)

```
42        // code here would not be reached; would cause compilation errors
43
44     } // end method throwException
45
46     // demonstrate finally when no exception occurs
47     public static void doesNotThrowException()
48     {
49        try // try block does not throw an exception
50        {
51           System.out.println( "Method doesNotThrowException" );
52        } // end try
53        catch ( Exception exception ) // does not execute
54        {
55           System.err.println( exception );
56        } // end catch
57        finally // executes regardless of what occurs in try...catch
58        {
59           System.err.println(
60              "Finally executed in doesNotThrowException" );
61        } // end finally
62
63        System.out.println( "End of method doesNotThrowException" );
64     } // end method doesNotThrowException
65  } // end class UsingExceptions
```

```
Method throwException
Exception handled in method throwException
Finally executed in throwException
Exception handled in main
Method doesNotThrowException
Finally executed in doesNotThrowException
End of method doesNotThrowException
```

Fig. H.3 | try...catch...finally exception-handling mechanism. (Part 2 of 2.)

System.out and System.err are **streams**—sequences of bytes. While System.out (known as the **standard output stream**) displays a program's output, System.err (known as the **standard error stream**) displays a program's errors. Output from these streams can be redirected (i.e., sent to somewhere other than the command prompt, such as to a file). Using two different streams enables you to easily separate error messages from other output. For instance, data output from System.err could be sent to a log file, while data output from System.out can be displayed on the screen. For simplicity, this appendix will not redirect output from System.err, but will display such messages to the command prompt. You'll learn more about streams in Appendix J.

*Throwing Exceptions Using the **throw** Statement*
Method main (Fig. H.3) begins executing, enters its try block and immediately calls method throwException (line 10). Method throwException throws an Exception. The statement at line 26 is known as a **throw statement**—it's executed to indicate that an exception has occurred. So far, you've only caught exceptions thrown by called methods.

You can throw exceptions yourself by using the throw statement. Just as with exceptions thrown by the Java API's methods, this indicates to client applications that an error has occurred. A throw statement specifies an object to be thrown. The operand of a throw can be of any class derived from class Throwable.

> **Software Engineering Observation H.5**
> *When toString is invoked on any Throwable object, its resulting string includes the descriptive string that was supplied to the constructor, or simply the class name if no string was supplied.*

> **Software Engineering Observation H.6**
> *An object can be thrown without containing information about the problem that occurred. In this case, simply knowing that an exception of a particular type occurred may provide sufficient information for the handler to process the problem correctly.*

> **Software Engineering Observation H.7**
> *Exceptions can be thrown from constructors. When an error is detected in a constructor, an exception should be thrown to avoid creating an improperly formed object.*

Rethrowing Exceptions

Line 32 of Fig. H.3 **rethrows the exception**. Exceptions are rethrown when a catch block, upon receiving an exception, decides either that it cannot process that exception or that it can only partially process it. Rethrowing an exception defers the exception handling (or perhaps a portion of it) to another catch block associated with an outer try statement. An exception is rethrown by using the **throw keyword**, followed by a reference to the exception object that was just caught. Exceptions cannot be rethrown from a finally block, as the exception parameter (a local variable) from the catch block no longer exists.

When a rethrow occurs, the *next enclosing try block* detects the rethrown exception, and that try block's catch blocks attempt to handle it. In this case, the next enclosing try block is found at lines 8–11 in method main. Before the rethrown exception is handled, however, the finally block (lines 37–40) executes. Then method main detects the rethrown exception in the try block and handles it in the catch block (lines 12–15).

Next, main calls method doesNotThrowException (line 17). No exception is thrown in doesNotThrowException's try block (lines 49–52), so the program skips the catch block (lines 53–56), but the finally block (lines 57–61) nevertheless executes. Control proceeds to the statement after the finally block (line 63). Then control returns to main and the program terminates.

> **Common Programming Error H.6**
> *If an exception has not been caught when control enters a finally block and the finally block throws an exception that's not caught in the finally block, the first exception will be lost and the exception from the finally block will be returned to the calling method.*

> **Error-Prevention Tip H.4**
> *Avoid placing code that can throw an exception in a finally block. If such code is required, enclose the code in a try...catch within the finally block.*

Common Programming Error H.7

Assuming that an exception thrown from a catch block will be processed by that catch block or any other catch block associated with the same try statement can lead to logic errors.

Good Programming Practice H.1

Exception handling is intended to remove error-processing code from the main line of a program's code to improve program clarity. Do not place try...catch...finally around every statement that may throw an exception. This makes programs difficult to read. Rather, place one try block around a significant portion of your code, follow that try block with catch blocks that handle each possible exception and follow the catch blocks with a single finally block (if one is required).

H.7 Stack Unwinding and Obtaining Information from an Exception Object

When an exception is thrown but not caught in a particular scope, the method-call stack is "unwound," and an attempt is made to catch the exception in the next outer try block. This process is called **stack unwinding**. Unwinding the method-call stack means that the method in which the exception was not caught *terminates*, all local variables in that method go out of scope and control returns to the statement that originally invoked that method. If a try block encloses that statement, an attempt is made to catch the exception. If a try block does not enclose that statement or if the exception is not caught, stack unwinding occurs again. Figure H.4 demonstrates stack unwinding, and the exception handler in main shows how to access the data in an exception object.

```java
1  // Fig. H.4: UsingExceptions.java
2  // Stack unwinding and obtaining data from an exception object.
3
4  public class UsingExceptions
5  {
6     public static void main( String[] args )
7     {
8        try
9        {
10          method1(); // call method1
11       } // end try
12       catch ( Exception exception ) // catch exception thrown in method1
13       {
14          System.err.printf( "%s\n\n", exception.getMessage() );
15          exception.printStackTrace(); // print exception stack trace
16
17          // obtain the stack-trace information
18          StackTraceElement[] traceElements = exception.getStackTrace();
19
20          System.out.println( "\nStack trace from getStackTrace:" );
21          System.out.println( "Class\t\tFile\t\t\tLine\tMethod" );
22
```

Fig. H.4 | Stack unwinding and obtaining data from an exception object. (Part 1 of 2.)

```
23              // loop through traceElements to get exception description
24              for ( StackTraceElement element : traceElements )
25              {
26                  System.out.printf( "%s\t", element.getClassName() );
27                  System.out.printf( "%s\t", element.getFileName() );
28                  System.out.printf( "%s\t", element.getLineNumber() );
29                  System.out.printf( "%s\n", element.getMethodName() );
30              } // end for
31          } // end catch
32      } // end main
33
34      // call method2; throw exceptions back to main
35      public static void method1() throws Exception
36      {
37          method2();
38      } // end method method1
39
40      // call method3; throw exceptions back to method1
41      public static void method2() throws Exception
42      {
43          method3();
44      } // end method method2
45
46      // throw Exception back to method2
47      public static void method3() throws Exception
48      {
49          throw new Exception( "Exception thrown in method3" );
50      } // end method method3
51  } // end class UsingExceptions
```

```
Exception thrown in method3

java.lang.Exception: Exception thrown in method3
        at UsingExceptions.method3(UsingExceptions.java:49)
        at UsingExceptions.method2(UsingExceptions.java:43)
        at UsingExceptions.method1(UsingExceptions.java:37)
        at UsingExceptions.main(UsingExceptions.java:10)

Stack trace from getStackTrace:
Class            File                  Line    Method
UsingExceptions  UsingExceptions.java  49      method3
UsingExceptions  UsingExceptions.java  43      method2
UsingExceptions  UsingExceptions.java  37      method1
UsingExceptions  UsingExceptions.java  10      main
```

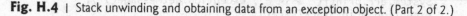

Fig. H.4 | Stack unwinding and obtaining data from an exception object. (Part 2 of 2.)

Stack Unwinding

In main, the try block (lines 8–11) calls method1 (declared at lines 35–38), which in turn calls method2 (declared at lines 41–44), which in turn calls method3 (declared at lines 47–50). Line 49 of method3 throws an Exception object—this is the *throw point*. Because the throw statement at line 49 is *not* enclosed in a try block, *stack unwinding* occurs— method3 terminates at line 49, then returns control to the statement in method2 that invoked method3 (i.e., line 43). Because *no* try block encloses line 43, *stack unwinding* occurs again—method2 terminates at line 43 and returns control to the statement in method1 that invoked method2 (i.e., line 37). Because *no* try block encloses line 37, *stack unwinding* occurs one more time—method1 terminates at line 37 and returns control to the statement in main that invoked method1 (i.e., line 10). The try block at lines 8–11 encloses this statement. The exception has not been handled, so the try block terminates and the first matching catch block (lines 12–31) catches and processes the exception. If there were no matching catch blocks, and the exception is not declared in each method that throws it, a compilation error would occur. Remember that this is not always the case—for *unchecked* exceptions, the application will compile, but it will run with unexpected results.

Obtaining Data from an Exception Object

Recall that exceptions derive from class Throwable. Class Throwable offers a **printStackTrace** method that outputs to the standard error stream the stack trace (discussed in Section H.2). Often, this is helpful in testing and debugging. Class Throwable also provides a **getStackTrace** method that retrieves the stack-trace information that might be printed by printStackTrace. Class Throwable's **getMessage** method returns the descriptive string stored in an exception.

> **Error-Prevention Tip H.5**
> *An exception that's not caught in an application causes Java's default exception handler to run. This displays the name of the exception, a descriptive message that indicates the problem that occurred and a complete execution stack trace. In an application with a single thread of execution, the application terminates. In an application with multiple threads, the thread that caused the exception terminates.*

> **Error-Prevention Tip H.6**
> Throwable *method* toString *(inherited by all* Throwable *subclasses) returns a* String *containing the name of the exception's class and a descriptive message.*

The catch handler in Fig. H.4 (lines 12–31) demonstrates getMessage, printStackTrace and getStackTrace. If we wanted to output the stack-trace information to streams other than the standard error stream, we could use the information returned from getStackTrace and output it to another stream or use one of the overloaded versions of method printStackTrace.

Line 14 invokes the exception's getMessage method to get the exception description. Line 15 invokes the exception's printStackTrace method to output the stack trace that indicates where the exception occurred. Line 18 invokes the exception's getStackTrace method to obtain the stack-trace information as an array of **StackTraceElement** objects. Lines 24–30 get each StackTraceElement in the array and invoke its methods **getClassName**, **getFileName**, **getLineNumber** and **getMethodName** to get the class name, file name, line number and method name, respectively, for that StackTraceElement. Each StackTraceElement represents one method call on the method-call stack.

The program's output shows that the stack-trace information printed by printStackTrace follows the pattern: *className.methodName(fileName:lineNumber)*, where *className*, *methodName* and *fileName* indicate the names of the class, method and file in which the exception occurred, respectively, and the *lineNumber* indicates where in the file the exception occurred. You saw this in the output for Fig. H.1. Method getStackTrace enables custom processing of the exception information. Compare the output of print-StackTrace with the output created from the StackTraceElements to see that both contain the same stack-trace information.

> **Software Engineering Observation H.8**
>
> *Never provide a catch handler with an empty body—this effectively ignores the exception. At least use printStackTrace to output an error message to indicate that a problem exists.*

H.8 Wrap-Up

In this appendix, you learned how to use exception handling to deal with errors. You learned that exception handling enables you to remove error-handling code from the "main line" of the program's execution. We showed how to use try blocks to enclose code that may throw an exception, and how to use catch blocks to deal with exceptions that may arise. You learned about the termination model of exception handling, which dictates that after an exception is handled, program control does not return to the throw point. We discussed checked vs. unchecked exceptions, and how to specify with the throws clause the exceptions that a method might throw. You learned how to use the finally block to release resources whether or not an exception occurs. You also learned how to throw and rethrow exceptions. We showed how to obtain information about an exception using methods printStackTrace, getStackTrace and getMessage. In the next appendix, we discuss graphical user interface concepts and explain the essentials of event handling.

Self-Review Exercises

H.1 List five common examples of exceptions.

H.2 Give several reasons why exception-handling techniques should not be used for conventional program control.

H.3 Why are exceptions particularly appropriate for dealing with errors produced by methods of classes in the Java API?

H.4 What is a "resource leak"?

H.5 If no exceptions are thrown in a try block, where does control proceed to when the try block completes execution?

H.6 Give a key advantage of using catch(Exception *exceptionName*).

H.7 Should a conventional application catch Error objects? Explain.

H.8 What happens if no catch handler matches the type of a thrown object?

H.9 What happens if several catch blocks match the type of the thrown object?

H.10 Why would a programmer specify a superclass type as the type in a catch block?

H.11 What is the key reason for using finally blocks?

H.12 What happens when a catch block throws an Exception?

H.13 What does the statement throw *exceptionReference* do in a catch block?

H.14 What happens to a local reference in a try block when that block throws an Exception?

Answers to Self-Review Exercises

H.1 Memory exhaustion, array index out of bounds, arithmetic overflow, division by zero, invalid method parameters.

H.2 (a) Exception handling is designed to handle infrequently occurring situations that often result in program termination, not situations that arise all the time. (b) Flow of control with conventional control structures is generally clearer and more efficient than with exceptions. (c) The additional exceptions can get in the way of genuine error-type exceptions. It becomes more difficult for you to keep track of the larger number of exception cases.

H.3 It's unlikely that methods of classes in the Java API could perform error processing that would meet the unique needs of all users.

H.4 A "resource leak" occurs when an executing program does not properly release a resource when it's no longer needed.

H.5 The catch blocks for that try statement are skipped, and the program resumes execution after the last catch block. If there's a finally block, it's executed first; then the program resumes execution after the finally block.

H.6 The form catch(Exception *exceptionName*) catches any type of exception thrown in a try block. An advantage is that no thrown Exception can slip by without being caught. You can then decide to handle the exception or possibly rethrow it.

H.7 Errors are usually serious problems with the underlying Java system; most programs will not want to catch Errors because they will not be able to recover from them.

H.8 This causes the search for a match to continue in the next enclosing try statement. If there's a finally block, it will be executed before the exception goes to the next enclosing try statement. If there are no enclosing try statements for which there are matching catch blocks and the exceptions are declared (or unchecked), a stack trace is printed and the current thread terminates early. If the exceptions are checked, but not caught or declared, compilation errors occur.

H.9 The first matching catch block after the try block is executed.

H.10 This enables a program to catch related types of exceptions and process them in a uniform manner. However, it's often useful to process the subclass types individually for more precise exception handling.

H.11 The finally block is the preferred means for releasing resources to prevent resource leaks.

H.12 First, control passes to the finally block if there is one. Then the exception will be processed by a catch block (if one exists) associated with an enclosing try block (if one exists).

H.13 It rethrows the exception for processing by an exception handler of an enclosing try statement, after the finally block of the current try statement executes.

H.14 The reference goes out of scope. If the referenced object becomes unreachable, the object can be garbage collected.

Exercises

H.15 *(Exceptional Conditions)* List the various exceptional conditions that have occurred in programs throughout the appendices so far. List as many additional exceptional conditions as you can. For each of these, describe briefly how a program typically would handle the exception by using the exception-handling techniques discussed in this appendix. Typical exceptions include division by zero and array index out of bounds.

H.16 *(Exceptions and Constructor Failure)* Until this appendix, we've found dealing with errors detected by constructors to be a bit awkward. Explain why exception handling is an effective means for dealing with constructor failure.

H.17 *(Catching Exceptions with Superclasses)* Use inheritance to create an exception superclass (called ExceptionA) and exception subclasses ExceptionB and ExceptionC, where ExceptionB inherits from ExceptionA and ExceptionC inherits from ExceptionB. Write a program to demonstrate that the catch block for type ExceptionA catches exceptions of types ExceptionB and ExceptionC.

H.18 *(Catching Exceptions Using Class Exception)* Write a program that demonstrates how various exceptions are caught with

    catch (Exception exception)

This time, define classes ExceptionA (which inherits from class Exception) and ExceptionB (which inherits from class ExceptionA). In your program, create try blocks that throw exceptions of types ExceptionA, ExceptionB, NullPointerException and IOException. All exceptions should be caught with catch blocks specifying type Exception.

H.19 *(Order of catch Blocks)* Write a program that shows that the order of catch blocks is important. If you try to catch a superclass exception type before a subclass type, the compiler should generate errors.

H.20 *(Constructor Failure)* Write a program that shows a constructor passing information about constructor failure to an exception handler. Define class SomeClass, which throws an Exception in the constructor. Your program should try to create an object of type SomeClass and catch the exception that's thrown from the constructor.

H.21 *(Rethrowing Exceptions)* Write a program that illustrates rethrowing an exception. Define methods someMethod and someMethod2. Method someMethod2 should initially throw an exception. Method someMethod should call someMethod2, catch the exception and rethrow it. Call someMethod from method main, and catch the rethrown exception. Print the stack trace of this exception.

H.22 *(Catching Exceptions Using Outer Scopes)* Write a program showing that a method with its own try block does not have to catch every possible error generated within the try. Some exceptions can slip through to, and be handled in, other scopes.

GUI Components and Event Handling

Objectives

In this appendix you'll learn:

- How to use Java's cross-platform Nimbus look-and-feel.
- To build GUIs and handle events generated by user interactions with GUIs.
- To use nested classes and anonymous inner classes to implement event handlers.

I.1 Introduction

A **graphical user interface (GUI)** presents a user-friendly mechanism for interacting with an app. A GUI (pronounced "GOO-ee") gives an app a distinctive "look-and-feel." GUIs are built from **GUI components**, such as labels, buttons, textboxes, menus scrollbars and more. These are sometimes called controls or widgets—short for window gadgets. A GUI component is an object with which the user interacts via the mouse, the keyboard or another form of input, such as voice recognition. In this appendix, we introduce a few basic GUI components and how to respond to user interactions with them—a technique known as event handling. We also discuss *nested classes* and *anonymous inner classes*, which are commonly used for event handling in Java and Android apps.

I.2 Nimbus Look-and-Feel

In our screen captures, we use Java's elegant **Nimbus** cross-platform look-and-feel. There are three ways that you can use Nimbus:

1. Set it as the default for all Java apps that run on your computer.
2. Set it as the look-and-feel at the time that you launch an app by passing a command-line argument to the java command.
3. Set it as the look-and-feel programatically in your app.

We set Nimbus as the default for all Java apps. To do so, you must create a text file named swing.properties in the lib folder of both your JDK installation folder and your JRE installation folder. Place the following line of code in the file:

```
swing.defaultlaf=com.sun.java.swing.plaf.nimbus.NimbusLookAndFeel
```

For more information on locating these installation folders visit

```
http://docs.oracle.com/javase/7/docs/webnotes/install/
```

In addition to the standalone JRE, there is a JRE nested in your JDK's installation folder. If you're using an IDE that depends on the JDK, you may also need to place the swing.properties file in the nested jre folder's lib folder.

If you prefer to select Nimbus on an app-by-app basis, place the following command-line argument after the java command and before the app's name when you run the app:

```
-Dswing.defaultlaf=com.sun.java.swing.plaf.nimbus.NimbusLookAndFeel
```

I.3 Text Fields and an Introduction to Event Handling with Nested Classes

Normally, a user interacts with an app's GUI to indicate the tasks that the app should perform. For example, when you write an e-mail in an e-mail app, clicking the **Send** button tells the app to send the e-mail to the specified e-mail addresses. GUIs are **event driven**. When the user interacts with a GUI component, the interaction—known as an **event**—drives the program to perform a task. Some common user interactions that cause an app to perform a task include clicking a button, typing in a text field, selecting an item from a menu, closing a window and moving the mouse. The code that performs a task in response to an event is called an **event handler**, and the overall process of responding to events is known as **event handling**.

Let's consider two GUI components that can generate events—**JTextFields** and **JPasswordFields** (package javax.swing). Class JTextField extends class **JTextComponent** (package javax.swing.text), which provides many features common to Swing's text-based components. Class JPasswordField extends JTextField and adds methods that are specific to processing passwords. Each of these components is a single-line area in which the user can enter text via the keyboard. Apps can also display text in a JTextField (see the output of Fig. I.2). A JPasswordField shows that characters are being typed as the user enters them, but hides the actual characters with an **echo character**, assuming that they represent a password that should remain known only to the user.

When the user types in a JTextField or a JPasswordField, then presses *Enter*, an event occurs. Our next example demonstrates how a program can perform a task in response to that event. The techniques shown here are applicable to all GUI components that generate events.

The app of Figs. I.1–I.2 uses classes JTextField and JPasswordField to create and manipulate four text fields. When the user types in one of the text fields, then presses *Enter*, the app displays a message dialog box containing the text the user typed. You can type only in the text field that's "in **focus**." When you click a component, it *receives the focus*. This is important, because the text field with the focus is the one that generates an event when you press *Enter*. In this example, you press *Enter* in the JPasswordField, the password is revealed. We begin by discussing the setup of the GUI, then discuss the event-handling code.

```
1   // Fig. I.1: TextFieldFrame.java
2   // JTextFields and JPasswordFields.
3   import java.awt.FlowLayout;
4   import java.awt.event.ActionListener;
5   import java.awt.event.ActionEvent;
6   import javax.swing.JFrame;
7   import javax.swing.JTextField;
8   import javax.swing.JPasswordField;
9   import javax.swing.JOptionPane;
10
11  public class TextFieldFrame extends JFrame
12  {
```

Fig. I.1 | JTextFields and JPasswordFields. (Part I of 3.)

```
13      private JTextField textField1; // text field with set size
14      private JTextField textField2; // text field constructed with text
15      private JTextField textField3; // text field with text and size
16      private JPasswordField passwordField; // password field with text
17
18      // TextFieldFrame constructor adds JTextFields to JFrame
19      public TextFieldFrame()
20      {
21         super( "Testing JTextField and JPasswordField" );
22         setLayout( new FlowLayout() ); // set frame layout
23
24         // construct textfield with 10 columns
25         textField1 = new JTextField( 10 );
26         add( textField1 ); // add textField1 to JFrame
27
28         // construct textfield with default text
29         textField2 = new JTextField( "Enter text here" );
30         add( textField2 ); // add textField2 to JFrame
31
32         // construct textfield with default text and 21 columns
33         textField3 = new JTextField( "Uneditable text field", 21 );
34         textField3.setEditable( false ); // disable editing
35         add( textField3 ); // add textField3 to JFrame
36
37         // construct passwordfield with default text
38         passwordField = new JPasswordField( "Hidden text" );
39         add( passwordField ); // add passwordField to JFrame
40
41         // register event handlers
42         TextFieldHandler handler = new TextFieldHandler();
43         textField1.addActionListener( handler );
44         textField2.addActionListener( handler );
45         textField3.addActionListener( handler );
46         passwordField.addActionListener( handler );
47      } // end TextFieldFrame constructor
48
49      // private inner class for event handling
50      private class TextFieldHandler implements ActionListener
51      {
52         // process text field events
53         public void actionPerformed( ActionEvent event )
54         {
55            String string = ""; // declare string to display
56
57            // user pressed Enter in JTextField textField1
58            if ( event.getSource() == textField1 )
59               string = String.format( "textField1: %s",
60                  event.getActionCommand() );
61
62            // user pressed Enter in JTextField textField2
63            else if ( event.getSource() == textField2 )
64               string = String.format( "textField2: %s",
65                  event.getActionCommand() );
```

Fig. I.1 | JTextFields and JPasswordFields. (Part 2 of 3.)

```
66
67          // user pressed Enter in JTextField textField3
68          else if ( event.getSource() == textField3 )
69             string = String.format( "textField3: %s",
70                event.getActionCommand() );
71
72          // user pressed Enter in JTextField passwordField
73          else if ( event.getSource() == passwordField )
74             string = String.format( "passwordField: %s",
75                event.getActionCommand() );
76
77          // display JTextField content
78          JOptionPane.showMessageDialog( null, string );
79       } // end method actionPerformed
80    } // end private inner class TextFieldHandler
81 } // end class TextFieldFrame
```

Fig. 1.1 | JTextFields and JPasswordFields. (Part 3 of 3.)

Lines 3–9 import the classes and interfaces we use in this example. Class TextField-Frame extends JFrame and declares three JTextField variables and a JPasswordField variable (lines 13–16). Each of the corresponding text fields is instantiated and attached to the TextFieldFrame in the constructor (lines 19–47).

Specifying the Layout
When building a GUI, you must attach each GUI component to a container, such as a window created with a JFrame. Also, you typically must decide *where* to position each GUI component—known as specifying the layout. Java provides several **layout managers** that can help you position components.

Many IDEs provide GUI design tools in which you can specify components' exact sizes and locations in a visual manner by using the mouse; then the IDE will generate the GUI code for you. Such IDEs can greatly simplify GUI creation.

To ensure that our GUIs can be used with *any* IDE, we did *not* use an IDE to create the GUI code. We use Java's layout managers to size and position components. With the **FlowLayout** layout manager, components are placed on a container from left to right in the order in which they're added. When no more components can fit on the current line, they continue to display left to right on the next line. If the container is resized, a Flow-Layout *reflows* the components, possibly with fewer or more rows based on the new container width. Every container has a default layout, which we're changing for TextFieldFrame to a FlowLayout (line 22). Method **setLayout** is inherited into class TextFieldFrame indirectly from class Container. The argument to the method must be an object of a class that implements the LayoutManager interface (e.g., FlowLayout). Line 22 creates a new FlowLayout object and passes its reference as the argument to setLayout.

Creating the GUI
Line 25 creates textField1 with 10 columns of text. A text column's width in *pixels* is determined by the average width of a character in the text field's current font. When text is displayed in a text field and the text is wider than the field itself, a portion of the text at the right side is not visible. If you're typing in a text field and the cursor reaches the right

edge, the text at the left edge is pushed off the left side of the field and is no longer visible. Users can use the left and right arrow keys to move through the complete text. Line 26 adds textField1 to the JFrame.

Line 29 creates textField2 with the initial text "Enter text here" to display in the text field. The width of the field is determined by the width of the default text specified in the constructor. Line 30 adds textField2 to the JFrame.

Line 33 creates textField3 and calls the JTextField constructor with two arguments—the default text "Uneditable text field" to display and the text field's width in columns (21). Line 34 uses method **setEditable** (inherited by JTextField from class JTextComponent) to make the text field *uneditable*—i.e., the user cannot modify the text in the field. Line 35 adds textField3 to the JFrame.

Line 38 creates passwordField with the text "Hidden text" to display in the text field. The width of the field is determined by the width of the default text. When you execute the app, notice that the text is displayed as a string of asterisks. Line 39 adds passwordField to the JFrame.

Steps Required to Set Up Event Handling for a GUI Component

This example should display a message dialog containing the text from a text field when the user presses *Enter* in that text field. Before an app can respond to an event for a particular GUI component, you must:

1. Create a class that represents the event handler and implements an appropriate interface—known as an **event-listener interface**.

2. Indicate that an object of the class from *Step 1* should be notified when the event occurs—known as **registering the event handler**.

Using a Nested Class to Implement an Event Handler

All the classes discussed so far were so-called **top-level classes**—that is, they were not declared inside another class. Java allows you to declare classes *inside* other classes—these are called **nested classes**. Nested classes can be static or non-static. Non-static nested classes are called **inner classes** and are frequently used to implement *event handlers*.

An inner-class object must be created by an object of the top-level class that contains the inner class. Each inner-class object *implicitly* has a reference to an object of its top-level class. The inner-class object is allowed to use this implicit reference to directly access all the variables and methods of the top-level class. A nested class that's static does not require an object of its top-level class and does not implicitly have a reference to an object of the top-level class.

Nested Class TextFieldHandler

The event handling in this example is performed by an object of the private inner class TextFieldHandler (lines 50–80). This class is private because it will be used only to create event handlers for the text fields in top-level class TextFieldFrame. As with other class members, *inner classes* can be declared public, protected or private. Since event handlers tend to be specific to the app in which they're defined, they're often implemented as private inner classes or as *anonymous inner classes* (Section I.7).

GUI components can generate many events in response to user interactions. Each event is represented by a class and can be processed only by the appropriate type of event handler. Normally, a component's supported events are described in the Java API documentation for that component's class and its superclasses. When the user presses *Enter* in a JTextField or JPasswordField, an **ActionEvent** (package java.awt.event) occurs. Such an event is processed by an object that implements the interface **ActionListener** (package java.awt.event). The information discussed here is available in the Java API documentation for classes JTextField and ActionEvent. Since JPasswordField is a subclass of JTextField, JPasswordField supports the same events.

To prepare to handle the events in this example, inner class TextFieldHandler implements interface ActionListener and declares the only method in that interface—actionPerformed (lines 53–79). This method specifies the tasks to perform when an ActionEvent occurs. So, inner class TextFieldHandler satisfies *Step 1* listed earlier in this section. We'll discuss the details of method actionPerformed shortly.

Registering the Event Handler for Each Text Field

In the TextFieldFrame constructor, line 42 creates a TextFieldHandler object and assigns it to variable handler. This object's actionPerformed method will be called automatically when the user presses *Enter* in any of the GUI's text fields. However, before this can occur, the program must register this object as the event handler for each text field. Lines 43–46 are the event-registration statements that specify handler as the event handler for the three JTextFields and the JPasswordField. The app calls JTextField method **addActionListener** to register the event handler for each component. This method receives as its argument an ActionListener object, which can be an object of any class that implements ActionListener. The object handler *is an* ActionListener, because class TextFieldHandler implements ActionListener. After lines 43–46 execute, the object handler **listens for events**. Now, when the user presses *Enter* in any of these four text fields, method actionPerformed (line 53–79) in class TextFieldHandler is called to handle the event. If an event handler is not registered for a particular text field, the event that occurs when the user presses *Enter* in that text field is **consumed**—i.e., it's simply ignored by the app.

Software Engineering Observation I.1

The event listener for an event must implement the appropriate event-listener interface.

Common Programming Error I.1

Forgetting to register an event-handler object for a particular GUI component's event type causes events of that type to be ignored.

Details of Class TextFieldHandler's actionPerformed Method

In this example, we're using one event-handling object's actionPerformed method (lines 53–79) to handle the events generated by four text fields. Since we'd like to output the name of each text field's instance variable for demonstration purposes, we must determine which text field generated the event each time actionPerformed is called. The **event source** is the GUI component with which the user interacted. When the user presses *Enter* while one of the text fields or the password field *has the focus*, the system creates a unique ActionEvent object that contains information about the event that just occurred, such as the event source and the text in the text field. The system passes this ActionEvent object to the event listener's actionPerformed method. Line 55 declares the String that will be displayed. The variable is initialized with the **empty string**—a String containing no characters. The compiler requires the variable to be initialized in case none of the branches of the nested if in lines 58–75 executes.

ActionEvent method getSource (called in lines 58, 63, 68 and 73) returns a reference to the event source. The condition in line 58 asks, "Is the event source textField1?" This condition compares references with the == operator to determine if they refer to the same object. If they *both* refer to textField1, the user pressed *Enter* in textField1. Then, lines 59–60 create a String containing the message that line 78 displays in a message dialog. Line 60 uses ActionEvent method **getActionCommand** to obtain the text the user typed in the text field that generated the event.

In this example, we display the text of the password in the JPasswordField when the user presses *Enter* in that field. Sometimes it's necessary to programatically process the characters in a password. Class JPasswordField method **getPassword** returns the password's characters as an array of type char.

Class *TextFieldTest*

Class TextFieldTest (Fig. I.2) contains the main method that executes this app and displays an object of class TextFieldFrame. When you execute the app, even the uneditable JText-Field (textField3) can generate an ActionEvent. To test this, click the text field to give it the focus, then press *Enter*. Also, the actual text of the password is displayed when you press *Enter* in the JPasswordField. Of course, you would normally not display the password!

This app used a single object of class TextFieldHandler as the event listener for four text fields. It's possible to declare several event-listener objects of the same type and register each object for a separate GUI component's event. This technique enables us to eliminate the if...else logic used in this example's event handler by providing separate event handlers for each component's events.

```
1   // Fig. I.2: TextFieldTest.java
2   // Testing TextFieldFrame.
3   import javax.swing.JFrame;
4
5   public class TextFieldTest
6   {
7      public static void main( String[] args )
8      {
9         TextFieldFrame textFieldFrame = new TextFieldFrame();
10        textFieldFrame.setDefaultCloseOperation( JFrame.EXIT_ON_CLOSE );
11        textFieldFrame.setSize( 350, 100 ); // set frame size
12        textFieldFrame.setVisible( true ); // display frame
13     } // end main
14  } // end class TextFieldTest
```

Fig. I.2 | Testing TextFieldFrame. (Part 1 of 2.)

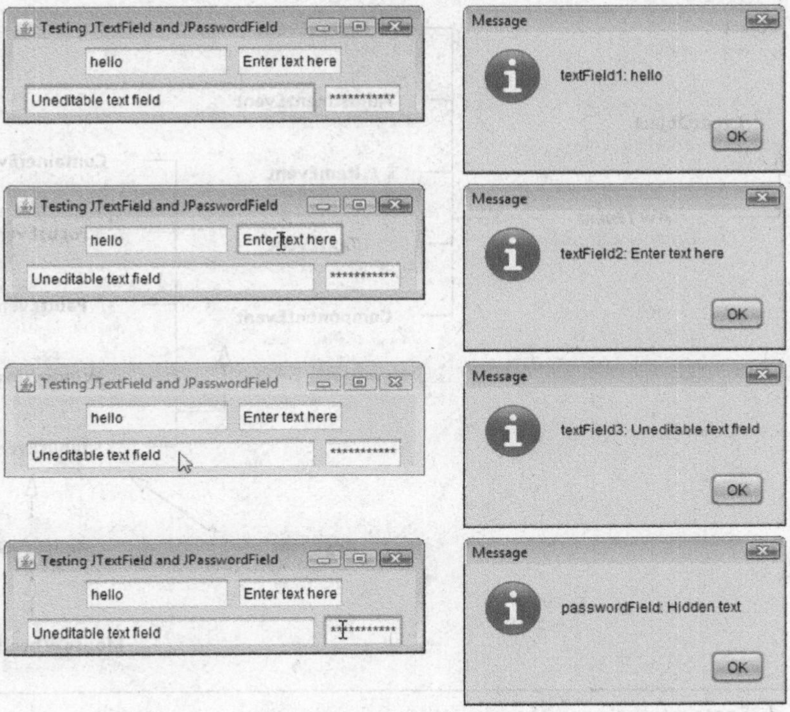

Fig. I.2 | Testing `TextFieldFrame`. (Part 2 of 2.)

I.4 Common GUI Event Types and Listener Interfaces

In Section I.3, you learned that information about the event that occurs when the user presses *Enter* in a text field is stored in an `ActionEvent` object. Many different types of events can occur when the user interacts with a GUI. The event information is stored in an object of a class that extends `AWTEvent` (from package `java.awt`). Figure I.3 illustrates a hierarchy containing many event classes from the package **java.awt.event**. Additional event types are declared in package **javax.swing.event**.

Let's summarize the three parts to the event-handling mechanism that you saw in Section I.3—the *event source*, the *event object* and the *event listener*. The event source is the GUI component with which the user interacts. The event object encapsulates information about the event that occurred, such as a reference to the event source and any event-specific information that may be required by the event listener for it to handle the event. The event listener is an object that's notified by the event source when an event occurs; in effect, it "listens" for an event, and one of its methods executes in response to the event. A method of the event listener receives an event object when the event listener is notified of the event. The event listener then uses the event object to respond to the event. This event-handling model is known as the **delegation event model**—an event's processing is delegated to an object (the event listener) in the app.

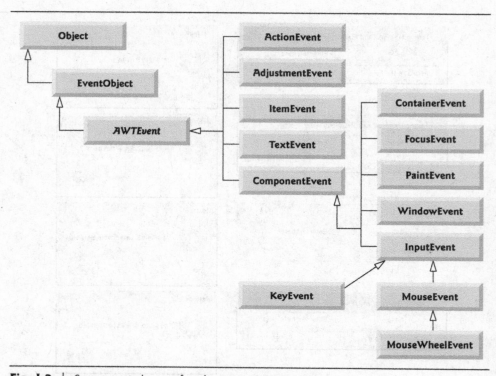

Fig. I.3 | Some event classes of package `java.awt.event`.

For each event-object type, there's typically a corresponding event-listener interface. An event listener for a GUI event is an object of a class that implements one or more of the event-listener interfaces.

Each event-listener interface specifies one or more event-handling methods that *must* be declared in the class that implements the interface. Recall from Section G.12 that any class which implements an interface must declare *all* the abstract methods of that interface; otherwise, the class is an abstract class and cannot be used to create objects.

When an event occurs, the GUI component with which the user interacted notifies its *registered listeners* by calling each listener's appropriate *event-handling method*. For example, when the user presses the *Enter* key in a `JTextField`, the registered listener's `actionPerformed` method is called. How did the event handler get registered? How does the GUI component know to call `actionPerformed` rather than another event-handling method? We answer these questions and diagram the interaction in the next section.

I.5 How Event Handling Works

Let's illustrate how the event-handling mechanism works, using `textField1` from the example of Fig. I.1. We have two remaining open questions from Section I.3:

1. How did the *event handler* get *registered*?

2. How does the GUI component know to call `actionPerformed` rather than some other event-handling method?

The first question is answered by the event registration performed in lines 43–46 of Fig. I.1. Figure I.4 diagrams JTextField variable textField1, TextFieldHandler variable handler and the objects to which they refer.

Registering Events

Every JComponent has an instance variable called listenerList that refers to an object of class **EventListenerList** (package javax.swing.event). Each object of a JComponent subclass maintains references to its registered listeners in the listenerList. For simplicity, we've diagrammed listenerList as an array below the JTextField object in Fig. I.4.

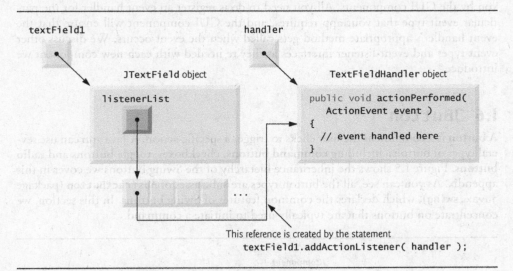

textField1   handler

JTextField object   TextFieldHandler object

listenerList

```
public void actionPerformed(
    ActionEvent event )
{
    // event handled here
}
```

This reference is created by the statement
textField1.addActionListener(handler);

Fig. I.4 | Event registration for JTextField textField1.

When line 43 of Fig. I.1

```
textField1.addActionListener( handler );
```

executes, a new entry containing a reference to the TextFieldHandler object is placed in textField1's listenerList. Although not shown in the diagram, this new entry also includes the listener's type (in this case, ActionListener). Using this mechanism, each lightweight Swing GUI component maintains its own list of *listeners* that were *registered* to *handle* the component's *events*.

Event-Handler Invocation

The event-listener type is important in answering the second question: How does the GUI component know to call actionPerformed rather than another method? Every GUI component supports several *event types*, including **mouse events**, **key events** and others. When an event occurs, the event is **dispatched** only to the *event listeners* of the appropriate type. Dispatching is simply the process by which the GUI component calls an event-handling method on each of its listeners that are registered for the event type that occurred.

Each *event type* has one or more corresponding *event-listener interfaces*. For example, ActionEvents are handled by ActionListeners, **MouseEvents** by **MouseListeners** and

MouseMotionListeners, and **KeyEvents** by **KeyListeners**. When an event occurs, the GUI component receives (from the JVM) a unique *event ID* specifying the event type. The GUI component uses the event ID to decide the listener type to which the event should be dispatched and to decide which method to call on each listener object. For an ActionEvent, the event is dispatched to *every* registered ActionListener's actionPerformed method (the only method in interface ActionListener). For a MouseEvent, the event is dispatched to *every* registered MouseListener or MouseMotionListener, depending on the mouse event that occurs. The MouseEvent's event ID determines which of the several mouse event-handling methods are called. All these decisions are handled for you by the GUI components. All you need to do is register an event handler for the particular event type that your app requires, and the GUI component will ensure that the event handler's appropriate method gets called when the event occurs. We discuss other event types and event-listener interfaces as they're needed with each new component we introduce.

I.6 JButton

A **button** is a component the user clicks to trigger a specific action. A Java app can use several types of buttons, including **command buttons**, **checkboxes**, **toggle buttons** and **radio buttons**. Figure I.5 shows the inheritance hierarchy of the Swing buttons we cover in this appendix. As you can see, all the button types are subclasses of **AbstractButton** (package javax.swing), which declares the common features of Swing buttons. In this section, we concentrate on buttons that are typically used to initiate a command.

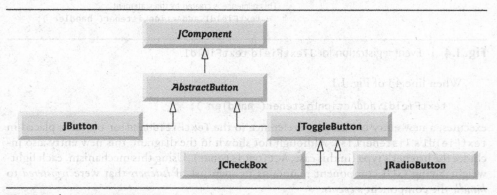

Fig. I.5 | Swing button hierarchy.

A command button (see Fig. I.7's output) generates an ActionEvent when the user clicks it. Command buttons are created with class **JButton**. The text on the face of a JButton is called a **button label**. A GUI can have many JButtons, but each button label should be unique in the portion of the GUI that's currently displayed.

> **Look-and-Feel Observation I.1**
> *The text on buttons typically uses book-title capitalization.*

Look-and-Feel Observation I.2

Having more than one JButton with the same label makes the JButtons ambiguous to the user. Provide a unique label for each button.

The app of Figs. I.6 and I.7 creates two JButtons and demonstrates that JButtons support the display of Icons. Event handling for the buttons is performed by a single instance of *inner class* ButtonHandler (lines 39–47).

```java
1   // Fig. I.6: ButtonFrame.java
2   // Command buttons and action events.
3   import java.awt.FlowLayout;
4   import java.awt.event.ActionListener;
5   import java.awt.event.ActionEvent;
6   import javax.swing.JFrame;
7   import javax.swing.JButton;
8   import javax.swing.Icon;
9   import javax.swing.ImageIcon;
10  import javax.swing.JOptionPane;
11
12  public class ButtonFrame extends JFrame
13  {
14     private JButton plainJButton; // button with just text
15     private JButton fancyJButton; // button with icons
16
17     // ButtonFrame adds JButtons to JFrame
18     public ButtonFrame()
19     {
20        super( "Testing Buttons" );
21        setLayout( new FlowLayout() ); // set frame layout
22
23        plainJButton = new JButton( "Plain Button" ); // button with text
24        add( plainJButton ); // add plainJButton to JFrame
25
26        Icon bug1 = new ImageIcon( getClass().getResource( "bug1.gif" ) );
27        Icon bug2 = new ImageIcon( getClass().getResource( "bug2.gif" ) );
28        fancyJButton = new JButton( "Fancy Button", bug1 ); // set image
29        fancyJButton.setRolloverIcon( bug2 ); // set rollover image
30        add( fancyJButton ); // add fancyJButton to JFrame
31
32        // create new ButtonHandler for button event handling
33        ButtonHandler handler = new ButtonHandler();
34        fancyJButton.addActionListener( handler );
35        plainJButton.addActionListener( handler );
36     } // end ButtonFrame constructor
37
38     // inner class for button event handling
39     private class ButtonHandler implements ActionListener
40     {
41        // handle button event
42        public void actionPerformed( ActionEvent event )
43        {
```

Fig. I.6 | Command buttons and action events. (Part I of 2.)

```
44              JOptionPane.showMessageDialog( ButtonFrame.this, String.format(
45                 "You pressed: %s", event.getActionCommand() ) );
46           } // end method actionPerformed
47        } // end private inner class ButtonHandler
48     } // end class ButtonFrame
```

Fig. I.6 | Command buttons and action events. (Part 2 of 2.)

```
1   // Fig. I.7: ButtonTest.java
2   // Testing ButtonFrame.
3   import javax.swing.JFrame;
4
5   public class ButtonTest
6   {
7      public static void main( String[] args )
8      {
9         ButtonFrame buttonFrame = new ButtonFrame(); // create ButtonFrame
10        buttonFrame.setDefaultCloseOperation( JFrame.EXIT_ON_CLOSE );
11        buttonFrame.setSize( 275, 110 ); // set frame size
12        buttonFrame.setVisible( true ); // display frame
13     } // end main
14  } // end class ButtonTest
```

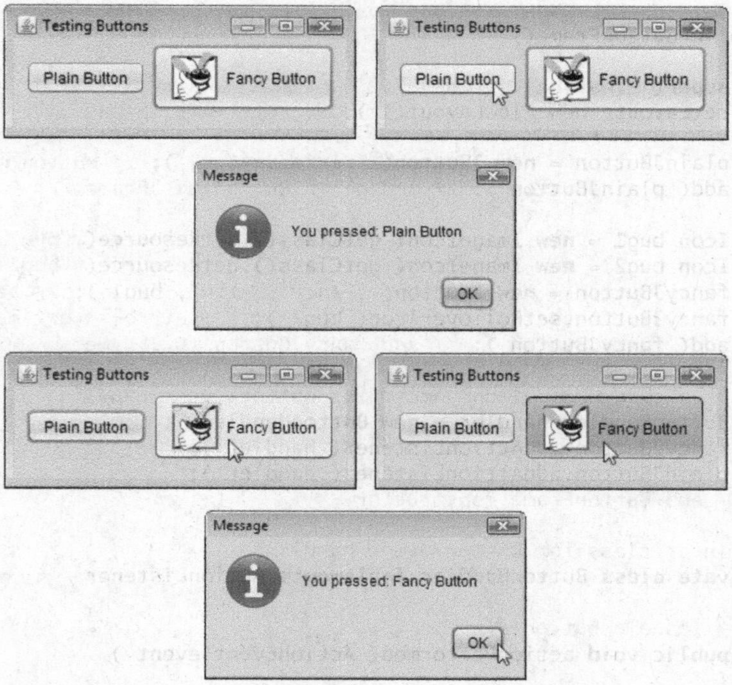

Fig. I.7 | Testing ButtonFrame.

Lines 14–15 of Fig. I.6 declare JButton variables plainJButton and fancyJButton. The corresponding objects are instantiated in the constructor. Line 23 creates plain-JButton with the button label "Plain Button". Line 24 adds the JButton to the JFrame.

A JButton can display an Icon. To provide the user with an extra level of visual interaction with the GUI, a JButton can also have a **rollover Icon**—an Icon that's displayed when the user positions the mouse over the JButton. The icon on the JButton changes as the mouse moves in and out of the JButton's area on the screen. Lines 26–27 (Fig. I.6) create two ImageIcon objects that represent the default Icon and rollover Icon for the JButton created at line 28. Both statements assume that the image files are stored in the same directory as the app. Images are commonly placed in the same directory as the app or a subdirectory like images). These image files have been provided for you with the example.

Line 28 creates fancyButton with the text "Fancy Button" and the icon bug1. By default, the text is displayed to the right of the icon. Line 29 uses **setRolloverIcon** (inherited from class AbstractButton) to specify the image displayed on the JButton when the user positions the mouse over it. Line 30 adds the JButton to the JFrame.

Look-and-Feel Observation I.3

Because class AbstractButton supports displaying text and images on a button, all subclasses of AbstractButton also support displaying text and images.

Look-and-Feel Observation I.4

Using rollover icons for JButtons provides users with visual feedback indicating that when they click the mouse while the cursor is positioned over the JButton, an action will occur.

JButtons, like JTextFields, generate ActionEvents that can be processed by any ActionListener object. Lines 33–35 create an object of private *inner class* ButtonHandler and use addActionListener to *register* it as the *event handler* for each JButton. Class ButtonHandler (lines 39–47) declares actionPerformed to display a message dialog box containing the label for the button the user pressed. For a JButton event, ActionEvent method getActionCommand returns the label on the JButton.

*Accessing the **this** Reference in an Object of a Top-Level Class From a Nested Class*
When you execute this app and click one of its buttons, notice that the message dialog that appears is centered over the app's window. This occurs because the call to JOptionPane method showMessageDialog (lines 44–45 of Fig. I.6) uses ButtonFrame.this rather than null as the first argument. When this argument is not null, it represents the so-called *parent GUI component* of the message dialog (in this case the app window is the parent component) and enables the dialog to be centered over that component when the dialog is displayed. ButtonFrame.this represents the this reference of the object of top-level class ButtonFrame.

Software Engineering Observation I.2

When used in an inner class, keyword this refers to the current inner-class object being manipulated. An inner-class method can use its outer-class object's this by preceding this with the outer-class name and a dot, as in ButtonFrame.this.

I.7 JComboBox; Using an Anonymous Inner Class for Event Handling

A combo box (sometimes called a **drop-down list**) enables the user to select one item from a list (Fig. I.9). Combo boxes are implemented with class **JComboBox**, which extends class JComponent. JComboBoxes generate ItemEvents just as JCheckBoxes and JRadioButtons do. This example also demonstrates a special form of inner class that's used frequently in event handling. The app (Figs. I.8–I.9) uses a JComboBox to provide a list of four image-file names from which the user can select one image to display. When the user selects a name, the app displays the corresponding image as an Icon on a JLabel. Class ComboBox-Test (Fig. I.9) contains the main method that executes this app. The screen captures for this app show the JComboBox list after the selection was made to illustrate which image-file name was selected.

Lines 19–23 (Fig. I.8) declare and initialize array icons with four new ImageIcon objects. String array names (lines 17–18) contains the names of the four image files that are stored in the same directory as the app.

```java
1   // Fig. I.8: ComboBoxFrame.java
2   // JComboBox that displays a list of image names.
3   import java.awt.FlowLayout;
4   import java.awt.event.ItemListener;
5   import java.awt.event.ItemEvent;
6   import javax.swing.JFrame;
7   import javax.swing.JLabel;
8   import javax.swing.JComboBox;
9   import javax.swing.Icon;
10  import javax.swing.ImageIcon;
11
12  public class ComboBoxFrame extends JFrame
13  {
14     private JComboBox imagesJComboBox; // combobox to hold names of icons
15     private JLabel label; // label to display selected icon
16
17     private static final String[] names =
18        { "bug1.gif", "bug2.gif",  "travelbug.gif", "buganim.gif" };
19     private Icon[] icons = {
20        new ImageIcon( getClass().getResource( names[ 0 ] ) ),
21        new ImageIcon( getClass().getResource( names[ 1 ] ) ),
22        new ImageIcon( getClass().getResource( names[ 2 ] ) ),
23        new ImageIcon( getClass().getResource( names[ 3 ] ) ) };
24
25     // ComboBoxFrame constructor adds JComboBox to JFrame
26     public ComboBoxFrame()
27     {
28        super( "Testing JComboBox" );
29        setLayout( new FlowLayout() ); // set frame layout
30
31        imagesJComboBox = new JComboBox( names ); // set up JComboBox
32        imagesJComboBox.setMaximumRowCount( 3 ); // display three rows
```

Fig. I.8 | JComboBox that displays a list of image names. (Part 1 of 2.)

```
33
34        imagesJComboBox.addItemListener(
35          new ItemListener() // anonymous inner class
36          {
37            // handle JComboBox event
38            public void itemStateChanged( ItemEvent event )
39            {
40              // determine whether item selected
41              if ( event.getStateChange() == ItemEvent.SELECTED )
42                label.setIcon( icons[
43                  imagesJComboBox.getSelectedIndex() ] );
44            } // end method itemStateChanged
45          } // end anonymous inner class
46        ); // end call to addItemListener
47
48        add( imagesJComboBox ); // add combobox to JFrame
49        label = new JLabel( icons[ 0 ] ); // display first icon
50        add( label ); // add label to JFrame
51      } // end ComboBoxFrame constructor
52    } // end class ComboBoxFrame
```

Fig. I.8 | JComboBox that displays a list of image names. (Part 2 of 2.)

```
 1    // Fig. I.9: ComboBoxTest.java
 2    // Testing ComboBoxFrame.
 3    import javax.swing.JFrame;
 4
 5    public class ComboBoxTest
 6    {
 7      public static void main( String[] args )
 8      {
 9        ComboBoxFrame comboBoxFrame = new ComboBoxFrame();
10        comboBoxFrame.setDefaultCloseOperation( JFrame.EXIT_ON_CLOSE );
11        comboBoxFrame.setSize( 350, 150 ); // set frame size
12        comboBoxFrame.setVisible( true ); // display frame
13      } // end main
14    } // end class ComboBoxTest
```

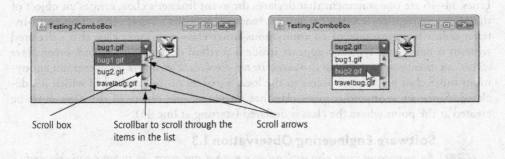

Fig. I.9 | Testing ComboBoxFrame. (Part I of 2.)

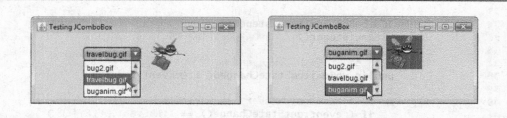

Fig. I.9 | Testing `ComboBoxFrame`. (Part 2 of 2.)

At line 31, the constructor initializes a `JComboBox` object with the `String`s in array names as the elements in the list. Each item in the list has an **index**. The first item is added at index 0, the next at index 1 and so forth. The first item added to a `JComboBox` appears as the currently selected item when the `JComboBox` is displayed. Other items are selected by clicking the `JComboBox`, then selecting an item from the list that appears.

Line 32 uses `JComboBox` method **setMaximumRowCount** to set the maximum number of elements that are displayed when the user clicks the `JComboBox`. If there are additional items, the `JComboBox` provides a **scrollbar** (see the first screen) that allows the user to scroll through all the elements in the list. The user can click the **scroll arrows** at the top and bottom of the scrollbar to move up and down through the list one element at a time, or else drag the **scroll box** in the middle of the scrollbar up and down. To drag the scroll box, position the mouse cursor on it, hold the mouse button down and move the mouse. In this example, the drop-down list is too short to drag the scroll box, so you can click the up and down arrows or use your mouse's wheel to scroll through the four items in the list.

Look-and-Feel Observation I.5
Set the maximum row count for a `JComboBox` to a number of rows that prevents the list from expanding outside the bounds of the window in which it's used.

Line 48 attaches the `JComboBox` to the `ComboBoxFrame`'s `FlowLayout` (set in line 29). Line 49 creates the `JLabel` that displays `ImageIcon`s and initializes it with the first `Image-Icon` in array `icons`. Line 50 attaches the `JLabel` to the `ComboBoxFrame`'s `FlowLayout`.

Using an Anonymous Inner Class for Event Handling

Lines 34–46 are one statement that declares the event listener's class, creates an object of that class and registers it as the listener for `images JComboBox`'s `ItemEvent`s. This event-listener object is an instance of an **anonymous inner class**—an inner class that's declared without a name and typically appears inside a method declaration. *As with other inner classes, an anonymous inner class can access its top-level class's members.* However, an anonymous inner class has limited access to the local variables of the method in which it's declared. Since an anonymous inner class has no name, one object of the class must be created at the point where the class is declared (starting at line 35).

Software Engineering Observation I.3
An anonymous inner class declared in a method can access the instance variables and methods of the top-level class object that declared it, as well as the method's `final` local variables, but cannot access the method's non-`final` local variables.

Lines 34–46 are a call to imagesJComboBox's addItemListener method. The argument to this method must be an object that *is an* ItemListener (i.e., any object of a class that implements ItemListener). Lines 35–45 are a class-instance creation expression that declares an anonymous inner class and creates one object of that class. A reference to that object is then passed as the argument to addItemListener. The syntax ItemListener() after new begins the declaration of an anonymous inner class that implements interface ItemListener. This is similar to beginning a class declaration with

> **public class** MyHandler **implements** ItemListener

The opening left brace at 36 and the closing right brace at line 45 delimit the body of the anonymous inner class. Lines 38–44 declare the ItemListener's itemStateChanged method. When the user makes a selection from imagesJComboBox, this method sets label's Icon. The Icon is selected from array icons by determining the index of the selected item in the JComboBox with method **getSelectedIndex** in line 43. For each item selected from a JComboBox, another item is first deselected—so two ItemEvents occur when an item is selected. We wish to display only the icon for the item the user just selected. For this reason, line 41 determines whether ItemEvent method **getStateChange** returns ItemEvent.SELECTED. If so, lines 42–43 set label's icon.

Software Engineering Observation I.4

Like any other class, when an anonymous inner class implements an interface, the class must implement every method in the interface.

The syntax shown in lines 35–45 for creating an event handler with an anonymous inner class is similar to the code that would be generated by a Java IDE. Typically, an IDE enables you to design a GUI visually, then it generates code that implements the GUI. You simply insert statements in the event-handling methods that declare how to handle each event.

I.8 Adapter Classes

Many event-listener interfaces, such as MouseListener and MouseMotionListener, contain multiple methods. It's not always desirable to declare every method in an event-listener interface. For instance, an app may need only the mouseClicked handler from MouseListener or the mouseDragged handler from MouseMotionListener. Interface WindowListener specifies seven window event-handling methods. For many of the listener interfaces that have multiple methods, packages java.awt.event and javax.swing.event provide event-listener adapter classes. An **adapter class** implements an interface and provides a default implementation (with an empty method body) of each method in the interface. You can extend an adapter class to inherit the default implementation of every method and subsequently override only the method(s) you need for event handling.

Software Engineering Observation I.5

When a class implements an interface, the class has an is-a *relationship with that interface. All direct and indirect subclasses of that class inherit this interface. Thus, an object of a class that extends an event-adapter class is an object of the corresponding event-listener type (e.g., an object of a subclass of MouseAdapter is a MouseListener).*

I.9 Wrap-Up

In this appendix, you learned about a few Java GUI components and how to implement event handlers using nested classes and anonymous inner classes. You saw the special relationship between an inner-class object and an object of its top-level class. You also learned how to create apps that execute in their own windows. We discussed class JFrame and components that enable a user to interact with an app.

Self-Review Exercises

I.1 Fill in the blanks in each of the following statements:
 a) A(n) _____ arranges GUI components in a Container.
 b) The add method for attaching GUI components is a method of class _____.
 c) GUI is an acronym for _____.
 d) Method _____ is used to specify the layout manager for a container.

I.2 Specify whether the following statement is *true* or *false* and if *false*, explain why: Inner classes are not allowed to access the members of the enclosing class.

Answers to Self-Review Exercises

I.1 a) layout manager. b) Container. c) graphical user interface. d) setLayout.

I.2 False. Inner classes have access to all members of the enclosing class declaration.

Exercises

I.3 *(Temperature Conversion)* Write a temperature-conversion app that converts from Fahrenheit to Celsius. The Fahrenheit temperature should be entered from the keyboard (via a JTextField). A JLabel should be used to display the converted temperature. Use the following formula for the conversion:

$$Celsius = \frac{5}{9} \times (\ Fahrenheit - 32\ )$$

I.4 *(Temperature-Conversion Modification)* Enhance the temperature-conversion app of Exercise I.3 by adding the Kelvin temperature scale. The app should also allow the user to make conversions between any two scales. Use the following formula for the conversion between Kelvin and Celsius (in addition to the formula in Exercise I.3):

$$Kelvin = Celsius + 273.15$$

I.5 *(Guess-the-Number Game)* Write an app that plays "guess the number" as follows: Your app chooses the number to be guessed by selecting an integer at random in the range 1–1000. The app then displays the following in a label:

```
I have a number between 1 and 1000. Can you guess my number?
Please enter your first guess.
```

A JTextField should be used to input the guess. As each guess is input, the background color should change to either red or blue. Red indicates that the user is getting "warmer," and blue, "colder." A JLabel should display either "Too High" or "Too Low" to help the user zero in. When the user gets the correct answer, "Correct!" should be displayed, and the JTextField used for input should be changed to be uneditable. A JButton should be provided to allow the user to play the game again. When the JButton is clicked, a new random number should be generated and the input JTextField changed to be editable.

Other Java Topics

Objectives

In this appendix you'll:

- Learn what collections are.
- Use class **Arrays** for array manipulations.
- Understand how type-wrapper classes enable programs to process primitive data values as objects.
- Use prebuilt generic data structures from the collections framework.
- Use iterators to "walk through" a collection.
- Learn fundamental file- and stream-processing concepts.
- What threads are and why they're useful.
- How threads enable you to manage concurrent activities.
- To create and execute **Runnables**.
- Fundamentals of thread synchronization.
- How multiple threads can update Swing GUI components in a thread-safe manner.

J.1 Introduction

This appendix presents several additional topics to support the Android portion of the book. Sections J.2–J.9 present an overview of the Java collections framework and several examples of working with various collections that we use in our Android apps. Sections J.10–J.12 introduce file and stream concepts, overview method of class File and discuss object-serialization for writing entire objects to streams and reading entire objects from streams. Finally, Sections J.13–J.17 present the fundamentals of multithreading.

J.2 Collections Overview

Section E.12 introduced the generic ArrayList collection—a resizable array-like data structure that stores references to objects of a type that you specify when you create the ArrayList. We now continue our discussion of the Java **collections framework**, which contains many other prebuilt generic data structures and various methods for manipulating them. We focus on those that are used in the Android chapters of this book and those that have close parallels in the Android APIs. For complete details of the collections framework, visit

docs.oracle.com/javase/7/docs/technotes/guides/collections/

A **collection** is a data structure—actually, an object—that can hold references to other objects. Usually, collections contain references to objects that are all of the same type. The collections-framework interfaces declare the operations to be performed generically on various types of collections. Figure J.1 lists some of the interfaces of the collections framework. Several implementations of these interfaces are provided within the framework. You may also provide implementations specific to your own requirements.

Because you specify the type to store in a collection at compile time, generic collections provide compile-time type safety that allows the compiler to catch attempts to use invalid types. For example, you cannot store Employees in a collection of Strings. Some

Interface	Description
Collection	The root interface in the collections hierarchy from which interfaces Set, Queue and List are derived.
Set	A collection that does not contain duplicates.
List	An ordered collection that can contain duplicate elements.
Map	A collection that associates keys to values and cannot contain duplicate keys.
Queue	Typically a first-in, first-out collection that models a waiting line; other orders can be specified.

Fig. J.1 | Some collections-framework interfaces.

examples of collections are the cards you hold in a card game, your favorite songs stored in your computer, the members of a sports team and the real-estate records in your local registry of deeds (which map book numbers and page numbers to property owners).

J.3 Type-Wrapper Classes for Primitive Types

Each primitive type (listed in Appendix L) has a corresponding **type-wrapper class** in package java.lang. These classes are called **Boolean**, **Byte**, **Character**, **Double**, **Float**, **Integer**, **Long** and **Short**. These enable you to manipulate primitive-type values as objects. Java's reusable data structures manipulate and share *objects*—they cannot manipulate variables of primitive types. However, they can manipulate objects of the type-wrapper classes, because every class ultimately derives from Object.

Each of the numeric type-wrapper classes—Byte, Short, Integer, Long, Float and Double—extends class Number. Also, the type-wrapper classes are final classes, so you cannot extend them.

Primitive types do not have methods, so the methods related to a primitive type are located in the corresponding type-wrapper class (e.g., method parseInt, which converts a String to an int value, is located in class Integer). If you need to manipulate a primitive value in your program, first refer to the documentation for the type-wrapper classes—the method you need might already be declared.

Autoboxing and Auto-Unboxing

Java provides *boxing* and *unboxing conversions* to automatically convert between primitive-type values and type-wrapper objects. A **boxing conversion** converts a value of a primitive type to an object of the corresponding type-wrapper class. An **unboxing conversion** converts an object of a type-wrapper class to a value of the corresponding primitive type. These conversions are performed automatically (called **autoboxing** and **auto-unboxing**), allowing primitive-type values to be used where type-wrapper objects are expected and vice versa.

J.4 Interface Collection and Class Collections

Interface **Collection** is the root interface in the collection hierarchy from which interfaces Set, Queue and List are derived. Interface **Set** defines a collection that does not contain duplicates. Interface **Queue** defines a collection that represents a waiting line—typically, insertions are made at the back of a queue and deletions from the front, though other orders can be specified. We discuss Queue and Set in Sections J.7—J.8. Interface Collection contains **bulk operations** (i.e., operations performed on an entire collection) for operations such as adding, clearing and comparing objects (or elements) in a collection. A Collection can also be converted to an array. In addition, interface Collection provides a method that returns an **Iterator** object, which allows a program to walk through the collection and remove elements from it during the iteration. We discuss class Iterator in Section J.5.1. Other methods of interface Collection enable a program to determine a collection's size and whether a collection is empty. Class **Collections** provides static methods that search, sort and perform other operations on collections. Section J.6 discusses the methods that are available in class Collections.

Software Engineering Observation J.1

Most collection implementations provide a constructor that takes a Collection argument, thereby allowing a new collection to be constructed containing the elements of the specified collection.

J.5 Lists

A List is an ordered Collection that can contain duplicate elements. Like array indices, List indices are zero based (i.e., the first element's index is zero). In addition to the methods inherited from Collection, interface List provides methods for manipulating elements via their indices, manipulating a specified range of elements, searching for elements and obtaining a **ListIterator** to access the elements.

Interface List is implemented by several classes, including **ArrayList** (introduced in Appendix E) and **LinkedList**. Class ArrayList is a resizable-array implementation of List. Inserting an element between existing elements of an ArrayList is an *inefficient* operation—all elements after the new one must be moved out of the way, which could be an expensive operation in a collection with a large number of elements. A LinkedList enables efficient insertion (or removal) of elements in the middle of a collection. The following two subsections demonstrate various List and Collection capabilities.

J.5.1 ArrayList and Iterator

Figure J.2 uses an ArrayList (introduced in Section E.12) to demonstrate several capabilities of interface Collection. The program places two Color arrays in ArrayLists and uses an Iterator to remove elements in the second ArrayList collection from the first.

```
1   // Fig. J.2: CollectionTest.java
2   // Collection interface demonstrated via an ArrayList object.
3   import java.util.List;
4   import java.util.ArrayList;
5   import java.util.Collection;
6   import java.util.Iterator;
7
8   public class CollectionTest
9   {
```

Fig. J.2 | Collection interface demonstrated via an ArrayList object. (Part 1 of 2.)

```
10      public static void main( String[] args )
11      {
12          // add elements in colors array to list
13          String[] colors = { "MAGENTA", "RED", "WHITE", "BLUE", "CYAN" };
14          List< String > list = new ArrayList< String >();
15
16          for ( String color : colors )
17              list.add( color ); // adds color to end of list
18
19          // add elements in removeColors array to removeList
20          String[] removeColors = { "RED", "WHITE", "BLUE" };
21          List< String > removeList = new ArrayList< String >();
22
23          for ( String color : removeColors )
24              removeList.add( color );
25
26          // output list contents
27          System.out.println( "ArrayList: " );
28
29          for ( int count = 0; count < list.size(); count++ )
30              System.out.printf( "%s ", list.get( count ) );
31
32          // remove from list the colors contained in removeList
33          removeColors( list, removeList );
34
35          // output list contents
36          System.out.println( "\n\nArrayList after calling removeColors: " );
37
38          for ( String color : list )
39              System.out.printf( "%s ", color );
40      } // end main
41
42      // remove colors specified in collection2 from collection1
43      private static void removeColors( Collection< String > collection1,
44          Collection< String > collection2 )
45      {
46          // get iterator
47          Iterator< String > iterator = collection1.iterator();
48
49          // loop while collection has items
50          while ( iterator.hasNext() )
51          {
52              if ( collection2.contains( iterator.next() ) )
53                  iterator.remove(); // remove current Color
54          } // end while
55      } // end method removeColors
56  } // end class CollectionTest
```

```
ArrayList:
MAGENTA RED WHITE BLUE CYAN

ArrayList after calling removeColors:
MAGENTA CYAN
```

Fig. J.2 | Collection interface demonstrated via an ArrayList object. (Part 2 of 2.)

Lines 13 and 20 declare and initialize String arrays colors and removeColors. Lines 14 and 21 create ArrayList<String> objects and assign their references to List<String> variables list and removeList, respectively. We refer to the ArrayLists in this example via List variables. This makes our code more flexible and easier to modify. If we later decide that LinkedLists would be more appropriate, we'll need to modify only lines 14 and 21 where we created the ArrayList objects.

Lines 16–17 populate list with Strings stored in array colors, and lines 23–24 populate removeList with Strings stored in array removeColors using **List method add**. Lines 29–30 output each element of list. Line 29 calls **List method size** to get the number of elements in the ArrayList. Line 30 uses **List method get** to retrieve individual element values. Lines 29–30 also could have used the enhanced for statement (which we'll demonstrate with collections in other examples).

Line 33 calls method removeColors (lines 43–55), passing list and removeList as arguments. Method removeColors deletes the Strings in removeList from the Strings in list. Lines 38–39 print list's elements after removeColors completes its task.

Method removeColors declares two Collection<String> parameters (lines 43–44) that allow any two Collections containing strings to be passed as arguments to this method. The method accesses the elements of the first Collection (collection1) via an Iterator. Line 47 calls Collection method **iterator** to get an Iterator for the Collection. Interfaces Collection and Iterator are generic types. The loop-continuation condition (line 50) calls Iterator method **hasNext** to determine whether the Collection contains more elements. Method hasNext returns true if another element exists and false otherwise.

The if condition in line 52 calls **Iterator method next** to obtain a reference to the next element, then uses method **contains** of the second Collection (collection2) to determine whether collection2 contains the element returned by next. If so, line 53 calls **Iterator method remove** to remove the element from the Collection collection1.

Common Programming Error J.1

If a collection is modified after an iterator is created for that collection, the iterator immediately becomes invalid—operations performed with the iterator after this point throw ConcurrentModificationExceptions. For this reason, iterators are said to be "fail fast."

J.5.2 LinkedList

Figure J.3 demonstrates various operations on LinkedLists. The program creates two LinkedLists of Strings. The elements of one List are added to the other. Then all the Strings are converted to uppercase, and a range of elements is deleted.

```
1   // Fig. J.3: ListTest.java
2   // Lists, LinkedLists and ListIterators.
3   import java.util.List;
4   import java.util.LinkedList;
5   import java.util.ListIterator;
6
7   public class ListTest
8   {
```

Fig. J.3 | Lists, LinkedLists and ListIterators. (Part 1 of 3.)

```
 9      public static void main( String[] args )
10      {
11         // add colors elements to list1
12         String[] colors =
13            { "black", "yellow", "green", "blue", "violet", "silver" };
14         List< String > list1 = new LinkedList< String >();
15
16         for ( String color : colors )
17            list1.add( color );
18
19         // add colors2 elements to list2
20         String[] colors2 =
21            { "gold", "white", "brown", "blue", "gray", "silver" };
22         List< String > list2 = new LinkedList< String >();
23
24         for ( String color : colors2 )
25            list2.add( color );
26
27         list1.addAll( list2 ); // concatenate lists
28         list2 = null; // release resources
29         printList( list1 ); // print list1 elements
30
31         convertToUppercaseStrings( list1 ); // convert to uppercase string
32         printList( list1 ); // print list1 elements
33
34         System.out.print( "\nDeleting elements 4 to 6..." );
35         removeItems( list1, 4, 7 ); // remove items 4-6 from list
36         printList( list1 ); // print list1 elements
37         printReversedList( list1 ); // print list in reverse order
38      } // end main
39
40      // output List contents
41      private static void printList( List< String > list )
42      {
43         System.out.println( "\nlist: " );
44
45         for ( String color : list )
46            System.out.printf( "%s ", color );
47
48         System.out.println();
49      } // end method printList
50
51      // locate String objects and convert to uppercase
52      private static void convertToUppercaseStrings( List< String > list )
53      {
54         ListIterator< String > iterator = list.listIterator();
55
56         while ( iterator.hasNext() )
57         {
58            String color = iterator.next(); // get item
59            iterator.set( color.toUpperCase() ); // convert to upper case
60         } // end while
61      } // end method convertToUppercaseStrings
```

Fig. J.3 | Lists, LinkedLists and ListIterators. (Part 2 of 3.)

```
62
63      // obtain sublist and use clear method to delete sublist items
64      private static void removeItems( List< String > list,
65         int start, int end )
66      {
67         list.subList( start, end ).clear(); // remove items
68      } // end method removeItems
69
70      // print reversed list
71      private static void printReversedList( List< String > list )
72      {
73         ListIterator< String > iterator = list.listIterator( list.size() );
74
75         System.out.println( "\nReversed List:" );
76
77         // print list in reverse order
78         while ( iterator.hasPrevious() )
79            System.out.printf( "%s ", iterator.previous() );
80      } // end method printReversedList
81   } // end class ListTest
```

```
list:
black yellow green blue violet silver gold white brown blue gray silver
list:
BLACK YELLOW GREEN BLUE VIOLET SILVER GOLD WHITE BROWN BLUE GRAY SILVER

Deleting elements 4 to 6...
list:
BLACK YELLOW GREEN BLUE WHITE BROWN BLUE GRAY SILVER

Reversed List:
SILVER GRAY BLUE BROWN WHITE BLUE GREEN YELLOW BLACK
```

Fig. J.3 | Lists, LinkedLists and ListIterators. (Part 3 of 3.)

Lines 14 and 22 create LinkedLists list1 and list2 of type String. LinkedList is a generic class that has one type parameter for which we specify the type argument String in this example. Lines 16–17 and 24–25 call List method add to append elements from arrays colors and colors2 to the end of list1 and list2, respectively.

Line 27 calls **List method addAll** to append all elements of list2 to the end of list1. Line 28 sets list2 to null, so the LinkedList to which list2 referred can be garbage collected. Line 29 calls method printList (lines 41–49) to output list1's contents. Line 31 calls method convertToUppercaseStrings (lines 52–61) to convert each String element to uppercase, then line 32 calls printList again to display the modified Strings. Line 35 calls method removeItems (lines 64–68) to remove the elements starting at index 4 up to, but not including, index 7 of the list. Line 37 calls method printReversedList (lines 71–80) to print the list in reverse order.

Method convertToUppercaseStrings
Method convertToUppercaseStrings (lines 52–61) changes lowercase String elements in its List argument to uppercase Strings. Line 54 calls **List method listIterator** to get the List's **bidirectional iterator** (i.e., one that can traverse a List backward or forward).

ListIterator is also a generic class. In this example, the ListIterator references String objects, because method listIterator is called on a List of Strings. Line 56 calls method hasNext to determine whether the List contains another element. Line 58 gets the next String in the List. Line 59 calls **String method toUpperCase** to get an uppercase version of the String and calls **ListIterator method set** to replace the current String to which iterator refers with the String returned by method toUpperCase. Like method toUpperCase, **String method toLowerCase** returns a lowercase version of the String.

Method removeItems
Method removeItems (lines 64–68) removes a range of items from the list. Line 67 calls **List method subList** to obtain a portion of the List (called a **sublist**). This is a so-called **range-view method**, which enables the program to view a portion of the list. The sublist is simply a view into the List on which subList is called. Method subList takes as arguments the beginning and ending index for the sublist. The ending index is not part of the range of the sublist. In this example, line 35 passes 4 for the beginning index and 7 for the ending index to subList. The sublist returned is the set of elements with indices 4 through 6. Next, the program calls **List method clear** on the sublist to remove the elements of the sublist from the List. Any changes made to a sublist are also made to the original List.

Method printReversedList
Method printReversedList (lines 71–80) prints the list backward. Line 73 calls List method listIterator with the starting position as an argument (in our case, the last element in the list) to get a bidirectional iterator for the list. **List method size** returns the number of items in the List. The while condition (line 78) calls **ListIterator's hasPrevious method** to determine whether there are more elements while traversing the list backward. Line 79 calls **ListIterator's previous method** to get the previous element from the list and outputs it to the standard output stream.

J.5.3 Views into Collections and Arrays Method asList
An important feature of the collections framework is the ability to manipulate the elements of one collection type (such as a set) through a different collection type (such as a list), regardless of the collection's internal implementation. The set of public methods through which collections are manipulated is called a **view**.

Class Arrays provides static method **asList** to view an array (sometimes called the **backing array**) as a List collection. A List view allows you to manipulate the array as if it were a list. This is useful for adding the elements in an array to a collection and for sorting array elements. The next example demonstrates how to create a LinkedList with a List view of an array, because we cannot pass the array to a LinkedList constructor. Any modifications made through the List view change the array, and any modifications made to the array change the List view. The only operation permitted on the view returned by asList is *set*, which changes the value of the view and the backing array. Any other attempts to change the view (such as adding or removing elements) result in an **UnsupportedOperationException**.

Viewing Arrays as Lists and Converting Lists to Arrays
Figure J.4 uses Arrays method asList to view an array as a List and uses **List method toArray** to get an array from a LinkedList collection. The program calls method asList to create a List view of an array, which is used to initialize a LinkedList object, then adds

```
1   // Fig. J.4: UsingToArray.java
2   // Viewing arrays as Lists and converting Lists to arrays.
3   import java.util.LinkedList;
4   import java.util.Arrays;
5
6   public class UsingToArray
7   {
8      // creates a LinkedList, adds elements and converts to array
9      public static void main( String[] args )
10     {
11        String[] colors = { "black", "blue", "yellow" };
12
13        LinkedList< String > links =
14           new LinkedList< String >( Arrays.asList( colors ) );
15
16        links.addLast( "red" ); // add as last item
17        links.add( "pink" ); // add to the end
18        links.add( 3, "green" ); // add at 3rd index
19        links.addFirst( "cyan" ); // add as first item
20
21        // get LinkedList elements as an array
22        colors = links.toArray( new String[ links.size() ] );
23
24        System.out.println( "colors: " );
25
26        for ( String color : colors )
27           System.out.println( color );
28     } // end main
29  } // end class UsingToArray
```

```
colors:
cyan
black
blue
yellow
green
red
pink
```

Fig. J.4 | Viewing arrays as Lists and converting Lists to arrays.

a series of strings to the LinkedList and calls method toArray to obtain an array containing references to the Strings.

Lines 13–14 construct a LinkedList of Strings containing the elements of array colors. Line 14 uses Arrays method asList to return a List view of the array, then uses that to initialize the LinkedList with its constructor that receives a Collection as an argument (a List *is a* Collection). Line 16 calls **LinkedList method addLast** to add "red" to the end of links. Lines 17–18 call **LinkedList method add** to add "pink" as the last element and "green" as the element at index 3 (i.e., the fourth element). Method addLast (line 16) functions identically to method add (line 17). Line 19 calls **LinkedList method add-First** to add "cyan" as the new first item in the LinkedList. The add operations are permitted because they operate on the LinkedList object, not the view returned by asList.

Line 22 calls the List interface's toArray method to get a String array from links. The array is a copy of the list's elements—modifying the array's contents does *not* modify the list. The array passed to method toArray is of the same type that you'd like method toArray to return. If the number of elements in that array is greater than or equal to the number of elements in the LinkedList, toArray copies the list's elements into its array argument and returns that array. If the LinkedList has more elements than the number of elements in the array passed to toArray, toArray allocates a new array of the same type it receives as an argument, copies the list's elements into the new array and returns the new array.

J.6 Collections Methods

Class Collections provides several high-performance algorithms (Fig. J.5) for manipulating collection elements. The algorithms are implemented as static methods. The methods sort, binarySearch, reverse, shuffle, fill and copy operate on Lists. Methods min, max and addAll operate on Collections.

Method	Description
sort	Sorts the elements of a List.
binarySearch	Locates an object in a List.
reverse	Reverses the elements of a List.
shuffle	Randomly orders a List's elements.
fill	Sets every List element to refer to a specified object.
copy	Copies references from one List into another.
min	Returns the smallest element in a Collection.
max	Returns the largest element in a Collection.
addAll	Appends all elements in an array to a Collection.

Fig. J.5 | Some methods of class Collections.

J.6.1 Method sort

Method **sort** sorts the elements of a List, which must implement the **Comparable** interface. The order is determined by the natural order of the elements' type as implemented by a compareTo method. Method compareTo is declared in interface Comparable and is sometimes called the **natural comparison method**. The sort call may specify as a second argument a **Comparator** object that determines an alternative ordering of the elements.

Sorting in Ascending or Descending Order
If list is a List of Comparable objects (such as Strings), you can use Collections method sort to order the elements in ascending order as follows:

```
Collections.sort( list ); // sort list into ascending order
```

You can sort the List in descending order as follows:

```
// sort list into descending order
Collections.sort( list, Collections.reverseOrder() );
```

The static **Collections** method **reverseOrder** returns a Comparator object that orders the collection's elements in reverse order.

Sorting with a Comparator

For objects that are not Comparable, you can create custom Comparators. Figure J.6 creates a custom Comparator class, named TimeComparator, that implements interface Comparator to compare two Time2 objects. Class Time2, declared in Fig. F.5, represents times with hours, minutes and seconds.

```
1   // Fig. J.6: TimeComparator.java
2   // Custom Comparator class that compares two Time2 objects.
3   import java.util.Comparator;
4
5   public class TimeComparator implements Comparator< Time2 >
6   {
7      public int compare( Time2 time1, Time2 time2 )
8      {
9         int hourCompare = time1.getHour() - time2.getHour(); // compare hour
10
11        // test the hour first
12        if ( hourCompare != 0 )
13           return hourCompare;
14
15        int minuteCompare =
16           time1.getMinute() - time2.getMinute(); // compare minute
17
18        // then test the minute
19        if ( minuteCompare != 0 )
20           return minuteCompare;
21
22        int secondCompare =
23           time1.getSecond() - time2.getSecond(); // compare second
24
25        return secondCompare; // return result of comparing seconds
26     } // end method compare
27  } // end class TimeComparator
```

Fig. J.6 | Custom Comparator class that compares two Time2 objects.

Class TimeComparator implements interface Comparator, a generic type that takes one type argument (in this case Time2). A class that implements Comparator must declare a compare method that receives two arguments and returns a negative integer if the first argument is less than the second, 0 if the arguments are equal or a positive integer if the first argument is greater than the second. Method compare (lines 7–26) performs comparisons between Time2 objects. Line 9 compares the two hours of the Time2 objects. If the hours are different (line 12), then we return this value. If this value is positive, then the first hour is greater than the second and the first time is greater than the second. If this value is negative, then the first hour is less than the second and the first time is less than the second. If this value is zero, the hours are the same and we must test the minutes (and maybe the seconds) to determine which time is greater.

Figure J.7 sorts a list using the custom Comparator class TimeComparator. Line 11 creates an ArrayList of Time2 objects. Recall that both ArrayList and List are generic types and accept a type argument that specifies the element type of the collection. Lines 13–17 create five Time2 objects and add them to this list. Line 23 calls method sort, passing it an object of our TimeComparator class (Fig. J.6).

```java
1   // Fig. J.7: Sort.java
2   // Collections method sort with a custom Comparator object.
3   import java.util.List;
4   import java.util.ArrayList;
5   import java.util.Collections;
6
7   public class Sort3
8   {
9      public static void main( String[] args )
10     {
11        List< Time2 > list = new ArrayList< Time2 >(); // create List
12
13        list.add( new Time2(  6, 24, 34 ) );
14        list.add( new Time2( 18, 14, 58 ) );
15        list.add( new Time2(  6, 05, 34 ) );
16        list.add( new Time2( 12, 14, 58 ) );
17        list.add( new Time2(  6, 24, 22 ) );
18
19        // output List elements
20        System.out.printf( "Unsorted array elements:\n%s\n", list );
21
22        // sort in order using a comparator
23        Collections.sort( list, new TimeComparator() );
24
25        // output List elements
26        System.out.printf( "Sorted list elements:\n%s\n", list );
27     } // end main
28  } // end class Sort3
```

```
Unsorted array elements:
[6:24:34 AM, 6:14:58 PM, 6:05:34 AM, 12:14:58 PM, 6:24:22 AM]
Sorted list elements:
[6:05:34 AM, 6:24:22 AM, 6:24:34 AM, 12:14:58 PM, 6:14:58 PM]
```

Fig. J.7 | Collections method sort with a custom Comparator object.

J.6.2 Method shuffle

Method **shuffle** randomly orders a List's elements. Appendix E presented a card shuffling and dealing simulation that shuffled a deck of cards with a loop. If you have an array of 52 Card objects, you can shuffle them with method shuffle as follows:

```java
List< Card > list = Arrays.asList( deck ); // get List
Collections.shuffle( list ); // shuffle deck
```

The second line above shuffles the array by calling static method shuffle of class Collections. Method shuffle requires a List argument, so we must obtain a List view of the array before we can shuffle it. The Arrays class's static method asList gets a List view of the deck array.

J.7 Interface Queue

A queue is a collection that represents a waiting line—typically, insertions are made at the back of a queue and deletions are made from the front. Interface **Queue** extends interface Collection and provides additional operations for inserting, removing and inspecting elements in a queue. You can view the details of interface Queue and the list of classes that implement it at

> http://docs.oracle.com/javase/7/docs/api/java/util/Queue.html

J.8 Sets

A **Set** is an unordered Collection of unique elements (i.e., no duplicate elements). The collections framework contains several Set implementations, including **HashSet** and **TreeSet**. HashSet stores its elements in a hash table, and TreeSet stores its elements in a tree. Hash tables are presented in Section J.9.

Figure J.8 uses a HashSet to remove duplicate strings from a List. Recall that both List and Collection are generic types, so line 16 creates a List that contains String objects, and line 20 passes a Collection of Strings to method printNonDuplicates.

```
1   // Fig. J.8: SetTest.java
2   // HashSet used to remove duplicate values from an array of strings.
3   import java.util.List;
4   import java.util.Arrays;
5   import java.util.HashSet;
6   import java.util.Set;
7   import java.util.Collection;
8
9   public class SetTest
10  {
11     public static void main( String[] args )
12     {
13        // create and display a List< String >
14        String[] colors = { "red", "white", "blue", "green", "gray",
15           "orange", "tan", "white", "cyan", "peach", "gray", "orange" };
16        List< String > list = Arrays.asList( colors );
17        System.out.printf( "List: %s\n", list );
18
19        // eliminate duplicates then print the unique values
20        printNonDuplicates( list );
21     } // end main
22
23     // create a Set from a Collection to eliminate duplicates
24     private static void printNonDuplicates( Collection< String > values )
25     {
26        // create a HashSet
27        Set< String > set = new HashSet< String >( values );
```

Fig. J.8 | HashSet used to remove duplicate values from an array of strings. (Part 1 of 2.)

```
28
29          System.out.print( "\nNonduplicates are: " );
30
31          for ( String value : set )
32             System.out.printf( "%s ", value );
33
34          System.out.println();
35       } // end method printNonDuplicates
36    } // end class SetTest
```

```
List: [red, white, blue, green, gray, orange, tan, white, cyan, peach, gray,
orange]

Nonduplicates are: orange green white peach gray cyan red blue tan
```

Fig. J.8 | HashSet used to remove duplicate values from an array of strings. (Part 2 of 2.)

Method printNonDuplicates (lines 24–35) takes a Collection argument. Line 27 constructs a HashSet<String> from the Collection<String> argument. By definition, Sets do not contain duplicates, so when the HashSet is constructed, it removes any duplicates in the Collection. Lines 31–32 output elements in the Set.

Sorted Sets

The collections framework also includes the **SortedSet interface** (which extends Set) for sets that maintain their elements in sorted order—either the elements' natural order (e.g., numbers are in ascending order) or an order specified by a Comparator. Class TreeSet implements SortedSet. Items placed in a TreeSet are sorted as they're added.

J.9 Maps

Maps associate keys to values. The keys in a Map must be unique, but the associated values need not be. If a Map contains both unique keys and unique values, it's said to implement a **one-to-one mapping**. If only the keys are unique, the Map is said to implement a **many-to-one mapping**—many keys can map to one value.

Maps differ from Sets in that Maps contain keys and values, whereas Sets contain only values. Three of the several classes that implement interface Map are **Hashtable**, **HashMap** and **TreeMap**, and maps are used extensively in Android. Hashtables and HashMaps store elements in hash tables, and TreeMaps store elements in trees—the details of the underlying data structures are beyond the scope of this book. **Interface SortedMap** extends Map and maintains its keys in sorted order—either the elements' natural order or an order specified by a Comparator. Class TreeMap implements SortedMap. Figure J.9 uses a HashMap to count the number of occurrences of each word in a string.

```
1    // Fig. J.9: WordTypeCount.java
2    // Program counts the number of occurrences of each word in a String.
3    import java.util.Map;
```

Fig. J.9 | Program counts the number of occurrences of each word in a String. (Part 1 of 3.)

```java
 4    import java.util.HashMap;
 5    import java.util.Set;
 6    import java.util.TreeSet;
 7    import java.util.Scanner;
 8
 9    public class WordTypeCount
10    {
11       public static void main( String[] args )
12       {
13          // create HashMap to store String keys and Integer values
14          Map< String, Integer > myMap = new HashMap< String, Integer >();
15
16          createMap( myMap ); // create map based on user input
17          displayMap( myMap ); // display map content
18       } // end main
19
20       // create map from user input
21       private static void createMap( Map< String, Integer > map )
22       {
23          Scanner scanner = new Scanner( System.in ); // create scanner
24          System.out.println( "Enter a string:" ); // prompt for user input
25          String input = scanner.nextLine();
26
27          // tokenize the input
28          String[] tokens = input.split( " " );
29
30          // processing input text
31          for ( String token : tokens )
32          {
33             String word = token.toLowerCase(); // get lowercase word
34
35             // if the map contains the word
36             if ( map.containsKey( word ) ) // is word in map
37             {
38                int count = map.get( word ); // get current count
39                map.put( word, count + 1 ); // increment count
40             } // end if
41             else
42                map.put( word, 1 ); // add new word with a count of 1 to map
43          } // end for
44       } // end method createMap
45
46       // display map content
47       private static void displayMap( Map< String, Integer > map )
48       {
49          Set< String > keys = map.keySet(); // get keys
50
51          // sort keys
52          TreeSet< String > sortedKeys = new TreeSet< String >( keys );
53
54          System.out.println( "\nMap contains:\nKey\t\tValue" );
55
```

Fig. J.9 | Program counts the number of occurrences of each word in a String. (Part 2 of 3.)

```
56          // generate output for each key in map
57          for ( String key : sortedKeys )
58              System.out.printf( "%-10s%10s\n", key, map.get( key ) );
59
60          System.out.printf(
61              "\nsize: %d\nisEmpty: %b\n", map.size(), map.isEmpty() );
62      } // end method displayMap
63 } // end class WordTypeCount
```

```
Enter a string:
this is a sample sentence with several words this is another sample
sentence with several different words

Map contains:
Key            Value
a                1
another          1
different        1
is               2
sample           2
sentence ·       2
several          2
this             2
with             2
words            2

size: 10
isEmpty: false
```

Fig. J.9 | Program counts the number of occurrences of each word in a String. (Part 3 of 3.)

Line 14 creates an empty HashMap with a default initial capacity (16 elements) and a default load factor (0.75)—these defaults are built into the implementation of HashMap. When the number of occupied slots in the HashMap becomes greater than the capacity times the load factor, the capacity is doubled automatically. HashMap is a generic class that takes two type arguments—the type of key (i.e., String) and the type of value (i.e., Integer). Recall that the type arguments passed to a generic class must be reference types, hence the second type argument is Integer, not int.

Line 16 calls method createMap (lines 21–44), which uses a map to store the number of occurrences of each word in the sentence. Line 25 obtains the user input, and line 28 tokenizes it. The loop in lines 31–43 converts the next token to lowercase letters (line 33), then calls **Map method containsKey** (line 36) to determine whether the word is in the map (and thus has occurred previously in the string). If the Map does not contain a mapping for the word, line 42 uses **Map method put** to create a new entry in the map, with the word as the key and an Integer object containing 1 as the value. Autoboxing occurs when the program passes integer 1 to method put, because the map stores the number of occurrences of the word as an Integer. If the word does exist in the map, line 38 uses **Map method get** to obtain the key's associated value (the count) in the map. Line 39 increments that value and uses put to replace the key's associated value in the map. Method put returns the key's prior associated value, or null if the key was not in the map.

Method displayMap (lines 47–62) displays all the entries in the map. It uses **HashMap method keySet** (line 49) to get a set of the keys. The keys have type String in the map, so method keySet returns a generic type Set with type parameter specified to be String. Line 52 creates a TreeSet of the keys, in which the keys are sorted. The loop in lines 57–58 accesses each key and its value in the map. Line 58 displays each key and its value using format specifier %-10s to left justify each key and format specifier %10s to right justify each value. The keys are displayed in ascending order. Line 61 calls **Map method size** to get the number of key/value pairs in the Map. Line 61 also calls **Map method isEmpty**, which returns a boolean indicating whether the Map is empty.

J.10 Introduction to Files and Streams

Data stored in variables and arrays is temporary—it's lost when a local variable goes out of scope or when the program terminates. For long-term retention of data, even after the programs that create the data terminate, computers use **files**. You use files every day for tasks such as writing a document or creating a spreadsheet. Data maintained in files is **persistent data**—it exists beyond the duration of program execution.

Files as Streams of Bytes

Java views each file as a sequential **stream of bytes** (Fig. J.10). Every operating system provides a mechanism to determine the end of a file, such as an **end-of-file marker** or a count of the total bytes in the file that's recorded in a system-maintained administrative data structure. A Java program processing a stream of bytes simply receives an indication from the operating system when it reaches the end of the stream—the program does *not* need to know how the underlying platform represents files or streams. In some cases, the end-of-file indication occurs as an exception. In other cases, the indication is a return value from a method invoked on a stream-processing object.

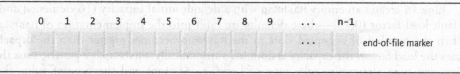

Fig. J.10 | Java's view of a file of *n* bytes.

Byte-Based and Character-Based Streams

Streams can be used to input and output data as bytes or characters. **Byte-based streams** input and output data in its binary format. **Character-based streams** input and output data as a sequence of characters. If the value 5 were being stored using a byte-based stream, it would be stored in the binary format of the numeric value 5, or 101. If the value 5 were being stored using a character-based stream, it would be stored in the binary format of the character 5, or 00000000 00110101 (this is the binary representation for the numeric value 53, which indicates the Unicode® character 5). The difference between the two forms is that the numeric value can be used as an integer in calculations, whereas the character 5 is simply a character that can be used in a string of text, as in "Sarah Miller is 15 years old". Files that are created using byte-based streams are referred to as **binary files**, while files created using character-based streams are referred to as **text files**. Text files can be read by text editors, while binary files are read by programs that understand the file's specific content and its ordering.

Opening a File
A Java program **opens** a file by creating an object and associating a stream of bytes or characters with it. The object's constructor interacts with the operating system to open the file.

The `java.io` Package
Java programs perform file processing by using classes from package **java.io**. This package includes definitions for stream classes, such as **FileInputStream** (for byte-based input from a file), **FileOutputStream** (for byte-based output to a file), **FileReader** (for character-based input from a file) and **FileWriter** (for character-based output to a file), which inherit from classes InputStream, OutputStream, Reader and Writer, respectively. Thus, the methods of the these stream classes can also be applied to file streams.

Java contains classes that enable you to perform input and output of objects or variables of primitive data types. The data will still be stored as bytes or characters behind the scenes, allowing you to read or write data in the form of ints, Strings, or other types without having to worry about the details of converting such values to byte format. To perform such input and output, objects of classes **ObjectInputStream** and **ObjectOutputStream** can be used together with the byte-based file stream classes FileInputStream and FileOutputStream (these classes will be discussed in more detail shortly). The complete hierarchy of types in package java.io can be viewed in the online documentation at

> docs.oracle.com/javase/7/docs/api/java/io/package-tree.html

Character-based input and output can also be performed with classes Scanner and **Formatter**. Class Scanner is used extensively to input data from the keyboard—it can also read data from a file. Class Formatter enables formatted data to be output to any text-based stream in a manner similar to method System.out.printf.

J.11 Class File

Class **File** is useful for retrieving information about files or directories from disk. File objects are used frequently with objects of other java.io classes to specify files or directories to manipulate.

Creating File Objects
Class File provides several constructors. The one with a String argument specifies the name of a file or directory to associate with the File object. The name can contain **path information** as well as a file or directory name. A file or directory's path specifies its location on disk. The path includes some or all of the directories leading to the file or directory. An **absolute path** contains all the directories, starting with the **root directory**, that lead to a specific file or directory. Every file or directory on a particular disk drive has the same root directory in its path. A **relative path** normally starts from the directory in which the application began executing and is therefore "relative" to the current directory. The constructor with two String arguments specifies an absolute or relative path as the first argument and the file or directory to associate with the File object as the second argument. The constructor with File and String arguments uses an existing File object that specifies the parent directory of the file or directory specified by the String argument. The fourth constructor uses a URI object to locate the file. A **Uniform Resource Identifier (URI)** is a more general form of the **Uniform Resource Locators (URLs)** that are used to locate websites.

For example, `http://www.deitel.com/` is the URL for the Deitel & Associates website. URIs for locating files vary across operating systems. On Windows platforms, the URI

```
file://C:/data.txt
```

identifies the file `data.txt` stored in the root directory of the C: drive. On UNIX/Linux platforms, the URI

```
file:/home/student/data.txt
```

identifies the file `data.txt` stored in the home directory of the user `student`.

Figure J.11 lists some common `File` methods. The complete list can be viewed at `docs.oracle.com/javase/7/docs/api/java/io/File.html`.

Method	Description
`boolean canRead()`	Returns `true` if a file is readable by the current application; `false` otherwise.
`boolean canWrite()`	Returns `true` if a file is writable by the current application; `false` otherwise.
`boolean exists()`	Returns `true` if the file or directory represented by the `File` object exists; `false` otherwise.
`boolean isFile()`	Returns `true` if the name specified as the argument to the `File` constructor is a file; `false` otherwise.
`boolean isDirectory()`	Returns `true` if the name specified as the argument to the `File` constructor is a directory; `false` otherwise.
`boolean isAbsolute()`	Returns `true` if the arguments specified to the `File` constructor indicate an absolute path to a file or directory; `false` otherwise.
`String getAbsolutePath()`	Returns a `String` with the absolute path of the file or directory.
`String getName()`	Returns a `String` with the name of the file or directory.
`String getPath()`	Returns a `String` with the path of the file or directory.
`String getParent()`	Returns a `String` with the parent directory of the file or directory (i.e., the directory in which the file or directory is located).
`long length()`	Returns the length of the file, in bytes. If the `File` object represents a directory, an unspecified value is returned.
`long lastModified()`	Returns a platform-dependent representation of the time at which the file or directory was last modified. The value returned is useful only for comparison with other values returned by this method.
`String[] list()`	Returns an array of `String`s representing a directory's contents. Returns `null` if the `File` object does not represent a directory.

Fig. J.11 | `File` methods.

J.12 Introduction to Object Serialization

Java provides **object serialization** for writing entire objects to a stream and reading entire objects from a stream. A so-called **serialized object** is an object represented as a sequence of bytes that includes the object's data as well as information about the object's type and the types of data stored in the object. After a serialized object has been written into a file, it can be read from the file and **deserialized**—that is, the type information and bytes that represent the object and its data can be used to recreate the object in memory.

Classes *ObjectInputStream* and *ObjectOutputStream*

Classes ObjectInputStream and ObjectOutputStream, which respectively implement the **ObjectInput** and **ObjectOutput** interfaces, enable entire objects to be read from or written to a stream (possibly a file). To use serialization with files, we initialize ObjectInput-Stream and ObjectOutputStream objects with stream objects that read from and write to files—objects of classes FileInputStream and FileOutputStream, respectively. Initializing stream objects with other stream objects in this manner is sometimes called **wrapping**—the new stream object being created wraps the stream object specified as a constructor argument. To wrap a FileInputStream in an ObjectInputStream, for instance, we pass the FileInputStream object to the ObjectInputStream's constructor.

Interfaces *ObjectOutput* and *ObjectInput*

The ObjectOutput interface contains method **writeObject**, which takes an Object as an argument and writes its information to an OutputStream. A class that implements interface ObjectOutput (such as ObjectOutputStream) declares this method and ensures that the object being output implements interface Serializable (discussed shortly). Correspondingly, the ObjectInput interface contains method **readObject**, which reads and returns a reference to an Object from an InputStream. After an object has been read, its reference can be cast to the object's actual type.

J.13 Introduction to Multithreading

It would be nice if we could focus our attention on performing only one action at a time and performing it well, but that's usually difficult to do. The human body performs a great variety of operations *in parallel*—or, as we say in programming, **concurrently**. Respiration, blood circulation, digestion, thinking and walking, for example, can occur concurrently, as can all the senses—sight, touch, smell, taste and hearing.

Computers, too, can perform operations concurrently. It's common for personal computers to compile a program, send a file to a printer and receive electronic mail messages over a network concurrently. Only computers that have multiple processors can truly execute multiple instructions concurrently. Operating systems on single-processor computers create the illusion of concurrent execution by rapidly switching between activities, but on such computers only a single instruction can execute at once. Today's multicore computers have multiple processors that enable computers to perform tasks truly concurrently. Multicore smartphones are starting to appear.

Java Concurrency

Java makes concurrency available to you through the language and APIs. Java programs can have multiple **threads of execution**, where each thread has its own method-call stack and program counter, allowing it to execute concurrently with other threads while sharing with them application-wide resources such as memory. This capability is called **multithreading**.

Performance Tip J.1

A problem with single-threaded applications that can lead to poor responsiveness is that lengthy activities must complete before others can begin. In a multithreaded application, threads can be distributed across multiple processors (if available) so that multiple tasks execute truly concurrently and the application can operate more efficiently. Multithreading can also increase performance on single-processor systems that simulate concurrency—when one thread cannot proceed (because, for example, it's waiting for the result of an I/O operation), another can use the processor.

Concurrent Programming Uses

We'll discuss many applications of **concurrent programming**. For example, when downloading a large file (e.g., an image, an audio clip or a video clip) over the Internet, the user may not want to wait until the entire clip downloads before starting the playback. To solve this problem, multiple threads can be used—one to download the clip, and another to play it. These activities proceed concurrently. To avoid choppy playback, the threads are **synchronized** (that is, their actions are coordinated) so that the player thread doesn't begin until there's a sufficient amount of the clip in memory to keep the player thread busy. The Java Virtual Machine (JVM) creates threads to run programs and threads to perform housekeeping tasks such as garbage collection.

Concurrent Programming Is Difficult

Writing multithreaded programs can be tricky. Although the human mind can perform functions concurrently, people find it difficult to jump between parallel trains of thought. To see why multithreaded programs can be difficult to write and understand, try the following experiment: Open three books to page 1, and try reading the books concurrently. Read a few words from the first book, then a few from the second, then a few from the third, then loop back and read the next few words from the first book, and so on. After this experiment, you'll appreciate many of the challenges of multithreading—switching between the books, reading briefly, remembering your place in each book, moving the book you're reading closer so that you can see it and pushing the books you're not reading aside—and, amid all this chaos, trying to comprehend the content of the books!

Use the Prebuilt Classes of the Concurrency APIs Whenever Possible

Programming concurrent applications is difficult and error prone. If you must use synchronization in a program, you should *use existing classes from the Concurrency APIs that manage synchronization for you*. These classes are written by experts, have been thoroughly tested and debugged, operate efficiently and help you avoid common traps and pitfalls.

J.14 Creating and Executing Threads with the Executor Framework

This section demonstrates how to perform concurrent tasks in an application by using Executors and Runnable objects.

Creating Concurrent Tasks with the Runnable Interface

You implement the **Runnable** interface (of package java.lang) to specify a task that can execute concurrently with other tasks. The Runnable interface declares the single method **run**, which contains the code that defines the task that a Runnable object should perform.

Executing Runnable Objects with an Executor

To allow a Runnable to perform its task, you must execute it. An **Executor** object executes Runnables. An Executor does this by creating and managing a group of threads called a **thread pool**. When an Executor begins executing a Runnable, the Executor calls the Runnable object's run method, which executes in the new thread.

The Executor interface declares a single method named **execute** which accepts a Runnable as an argument. The Executor assigns every Runnable passed to its execute method to one of the available threads in the thread pool. If there are no available threads, the Executor creates a new thread or waits for a thread to become available and assigns that thread the Runnable that was passed to method execute.

Using an Executor has many advantages over creating threads yourself. Executors can *reuse existing threads* to eliminate the overhead of creating a new thread for each task and can improve performance by *optimizing the number of threads* to ensure that the processor stays busy, without creating so many threads that the application runs out of resources.

Software Engineering Observation J.2

Though it's possible to create threads explicitly, it's recommended that you use the Executor interface to manage the execution of Runnable objects.

Using Class Executors to Obtain an ExecutorService

The **ExecutorService** interface (of package java.util.concurrent) *extends* Executor and declares various methods for managing the life cycle of an Executor. An object that implements the ExecutorService interface can be created using static methods declared in class **Executors** (of package java.util.concurrent). We use interface ExecutorService and a method of class Executors in our example, which executes three tasks.

Implementing the Runnable Interface

Class PrintTask (Fig. J.12) implements Runnable (line 5), *so that multiple PrintTasks can execute concurrently*. Variable sleepTime (line 7) stores a random integer value from 0 to 5 seconds created in the PrintTask constructor (line 17). Each thread running a Print-Task sleeps for the amount of time specified by sleepTime, then outputs its task's name and a message indicating that it's done sleeping.

```
1   // Fig. J.12: PrintTask.java
2   // PrintTask class sleeps for a random time from 0 to 5 seconds
3   import java.util.Random;
4
5   public class PrintTask implements Runnable
6   {
7      private final int sleepTime; // random sleep time for thread
8      private final String taskName; // name of task
9      private final static Random generator = new Random();
10
11     // constructor
12     public PrintTask( String name )
13     {
14        taskName = name; // set task name
```

Fig. J.12 | PrintTask class sleeps for a random time from 0 to 5 seconds. (Part 1 of 2.)

```
15
16        // pick random sleep time between 0 and 5 seconds
17        sleepTime = generator.nextInt( 5000 ); // milliseconds
18    } // end PrintTask constructor
19
20    // method run contains the code that a thread will execute
21    public void run()
22    {
23        try // put thread to sleep for sleepTime amount of time
24        {
25            System.out.printf( "%s going to sleep for %d milliseconds.\n",
26                taskName, sleepTime );
27            Thread.sleep( sleepTime ); // put thread to sleep
28        } // end try
29        catch ( InterruptedException exception )
30        {
31            System.out.printf( "%s %s\n", taskName,
32                "terminated prematurely due to interruption" );
33        } // end catch
34
35        // print task name
36        System.out.printf( "%s done sleeping\n", taskName );
37    } // end method run
38 } // end class PrintTask
```

Fig. J.12 | PrintTask class sleeps for a random time from 0 to 5 seconds. (Part 2 of 2.)

A PrintTask executes when a thread calls the PrintTask's run method. Lines 25–26 display a message indicating the name of the currently executing task and that the task is going to sleep for sleepTime milliseconds. Line 27 invokes static method **sleep** of class Thread to place the thread in the *timed waiting* state for the specified amount of time. At this point, the thread loses the processor, and the system allows another thread to execute. When the thread awakens, it reenters the *runnable* state. When the PrintTask is assigned to a processor again, line 36 outputs a message indicating that the task is done sleeping, then method run terminates. The catch at lines 29–33 is required because method sleep might throw a *checked* exception of type **InterruptedException** if a sleeping thread's **interrupt** method is called.

Using the ExecutorService to Manage Threads that Execute PrintTasks

Figure J.13 uses an ExecutorService object to manage threads that execute PrintTasks (as defined in Fig. J.12). Lines 11–13 create and name three PrintTasks to execute. Line 18 uses Executors method **newCachedThreadPool** to obtain an ExecutorService that's capable of creating new threads as they're needed by the application. These threads are used by ExecutorService (threadExecutor) to execute the Runnables.

```
1  // Fig. J.13: TaskExecutor.java
2  // Using an ExecutorService to execute Runnables.
3  import java.util.concurrent.Executors;
4  import java.util.concurrent.ExecutorService;
```

Fig. J.13 | Using an ExecutorService to execute Runnables. (Part 1 of 2.)

```
5
6    public class TaskExecutor
7    {
8       public static void main( String[] args )
9       {
10          // create and name each runnable
11          PrintTask task1 = new PrintTask( "task1" );
12          PrintTask task2 = new PrintTask( "task2" );
13          PrintTask task3 = new PrintTask( "task3" );
14
15          System.out.println( "Starting Executor" );
16
17          // create ExecutorService to manage threads
18          ExecutorService threadExecutor = Executors.newCachedThreadPool();
19
20          // start threads and place in runnable state
21          threadExecutor.execute( task1 ); // start task1
22          threadExecutor.execute( task2 ); // start task2
23          threadExecutor.execute( task3 ); // start task3
24
25          // shut down worker threads when their tasks complete
26          threadExecutor.shutdown();
27
28          System.out.println( "Tasks started, main ends.\n" );
29       } // end main
30    } // end class TaskExecutor
```

```
Starting Executor
Tasks started, main ends

task1 going to sleep for 4806 milliseconds
task2 going to sleep for 2513 milliseconds
task3 going to sleep for 1132 milliseconds
task3 done sleeping
task2 done sleeping
task1 done sleeping
```

```
Starting Executor
task1 going to sleep for 3161 milliseconds.
task3 going to sleep for 532 milliseconds.
task2 going to sleep for 3440 milliseconds.
Tasks started, main ends.

task3 done sleeping
task1 done sleeping
task2 done sleeping
```

Fig. J.13 | Using an ExecutorService to execute Runnables. (Part 2 of 2.)

Lines 21–23 each invoke the ExecutorService's execute method, which executes the Runnable passed to it as an argument (in this case a PrintTask) some time in the future. The specified task may execute in one of the threads in the ExecutorService's thread pool, in a new thread created to execute it, or in the thread that called the execute method—the ExecutorService manages these details. Method execute returns immediately from each invocation—the program does *not* wait for each PrintTask to finish. Line 26 calls ExecutorService method **shutdown**, which notifies the ExecutorService to *stop accepting new tasks, but continues executing tasks that have already been submitted*. Once all of the previously submitted Runnables have completed, the threadExecutor terminates. Line 28 outputs a message indicating that the tasks were started and the main thread is finishing its execution.

The code in main executes in the **main thread**, a thread created by the JVM. The code in the run method of PrintTask (lines 21–37 of Fig. J.12) executes whenever the Executor starts each PrintTask—again, this is sometime after they're passed to the ExecutorService's execute method (Fig. J.13, lines 21–23). When main terminates, the program itself continues running because there are still tasks that must finish executing. The program will not terminate until these tasks complete.

The sample outputs show each task's name and sleep time as the thread goes to sleep. The one with the shortest sleep time *normally* awakens first, indicates that it's done sleeping and terminates. In the first output, the main thread terminates *before* any of the PrintTasks output their names and sleep times. This shows that the main thread runs to completion before the PrintTasks get a chance to run. In the second output, all of the PrintTasks output their names and sleep times *before* the main thread terminates. Also, notice in the second example output, task3 goes to sleep before task2, even though we passed task2 to the ExecutorService's execute method before task3. This illustrates the fact that *we cannot predict the order in which the tasks will start executing, even if we know the order in which they were created and started.*

J.15 Overview of Thread Synchronization

When multiple threads share an object and it's modified by one or more of them, indeterminate results may occur unless access to the shared object is managed properly. If one thread is in the process of updating a shared object and another thread also tries to update it, it's unclear which thread's update takes effect. When this happens, the program's behavior cannot be trusted—sometimes the program will produce the correct results, and sometimes it won't. In either case, there'll be no indication that the shared object was manipulated incorrectly.

The problem can be solved by giving only one thread at a time *exclusive access* to code that manipulates the shared object. During that time, other threads desiring to manipulate the object are kept waiting. When the thread with exclusive access to the object finishes manipulating it, one of the threads that was waiting is allowed to proceed. This process, called **thread synchronization**, coordinates access to shared data by multiple concurrent threads. By synchronizing threads in this manner, you can ensure that each thread accessing a shared object excludes all other threads from doing so simultaneously—this is called **mutual exclusion**.

Monitors

A common way to perform synchronization is to use Java's built-in **monitors**. Every object has a monitor and a **monitor lock** (or **intrinsic lock**). The monitor ensures that its object's monitor lock is held by a maximum of only one thread at any time, and thus can be used to enforce mutual exclusion. If an operation requires the executing thread to hold a lock while the operation is performed, a thread must acquire the lock before proceeding with the operation. Other threads attempting to perform an operation that requires the same lock will be *blocked* until the first thread releases the lock, at which point the *blocked* threads may attempt to acquire the lock and proceed with the operation.

To specify that a thread must hold a monitor lock to execute a block of code, the code should be placed in a **synchronized statement**. Such code is said to be **guarded** by the monitor lock; a thread must **acquire the lock** to execute the guarded statements. The monitor allows only one thread at a time to execute statements within synchronized statements that lock on the same object, as only one thread at a time can hold the monitor lock. The synchronized statements are declared using the **synchronized keyword**:

```
synchronized ( object )
{
    statements
} // end synchronized statement
```

where *object* is the object whose monitor lock will be acquired; *object* is normally this if it's the object in which the synchronized statement appears. If several synchronized statements are trying to execute on an object at the same time, only one of them may be active on the object—all the other threads attempting to enter a synchronized statement on the same object are temporarily *blocked* from executing.

When a synchronized statement finishes executing, the object's monitor lock is released and one of the *blocked* threads attempting to enter a synchronized statement can be allowed to acquire the lock to proceed. Java also allows **synchronized methods**. Before executing, a non-static synchronized method must acquire the lock on the object that's used to call the method. Similarly, a static synchronized method must acquire the lock on the class that's used to call the method.

J.16 Concurrent Collections Overview

Earlier in this appendix, we introduced various collections from the Java Collections API. The collections from the java.util.concurrent package are specifically designed and optimized for use in programs that share collections among multiple threads. For information on the many concurrent collections in package java.util.concurrent, visit

```
docs.oracle.com/javase/7/docs/api/java/util/concurrent/package-
    summary.html
```

J.17 Multithreading with GUI

Swing applications present a unique set of challenges for multithreaded programming. All Swing applications have an **event dispatch thread** to handle interactions with the GUI components. Typical interactions include *updating GUI components* or *processing user actions* such as mouse clicks. All tasks that require interaction with an application's GUI are placed in an *event queue* and are executed sequentially by the event dispatch thread.

Swing GUI components are not thread safe—they cannot be manipulated by multiple threads without the risk of incorrect results. Thread safety in GUI applications is achieved not by synchronizing thread actions, but by *ensuring that Swing components are accessed from the event dispatch thread*—a technique called **thread confinement**.

Usually it's sufficient to perform simple tasks on the event dispatch thread in sequence with GUI component manipulations. If a lengthy task is performed in the event dispatch thread, it cannot attend to other tasks in the event queue while it's tied up in that task. This causes the GUI to become unresponsive. *Long-running tasks should be handled in separate threads*, freeing the event dispatch thread to continue managing other GUI interactions. Of course, to update the GUI based on the tasks's results, you must use the event dispatch thread, rather than from the worker thread that performed the computation.

Class SwingWorker

Class **SwingWorker** (in package javax.swing) perform long-running tasks in a worker thread and to update Swing components from the event dispatch thread based on the tasks' results. SwingWorker implements the Runnable interface, meaning that *a SwingWorker object can be scheduled to execute in a separate thread*. The SwingWorker class provides several methods to simplify performing tasks in a worker thread and making the results available for display in a GUI. Some common SwingWorker methods are described in Fig. J.14. Class SwingWorker is similar to class AsyncTask, which is used frequently in Android apps.

Method	Description
doInBackground	Defines a long task and is called in a worker thread.
done	Executes on the event dispatch thread when doInBackground returns.
execute	Schedules the SwingWorker object to be executed in a worker thread.
get	Waits for the task to complete, then returns the result of the task (i.e., the return value of doInBackground).
publish	Sends intermediate results from the doInBackground method to the process method for processing on the event dispatch thread.
process	Receives intermediate results from the publish method and processes these results on the event dispatch thread.
setProgress	Sets the progress property to notify any property change listeners on the event dispatch thread of progress bar updates.

Fig. J.14 | Commonly used SwingWorker methods.

Performing Tasks in a Worker Thread

In the next example, the user enters a number *n* and the program gets the *n*th Fibonacci number, which we calculate using a recursive algorithm. The algorithm is time consuming for large values, so we use a SwingWorker object to perform the calculation in a worker thread. The GUI also allows the user to get the next Fibonacci number in the sequence with each click of a button, beginning with fibonacci(1). This short calculation is performed directly in the event dispatch thread. The program is capable of producing up to the 92nd Fibonacci number—subsequent values are outside the range that can be represented by a long. You can use class BigInteger to represent arbitrarily large integer values.

Class BackgroundCalculator (Fig. J.15) performs the recursive Fibonacci calculation in a *worker thread*. This class extends SwingWorker (line 8), overriding the methods doInBackground and done. Method doInBackground (lines 21–24) computes the *n*th Fibonacci number in a worker thread and returns the result. Method done (lines 27–43) displays the result in a JLabel.

```
1   // Fig. J.15: BackgroundCalculator.java
2   // SwingWorker subclass for calculating Fibonacci numbers
3   // in a worker thread.
4   import javax.swing.SwingWorker;
5   import javax.swing.JLabel;
6   import java.util.concurrent.ExecutionException;
7
8   public class BackgroundCalculator extends SwingWorker< Long, Object >
9   {
10      private final int n; // Fibonacci number to calculate
11      private final JLabel resultJLabel; // JLabel to display the result
12
13      // constructor
14      public BackgroundCalculator( int number, JLabel label )
15      {
16         n = number;
17         resultJLabel = label;
18      } // end BackgroundCalculator constructor
19
20      // long-running code to be run in a worker thread
21      public Long doInBackground()
22      {
23         return nthFib = fibonacci( n );
24      } // end method doInBackground
25
26      // code to run on the event dispatch thread when doInBackground returns
27      protected void done()
28      {
29         try
30         {
31            // get the result of doInBackground and display it
32            resultJLabel.setText( get().toString() );
33         } // end try
34         catch ( InterruptedException ex )
35         {
36            resultJLabel.setText( "Interrupted while waiting for results." );
37         } // end catch
38         catch ( ExecutionException ex )
39         {
40            resultJLabel.setText(
41               "Error encountered while performing calculation." );
42         } // end catch
43      } // end method done
44
45      // recursive method fibonacci; calculates nth Fibonacci number
46      public long fibonacci( long number )
47      {
48         if ( number == 0 || number == 1 )
49            return number;
50         else
51            return fibonacci( number - 1 ) + fibonacci( number - 2 );
52      } // end method fibonacci
53   } // end class BackgroundCalculator
```

Fig. J.15 | SwingWorker subclass for calculating Fibonacci numbers in a worker thread.

SwingWorker is a *generic class*. In line 8, the first type parameter is Long and the second is Object. The first type parameter indicates the type returned by the doInBackground method; the second indicates the type that's passed between the publish and process methods to handle intermediate results. Since we do not use publish and process in this example, we simply use Object as the second type parameter.

A BackgroundCalculator object can be instantiated from a class that controls a GUI. A BackgroundCalculator maintains instance variables for an integer that represents the Fibonacci number to be calculated and a JLabel that displays the results of the calculation (lines 10–11). The BackgroundCalculator constructor (lines 14–18) initializes these instance variables with the arguments that are passed to the constructor.

> ### Software Engineering Observation J.3
> *Any GUI components that will be manipulated by SwingWorker methods, such as components that will be updated from methods process or done, should be passed to the SwingWorker subclass's constructor and stored in the subclass object. This gives these methods access to the GUI components they'll manipulate.*

When method execute is called on a BackgroundCalculator object, the object is scheduled for execution in a worker thread. Method doInBackground is called from the worker thread and invokes the fibonacci method (lines 46–52), passing instance variable n as an argument (line 23). Method fibonacci uses recursion to compute the Fibonacci of n. When fibonacci returns, method doInBackground returns the result.

After doInBackground returns, method done is automatically called from the event dispatch thread. This method attempts to set the result JLabel to the return value of doInBackground by calling method get to retrieve this return value (line 32). Method get waits for the result to be ready if necessary, but since we call it from method done, the computation will be complete before get is called. Lines 34–37 catch InterruptedException if the current thread is interrupted while waiting for get to return. This exception will not occur in this example since the calculation will have already completed by the time get is called. Lines 38–42 catch ExecutionException, which is thrown if an exception occurs during the computation.

Class FibonacciNumbers

Class FibonacciNumbers (Fig. J.16) displays a window containing two sets of GUI components—one set to compute a Fibonacci number in a worker thread and another to get the next Fibonacci number in response to the user's clicking a JButton. The constructor (lines 38–109) places these components in separate titled JPanels. Lines 46–47 and 78–79 add two JLabels, a JTextField and a JButton to the workerJPanel to allow the user to enter an integer whose Fibonacci number will be calculated by the BackgroundWorker. Lines 84–85 and 103 add two JLabels and a JButton to the event dispatch thread panel to allow the user to get the next Fibonacci number in the sequence. Instance variables n1 and n2 contain the previous two Fibonacci numbers in the sequence and are initialized to 0 and 1, respectively (lines 29–30). Instance variable count stores the most recently computed sequence number and is initialized to 1 (line 31). The two JLabels display count and n2 initially, so that the user will see the text Fibonacci of 1: 1 in the eventThread-JPanel when the GUI starts.

```java
 1   // Fig. J.16: FibonacciNumbers.java
 2   // Using SwingWorker to perform a long calculation with
 3   // results displayed in a GUI.
 4   import java.awt.GridLayout;
 5   import java.awt.event.ActionEvent;
 6   import java.awt.event.ActionListener;
 7   import javax.swing.JButton;
 8   import javax.swing.JFrame;
 9   import javax.swing.JPanel;
10   import javax.swing.JLabel;
11   import javax.swing.JTextField;
12   import javax.swing.border.TitledBorder;
13   import javax.swing.border.LineBorder;
14   import java.awt.Color;
15   import java.util.concurrent.ExecutionException;
16
17   public class FibonacciNumbers extends JFrame
18   {
19      // components for calculating the Fibonacci of a user-entered number
20      private final JPanel workerJPanel =
21         new JPanel( new GridLayout( 2, 2, 5, 5 ) );
22      private final JTextField numberJTextField = new JTextField();
23      private final JButton goJButton = new JButton( "Go" );
24      private final JLabel fibonacciJLabel = new JLabel();
25
26      // components and variables for getting the next Fibonacci number
27      private final JPanel eventThreadJPanel =
28         new JPanel( new GridLayout( 2, 2, 5, 5 ) );
29      private long n1 = 0; // initialize with first Fibonacci number
30      private long n2 = 1; // initialize with second Fibonacci number
31      private int count = 1; // current Fibonacci number to display
32      private final JLabel nJLabel = new JLabel( "Fibonacci of 1: " );
33      private final JLabel nFibonacciJLabel =
34         new JLabel( String.valueOf( n2 ) );
35      private final JButton nextNumberJButton = new JButton( "Next Number" );
36
37      // constructor
38      public FibonacciNumbers()
39      {
40         super( "Fibonacci Numbers" );
41         setLayout( new GridLayout( 2, 1, 10, 10 ) );
42
43         // add GUI components to the SwingWorker panel
44         workerJPanel.setBorder( new TitledBorder(
45            new LineBorder( Color.BLACK ), "With SwingWorker" ) );
46         workerJPanel.add( new JLabel( "Get Fibonacci of:" ) );
47         workerJPanel.add( numberJTextField );
48         goJButton.addActionListener(
49            new ActionListener()
50            {
```

Fig. J.16 | Using SwingWorker to perform a long calculation with results displayed in a GUI. (Part 1 of 3.)

```java
51          public void actionPerformed( ActionEvent event )
52          {
53             int n;
54
55             try
56             {
57                // retrieve user's input as an integer
58                n = Integer.parseInt( numberJTextField.getText() );
59             } // end try
60             catch( NumberFormatException ex )
61             {
62                // display an error message if the user did not
63                // enter an integer
64                fibonacciJLabel.setText( "Enter an integer." );
65                return;
66             } // end catch
67
68             // indicate that the calculation has begun
69             fibonacciJLabel.setText( "Calculating..." );
70
71             // create a task to perform calculation in background
72             BackgroundCalculator task =
73                new BackgroundCalculator( n, fibonacciJLabel );
74             task.execute(); // execute the task
75          } // end method actionPerformed
76       } // end anonymous inner class
77    ); // end call to addActionListener
78    workerJPanel.add( goJButton );
79    workerJPanel.add( fibonacciJLabel );
80
81    // add GUI components to the event-dispatching thread panel
82    eventThreadJPanel.setBorder( new TitledBorder(
83       new LineBorder( Color.BLACK ), "Without SwingWorker" ) );
84    eventThreadJPanel.add( nJLabel );
85    eventThreadJPanel.add( nFibonacciJLabel );
86    nextNumberJButton.addActionListener(
87       new ActionListener()
88       {
89          public void actionPerformed( ActionEvent event )
90          {
91             // calculate the Fibonacci number after n2
92             long temp = n1 + n2;
93             n1 = n2;
94             n2 = temp;
95             ++count;
96
97             // display the next Fibonacci number
98             nJLabel.setText( "Fibonacci of " + count + ": " );
99             nFibonacciJLabel.setText( String.valueOf( n2 ) );
100         } // end method actionPerformed
101      } // end anonymous inner class
102   ); // end call to addActionListener
```

Fig. J.16 | Using SwingWorker to perform a long calculation with results displayed in a GUI. (Part 2 of 3.)

```
103          eventThreadJPanel.add( nextNumberJButton );
104
105       add( workerJPanel );
106       add( eventThreadJPanel );
107       setSize( 275, 200 );
108       setVisible( true );
109    } // end constructor
110
111    // main method begins program execution
112    public static void main( String[] args )
113    {
114       FibonacciNumbers application = new FibonacciNumbers();
115       application.setDefaultCloseOperation( EXIT_ON_CLOSE );
116    } // end main
117 } // end class FibonacciNumbers
```

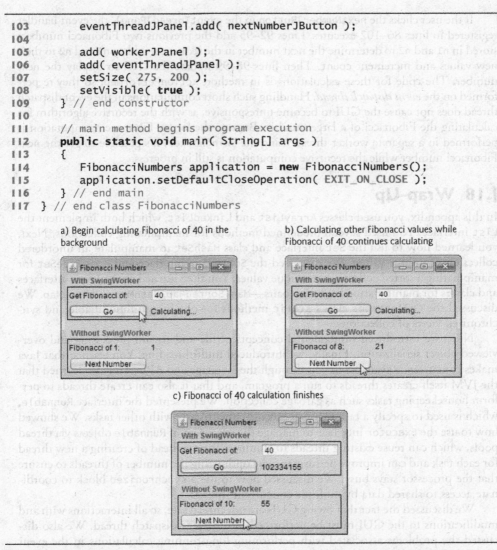

a) Begin calculating Fibonacci of 40 in the background

b) Calculating other Fibonacci values while Fibonacci of 40 continues calculating

c) Fibonacci of 40 calculation finishes

Fig. J.16 | Using SwingWorker to perform a long calculation with results displayed in a GUI. (Part 3 of 3.)

Lines 48–77 register the event handler for the goJButton. If the user clicks this JButton, line 58 gets the value entered in the numberJTextField and attempts to parse it as an integer. Lines 72–73 create a new BackgroundCalculator object, passing in the user-entered value and the fibonacciJLabel that's used to display the calculation's results. Line 74 calls method execute on the BackgroundCalculator, scheduling it for execution in a separate worker thread. Method execute does not wait for the BackgroundCalculator to finish executing. It returns immediately, allowing the GUI to continue processing other events while the computation is performed.

If the user clicks the nextNumberJButton in the eventThreadJPanel, the event handler registered in lines 86–102 executes. Lines 92–95 add the previous two Fibonacci numbers stored in n1 and n2 to determine the next number in the sequence, update n1 and n2 to their new values and increment count. Then lines 98–99 update the GUI to display the next number. The code for these calculations is in method actionPerformed, so they're performed on the *event dispatch thread*. Handling such short computations in the event dispatch thread does not cause the GUI to become unresponsive, as with the recursive algorithm for calculating the Fibonacci of a large number. Because the longer Fibonacci computation is performed in a separate worker thread using the SwingWorker, it's possible to get the next Fibonacci number while the recursive computation is still in progress.

J.18 Wrap-Up

In this appendix, you used classes ArrayList and LinkedList, which both implement the List interface. You used several predefined methods for manipulating collections. Next, you learned how to use the Set interface and class HashSet to manipulate an unordered collection of unique values. We discussed the SortedSet interface and class TreeSet for manipulating a sorted collection of unique values. You then learned about Java's interfaces and classes for manipulating key/value pairs—Map, SortedMap, HashMap and TreeMap. We discussed the Collections class's static methods for obtaining unmodifiable and synchronized views of collections.

Next, we introduced fundamental concepts of file and stream processing and overviewed object serialization. Finally, we introduced multithreading. You learned that Java makes concurrency available to you through the language and APIs. You also learned that the JVM itself creates threads to run a program, and that it also can create threads to perform housekeeping tasks such as garbage collection. We presented the interface Runnable, which is used to specify a task that can execute concurrently with other tasks. We showed how to use the Executor interface to manage the execution of Runnable objects via thread pools, which can reuse existing threads to eliminate the overhead of creating a new thread for each task and can improve performance by optimizing the number of threads to ensure that the processor stays busy. We discussed how to use a synchronized block to coordinate access to shared data by multiple concurrent threads.

We discussed the fact that Swing GUIs are not thread safe, so all interactions with and modifications to the GUI must be performed in the event dispatch thread. We also discussed the problems associated with performing long-running calculations in the event dispatch thread. Then we showed how you can use the SwingWorker class to perform long-running calculations in worker threads and how to display the results of a SwingWorker in a GUI when the calculation completed.

Self-Review Exercises

J.1   Fill in the blanks in each of the following statements:
   a) A(n) _____ is used to iterate through a collection and can remove elements from the collection during the iteration.
   b) An element in a List can be accessed by using the element's _____.
   c) Assuming that myArray contains references to Double objects, _____ occurs when the statement "myArray[0] = 1.25;" executes.

    d) Java classes _____ and _____ provide the capabilities of arraylike data structures that can resize themselves dynamically.

    e) Assuming that `myArray` contains references to `Double` objects, _____ occurs when the statement `"double number = myArray[ 0 ];"` executes.

    f) `ExecutorService` method _____ ends each thread in an `ExecutorService` as soon as it finishes executing its current `Runnable`, if any.

    g) Keyword _____ indicates that only one thread at a time should execute on an object.

J.2   Determine whether each statement is *true* or *false*. If *false*, explain why.

    a) Values of primitive types may be stored directly in a collection.

    b) A `Set` can contain duplicate values.

    c) A `Map` can contain duplicate keys.

    d) A `LinkedList` can contain duplicate values.

    e) `Collections` is an interface.

    f) `Iterators` can remove elements.

    g) Method `exists` of class `File` returns `true` if the name specified as the argument to the `File` constructor is a file or directory in the specified path.

    h) Binary files are human readable in a text editor.

    i) An absolute path contains all the directories, starting with the root directory, that lead to a specific file or directory.

Answers to Self-Review Exercises

J.1   a) `Iterator`. b) index. c) autoboxing. d) `ArrayList`, `Vector`. e) auto-unboxing. f) `shutdown`. g) `synchronized`.

J.2   a) False. Autoboxing occurs when adding a primitive type to a collection, which means the primitive type is converted to its corresponding type-wrapper class. b) False. A `Set` cannot contain duplicate values. c) False. A `Map` cannot contain duplicate keys. d) True. e) False. `Collections` is a class; `Collection` is an interface. f) True. g) True. h) False. Text files are human readable in a text editor. Binary files might be human readable, but only if the bytes in the file represent ASCII characters. i) True.

Execises

J.3   Define each of the following terms:

    a) `Collection`

    b) `Collections`

    c) `Comparator`

    d) `List`

    e) `HashMap`

    f) `ObjectOutputStream`

    g) `File`

    h) `ObjectOutputStream`

    i) byte-based stream

    j) character-based stream

J.4   Briefly answer the following questions:

    a) What is the primary difference between a `Set` and a `Map`?

    b) What happens when you add a primitive type (e.g., `double`) value to a collection?

    c) Can you print all the elements in a collection without using an `Iterator`? If yes, how?

J.5   *(Duplicate Elimination)* Write a program that reads in a series of first names and eliminates duplicates by storing them in a `Set`. Allow the user to search for a first name.

J.6 *(Counting Letters)* Modify the program of Fig. J.9 to count the number of occurrences of each letter rather than of each word. For example, the string "HELLO THERE" contains two Hs, three Es, two Ls, one O, one T and one R. Display the results.

J.7 *(Color Chooser)* Use a HashMap to create a reusable class for choosing one of the 13 predefined colors in class Color. The names of the colors should be used as keys, and the predefined Color objects should be used as values. Place this class in a package that can be imported into any Java program. Use your new class in an application that allows the user to select a color and draw a shape in that color.

J.8 *(Counting Duplicate Words)* Write a program that determines and prints the number of duplicate words in a sentence. Treat uppercase and lowercase letters the same. Ignore punctuation.

J.9 *(Prime Numbers and Prime Factors)* Write a program that takes a whole number input from a user and determines whether it's prime. If the number is not prime, display its unique prime factors. Remember that a prime number's factors are only 1 and the prime number itself. Every number that is not prime has a unique prime factorization. For example, consider the number 54. The prime factors of 54 are 2, 3, 3 and 3. When the values are multiplied together, the result is 54. For the number 54, the prime factors output should be 2 and 3. Use Sets as part of your solution.

J.10 *(Sorting Words with a TreeSet)* Write a program that uses a String method split to tokenize a line of text input by the user and places each token in a TreeSet. Print the elements of the TreeSet. [*Note:* This should cause the elements to be printed in ascending sorted order.]

J.11 *(Bouncing Ball)* Write a program that bounces a blue ball inside a JPanel. The ball should begin moving with a mousePressed event. When the ball hits the edge of the JPanel, it should bounce off the edge and continue in the opposite direction. The ball should be updated using a Runnable.

Operator Precedence Chart

Operators are shown in decreasing order of precedence from top to bottom (Fig. K.1).

Operator	Description	Associativity
++ --	unary postfix increment unary postfix decrement	right to left
++ -- + - ! ~ (*type*)	unary prefix increment unary prefix decrement unary plus unary minus unary logical negation unary bitwise complement unary cast	right to left
* / %	multiplication division remainder	left to right
+ -	addition or string concatenation subtraction	left to right
<< >> >>>	left shift signed right shift unsigned right shift	left to right
< <= > >= instanceof	less than less than or equal to greater than greater than or equal to type comparison	left to right
== !=	is equal to is not equal to	left to right
&	bitwise AND boolean logical AND	left to right
^	bitwise exclusive OR boolean logical exclusive OR	left to right

Fig. K.1 | Operator precedence chart. (Part 1 of 2.)

Operator	Description	Associativity
|	bitwise inclusive OR boolean logical inclusive OR	left to right
&&	conditional AND	left to right
||	conditional OR	left to right
?:	conditional	right to left
=	assignment	right to left
+=	addition assignment	
-=	subtraction assignment	
*=	multiplication assignment	
/=	division assignment	
%=	remainder assignment	
&=	bitwise AND assignment	
^=	bitwise exclusive OR assignment	
|=	bitwise inclusive OR assignment	
<<=	bitwise left-shift assignment	
>>=	bitwise signed-right-shift assignment	
>>>=	bitwise unsigned-right-shift assignment	

Fig. K.1 | Operator precedence chart. (Part 2 of 2.)

Primitive Types

Type	Size in bits	Values	Standard
boolean		true or false	
[*Note:* A boolean's representation is specific to the Java Virtual Machine on each platform.]			
char	16	'\u0000' to '\uFFFF' (0 to 65535)	(ISO Unicode character set)
byte	8	-128 to $+127$ (-2^7 to $2^7 - 1$)	
short	16	$-32,768$ to $+32,767$ (-2^{15} to $2^{15} - 1$)	
int	32	$-2,147,483,648$ to $+2,147,483,647$ (-2^{31} to $2^{31} - 1$)	
long	64	$-9,223,372,036,854,775,808$ to $+9,223,372,036,854,775,807$ (-2^{63} to $2^{63} - 1$)	
float	32	*Negative range:* $-3.4028234663852886E+38$ to $-1.40129846432481707e-45$ *Positive range:* $1.40129846432481707e-45$ to $3.4028234663852886E+38$	(IEEE 754 floating point)
double	64	*Negative range:* $-1.7976931348623157E+308$ to $-4.94065645841246544e-324$ *Positive range:* $4.94065645841246544e-324$ to $1.7976931348623157E+308$	(IEEE 754 floating point)

Fig. L.1 | Java primitive types.

For more information on IEEE 754 visit grouper.ieee.org/groups/754/.

Index